Cultural Studies – The Basics

Cultural Studies – The Basics

Jeff Lewis

SAGE Publications
London • Thousand Oaks • New Delhi

First published 2002

 SAGE Publications Ltd
6 Bonhill Street
London EC2A 4PU

SAGE Publications Inc
2455 Teller Road
Thousand Oaks, California 91320

SAGE Publications India Pvt Ltd
32, M-Block Market
Greater Kailash - I
New Delhi 110 048

British Library Cataloguing in Publication data

ISBN 0 7619 6324 3
    0 7619 6325 1

Library of Congress Catalog Control Number 2001 135323

Typeset by SIVA Math Setters, Chennai, India
Printed in Great Britain by The Cromwell Press Ltd,
Trowbridge, Wiltshire

Contents

Contents

Contents

Contents

To my parents, Norma and Allen Lewis

List of Tables, Figures and Plates

TABLES

FIGURES

PLATES

Preface

Together we weave what we can from the warp and woof of one another's experience. For the scholar, I suspect that he had unburdened himself of what had been haunting him. He left here knowing that he had contributed important information to the map I had in mind. … I felt that this would turn out to be an interesting headland for us both to visit in our pursuit of respective havens.

James Cowan, *A Mapmaker's Dream*

Cultural Studies – The Basics has been written for a general and diverse academic audience, with a particular focus on readers who are new to the field. My principal aim in writing this book has been to bring together the various lineages and perspectives that comprise contemporary cultural analysis and which form our understanding of contemporary culture itself. The book, that is, combines an interest in the analysis and theorizing of culture with an elucidation of contemporary culture and meaning-making processes. To achieve this end, the book has been designed with multiple levels of access, entry and engagement. At all times, my aim has been to allow readers to form their own judgements and create their own pathways to understanding and knowledge.

The book brings together the major lineages that form contemporary cultural analysis: sociology, anthropology, politics and textual studies (literature, art, architecture, film and media studies). While giving voice to these various approaches and perspectives, I have attempted to construct a transdisciplinary analysis which combines an interest in issues of ideology, power, everyday meaning-making and cultural practices, and the media. The book weaves together an interrogation of various foundational theories and modes of cultural analysis with an investigation of substantive zones of cultural interest and activity. At all times, it treats theory as an important and exhilarating form of cartography or map-making – these maps, however, will always return the reader to the direction of home and the familiar plane of lived experience.

The book is divided into two broad sections: 'Forming Culture/Informing Cultural Theory' and 'Cultural Locations'. Part One examines the ways in which the concept of culture has been problematized and theorized. It provides a critical reading of these various theories and modes of analysis, measuring them against the transdisciplinary and language-based model outlined in Chapter 1. Part Two develops this model through a more specific reading of contemporary culture.

Each individual chapter in the book has been structured in a similar way. A chapter outline presents the principal ideas and issues to be covered. This is followed by a general introduction which provides significant background to the themes and ideas, and the ways in which the discussion will proceed. The discussion incorporates specific examples which are designed to illustrate and elucidate particular points of investigation. Each chapter concludes with a substantive analysis of some of the more problematic and pertinent issues raised in the course of the discussion.

Acknowledgements

I wish to thank and acknowledge Kirsty Best for her substantial contributions to this book. I would also like to thank Belinda Lewis, whose support and assistance remain immeasurable. I need to thank other colleagues – Brian Henderson, Jack Clancy, Judith Smart and Sheldon Harsel – who have always demonstrated for me the great value and decency of a scholarly life. I want to thank my students, who remain the inspiration for these efforts. Particular thanks to Chris Rojek of Sage who has supported this project since its inception.

I would also like to thank Terry Batt for permission to use his painting *The Dada Cowboy Rides Again* (Plate 7.1). Thanks to Thea Linke (cremation ceremony, Plate 1.2) and Carolyn Lewis (Sydney Olympics, Plate 1.1) for permission to use photographs. Thanks to Michelle Gregson (Plate 4.1), Belinda Rikard-Bell (Plate 9.1) and Stelarc (Plate 9.1) for their kind assistance with these photographs.

I wish to acknowledge the School of Applied Communication and the Faculty of Art, Design and Communication at RMIT University for granting leave time which assisted in the writing of this book. Thanks also to the many staff and students of RMIT who have contributed to the ideas, research and editing which have helped shape this book. Thanks especially to Jess Raschke.

Part One

Forming Culture/ Informing Cultural Theory

Part Contents

1

Defining Culture:

The Scope of the Task

Outline of the chapter

Cultures are formed around the meanings people construct and share. Contemporary First World cultures, in particular, are formed through televisual media experiences and other everyday practices (activities). These 'mediation' processes can be understood as the interaction between the text, the text producers and the text audiences. This relationship operates within an encompassing and dynamic cultural context. Culture, therefore, is both the context of existing meanings and the dynamic which stimulates the production and dissemination of new meanings. Culture, in fact, is best understood as the processes of meaning-making within a given social group. Culture may be formed and operate through a broad range of social groupings and social practices: for example, family, neighbourhood, age-group, ethnic group, religion, workplace, text style, clothing style, nation, globe, and so on.

Cultural theory and cultural studies are about culture, but these academic disciplines themselves also operate within a particular cultural context. They function and exist within an existing framework of meanings and knowledge, and they attempt to stimulate new ideas and meanings. Cultural studies and cultural theory, therefore, need to be understood and analysed in terms of their own cultural context. The two principal aims of this book are to:

(a) explore and explain the development and genealogy of cultural theory and cultural studies; and
(b) explore and explain these analyses in relation to contemporary cultural processes.

In particular, we will examine the formation of contemporary culture and cultural analysis in relation to notions of modernism and postmodernism. Through these studies we will consider the implications of power and cultural politics. Our critique of the various theorizations of culture will consistently return to the question of how language, discourse and the media operate within the contexts of multiplying social interests and practices, and the dynamics of meaning-making processes. These examinations will lead to a broader interrogation of cultural analysis and culture itself.

TELEVISUAL CULTURE

In 1997 Diana Spencer, Princess of Wales, was killed in a car accident in Paris. The driver was well over the legal alcohol limit and was travelling at speeds in excess of 200 kilometres an hour. While we might condemn the recklessness of the group, a global audience of around 2.5 billion people watched the laying to rest of the 'People's Princess', making it the most watched event in all human history. In 1998 the annual earnings of the North American pop singer Celine Dion was $55.5 million, though this figure was still well short of the Rolling Stones' earnings for that year: $94.5 million. The stars of the TV series *Friends* signed contracts in 2000 of around $1 million per twenty-minute episode. In 1999 the US/UK-led forces of the North Atlantic Treaty Organization began an intense bombing campaign on the small Balkans state of Kosovo. As with the Gulf War (1990–1), global TV audiences were exposed nightly to a highly polemicized war between the forces of good and the forces of evil; the military war, that is, was accompanied by a language war in which the NATO forces were presented as morally, militarily and technologically superior to their enemies. Later that year, two teenage boys opened fire on their classmates at a small provincial public school in Columbine, USA. Thirty-six children were seriously or critically wounded, provoking a revival of political and public debates over the harm being caused by violent TV, film and video programmes. At the time of these killings the Hollywood blockbuster *Titanic* had become the world's highest grossing film ($1.83 billion). In September 2000 another global audience of around 2–3 billion people watched 'the world's greatest athletes' performing at the Sydney Olympics; twelve months later a similar audience was stunned by the vision of 'terrorist' attacks on the World Trade Center in New York.

Many people speculated that Diana's death was caused by the media, both literally and metaphorically. At the time of the accident, Diana and her companions were attempting to escape the intrusions of the rogue celebrity press, the paparazzi. Of course, Diana was also part of a broader public interest and imagining. She had appeared often in the major, mainstream media, and her life and personal struggles had become a significant part of the everyday lives and experiences of 'ordinary' people. To this extent, Diana was a media and cultural product like any other. However partially or impermanently, the characters, events, celebrities and texts that are constituted through the media are a fundamental part of our culture. Warfare, tragedy, love, desire, struggle, relationships – all are mediated for us and implicated in our everyday experiences. The Rolling Stones, Leonardo DiCaprio, the attack on the Twin Towers in New York and the Columbine killings become real for us – emotionally and cognitively present in our daily contemplations, conversations, pleasures and pains. They provide a resource for the management of our own problems, our own relationships, our own politics and processes of persuasion. They become part of who we are and how we understand the world around us.

Thus, the media 'mediate meaning'. The media don't exist 'out there', but are implicated in the way we make sense of things, the way we make meanings, the way we construct culture. To achieve this confluence of meaning-making, there must be some significant proximity or contiguity in the relationship between media and audiences: there must be some overlapping

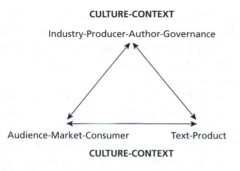

CULTURE-CONTEXT

Industry-Producer-Author-Governance

Audience-Market-Consumer   Text-Product

CULTURE-CONTEXT

Figure 1.1 Culture, the media and meaning-making

or mutual imagining. Culture is that shared space of imagining where the media and audiences interact. Figure 1.1 gives us some sense of how this interaction takes place.

Media producers include all those people, institutions, regulations and processes who/which contribute to the formation of texts. Texts include every form of mediation in language, sound, smell and image. Media texts may include handycam home videos, garage music, blockbuster movies, websites, books, TV news, and so on. Audiences include any form of text consumer at any level of production or reception. At all points, each of the elements in Figure 1.1 is interacting with all other elements. Culture is constructed out of the triad of mediation, though it is also the fundamental resource for the formation of those mediations. That is, this mediation relationship operates within a context of existing meanings, though it is also active in the dynamic which stimulates the construction and dissemination of new meanings. This 'construction' and 'dissemination' process is as much a part of audience activities and practices as it is the role and responsibility of the text producers. Audiences, that is, construct meanings as much as they consume them.

Capital and Culture

Pierre Bourdieu (1977, 1984, 1990; see also Baudrillard, 1981) argues that capitalism and culture change markedly during the course of the twentieth century. According to Bourdieu, capitalist production and consumption become less needs-based and more concentrated through symbolic exchange. That is, by the beginning of the twentieth century capitalism had pretty much supplied the citizens of developed societies with the things they needed for basic survival: food, clothing and shelter. In order to sustain itself, capitalism had to create new needs and new motivations for consumption. Capitalism had developed, of course, through a delicate balancing of demand and supply: its system of differential rewards facilitated differential demand and supply. In other words, capitalism produces a hierarchy of wealth; competition between consumers means that only some products can be afforded by some consumers. This competition produces scarcity: a mansion is more expensive than a hovel because of scarcity of supply and competitive demand. Individuals are motivated to participate in capitalist economy because they see opportunities for satisfaction of their demands and an improvement in their competitive position.

Bourdieu argues that these differential rewards are socially and politically constructed. The various positions on the hierarchy of individuals and groups are determined and fixed within the demand system. Even so, capitalism had created a reasonable level of demand satisfaction across modern societies by the beginning of the twentieth century. While most people didn't own a mansion, they had an income, a dwelling and a level of political representation. New forms of demand could be stimulated through new forms of products and the meanings of these products. For Bourdieu and other commentators these new demands are constituted through the formation of a 'consumer society'. That is, capitalism shifts more toward the exchange of meanings, as products became more intensely symbolized through advertising and the social discourse of 'taste'. Value is placed on products according to their social status, as well as their cost and scarcity. Products (and services) begin to attract a 'symbolic' value which can then be attached to the owner. Thus, while one person might travel to work in a late model BMW, another might ride a Vespa or catch the public bus. In Bourdieu's terms, these symbolic distinctions apply through a broad spectrum of social products and activities, fixing people's status in terms of their 'taste'. Individuals and groups identify each other and their social positioning according to their taste, including their taste in music and clothing styles. Of course there had always been a level of symbolic value attached to products, but through the emergence of consumer society, these symbolic values proliferate along with the proliferation of products and consumer activities.

Bourdieu argues that these discriminations are socially constructed and have no basis in the underlying realities of human existence. People are not born with superior or inferior tastes in cultural products; rather, the economic system of capitalism requires distinctions in order to operate. According to Bourdieu, these operations rely on, and in fact help to create, a system of class discrimination where privilege is maintained over underprivilege. Jean Baudrillard (esp. 1981, 1984a), however, is critical of Bourdieu's reading of symbols and social distinction, arguing that contemporary sign systems cannot be so simply correlated with forms of social power. For Baudrillard, the symbolic force of a BMW is created less through the discrimination of consumption and more through its ability to 'arouse' consumers.

Baudrillard, in fact, begins from a rather different perspective to that of Bourdieu. For Baudrillard, contemporary culture is a deluge of signs, symbols and images. These signs (anything that carries meaning) are proliferating through the volumes of media and informational processes that now distinguish and create contemporary culture. The Princess Di phenomenon, the killings at Columbine, the love affairs of Leonardo DiCaprio – all are constituted through a new, televisual culture, a new reality, a hyperreality, which has no substance and no fixed form. This hyperreality creates new forms of stimulation, new forms of arousal and demand, new forms of erratic consumption. The product becomes intensely sexualized, often through the deployment of a young female body – but this arousal is a simulation and can never be satisfied. The consumer is prompted to act and consume; however, the deluge of images and signs is unending and the urge to consume is never consummated, never quite complete.

In Baudrillard's terms, therefore, the sign overtakes the product as the primary source of arousal and action. Because it is nothing more than a sign, a powerfully sexualized sign, the consumer can never escape its abstraction. The proliferation of signs continues to stimulate. The BMW is sexually imaged and motivates some form of consumption – if not the car, then something else. But ultimately, there is nothing there. The sign is vacant, leading merely to another sign, another amorphous arousal, another vacuous avatar. For Baudrillard, contemporary culture is marked by this absence of material reality. Everything is mediated, and in Baudrillard's extreme view this means that everything is an imitation of an imitation – a simulacra. In these terms, it is possible for Baudrillard (1995) to contend very seriously that 'the Gulf War did not take place' because the whole event was pre-prepared for televisual consumption, pre-digested and presupposed in its outcomes.

Fredric Jameson (1990, 1991) suggests, however, that this new culture betrays itself in a deeper logic whereby the news media are constantly reconstituting themselves in the condition of 'the perpetually new'. The electronic media and the proliferation of signs and symbols actually reduce human value and human culture by compressing time and space. According to Jameson, contemporary culture has 'finally transcended the capacities of the individual human body to locate itself, to organize its immediate surroundings perceptually, and cognitively to map its position in a mappable external world' (1990: 85). The news media, that is, function to concentrate time and information in particular ways that separate us from the past, constituting all knowledge as an historical amnesia. Mediated culture, in this sense, is both a phantasm and a condition of severe loss. Our sense of presence in the culture and in meaning-making has been seriously compromised by the proliferating omnipresence of the media and information systems.

While many analysts of contemporary culture share Jameson's critical concerns, others treat the proliferation of signs and images more optimistically. Richard Dyer (1985), John Fiske (1987, 1989b) and Henry Jenkins (1992), for example, have seen significant connections between the production of popular media texts, especially narrative fictions, and the cognitive and sensual satisfactions of audiences. 'Celebrity', in particular, is identified as the communal link that reconciles consumption

capitalism with the everyday practices and pleasures of individuals within mass, contemporary society. For these authors, and many others impressed by the social and personal potential of popular media, the rendering of human experience in images and information is not to be feared, but to be explored, enjoyed and used by the people who integrate these texts into their own lifeworlds and imaginations.

Experiencing Culture

These varying perspectives represent divergent approaches to the mediation of culture. Roland Barthes (1975) has explained that any representation or symbolization necessarily constitutes a 'text', or system of meanings. For Barthes and other cultural theorists there can be no reality outside the text. In other words, an individual can only relate to, or know, the world around him or her through some form of mediation. In Barthes's sense, everything constitutes a text or sign system: a stop sign, an article of clothing, conversation, a bottle of wine, a tree, a Hollywood movie, a newspaper. Of course, things exist outside the representations of text, but they can have no meaning until they are captured by culture. This means that a distinction between nature and culture is no longer valid, since even natural objects (water, stars, trees) are rendered meaningful by human sign systems.

Thus, all objects in the universe become available to human knowledge and the human mind when they are represented as texts. It should be noted that cultural theorists use various concepts to describe a similar thing: representation, construction, constituitivity, text, discourse, sign, symbolization, language, and signification all refer to the process of mediating the world of actual phenomena in some sort of meaning system. For this book, we will use these concepts pretty much interchangeably, unless otherwise specified through the analysis of a particular theorist. The important thing for cultural analysis is that the world of actual phenomena has no meaning until it is represented. Barthes and others believe, therefore, that we can read or interpret all aspects of human life – including objects, beliefs, ideas, attitudes, behaviours and everyday practices – as we would read any other form of text. For Barthes and others who follow this lead, all aspects of human experience are formed through culture and are therefore 'constructed' or 'mediated' just like a novel or a film.

As we have seen, there are varying perspectives on how culture is formed and mediated, and how these mediations are themselves constituted in relation to social relationships, practices, power and the material conditions in which people live. It is worth noting, in fact, that some cultural analysts emphasize language and meaning-making over material conditions, while others take an opposite view. That is, theorists like Baudrillard believe that the physical conditions of our reality, while important, are determined by the hyper-reality of televisual mediation. Others, such as David Harvey (1989) and Jim McGuigan (1996), argue that it is the actual operations of institutions and their productive capacities which determine the shape and character of culture and meaning-making. As we shall see in the discussions that follow, this variation in emphasis is evident from the very beginnings of cultural theory and analysis, and continues to be a significant point of debate within contemporary cultural studies.

In either case, there is a general agreement among contemporary cultural theorists that the process of mediation is central to our understanding of culture. Culture is formed out of the 'condition' of human experience and human imagining. Experience, practices and artefacts (things) become meaningful when they enter a subject's symbolic order: that is, when they become 'represented' within a general system of meaning. A few points should be noted here:

1 Just as human experiences change over time, so too do our ways of thinking, imagining and making meaning. Culture, therefore, is highly dynamic. For this reason we relate culture to the *processes* of meaning-making; culture is never fixed but is always subject to change.

2 Culture is not the synonym of society, even though the formation of social groupings is critical to the formation of cultural meanings. Thus, while sometimes we might talk about 'a culture', we are generally referring to the meanings that are formed around a particular social grouping. These meanings are implicated in the experiences and imaginings of the individuals who make up the group. The concept 'a culture', therefore, is merely a shorthand description and should not be read simply as 'a society'.

3 Meaning-making involves a complex interaction of social and individual practices and modes of thinking (cognition). It is also critically embedded in the material and historical conditions in which the culture is formed.

4 Culture, therefore, is experienced through rational, emotional, sensate and aesthetic processes.

The concept of 'imagining' usefully summarizes the ways in which we experience culture: the imagination is the space in which all our thoughts and experiences congregate in order to form our meanings. Clearly, this use of the concept of imagining distinguishes it from those conceptions which place imagining in opposition to knowledge, reason, science or facts. That is, just as all things may be text or discourse, all things rely on the forming power of human imagining. Science, while claiming to be objective and disengaged from fiction, sensation or emotions, is nevertheless imagined at its source; it is another mediation, another forming of reality through language and discourse.

The concept of imagining therefore permits a confluence of human processing: rational, cognitive, epistemological (knowing), sensate, emotional, creative. It facilitates the emergence and convergence of meaning-making, social practices and material conditions within the dynamic of human experience. Thus, we can re-configure or re-imagine our relationship with another human being, a former lover, for example, toward whom we have become indifferent or even hostile. The concept of imagining might also help to explain the reconstruction of our individual identities through different social and temporal contexts: for example, through the experiences of migration or education. It explains how an industrial, working-class slum can be re-configured and re-imagined as a trendy, inner-city housing development. The physical space may be only moderately changed, but the cultural imagining is radically altered.

Defining Di

It must be already clear that this assemblage of cultural discourses and imaginings can never be one thing that is easily summarized and explained. In fact, one of the other great points of agreement amongst recent cultural theorists is that contemporary culture is multi-forming, divergent and constantly in dispute. Language wars are present, that is, not only through the engagement of military forces as in Middle East conflicts, but in all forms of meaning-making and culture. The celebrity status of Princess Diana serves to illustrate this point, even though, on the surface, the Diana funeral appears to be one of the most unifying experiences in human history. The life and death of Diana Spencer need to be understood as a series of calamitous and struggling discourses which engage with an enormous number of people's pleasures and pains. The person of Diana – whoever that might have been – is represented or constructed through the mass media and through general public discourses that interact with media texts (Davies, 1999). Her clothes, her hair, her palace, her title, her 'image', her sex, her relationships – all are representations or texts in as much as we attach meaning to them in our everyday practices and communicative encounters. And while this is true for each of us and has always been the defining feature of culture, the Princess Diana phenomenon illustrates the particular capacity of contemporary culture to construct and radiate meanings even through the vacuum of personal knowing. That is to say, our society and culture can function as a mass of accumulated parts because mediated knowing has been able to replace immediate or personal knowing of the other members of that huge communal formation (modern society). Though we know relatively few members of that mass group personally, we are nevertheless able to imagine and identify with a culture or community of other humans because of the mass media, their images, narratives and information. We didn't know Diana personally, but we developed a personal knowing and an emotional engagement through the operations of the media.

The position of the celebrity is therefore fundamentally paradoxical (see Marshall, 1997). Diana is 'of the people' and yet prominent among us. She is constructed by our own capacity for meaning-making and yet delivered to us through the dissemination power of the mass media. Whoever-she-is must respond to what we think and feel she is, and yet we contribute significantly to the discourses that surround, attach themselves to, and produce her. The Diana we know and respond to becomes implicated in our own life experiences; she is not 'out there' as a distinctive, singular and objective fact. Rather, Diana is known only as she is 'mediated' through the texts and discourses that produce her. Thus, she becomes one of us, a living being in the fold of our own relationships, loves, fears, and homes.

Let's consider this in more detail. At the simplest level, of course, Diana Spencer came to represent charm, spontaneity and glamour for the popular imagination (Drew, 1998). This regal beauty hearkens to a range of already existing texts, images and imaginings that have been drawn through the fairytale and popular texts of childhood and beyond. Jacques Derrida (see 1979, 1981) calls this linking of texts and the accumulating of interdependent meanings 'intertextuality'. Thus, our sense of Diana is built around other texts and textual experiences, some of which we might regard as adapted mythologies: narratives that are so frequently repeated that they become embedded in our belief systems or taken-for-granted truths and ideologies. The mass media also rely on, and textually appropriate (borrow from), these textual experiences to enrich, enliven and emotionally inscribe their own particular stories of Diana and her life (see Richards et al., 1999).

The 'celebration' and celebrity-making of Diana can only be understood in terms of these other texts and the propensity of a consumer capitalist culture to *commodify* people as media products. As John Taylor (2000) argues, Diana's appeal is certainly driven by the imaging of regal grace, beauty and charity, though inevitably this commodification implicates certain political and ideological considerations. Specifically, the image is self-legitimating: it confirms its own value and right to give pleasure to its audiences as indeed it confirms the validity of capitalism, capitalist institutions and its media, and the status and substance of the royal heritage itself. John Hartley (1996) has argued that the very idea of a constitutional monarchy continues to be legitimated through the popular media's continual re-presentation of the royal family: 'The "tabloid" and "gossip" media's obsession with the royal gonads is at the cutting edge, as it were, of political journalism in this context' (Hartley, 1996: 12). The image and the institutions which support it are entirely self-interested, driven by an ideology that is predicated on production, consumption, power and profit. Politics and ideology, that is, are necessarily implicated in the construction of the Diana character in the same way as they are implicated in the celebrity creation of movie and popular music stars.

However, and as Hartley himself goes on to ponder, the ideological context of the culture is itself formidably ambiguous. The Diana image is delivered to us by a plutocratic institution which might well have vested interests in the maintenance of elite power formations – celebrity sells and social hierarchies confirm the privilege and media owners. Even so, we need to recognize that it is the interests and consumption practices of ordinary people which actually determine the 'success' of those constructed images. The people ultimately select the image for their own everyday purposes and pleasures. Diana's privilege and power within the culture are sanctioned and permitted, that is, by the interests of her audience – her media subjects (Turnock, 2000).

But even this does not explain the incredible popularity of the image in life and in death. As we examine it more closely, the Diana character was constructed through a remarkable range of competing signs and symbols. Yes, she was charming, gracious and beautiful, and ultimately these qualities were able to evolve into more mature narratives of maternity, abandonment and profound feminine integrity. But equally, Diana's political presence seemed strangely reconciling. The iniquities of inherited privilege and despotic rule are neutralized through the popular imaginings and presentation of Diana's more charitable and democratic demeanour. Those tiaras and dresses that might have radically distanced Diana from her consuming public became relativized: symbols of her charity, her work for the poor and impoverished of the world. As befitting the mythologies of benevolent authority, Diana's charity was both a demonstration of popular and community participation and a validation of her right to prominence and privilege. This 'charitable' demeanour was able to camouflage, it would seem, the social privilege which facilitated the sale in 1997 of one of Diana's dresses for over $200,000 (a silk gown Diana wore when dancing with John Travolta at the White House).

Diana's celebrity, therefore, was intensely political, although the direction and exercise of that 'power' remain invisible or at least evasive. In the clamouring of grief that followed her death, there seemed no space at all for criticism or negative review. The opulent lifestyle and the inebriant circumstances of the accident were largely ignored by the serious and popular press, though had the same fate befallen

socially ascribed villains – criminals, blacks, poor single mothers – the treatment of the issue would have been entirely different. In Diana's case the paparazzi, those voracious and marauding media hyenas, provided an effective focus for public blame – the paparazzi refused to comply with Diana's highly managed image manufacture. The public seemed strangely to forget that the paparazzi and the official press were merely the conduits for its own rabid consumption of the Diana narratives.

Indeed, one of the most telling features of Diana's celebrity was the ongoing battle for control of her image and representation. While the Diana celebrity had an immense capacity to increase audience ratings and circulation figures, control of the image was more extensively waged between different commercial, ethical and institutional interests. This 'struggle to signify', as Stuart Hall calls it, was most intensely manifest in the aftermath of Diana's death when the official Diana media machine was railing against the tabloid press, which was in turn railing against the paparazzi. For their part, the paparazzi, or unofficial celebrity press, represented themselves as the defenders of 'free speech' and editorial independence; they told the true stories because they weren't constrained by Diana's public relations machinery. It was the paparazzi who released 'unofficial' photographs of Diana's life for the intrigue and pleasures of the general public. The paparazzi fed the rabid and salacious interests of Diana's public, contributing to her fame and her celebrity mystique.

These internal media ructions seemed peculiarly subdued during the period immediately following Diana's death. As Mick Hume (1998) has pointed out, the petty ethical squabbling turned to a general mood of embarrassment, if not shame. The Diana consumers articulated their grief through blame of others. The media culture that pursued all in order to make it available for the sensate pleasures of the consumer was suddenly under scrutiny. The media were blamed for Diana's death and an ethical truce was called as 2.5 billion people watched the regal coffin as it was charioted through the streets to Westminster. The media had gone too far and brought about her death, but at least they were available for our own personal grieving.

What is clear, then, is that our ability to make sense of the world we live in is now absolutely dependent on our relationship with the media. It is not that we are 'conditioned' by the various information and entertainment media, but rather that we are a part of them since our knowledge of ourselves and our world is filtered through their images and language. It may well be that the increasing abstractness of the world actually elicits an equally strong, though contradictory and unconscious, desire for moral and ideological substance – a 'grounded' reality that is not so evanescent, ephemeral and contingent. The mythology of Diana, her regality and substantive links with the deep past, represent a way of imagining the world as a 'community' of subjects or citizens. The Diana narrative, that is, may well provide for people that sense of community and social consensus which contemporary culture, for all its pleasures, plenitude and possibilities, has rendered more abstract, if not elusive.

National Culture and Televisual Culture

Benedict Anderson (1991) has argued that the formation of 'nation', national community and national identity is intrinsically linked to the development of the print media. It was possible for individuals to imagine their participation in a national community because mass printing enabled the broad distribution of common language, values, ideas, norms, practices and ideologies. In other words, a national culture was formed in relation to the medium of print. From all that we have said about a televisual culture assembling around celebrity figures like Princess Diana and global events like the Sydney 2000 Olympic Games, it might seem that the notion of a national culture is in sharp decline. However, the concept of culture we have been developing in this chapter accommodates various levels of formation and location. Indeed, nation continues as a primary cultural definer for many people, even in the context of an increasingly globalized, postmodern world. Many people would continue to answer the question, 'What is your culture?' with a response embedded in the concept of nation and national characteristics. For many people the nation-state continues as the pre-eminent social, economic and institutional referent – culture is primarily articulated through state-sponsored norms, values and ideologies.

The point here, and indeed the point of our discussion of Diana as an example of televisual global culture, is that meanings cluster through various levels of human experience and practice. The nation-state may represent one significant level of human culture, but an individual can participate in a wide range of social groupings and their cultures: family, friendship group, religion, nation and the world. Televisual culture transacts these various social groupings so that such things as ethics, political beliefs and practices may be influenced by the meanings that are formed and distributed through mediated imagery and information. Our relationship with televisual cultural phenomena like Diana is constituted in terms of, and in conjunction with, all our other cultural layers, levels and experiences. We cannot, therefore, draw simple boundaries around culture. The lines we do draw must be open, porous and evanescent, ready to absorb new meanings and texts, new practices and ideologies. Culture cannot be simply located within a geography, social group, organization or informational flow. Rather, culture is to be located as a transitory and open category – an assemblage of meanings and practices which become available to our understanding and investigation. In this sense a national culture can exist; a family culture can exist. Equally, a televisual culture can exist, as can a culture shaped around media texts like The Beatles, *The Simpsons* or gothic street culture. Individuals can be 'located' within any number of these formations at any time.

WHAT IS CULTURE?

We have talked generally about culture in terms of meaning-making and human imagining. As we shall discover in the course of this book, however, there are numerous ways of defining and elucidating culture. Our own examination of these theories will be based on a rather inclusive approach to culture. This approach will be constructed around the following definitions:

1   *Culture is an assemblage of imaginings and meanings*. Culture is constructed by humans in order to communicate and create community. While society and community are assemblages of people, culture is an assemblage of imaginings and meanings. Culture begins with an imagining of the world about us; these imaginings are represented in some way. That is, they are formed in discourse, language, symbols, signs and texts – all concepts applied to meaning systems. These imaginings and meanings, however, can never be fixed or solidified, but remain assemblages that can be dismantled through time, space and human action. That is, the 'system' into which meanings are formed is far from absolute and immutable. The meanings are put together for a purpose within a particular historical and spatial (material) context. Meaning systems are always subject to the return of imagining and vice versa. Imagining and meanings operate to form one another, but they can never be relied on as stable and sustaining formations. Meaning and imagining can at any time confirm or destabilize one another.

2   *Culture is an assemblage of imaginings and meanings that may be consonant, disjunctive, overlapping, contentious, continuous or discontinuous*. In other words culture is always transitional, open and unstable. As we shall see, language and meaning systems have often been treated as solid and fixed formations. However, meaning systems like language are capable of producing misunderstandings and non-meaning as well as meanings. At any one time, a culture can be subject to an infinite array of meaning disputes and gaps. There may be a 'dominant' meaning or 'dominant' ideology which attempts to direct meanings in particular ways, but a culture can never be closed since it is made up of competing interests and many different individuals (subjects) and groups.

3   *Culture is an assemblage of imaginings and meanings that may be consonant, disjunctive, overlapping, contentious, continuous or discontinuous. These assemblages may operate through a wide variety of human social groupings and social practices*. This means that we can speak of a family culture, a national culture, an ethnic culture, a global culture, a work culture, a religious culture, a university culture, a football culture, a

Plates 1.1 and 1.2 Culture is formed through various levels of human social groupings and communities. The 2000 Sydney Olympic Games (Plate 1.1) brought together around 3.5 billion people into a single global televisual

technological culture, a gay culture, and so on. Some cultural analysts refer to these social groupings, or some of them, as 'institutions'; to this extent, individuals may be subject to the cultural meanings that are produced and imposed by large and historically enduring institutions such as governmental institutions, the 'family', or media corporations.

An individual human subject may participate in many different cultures simultaneously. Each of these cultures may have its own system of meanings which articulates itself through norms and values, beliefs, political ideals, rituals (repeated behaviours), clothing styles, vocabulary, status positions, and so on. A meaning system, that is, has many different dimensions which are formed through various levels of dominant values. In fact, each culture may be more or less rigid in the structure of its associations or assemblages. Rigid rules, for example, may apply to the culture of the biker gang; these rules may define power relationships, economy, the position of the rider in the road line, sexual practices and clothing styles. Individuals may experience severe dissonance through their participation in different cultures. A Muslim living in the United States, for example, may wish to practise polygamy, even though this transgresses the rules and dominant ideologies of the national culture. Equally, a heroin user may experience significant dissonance in a professional workplace.

A perpetual problem for the study of culture(s) is the question of dominant and subordinate or marginal cultures. The meanings that are constituted within these smaller social groupings and their cultures may operate as part of a much larger social grouping such as nation or 'modern Western culture'. These prevailing or 'dominant' cultures with their dominant meanings may be articulated through dominant belief systems, ritualized practices and ideologies. The relationship between dominant and subordinate/marginal cultures is a principal theme in cultural theory and cultural analysis.

4 *Culture is an assemblage of imaginings and meanings that may be consonant, disjunctive, overlapping, contentious, continuous or discontinuous. These assemblages may operate through a wide variety of human social groupings and social practices. In contemporary culture these experiences of imagining and meaning-making are intensified through the proliferation of mass media images and information. As we have discussed*

Plates 1.1 and 1.2 (*Continued*)

community. For all their immense diversity, the members of this televisual community nonetheless shared significant practices, values and meanings through their experience of the Olympics text. Plate 1.2 presents a cremation ritual on the Indonesian island of Nusa Lembongan. The cremation was witnessed by the island's community of around 150 people. This highly localized custom has been practised for centuries, having been adapted from the Hindu rituals of neighbouring Bali. Unlike Bali, however, Nusa Lembongan's community and practices are yet to be fully conscripted into the cultural net of global tourism. Impecunious mourners on Lembongan may have to wait several years to be able to afford the cremation of a family member. On Bali cremations are frequently funded by the major international hotels in order to ensure 'authentic' cultural entertainment for their guests.

above, the electronic media have intensified particular cultural trends and processes during the twentieth century. The particular characteristics of electronic communication have rendered the problem of cultural dispute, dissonance, instability and transition more acute. Previously distant human cultural formations have been brought into greater propinquity, creating the circumstances for a proliferation of cultural discourses. These proliferating discourses stimulate ever-increasing possibilities for new meanings and new non-meanings or communication gaps.

For example, as the media products of the United States penetrate non-Anglo/European cultures, there is a remarkable proliferation of new discourses and disputes. In the period since World War II (1939–45), American films have introduced the discourse of romantic love and mouth kissing to cultures which had only deployed it as a marginal or fetishistic practice. The meaning of mouth kissing and the sexual mores associated with its deployment have been widely contested in countries like Japan, Korea and Vietnam.

CONTEMPORARY THEORY AND CULTURAL STUDIES

Focus and Structure of the Book

The three principal aims of this book are as follows:

1 To outline and elucidate the intellectual lineages which lead to contemporary cultural theory and cultural studies. In particular, this book seeks to provide a framework for understanding, comparing and assessing these modes of theory and analysis.

2 To elucidate the principal approaches deployed in contemporary cultural theory and analysis. These approaches inform much of the analysis of specific cultural sites and phenomena.
3 To identify key locations and issues in contemporary cultural analysis and thus present insights into the nature and operations of contemporary culture.

The current book, therefore, presents a comprehensive vision of culture and cultural studies. To this extent, it is presented in two parts. Part One examines the ways in which culture is formed and analysed. This part examines, in particular, the ways in which the concept of culture is problematized in humanities and social science research. Specifically, Part One traces how theorists seek to explain society in terms of a 'symbolic order': the ways in which the organization of people into large social groups is facilitated through 'orderly' and systematic processes of meaning-making. This notion of a symbolic order is translated into the broader notion of culture. Part One also demonstrates how culture becomes implicated in the complex relationships of power, ideology and signification. The part measures these various theories and modes of analysis against the transdisciplinary and language-based model outlined above. Part Two develops this model through a more specific reading of contemporary culture. These modes of analysis are deployed through specific cultural locations: cultural geography, identity and subjectivity, the body, new communications technology, and culture and government. In a very real sense, this part maps the terrain of cultural theory and cultural studies, providing models for specific modes of analysis.

It is important to note that the current book proceeds from a particular theoretical and ideological premise. To this extent, it is like any other text and needs to be read

Table 1.1   *The Modern/The Postmodern*

The modern	The postmodern
Enlightenment	Post-Enlightenment
Logic-centred	Image/media
Scientific method	Chaos/Quantum
Absolute truth	Relativism
Humanism/liberalism	Cultural specificity
Homogeneous	Heterogeneous
Europe-centred	Global/multicultural
Universal laws	Deconstruction
Social structure	Individual pleasure
Industrialism	Post-industrialism
Materialism	Symbolism
Atoms	Information
Patriarchy	Sexual fluidity
High art	Popular media
Chronology	Time/space compression
Broadcast	Multiple creators
Reality	Simulation
Conclusion	Inconclusive/language play

with the same critical sensitivity that is recommended for all cultural analysis. Thus, our presentation of the broad field of cultural theories and modes of analysis is informed by a specific critical perspective, one that is clearly constituted around the definition of culture we have outlined above. While the actual character of contemporary culture will be discussed in considerable detail, most particularly in the second part, a few preliminary remarks about the focus and direction of the current book are worth making.

Modernism and Postmodernism

Contemporary cultural theory and cultural studies derive from a broad range of academic and intellectual sources: various zones of social theory, anthropology, Marxism, feminism and language theory. While this book examines these sources as part of a general lineage, a number of recent studies

have suggested that contemporary cultural analysis is formed around a distinct intellectual and cultural break with older areas of social inquiry and outmoded forms of thinking. Most commonly, these studies have suggested that contemporary analysis is fundamentally a 'postmodern' activity which focuses on the general condition of a postmodern, global culture: that is, cultural studies is a postmodern discipline which analyses postmodern culture. Often, these studies place postmodern culture in opposition to an older modern culture. The differences between the two can be summarized as in Table 1.1.

A good deal will be said about this putative cultural and historical divide and the mode of analysis which constitutes it. However, it is important to establish at the outset that the approach of the current book is a little different. Specifically, we will accept the notion of cultural and historical specificity and the general argument which suggests that history may be discontinuous as much as continuous. We would also agree that contemporary cultural analysis should interrogate the problematics of diversity and difference, and the significant characteristics of the electronic media in the formation of contemporary culture. Our dispute with the cultural divide argument is simply one of emphasis or focus. Just as there can be little doubt that contemporary culture derives from previous cultural experiences, so contemporary analysis derives from previous intellectual traditions. Even when current ideas reject earlier ones, there remains a significant degree of indebtedness. To this extent, we would suggest that all categories of history or ideas are 'relative' rather than 'absolute' since they are ultimately and inevitably connected to all other history and ideas. While it thus disputes with the modern in important ways, the postmodern is nevertheless connected to and derives from the modern.

The emphasis of the current book, therefore, is on the connections as well as the points of divergence in the reading and analysis of culture. Our study incorporates a broad discussion of the foundation and formation of culture as a matter of knowledge and dispute. In our view, the genesis of cultural theory is formed within the genesis of culture itself. It is only when culture becomes problematized – when it can no longer be assumed or taken for granted – that the concept of 'culture' congeals as a necessary analytical tool. That is, the crisis of understanding that accompanies modernization has sensitized many intellectuals to the problems associated with meaning-making, communication, social practices and society generally. To this extent, the concept of culture is developed as a way of accessing and interrogating this broad assemblage of issues and problems. In many ways, culture comes into existence when it is identified and articulated as a

concept; culture is 'uncovered' in the formative work of cultural theory and cultural analysis. Of course, more recent changes ('postmodernization') continue to place pressure on the concept and our capacity to know and understand our contemporary world. The increasing diversity and differentiations within developed societies have prompted many disciplines to adopt the concept as an analytical tool. Our aim is to present 'culture' through these diverse paradigms and theories, measuring their respective strengths and weaknesses. We would seek, that is, to illuminate the links and disputes that exist within the broad field of cultural analysis in order to contribute, finally, to a more thorough understanding of our culture(s).

The Individual – Collective Tension

Table 1.1 clearly illustrates the perceived differences between a modern and a postmodern culture. This characterization of the two historical formations suggests that modernism is fundamentally universal, absolute, homogenizing, statically structured and founded on notions of an absolute truth. Postmodernism, on the other hand, is a culture replete with pluralism and relative truths. Postmodernism is clearly related to the conditions of an electronically mediated culture. In many ways, the concept of postmodernism appears to approximate the mediated culture described in our Princess Diana story: the people may be mourning the passing of modernism with its great promise of cultural solidity, social stability and the perpetuity of a utopian ideal. The passing of Diana may be a microcosm for the passing of integrity, morality and absolute truth. The mediated culture that is expressed through the Diana funeral, with its audience of around 2.5 billion people, represents a perpetual nostalgia of the postmodern age.

In Chapter 7 we will discuss in detail the validity of the modern-postmodern great divide theory. For the moment, however, it is worth focusing on one particular aspect of the divide, one which returns perpetually as a problematic in the general theorizing and analysis of culture. Specifically, the tension between the individual and the group or collective appears as a constant theme in cultural and social analysis from its very beginnings. In many respects, this should not surprise us since the whole structure and orientation of contemporary culture have been built around the resolution of individual and collective needs, laws, meanings and interests.

Many of the theorists who celebrate the arrival of a postmodern culture argue that the modern period articulated this problem, but failed dismally to overcome it. If we refer again to Table 1.1, we can see that the postmodern is characterized by an embrace of particularities and pluralism as it rejects the homogeneity and universalism of modernism. That is, modernism is supposed to have attempted to reconcile the problem of individual and collective needs through the establishment of universal rules. Scientific method, mathematics, theories of a cohesive and ordered society, democratic institutions – all are designed to resolve particularity through its incorporation in a universal system governed by logical rules. The celebrants of postmodernism argue that this modernist approach has failed us because it subsumes individualism and freedom beneath the weight of universal interests. Postmodernism celebrates difference and diversity. The appropriate subject of cultural studies is, therefore, centered on diversity, rather than commonality.

The problem with this approach is that it tends to simplify excessively the character and complexity of modernism through its celebration of a postmodern alternative. Modernism and the rise of mass society and mass culture clearly implicate the tension between individual and collective interests. Modernism has made numerous attempts to overcome this problem, but every attempt seems to have been frustrated by the problem's persistence. In fact, at every point the increasing 'massification' of society with its constant requirements of maintenance, order and cohesion is confronted by an equally persistent individualism. Not surprisingly, therefore, the rise of theories of collectivity is accompanied by equally potent theories of individualism. The celebrants of postmodernism claim to have resolved the problem through a complete jettison of collective interests, except inasmuch as they are an incidental outcome of the liberation of individual pleasures, interests and the capacity for self-determination.

Our aim here is not to resolve this debate, but rather to highlight it in relation to the focus of our study. Specifically, this tension between individual and collective interests lies behind many of the debates about culture, power and meaning-making. It is present, for example, in the story of Diana, where the collective of the audience might seem to constitute a particularly homogeneous formation, and where Diana herself might appear to constitute a single, shared institution of power. Diana's privilege may be justified in terms of her own personal pleasure as well as in the personal pleasures rendered to the celebrity consumers. We might ask critical questions, however, about a culture which so expansively mourns the passing of one person, but which obliterates thousands in Kosovo or Iraq with barely a murmur. We might compare critically the extravagant rewards and pleasures of a few celebrity musicians in the First World with the starvation of millions of children in the Third World. We might ask how it is possible in the US for two juveniles to go on a mad killing rampage, while gun lobbyists continue to proclaim a generic right to 'bear arms'.

Disputes over power and language are central, therefore, to the individual–collective tension. This theme will return to us many times during the course of this book, not merely as a problematic of contemporary cultural theorizing, but also as an active component of the imaginings that bind and divide us.

MODERNISM

While some theorists see postmodernism as part of a great divide, others regard it as a footnote to the continuation of the modern. Still others dismiss the concept altogether, even though they may agree with its general description of the contemporary cultural landscape. In any case, an understanding of modernism is necessary for our broader reading of contemporary culture and its theorization. The key characteristics and contradictions of modernism are outlined below.

Capitalism

Capitalism developed as the primary economic system in Europe from the seventeenth century onwards. Capitalism involves the manufacture, sale and consumption of products and the development of a mercantile or trading class of people. These products attract value because they are needed by consumers; the products attract a higher or lower value depending on the level of demand and supply. Generally speaking, the higher the demand, the higher the value (price), and vice versa. Classical economics tells us that the market (level of demand and competition between consumers) will ultimately determine the value of any product.

There is a paradox operating here, though. Capitalism is a collective system which depends on competition between individuals and groups in order to function. These hierarchies of ability to pay will be corrupted by any external interference to the 'free' market process. Collective forms of behaviour (cartels, monopolies, tariffs, public enterprises, etc.) can disturb the greater collectivity of the system. Moreover, there is a fine balance between sufficient scarcity of supply and sufficient demand both for individual products and services and in the overall 'economy' (exchange system). This fine balance is problematized in the following ways:

1 The market system assumes a level of competitive equality. In fact the competitive position of capitalist players is uneven from the beginning of a life to its conclusion. Individuals and groups use their competitive advantage to maintain and enhance their own, and their group's, relative advantage in the hierarchy.

2 Capitalists manipulate these advantages in order to enhance their own and their products' strategic position. Scarcity of supply is manipulated in order to increase product value. Of course there is a danger that this limiting of access to products might risk the loss of demand altogether.

3 Across the broader span of the capitalist system, this manipulation of supply – demand leads frequently to excessive (inflation) and depressive (recession) levels of demand.

4 Capitalism is always seeking to increase value by reducing costs involved in production. In particular, capitalism seeks to remove the cost of labour in production; however, labour provides the income necessary for workers to demand products. Capitalism, therefore, perpetually defers the obliteration of labour,

consoling itself through the constant constraint of wages and salaries.

5 More broadly, political and ethical challenges are posed to capitalism because some people have greater access to capitalist pleasures than others. Thus, while everyone may want access to a Rolls-Royce, capitalism determines that only a few people can afford it. This limited access increases value and profit for the producer as it necessarily limits the life pleasures of the majority of consumers.

Liberal Humanism and Democracy

The political philosophy of liberalism developed in Europe during the eighteenth and nineteenth centuries. Essentially liberalism (being liberal or free) emphasizes the dignity of the individual, individual rights and freedoms (see Mill, 1971). Humanism is an ethical philosophy which also became increasingly important during the rise of modernism. Compassion, justice, equality, respect and a belief in the fundamental goodness of human beings are the chief characteristic of humanism. For some thinkers (e.g., Aldous Huxley) humanism is a secular ethics, while others (e.g., Matthew Arnold) believe that humanism is the fundamental value of Christianity. Liberal humanism combines compassion and respect with a belief in individual freedom; it informs much of the political debate over manhood and universal suffrage during the nineteenth century.

During this period, democratic institutions became the physical expression of the liberal humanist ideal. Social cohesion was supposedly achieved through the reconciliation of individual and collective interests. Each person would vote for his or her representative, and differences would be resolved through parliamentary debate. Social order, law and governmental authority were the physical expression of the ideology of democracy and liberal humanism. The state, paradoxically, became the protector of individual rights and freedoms, even though these freedoms might at any point be forfeited through the greater interests of the state: for example, in war or through criminal actions. Beyond these extreme conditions, however, the state, along with its laws, becomes self-confirming and self-aggregating in ways that take it well away from the personal lives of those it claims to represent. The freedom it claims to protect is therefore threatened by the authority it wields.

While this system of representation aims to reconcile collective and individual interests, power is not evenly distributed and remains more or less the privilege of particular social elites. White, educated and middle-class men who are predisposed to public oratory and adversarial debate continue to predominate in contemporary parliaments; women, particular migrant groups, youth, indigenous peoples and the unemployed are significantly under-represented. Edward Said (1993) argues that this devolution of power through the ethos of liberal humanism obscures the historical exclusion of colonized people from its ambit. The wealth of European nations which coupled liberal humanism and democracy was forged, Said claims, on the slavery and impoverishment of the colonized peoples, who were not part of the representative system (see Chapter 10).

Mass Media

A number of cultural historians and theorists have identified a significant relationship between social and cultural change, and the development of new communications technologies and communicative practices (e.g., McLuhan, 1964; Marvin,

1988; Carey, 1989; Negroponte, 1995). Benedict Anderson (1991; see also Eisenstein, 1983) has traced the development of nation and national consciousness through the dissemination of high-speed printing and the emergence of the mass media. He demonstrates that the formation of nation as a linguistical or discursive possibility was necessarily associated with the means of mass societal communication. With significantly expanding populations, trade and urbanization, social networks required mechanisms for access and dissemination of information, socialization and identity-building. Books, newspapers and electrical communication systems enabled the vast tension between social structures and individuals to be mediated. The mass media, in fact, became the institutional fabric of that 'massification', facilitating the 'liberation' of individuals and the formation of democratic structures. Not surprisingly, however, this powerful communication facility has been subject to assertions of control and institutional processes of persuasion and deceit. The mass media, therefore, allow for greater homogeneity as well as the possibility of individual freedom and the broader distribution of alternative ideas and ideologies. As we shall see in subsequent discussions of the media and popular culture, this paradox manifests itself in the relationship between audiences and the texts of the mass media. In this sense, we could ask, are the Diana audiences free in their choosing and pleasures, or are they the dupes of marketing and media organizations?

intellectual and aesthetic conventions, Romanticism is itself a confluence of numerous positions and perspectives, some of which are entirely at odds with one another. In particular, the idealism, individualism and imagination celebrated by the Romantics is implicated in the political and social conditions of the times, including the substantial logics that produced the Enlightenment and the politics of liberal humanism. Thus, while scholars often conceive of Romanticism in opposition to industrialism and the decaying environments of urbanized Europe, it is also true that the Romantic solutions to these serious social problems tended to intensify, rather than relieve, the capitalist imperatives of individualism and self-interest. Romanticism challenged the alienating and dehumanizing effects of technology and industrialization, but it did so through a general rendering of individualism and individual freedom and not through a more substantive questioning of the capitalist or modernist projects. Romanticism celebrated the moral possibilities of personal and spiritual transcendence; it praised the virtues of nature, naturalism, the imagination and reason, though some significant Romantic writers remained deeply suspicious of direct political activism, the industrial working classes, Marxism and the French Revolution. Even so, there were a number of Romantic writers, social theorists and artists who were politically utopian, seeking a social formation that would release humans from spiritual and moral ignominy and social decay.

Romanticism

Modernism is also characterized by sets of ideas and ideals, the most formidable and persistent of which is Romanticism (see Chapters 2 and 3). However, like all great

Enlightenment

The Enlightenment or 'bringing the light' is, like Romanticism, a constant of modernism. Rising through the Mediterranean Renaissance and Elizabethan England, the

Enlightenment revives and extends Classical (Greek and Roman) principles of value and learning. The pinnacle of such learning is science and the philosophy of science (nature). Nature, that is, becomes ideologized as the ideal toward which human society should aspire. To know nature was to know the human condition. Descartes, Hume, Locke, Kant and even Hegel, each in his own different way, drew parallels between nature and the human, urging a form of universal knowledge (and language) that would facilitate human access to the source of 'all-knowing'. This knowledge, however, requires descriptions of the universe which separate the human self – with all its emotions, psychological and communicative inconsistencies – from the operations of the external world of nature and material phenomena. What is generally referred to as the subject–object split occurs as the Enlightenment seeks to explain humans in terms of natural laws. The logical operations of the mind (reason) become the fount of all knowledge.

This persistent interest in scientific knowledge or truth underpins many of the substantial ideologies of modernism. In its ideal form, democracy is based on the general distribution of truth through public education and the news media. The rational operation of systems – including systems of economy and government – is based on notions of truth. Our world seems bound by debates which continue to assume the existence of truth, even though much of what passes as objective truth is a positioned form of persuasion, or relative truth (one which is more true than another claim).

Consciousness, Epistemology, Ontology, Universalism

Modernism and the Enlightenment became particularly interested in the problems of reality and how humans know and understand that reality. As we shall see in Chapter 2, philosophy developed various concepts in order to explain the process of 'knowing' the world, many of which combined elements of reason, scientific methods, mysticism and Romanticism. Some of these concepts are outlined here:

1. Consciousness refers to the processes of knowing or being aware of the world. Some theorists use the term to refer to an awareness or knowledge of the non-visible or non-material dimensions of the world. When defined in this way, consciousness becomes more mystical and has a spiritual or theological component. Many modernists believe that consciousness is something which humans share as a sub-surface or spiritual awareness of the essential fabric of themselves and the world around them. This consciousness of the non-material conditions of the universe, according to some theories, binds us to one another and to the world of objects.

2. Epistemology is the study of knowledge. Eighteenth- and nineteenth-century philosophy was particularly interested in the problem of knowledge and how we know the world. Epistemology invariably theorizes notions of 'reason' and 'the mind', which are central concepts in the formation of modernism.

3. Ontology, or the study of essence, refers generally to the idea that there is a dimension of reality which exists below the visible, material surface. Again, this idea suggests that the universe has a 'metaphysical' dimension which is its true or essential character.

4. Universalism suggests that all things in the universe or in the human world can be explained by a single, inclusive theory. Modernism offers various types

of universalistic theories. Karl Marx, for example, developed a theory which could explain all of human history and the state of society. G.W.F. Hegel offered an explanation for all history and all nature. Scientific method was developed as a universal approach to knowledge and truth.

Freedom

The question of freedom is central to all the other contradictions outlined above. Quite obviously, the freedom explicated through the liberal democratic tradition has been built around institutional and representative political systems, as well as the morals and values that have been generally attributed to humanist individualism. Immanuel Kant, like Descartes and other Enlightenment philosophers, saw morality as an imperative of nature; the task of science and art was to reveal these imperatives for human instruction. Clearly, the tension between individual and collective rights is central to the formation of 'freedom'. The French Romantic philosopher Jean-Jacques Rousseau articulates this conundrum, attempting to essentialize individual freedom through the rational reconstruction of the state. Rousseau rejects medieval conceptions of 'man' as the Fallen who must be taught goodness. Rousseau recalls the day he had sat beneath a tree and envisioned man's natural goodness:

Oh, sir, if ever I could have written even the quarter of what I saw and felt under that tree, with what clarity should I have revealed all the contradictions of the social system, with what force would I have exposed all the abuse of our institutions, in what simple terms would I have demonstrated that man is naturally good, and that it is through these institutions alone that man becomes bad. (from Hendel, 1937: 208)

The innate goodness of man, therefore, can be expressed through the moral integrity of the parliament and state. The difficulty of reconciling the needs of a society's aggregation of groups and individuals is largely overcome through the ideal of mutuality and free will. According to Rousseau, the constant will of all the members of the state represents the 'general will of all'. The interests of an individual citizen are never overridden by parliament; these interests are incorporated into the general interests of the state. In other words, parliament's particular decision over a particular problem is less important than the action of making that decision – freedom is constituted and assured in the very act of making a decision. An individual's freedom is confirmed every time parliament makes a decision, even if that decision on the surface seems to transgress the interests of an individual. The individual is supreme, but this supremacy is articulated exclusively through democracy and democratic institutions. The modernist project, therefore, is completed through the reconciliation of the individual and the system. Cultural studies revisits this problem, asking directly whether reconciliation is ever possible. For cultural studies, freedom becomes much more than the process of institutional representation, which is a single and highly localized perspective of what it means to be free (emancipated, liberated). Questions of freedom and governmentality are consistently present in contemporary cultural analysis. An emphasis on difference, identity and individual subjectivity seeks to extend Rousseau's Romantic reconciliation.

KEY CONCEPTS

Modernism informs many of the debates and discussions in contemporary cultural theory, including discussions on postmodernism and its various interests. In the chapters that follow we will confront a substantial variety of ideas, perspectives and approaches to culture. The following definitions provide a basis for dealing with these many contending readings of contemporary culture.

Discourse

Discourse is a common concept in cultural theory and cultural studies. For most theorists it simply means a 'regulated' system of meanings or representations. Discourse produces the meanings of the world (knowledge) in an intelligible way; we understand an object, event, person or practice because it is placed within the symbolic or discursive order. It is important to note that this discursive order actually excludes alternative meanings and meaning possibilities. A pen, for example, has meaning within the discursive order of modern society. The same artefact, however, may have no meaning in the culture of tribal or other pre-modern societies. Similarly, non-marital sex may be constituted as 'good' within particular discursive systems, but may be excluded entirely from the discursive order of other cultures.

Language, images, song lyrics and musical patterns, traffic signals – all constitute forms of discourse. These meaning systems are generally studied in operation. That is, cultural analysts will look, for example, at the discourses employed in a particular form of advertising; we may also look at particular themes such as contemporary discourses on gender. As noted above, discourse is sometimes used interchangeably with similar concepts such as representation, textualization, language and signification. Some theorists prefer to treat discourse as the more micro or local

operations of a text; that is, a text is the meaning system and the discourses are its individual constituencies. Thus, we might talk about the discourses on race that are deployed in the film (text) *Chinatown*; we might also talk in terms of discourses on violence or criminality.

Michel Foucault, a French language theorist and historian, believes that the operations of meaning-making (discourse) are always associated with relationships of power (see Chapter 5). For Foucault and others who follow this perspective, discourse and power are so thoroughly interrelated that they constitute a virtual compound: 'discourse/power'. One must always operate in reference to the other. Discourse, therefore, is an essential part of human relationships and human knowledge. 'Knowledge/power' can only exist in relation to discourse.

Power

Power is generally considered to be something which enables one person or group to exert their will and interests over others. There are two general approaches to power in cultural theory. First, it is considered to be attached to social structures like class, ethnicity and gender; this is often regarded as a modernist approach. It claims that power is a facility of the capitalist hierarchy whereby certain groups maintain privilege in a relatively ongoing manner. Marxists, for example, believe that this power is unjustly and disproportionately exerted by an elite ruling class over subordinate classes (see Chapter 3). Liberal humanists believe that these variations in power need to be checked and continually reconciled with the needs of subjugant groups; democracy and public education have been the most commonly cited mechanisms for managing the unevenness of power.

The second approach to power is less concerned with major social structures and more concerned with personal manifestations and experiences of power. This 'microphysics' sees power in terms of process and exchangeability. All people are engaged in relationships that involve power. However, power, as it is experienced at the level of the individual body, is quite unstable and may be deployed and redeployed in an infinite series of processes and exchanges. Even a conversation can involve disruptions and exchanges of power. Sexuality is experienced through power. Consumption and media viewing will also involve differentials and exchanges of interest, acceptance, negation, taste – all of which are informed by power. For example, power may be mobilized in a text – viewer relationship when the viewer chooses to watch or not watch a particular programme. Power may also be mobilized when a viewer discusses programmes with partners and friends. Debates about which movie to see, which seat to take, which confectionery to eat, whether to kiss on the first date – all involve the microphysics of power.

Modernism, Modern Society, Contemporary Culture

The term 'modern' is used in various ways in cultural studies and cultural theory. Its general definition, 'of recent times', became corrupted during the 1960s when art and literature critics began to speak of a 'postmodern' aesthetics. Clearly this post-modernism refers to an aesthetics which is 'more recent' (avant–garde) and more adventurous than the aesthetics of modernism. In this usage, 'the modern' is often restricted to a particular style of art, literature and architecture which is predominant in the nineteenth century: for example,

Dickens, Thackeray, George Eliot, Zola, Maupassant, Whitman. High modernism generally refers to the predominant aesthetics of the early to mid-twentieth century: for example, Joyce, Camus, Dostoevsky, Faulkner, Picasso, Braque, Goya.

As we have noted above, this aesthetic description has been transformed by social criticism and areas of cultural studies. A number of critics now apply the modern and the postmodern as divisions in chronology (sometimes called periodization). The move from a modern to a postmodern historical phase is often associated with the arrival and deployment of particular forms of communication technology – especially the widespread deployment of satellite technology and the computer. In this sense, the modern is replaced by the postmodern around two to three decades ago. By and large, we will try to minimize confusion by using the terms 'modern' and 'postmodern' only in relation to one another.

When speaking about today's cultural experiences, we will most often use the term 'contemporary culture' or 'contemporary society'. This is a shorthand reference to the very complex associations, assemblages and meaning-making processes which constitute today's various cultural forms and cultures.

Ideology

There are various ways of using and defining the concept of ideology. In general use, ideology refers to a set of politically related beliefs. In this sense, there may be an ideology which informs conservative, liberal and labour-based political parties. There may be a communist, Nazi or feminist ideology. We may have a personal political ideology which leads us to make particular choices.

As it is used in cultural studies, however, ideology can take a more specialized meaning. Mostly, this meaning derives from Karl Marx's social and political theories. Marx believed that ideology was a kind of 'false consciousness', a set of beliefs which are propagated by the ruling classes and which the underclasses take up as their own. That is, the interests of the ruling classes become part of a generalized social belief system. Later Marxists have offered some extensions and variations on Marx's original definition, most particularly in relation to the operations of a culture's belief system. Louis Althusser (1971), for example, seeks to understand why subordinate groups in a society appear to be so compliant with their oppression. His answer is basically that a 'dominant ideology' exists in the culture. This dominant ideology informs the 'dominant culture', which, according to Althusser, constrains human liberation. Subordinate classes comply with their oppression because they have absorbed the interests and beliefs of the ruling classes into their own common-sense view of things.

Seattle Under Siege

Protesters continued to blockade the World Economic Forum, bringing chaos to the streets of Seattle. Authorities have condemned the action, describing it as a futile and ignorant assault on the undeniable benefits of free trade. Forum organizer Hermolt Schmidt has told the protesters that violence could offer no solutions. 'We have invited protesters to submit their concerns in an orderly and peaceful manner. In fact many of the concerns of anti-globalists are discussed inside the Forum,' Mr Schmidt explained. 'This is a forum for the sharing of ideas. The protesters' blockade is infringing our rights to free speech and the orderly conduct of our business'.

The World Economic Forum was addressed last night by the world's richest man, Bill Gates. Mr Gates, head of software super-giant Microsoft, explained to the Forum that the opening up of world trade would benefit all members of the global community. With the success of the Internet new ways of buying and selling goods were being opened up all the time. The poorest people of the world would undoubtedly benefit from more open trade, Mr Gates said.

US president, Bill Clinton, described the Seattle protesters as an embarrassment to the nation and national interest. Speaking from the White House, Mr Clinton expressed 'serious disappointment' in those citizens who had resorted to violence in order to make their point. A spokesman for Mr Clinton said that the 'citizens of the world's most powerful nation should be setting an example, rather than engaging in riots and illegal acts.'

Shop windows were broken and fires were set alight in Seattle last night as protesters continued their all-night vigil. The police department has made several arrests.

Analysis

The writer of this article is drawing on cultural resources to represent (re-present) the story of the World Economic Forum (WEF). These cultural resources include, obviously, the event itself and the institutional machinery which facilitates the production and distribution of the story. There are also less visible resources, including pre-existing ideas, political values and discourses; these less visible resources give the journalist and the article their particular 'perspective'. Readers of the article may understand and agree with this perspective since they also draw on similar cultural resources. The concept of ideology is often used in cultural studies to refer to those predominant ideas and values which may influence the way a text is created and interpreted. It is argued that powerful social groups are able to exert their influence over cultural resources, leading to the widespread acceptance of the groups' ideas, values and political perspectives. That is, these groups are able to represent the world according to their own interests and 'ideology'.

The Seattle article may be analysed in terms of this 'dominant ideology' thesis. For example, the ideology of globalization is reinforced in the article. Global capitalism is seen as a good thing and various authoritative voices – Hermolt Schmidt, Bill Gates and Bill Clinton – are used to support this ideology. The protesters are seen as riotous and ignorant, their perspective is dismissed out of hand. The ideology of capitalist and social hierarchy is also confirmed in the story. Authority is validated, while the challenge to that authority is defined in terms of chaos and criminal activities. The banner 'Seattle Under Siege' positions the reader and tells him or her how the WEF and the protesters should be interpreted. Any sympathy the reader may hold for the protests is undermined by the claim that the protesters' views are being considered within the framework of a lawful assembly. The protest, in fact, threatens 'free speech' and may be interpreted therefore as anti-American, seditious and anti-democratic. The ideology of nation is also inscribed in the voice of the US President, who presides over 'the most powerful nation on earth'. Of course, these are not the words of the journalist, but the selection of items. The 'angle' and the privileging of particular perspectives and voices over others clearly position the author and the text in terms of dominant ideologies. How could anyone dare to question such authority?

In cultural studies the concept of 'domination' is highly contested. A number of (especially celebrational postmodern) theorists reject the idea, arguing that it does not acknowledge sufficiently the great diversities and differences that operate within a social group. Postmodernists argue that the 'dominant ideology' thesis and Marxism more generally are too pessimistic and fail to appreciate the liberational potential of contemporary culture (see Chapters 7–9).

For the purposes of this book, we will be using a relatively open approach to the concept of ideology. That is, we would tend to see ideology in terms of culture's struggle to signify. Like power, ideology is forever forming and never complete; it is challenged at the moment of its formation. Even ideologies that have a pre-eminent position in contemporary culture (capitalism, liberal democracy, technological progressivism) are subject to dynamic cultural forces, including internal and external modifications, challenges and remediations. In this sense, the concept of 'ideology' will be carefully deployed, referring to specific instances and theoretical paradigms.

Preferred Reading/ Dominant Reading

This approach is closely related to Althusser's notion of a 'dominant' ideology. Basically, audiences are infused with the dominant values, ideals, beliefs and meanings of a large social grouping such as a nation or Western culture. Audiences draw on these pre-existing meanings to interpret or 'read' a media text. The text, of course, has also been formed out of the raw materials of this dominant culture. Therefore, there is a high degree of agreement between audience members regarding the 'meaning' of a text. Of course texts may carry a range of meaning possibilities, but the text's interaction with the audience leads to a general consensus position: this agreement constitutes a 'preferred' or 'dominant' reading of the text (see Chapter 8). Like the concept of ideology, however, the notion of preferred reading is challenged by those theorists who seek to emphasize the freedoms and differences that individual subjects experience across their various levels of culture.

Dominant Culture, Sub-culture, Subaltern Culture

Different concepts have been developed in order to explain the relationship between the various levels of culture. As indicated above, we might choose to analyse large social groupings and their culture (nation, Western culture, global culture), or smaller levels (neighbourhood, the family, local communities). Sociologists developed the concept of 'sub-culture' in the 1960s in order to locate their studies in these smaller zones. However, these studies often conceived of the sub-culture as a 'deviation' (deviant sub-group) from the larger, mainstream grouping. Therefore, studies on biker groups, youth culture, drug-takers, and so on, tended to re-confirm the deviant status of the sub-culture.

Other forms of cultural analysis have identified modern Western societies as constituting a dominant global culture. 'Subaltern' cultures are those that exist at the margins of the dominant culture; this includes postcolonial cultures, migrants and non-Westerners. There are other comparable cultural divisions such as East–West, North–South, developed–Third World, colonizer–colonized (see Chapter 10).

The notion of dominant and marginalized cultures is generally applied within the one national grouping. In the United States, for example, we might conceive of a dominant, English-speaking, heterosexual, middle-class, white culture which constitutes the norm or standard by which all other social groupings are measured. At the margins of this dominant culture are groups such as gays and lesbians, black Africans, Hispanic immigrants, indigenous people, and so on. Very often these marginal groups are conceived as the 'other': the means by which the dominant group conceives of its normality ('I know who I am because I am not the other').

Diversity, Difference, Multiculturalism

The problem with the divisions of dominant and subordinate (subaltern, margin, other) is that it tends to re-confirm the division which oppresses and subjugates the lower-status group. Cultural studies, therefore, has developed a discourse of otherness which is more celebratory and relies less on divisions of status. Pluralism, diversity, difference and multiculuralism are terms which basically reject the notion of normality or domination, replacing it with a description of culture as fundamentally diverse. Often, these concepts are associated with a post-modern politics which insists on the capacity of individual subjects to choose their lifestyles and identities.

Identity, Subjectivity

We have always had theories about what it means to be a human being, and more particularly what it means to be an 'individual' human being. Theology and philosophy have speculated about the individual and the individual soul. Early modern theories suggested that each individual constitutes a natural and spiritual essence which is more or less fixed from the time of birth. Experience tends merely to write on the bare spaces of the mind, or connect with pre-existing frameworks (see Chapter 2). Many of these theories were developed as justifications for capitalist hierarchies, arguing that individuals are naturally inferior or superior to their fellows. The disciplines of psychology and psychoanalysis sought to explain individuals in terms of personal encounters with the outside world; in either case, an individual's 'personality' was largely fixed by the time he or she reached adulthood.

Language theory and cultural studies have suggested that an individual is not fixed but develops in relation to cultural meaning-making contexts and mediations. In other words, there is nothing fixed about an individual, nothing essential. The concept of subjectivity (being a subject) is offered as a way of acknowledging the mutability, openness and dynamism of individuals. An individual's 'identity' is constructed in the same way as a text is constructed. There are two sides to this:

1   A subject or subjectivity may be 'positioned' (constituted, created) in relation to a given text or discourse. This argument suggests that readers and viewers are critically influenced by a text's ideology, beliefs, emotional and aesthetic content. In cultural studies' terms, this means that our knowledge of the world and our construction of ourselves are formed in relation to texts (cf. dominant reading argument).
2   More recent arguments suggest that the interaction between reader and text is far more fluid than argument (1) appreciates. Subjectivity is an open process which allows us to choose who we want to be.

In this latter argument, the individual will have some level of choice over the subjectivity and identity he or she wishes to present to the world. Thus, an individual subject may choose to construct his or her identity in relation to ethnicity, religious interests, sexuality, politics, preferred sport or recreational activity, occupation, particular media texts or admired celebrity, and so on. These elements of cultural choice may be mixed or restricted; an individual might change identities according to particular contexts. The identity itself might be articulated through clothing, vocabulary, social practices, modes of association, and choice in consumer products. For many cultural theorists identity is also the central focus of a resistant or radical cultural politics.

Hegemony

Hegemony is a concept developed by the Italian communist Antonio Gramsci (1971) to describe the way relations of power operate. According to Gramsci, ruling groups (organic intellectuals) maintain their power through a process of negotiation with subordinate groups. The subordinates are more willing to go along with their oppression when they have been part of the 'negotiations' of control. Leadership operates through a little give and take. Contemporary cultural theory has adapted Gramsci's approach to power and hegemony for the study of cultural and media processes. For writers like Stuart Hall (1982), the concept of hegemony is better suited to the study of the media than is Althusser's notion of ideology (see Chapter 4). Hegemony operates, for example, as media-makers (institutions and producers) directly or indirectly consult their audiences about the formation of particular texts. Market research is the most clear example of this process, although media-makers are constantly seeking to identify audience experiences and moods through the propagation of feedback lines, fan clubs and other modes of interaction.

Moreover, audiences are active creators of meaning and their approach to textual interpretation is often complex and difficult easily to summarize. Interpretations or 'readings' of texts vary between different individuals and audience groups. In other words, meanings are 'negotiated' between producers, audiences and texts, even though powerful groups in the community have the capacity to exert greater cultural influence. The extent to which these negotiations are balanced between the producer and the consumer remains a point of considerable debate. Some theorists emphasize the 'dominant reading' thesis, while others are more interested in interpretive and cultural diversity.

Popular Culture

There are continuing debates about the concept of culture and the discipline of cultural studies. 'Culture' continues to be used as:

(a) a synonym for 'the arts', especially the high arts;

(b) a cognitive category which refers to an individual's state of learning, sophistication or 'cultivation'; and

(c) an anthropological concept referring broadly to a collective 'way of life'.

A number of cultural theorists have sought to describe contemporary culture in opposition to the first two of these definitions. That is, they have sought to describe and analyse culture against elitist valorizations of high art and individual intellectual and aesthetic elevations. Cultural studies in this sense become an interrogation of the everyday lives of everyday people; it is an egalitarian or democratic activity which aims to destabilize hierarchical modes of human meaning-making.

This approach to cultural studies tends to centralize popular media texts as though they were tantamount to culture itself. That is, the production and consumption of popular media texts is more than a methodology; it is the essence of a *popular* cultural studies. 'The popular', in this sense, means more than 'popularity' or widely consumed. As we shall see, for a number of popular culture theorists 'the popular' becomes a more or less political category which centralizes and celebrates popular media texts and their consumption; popular texts and consumer practices provide the political framework for the resolution of many serious social, economic and cultural problems. In particular, the practice of everyday consumption of media and other cultural products constitutes the expression of diversity and individual freedom.

Among many others, for example, Jim Collins argues that postmodern popular culture is characterized by 'the fragmentation of a unitary public sphere into multiple reading publics and diverse forms of narrative' (1989: 7). Popular culture, in this sense, may be understood as the interaction between commonly mediated texts and the everyday meaning-making and practices of ordinary people. That is to say, participation in culture may include the creative and active 'reading' and using of texts for the pleasures and practices of ordinary people. John Fiske argues, therefore, that popular culture is a set of practices rather than a set of texts; these practices or positionings are fundamentally political:

> There can be no popular dominant culture, for popular culture is formed always in relation to, and never as part of, the forces of domination. ... The business man entertaining his friends in a private box at a football game is not participating in popular culture; the same man, however, devoid of his business suit and sporting the favours of his local team as he cheers them on from the bleachers, can be. (Fiske, 1989b: 44)

There have, of course, been numerous objections to this approach to culture, most specifically in relation to the political efficacy of popular media texts and their consumption (see Chapter 8). Jim McGuigan (1992, 1996) has been stinging in his condemnation of a cultural theory which, as he sees it, reduces politics and power to a form of celebratory hedonism.

Post-Fordism, Post-Industrialism, Information Age

These are concepts used in order to describe some substantial changes in the operations of economy, society and culture. The concept of post-Fordism (see Harvey, 1989) suggests that the peak of industrial development was achieved in the early twentieth century when Henry Ford introduced the processes of mass production to the automobile industry. Ford believed that his techniques of mass production would provide an affordable motor car for every household in America. A post-Fordist age suggests that we have now moved into a more 'flexible' and service-oriented economy. Daniel Bell (1973, 1976) was among the first social theorists to suggest that this new age was, in fact, 'post-industrial'; a new society would be constructed, Bell argued, around science and rational thinking.

With the arrival of micro-digital computer technology from the 1980s, this new epoch came to be identified as 'the information age'. Recent theorists have argued that micro-computers and networking have revolutionized communications, economy and society more generally. Along with the density and proliferation of televisual imagery, these informate facilities are transforming the way we live and the way we conceive of our reality. These theories are often articulated in relation to the ideas of postmodernism and the related historical phase many theorists call postmodern*ity*.

INTERROGATING CULTURE: METHODOLOGIES

Our task in this book is to interrogate the various ways in which culture is formed, theorized and studied. An important part of this project is to present the most significant models of cultural analysis and methodologies. While some cultural studies practitioners use various combinations of these models, others tend to privilege specific techniques and methods of analysis (see McGuigan, 1997; Giles and Middleton, 1999). Cultural studies, in fact, is noteworthy in terms of its deployment of diverse methodological designs. This 'interdisciplinary' approach to the study of culture brings together many of the intellectual and methodological traditions of the humanities (literature, media studies, history, aesthetics, philosophy) and the social sciences (sociology, anthropology, political science). While these different traditions have produced some quite passionate debates and disagreements about the 'true mission' of cultural studies, their confluence has also produced an extraordinarily fertile and productive body of work. These methodological models can be summarized in terms of theoretical analysis, critical investigation, deconstruction, textual studies, empirical studies and policy-based research.

Theoretical Analysis

Most cultural analysts use theory and conceptual frameworks in order to identify, clarify and speculate over specific cultural sites and issues. Some cultural theorists seek to establish the conceptual parameters within which cultural analysis should take place. They raise questions such as: What is culture? What is the appropriate focus of cultural studies? What is the relationship between power and culture? What role do the media play in constructing culture? Are social practices more or less important than textual analysis? These sorts of questions have already been raised in this chapter. In this sense, we can define theory as a form of conceptualization in language.

Other cultural analysts (e.g., Hall, 1991a, 1991b) argue that theory is only a means to an end: it frames the questions which should then be directed toward specific research of specific texts, social practices, institutions and relationships. In either case, theory is no more and no less than our way of knowing the world through its transformation into language. It takes us out of the quotidian immediacy of experience and allows us to see how various elements relate and intersect with one another. In other words, theory operates like a cognitive map. Our immersion in the world of action is relieved by theorization: by our capacity to step back and frame our contemplations in an orderly, established and systematic way. We can use this framing to judge the value, efficacy and accuracy of other frames of reference, ideas and theories, as well as more specific analyses of cultural phenomena. That is, we need to theorize in order to produce understanding, judgement and worthwhile action.

Critical Investigation

As we have claimed in our own theorizations, cultural studies is embedded in questions of power and ideology. These questions of power and ideology are articulated through symbolic forms of social practice, institutions and texts. As indicated above, some theorists prefer to keep these categories of articulation separate, while others regard all things as symbolic and therefore as 'discourse' or 'text'. While we shall say more about this shortly, it is worth noting that the critical evaluation of these symbolic forms is central to the cultural studies project. Thus, beyond the speculations of theory, cultural analysis has developed and deployed quite potent techniques of critical analysis, most particularly in terms of identifiable differentiations in economic, social and cultural power. In many areas, such as feminism, postcolonial studies and gay liberationism, cultural studies has sought to overthrow particular regimes of power, particularly as they are expressed in discourse and texts. At their most polemical and overt, these critical studies begin from a specific oppositional position and 'criticize' the orthodoxies of dominant and oppressive ideologies.

To this extent, critical cultural studies is embedded in questions of liberation and identity. As we have noted, identity is formed around cultural experiences and facilitates some level of subjective choice in determining 'who I am'. This identity politics often examines the 'representation' of particular social groups in terms of a dominant ideology. This dominant ideology attempts to prescribe identity for the individual (cultural agent) which the analyst in turn seeks to overthrow. A feminist reading of the Diana story may, for example, emphasize the political construction of female identity and the limits that are placed on Diana's (and other women's) subjectivity.

More generally, the current book will apply a critical model in order to interrogate significant issues of power. As we have suggested, culture cannot be disengaged from its symbolization and imagining, nor can these imaginings be disengaged from the power relationships that form and inform them. To this extent, then, our interrogations of culture will regularly encounter questions of power, liberation and resistance. Power is ubiquitous, as Michel Foucault claims, and all power involves the struggle to signify, construct meanings and control language and mediation generally. Politics and power, therefore, are not simply contingencies of democratic processes or governance. Power, as we have suggested above, is a

fluid presence in the processes of forming, producing and consuming (interpreting/creating) meaning. As we shall see throughout this book, questions of power and ideology arise at the moment of utterance, the moment of forming the imagination in discourse. Whether they concede it or not, all cultural theorists and analysts are engaged in the operations of language struggles and language war.

Deconstruction

The technique of deconstruction has become an important and distinct part of the critical lexicon. Jacques Derrida (1974, 1979) pioneered the technique, applying it to the study of Western philosophy. Basically, Derrida seeks to illuminate the historical and linguistic assumptions which underpin the formation and cultural legitimacy of certain dominant ideas. Derrida examines the 'construction' of these ideas by questioning their underlying legitimacy; once the social legitimacy is cast into doubt, then the idea begins to unravel or become 'deconstructed'. Derrida's strategy of deconstruction points specifically to the language structures and rhetorical techniques used in Western philosophy. This rhetoric, Derrida argues, is based on forms of 'binary opposition' where two elements are juxtaposed in order to demonstrate the superiority of one over the other: for example, reason over unreason, civilization over nature, man over woman, West over East, speech over writing, and so on. Deconstruction seeks to dissolve these binary formations by showing that, since everything is a mere construction of language, neither of the binary opponents can exist without reference to the other. Both sides of the opposition are relative to one another so neither can be absolutely and everlastingly true:

their 'truth' is only a claim against the other pole. As language unravels, so does truth.

Cultural studies practitioners have adapted Derrida's methods for a more general analysis of cultural phenomena. In particular, analysts have sought to expose and deconstruct the discourses (power and language) which inform particular texts, institutions and social practices. Edward Said (1993), for example, has demonstrated how the liberalist and bourgeois morality that underpins nineteenth-century English literature was informed by imperialist, xenophobic and racist ideology. Similarly, the representation of Princess Diana confirms particular political and social attitudes, most particularly the legitimacy of capitalist hierarchy and the mediated artifice of feminine glamour. Deconstruction techniques can also be applied to less obviously polemic conditions such as the representation of specific racial groups in various forms of contemporary advertising. The deployment of a Japanese person in English-speaking advertisements, for example, is not necessarily Orientalist or overtly racist, but may configure a new kind of ethnic typology: it may represent innovation, digital expertise and efficiency. Deconstruction seeks out the assumptions which lead to the formation of typologies in this kind of textualization.

Textual Studies

The study of texts such as books, films, TV programmes and musical recordings has emerged as a significant part of the humanities. Cultural studies, however, has developed a particular technique of textual analysis, one which seeks to locate the text within its historical, material and cultural context. Thus, rather than consider meaning to be something immanent in the text

or as something which elevates art over all other aspects of life, cultural studies has treated texts as cultural documents. These documents cannot be separated from the circumstances and conditions of their production and consumption. Thus, cultural texts are fundamentally and inescapably embedded in social practices, institutional processes, politics and economy. The meanings of texts cannot be treated as independent of the broader flows and operations of the culture in which the text exists.

As we have already noted, of course, this interconnectedness of text and context may be studied in many ways; equally the definition of what constitutes 'a text' is also quite variable. Some analysts seek to separate media texts from everyday practices and experiences. Others, like Barthes, claim that since everything is symbolic or meaningful, everything can be treated as text. For Michel Foucault (1974, 1977a, 1980), everything is mediated in terms of power relationships and so everything can be regarded as 'discourse' (language and power). In any case, the symbolic conditions of textuality remain a central and critical focus for cultural studies. For some analysts the text is a primary indicator of the context; for others the context presents insights into the text and its representations.

In cultural studies, popular media texts are as significant as the more complex and abstruse art forms. TV soap operas and commercials reflect important aspects of everyday culture. Some forms of cultural inquiry concern themselves with the structure of textual narratives (story-telling), most particularly as these narratives reflect broader cultural patterns and processes of conflict resolution. This 'structuralist' or 'semiological' approach suggests that textual narratives are the aesthetic manifestation of deeply rooted cultural patterns: 'myths', for example, which are part of the essential patterning of a given culture (see Barthes, 1973; Fiske et al., 1987). More recent analysis has tended to move away from this approach, adopting a more open and fluid analysis of representation and culture. This approach may be critical or deconstructive, or it may be designed to elucidate the complex interrelationships that operate through culture. Our analysis of the Diana story constitutes a textual analysis which seeks to illuminate the complex nature of identity construction, textual representation and textual reception. It also reflects on the institutional processes that are engaged in the promotion of a celebrity.

Empiricism

Empiricism is a method of recording and analysing natural and social phenomena. It may be understood simply as the objective recording of 'experience'. As early forms of social science became more interested in the symbolic dimensions of social experience, a range of empirical methods were developed and applied (Alasuutari, 1995). In particular, anthropology and sociology became interested in recording the social and symbolic practices – that is, the 'way of life' – of specific social groups. This 'way of life' included all symbolic activities (e.g., rituals and economic activities) and artefacts (e.g., implements, art objects, paintings), both of which carry significant meaning. Particular areas of cultural studies, most particularly those arising out of sociology, have continued to distinguish between cultural practices and cultural texts, applying various forms of empirical research to explain the relationship between the two.

Sociological analysis of so-called 'deviant sub-cultures' (e.g., biker gangs, drug users, naturists) sought to describe the groups' way of life. In work more directly articulated through cultural theory, Dick Hebdige (1979, 1988) adapted these methods for the study of youth culture and 'style' in the United Kingdom. Similarly, some areas of audience studies have sought to elucidate the ways in which audiences 'consume' and use media texts in their everyday lives. This 'ethnography', as it is often called, records ordinary people's practices and application of texts. Morley and Silverstone (1990), for example, have used empirical methods to show how audience/consumers use the technology of the TV in their normal, domestic lives. Video recordings, questionnaires and focus groups are all commonly used to study people and their relationship to texts within a given cultural context.

Ethnography of this kind tends to produce very descriptive or 'qualitative' data. This approach is achieving considerable popularity within cultural studies as it remains embedded in a notion of 'way of life'. Ien Ang's study of the audiences of *Dallas* (Ang, 1985) was not ethnographic, but nevertheless sought information about the experience of ordinary viewers. Some research, however, applies more rigorous quantitative or statistical methods to gather data. These sorts of studies use, for example, extensive survey techniques and statistical data gathered from TV ratings or from government bureaus. These sorts of research models have difficulty justifying their theoretical connection to cultural studies since they present such data in terms of objective truth. Cultural studies tends to treat reality and truth as a form of cultural construction: that is, the truth is only ever partial as it is formed in the unstable and uncertain materials of language and culture.

Policy-based Studies

Policy-based studies are becoming increasingly popular in cultural and media studies, especially in terms of major technologies such as TV and digital communications. There may be many reasons for this increased popularity, not the least of which is the propensity of governments to fund empirical and policy-directed social science. Policy research applies a range of strategies in order to elucidate the economic, social and cultural implications of some more or less specific cultural/media issue. For example, the public anguish over the death of Princess Diana prompted various governments to consider the question of individual privacy and the media. Cultural studies presented various perspectives on the issue of privacy and the popular media; cultural policy research asked whether some greater level of regulatory protection was required. Cultural policy studies have also examined issues such as the public funding of national film and television programmes, funding of public and community broadcasters, ownership of media corporations, and public ownership of telephone services. Issues of access, surveillance and censorship have also been regularly canvassed in policy-based cultural research.

Empirical and statistical methods, case studies and direct interviews are all common strategies in policy research. Close reading, textual analysis and deconstruction are less common in research, which is often directed toward 'reports' and audiences outside the academy.

ADVANTAGES OF THE CULTURAL STUDIES APPROACH

As we have noted throughout this chapter, contemporary developed societies are characterized by the following:

1 *Increasing differentiation and diversity.* There are increasing levels of social, economic and cultural interaction between humans across the globe. Migration, workplace structures and practices, tourism, business travel, education exchange and global communications are creating more varied and less unitary social and cultural conditions. Individual human subjects live in increasingly complex circumstances where they are constantly exposed to alternative ways of living, acting and making meaning.
2 *Increasing consumerism.* Capitalism continues to mutate as it seeks out new and different products for new and different markets. The practices of consumption lead onward to problematics of newness, taste and fashion, sexualization, and environmental calamity.
3 *Increasing density of televisual product and modes of knowing.* The proliferation of the visual image has led to new problematics in thinking and experiencing the world. The culture is saturated with aural and visual images. Digitization and computer networking are contributing to the transformation of work and of information and entertainment-based practices. Subjects are exposed daily to multiplying modes of televisual stimulus.

As we have outlined in this chapter, the concept of culture provides an invaluable tool for the exposition and analysis of these characteristics and of the contemporary world more generally. Of course, our task of explaining and analysing culture is a formidable one: culture is a work in progress which is thoroughly implicated in all matters of human activity and thinking. Yet the magnitude of the task is commensurate with the rewards. Culture, as a diverse assemblage of meanings and meaning-making processes and practices, is an enthralling and extremely rewarding field of inquiry. This chapter has established the scope of our challenge; the remaining chapters in Part One will examine in more detail how culture came to be formed in various modes of analysis and theory.

2

Society and Culture

Outline of the chapter

This chapter examines the development of a cultural studies perspective in social theory and sociology. The concept 'society' refers generally to assemblages of people, while 'culture' refers to assemblages of meanings and meaning-making processes.

This chapter looks at Enlightenment and modernist theories of knowledge, most particularly as they were developed through German and British Idealism (also called Romanticism). German Idealism, in particular, remains forceful as it informs a good deal of contemporary society's modes of thought and analysis. Idealism brings together the experiences of spiritualism, scientific rationalism, and notions of freedom and imagination. Culture, as a symbolic or aesthetic activity, is distinguished from the concept of society, which is the general aggregation of people into a more or less homogeneous formation.

Émile Durkheim and Max Weber, the so-called 'fathers of sociology', apply these theories to the study of society. In fact, they establish an heuristic relationship between society, social action and social structure, on the one hand, and symbolic practices (culture), on the other. While it is true that these earlier forms of social theory and sociology tended to treat culture as the servant of 'society', Durkheim and Weber nevertheless developed a systematic and thoughtful account of how symbols and meaning-making practices are shaped in relation to social organizations and institutions. The work of Durkheim, in particular, establishes the methods and rationale for anthropological investigations of social groups and their symbolic activities.

Durkheim and Weber's seminal studies also provide a paradigm for the development of a 'pragmatic' sociology at the University of Chicago. Early in the twentieth century, Chicago sociologists like Robert Park brought together a variety of investigative methods to form a pragmatic, empirical sociology. These methods, which incorporated various forms of anthropology and everyday journalism, were central to the development of a sociology of sub-groups. As sociology developed during the twentieth century, the Chicago approach also became involved in the application of 'phenomenology' for the study of society. Phenomenology – the study of 'phenomena' in their most obvious, everyday and accessible form – became a distinct sociological enterprise. It allows sociology to interact with the social world through an engagement with everyday practices; it also emphasizes the very important idea of 'difference' in the way social actors make sense of social phenomena. Recent sociology has begun to move away from its conceptualizations of society as an homogenized human system toward a greater interest in diversity, mediation and meaning-making. During the course of these changes, social theory and sociology have had to adapt the older theories of knowledge, the self and society in order to accommodate these new ideas on mediation and difference.

GENERAL INTRODUCTION

This chapter examines the relationship between theories of society and theories of culture. While it is difficult for us to appreciate today, the concepts of 'society' and 'culture' are relatively new, appearing as important modes of description from the nineteenth century. The need for new concepts and new ways of thinking about 'society' arose, however, during the previous centuries as humans in the advanced world began to leave their rural communities to form large, urban-based, industrial cities and nation-states. Print technologies facilitated the formation of new communicative modes where information could be sorted and conveyed over vast distances. This separation of information from the informant also facilitated the creation of new social relationships, symbolic relationships that were no longer reliant on the actual presence of a speaker. In this new mediated community individuals could be aware of the existence of many other members of the community without having a direct or personal interaction with them. Society, therefore, comes to be created through symbolic modes and relationships as much as through the sheer congregation of human beings. Modernist ideas – epistemology, Romanticism, Idealism, empiricism and scientific positivism – contributed

to the development of new theories of social reality (society) and the symbolic relationships (culture) which inform that reality.

Some areas of contemporary cultural analysis position themselves in opposition to modernism, most especially modernism's predisposition toward homogeneity, universalism and the unitary and integrated subject. In particular, and as we noted in the previous chapter, the emergence of new social forms and ideas commonly referred to as postmodernism has led cultural studies to a critical revision of earlier modernist modes of thinking. Paradoxically, however, these modernist conceptions form an important part of the genealogy that has produced contemporary cultural analysis. These theories are quite complex as they ask very profound questions about the relationship between the human mind and its external reality: that is, about the relationship between the subject and the object. Whether we accept or reject these arguments, they form the basis of our own knowledge about ourselves and our symbolic interactions with one another. This chapter examines the relationship between theories of society and theories of culture. In particular, we trace the ways in which symbolic practices and artefacts become increasingly integrated into theories of society and social organization.

MODERNISM AND SOCIAL REALITY

During the eighteenth and nineteenth centuries the notion of 'society' generally referred to the elite community of landed aristocrats who presided over a hierarchy of people, manners and relationships. The literature of Jane Austen, George Eliot and Oscar Wilde illustrates how these social elites viciously guarded the territories of their privilege and power. These works, however, also document the fracturing of these plutocracies as they are challenged and eventually overrun by the interests of the mercantile middle classes (the bourgeoisie). As we shall see, a number of theorists contributed to the development of a new conception of 'society', one which encompassed a much broader span of human community. This overhaul of notions of community and society was necessary for a social system which had grown well beyond the proportions of personal interaction and personal relationships. This new society was constructed, therefore, out of the symbolic, as well as the material, conditions of human organization. 'Symbolism' refers to the extension and abstraction of meanings beyond the immediate or literal; in order for this new society to exist at all, humans had to construct a symbolic connection between themselves and for the institutions which sustained them. In acknowledging the symbolic dimensions of human community, however, these new social theories had to overcome a number of significant theoretical problems.

Reason and Order

One of the most persistent of these problems refers to the relationship between the subject (I, me) and the object (external reality, others). 'What is real' emerges as a significant problem for philosophers and theorists from the late sixteenth and seventeenth centuries and continues today. There is no doubt that this question has always plagued human groups and the answers have often resolved themselves through theology and metaphysics. This period of European history is noteworthy, however, as it attempts to advance new theories of reality beyond a simple reference to a deity or cosmological system. Specifically, the human mind becomes centralized in terms of explaining how the world is formed and how individuals and social groups should function in relation to that 'reality'. There are a number of reasons for this:

1 Significant advances in technology and techniques of economic production are associated with the way humans conceived of themselves, their physical environment and their relationship to nature. In particular, the notion of humans confronting and overcoming nature and natural forces became part of this conceit. The natural world was a 'mechanism' that obeyed natural laws; these laws could be measured and mastered. Human reason and a capacity for order and organizational management became central to these processes of understanding and controlling nature, especially through the development and application of technology.

2 This new relationship with nature, along with the accelerating changes being brought by industrialization and urbanization, seriously strained social relationships, social laws, political organization and concepts of morality. The combination of these dislocations

and the desire for order and stability contributed to the formation of social and political idealism. Michel Foucault (1974) suggests that these unstable social conditions, in fact, contributed to the development of theories of order and stability during the early period of modernity. Thomas Hobbes (1588–1679), for example, believed that the universe was comprised of 'bodies in motion' and that the human mind was just another body in motion. Society needed to mimic the logical pattern of the universe in order to sustain itself in an orderly manner. In many respects, the human mind and the functioning of 'reason' provided a point of reference from which social, economic and technological change could proceed in a measured and sensible way.

3 The economic system of capitalism further problematizes the individual and his/her relationships with others. Capitalism supports individual prosperity, though in practice an individual's triumph necessitates the failure, or even the oppression, of others. The individual is therefore constituted through complex processes of interaction and differentiation. To this extent, an individual's reality is negotiated in terms of his/her economic and social position within a broader social hierarchy. This negotiation is distinctly political, ideological and contradictory. The human mind is central to these processes as it overlays a discourse of order onto what are often brutish and sense-driven processes of self-preservation and self-gratification.

4 As noted above, the new and more abstracted forms of social organization are possible only through the exertion of symbolizing processes. Language – in particular, written language – becomes the primary facility and technology for the mass organization of people. We know others and we know our world because we are able to conceive of them symbolically. Benedict Anderson (1991) speaks quite specifically of 'imagined communities', the new nation-states of the modern era which are formed through the broad distribution of printed information. Print allows governments to administer populations and citizens; it also allows citizens to share important knowledge, language and ideologies which define them as citizens. Clearly, the rational ordering of human communication systems is central to this process. Even so, the dislocating effects of industrialization and capitalist differentiation continually threaten this integrated order; the communications systems enabled the proliferation of challenges and alternative ideologies as much as they facilitated the exertion of unity and control. An attempt to assert rational and integrated theory over this diverse and threatening social landscape appears to have motivated many of the social theories during the period of modernity.

The Subject and the Object

This centralization of the self and the rational mind occurs within a general context of threat to individual identity, dignity and sense of community belonging. The 'massification' of society problematizes the relationship between the subject (self) and the object (external reality). In this sense, the question of perception (how I see things) becomes increasingly pertinent in terms of two distinct trends:

1 The world becomes formed increasingly through abstract and symbolic processes. As communication is removed from the

immediacy of interaction, it relies increasingly on processes of interpretation and shared knowledge. The more abstract a communicative exchange, the greater the possibility of alternative interpretations and meaning-making.

2   Individuals and their relationships become more complex and subject to increasing differentiations in social rules, knowledge and protocols. When the technology of telegraphy was introduced in the nineteenth century, for example, a whole new set of protocols and modes of language-sharing had to be introduced. People from different social levels, time zones, countries, cultural backgrounds and language aptitudes were suddenly brought into an interactive community.

Clearly, people from different social and community backgrounds will see the world in rather different ways. The reality of the world, therefore, becomes implicated in matters of perception, symbolism and the symbolic ordering of knowledge.

Modern philosophy, in fact, became fascinated with this very problem of how we know the world. This is the essence of the philosophy of epistemology. At the centre of this question is the relationship between the subject and the object. The following is a very brief account of some of the more significant theories of knowing as they emerged from the period of the Enlightenment.

1   René Descartes (1596–1650) wanted to theorize the whole of human existence by rendering it 'knowable'. Knowledge of 'man' and 'nature' was possible, according to Descartes, provided we first doubted its existence. From the position of doubt we would apply a method of proof. Anything could be proven and known through the rendering of its laws of action; mathematics provided the ideal language for presenting these laws since it was universal and not tied to particular nations and speakers.

2   According to John Locke (1632–1704), the universe is a self-adjusting system which is informed by logical processes. Locke's *An Essay Concerning Human Understanding* (1950, orig. 1690) attempts to explain how human minds are able to enclose the spatiality of the universe and its logical patterns. Experience provides us with the sensate resources necessary for understanding nature. Beginning as a blank sheet, the mind is inscribed with the ideas necessary for knowledge and comprehension. Locke and Descartes provide the foundations for the development of empirical research methods (see Chapter 1).

3   Descartes and Locke inadvertently divide the universe into two distinct parts – the subject and the object. This is known as Cartesian dualism, and many of the philosophers of the eighteenth and nineteenth centuries sought to re-bond the two parts so that the subject could be treated as a 'unitary whole'. Romantic philosophy attempts to reconcile the rational dimensions of the human mind with the more mystical aspects of spirit and nature. This form of philosophy, which concerns itself with the essential patterns of nature, is also often referred to as ontology (of essences). The task, for Romantic phlilosopher like Immanuel Kant (1724–1804), was to reconcile the human in the universal conditions of time, space and ultimately causality. This 'universalism' sought to identify the ways in which we are able to know the reality of the world; this is possible, Kant argues, because there are non-physical (spiritual) patterns which exist

both in nature and in the human mind. The human mind, most particularly the faculty of reason, is able to recognize these patterns and therefore comprehend, manage and articulate universal knowledge, including a universal morality.

4 Kant's attempt to reconcile the subject and object lionizes reason and the human mind. However, this centralization of the mind as the spiritual host of universal patterns and knowledge creates a further division between the mind and the body. Even so, Kant's scepticism has provided a theoretical foundation for the positivism (mathematical analysis) which developed in the social sciences, while his notion of the spirit or *Geist* has influenced Romantic literature and philosophy, including G.W.F. Hegel's (1770–1831) transcendental rationalism. Hegel's grand project was to explain all phenomena in terms of a highly integrated and systematic logics of order. Hegel's dialectical order informs Karl Marx's account of history as 'teleology' – a series of structural conflicts with a causal and predetermined outcome (see Chapter 3). Hegel's Idealism, however, reaches well beyond history; for Hegel, the unity of dialectical tension (unity in opposition) constitutes the fundamental order which underpins the whole universe and which reintegrates humans with external nature. Reality, therefore, is formed around elements in conflict; these elements are reconciled or 'synthesized' by the conditions of what Hegel calls 'the actual' or the spiritual. Hegel's grand scheme, like Kant's, creates yet another dualism, this time between the real (what appears) and the actual (the non-physical patterns which exist as the essence of material reality).

Criticisms of Epistemology

The attempt by various forms of epistemology and ontology to reconcile the division between subject and object is often criticized for its universalism – its claim that all nature, human existence and social phenomena can be explained and integrated into a single theory of everything. How we know ourselves and experience the world is clearly a contingency of many complex social and symbolic processes. Ontological explanations and the tendency to separate mind and body, however, have tended to reduce these complexities, subsuming them within an abstruse theory of how subjects experience and know their reality. Questions of politics, social relationships and symbolic systems are negated or overlooked in a theoretical reaction to what might be seen as the shock of modernization. This shock or 'crisis of understanding' is clearly related to the radical separation of human spirituality from the material and technological conditions of the eighteenth and nineteenth centuries. The rationality that had contributed to the 'schizophrenia' of the modern state – progress and dissolution – had turned its cold eyes on the referential status of God. That is, God and spirituality were besieged by various forms of instrumental rationality (technology, the mass organization of the state, capitalism); Romantic philosophy attempted to restore the possibilities of spirituality with the possibilities of social, technical and economic progress. It was hoped that the human mind – reason, spirit, imagination – would draw all humanity together into a civilized and elevated spiritual community.

Of course, there are many schools of thought which continue to support the notion of an objective and sharable reality; however, the idea that this reality is founded on a non-material or spiritual essence has been critically challenged. In particular, various forms of sociology and cultural studies criticize the universalism of a Romantic theory which overlooks the specific historical, material and symbolic conditions in which people live their lives. According to this view, the important reality for social agents is the one in which they live and with which they engage. Thus, while the idea of social unity remains important for many early sociologists and cultural analysts, their interest is centred on how this unity is expressed and made possible by distinct social processes rather than on the underlying patterns of nature and the human mind. The underlying patterns or structures of nature are less relevant than the underlying patterns of society itself. These patterns or 'structures' become the focus of early social and cultural analysis since these are the things which give shape and reality to 'society' and people's everyday existence within it.

STRUCTURE AND CULTURAL SOCIOLOGY

As we shall see, Hegel's theories were important in the formation of Karl Marx's social and historical analysis. More generally, however, Descartes' scientific method, Locke's empiricism, Hobbes' materialism and the Idealists' attempt at 'grounding' science and reason all contributed significantly to the formation of the human and social sciences. The science of society, therefore, was shaped through the hybridization of the natural sciences and the philosophical traditions of empiricism and epistemology. This important concept, 'society', had once been restricted to the social elite, as in 'high society'. Increasingly, however, the need to understand and

conceptualize the greater human mass led to a more inclusive deployment of the concept. Urbanization, the broadening reach of communications and transport technologies, widening electoral suffrage, and the expansion of ideologies such as nationalism and imperialism, all contributed to a widening of the conception of 'the society of man'.

Karl Marx (1818–83) (see Chapter 3) conceived of this great human mass as the outcome of distinct social and historical forces. In particular, he regarded this new human formation, mass society, as being characterized by struggle and conflict. Large groupings within the social formation struggled against one another until social change was achieved; this change, however, brought new groups into conflict. Marx's model of social and historical conflict contrasted with other theorists who believed that stability, perhaps a dynamic stability, was the most notable feature of the society of man. Auguste Comte (1798–1857) was among the earliest theorists to consider 'the society of man' in terms of empirical enquiry. Comte's aim was to produce a naturalistic science of society which would account for the stability of society at any given moment, but which would also explain its change over time. Comte applied the principles and methods of the natural sciences – observation, experimentation and comparison – for the study of the *laws* which govern human society.

Émile Durkheim and Social Structure

Perhaps more than any other scholar of the time, Émile Durkheim (1858–1917) is responsible for establishing the theoretical parameters of the science of society, directing both the focus and methodology of enquiry. Thus, while 'culture' remains a somewhat amorphous concept for Durkheim, 'society' is more clearly defined as a generally cohesive and integrated organization of people into a locatable, hermetic form. Durkheim's approach to the study of society, however, contributes directly to the evolution of a cultural sociology in two significant ways: first, in his account of social structure; and secondly, through the analysis of symbolism and religion which takes place in his later works. It is certainly true that Durkheim's early analysis of social structure is characterized by a significant devotion to the externality of social structure, quantification and data collection. His work at this level appears to be invested in Cartesian methodologies, maintaining its adherence to the trajectory of Enlightenment scientific rationalism. Even so, the concept of social structure – the invisible pillars that hold society together – is one of the most important in sociology, providing the focus and raw materials for much of the discipline's development during the twentieth century.

Structure is a rather elusive concept since it refers to phenomena which are not in themselves visible, but which are known through their effects on human action. Social structures are the building blocks (frameworks or pillars) of social bonds and interrelationships. In his explanations of the functioning of integrated social systems, Talcott Parsons (1961: 36–7) adapted Durkheim's notion of structure in his own explanation of social action and how integrated social systems function for the satisfaction of individual and collective needs. According to Parsons, structure is able to influence the thinking, attitudes and behaviours of social actors (individuals engaged in action in society). Structures are large, slow-moving and constant when compared with the rapid and ever-fluctuating 'empirical' experience of everyday life. Moreover, these structures are external and objective, impervious therefore to the caprice and control of small groups and individuals. Even so, structures and social systems are stable because they correspond to the interests and the shared, normative expectations (what is expected and normal) and values of individuals within the society.

What constituted society for Durkheim was not so much the attributes of individuals, but rather the social and historical forces that bring a group and its structure into being. This is something more than the assemblage of individual consciousnesses; the group comes to take a life of its own.

> The determining cause of a social fact should be sought amongst the social facts preceding it and not among the states of the individual consciousness. (Durkheim, 1960: 110)

If we were considering a political party as a structure, then the social facts of that party would be constituted from those forces which brought the party into being and which sustain it through the present. Social facts could not be determined by the individual party member's consciousness, personal attributes or moral perspectives. While the collective of these elements may contribute to the sustainability of the party, they cannot, of themselves, explain its existence.

Talcott Parsons and Social Structure

The concept of culture, as the assemblage of a people's symbolic way of life, has only limited value for this part of Durkheim's work. That is, while culture might incorporate all the values that exist within a given human group, only some of these values are shared and form the basis of institutions (e.g., morality, law, family values, etc.). For Durkheim, these institutional values form the basis of ongoing social structures. Talcott Parsons' work significantly extends Durkheim's original ideas: the interest in structure derives from, and supports, a substantial investment in the notion of an integrated and cohesive society. Certainly, this phase of Durkheim's work investigates and confirms a form of social order that is fundamentally objective and accessible to positivist and statistical analysis.

Parsons' own work, which dominated sociology over half a century later, was perhaps even more formidable in its theoretical insistence that 'macro' society was the primary investigative unit, and social or cultural *integration* was the primary sociological enterprise. What was significant about society was its durability, its capacity for order and systematic self-maintenance. As with the earlier Durkheim, Parsons argued that culture was like flesh on the bone, the covering of the substance of social structure. Culture, in fact, provided the possibilities of 'goal attainment' for social actors. That is, the cultural system facilitates for actors the attainment of their material, sensual and moral gratifications; in addition the symbol system helps neutralize the conflicts and problems associated with this attainment by restoring actors to an integrated and stable set of values which they inevitably share with other social actors.

Parsons' approach to the study of society and culture might be summarized as follows:

1 Parsons is concerned with the universal conditions which hold a society together. To this extent, his concern is not particularly with the factors which make an historical epoch unique but rather with the universal human qualities which maintain social cohesion.

2 Parsons is particularly interested in social constraints. He agrees with the early Durkheim that human desire is more or less insatiable, and that society must impose limits on the gratification of those desires if it is to sustain itself.

3 Parsons' methods are built around a fundamental Cartesian belief in the capacity of phenomena to be objectified. That is, his statistical methodology is itself an integrated system which highlights the most prominent and significant features of a society. Parsons' conclusions are built around an absolutist and universal principle of truth.

4 This approach to the study of society rarefies, abstracts and objectifies the phenomena it is studying. That is, Parsons' positivism reconstructs the social world in terms of hypotheses, methods, data and conclusions. Using the language of scientific method, Parsons and his followers create a descriptive and analytical language that is far removed from everyday social discourse and the social phenomena it is investigating.

5 For Parsons, the concept of 'society' as an integrated whole is far more important than the concept of a cultural system. This cultural *system* merely supports the structures of society. In either case, it is the system which is of paramount importance. the parts merely support the organizational whole; culture supports society. Parsons' work demonstrates a significant lack of interest in the notion of cultural parts or cultural diversity except in as much as they complement the functioning of the social system.

Parsons' view of a stable and cohesive sign system reflects the ascendant intellectual and ideological conditions of the Cold War, especially in the United States. In fact, 1950s America, which seems on the surface to be so secure, cohesive and stable, was being tortured by its own self-doubt and internal paranoias. This so-called pluralist, liberalist society seemed to lose confidence as it pursued its anti-communist foreign policy, madly accumulating nuclear weaponry and viciously repressing any hint of internal dissent. The anti-communist trials established by Senator McCarthy indicate just how oppressive and paranoid American conservatism had become. Parsons' pedestrian and methodical approach to social cohesion, and his implacable allegiance to the concept of symbolic order, seem to have served the interests of the intellectual conservatism and prevailing social values of the times.

Parsons' extension of Durkheim's structuralist approach to the study of society not only reinforces the notion of social cohesion, it actively seeks to homogenize and stabilize social life. The absence of discussions of power in his work has been widely criticized, as indeed have his positivist (statistical) methods. Even so, what is significant about Parsons is his attempt to draw together the major strands of sociological enquiry: social structure, social action and symbolic systems. The weakest area of these studies, however, is certainly his analysis of the symbolic system. Parsons' notion of culture was limited by his devotion to social conformity. While a form of cultural analysis had appeared in the US early in the twentieth century, it was not until the emergence of a more fully theorized British cultural studies and American cultural sociology that the true limits of Parsons' approach became obvious.

DURKHEIM AND SYMBOLISM

Durkheim's second major contribution to the development of cultural studies and cultural theory came in his later works on primitive religion and symbolism. While there are various ways of defining symbolism, Durkheim applies the concept as a set of complex associations where religious rituals, icons and artefacts were interpreted by members of the social groups (tribe, community, congregation). Meaning, therefore, was a matter of interaction between the symbol, the group and individuals within the group. This hermeneutic or interpretive definition of symbolism suggests an open, relative and flexible relationship between the cultural artefact and its meaning. It may be contrasted to a more deterministic definition of symbol which suggests an absolute relationship between the two. In this latter application the symbol is treated as a sign which has a fixed relationship with the thing it represents: that is, there is a direct line between the sign and its referent. Talcott Parsons' application of signs within an integrated symbolic system tends to be more fixed and absolute; Durkheim's notion of the symbolic tends to be more open and flexible. Parsons would be interested in the ways a particular sign – the value placed on a new automobile, for example – fits into a generalized system of social order and how the sign motivates and directs individuals' goal attainment. Durkheim was more interested in the way a ritual may be interpreted and used to explain the complex matrices and interrelationships of life.

Durkheim's theory of symbolic or cultural sociology appeared most earnestly from the 1890s and dominated his work until his death in 1917. While distinguishing between the profane and the sacred,

Durkheim nevertheless insisted that an analysis of religion would necessarily illuminate a culture's general symbolic environment: 'A great number of problems change their aspects as soon as their connections with the sociology of religion are recognized' (Durkheim, 1960: 351). Thus, while Durkheim's interest in primitive religions may appear to invest itself in the more comparative or anthropological dimensions of sociology, his intention was to use the particular instances of his investigations to illuminate the symbolic and cultural character of modern society as well. Certainly, the posthumous publication of many of Durkheim's lectures demonstrates quite directly that symbolic systems, subjectivity and solidarity were central issues for the analysis of contemporary as well as primitive human groups. Issues of education, politics, professional organizations, morality and the law were all appropriate for analysis within the general sphere of symbolic classification (see, e.g., Durkheim, 1977).

It is this classificatory system which problematizes the relationship between symbolic culture and social structure. In particular, Durkheim suggests that there is an emotional hierarchy which symbolizes human relationships within social groups. While this is most obvious in primitive societies, symbolic relationships are also discernible within complex societies: we may feel closest to our immediate family, less so to cousins and less so to neighbours and associates. This emotional or 'affective' hierarchy parallels broader social and cosmological hierarchies which are ordered and articulated according to principles of thought or 'cognition'. In other words, the cosmos can be divided between the most intimate and least intimate intensities – from the sacred to the profane. The sacred, through its symbology, is condensed, solid, pure and unifying; the profane is diffuse,

potentially threatening, disruptive and precarious. Durkheim goes on to explain that many primitive religions also employ forms of naturalistic totems which symbolize particular familial groups or clans, and which locate that group within a geographical and social/symbolic system. Totems provide temporal, spiritual and socio-economic identity for the group, setting them in a fixed relationship with other groups and within the broader natural and cosmological order.

While it is important not to conclude that Durkheim's symbolism constitutes a radical break from the epistemological heritage of German Idealism, it is certainly true that Durkheim raises important questions about the relationship between symbolism and social structure. Therefore, while he readily concedes that not all societies share the same classificatory symbolic system, Durkheim does privilege the notion of a social unity built around a common symbolic system. Thus, even though there are patterns of classification common to all (sacred – profane most obviously), Durkheim attempts to maintain the specificity of different social groups by admitting a certain flexibility into the interpretation process. Certainly, as he considers the more open and complex conditions of modern society, he readily concedes that the classificatory system is necessarily subject to more challenging and disruptive hermeneutic processes. This dualism in Durkheim's work has been recognized by his followers, including Talcott Parsons. Thus, while praising the attention Durkheim pays to symbolic and cultural systems, Parsons (1967) is critical of the later works' emphasis on autonomous symbolic processes rather than values and their institutionalization. The work of Durkheim's more immediate associates and students demonstrates the same shifting emphasis from systemic social order to autonomous and free-functioning hermeneutics: Halbwach (working-class consumption), Mauss (exchange) and Bougle (caste) have all demonstrated that symbolic culture is not merely the servant of social structure and social system, as Parsons claims.

It should be remembered, of course, that these are the seminal years of socio-logical research and it was not until the rise of Parsons' empirical positivism during the 1940s through to the 1950s that the discipline was really able to declare itself as a cohesive and formidable body of knowledge. Until that time, the research fields were sporadic and some-what inchoate. Alexander (1988) points out that sociology's interest in Durkheim diminished somewhat during this period, though his influence continued to develop in other theoretical and heuristic fields interested in culture and symbolism. The work of French structural anthropology and linguistics (see Chapter 5) and American anthropology, for example, absorbed significant aspects of Durkheim's later work in the development of their own definitions and deployments of the notion of culture. Thus, while it is fair to say that Durkheim's dual interest in social structure and symbolic processes is never fully realized as an integrated theory of modern culture, the work provided a framework for elaborations by later cultural theorists.

MAX WEBER

As mentioned in Chapter 1, one of the great problems for modernism has been the persistent tension between collective and individual interests – between the macro and micro levels of society and culture. This tension has underpinned, yet continued to

trouble, a whole range of philosophical and empirical investigations into the human condition. It lies behind the universal – par-ticular tension that Kant and Hegel attempted to reconcile; it persists in the structure – symbolism dualities of Durkheim; and it is again central to the methodological precepts outlined by Max Weber (1864–1920). Along with Durkheim, Weber is generally cited as one of the founders of modern sociology, and is a major contributor to the development of cultural theory based around the concept of social action. Weber's major contribu-tions to the development of cultural sociology are as follows:

1 The development of sociological methods which are not grounded in the assumptions of natural science but which are directed specifically toward the study of human society. These methods, while constituted around reason and objectivity, are specifically designed to account for the investigation of social actors in action.

2 The development of a social theory which centres on the subjective mean-ings social actors attach to social action. These actions (and their meanings) are directed toward mutual interests, and they always occur within a particular social and historical context. Behaviour that falls outside these parameters is not available to sociology.

According to Weber, there are four types of social action:

(a) purposeful or goal-oriented rational action, such as the construction of a steam engine to carry goods and people over vast distances;

(b) value-oriented rational action, such as the pursuit of an ascetic lifestyle for the sake of (irrational) salvation;

(c) emotional or affective social action, such as committing murder in a fit of rage; and

(d) traditional action, such as the reproduction of traditional artefacts or enactment of traditional rituals.

While there may be some level of overlap in these categories, Weber was most intrigued by the rising predominance of purposive action in modern society. In many respects, Weber's analysis of law, economics, politics and personal relationships returned to the question of how modern society had come to be dominated by goal-oriented rationalization. As frequently, the answer centred on the ways in which human action and social and historical contexts shifted in relation to one another. Weber could not settle on a (Hobbesian) materialist version of social reality, nor on a (Kantian) idealist version. Instead, he fixed his analysis on the concrete experience of the common subject as the fundamental unit of sociological enquiry:

> Interpretive sociology considers the individual and his action as the basic unit, as its 'atom'.... The individual is ... the upper limit and the sole carrier of meaningful conduct.... Such concepts as 'state', 'association', 'feudalism' and the like, designate certain categories of human interaction. Hence it is the task of sociology to reduce these concepts to 'understandable' action, that is, without exception to the actions of participating individual men. (Weber, 1946: 55).

For Weber, a method of social enquiry must account for the problem of 'facts'. Social and cultural enquiry cannot be directly paralleled with the laws and methodologies of 'natural' science since nature is largely static, material and presumes a certain determinacy or directly observable causality. While the laws of nature cannot entirely exhaust all there is to know about nature, they function sufficiently as 'representations' of nature – as 'reality'. Humans, however, are more complicated. Their behaviour, knowledge and symbolization cannot be treated or 'revealed' as a mere mirror of reality. Indeed, following Kant, Weber believed that the essences of culture and nature could not be revealed; only the phenomenal or surface forms of that reality were available to enquiry and observation. It was not appropriate, therefore, for cultural or social science to seek laws or empirical generalizations which would elucidate phenomenal essence. Rather, it was the task of the researcher to reveal phenomena as *social action* within the realm of reason and reasoned investigative frameworks.

Reason is absolutely critical to Weber's schema, not because he wanted to mimic the natural sciences and their positivist empirical frameworks, but because he recognized the theoretical and heuristic dangers of his own departure from generalized facticity. That is, if facts are not to be regarded as universal and absolute representations of reality, then it becomes immediately possible that social and cultural enquiry could be no more than a series of dissociated and limitless accounts of a purely individual or idiosyncratic version of the world. Weber's deviation from the standards of empirical science and the assumption of its reality opened his work to a twofold problem:

1 Is the social and cultural merely a dissociated collection of individual perceptions of the real constituted by wholly separate and individualized particles of knowledge? Is the social world a loose assemblage of subjective experiences that have no greater bond than the assumption of a shared reality?

2 Is the social researcher reduced to a mere recording function for these

particularized bits of knowledge, with his or her own work constituting merely one more version of the idiosyncratic?

In response Weber argues that cultural and social knowledge are formed through a kind of intersubjective consensus, a consciousness that is constituted in the interests of collective gratification. 'Knowing' is thus a form of cultural action which is constrained, as it is constituted, by morality, heritage, tradition, conventions and reason. Members of a social group 'create' a reality for a given purpose at a given time. This intersubjective reality is not haphazard or speculative, but operates through the collective consciousness of individuals in action.

Equally, cultural analysis is shaped and informed by its own historical conditions; it too is subject to the collective values that are ascendant and which operate through institutional conventions. That is, cultural and social research are very much 'of their times', part of the context they themselves are investigating. For Weber, this 'empathy' between cultural analysis and its focus does not reduce the need for researchers to be 'value'-sensitive in their work. Rather, it inclines social science away from relativism and toward a paradigm of 'consensual' truth where 'values' are acknowledged and interpretation is a delicate process of judgement and discrimination. Weber's empirical social and cultural science is, therefore, a finely positioned methodology which distinguishes between relativism, on the one hand, and numerical positivism, on the other. It is science because it is constituted through rigorous, repeatable and agreed standards of 'data' collection and analysis. It is 'objective' yet subject to the particular conditions prevalent in a particular place at a particular moment in history. Weber attempts, that is, to mediate polarities of knowledge: one which is universal

and applicable in all circumstances, and the other which has particular paradigmatic value for a particular social group at a particular moment.

While Weber's essays on methodology (Weber, 1949) have contributed significantly to the evolution of social science and its research strategies, considerable debate surrounds the theoretical and ideological efficacy of the overall body of his writing. In particular, Marxist critics are suspicious of Weber's neo-Kantianism, which consistently integrates social values, and which places the concept of culture before the structural discriminations of class and production. Weber, like Kant, seeks an almost Romantic solution to the problem of collective and individual interests. His emphasis on social action tends to privilege individual subjectivity over and above the sorts of structured discriminations and politics that surround capitalism. Indeed, the belief that society and culture are constituted forms of consensus tends to camouflage the conflicts and antagonisms which persist in all social formations, especially mass society.

In fact, Weber employs a particular concept, the 'ideal type', which is designed to reconcile the tension between universal typologies and the actuality of individual actors. Numerous critics have suggested that this utopianism actually distracts social enquiry from the specific disorders and oppressions that are suffered by particular social groups. To this extent, the ideal type acts as a metaphor for Weber's notion of a culture built around discrete values: culture is not the mirror or superstructure of economy or politics, but is rather an autonomous producer and reproducer of social order and social relationships as they are structured through social action. Culture is, therefore, a cognitive rather than a material category. It is a way of thinking which consistently returns from a potentially threatening diversity into a more comforting mode of consensuality and collective consciousness.

Not surprisingly, a number of modern Marxists have been highly critical of texts like *The Protestant Ethic and the Spirit of Capitalism* (1930), in which Weber attempts to explain the 'culture' of capitalism in distinctly Kantian terms. Thus, the 'spirit' of capitalism refers to a way of being in the world which is predicated on values, morality and rationality. This complex of rationalized and rationalizing values is reciprocally experienced by entrepreneurs seeking profit and workers seeking to articulate themselves in labour. Culture is present in every act and cannot be treated as divisible, a separate modality, or mirror of economic imperatives. For the Marxist commentators, however, Weber's account is not merely a description of capitalist cultural processes, but is informed by intense ideological presuppositions. In accordance with his own methodological precepts, Weber's description of capitalism and Protestantism is value-neutral, or at least embedded in the values of his times. Marxism, as we shall see in the following chapter, regards this value-neutrality as a capitulation to the dominant values and ideology upon which it supposedly focuses.

THE CHICAGO SCHOOL

As Charles Turner (1992) has argued, Weber's approach to culture clearly derives from German Idealism. As with the Idealists, Weber believes that culture can be distinguished as an ontological phenomenon signifying 'depth of feeling, immersion in books, development of the individual personality' (Turner, 1992: 35). The notion of culture or cultivation, as it is used by Immanuel Kant, is fundamentally about learning, knowledge, consciousness and the symbolic system which more or less bonds society as 'civilization'. More importantly, though, culture for Kant and later Weber is a social category which seems capable of resolving the ongoing tension between collective and subjective interests. Weber assumes this reconciliation can take place through the operations of action, which are the outward demonstrations of a collective motivation, intersubjective consensus or consciousness. As we have noted in Chapter 1, this approach to culture attempts to synthesize the particularities, differences and even chaotic impulses of varying social elements.

Thus, for all their differences, Durkheim, Weber and Parsons share a similar notion of culture as a synthesizing symbolic system. Indeed, while Karl Marx and other social reformers were analysing modern society in terms of suffering and conflict, Durkheim, Parsons and Weber were seeking to understand the ways in which society holds itself together and the role that culture plays in maintaining social order and cohesion. Reason, order and stability are regarded as positive values by all three sociologists. Symbolic systems serve to validate goal-attainment, rationality and the assimilation of social differences into an integrative social and cultural system. Capitalism and capitalist ideology escape serious critique; capitalism, in fact is presented as a functioning and satisfying context for social action, structure and symbolic order. Parsons, most especially, draws the particulates of social action into a highly integrative conception of system and structure, re-confirming continually the value system and symbolic heritage that support modern capitalism, and the social and economic gratifications offered by contemporary economy. Weber, for his part, might reject a notion that culture and symbolic systems exist as the sub-strata of economy, but there is little in his work that would seem to support a critical engagement with cultural or economic processes. All three sociologists share a substantial commitment to the ideology of dominant value systems, integrative social or symbolic structures and systems, (Western) rationality, universalism and the status of the intellectual as social leader.

Undoubtedly, an interest in social processes, structures and institutions has substantively defined the territory of sociology. The standards of interest established in the nineteenth century persisted into the twentieth century; the concepts of culture, discourse and symbolization were subordinated to the fundamental precepts of social structure and social action. Even so, the twentieth century also announces a new kind of social enquiry, one which emerges significantly in the New World and which begins to address the problematic of the individual – collective tension through a somewhat different lens. Thus, while the sociology of Europe is beset by the problematics of social order and social function, American sociology at the beginning of the twentieth century presents a new and quite pragmatic approach to the question of social sub-groups and individualist interests.

Indeed, in an emerging national culture which seems obsessed by individual rights and individual prosperity, American sociology might seem to have been ideologically impelled to create a new way of studying the composition of its society. Certainly, Romanticism had provided a metaphysical grounding for the reconciliation of individual and collective interests, and this grounding had been adapted by European social research. Even so, the European intellectual tradition remained somewhat suspicious of individualism, perhaps because of its potential for radical deviation from ordered social change and the paternalism of

the aristocratic heritage. Either way, the new world of the United States seemed to embrace individualism as the basis of a national ideology. Laissez-faire capitalism and a diverse population base provided the conditions necessary for the formation of a society which was distinctly different from the European heritage. Not surprisingly, these new social conditions required new ways of researching and uncovering their meanings.

The sociology that developed in and around the University of Chicago was concerned with the transmission of broader value systems and their effects on the actions, attitudes and practices of smaller sub-groups. This more inclusive approach to sociological inquiry marks a significant realignment of academic and institutional thinking, most particularly in terms of symbolization processes and the experience of a culture in flux. The fluid and formative conditions of the United States – with its significant social investments in immigration, class mobility, pluralism and individualism – seem to have provided an effective context for the development of more expansive ways of thinking about society and culture. In the early part of the twentieth century, during a period of sustained economic prosperity, population growth and millenial revisionism, the notions of 'America', of mass society and of mass communication were extremely potent.

The Polish Peasant

Among the most significant of the Chicago School studies is *The Polish Peasant in Europe and America*, an astonishingly rich and complete analysis of the experiences of Polish immigrants, published in five volumes between 1918 and 1920. The authors, W.I. Thomas and Florian Znaniecki, felt impelled to explore these experiences through the analysis of personal writings, newspaper clippings, parish reports, immigrant, bureaucratic and welfare documents, material from migrant associations and case studies. To this extent, *The Polish Peasant* directs sociological enquiry into a more subjective field of study, one which concerns itself with social change and the pyscho-social effects of 'disorganization' and 'reorganization'. Unlike histories of prominent people and dramatic events, *The Polish Peasant* awakened social enquiry to the significant experiences of ordinary people; these experiences and perspectives illuminated broader cultural patterns where values, rituals and ways of conceiving of self, identity and meaning were seriously challenged through the experience of migration. Culture itself became the critical component of human life.

In many respects *The Polish Peasant* announced the beginning of a new approach to social research. While it lacked the sort of theoretical density with which Durkheim and Weber presented their field studies, *The Polish Peasant* represented a significant step forward for sociology. Its assemblage of various perspectives on a particular phenomenon, the migration of Polish peasants to America, illuminated the complexity and multi-dimensionality of culture. Although American sociology remained fragmented until the 1950s and 1960s, the work of Thomas and Znaniecki provided a useful model for the development of sociological research. In particular, Thomas and Znaniecki's work provided a grounding for the emergence of the subjectivist approach to the analysis of individual experience, sub-cultures and cultural diversity which was to flourish later in the century. This strand of American sociology constitutes

a precursor to the theories of symbolic interactionism and phenomenology.

Robert Park

Robert Park (1864–1944) joined the University of Chicago in 1914 as a replacement teacher. Park was already fifty, and had spent a good deal of his professional life as a journalist and social reformer. Like his mentor William Thomas, Park was profoundly interested in the experiences of the poor, oppressed and underprivileged. However, Park's earlier training in German philosophy provided the grounding for the development of concepts and approaches which the Chicago sociology required if it were to move from being a social movement to becoming a rigorous academic department. Thomas and Znaniecki had presented a methodology which was descriptive, but Park sought to analyse the phenomena of the urban world in a way that was consistent and systematic, and which would render substantive explanations. To this extent, Park (Park and Burgess, 1921) distinguishes four major social processes:

1 *Competition* is the fundamental, elementary and universal principle of human interaction. It is consistent and permeates all areas of human life. It tends to position people within their known community.

2 *Conflict* is intermittent and personal. While competition determines an individual's place in the ecological or economic order, rivalry and conflict determine one's position in the broader social order, in society itself.

3 *Accommodation* implies a cessation of conflict which comes about by the final fixing of an individual's position in

society. The forces which allocate status and power in a society temporarily fix the person in his or her hierarchical position. Accommodation, like conflict, is fragile and easily upset. Any kind of change in a person's life conditions (such as migration) might alter radically his or her status of accommodation.

4 *Assimilation* is the process by which individuals and groups acquire the sentiments, attitudes and characteristics of other people. By sharing the other group's experiences and history, the assimilating individual can engage with them in a common culture.

Park's work on immigration and urban life generally applies these concepts in order to produce a more complete understanding of the processes of social change and cultural dislocation. While Thomas and Znaniecki's work remains memorable for its documentary density, Robert Park more fully theorized the orientation and value of sub-cultural sociological analysis. He sought to articulate the various enclaves, institutional, ethnic and social sub-groups which constituted the fabric of urban life. He wants to explore urban life as 'a state of mind, a body of customs and traditions, and of the organized attitudes and sentiments that inhere in these customs and traditions' (1969: 91). This 'state of mind and body' might seem to revivify the Kantian/Weberian notion of a social 'web' which functions at the level of a shared consciousness. However, unlike the Kantian/Weberian web of consciousness, Park's work was designed as a 'living' or extant sociology which transforms the anthropological conception of tribal life into an urban documentary, one which provides a textured image of the contemporary environment.

Park's precepts influenced several generations of Chicago and other American sociologists. The Chicago School developed significant strategies for the investigations of ethnic and 'deviant' sub-groups, illuminating, in particular, the rituals, customs and value systems which defined the fabric and constituency of the group. The Chicago School were significant in that they established an unashamedly popular culturalist paradigm for the study of society. Notions of power, hierarchy and ideology were present in their work, though they generally resisted an elaborate Marxist analysis of social problems and social injustice. Park's interest in Marxism was more intellectual than political, and in most cases the Chicago School maintained a powerful liberalist perspective on the phenomena they studied. Park's own journalistic ethics seemed to underlie the formulations of his projects and analyses. In particular, he believed that the objective rendering of the complex details of everyday life would contribute more to the alleviation of social problems and social injustice than to the overthrow of governments. The task was to illuminate, and the techniques of observation and recording were not dissimilar to those employed by the journalist. Park's own interest in radio and the popular media, and the wider patterns of investigations within the School, reflected a substantial confluence with the ethics and heritage of modern journalism – a ground-level, real-life humanism that protected the interests of the everyday citizen, as well as the institutions of democratic liberalism.

COMMUNICATION AND THE PAYNE FUND STUDIES

Stuart Hall (1982) has identified within American social and communications research a marked disinclination to questions of ideology and power. And indeed, the ascendancy of Parsons' positivism during the 1950s and 1960s is often seen as a significantly reactionary phase in American sociology. Elizabeth Long (1997) has suggested that the ascent of Parsons' structural functionalism actually subsumed American sociology's more usual interest in the popular and everyday, reflecting perhaps the arrival of significant numbers of intellectuals from Europe during the 1930s. While it is certainly true that intellectual life in America was significantly affected by the presence of European intellectuals like Parsons and the Frankfurt School (see Chapter 3), it is also true that even before Parsons' ascent American social research was as interested in large social institutions and statistical methods (positivism) as it was in popular perspectives and ethnographic/discursive methods of enquiry. Indeed, during the 1920s, as statistical methods became more sophisticated, it seemed inevitable that the clarity promised by numerical investigation should prove alluring to the fields of behavioural and sociological science.

It was also during this period that communications departments were being established across the United States. While mostly these schools were dedicated to the professional training of journalists, there was also a ferment of academic interest in the effects of the new mass media on individual US citizens. Ideas on mass society and mass media led to the formulation of theories such as 'the theory of uniform effects', 'selective influence' and 'indirect influence'. All of these theories attempt, with increasing levels of sophistication, to explain the effect of mass media and their messages on individuals, their attitudes and behaviour. This academic interest, in fact, echoed broader public and governmental concerns about the impact of the mass media, especially on children.

The genesis of social research into the mass media reflects the growing significance of the media in American cultural life. Equally, academic interest in communications and the media marks an important moment for the development of cultural studies, reflecting the significant role the media play in the formation of contemporary culture. In the post-World War I period, with American films dominating global markets and the system of mass-produced talkies imminent, serious consternation about the new medium was being expressed in editorials, sermons, magazines and other public forums. In 1928 William H. Short, executive director of the Motion Picture Research Council, invited a group of university psychologists, sociologists and educators to design a research project that would assess the influence of movies on children. With no government funds available, the group received funding from a private philanthropic organization, the Payne Fund, to conduct the studies from 1929 to 1932. Publication of the ten-volume Payne Fund Studies began in 1933, establishing a significant pattern for mass communications research in the United States.

While cultural studies has largely rejected the Payne Fund research model, the studies do demonstrate the centrality of popular media in culture and the variability of their influence on audiences. In a sense, the studies articulated the deficiencies of a simple transmission model of mass media message-sending (see Figure 2.1); as Lowery and De Fleur concede, '[o]ne of the great disappointments of mass communications research as it accumulated was that it seemed to show that media had only limited influences on their audiences, rather than the powerful influences feared by their critics' (1983: 27). While the modelling for this kind of research has grown increasingly complicated during and since

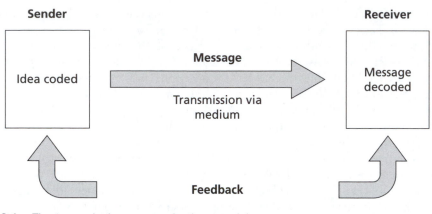

Figure 2.1   The transmission communications model

the Payne Fund research, there remains a common belief that media institutions construct messages that are transmitted through channels and received by audiences. The Payne Fund studies found that this transmission–reception process was largely elusive; they draw the inevitable conclusion that if effects are discernible at all, they are longevous, indirect and difficult to study. Blumer (1933) found, for example, that the impact of film on criminality may be varied or even contradictory, depending on the diversity of themes depicted and the social environment, attitudes and interests of the specific audience member.

There is little doubt that the effects tradition, which continues in America and elsewhere today, has strong attachments to cognitive or psychological approaches to human experience. Its primary focus is on the relationship between major social institutions and their value systems, on the one hand, and individuals, on the other. Thus, while the power of institutions and the broad reach of their messages are critically examined in effects research, there is no impulse to challenge the underlying ideologies that inform these institutions. If

anything, the postivist approach to social and cultural research tends to assume, if not reinforce, the values of social stability and social order. Even so, the Payne Fund studies were at least sensible to the importance of the new forms of electrical media, recognizing that the way people lived, thought and behaved was inevitably linked to the modes of information, imagery and narratives to which they were exposed. A more complete understanding of the popular media would require a more complete theorizing of the notions of culture and language. British/Birmingham cultural studies (see Chapter 4) looked directly toward the Payne Fund and other forms of cognitive media research in order to construct a more complex and politically informed analysis of the popular media.

PHENOMENOLOGY

Sociological Roots

The philosophical tradition of phenomenology – the investigation of phenomena in the world – was largely adapted into sociology through the writings of Peter Berger in the 1960s. However, the work of the Chicago School and their descendants might well be identified as confluents of a phenomenological tradition. In particular, the face-to-face, ground-level research of sociologists like the Lynds (*Middletown*, 1929) and William Whyte (*Street Corner Society*, 1943) maintained, and indeed enhanced, the interests of community-based social enquiry. While it is true that the Lynds excluded marginal groups (African Americans, divorcees) from their snapshot of community life, Whyte was much more adventurous in his explorations of the street-life textures of Boston's North End, and his examination of everyday Bostonian life drew on the anthropological precepts of inclusiveness and ritualized power. The social mapping of later sociologists such as Elliot Liebow (*Tally's Corner*, 1967), Kai Erikson (*Everything in its Path*, 1976) and Berger himself, owes much to the evolution of urban anthropological methods.

Edmund Husserl

As a theory, however, phenomenology remains both marginal in sociology and somewhat elusive. This is partly because the two great progenitors of phenomenology, Edmund Husserl (1859–1938) and his student Martin Heidegger (1889–1976), held quite divergent positions on the definition and application of the concept. What is common to both positions, however, is the restoration of the subjective ('I', 'me') over the objective (all that is external and real). Husserl, in fact, rejects Hegel's transcendental rationalism, which privileges the objective as the central sphere of ontology (being in the world). Instead, he revives René Descartes' epistemology (account of knowledge), which sought to

confirm the substantiveness of knowledge by the method of doubt: to doubt is to render knowledge ultimately immune from scepticism. To achieve this level of scientific knowledge, Husserl argues, the knowing subject or 'knower' must be centralized in the process of knowing. That is, the knowing subject must precede the externality of the world of objects.

Like Descartes and Hume and unlike Kant, Husserl does not subscribe to the notion that consciousness or *a priori* Truth precedes experience and evidence. However, like Kant, Husserl's phenomenology is also transcendental or 'eidetic'; its primary concerns are with the transcendental structures of consciousness which derive from the knowing subject and essential types of things. The word 'phenomena' derives from the Greek, 'that which appears'. For Husserl, the knowing subject must have consciousness of something; an individual cannot have consciousness that is not about something. Phenomenology claims to reveal the underlying nature of phenomena and the essence of human consciousness. In Husserl's own words, 'Phenomenology aims at being a descriptive theory of pure transcendental experience' (1931: 191). Husserl's interest in the structures of pure or transcendent experience constitutes the sort of idealist universalism which might distinguish between the phenomenological and the ordinary. Husserl refers to the experience of the ordinary as incorporating usual judgements and 'natural' standpoints which cannot be in themselves phenomenological. When, however, all unproven or ordinary judgements are put aside or parenthesized, then the true nature of phenomena is revealed in the consciousness of the subject. Alternatively, proven judgements are implicated in the revelation of the true nature of phenomena.

Husserl, therefore, never exempts his phenomenological philosophy from rationalism or empiricism (experience). In fact, the enterprise of phenomenology is to reveal the true nature of things, the true nature of phenomena. Ordinary judgements are no more than unproven positions. Phenomenology, on the other hand, represents an investigation of the ontology that lies within a subject's consciousness of something. The true nature of our knowing a tree, for example, cannot be adduced by examining the tree or by assuming the tree simply exists. The phenomenology of the tree exists only as the tree is embedded in the consciousness of the knower. Rational investigation reveals for us the true structure or being of the tree as it is known.

Martin Heidegger

Heidegger rejects Husserl's transcendental Idealism and with it the transcendental ego. For Heidegger, it is not the irreducible and ultimate fact that 'man' exists in a world that transcends him; rather he exists in a state of 'givenness': *Dassein* or 'there-being'. For Heidegger, the question of what it is *to be* must be continually raised because Idealism fails to present it. We find ourselves 'flung down' into the world and into a time and place we did not choose. We cannot adopt the perspective of disinterested observer because we are always and forever part of the fabric of objects that exist in and of our own consciousness. It is this being-in-the-world which Heidegger claims to be constrained by the Idealist ego and its essentialism. The only significant standpoint, the only one open to investigation, is the one Husserl describes as 'natural' where the subject remains fixed in ordinary judgements with other ordinary people. Phenomenology, in this sense, becomes a way of being and a methodology rather than a transcendent experience:

The expression 'phenomenology' ... signifies primarily a methodological concept. This expression does not characterize the *what* of the objects of philosophical research as subject-matter, but rather the *how* of the research. (Heidegger, 1952: 50)

Heidegger's version of phenomenology differs markedly from Husserl's in as much as the ordinary experience of phenomena is its primary focus. Our experience of a tree is determined not by its transcendent presence in our consciousness, but by the mere fact of its existence in relation to ourselves. Heidegger's view that we are 'flung down' into the world of phenomena heralds the sort of existence-in-the-world thesis presented by existential philosophy. Søren Kierkegaard, Jean-Paul Sartre, Friedrich Nietzsche and Heidegger himself all share a view that the mere fact that we are here in the world is the fundamental fact. The Viennese philosopher Alfred Schütz brought these notions of phenomenology into the realm of social enquiry, adding a further level of sophistication to the Chicago School approach to everyday life.

Alfred Schütz

After his arrival in the United States from Vienna in 1939, Alfred Schütz made a significant contribution to the development of a phenomenological perspective in American sociology. He combined aspects of phenomenology with Weber's theory of intersubjectivity. Schütz was interested in developing a social theory which, focusing on social action, could account for the capacity of subjects to be conscious of themselves in relation to others. That is, subjectivity, since it had to be conscious of something, would necessarily be involved in 'constructing' meaning *of something*. Subjects would construct meaning through their everyday practices and in relation to other constructing, conscious subjects. Again following Weber, Schütz was interested in the notion of intersubjectivity: that is, subjects interact and communicate in order to produce some sharable meaning or meaning consensus. Schütz provides for later sociologists a theoretical grounding for the analysis of a social reality that is shaped by subjects' interaction in everyday contexts.

Peter Berger

Much of Schütz's work resembles earlier phenomenology, most especially in its ontological, almost theological, interest in 'ultimate' questions of being, existence and the meanings that constitute human consciousness. While Schütz's work draws these questions more fully toward matters of society and social interaction, the more complete translation of phenomenology as a sociology of subjectivity is provided by Maurice Merleau-Ponty and Peter Berger. Like Schütz, Berger was born in Vienna and was heavily influenced by notions of 'intersubjectivity' as the basis of social construction of meaning. That is, our awareness of the world of objects (our consciousness) is largely facilitated through our mutual interests with other conscious subjects; we work together to create our version of the world. Also like Schütz, Berger emigrated to the United States, and in his prolific writings dating from the 1960s, he urged a mode of empirically grounded sociological research which described the 'phenomena' of everyday actors in everyday life. Berger's greatest contribution to contemporary sociology and cultural analysis resides in a theoretical competence which facilitated the study of microtic experiences such as the internalization of values, as well as macrotic phenomena such as the social construction of

institutions (see Berger, 1967; Berger and Luckman, 1966).

Berger does not offer us a distinct and detailed theory of culture, though his philosophical assumptions and the character of his work certainly expresses a fundamental interest in the processes of meaning-making and the 'consciousness' that underpins everyday social experiences. Essentially, culture for Berger may be summarized as 'the totality of man's problems' (1967: 6). Such a totalizing definition is typical of phenomenological thinking; society is merely a portion of culture, and culture appears as the reflection of the ontological dimensions of all human consciousness. What it is to be human continues to preoccupy the phenomenologist, framing the content and conceptual analyses the empirical researcher presents. For the phenomenologist, culture exists only in as much as people are conscious of it (Berger and Luckmann, 1966: 78). Sign systems and language, in particular, are seen as the primary conduits of intersubjectivity and meaning (Berger and Luckmann, 1966).

Central to this conception of language is the notion of dialectic, which Berger uses (unlike Hegel and Marx) to denominate a form of subjective interplay. These interplays exist in many forms, though the interplay of self and body and self and the socio-cultural world are fundamental to Berger's understanding of culture. Berger's discussions of the body and organicism, for example, lay the foundations for more recent cultural studies interest in the body and bodily inscriptions of meaning (see Chapter 9). Most importantly, Berger explains how a person's individual biology can limit his or her experiences in life, noting that the world one has created also acts in return upon the body (Berger and Luckmann, 1966: 181). Sexuality and intake of food are necessities of biological existence; the body lives, seeks sexual release and nourishment, but particular circumstances of life impact upon the behaviours that determine how these phenomena are experienced. Humans are socially conditioned into certain values, belief systems and behaviours, and these socio-cultural forms will necessarily determine the means by which individuals experience nourishment and sexual release.

The interplay of body and self parallels the broader interplay of self and general socio-cultural forms. By and large, Berger is arguing here that society and culture are the collective manifestations of the inherent interests of individuals. Society and culture and the individual necessitate each other. Individuals do not create reality in their own terms but must always and inevitably refer to the collective conditions of their world. Socialization conveys to the individual all the knowledge that is required for social functioning. Individuals create culture out of what is passed on to them; they are motivated to do this, Berger argues, as a substitute for what is denied them by their instinctually deprived organicism. In other words, society and the individual are both manifestations and constructions of each other. This fundamentally dialectical relationship, Berger claims, draws together the two opposing pillars of social theory: the Weberian notion of individual meaning and the Durkheimian interest in facts and social structures. In fact, they are two sides of the same coin, and each must be understood in terms of the other.

There is no doubting the significant contribution that Berger's work has made to the development of sociology and a sociological form of cultural studies. Berger's work needs to be understood, however, as a fundamentally humanist and ontological pursuit. There is little in the work that

demonstrates a significant commitment to radical social reform, nor indeed to the political dimensions of social and cultural experience. Indeed, while Berger's writings during the early 1970s betray a level of political awareness (*The Homeless Mind*, and *Pyramids of Sacrifice*, 1973), his discussions of language and social reality fail to acknowledge the significant relationship between culture and power that was being pursued by his contemporaries in Britain and continental Europe. The controversies surrounding Berger's work, like that of his symbolic interactionist colleagues, related more to the validity of method. Berger's phenomenological methods presented a significant challenge to those forms of quantitative and objectivist social science that had been popularized by Talcott Parsons and his followers. Berger's interest in ethnographic mapping and speculative phenomenology are characterized by positivism as a form of intuitive and descriptive narrative which lacks empirical or scientific precision.

As sociology has begun to incorporate more fully a cultural perspective, various theorists and empirical researchers have integrated theories of language with the phenomenological lineage. Phenomenology, in fact, provides a quite particular account of culture, one which identifies the *essential* features of a context and the invisible *consciousness* of everyday social actors. The collective of these individual consciousnesses comprises the 'lifeworld' of a culture. In textual studies critics have often concentrated on the 'lifeworld' of characters within the text (e.g. the Geneva School of literary critics), though more recent work has attempted to account for the interplay between text and reader/audience (see Wilson, 1993, 1995). In a sense, this shift from a text-centred criticism to an investigation of the subjectivities of audiences reflects a similar move in phenomenology from Husserl's more scientific or objectivist interests to Heidegger's more free-flowing adventures into the lifeworld of everyday people.

Phenomenology and *Blade Runner*

Phenomenology has been adapted into various forms of literary and film studies. From its Greek derivation, phenomena refers to 'that which appears'. In early adaptations of phenomenology for the study of texts, critics sought to reveal the essential character or underlying consciousness which patterns the aestheticized world. Phenomenology at this level is really attempting to reveal some fundamental qualities which are shared by human minds and their consciousness (awareness or knowledge) of the world. J. Hillis Miller, for example, examines Thomas Hardy's novels to reveal certain repeated patterns of the author's consciousness; these patterns are formed through metaphors of distance and desire. Similarly, a phenomenological analysis of the fantasy science-fiction film *Blade Runner* might reveal the patterns of consciousness which produce a sense of alienation and desire. *Blade Runner* depicts a perfected but tragically constricted human evolution. The Replicant reflects a deeply shared desire to extend and complete our humanity while at the same time acknowledging the inevitability of its impossibility.

While this 'web of consciousness' approach is drawn from Husserl's phenomenology, a more subjectivist approach has been adapted from the work of Martin Heidegger. Heidegger was more interested in the facts of our existence. For Heidegger, being present in the world of objects is a 'given'; an individual subject will find himself or herself merging with the objects with which they interact. That is, our minds merge with those things of which we are conscious. This insight has led many textual critics to become more interested in the audience's experience of the phenomena of a text. An analysis of *Blade Runner* in this more audience-centred approach would seek to explain how an audience member (or audience group) would respond to the things revealed: the alienation, social hierarchies, degradation and conflicts between base and super humanity. In particular, this form of analysis would be interested in the 'situation' in which the text is viewed, in terms of both the physical environment and the life conditions of the viewer.

Wolfgang Iser's literary phenomenological criticism can be usefully applied to film texts. Iser (1978) believed that the work of a critic was to reveal the ways in which a reader makes sense of a literary text. In the case of *Blade Runner*, phenomenology would be interested in the ways in which an audience member may draw on his/her own memory of characters, events and experiences in order to make sense of the fictional world of the text. The audience member's first impression of Deckard, for example, will apply his/her pre-existing memory in order to make sense of the character's appearance, values and actions. In particular, this memory may invoke real people whom the audience member knows or other characters from film. In either case, the memory engages with the filmic revelation; the audience member makes adjustments to his/her own understanding of the text as well as the memory. Deckard's resemblance to the commonly deployed crime fiction character 'the gritty cop', for example, may be brought into play as the audience member seeks to understand Deckard's appearance in the subterranean social conditions of the future world. As new aspects of character are revealed and as the events of the film unfold, the audience continues to make adjustments in order to make sense of the character and the context of *Blade Runner*. The complexity of character, most especially as it is articulated through the ambiguous status of Deckard's Replicant girlfriend, forces the audience member continually to modify his/her understanding and memory.

Clearly, each audience member will have different expectations and experiences of the text. Sometimes these differences can be very marked (e.g. between different gender, class-groups, ethnicities, age-groups), while in other situations the differences may be less significant. In either case, the audience member will not have a fixed experience of the text; rather, audience members will experience the text through changing and adjusting points of view. Within these modifying viewpoints, the audience member also confers with the norms and morality of the film, filtering and making judgements about characters and their actions. The question of whether Deckard should kill his Replican girlfriend, for example, looms large in the film, and audiences will be impelled to make their own moral judgements about Deckard's decision. The resolution of the dilemma that is offered by the film is only pertinent in terms of the audience member's own moral frame of reference. This frame of reference, however, is forced to adjust to the new circumstances and the particular instance of Deckard's position. In this sense, Iser argues, an audience/reader may be forced to adjust his or her own moral schema, his or her own 'world view', as it engages with the film's narratives, norms and values.

Phenomenology and TV

While a phenomenological perspective has been evident in film studies, recent studies in television appear to be embracing and adapting the work of Ricoeur (1981) as a form of hermeneutic or interpretive phenomenology. More than any other medium, television has been integrated into the everyday practices and experiences of people; for phenomenologists of contemporary culture, the TV would constitute a central indicator in the reality-making and consciousness of social actors. Thus, TV is constituitive of meanings and social practices in two ways: first, as the conduit of externally constructed and domestically interpreted texts; and, secondly, as a domestic technology which of itself engages with the everyday practices, schedules, relationships, social rituals, and so on, of the people in a household. Phenomenology would aim to elucidate these two arenas of culture and meaning-making through its empirical techniques of participation, observation and recording. While a good deal more will be said about audiences and their practices in later chapters (see Chapter 8), it is worth noting that phenomenology, and its various contemporary permutations, does not of itself provide an account of political divisions, nor does it constitute the sort of reformist agenda that informs British cultural studies.

Tony Wilson (1993, 1995) argues, in fact, that contemporary TV analysis, drawing on British cultural studies and French poststructuralism, has found itself in a serious theoretical bind. According to him, contemporary cultural analysis of TV has lost its ability to analyse the meaning of a text, concerning itself with ideological contexts in which the medium operates. These contexts are only part of the process of meaning-making; analysis must also examine the relationship between a text and its audience, and the ways in which an audience constructs its meanings. Phenomenology allows texts to conduct meaning (something poststructuralism denies), but only in terms of the intersubjectivity of audiences. That is, the audience of a TV text will construct meanings in relation to each other's subjective orientations and consciousness. Knowing, or being conscious of, the TV text allows the text to exist for these audiences. The role of the researcher is to uncover the processes and internal structures which facilitate particular meanings in relation to the audience's lifeworld. For Wilson, therefore, there are no theoretical problems in reporting the variations and similarities in meaning-making between individual audience members and between different audience groups. The meaning of a TV text exists in relation to the variant lifeworlds of the various audience members. Different ethnic groups, for example, will experience the 'phenomena'

of a TV text like *Friends* in an infinite variety of ways – nevertheless meaning remains a direct consequence of intersubjective communication.

SYMBOLIC INTERACTION

Symbolic interaction(ism) is another branch of sociology which derives from Chicago-style subjectivism, psychology and a general reaction against the ascendancy of structural functionalism. Denzin (1992: 3) explains that symbolic interaction combines aspects of behaviourist language theory with interpretive phenomenology; the major distinction between phenomenological approaches and interactionism rests primarily in the latter's greater interest in the microcosm of individual social actors' participation in specific situations where meaning is negotiated and exchanged. While Denzin (1992) and Becker and McCall (1990) have traced the emergence and development of symbolic interactionism through social psychology (esp. George Herbert Mead), anthropology and philosophical pragmatism (esp. John Dewey), it was not until the 1950s and 1960s that a fully theorized interactionist approach became available to sociological enquiry. Most notably, the new symbolic interactionists brought a more systematic empirical methodology to the study of meaning exchange, as well as a more sustained substantive cohesion to the notion of symbolism and meaning construction.

In *The Presentation of Self in Everyday Life*, Erving Goffman (1959) suggested in a vaguely ironical way that the modern self was, in fact, a series of responses to given symbolic contexts. That is, notions of an essential self needed to be measured against the tendency for individuals to 'dress themselves up' in order to satisfy the requirements of a particular situation. Goffman constructed a framework, for example, for reading the 'man in the grey flannel suit', observing that social status could be dressed up according to norms and expectations of a particular situation. While Goffman's analysis may seem rather tame when measured against the radical subjectivities discussed in current cultural analysis, his work did lay the foundations for new ways of understanding social contexts.

During the 1960s Howard Becker's work on deviance brought symbolic interactionism into the mainstream of a more inclusive and expanding field of sociological enquiry. This invigoration of sociology, in fact, accompanied wider social trends of the 1960s and early 1970s whereby particular areas of public discourses were engaging with ideas of socialization, alternative lifestyles, youth culture and the questioning of value-systems that had led to the Vietnam War and the threat of a nuclear Armageddon. Popular films such as *The Wild One* and *Rebel without a Cause* and the rise of youth music had alerted sociologists and the general public to the paradoxes and potential efficacies of social deviance. Reaction against McCarthyist conservatism and Parsons' positivism drew sociologists out of obscurity, stimulating a more widespread engagement with phenomenological and symbolic interactionist theories and methods.

There can be little doubt that the work of phenomenology and symbolic interaction on deviance and sub-culture influenced the work of British cultural theorists like Raymond Williams, Dick Hebdige and Stuart Hall (see Chapter 4). Even so, these methods and theories may, in a sense, have reached their pinnacle in Becker's work, and while interactionism continues today, recent developments in language or discourse theories have highlighted the limitations of a social psychological approach which emphasizes the microcosm of interaction as the central unit in cultural enquiry. Becker's own work on deviance in a sense legitimates the whole notion of normalcy and deviance; a cultural studies perspective would certainly reject that sort of dualism as it would reject the very idea of 'difference' being articulated as negative or aberrant. Clearly Becker's point is that society constructs notions of deviance, but for the current generation of cultural criticism, such an approach would be the 'bottom-line' or 'given' of any form of cultural enquiry. More generally, the belief that 'society' is a constitution of individual meaning exchanges is never fully realized in the interactionist analysis. The body of qualitative research which comprises the interactionist tradition never actually conceives of, nor adequately accounts for, 'culture' as such. Discussions and analysis satisfy themselves with the minimalist position; the psychological condition of the individual actor seems never to escape into the broadening processes of the 'lifeworld'. The interactionist analysis of deviance, for example, seems satisfied in its reports of the psychological state of interacting subjects and the ways in which their meanings are coded within a highly localized context of interaction – the sharing of drugs, the purchase of a new motorbike.

While some interactionists claim that their approach does indeed facilitate an investigation of social structure (see Denzin, 1992: 61–2), there is no doubt that any attention paid to broader social formations is incidental to the primary and microscopic view of specific social exchanges. Some critics have also suggested that interactionism tends to reproduce, in fact, microtic versions of larger social structures, forming as a consequence a reification of structure as 'context', 'meaning' or 'activity' (Prendergast and Knotternust, 1990). This reduction of larger systems produces a rationalistic, cognitive and emotionless rendering of the meaning exchange process.

Above all, however, the interactionists remain fundamentally liberal and indeed politically neutral (see Reynolds, 1990). While this criticism was common in neo-Marxist writings of the 1950s and 1960s, most especially in the work of C. Wright Mills, the complaint persists in the writings of more culturally oriented commentators like James Carey in the United States and Stuart Hall in Britain. Moreover, recent language theory (poststructuralism and postmodernism) has argued that all texts are problematical renderings or constructions of reality, rather than mirrors of reality itself. While phenomenology grounds itself in fundamental ontologies (essential truths), symbolic interactionism satisfies itself with an empiricism which it claims will produce its own conceptual or theoretical groundings. The methodologies (ethnography or participant observation) of symbolic interactionism are offered as the epistemological substance of the world as experienced. The theory or way of framing and understanding an event will necessarily arise through the data collection process – all will be revealed. Contemporary language theory, however, argues that such renderings are themselves supplements to the original experience: that is, they mediate rather than mirror reality, forming a secondary text which is itself subject to construction and interpretation. What is revealed in symbolic interaction research is an interpretation of an interpretation, and barely constitutes an empirical fact. This problem of methodology continues to haunt sociology, even as it has embraced many of the principles and precepts of cultural analysis.

ANTHROPOLOGY

Anthropology can be understood as a form of comparative sociology. Generally speaking, the discipline emerged out of an interest by European and American scholars in the cultures of colonized peoples. During the eighteenth and nineteenth centuries, the various fields of naturalism, philology (study of languages), archaeology and anthropology were not distinctly bordered; the invading nations sanctioned and encouraged the examination of the conquered people not merely to substantiate military, commercial and administrative efficiency, but also to fortify the conquering civilization's intellectual superiority. Artefacts, biological samples, primitive peoples themselves, were all treated as specimens or curiosities, and were appropriated for the universities, museums and private collections of the conquering country. The moral legitimation of this barbarism was provided by intellectuals like Adam Smith (1723–90) Herbert Spencer (1820–1903) and Robert Malthus (1766–1834), whose ideas on self-interest became vulcanized to Charles Darwin's evolutionism to produce the first major globalization theories: the survival of the fittest nation or civilization. We have already seen that nineteenth-century German philosophy was very much entranced with the idea of *Kultur* or the advance of individuals and civilizations. Nineteenth-century British philosophy articulated a more pragmatic though equally forceful interest in the necessities of usefulness, prosperity and the advance of superior nations.

Edward Said (1978, 1993) has mapped the discourses of colonizing nations, arguing that the entire culture of the conquering nations was predicated on differentials of power that incorporated the territories and cultures of invaded peoples. For Said, the production of nineteenth-century art and scholarship was bound by an identity which distinguished the civility of the home culture from the primitivism of alien 'others'; the discipline of anthropology emerges out of that dualism, that sense of curiosity, Romanticism and even guilt. Whether motivated by compassion, dispassion or celebration, the very presence of the Westerner in the alien culture, Said argues, served merely to reinforce the privilege and status of the investigator over the investigated. The ethic of liberal humanism – democracy and freedom – seemed never to extend to the interests and dignity of the conquered people, except in terms of philanthropy or charity, which were themselves markers of a superior condition.

From these beginnings, however, anthropology has developed sophisticated techniques of analysis and societal comparison. Into the twentieth century, anthropology generally evolved into two broad fields of analysis:

1 Structural or cultural anthropology, as practised by Claude Lévi-Strauss, Ferdinand de Saussure and Mary Douglas, examines the cognitive structures that distinguish cultures. These structures arise through language systems and may be manifest as mythology, kinship or, in the case of contemporary culture, consumer goods (see Douglas, 1978). We will examine this field of structural anthropology in detail in Chapter 5.
2 Interpretive anthropologists are more keenly interested in cultural textures and forms of cultural relativism; the methods, which are far less scientifically precise, seek to elucidate the personal and subjective sensibilities which constitute meaning-making. This field of anthropology, examined in detail below, is closest to the humanist subjectivism and phenomenology which rises through Chicago sociology and blooms during the 1960s and 1970s.

Clifford Geertz

The work of American anthropologist Clifford Geertz has been most frequently presented as seminal in the development of interpretive anthropology. Underpinning Geertz's work is a reading of Weber's famous description of society in which 'man is an animal suspended in webs of significance he himself has spun'. Geertz takes 'culture to be those webs, and the analysis of it to be, therefore, not an experimental science in search of law, but an interpretive one in search of meaning' (1973: 5). Geertz's work demonstrates, in fact, a blurring of cultural boundaries whereby the researcher as interpreter invokes his/her own experiential knowledge in order to elucidate the text of his/her investigations. Thus, in his famous essay on Balinese cockfighting (see insert) Geertz invokes the non-Balinese texts of psychology and aesthetics (*King Lear*) in order to explain significant social relationships and 'personalities' in Balinese culture. Anthropology, according to Geertz, is a multidisciplinary activity which must confront the wide range of human activities – including 'power, change, faith, oppression, work, passion, authority, beauty, violence, love, prestige' – within the context of their doing (Geertz, 1973: 21; see also 1988).

The Balinese Cockfight

Clifford Geertz's anthropological studies of non-modern societies have provided a useful methodological and theoretical paradigm for contemporary cultural studies. In particular, Geertz seeks to illuminate the 'web of meaning' by which members of a given social group are bonded. These meanings, however, are not unitary or homogeneous, but are formed through struggle and conflict as well as consensus. Geertz's studies constitute a form of 'ethnography': a mapping of people, practices, artefacts and meaning-making processes. The following excerpt is taken from Geertz's study of the Balinese cockfight. The meaning of the fight is not immediately obvious; the task of the analyst is to draw these meanings into the light and interpret them for the non-Balinese.

Of cocks and men

To anyone who has been in Bali any length of time, the deep psychological identification of men with their cocks is unmistakable. It works in exactly the same way in Balinese as it does in English, even to producing the same tired jokes, strained puns, and uninventive obscenities. Bateson and Mead have even suggested that, in line with the Balinese conception of the body as a set of separately animated parts, cocks are viewed as detachable, self-operating penises, ambulant genitals with a life of their own...

In the cockfight, man and beast, good and evil, ego and id, the creative power of masculinity and the destructive power of loosened animality fuse in a bloody drama of hatred, cruelty, violence, and death. It is little wonder that when, as is the inevitable rule, the owner of the winning cock takes the carcass of the loser – often torn limb from limb by its enraged owner – home to eat, he does so with a mixture of social embarrassment, moral satisfaction, aesthetic disgust, and cannibal joy. Or that a man who has lost an important fight is sometimes driven to wreck the family shrines and curse the gods, an act of metaphysical (and social) suicide. Or that in seeking earthly analogues for heaven and hell the Balinese compare the former to the mood of a man whose cock has just won, the latter to that of a man whose cock has just lost. (Geertz, 1991: 243–4, 245)

Geertz's work, while distinguishing between society (social relationships) and culture (symbols), confirms the significance of their interaction. Indeed, as we consider the deployment of the concept of culture as 'way of life', Geertz's studies on Bali raise the important question: is culture no more than an expression, mirror or confirmation of existing social order? In reply Geertz suggests that culture actually and actively constructs meaning by providing social actors with the space for considering, reviewing and feeling what it is to be Balinese. That is, culture is not merely a confirmation of social and personality processes, but a field of creativity and production: symbolic production. Thus, art and all other expressive modes become forms of collective thought-experiment where members of the group can explore and wonder about the many things that perplex and intrigue them: works of art 'materialize a way of experiencing, bring a particular cast of mind into the world of objects, where men can look at it' (Geertz, 1976: 1478).

Geertz's own methodology of interpretation and elucidation is characterized as 'thick description' (1973), a form of ethnography adapted from literature studies as much as from the sociological analyses of Durkheim, Weber or his more immediate mentor, Gilbert Ryle. For Geertz, this ethnography may in fact apply the broadest range of data-collecting techniques in order to grasp and then render the complex of cultural meaning-making comprehensible to outsiders:

[I]nterviewing informants, observing rituals, eliciting kin terms, tracing property lines, censusing households.... Tracing his journal. Doing ethnography is like trying to read (in the sense of construct a reading of) a manuscript – foreign, faded, full of ellipses, incoherences, suspicious emendations, and tendentious commentaries, but written not in conventionalized graphs of sound but in transient examples of shaped behavior. (Geertz, 1973: 10)

Geertz's work is mobilized through this form of investigative and interpretive practice, allowing the theoretical dimensions of his analysis to emerge in context. Just as culture is relativistic, so theory is multi-layered and expressive of the texture of the investigative focus – that is, of culture itself. Theory is bound by culture. The best thing about interpretation techniques, according to Geertz, is that they eschew the necessities of conceptualization and therefore they are able to resist 'systematic modes of assessment' (Geertz, 1973: 24). Geertz insists that the whole point of a semiotic investigation is that it elucidates the signs and *concepts* as they are used by the subjects of the study, thus enabling access and 'conversation'. In other words, Geertz is recommending a theory or conceptual framework that is 'grounded' in the field, that arises from the data rather than being imposed upon them by the theoretician, abstractionist or scientist. While invoking the theories of key sociologists, Geertz's approach resembles the sort of thinking that informed Robert Park and others of the Chicago School. Geertz prefers to map his cultural subjects, allowing the descriptions to run as closely as possible to the texture of their lives.

Ethnography and Culture

While notions of grounded theory and ethnographic research paradigms have filtered into a range of contemporary social research fields, the democratic openness of Geertz's approach has been particularly appealing to the current generation of cultural studies researchers. In particular, Geertz's heuristic flexibility, his willingness to move unrestrainedly through a range of research fields and topics, and his democratic and relativistic approach to culture itself have proven alluring to those ehtnographers and sociologists who feel constrained by the theoretical density of the more linguistic and abstract areas of cultural studies. Certainly, the methods of ethnography (grounded people-mapping) resemble literary journalism and literature as much as discursive empiricism. The quality of Geertz's work is as much an outcome of his narrative style as of his powers of observation and analysis. Even so, his ethnographies have irritated other, perhaps more systematically inclined, scholars who find his work unpredictable, lacking in direct evidence, overly speculative and even mystical in its renderings of 'traditional culture'.

On the other hand, Geertz's work, while never approximating the sort of celebratory and homogenizing demeanour of Durkheim or Victor Turner, nevertheless tends to privilege notions of social order and systematically constituted social values within a culture. Social order conveys and is conveyed by the symbol system. Of course, Geertz pays attention to the social divisions and disharmonies that are manifest in a social group, but his work tends inevitably toward those symbolic practices which contribute to social maintenance and solidarity. The Balinese cockfight, for example, is seen as a confluence of harmonies and disharmonies, but the social order prevails because the text of the cockfight facilitates an important psychological dialogue, a playing out of fear, aggression and desire. In particular, Geertz elucidates the significant psychological connection between the men and their 'cocks' (fowls/phalluses) and the brutal combat that is played out as an emanation of power and potency. This sexual potency and the social rituals that are attached to it are mythologized through the Balinese conceptions of demonic

power. As though to acknowledge the dangers associated with excessive carnality, excessive potency, the cockfights are also imbued with the cyclical forcefulness of animistic and Hinduistic tensions which, in turn, reflect the moral and communal tensions which perpetually beset human social order.

In interpreting this bloody drama, Geertz resembles the literary or film critic as much as the ethnographer. The meaning of the text, as it is interpreted by the observer, returns to a form of microtic functionalism; the actors perform the ritual tasks in order to sustain the community and its social order. It is for this reason that Geertz represents the victorious cock-owner as performing a cathartic ritual of appeasement as he takes home the vanquished cock to eat: 'in seeking earthly analogues for heaven and hell the Balinese compare the former to the mood of a man whose cock has just won, the latter to a man whose cock has lost' (Geertz, 1991: 245).

DISCUSSION: SYMBOLIC ORDER AND NATION-STATE SOCIETY

Through their various permutations, social theory and sociology have made significant contributions to our understanding of how social groups form and function. In particular, sociology identified symbolic systems as a central facility for social organization. Along with shared values, practices and norms, shared symbols and meanings were seen to make a major contribution to the formation of social order. Both anthropology and sociology recognized that a symbolic order was necessary for the establishment and maintenance of a general social order. The nation-state, which has emerged as a central organizing unit in the modern world, relied on a system of shared meanings or symbols in order to ensure its continued viability. As we noted in Chapter 1, a notion of common culture became a central feature of the nation-state. As well as a common geography, language and political institutions, the modern, nation-based society maintained its collective exigency through the force and promotion of a national culture. Sociology contributed enormously to our understanding of these symbolic social processes.

Until relatively recently, however, sociology has not only been implicated in the identification and analysis of 'society'; it has also been engaged in its production, promotion and maintenance. That is, sociology has directly and indirectly contributed to the confirmation of the concept and ideology of an orderly national society. While, of course, there are many social members who may be extremely grateful for this, there are others who have become highly critical of sociology's underlying assumptions. We can summarize these criticisms in the following terms:

1 *Symbolic and social order*. As we shall see in later chapters, the notion of a symbolic order has been critically revised, most particularly by poststructural and postmodern theorists (see Chapters 5 and 7) who argue that language and culture are highly unstable and often unsystematic. For poststructuralists, language is volatile and transitory; its meanings are formed around complex and changeable historical and cultural circumstances. Jacques Derrida (1974) argues, for example, that words and their meanings do not exist in a fixed relationship, but are constantly shifting. Each word relies on other words to explain it; these words in turn rely on other words, and so on. Meaning, therefore, is perpetually deferred since there can never be a stable and perpetual origin to any word's meaning. In such a precarious symbolic environment, the whole notion of 'order' is cast into doubt.

2 *Social homogeneity*. Notions of social order, organization, symbolic order and social system clearly inform a good deal of social enquiry. Social and cultural theories which seek to explain 'systems' tend to treat those systems as valuable; their work is often informed by a more or less explicit desire to improve the functioning of these systems. To this extent, social enquiry has a substantial tradition of pragmatism and functionalism which often supports the maintenance of prevailing values. Postmodernism also casts doubt over the validity of these assumptions, arguing that an excessive devotion to the collective order subjugates the constituent parts of a social formation. That is, the social whole subjugates the interests, beliefs and dignity of individuals and minority groups.

Postmodernism and cultural theory more broadly have argued that the emphasis on the systematic functioning of the nation-state society has served to diminish the intrinsic diversity of human social groupings. The notion of multiculturalism, therefore, challenges the homogenizing impetus of the nation-state. A postmodern collective privileges the diversity of the constituent social parts over the solidity of a monolithic concept like society.

3 *Imposed authority and ideology*. The development of new modes of social enquiry during the 1960s and 1970s – ethnomethodology, symbolic interactionism and phenomenology – also

exposed significant deficiencies in mainstream sociology and its principal working concept, 'society'. While each of these new strategies of enquiry sought to illuminate lower gradients of social groupings and their experience of social reality, they remained, for the most part, ideologically and intellectually committed to the notion of a pluralist, though largely centralist, national society. Even so-called 'radical sociology', a cluster of neo-Marxist social theorists, remained only vaguely interested in the potential of cultural diversity and the deconstruction of the concept of nation. As with most neo-Marxists, radical sociologists conceived of society in terms of structural conflict; their radical objective was to replace an hierarchical system with a more egalitarian one.

Clearly, the authority of the nation-state and its fundamental ideologies are not substantially challenged by sociology. Of course specific permutations of government and governmental policies were challenged, but the authority of the state and the nation remained largely untouched. It is not until the emergence of an oppositional cultural studies that the underlying authority of the state and society are critically examined.

4 *Anthropology – speaking for others.* There are specific issues relating to the disciplinary objectives and methods of anthropology (comparative sociology). The most prominent of these relate to the presence of First World scholars in less developed parts of the world, and the propensity and power of these scholars to 'speak about and for others'. Eighteenth- and nineteenth-century 'anthropologists' are rightly criticized for their habit of appropriating the artefacts and artworks of less economically and militarily powerful peoples and placing them in private and public collections in the imperial world. The social Darwinism which supported this sort of colonialist pillaging has been replaced in more recent times by a less tyrannical code of scholarly behaviour. Even so, anthropology continues to be criticized for engaging in neo-imperialist and exploitative activities. Thus, the rituals, artefacts and practices of less developed peoples are transformed into 'intellectual property' as they are symbolically integrated into First World culture. Put simply, the cultural knowledge of less developed peoples exists for the satisfaction of First World curiosity.

Edward Said (1993) suggests, in fact, that the very presence of an anthropologist from a wealthy, alien culture serves merely to confirm the inferior status of the people being studied. The social power of the First World citizen is maintained and confirmed through the activities of anthropology. Rather than enhance diversity, anthropology serves only to enhance First World curiosity.

Sociology has sought to overcome these deficiencies by engaging more fully in cultural studies modes of theory and analysis. In fact, while we have identified specific strands of social enquiry which have been interested in symbols and symbolic patterns, there is now a greater interest amongst sociologists in issues of language, power and cultural diversity. To this extent, cultural studies deviates from traditional forms of social enquiry as it seeks to expose the meanings and articulations of ordinary people in their everyday lives. This oppositional cultural studies eventually overthrows simplistic notions of society, and social and symbolic order, as it strives to locate culture within the complex interactions and mediations of discourse rather than in presumed social structures and systems.

3

Marxism and the Formation of Cultural Ideology

Outline of the chapter

This chapter examines the influence of Marxism on contemporary cultural theory and cultural studies. We begin with an examination of Marx himself, and in particular Marx's approach to ideology and the base–superstructure model. While the vast majority of Marx's work is devoted to questions of politics and economy, the concepts of ideology and the superstructure provide an important basis for an understanding of the relationship between meaning-making and power. In particular, literary theorists like Georg Lukács and Bertolt Brecht adapted Marx's ideas for an analysis of textual representation; both theorists argue that literature and art have a responsibility to oppose dominant ideologies, and to reform society and culture. The Frankfurt School of Marxist social and cultural critics argue similarly that representational texts (literature, film, music, etc.) can be agents of oppression or liberation. Mass-produced culture, according to the Frankfurt School, tends to control and limit the potential for human agency and intellectual growth.

The Frankfurt School approach reflects a central tension for Marxist analysis: if representations, texts and dominant ideologies are so prevalent and dominant in capitalist society, how is it possible to think our way out of these controlling discourses? Louis Althusser and Antonio Gramsci were particularly influential in the development of a political cultural studies, and most particularly in the project of addressing this central Marxist dilemma. Both Althusser and Gramsci seek to understand how it is that the subordinate classes seem so compliant with their own oppression. For Althusser the answer presents itself in the concept of 'ideology'; Althusser reverses Marx's preoccupation with political economy by centralizing the cultural forces of 'belief' and meaning-making. Gramsci's concept of hegemony or leadership suggests that the relationship between rulers and ruled is more complex and interactive than Marx appreciated. This concept of hegemony was especially important for the development of a 'popular' cultural studies as it moved away from the Frankfurt School's somewhat simplistic approach to the power of mass-produced culture. According to contemporary hegemony theory, consumers of popular cultural texts have a considerable degree of agency (capacity to act and think independently) in the selection and interpretation of media texts. This agency or autonomy provides the basis for the development of new theories of politics and culture.

GENERAL INTRODUCTION

The concepts of power and social reform remain central to many areas of contemporary cultural analysis. While the actual nature and definition of power and politics continue to change, Marx and Marxism, as Stuart Hall suggests, are never far away from contemporary cultural politics. Karl Marx (1818–83) remains a towering figure in modern social and political theory. His revolutionary views on power and social relationships have influenced many generations of radicals and critical thinkers. His work continues as a point of reference in academic and public discourse, even as his followers adjust to dramatically altered historical circumstances. The collapse of the USSR and communist states in Eastern Europe, the liberalization of the Chinese and Vietnamese economies, the contraction of communist revolutionism in the developing world, and the fragmentation of the reformist agenda in developed democracies are all cited as evidence of the demise of Marxist ideals. Marx's theories on the mode of production, division of labour and class warfare seem no longer relevant in a culture so far removed from the conditions of nineteenth-century Europe. Even so, the philosophical underpinnings of Marx's critique continue to attract interest, most particularly as theorists attempt to understand the evolution of privilege, oppression and social hierarchy in contemporary culture.

Of course, it would be entirely unfair to expect that any social commentary could survive in its literal form much beyond its own immediate historical context. The power of Marx's analysis rests in its compassion and its recognition that the new economic system of capitalism created great comfort and pleasure for some but great injustice and hardship for the majority.

Thus, while moving beyond the literalism of Marx's political prescience, contemporary cultural theorists have found Marxist notions of power and ideology particularly valuable for the development of their own critical perspectives. The substance of this influence is quite variable. American pluralist/liberalist cultural theory has tended to resist issues of power, at least until relatively recently. British cultural studies (see Chapter 4) has been strongly influenced by the neo-Marxist analyses of Louis Althusser and Antonio Gramsci. More recent forms of postmodern cultural theory have tended to extend the French post-structuralist critique of Marxist analysis, rejecting in particular the austerity and class basis of Marxist analysis.

MARX AND HEGEL

Marx was born in Germany, but after suffering the indignities of social exclusion and anti-semitic prejudices moved to France and on to London, where he spent most of his adult life. While Marx himself was not a member of the working class or proletariat, he identified this social group as the victim of oppressive social conditions. Throughout his writing career, Marx worked toward the emancipation of society through the formulation of a self-consciously radical programme which would liberate all society from the ills of industrial capitalism. In reading Marx, however, we must remember that his ideas changed, as indeed did his social and intellectual circumstances; we shouldn't expect too absolute a consistency in the overall body of his work. Some of the most interesting and important aspects of Marx's thought are to be found in the earlier writings, where he struggles to liberate his own theorizing from that of his major mentor, G.W.F. Hegel. In order to

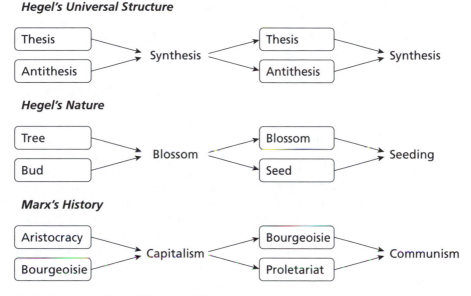

Figure 3.1   The dialectics of Hegel and Marx

understand some of the complexity in Marx's approach to culture, we need to appreciate Marx's intellectual relationship to Hegel's dialectics and the transcendental rationalism which underpins his work.

Hegel's Dialectics

In Chapter 2 we discussed the formation of Hegel's transcendental rationality, a view which sees the real world as merely an appearance of underlying epistemological structures (the 'actual'). Hegel, we recall, thought that the real and actual worlds could only be resolved through a spiritual ascent, a form of self-consciousness which would allow a complete reconciliation of human thinking (concepts) with the actual conditions of nature. This synthesis would finally reconnect the human mind (subjectivity) with the world of objects (objectivity). Reason and reasoned thinking lay at the centre of this progress.

Marx rejects the idea that the essential character of reality is spiritual, and that freedom and conflict in the world might be resolved through reference to the synthesizing power of essential nature. He does not accept Hegel's reduction of things and human activities to modes of consciousness, nor does he accept the distraction of human suffering from the real conditions of politics and economy. Hegel's dialectical theory, in fact, describes nature as a series of perpetually evolving conflicts and resolutions: all phenomena present themselves as thesis for which there is a natural and inevitable antithesis; the eventual crisis of opposition leads inevitably to synthesis. This synthesis ultimately expresses itself as a further thesis with consequent antithesis. Moral wisdom and freedom, according to Hegel, are achieved via an evolutionary progress through oppositional claims or conflicts to wisdom as consciousness and knowledge. Put simply, Hegel's dialectics in nature function as shown in Figure 3.1.

Hegel claims that this fundamental structure of nature compares with the spiritual ascent of human subjects. The principal difference, however, is that human morality can aspire to the bosom of God and ultimate spiritual/moral knowing.

Marx's Materialism

Marx's materialism is material in as much as it questions the value of such theories for the real-life attainment of human values and liberation. In the context of social and environmental dissolution, Marx sought to break with the metaphysics of Hegel and his philosophical tradition. In fact, while acknowledging the brilliance with which Hegel pursued the logical conclusions of this tradition, Marx wanted to install a form of philosophical naturalism. In the *Critique of Hegel's Philosophy of Right* (1970), Marx claims, against Hegel's notion that 'man' is essentially spirit, that he is rather 'real, corporeal man with his feet firmly planted on the solid ground, inhaling and exhaling all the powers of nature' (orig. 1843, 1970: 206). Marx takes this metaphor of nature to express the suffering of 'man' as much as his capacity for self-assertion and pleasure beyond the mere abstractness of Hegel's conception:

> As a ... natural, sentient, objective being, he is a suffering, conditioned and limited being, like animals and plants. ... The fact that man is an embodied, living being with natural powers means that he has real, sensuous objects as the objects of his being. (Marx, 1970: 206–7)

Hegel's idealism, therefore, is brilliant but overly abstracted (or in Marx's terms 'alienated') thought. And while Marx himself adapts the dialectical model (thesis–antithesis) for a reading of the major movements and conflicts of history, his ultimate aim is to ensure a perspective of the human experience which is grounded in the real conditions of human life.

Marx's Naturalism

Marx's naturalism, however, indicates a certain ambivalence (or internal dilemma) which persists through much of his work and which continues to plague critical writing today. This is the question of determinism and free will. Marx offers for us an image of history and of the human experience which is coloured by suffering and structurally determined oppression. The lasting impression of Marx's work is of an alienated individual and social class whose only possibilities for freedom are revolutionary uprising. Free will, most particularly as it is envisaged in *The Communist Manifesto* (1848), is an act of collective determination, though even here the collectivity is conditioned by 'class struggle' and the inevitability of dialectic determinism. Yet pencilled through the writings is a naturalism which, like the naturalism and idealism of particular Romantic writings, opens a space for individualized pleasures, including the pleasures of aestheticism. In opposing the alienating effects of industrialization by which the product of labour belongs to the capitalist, Marx refers to the possibilities of creative and natural being. In *The Economic and Philosophical Manuscripts* (1844) he refers specifically to the 'species being' by which humans confirm their uniqueness as animals by aestheticizing the products of their labour 'according to the laws of beauty'.

Thus, while Marx generally rejects Hegel's notions of spiritual nature, he clearly articulates in some of his writings the belief that humans must satisfy bodily and social needs. That is, while history is shaped by struggle, the end of these conflicts is the completion of their natural as well as human needs. Nature is ontological and independent of consciousness. Its value for human life is twofold: it provides resources for the satisfaction of needs, and it provides an aesthetic resource for the gratification of sense and individual pleasure. At this point, however, Marx again resists the Idealism and Romanticism of Hegel and philosophers like Jean-Jacques Rousseau, both of whom implicate human consciousness and freedom in the spiritual exigencies of nature. For Marx, nature does not hold the promise of pure reason nor spiritual ascent, but it does offer the individual the opportunity to shape and experience his or her humanity in the fullness of aestheticized sense.

Above all things, Marx's ideal brings history to account. While Hegel posits a utopia of pure reason, Marx's own logics lead him to the actualization of an egalitarian condition, where humanism and nature are fully resolved and mutually supportive. This new communalism is achieved through the real struggles of real human beings; there can be no recourse to the imagining of the spirit.

> Communism is the positive supersession of private property, of human self-alienation, and thus the real appropriation of human nature through and for man. It is, therefore, the return of man himself as a social, i.e. really human, being. ... Communism as a fully developed naturalism is humanism and as a fully developed humanism is naturalism. It is the definitive resolution of the antagonism between man and nature, and between man and man. It is the true solution of the conflict between existence and essence, between objectification and self-affirmation ... between individual and species. It is the solution of the riddle of history, and knows itself to be the solution. (Marx, 1963: 155)

Marx's answers to the problem of history and conflict, therefore, are political.

Communism promises the 'complete emancipation of human qualities and senses', including 'not only the five senses, but also the so-called spiritual senses, the practical senses [of] desiring, loving' (Marx, 1963: 160). While these largely incidental comments about the liberation of the senses appear at various points in Marx's writings, his most significant contribution to the theory of symbolization and meaning-making appears in his discussions of the relationship between economy and culture, most notably through the theory of ideology and the base–superstructure model.

SYMBOLIC CONTROL

Marx's somewhat sporadic discussions on naturalism and individual fulfilment present a rather limited perspective of free will. As with numerous other social commentators of the nineteenth century, Marx's structuralism tends to limit opportunities for the exertion of individual will, presenting a view of humans as victims of history, large social movements and institutionalized structures such as class. As we shall see, this problem of how individuals and groups might construct their freedom remains a problem for many other critics influenced by Marxist reformism. But for Marx himself it is particularly problematic, given that his liberationism is vested in a class of people of which he is not even a member. If the working classes are to act upon and achieve their freedom, then presumably they must be able to conceive of it in some way. Marx claims to resolve this question by producing his dialectical version of human history: it appears that the working classes must necessarily rise up against their oppression because history compels them. In other words, the proletariat's history appears to be pre-destined, a template that determines their actions.

The German Ideology

There is a logical problem here, for if the working classes are able to conceive of their freedom, it may be that they have already reduced their oppression. That is, the very act of thinking may constitute an overcoming of the limits of oppression. Freedom is difficult to conceive when we don't have it; it's a lack, an absence, an abstraction. If we can conceive of what we don't have, then perhaps it is the oppression that is the abstraction, an imagination of our present condition. In *The German Ideology* (1932) Marx attempts to articulate this conundrum by suggesting that our capacity to 'think' our freedom is itself determined by the ruling classes. These classes, who have a vested interest in extinguishing challenges to the validity or actuality of their 'right to rule', actively construct modes of compliance through the promotion of ideology (ideas, beliefs, values). To achieve this, the rulers attempt to transform the conditions of their self-interest into 'universal' social values. That is, social values which encourage obedience, loyalty to authority, legitimacies of blood, religion, social pragmatism, commercialism, and so on, are disseminated as the general conditions of goodness.

Ideology, therefore, is false consciousness because it derives from the interests of the present ruling class. In aristocratic times regal imagery and rituals confirmed the status and superiority of the aristocrats. The notion of 'blue blood' was conceived as a restrictive analogue, a means of distinguishing ruler from ruled. Shakespeare's plays are riddled with evidence of royal patronage, praise for kings and kingly deeds, and persistent reminders of the sacred lineage of royal blood. In Marx's time, the bourgeoisie constituted their power through public and popular discourses. Street signs, coins, education institutions, public hangings, all legitimated the rule of plutocrats. The obedience of the proletariat was constituted through this false consciousness, a belief that things were as they should be and that the proletariat's social, political and economic privations were justly ordered, if not ordained. Only in times of significant social stress can these ideologies be stripped bare and recognized as class-based rather than universal. Thus, in Marx's dialectics of history, the transformation from aristocratic pre-eminence to bourgeois pre-eminence would have been accompanied by a significant re-alignment of social values and ideology.

The imposition of ideologies, therefore, cannot extinguish entirely the possibilities of change and reform. Even so, Marx's description gives us a particular insight into the operations of culture as directing and determining human 'nature'. But his position is incomplete. His naturalism suggests that humans will inevitably suffer and experience pleasure and that culture will both provide the expression of that suffering and the source of its overcoming. In the midst of this uncertainty Marx continually returns to generalized explanations of determining social structures. These structures, as we have noted, are built around economy and labour, rather than its expressive or aesthetic modes. In conceding that ideology is the construct of class interests, Marx opens the way for a full account of symbolization and meaning construction. However, he lacks the conceptual armoury needed to attack this problem as fully as have later analysts. That is, he travels to the edge of some extremely incisive analysis of the political operations of language, symbolization and ideology. However, there are simply not enough intellectual resources, not enough concepts and theories available to him in

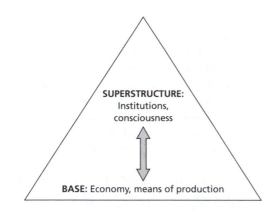

SUPERSTRUCTURE:
Institutions,
consciousness

BASE: Economy, means of production

Figure 3.2 Marx's base–superstructure model

order to take the next step. Rather, he confines himself to a more concentrated rendering of the economic structures which determine human suffering and oppression.

The Base and the Superstructure

The base–superstructure model outlined in *A Contribution to the Critique of Political Economy* (1976, orig. 1859) was designed to elucidate the relationship between the distinctly economic structures of a society and the institutional and behavioural articulations of those structures. The 'base' refers to 'forces' of economy and production (tools, technology, workers' skills) and the relationships of class that are mobilized in the application of those forces. The superstructure refers to institutions (political, educational, legal, etc.) and the forms of 'consciousness' that are the expression or outcome of these institutions. (see Figure 3.2.) These 'expressions' might be understood as ethics, values and ideology, though Marx and Engels never adequately explain the relationship between these categories. This elision has given rise to a multitude of subsequent interpretations, debates and applications.

Importantly, however, Marx and Engels' perspective in the *Critique* most certainly presents culture as the expression and servant of economy. Engels himself attempted to clarify the idea after Marx's death, suggesting that the relationship between the base and superstructure (economy and meaning-making) was not entirely deterministic because there is a degree of reciprocity: 'The economic situation is the basis, but the various components of the superstructure ... also exercise their influence upon the course of the historical struggles and in many cases determine their form' (1994: 194). Engels suggests here that the superstructure does more than just reflect the underlying determinations of economy. Rather, the superstructure – institutions, symbolizations, culture – actively participates in the form and shape of society and political relationships. That is, the base produces the actual character of a particular superstructure (feudal, agrarian, industrial), but the relationships between institutions and individuals inside the superstructure will clearly produce their own effects. Engels, that is, permits a level of 'free will' within the superstructure which, presumably, provides the opportunity for resistance, class warfare and revolution. Ultimately, however, this free will is limited by the underlying character of history and political economy. Only certain things are possible within the superstructure, and these are the limits set by the economic base.

The primacy of economy in Marx's theoretics limits his view of culture and symbolization. His unyielding resistance to Romanticism and the ideals of transcendent consciousness perhaps impair his ability to think outside the limits of that particular epistemology. It's not consciousness that determines life, but life that determines consciousness, Marx argues. But in many ways his view of consciousness, as a way of knowing that is thoroughly implicated in economy and relationships of production, restricts his conception of how that knowing might proceed. In particular, Marx fails to see how knowing and symbolization might create the circumstances of the liberation he seeks. Even so, while other nineteenth-century social theorists were formulating a disinterested, 'scientific' account of human experience, Marx was cognizant of the influences of power and politics in all realms of human activity. He believed that power was fundamentally embedded in culture, and it was this point that was to be elaborated by later theorists.

CRITICISMS OF MARX AND MARXIST ASSUMPTIONS

The cultural critique of Marx's theories can be summarized in the following terms:

1   Marx conceived of human relationships primarily in terms of political economy and materialism. For cultural theory this emphasis limits the possibilities of analysis to investigate abstract forms of symbolization.
2   This materialism is essentialized in Marx's theory of labour and the mode of production. Marx tends to restrict analysis by treating all social and cultural processes as fundamentally associated with relationships to capital. A person is located in a social class, depending on whether he or she owns capital or is 'owned' by capital. Class is the major social determinant, and constitutes foundational social structures. Marx, like the social theorist Émile Durkheim (see Chapter 2), is a structuralist.
3   This tendency to view the world in terms of class or collective groups has restricted Marx's analytical breadth. In particular, Marx constructs a limited

perspective of the individual, and of individual pleasures and gratifications. He does have a vision of individualism, though cultural critics have tended to see this purely in negative terms: the individual is set against the polemic of laissez-faire capitalism and utilitarianism. For cultural critics Marx's individual appears to be constrained by capitalism, an alienated victim who lives beneath the shadow of a capitalist smoke-stack. Individualism is configured as a misery, a symptom of the de-communalizing effects of mass urbanization.

4   Marx's theory of alienation suggests that the mode of production and the conditions of labour reduce individuals (and their subjectivity) to the condition of 'commodity' (a thing to be bought and sold). The sense of being 'alien' is a consequence of becoming nothing more than an oppressed unit in economic exchange; humans are deprived of the things they create and their value is estimated only in terms of what their labour can produce. In other words, their humanity is sacrificed in the process of commodification. The corollary of commodification is consumerism. Numerous critics believe that Marx's view on consumption fails to acknowledge the pleasures and gratifications that may be attached to consumption and commodification processes.
5   Marx's account of history tends to *totalize* or *universalize* all human experience in a single, grand theory that explains everything. Marx sees all human history in terms of class and conflict. History is teleological or determined by major social causes and effects. As we shall see shortly, Marx applies Hegel's notion of dialectics or opposition to construct a theory of class warfare. In history, one class is

always set against another. Inevitably, they conflict and a new class is ascendant. This class is challenged by a rising new class. There is another clash and another resolution. Social history, therefore, is always defined in terms of major social divisions, allowing virtually no space at all for any other human experiences.

6 Marx relies on the Cartesian/Kantian view of the split between the subjective and objective worlds. He sees humans in terms of external or objective forces which determine subjective experiences and actions. He devotes the majority of his interest and work to these external conditions and to the possibilities of class action.

Karl Marx and Homer Simpson

Karl Marx's *Communist Manifesto* provided the basis for a good deal of reformist thinking during the nineteenth and early twentieth centuries. The *Manifesto* explains how the revolutionary overthrow of the ruling classes by the proletariat or working classes will lead to a ruler-less utopia (anarchic communalism). The communist state, temporarily governed by the proletariat, will ultimately dissolve into a global community in which individual autonomy and collective responsibility will be reconciled and meld harmoniously into one another.

Of course, Marx's ideals have never been realized. The communist state was to evolve out of the ruins of bourgeois, industrial capitalism. In fact, social experiments with communism have emerged in largely pre-industrial states during times of severe social crisis, usually precipitated by some form of imperial war (e.g., Russia, China, Vietnam). In modern, industrialized capitalist states the concept of 'class' has become increasingly problematic and difficult to define. In the United States, for example, a country which has never developed a strong labour politics, the idea of class consciousness appears particularly dubious. Pre-eminent ideologies constituted around capitalist consumerism, individual prosperity and success, and social pluralism seem to have muted any significant formulations of class. If ever there was a strong identification with social class, it is seriously threatened by new forms of social fluidity and cultural imagining. The contraction of manufacturing and heavy industry has been accompanied by new informational and entertainment economies and lifestyles.

Homer Simpson, the hapless nuclear power plant worker from the animated TV series *The Simpsons*, personifies the condition of the working class in contemporary culture. Homer is the source of much of the programme's comic despair. He appears almost entirely unaware of the iniquitous social forces that oppress him, preferring a televisual bliss to the cold realities of his condition. Homer is a perpetual loser, unable to organize industrially, unable to deal with the grotesque perversities of his boss at the nuclear power plant. Instead, he barely acknowledges the truth of his oppression, escaping into sport, TV and the quotidian trials of family life. The popularity of *The Simpsons* over a very long period derives largely from its subtle interplay of pathos and ridicule. We sympathize with Homer, but we examine him from the safe distance of a middle-class, consumerist lifestyle. Homer inevitably belongs to some other social group, some other epoch; he is not a member of a social class with which the audience can identify. He is merely Homer Simpson – comic, pathetic, ignorant, and a true representative of Marx's proletariat 'false consciousness'.

7 Marx views ideology as false consciousness. He is suspicious of belief systems that are built on non-rational or excessively emotional, spiritual or artificial grounds. Marx's view that religion is the 'opiate of the masses' indicates a general suspicion of abstractionism and irrationality. His work is very much embedded in the traditions of scientific rationalism; his followers have consistently struggled with his limited perspective of symbolization, spiritualism and metaphor.

8 Marx directs his hopes for emancipation in the actions of the proletariat or working class. Emancipation is a contingency of the conditions of oppression. The working class will rise against the conditions of oppression and replace them with a utopian equality which will remove the dialectics of social division. The mode of production will be replaced by conditions of equal participation and ownership. Capital and individual ownership will be replaced by a non-acquisitive freedom by which all materials are shared equally. Critics have argued that this utopianism relies excessively on the leadership of intellectuals – one group speaking for the oppression of another. It is naively misguided about the capacity of humans to share and be non-competitive. It misunderstands the

desire of individuals to speak for themselves and seek gratification in terms of their own individualism and identity.

The complaints against Marx by cultural theorists are generally threaded through a more substantive interest in symbolization, a more complex view of power, and a greater sense that capitalism is more perplexing and complex than Marx had appreciated. While some theorists claim to have rejected Marxian views outright, others have attempted to manipulate and adjust the theories in order to embrace more contemporary intellectual and social conditions. In the remainder of this chapter we shall examine how Marx's theories have been adapted, most especially for a broad understanding of power, symbolization and culture.

MARXIST AND SOVIET LITERATURE

Russian Formalism

Marx's work, as with other areas of social and political theory, uncovered significant connections between society and culture. And while Marx could not have conceived of a generalized theory of culture which engaged with all levels of symbolic, ideological and everyday practices, his writings were incisive enough to acknowledge the important links between social structures and the articulation of relationships and social forms. The application of Marxist social theory as the foundation of the Russian Revolution (1917–19) forced the reformers and intellectuals of the new government to consider very specifically the role culture could play in the communist utopia they were constructing. In *Literature and Revolution* (1924) Leon Trotsky (1879–1940), the leading intellectual in the revolutionary government, conceded that literature and art transformed reality according to the peculiar laws of aesthetics, but this was only the formal and less important dimension of artistic works. Against the intellectual pre-eminence of Russian Formalism, Trotsky and other writers, like Georgy Plekhanov (1856–1918) and A.A. Zhdanov (1896–1948), sought to construct a theory of culture which insisted on the continuity of art and life, and which (re)informed readers of the plight and suffering of the social underclass.

These ideas were transformed into official Soviet policy during the period of Joseph Stalin's rule. Articulated by the Union of Soviet Writers (1932–4), these doctrines privileged realism above all other artistic forms, viewing the formal experimentations of Picasso, T.S. Eliot and Stravinsky as bourgeois decadence, the indulgence of modernist capitalism. Art, therefore, was seen as the necessary servant of the revolution, providing the cultural link between government and the people; folk art, the art of the people, would be privileged, therefore, over 'high art', which was regarded as complex, elitist and restricted to the interests of intellectuals. Indeed, for the revolutionary critic, the distance between the mind and the body – intellect and manual labour – should be dissolved.

Georg Lukács

Georg Lukács (1885–1971), an Hungarian-born, Germanic, social theorist, argued that art and literature should 'reflect' the real conditions of social living. In *History and Class Consciousness* (1923), Lukács, reflecting both the Hegelian dimensions of Marx and Weberian notions of consciousness and causality, claimed that this reality should be understood as a dialectical and unfolding system. Like his Soviet peers, Lukács's aesthetics was prescriptive, though he rejected the surface reality depicted in recent European naturalistic novels (e.g., Balzac and Zola) in favour of a more complete rendering of the subtle interplay of power, social relationships and class. Naturalism tends to rely on common-sense realities and apprehensions; a more complete rendering of human experience would also include the depths of human consciousness. This is not to say that a novel should indulge itself either in mere mimesis (imitation of mind) or in pure subjectivity, as was becoming fashionable in twentieth-century modernist literature. But somehow realism must mediate consciousness and surface appearances in order to produce a full vision of the human condition. This condition, as in the Hegelian sense of reality, is predicated ultimately on patterns of conflict and eventual order. Lukács insisted that artistic realism was the most fulsome and complete rendering of this ultimate order. A Soviet socialist order was implied in the social conditions of the novel's dialectic. That is, the best and most realistic novels would tell their stories in accordance with the genuine conflicts of the times in which they were set; the reader would be led to a resolution that was a predetermind outcome of the conflict.

Bertolt Brecht

Lukács's work was in many respects less literal and more Hegelian than that of many of his fellow soviet critics. Like Bertolt Brecht (1898–1956), Lukács understood the value of conflict and the means by which ideology could be created and contested in a culture. Unlike Brecht, however, Lukács was incapable of appreciating the complex formal experiments and techniques which were informing Western modernist aesthetics. Brecht's obedience to socialist ideological and moral paradigms was tempered continually by his willingness to challenge orthodoxy. The dialectical conflicts which patterned his plays were evident also in his formal conceits, most particularly those which undermined the taken-for-grantedness of his reality construction. Brecht's regular interruption of the narrative of his plays functions as a self-conscious attempt to disturb the expectations of his audience and to remind them of the other side of his reality, the life-as-lived reality. In a way that anticipates postmodernism, Brecht refuses to allow his actors to assume heroic, disproportionate or star status. Rather, in keeping with the overall anti-aesthetic of his aesthetic, the actors become self-mimicking, parodic reflections of the horrors of true life.

In *The Caucasian Chalk Circle* (1948), for example, Brecht uses the singers as a parodic form of Chorus, providing for the audience an insight into the political conditions in which the narrative, and their own lives, are taking place. The play interrogates the validity of authority through a classical Marxist polemic. However, Brecht is aware of the resilience of despotism and rather than conclude the play with the rise and reign of the proletariat, the play's victors are young peasant lovers who adopt the child of the former dictator. Government returns after a brief phase of anti-rule, the sort of carnival inversion typical of Shakespeare's festival plays. The absurd character of Azdak, who is mistakenly installed as 'authority' during a time of revolution, constitutes a parody of all authority, conventions and orthodoxies. Brecht's faith in Marxist revolutionism is tempered by a vision of comic doubt, a sense that the sensual and pleasurable, laughter and love, constitute the genuine mode of human liberation. This more purely naturalistic and individualistic emancipation represents an aesthetic variant of Marx's own naturalism. Indeed, Brecht's iconoclastic Marxism is profoundly compassionate, and it barely constitutes the revolutionary orthodoxy prescribed by Stalin and other soviet or communist authorities.

The significance of Lukács and Brecht for cultural theory rests primarily in their conception of reality and its relationship to symbolization and ideology. Theirs is not a simple didacticism, but a subtle and considered rendering of social critique. Marxist economy remains significant, but both Lukács and Brecht directed their social criticism toward the immense potentialities of culture. In an attempt to comprehend the more invisible dominions of human experience through a generalized construction and application of cultural politics, they found themselves returning to Hegelian idealist theories of subjectivity. The relationship between the external or objective world and the internal processing of that world was never adequately resolved. Indeed, the entire Soviet project and its vision of 'reality' remains troublesome, if not debilitating. When the Frankfurt School took up the challenge of constructing a cultural politics, they understood that somehow they would need to reconcile their critique of powerful social structures with the elusive character of everyday experiences, including those which seemed predicated on personal pleasure and social conformity.

THE FRANKFURT SCHOOL

The Frankfurt School is the name given to the group of Marxist scholars who were exiled from Nazi Germany in 1933. The group worked in New York before returning to Frankfurt in 1950. The Institute for Social Research at Frankfurt practised a 'Critical Theory' which rejected notions of realism in favour of a blend of Marxist social criticism, aesthetics and Freudian psychoanalysis. Among the major members of the group were Max Horkheimer (1895–1973), Theodor Adorno (1903–69) and Herbert Marcuse (1898–1979). Walter Benjamin (1892–1940), who committed suicide after failing to escape to Spain and freedom from the Nazis, is also associated with the Frankfurt School, though his work and experiences remain distinct. With the exception of Benjamin, whom we will deal with separately, the Frankfurt School members were particularly interested in the relationship between the mass media as a 'culture industry' and the working classes.

Distinctively, the group focused attention on popular culture and popular media texts. However, unlike earlier work done through the Payne Fund and the Chicago School of sociology, the Frankfurt group brought a far more radical approach to the critique of the (American) mass media. The cognitive effects model, which investigated the media's impact on individuals, and the anthropological inquiries of Chicago-style sociology were suddenly overwhelmed by the systematic and substantially theorized critique of the modern media and the culture in which they operated. As Lukács and Brecht had argued, culture could work against oppression; the Frankfurt School focused on mass culture and its propensity for social control. Culture was therefore foregrounded in the revolutionary struggle. Undoubtedly, the work of the Frankfurt School provided a basis for a new and more radical approach to the sociology of culture and the media.

ADORNO, FROMM AND THE AUTHORITARIAN PERSONALITY

Adorno and Horkheimer wanted to understand how and why the masses were so compliant with their oppression. For Adorno and Horkheimer, the monstrousness of the Third Reich was perhaps less terrible than the mindless acquiescence of the German people, a people who had prided themselves on their intellectual, technological and social potency. As we have noted, the German word for culture is a synonym for civilization. For the members of the Frankfurt School, Germany's great tradition of civility and social advance had been wiped away in a single, generational gesture – the surrender of culture and morality to the obscenity of absolute power. The German devotion to the Führer, the Father, seemed to represent the fundamental flaw in the German personality: an obedience to authority, no matter how demonic or debased, provided it was potent.

In *The Authoritarian Personality* (1950) Adorno and his colleagues argue, along the lines of the psychoanalytic theorist Eric Fromm, that the German people failed to achieve their 'objective' revolutionary potential because they had become trapped in what he and others called 'a false rebellion'. To appreciate this concept fully we need to understand the fundamental argument of Freudian Oedipal theory by which sons achieve sexual maturity by disengaging themselves from the sexual identity of their fathers. This 'Oedipus Complex' is named after the character in Greek tragedy who mistakenly kills his father and marries his mother (see Sophocles, *Oedipus Rex*). The rise of Adolf Hitler to the ascendant position of Imperial Father or Führer is directly attributable to the conditions of unresolved Oedipal tensions, according to Fromm. A resentful or masochistic submission to the father was being redirected to the entire social system, a social system which had been strained to breaking by an internationally generated impoverishment and moral dishonour.

Fromm argued that irrational authority derives from individuals' incapacity to relate to one another in love and labour. Conventional Marxism sees alienation – the separation of an individual from the product of his or her labour – as a critical deficiency of capitalism. Fromm suggests further that the inability to love and be loved creates severe psychic disjunctures. In particular, the alienation of sex drives would lead to their redirection away from the natural object and towards some 'fantastic' alternative: God, authority, the German hero, charismatic rulers, and so on. This process of displacement and rationalization is basically the function of ideology: the child continues to identify with the father because of the potency of ideology; the rejection of the father is internalized as it turns against the child's own ego; here it is controlled by the superego or ego-ideal, which is no longer the father but which, as Freud points out, may be a manifestation of other individuals, groups or classes. Hence the child's rebellion is sadomasochistic or false, and the outcome is a perverse obedience, a form of aggressive conformity.

Rebellion, therefore, shifts from a rebellion against the father toward a rebellion against those external authorities who have inflicted pain. Germany's reparation payments following World War I become the site of pain, and the foreign powers of France and Britain become the focus of rebellion. That is, the Oedipal rebellion is redirected against the foreign powers whose polices of reparation and the continuing dishonour of Germany could be challenged and defeated by the authority of the German hero, now embodied in the figure of the Führer. Through a manipulation of the sex drives, social classes can become emotionally attached to the authority that controls them. This alienation is more profoundly experienced in troubled times when the personality is weak. The displacement of the ego ideal to the wider society and to 'the Father' is particularly redolent for a capitalist society that has no way of restoring the integrity of the individual but which labours under the weight of patriarchal mechanization, institutionalization and the general hollowing out of the family.

This almost pathological dread of authority constitutes an interesting paradox in the Frankfurt School's political project. In considering the authoritarian personality, Adorno, in particular, expresses deep misgivings about the cultural representation of German history and its heroes. That is, the popular imagination seems to offer no real resistance to the imposition of oppressive social structures. The solution to this mass obedience appears to lie outside the capacities of the proletariat, who are as attracted to authority as are the bourgeoisie. A deep and pessimistic shadow falls across the Frankfurt School's work as they seek some escape from the conditions of oppression. Like Marx, Adorno recognizes that oppression is linked to substantial social and historical forces. But unlike Marx, Adorno and the other Frankfurt members locate this oppression primarily in the conditions created by culture. In this sense, consciousness precedes economy as the determinant of human experience. The German people are the victims of culture as much as they are victims of economy; the limits of their consciousness are the limits of their freedom. And while Adorno seeks the possibilities of liberation from within culture – through the transcendent experience of high art and intellect – there remains little hope for a people who have surrendered themselves so fully to the general conditions of a self-imposed ideology.

Adorno and Mass Culture

This apprehension of the mass-mindedness and social acquiescence that had led so easily to the disintegration of German culture was rendered even more disturbing by the School's engagement with American mass consumerism. In particular, the 'culture industry', with its capacity for the delivery of messages to mass audiences, was considered the principal agent of control and social conditioning. The masses' immersion in highly schematized popular culture texts paralleled for Adorno the 'opiate of the masses' thesis outlined by Marx. That is, entertainment texts such as film, radio and later television stifle the political imagination. Herbert Marcuse made a similar point in *One Dimensional Man* (1964), suggesting that popular culture texts indoctrinate and manipulate people into glib gratifications that ultimately create a 'false consciousness', an ideological positioning which accords with the interests of the ruling classes. In fact, a common theme in Frankfurt School writing on popular American culture is that social classes and individuals will necessarily be distracted from serious social and political issues as they are constantly seduced by superficial entertainments and consumer hedonism. The culture industry, like all other capitalist institutions, has a vested interest in hierarchies of power and the control of messages and ideologies supporting capitalist economics and the rights of privileged elites.

Populism in Popular Culture

Significant arguments continue to be made against the controlling effects of the mass media. Media analysts such as Noam Chomsky (1988) argue that the popular media, and especially the popular news media, create the conditions of consent. Powerful institutions control the media, and it is in these institutions' interests to promote certain types of social conformity. Neil Postman (1993) claims that contemporary media technologies have been designed to limit our thinking and promote highly particularized forms of consumerism. We can only think and feel certain things because the media provide us with the content and the frames of reference by which that content can be judged. Our emotions are constantly engaged by sentimental and formulaic narratives. John Stauber (1995) argues that even our news services are dominated by the interests of corporate nodes of power. According to Stauber, not only is the great proportion of news constructed according to highly stylized frames of reference – images and personalities – but most news is sourced through large corporate public relations companies. Stauber argues that audiences are persistently duped into thinking that they are receiving objective accounts of the world, whereas in fact most news is a projection of the interests of a powerful and highly influential elite.

This notion of social control is pertinent to our understanding of the political and social spheres. The whole notion of the democratic state is founded on the idea of an informed and educated electorate. With free public education and continued access to 'objective' information, citizens can make rational and clear-minded decisions about specific issues. Voters can put pressure on governments in order to influence public policy. News journalism has been regarded as a central institution in the modern, democratic state (the so-called 'fourth estate') since it provides checks and balances on governments in the exercise of their power. Investigative political journalism, in particular, exposes governments and other powerful institutions to the scrutiny of the public. According to Stauber, the dilution of journalism and news practices in an increasingly media-dense culture threatens the capacity of the media to provide these checks and balances. This weakens the fabric of democracy and the freedom of individual citizens. Stauber, like Chomsky and Postman, believes that the reformulation of news as entertainment seriously limits our ability to analyse social and political issues critically.

In *Dialectic of Enlightenment* (1972, orig. 1944) and a range of other writings, Adorno claims that the actual narratives of popular texts distort reality in order to obscure the real conditions of human life. Social conflict is resolved through the production of popular narratives and melodramas. The privileging of narratives of authority, control, heroics, the moral primacy of the bourgeois family and the myth of success tend inevitably to neutralize opposition by constituting a false ideology. These distorted ideologies are supported by what Adorno calls an 'instrumental rationality', which is the rationalization of human behaviours through schedules and technology. The peculiar power of the leisure and entertainment industry is that it is able to reproduce the same schedules and controls that are prevalent in workplaces. Individuals are obedient to the work schedule and to the TV and radio programme guides, sitting passively and attentively in front of the medium when the programme and time slot commands. That is, the radio, cinema and television construct a rationalized environment in which time and behaviours are controlled by the owners of capital, who are also the owners of time. Freedom, therefore, is surrendered through the momentum of technology and rationalized social authority. Thus, mass society itself replaces the ego-ideal of the father; people come to obey and are controlled by the 'massification' of society and the capitalist forces that lie behind it.

Clearly Adorno, Horkheimer and Marcuse do not equate the modern consumerist culture with the folk culture and folk art of the past. Indeed, the Frankfurt School regard popular culture generally as an illusion created by the owners of capital in order to maintain their own privileges. Folk art comes from the people; modern popular art comes from the large capitalist institutions. A number of more recent cultural theorists have argued that the Frankfurt School's distinction between folk and commercial, popular culture is excessively simplistic and elistist. In particular, The Frankfurt School's disavowal of popular music misunderstands critically the complex relationship between text, audiences and ideology (see Chapter 8). Critics like Frith and Horn (1987, see also Bennett et al., 1993), for example, regard Adorno's essay 'On popular music' as a privileging of elite and intellectual tastes over the interests and aesthetic preferences of ordinary people: the classical music Adorno admires has little to do with the lives of the 'folk' whom Adorno claims to defend.

Adorno argues in this essay that the mass production of musical texts tends to produce a constraining effect on imagination. Texts are thus standardized in a cyclical process whereby successful lyrical and melodic patterns are copied and repeated in order to satisfy the 'conditioned' tastes of audience consumers. These audience consumers are thus conditioned by the repeated patterns and seek nothing more than the replication of these familiar and comfortable, if unimaginative, gratifications. These gratifications, Adorno argues, derive from certain psycho-sociological needs within audiences, most particularly those relating to affiliations with dominant social structures. As with his other writings on popular culture, Adorno claims that popular music inclines audiences toward a form of obedience or capitulation that may be either a distraction from more serious or troubling aspects of life (rhythmic obedience), or a more complete immersion in the sentimentalism of the text (emotional obedience).

There is a certain and often cited pessimism about the Frankfurt School's account of the social world and its cultural conditions. Adorno and Horkheimer do, however, offer some possibilities of escape but this tends to parallel both the Romanticism of nineteenth-century literary theory and Hegelian Idealism. Specifically, Adorno locates freedom in the fissures of dialectical conflict which will be most evident in complex forms of art. The prevailing ideologies (or false consciousness) can be challenged by an art form that does not have to collude with dominant economic structures. Unlike popular cultural products, therefore, art and literature are distanced from reality and are capable of exposing the serious deficiencies of economy and dominant social forms. Thus, while Lukács criticizes modernist texts for reflecting the alienating conditions of modern existence, Adorno praises the avant-garde for challenging orthodoxies and creating 'negative knowledge'. The experimentation of modernist texts is seen as a virtue precisely because it is distanced from reality and because it attempts to re-form and restructure that reality. It is crucial, Adorno claims, for art to make the downtrodden aware of the real conditions of their existence and to make them angry about it. Both in content and in form, the modernism of Proust, Beckett and Schoenberg demonstrates for Adorno the power of alienation in modern times. The subjective experience of an individual's alienation is thus rendered objective by the work of art, creating new possibilities for resistance and change.

WALTER BENJAMIN AND
MECHANICAL REPRODUCTION

While Lukács emphasized the value of proletarian engagement in the formation of realistic art, and Adorno emphasized the importance of modernist techniques in the construction of complex, liberational avant-garde art, Walter Benjamin sought to mediate significant areas of both. Benjamin's famous essay 'The work of art in the age of mechanical reproduction' (1977, orig. 1935) acknowledges the role of art in social criticism and culture. However, Benjamin does not share Adorno's outright rejection of the new technologies and their particular modes of communication: radio, cinema, telephone and gramophone. Benjamin, in fact, inverts the focus of Adorno's work, arguing that the new technologies release art from the possession and control of the bourgeoisie. The notion of an authentic and unique work of art must be rethought because art now can be mechanically reproduced and multiply distributed. Audiences can experience a film or photograph simultaneously across the globe and across social borders.

Benjamin's theories have been highly influential in cinema and more latterly cultural studies, most particularly as they resonate with an egalitarianism rooted in the everyday practices of ordinary people. Benjamin argues that the 'aura' of a work of art – that unique, perhaps mystical, power which separates the art work from the everyday fleshliness of its audience – is irretrievably compromised by the work's reproducibility. The authority (the author) of the text and its ritualized aesthetic integrity can no longer be sustained in the face of mass distribution and mass consumption. The deconstruction of rituals and the dimming of aura, Benjamin argues, release the text to politics at the level of consumption. Thus, while Adorno maintains that the content and form of the art object hold the promise of politics, Benjamin sees this promise in the action of consumption. While Adorno fears the power of the culture industry to create standardized texts for obedient audiences, Benjamin identifies in capitalism itself the potentialities for its own demise.

Meaning, therefore, is less a contingency of mode of production than a participatory process, engaging producers, texts and audiences. Once meaning is released from the localized control of bourgeois ritual, the revolutionary potential of the text is released to audiences. In ways that parallel the interests of Weberianism, symbolic interaction and phenomenology, Benjamin's contemplations on meaning provide a more optimistic vision of everyday practices and the potential for humans to create their own freedom. In a more practical sense, Benjamin also locates this potential in text-writers and film-makers, who, within the confines and constraints of their own historical contexts, have the capacity to liberate ideas from the prevailing economic structures. Like Brecht, Benjamin suggests that socialist artists and writers should, in fact, become 'producers', and where possible take responsibility for the whole process of text-making. An artist, therefore, would actively revolutionize text production using the correct 'techniques'; these techniques, however, will always be subject to the complex set of associations, influences and constraints of the times.

LOUIS ALTHUSSER AND
STRUCTURALIST MARXISM

From Lukács through the Frankfurt School, and including the Second and Third Communist and Socialist Internationals,

Marxism was continually reviewing its origins in economics and scientific rationalism. Thus, the interest in the base–superstructure model was supplemented by increasing fascination with the ways in which the superstructure operated as ideology and within the general frame of culture. Unlike many other Western Marxists, Louis Althusser (1918–90) determined to rethink significant issues of structure and ideology from within the French Communist Party. Althusser's significant contribution to the development of a critical cultural studies, therefore, emerges through his commitment to a 'scientific' re-rendering of Marxist historical materialism, most particularly through the perspective of a 1960s French philosophy that was turning against existentialism and phenomenology. Paradoxically, and as Gregory Elliott (1994) has argued, Althusser's efforts to renovate Marxist structuralism contributed to the ferment of post-Marxist thinking that seized Parisian intellectual life after the débâcles of the 1968 revolutionary skirmishes. Althusser's revision of Marxist precepts is characterized by its remarkable eclecticism:

> [E]xpelling ... the Hegelian heritage, renouncing autarky, and restoring dialogue with non (or even anti) Marxist traditions, assimilating 'Nietzschean-Heideggerian, as well as Spinozist-Bachelardian, motifs, the Althusserian renovation of historical materialism intersected with broader currents in Celtic philosophical culture, associated with the names of Claude Lévi-Strauss, or Jacques Lacan, Michel Foucault, or Jacques Derrida ... assembled under the flag of ... theoretical anti-humanism. (Elliott, 1994: viii–ix)

Overdetermination

In his review of Marx and Engels' base–superstructure model, Althusser borrows from Freud's concept of overdetermination. Thus, while Marx and Engels saw economy as the fundamental determinant of the superstructure (social and cultural features of a people), Althusser imagined that the superstructure could function independently from, though in concert with, the economic base. In *For Marx*, Althusser refers to Lenin's question on why the socialist revolution occurred in Russia, which was not the most advanced industrial state (where Marx had predicted revolution would occur). Althusser answers that the revolution was not determined by economy alone, but was acting in concert with other significant cultural features not necessarily determined by economy at all – national character, traditions, history, international events and 'accidents' of history. Economy works with 'various levels and instances of the social formation' (Althusser, 1969: 101).

Overdetermination, then, refers to the complex set of elements and associations that comprise the social formation. Economy may ultimately be a determinant of these complex forms of life, but it doesn't and can't stand alone; it must interact with and diffuse itself through all other elements in social life, and as such forms part of the matrix of overdetermination. For Althusser, these social formations may be broadly categorized into three levels: the economic, the political and the ideological. In any given historical epoch, one level may have greater influence and determinacy than the others. Althusser's thesis significantly modifies Marx's original conception of base and superstructure, opening the way for a more considered approach to the influence of language and symbolization.

Significantly, Althusser distinguishes his own version of Marxist scientific analysis from Hegel's dialecticism, which he sees as overly totalistic and unitary. Althusser's reading of Hegel is significant because it provides the foundation for his own identification of contradictions and complexities in the relationship between the base and the superstructure. According to Althusser, Hegel sees history in terms of substantive phases that are dominated by a single idea. This single idea is informed by an overriding spiritual principle, which is the most abstract form of consciousness of itself. That is, an historical phase will know itself by being aware of itself in terms of an abstract philosophical or religious consciousness. This internal and mystical knowing will necessarily constitute the 'ideology' of that epoch (Althusser, 1969: 103). Althusser contrasts Hegel's understanding of history with his own Marxist conception of the base–superstructure relationship. The Hegelian conception of an historical epoch, Althusser claims, will be necessarily unitary and governed by one significant causality with one overriding idea. Althusser, echoing Antonio Gramsci (see below), rejects this unitary and totalistic notion of history, as he also rejects the mechanistic or deterministic views of particular Marxists who imagine history and social change to be a linear and uncomplicated function of will.

Althusser, therefore, seeks an explanation of the complex associations in a society, avoiding a conception of the social formation which is excessively homogenizing, unitary or simplistic. In fact, he is careful to avoid concepts like 'social system' which suggest a uniformity and level of integration, functionalism and co-operation which is both false and overly compliant. He recognizes that a social formation is an aggregate of people, elements and structures, and that an explanation of the processes which constitute hierarchical relationships within the formation can't be reduced to single causes. Althusser offers

various perspectives on oppression and emancipation; his notion of 'ideology', however, has provided one of the most important analytical concepts for the development of a critical cultural studies.

Althusser's Ideology

Althusser's concept of ideology was developed to articulate more fully these complex and contradictory associations which function through the various structures of a social formation. While the term has been adapted from Althusser by more recent British cultural studies, its use by Althusser is relatively consistent, emphasizing the capacity of a set of ideas to predominate within a social formation. In particular, he identifies ideology as a 'system' of practices and representations by which people 'imagine' the conditions of their life: 'By practice in general I shall mean any process of transformation of a determining given raw material into a determinate product, a transformation effected by a determinate human labour, using determinate means' (Althusser, 1969: 166). Practice, however, does not refer solely to labour and the means of production; practice may transform aspects of political life, and ideological practice may transform a person's relationship to the general conditions of the social formation.

Ideology might best be understood, then, as 'a representation of the imaginary relationship of individuals to their real conditions of existence' (Althusser, 1971: 152). To put this another way, ideology refers to the way we live out the real conditions of our life at the level of its representation in discourses and texts. Our imaginations are mobilized through the 'superstructure' which convinces us that our lives are better than they really are. It is important to consider this idea carefully because the relationship between the real and imaginary remains significant for cultural studies, most especially as it has integrated important areas of language theory. Althusser asks the question: why is there a need to represent the real conditions of life at all? Why not deal directly with the source? His answer takes the notion of ideology beyond mechanistic interpretations which might say simply that the powerful install these ideologies in order to control the less powerful. In fact, Althusser suggests that ideology functions across all levels of the social formation, influencing the practices, imaginations and belief systems of both ruling and subordinate classes.

Ideology, therefore, constitutes a 'closed' system: there can be no 'distance' from its influence, no identification of the 'real' except by virtue of a scientific, analytical, Marxist discourse. The notion of 'imagined relations' is critical because it limits the escape and the possibility of a critical distance and knowing. We cannot interpret the relation of people's imagination to their real conditions because the conduit between the two is also imagined or represented. Althusser (1971: 155) suggests, then, that the question of interpretation must be replaced by questions: why is representation necessary at all, and what is the nature of these imaginings? In terms of text analysis, Althusser applies the concept of the 'problematic' by which a text will frame and organize its ideas according to ideology; the problematic of a text must, in fact, function according to the information it includes (answers to questions it poses), as well as the information it does not include. The task of the Marxist analyst is to elucidate these inclusions and exclusions, illuminating the ideology by which the text is constructed.

Subject Positions

Althusser's use of the concept of ideology, therefore, differs from Marx's in at least one very important way. For Althusser, ideology is not so much 'false' consciousness, as Marx claims; rather, ideology constitutes a sort of 'misrecognition' of the real condition of one's existence. To this extent, ideology returns important information or knowledge about the world to the reader/viewer of a representational text. The reader/viewer is to an important extent 'created' or at least 'positioned' by this information. In his essay 'Ideology and the Ideological State Apparatuses' (1971) Althusser argues that ideology interpellates concrete individuals as concrete subjects. In other words, individuals are effectively transformed into 'ideological subjects through their engagement with the imaginary world created through representation. The world is rendered intelligible for the subject as s/he takes up a position provided by the text. In very important ways, texts provide subjects with the discursive resources necessary for comprehension of themselves and the world – but both the subjectivity and the world can only exist in terms of representation and the 'imaginary'.

Again, unlike the German Idealists and Romantic philosophers, Althusser presents an image of individuals and their subjectivity as multi-forming and 'fragmentary'. That is, human subjects are not unitary and integrated through the function of reason or spiritual essence. Different modes of representation create different subject positions; subjects encounter various ideologies and subject positions through class, gender, race and social position. For example, class is not a singular and fixed condition that may be objectively recounted; rather, it is constituted through a range of representational processes by which the subject comes to identify a certain reality. This class awareness or consciousness is shaped by ideology which necessarily produces gaps between the imagined and real conditions of life. A subject and his/her consciousness, therefore, will be only partial or incomplete since these gaps, along with the ever-unfolding of new or alternative representations, will frustrate any attempts at complete integration.

Ideological State Apparatuses

The principal problems with Althusser's approach to ideology have been well canvassed (see esp. Hall, 1982). We can, however, summarize these difficulties by highlighting the two somewhat irreconcilable aims of Althusser's deployment of the concept:

1   Ideology is understood as the representation of the imaginary relationship of individuals to their real conditions of existence. The world, therefore, is a vortex of representation in which the subject is positioned and repositioned by an ineluctable symbolic order. At this level, ideology constitutes an essential process by which individuals live their lives and make sense of the world.
2   Ideology is produced by the superstructure in relation to the conditions of overdetermination. Althusser's political position, therefore, seeks to identify the operations of representation, not merely to identify the reality beyond representation, but to clarify the question: why represent the world at all? His scientific, Marxist analysis becomes the only valid tool for irrupting the ideological nexus of imagination and reality. At this level, ideology becomes far more than a matter of imagination, fragmentation or misrecognition. Ideology is a

systematic mode of oppression which operates through significant and powerful social and economic 'apparatuses'.

Althusser's work has been most influential in cultural studies largely through this latter deployment of the concept of ideology. Althusser writes quite specifically about Ideological State Apparatuses (ISAs) which promote and distribute various forms of ideology through the dominant context of economic capitalism. As we noted above, the processes of overdetermination are formed through these apparatuses: family, education system, church and mass media. These apparatuses have become ubiquitous and effective in promoting and maintaining dominant order and the interests of powerful oligarchies. According to Althusser and other Marxists interested in the symbolic patterning of ideology, ISAs operate to supplement and often lead the social controls of threat and physical coercion.

The analysis and exposure of ISAs and ideological processes more generally have continued to be an important part of the work of cultural studies. There have been various attempts to integrate Althusserian theory into a more consistent and flexible analytical paradigm (see Hall, 1982; Laclau and Mouffe, 1985). In particular, and as we shall see below, the coupling of ideology with Gramsci's notion of hegemony has enabled cultural analysis to elucidate some significant and complex representations of power and power relationships. In a film like *Toy Story 2*, for example, we might identify ideologies which support patriarchal and capitalist interests. Even toys, it seems, are distinguished by gender (the cultural construction of sex typologies). The male heroes save the victim/female from the evils of exploitation. Family and middle-class values are restored through a symbolic order which confirms for children that women and men are necessarily constituted in this way. The subject/viewer is thus positioned by the film's narratized ideology; both the positioning and the ideology clearly serve the interests of the media-based, corporate ISA which produced the film in the first place. In this way, the legitimacy of capitalism, consumption, industrial cartels, social hierarchy and fixed labour are confirmed. Viewers anticipate a life in which they are placed as gendered and class-directed labour within a confined and highly managed social order. The fantasy of the film operates as a solution to the complex relationships and ideological forces that surround and challenge the subject/viewer.

Liberation and Literature

Part of the problem for an Althusserian analysis is that ideology appears to be too successful, providing little space for escape from its control. To a degree, however, art and literature are capable of creating a critical distance by which the subject may at least partially escape the controlling power of the ideological imaginary. The great work of art is, of course, subject to the predominance of epochal ideology; but the relationship between the imagined and real conditions of life, though it is itself 'imagined', can somehow fracture the substance of the ideology by making us 'see'. Althusser's essay 'Letter on art' (1971) has provided the analytical paradigm for Pierre Macherey's (1978) outline of literary theory. Rather than treat a text as an autonomous and integrated (unique) artefact, Macherey sees the work as a 'product', the outcome of a wide range of crisscrossing processes and elements. These processes constitute a form of social 'unconscious'. As Althusser explains, ideology normally functions to subsume social contradictions in an apparent harmony, a common-sense and naturalistic view of

reality. As Macherey argues, however, once the ideology is aestheticized, its inconsistencies, fissures and contradictions become obvious once again. Most particularly, the 'absences' or excluded information which corresponds to the ideological interests and failings of the text become available for elucidation by the critic. The task of analysis, therefore, is not to harmonize the fissures and absences of a text, but to illuminate them and their ideological sources.

ANTONIO GRAMSCI

One of the major questions posed by the social theorists who followed Marx concerned the apparent willingness of subordinate classes to co-operate with the means of their oppression. In his discussions on bureaucracy and capitalism, the liberal sociologist Max Weber (see Chapter 2) surmised that much of the symbolic activity of modern society was devoted to the legitimation of economy and politics; Adorno argued that popular culture and its institutions consciously sought to control the 'thinking' of audiences; and Althusser demonstrated that dominant ideologies were capable of diverting individuals' imaginations and practices away from the real conditions of their existence. While it is true that Marxism concerned itself with matters of violence, threat and social coercion, it is equally true that the left-wing lineage continued to puzzle over the apparent consensus which enabled capitalism to advance, despite the obvious and often brutal discrepancies in the distribution of its prosperity.

Hegemony

The work of Antonio Gramsci (1891–1937) was adapted into cultural studies in an attempt to overcome the limitations of Althusser's ideology. Stuart Hall (1982) and others in the Birmingham Centre for Contemporary Cultural Studies (see Chapter 4) identified particular value in Gramsci's somewhat more flexible approach to the operations of ideology and power. Gramsci saw the relationship between state coercion and legitimation as central to an understanding of constituted consensus and co-operation. Gramsci, a revolutionary and founding member of the Italian Communist Party, saw leadership or 'hegemony' as the pivotal issue. Gramsci, who had himself been imprisoned by the Fascists in 1926, argued that the state and other hegemonic institutions could not rely on force or coercion to control opposition and challenge to authority. The maintenance of social order or consensus is achieved by 'strategic management'. In a point later taken up by Althusser, Gramsci claims that social elites constitute their leadership through the universalizing of their own class-based self-interests. These self-interests are adopted by the greater majority of people, who apprehend them as natural or universal standards of value (common sense). This 'hegemony' neutralizes dissent, instilling the values, beliefs and cultural meanings into the generalized social structures. Althusser's notion of Ideological State Apparatuses of family, education, media, legal institutions, and so on, echoes Gramsci's belief that consensus is achieved through the general distribution of values, beliefs and cultural practices. The stability and normality of capitalism in Western democratic states has been achieved, according to the Gramscian theory, by this consolidation of the conditions of hegemony.

The Organic Intellectual

This universalizing is not, however, a simple act of coercion or imposition. To this extent, Gramsci transforms Marx's base–superstructure model into something that Marx himself (following Hegel also) considered: the state = political society + civil society. In this famous formulation political society refers to the coercive elements within the social totality, and civil society refers to the non-coercive elements which produce the conditions for the absorption and generalized dissemination of values, behaviours and beliefs. Part of this dissemination is achieved through the function of what Gramsci calls the 'organic intellectual'. While everyone has the potential for intellect, Gramsci insists, only particular people perform the function of intellectual leadership. All social groups produce their own organic leaders whose role it is to organize, negotiate, reform and distribute values and behaviours within their group or class. That is, the organic intellectual will construct the group's identity by giving 'it homogeneity and awareness of its own function' (Gramsci, 1971: 5).

Importantly, organic intellectuals are responsible for 'negotiating' consensus and the distribution of values throughout their constituency. This negotiation implies processes of cajolement, persuasion and threat, on the one hand, and resistance, engagement and incorporation, on the other. It may of course involve some levels of compromise and reform, and will always carry with it the possibility of violence, coercion and subjugation. The economic interests of the controlling group will always be the central, if subliminal, issue, but this interest may be achieved through a range of strategies, including the promise of some forms of personal or collective gratification in the present and future. This 'compromise equilibrium', as Gramsci calls it, though it may give the impression of completion, allows for the possibility of challenge and resistance.

In fact, hegemony can never entirely erase the discrepancies created by an unequal system of power and reward. In the flow of capital and imperial power into the non-European world, this hegemony might stimulate the paradox of an armed resistance movement which mimics the political character and institutions of its oppressors. Ho Chi Minh's nationalist uprisings which led to the Vietnam War were formed around a constellation of militarism, nationalism and administrative processes, all adapted from the French and US occupiers. On the other hand, the consensus might be more clearly negotiated, and armed resistance avoided, through the compromise equilibrium. In British colonies like Australia, New Zealand and Canada, for example, this equilibrium was facilitated through a torpid but constant release of imperial power. The economic interests of the oppressing group remained intact though the direct control of the territories was surrendered. In other words, a 'negotiated leadership' maintained the interests of the oppressors while presenting an impression of self-determination for the oppressed.

Gramsci and Cultural Studies

Resistance, however, was not guaranteed, and Gramsci himself identified a 'traditional intellectual' who might have sustained some level of historical continuity or critical distance beyond the class interests of the organic intellectual (Gramsci, 1971: 7). This distinction, however, proved ultimately unsatisfactory and Gramsci's hope for reform rested finally with the formation of a working-class organic intellectual. Raymond Williams (see 1981: 214–17), one of the founders of British cultural studies (see Chapter 4), adopted the theory of hegemony for a more broadly encompassing

analysis of culture and the media. Williams attempts to expand Gramsci's notion of an intellectual and the potential for resistance across culture. For Williams and other cultural commentators interested in popular media texts, Gramsci's notion of hegemony provides a Marxist framework for elucidating power relationships, but without the pre-eminence of economy and the mode of production thesis. The intellectual might constitute himself or herself through a productive relationship with consumers of media culture. Unlike Adorno's analysis, which is so scornful of the popular text's imposition of meaning, and the instrumental rationality and institutionalized structures it represents, Williams' Gramscian approach to text allows more room for the 'negotiation of meaning'. The popular text is not a simple coercion or exertion of cultural control; text consumers have a good deal more say in the way the text and its meanings operate.

Stuart Hall (1982), also from the British cultural studies lineage, argues that Gramsci's hegemony is ultimately a far more productive concept than Althusser's ideology. Hall claims that Althusser's ideology leaves far less room for resistance and agency than does Gramsci's negotiated hegemony. In either case, Gramsci's notion of hegemony provides a useful insight into the complex exchanges that take place within the broad dominion of the 'superstructure'. It provides that important space, missing in Marx's original thesis, in which control by powerful groups and institutions remains incomplete. Culture thus provides the means of oppression but also the means of liberation.

The organic intellectual might therefore emerge from within the ranks of any social interest group or movement since the 'common sense' by which people organize their everyday lives is fundamentally embedded within popular culture. While

Gramsci invested his resistance in the organic working-class intellectual, cultural studies has widened the scope of this liberationism, most especially through the construction of identity and other forms of popular cultural politics. Acknowledging the importance of subject positioning, the formation of identity through representation, and the centrality of popular media for the organization and intelligibility of everyday life, cultural studies has focused its attention on the ways in which meanings are negotiated through complex relationships of power and resistance. In many respects, and as Stuart Hall (1996) himself concedes, cultural studies intellectuals sought the common ground of the everyday people and practices they studied; they sought to arise from the ranks of the oppressed in order to liberate their voices. In other words, in the great contest of meaning-making they hoped to be organic intellectuals who would lead the charge of resistance. Some examples of this sort of work include studies by Judith Williamson on advertising (1978), David Morley on news and current affairs (1980a), and Tony Bennett et al. (1986) on popular film.

SCIENCE, LANGUAGE AND CRITICAL THEORY

The influence of the Marxist intellectual heritage remains evident in cultural studies, most particularly as it has been filtered through radical sociology, feminism, the Birmingham Centre for Contemporary Cultural Studies and the various permutations of postcolonial theory. This filtering process, most particularly as it has been influenced by the work of Gramsci and Althusser, has shifted the Marxist project away from economic politics toward a more generalized cultural politics. Even so,

this greater interest in language and symbolization has led to an even more sustained interrogation of the new or neo-Marxist project. Coming through the broad sweep of cultural theory, the source of these challenges can be summarized as follows:

1 *Fragmentation of the political field.* Marxist concentration on class has overemphasized a dialectical or dualistic conception of the social formation. Liberation has been defined in unacceptably narrow terms, neglecting the emancipatory claims of women, colonized peoples, ethnic minorities, gays, the disabled and other social sub-groups.

2 *The extension of interest in popular culture and consumption as pleasure.* Marxist denunciation of capitalism, and especially the austerity of theorists like Adorno, tends to overstate the vulnerability of ordinary people and their everyday practices. Mikhail Bakhtin (1984) provided some insights into the possibilities of the 'carnivalesque' or folk culture as a site of people's pleasure and hence resistance to dominant rationalities of order and control. In contemporary culture, these pleasures and consumption practices have led many social reformers to seek liberation in theory which embraces rather than entirely denounces the 'practices of capital'.

3 *The challenge of poststructuralism.* Poststructuralism and other recent developments in language theory (areas of postmodernism, discourse theory, reading theory, etc.) challenge the material and rational basis of Marxism and liberal humanism by shearing away the notion of a grounded or substantial and absolute truth.

Jürgen Habermas:
Communicative Action

While we will pursue all of these challenges in their own terms in later chapters, the attempts by Marxist-derived analysis to resist or accommodate the challenges are worth investigating as they herald a new phase of critical study. Jürgen Habermas (1983; see also Chapter 7) has argued, in fact, that the retreat from the purity of the Marxist paradigm constitutes a retreat from modernity and its unfinished project. In a significant debate with the French poststructuralist philosopher Jean-François Lyotard, Habermas argues that the filtering out of modernity's rational project of reform leaves the contemporary condition vulnerable to ongoing modes of oppression and social disorder. The Habermas–Lyotard debate centres on the two theorists' respective approach to language, truth and social criticism. Poststructuralists believe that all reality is formed through the mediation of language and therefore there can be no absolute or universal reality. The question of social criticism is opened up because no critical position is grounded in truth – critique only exists in the ungrounded perspective of the critic. Habermas argues, on the contrary, that a rationally derived truth, and hence critique, is both possible and desirable. A rationally derived truth remains the ultimate object of knowledge, Habermas maintains, but the fascination with poststructural and postmodern theoretics exposes philosophy and social science to substantial accusations of political and intellectual capitulation (if not conservatism).

While Habermas's conclusions remain problematic, his identification of the challenges of poststructuralism to the solidity of the Marxist project are significant, and have been central to many of the debates surrounding the respective theoretical claims during the past two decades. Habermas's utopianism attempts to integrate aspects of language theory with more conventional modes of historical materialism. While he begins with Max Weber's theory of modernity, he rejects the notion of consciousness as the central feature of modernist reality, the transcendent unity by which reality is ultimately experienced and known. For Habermas, the limitations of critical theory, most especially as it was articulated in the work of Adorno and Horkheimer, rests on their reliance on Hegelian/Marxist modes of dialectics and transcendent epistemology (modes of knowing). Habermas, therefore, wants to restore the power of a grounded, absolute, rational truth for a critical theory which could provide the directions for a better society.

As we recall, the principal focus of Frankfurt-style theories of consciousness rests on the separation of the subject (the individual who will know) from the object (the external phenomena that is to be known). The relationship between the subject and object is resolved, first, through *cognition*, where the object is represented to the subject as it really is; and, secondly, through *action*, whereby the object is transformed by the things the subject will do. These functions will always take place within the context of self-preservation. Cognition and action, then, implicate the mentality of 'survival of the fittest' – competition for control. From Weber through to the Frankfurt School this pessimistic vision seems to underpin theories of society. Habermas, however, attempts to construct a more optimistic and pragmatic social vision which is not dependent on notions of transcendent consciousness, or on relationships of power (control and manipulation). Like the intersubjectivity of Schütz's phenomenology, though without the unifying consciousness, Habermas creates a notion of consensus that is formed around communication between subjects. This 'intersubjectivity' is formed through a mediated reality that operates necessarily through human communicative action. The key is the collective constitution of shared reality, including the meaning that is attached to processes of cognition and action. Communicative action becomes the central theme of human truth-value:

> If we assume that the human species maintains itself through the socially co-ordinated activities of its members and that this co-ordination has to be established through communication – and in certain central spheres through communication aimed at reaching agreement – then the reproduction of the species also requires satisfying the conditions of a rationality that is inherent in communicative action. (Habermas, 1984a: 397)

Rationality remains central to Habermas's theory of modernity and to the utopianism which, he claims, would take modernity beyond the threshold of despair. Thus, Habermas conceives of modernity in Weberian terms as the differentiation of science, morality and art into relatively autonomous zones. The advance, 'perfection' and integration of these various spheres into the everyday experiences or *lifeworld* of ordinary people would mark the completion of the modernist project. The means by which these spheres could achieve perfection was never provided by Weber. Habermas, however, explains that rationality and the liberation of communicative action within the public sphere would certainly provide the appropriate conditions for a true human emancipation.

This rationality, however, was not the 'instrumental' or technical rationality to which Weber refers. Such a rationality, deriving from institutions, economy and bureaucracy, always risks the imposition of the will of the state over the potentialities of liberation. Habermas, therefore, follows Weber in distinguishing between instrumental rationality and communicative rationality, which functions most directly in the lifeworld of everyday practices and representations. That is, Habermas's communicative rationality is the site of culture and cultural exchange. This public sphere facilitates the free presentation of truth or validity claims which are challenged and modified in order to produce the effect of consensual, rationalized truth. In the utopian circumstances, this free exchange produces the best possible conditions – the 'ideal speech situation' – for the perfection of art, science and morality, and hence liberation. This ideal speech situation lies effectively outside history and is therefore universal in its intent. Habermas assures us that humans will naturally and inexorably seek to represent themselves and their culture in language, and that these representations are the fundamental constituencies of society. Of course, the lifeworld is bound by specific historical contexts, but in the 'dynamics of development', circumstances will necessarily be impelled toward the ultimate rationality of language and the formation of a situation in which this rationality can be expressed. So, beyond the specifics of the particular language interaction, the ideal speech situation becomes a universal ideal.

Habermas's views on various aspects of social and critical theory appear to have shifted during the course of his writing career. Some commentators would even challenge the suitability of the appellation 'Marxist' as applied to Habermas's theories, most especially as he has moved away from the base–superstructure model in favour of a more language-oriented theory of action. Indeed, Habermas has claimed quite explicitly that notions of a working-class politics must yield to a more complex assemblage of political and scientific discourses, most particularly as they are built around the notion of 'the public sphere' and universalized notions of communication, 'symbolic interaction' and language. On the surface, it may appear that Habermas is subscribing to those theories of language like poststrucutralism which place language at the centre of culture and which accept the fracturing of social agency and ideology. However, Habermas remains fixed in his view that communication is a rationality that is historically patterned, if not inevitable. He would take history beyond the causal structures of Marxist dialectics, but his vision remains centred in the logics of scientific discourse. 'Modern science ... [is] governed by ideals of an objectivity and impartiality secured through unrestricted discussion' (Habermas, 1987b: 291). Lyotard (1984a) disputes this point, arguing that modern science is a positioned and self-legitimating narrative, comparable in many respects to the narratives of literature or politics.

Paul Ricoeur: Hermeneutic Phenomenology

The French critical phenomenologist Paul Ricoeur shares Habermas's interest in science, language theory and emancipation. However, Ricoeur goes further than Habermas in rejecting critical theory's maintenance of historical teleology (structural causality) and the pessimism of a structuralist analytical paradigm. Ricoeur's phenomenological hermeneutics combines Heidegger's theory of being with the tradition of aesthetic and philosophical interpretation. Ricoeur, in fact, seeks a critical perspective that is optimistic without being glib or excessively idealist. As part of his general strategy of elucidation, Ricoeur argues that the interpretation of texts or

actions is fundamentally dialectical: that is, it is constituted through two distinct movements. The first allows for the plurality of texts whereby any given action of text may have innumerable meanings and possible interpretations. The second movement involves the ordered and contextualized examination of these meanings in order to exact the limits of interpretation. These limits constitute the validity of an interpretive schema for any given text. The 'meaning' of the text, therefore, places it within the context of historical consciousness which ultimately represents its objectification, that is, its existence as text/meaning which is objective and free from the eternal circle of subjective claims and distortions.

Thus, in terms of human action and the everyday sphere of reference, Ricoeur aims to resolve the putative tension between critical and interpretation theories. He presents this tension in terms of participation and alienation: hermeneutic theory regards tradition as a matter of the individual subject's participation in 'consciousness' (general knowing or self-awareness as it derives from an historical context). Tradition also implicates the subject's contribution to the collective consciousness of culture and history (i.e. the total knowing of the whole group). Critical theory, most especially as it is practised through the Frankfurt School and its antecedents, sees history in terms of the alienation of individuals and classes who struggle to be free within a context of ideological distortion and communicative constraint (see Ricoeur, 1974). That is, there is a tension between an individual's consciousness as derived from his/her social conditions, the individual's own contribution to the collective of those social conditions, and the limits placed on the individual's freedom by those social conditions.

Fundamentally, Ricoeur suggests that this tension is dissolved when hermeneutics assumes a critical 'distance' that is not predicated on an objectifiable social science free of values, but which rather accounts for its values through the fulsome embrace of text and depth interpretation. A depth interpretation releases the possibilities of the reader's projection to 'other worlds' and 'new horizons'. This engagement with consciousness predisposes against any particular or given 'reality', allowing the subject to contemplate and critique the nature of the real itself. The depth interpretation, therefore, inclines the reader to a more lucid self-examination, a form of self-critique against egotistical illusions and ideological distortions. This release to consciousness illuminates the phenomena of the world and creates, however temporarily, a significant moment of objectivity. Ricoeur, in fact, engages directly with the thesis of communicative action posited by Habermas, arguing finally that the critique of ideologies is only possible with the framework of a 'reinterpretation' of history. Social science's ideal of communication is only possible, Ricoeur argues, when the past itself is reinterpreted. The critical sciences can only function successfully when they are operating in accord with an interpretive paradigm and a theory of consciousness which would restore the ultimate conditions of objectivity for the emancipation of the subject.

FORESTALLING FRAGMENTATION: POSTMODERN MARXISM

Habermas's attempt to integrate new forms of language theory into his critical perspective has met with varied responses, not the least from French poststructuralists, who have broadly condemned the move (see Thompson and Held, 1982; Bernstein, 1985). Other Marxist cultural critics, such as Fredric Jameson and Terry Eagleton, have followed Habermas and Ricoeur by integrating important aspects of Marxist critique into a reformulated language theory. Specifically, both Jameson and Eagleton have been convinced by key elements in the structuralist and poststructuralist perspectives, but have resisted other elements which they see as capitulating to reactionary conclusions. Derrida's analytical strategy of deconstruction, for example, a technique which exposes the underlying historical and textual principles that produce a given body of writing, is seen as an extremely valuable contribution to critical reading. However, as the critics of deconstruction have pointed out, the method may lead to a sophisticated but interminable train of other texts (what Derrida calls intertextuality); or it may lead to the exposure of a substantive 'political unconscious' (Jameson, 1981), the cultural realm in which power and ideology are distributed.

Fredric Jameson

Fredric Jameson has identified substantial value in the deconstruction model, combining it with a more generalized Althusserian mode of analysis. In order to achieve this communion of structuralist and poststructuralist perspectives, Jameson has to reconcile substantially opposing approaches to the problem of structure. Althusser, we recall, conceives of language in terms of institutionally and structurally formed ideology. Poststructuralism, however, is deeply suspicious of any notions of structure and 'dominant ideology'. For poststructuralists, Althusser's notion of ideology is too totalistic and ubiquitous, forming relationships of power that misconstrue the precariousness of language and power, and the limits of knowledge. In celebrating the particulates of culture, poststructuralism is averse to universalisms of any kind, including the universal reformist solutions offered by neo-Marxism.

Even so, Jameson offers a significant theory of the political unconscious which eventually turns its focus on the condition of political postmodernism. Following Althusser and his other mentor, Pierre Macherey, Jameson is careful with the notion of a transcendent consciousness which would mystically restore the 'system' in its entirety at every particular moment to the individual's own, singular consciousness. Equally, Jameson shares the poststructuralist disavowal of interpretation which inevitably clusters disparate elements of an historical period into substantive categories. In its zeal to explain causal links, interpretation dismisses or distorts the dissimilarities constituted by historical discontinuities (elements in culture that are short-lived and unconnected to major or minor 'trends'). In *The Political Unconscious* (1981) Jameson sympathizes with Gilles Deleuze and Félix Guattari's suspicion of grand interpretations which summarize and categorize particular themes into heuristic codes. Deleuze and Guattari critique

> Freudian interpretation, which is characterized as a reduction, a rewriting of the whole rich and random multiple realities of concrete everyday experience into the contained, strategically prelimited terms of the family narrative – whether this be seen as myth, Greek tragedy, 'family romance', or even the Lacanian version of the Oedipus complex. What is denounced is therefore a system of allegorical interpretation in which the data of one narrative line are radically impoverished by their rewriting according to the paradigm of another narrative. (Jameson, 1981: 21–2)

Deleuze and Guattari's new form of interpretation, known as 'deconstruction', aims therefore to illuminate the processes of traditional interpretation which constitute a distortion or re-creation of the original text according to the interpreter's own schematic interests.

While Jameson agrees with the deconstructive technique, his primary aim is to indicate how these 're-creations' constitute a particular ideology, or at least function according to a particular ideological interest. Cultural texts, and the consummate history/culture which are built around and through those texts, operate according to certain ideological precepts, most particularly those which distinguish the powerful (bourgeoisie) from the less powerful. Marxism, according to Jameson, provides the most coherent and substantial analytical programme for the deconstruction of cultural texts and for an understanding of the broader patterns of cultural history. Against the trend of obsessive individualism and privatization (disguises for increased social differentiation), Jameson recommends that 'the only effective liberation from such constraints begins with the recognition that there is nothing that is not social and historical – indeed, that everything is in the last analysis political' (1981: 20).

An adapted Althusserian model of interpretation allows for the mediation of disparate elements in a text (film, literary work, art object, building) while maintaining the text's connection to social and historical structures. Also, following Macherey, Jameson suggests that the structuralist interpretation in fact demands that the 'apparent' formal unification of the text merely camouflages the internal gaps and fissures that reflect the ideological absences of the text. Unlike poststructuralist theory, however (and this is the point that Jameson himself would find most contentious), these disparate elements, discontinuities and contradictions are themselves interpreted as 'patterned' or schematized in relation to culture and ideology. While Jacques Derrida, for example, might see these elements as entirely random or existing only in relation to other texts, Jameson insists on their relationship with Marxist conceptions of structure and social hierarchy. They exist as extrinsic elements which are restored to the text by the act of (Marxist) interpretation (Jameson, 1981: 57). That is, the various particulates which exist independently and without recourse to major trends and causalities are nevertheless available for a Marxist reading of history; they become patterned through their recognition as independent in a general framework of oppression and discrimination.

Jameson's attempts to integrate the poststructuralist conception of language and his Marxist reform agenda crystallize even more cogently in his writings on postmodernism and consumer culture (Jameson, 1983, 1984, 1991). In these writings Jameson outlines his theory of consumer culture, observing that the 'political form of postmodernism ... will have as its vocation the invention and projection of a global cognitive mapping' (1984: 92). The postmodern consumerist theoretic, in fact, would alleviate the confusion of contemporary culture, and, significantly, the limitations of Jameson's own Marxist modelling. Jameson's work in this area has been telling, but like other Marxists who are tackling the conception of postmodernism and global capitalist consumerism, there remains a sense in which the whole enterprise threatens to undermine the capacity of the Marxist critique to function alone. In later sections we will examine more fully this attempt to provide a critical perspective from within the general fields of poststructuralism and postmodernism. As we shall see, contemporary culture is characterized by radical fragmentations, heterologies and dislocations. As theorists attempt

to account for the problematic of this fragmentalism, they have had to reshape and at times abandon older heuristic, political and theoretical frames of reference.

DISCUSSION: THE SURVIVAL OF THE MARXIST CRITIQUE

Not surprisingly, it has become increasingly difficult for Marxists to maintain the integrity of their origins. Like those of other Marxist theorists, Jameson's most recent writings have been forced to surrender much of their radical heritage. The question arises as to whether the work can be justifiably categorized as Marxist at all. Ernesto Laclau and Chantal Mouffe (1985) have attempted to extend the Marxist/Gramscian concept of hegemony both for a critique of contemporary cultural politics and for a reconstruction of a 'pluralist, radical democracy'. Hegemony becomes more than institutional or discursive leadership for Laclau and Mouffe; it becomes the source of a fragmented social democracy whereby all political claims and discourses are legitimated without the recourse to assemblages of class or totalizing social structures. Contemporary social movements inspired by a more ecological, sexual, personal or community-level emancipation cannot be simply attached to the differentiations elicited through the mode of production:

> What interests us about these new social movements, then, is not the idea of arbitrarily grouping them into a category opposed to social class, but the *novel* role they play in articulating that rapid diffusion of social conflictuality to more and more numerous relations which is characteristic today of advanced industrial societies. (Laclau and Mouffe, 1985: 159–60)

For Laclau and Mouffe these proliferating social relations represent an extension of what they call the 'democratic revolution'. This is not the 'end of ideology' as Daniel Bell (1973, 1976) conceives, nor has it led to the creation of Marcuse's one-dimensional man. Rather, ideology has fractured. The older versions of Marxism with their substantial investment in class, structure, grounded ontologies and universal notions of causality can no longer be relied upon either for diagnosis or for cure. According to Laclau and Mouffe, crisis in theory has replaced the older sureties, such that all theorization must take place within the general terrain of post-Marxism:

> Only if we renounce any epistemological prerogative based upon the ontologically privileged position of 'class', will it be possible seriously to discuss the present degree of validity of the Marxist categories. At this point we should state quite plainly that we are situated in a *post*-Marxist terrain. It is no longer possible to maintain the conception of subjectivity and class elaborated by Marxism, nor its vision of the historical course of capitalist development, nor, of course, the conception of communism as a transparent society from which antagonisms have disappeared. (Laclau and Mouffe, 1985: 4)

While we will look more closely in later chapters at Laclau and Mouffe's solutions to the theoretical crisis in cultural politics, their surrender of Marxist conceptualizations is telling. The search for a form of radical cultural politics which engages with cultural fragmentation and poststructuralism is leading theory to question the relevance of the Marxist appellation. While of course there are those who would never have accepted the appellation in the first place, preferring a reformism based around notions of liberal humanism or democratic principles, theorists like Jameson and Eagleton would deplore the surrender of the Marxist lineage.

The alteration in the political scene is associated with major social, cultural and political trends. Changes in the social hierarchy and the ascendancy of the ideologies of democracy and freedom have been widely discussed. In many respects the horrors of capitalism have been ameliorated through processes of 'embourgeoisement' or the transformation of the proletariat–bourgeois opposition into a more amorphous and inclusive middle class. Less privileged enclaves continue in the developed world: particular migrant groups, indigenous peoples, single mothers, the chronically unemployed, the disabled. These groups are politically and culturally disparate and function at the margins of the broader middle class. Indeed, many of the most politically active social groups, such as environmentalists, feminists and gays, are cognitively rather than materially oppressed, conservative in many realms of their lives except on the particular issue about which they are resistant. The radical potential of the Left has been softened, that is, by the fracturing of the reform agenda; trade unionism is in decline and there has been a broad feminization of the workplace. Postmodern perspectives have tended to divide the political agenda even further, raising the possibilities of a consumption-based emancipation (see Chapter 8). Recognizing this potential, and the prospect of an ever-dividing political agenda, Fredric Jameson has questioned the validity of his own Marxist convictions and the possibilities of a general social overhaul.

Of equal significance, however, has been the transformation of the problem of alienation. Marx conceived of alienation as the fundamental separation of individuals from the community and the product of their labour. While he identified alienation as a critical feature of social division, since the twentieth century we have seen the broadening of this process. In particular, concerns about the inequities of the mode of production, labour and capital have evolved into broader concerns over the distribution of information and imagery. The proliferation of images and the ascendancy of televisual and digital reality has hollowed out the discourses of alienation. As we shall see in subsequent chapters, the rise of televisual and digital culture has demanded a re-conceptualization of the relationship between language and power. The new cultural politics that has developed over the past two to three decades has been forced to account for the problematic of the popular media. The rebuilding of community and the continuing interrogation of concepts of culture and individualism resist a simple formulation of social control. Nevertheless, the relationship between language, power and culture dominates the progress and development of cultural theory.

4

British Cultural Studies

Outline of the chapter

The term 'cultural studies' was first used to denote a distinct academic discipline by the British critic Raymond Williams. For many commentators, in fact, cultural studies begins in the 1960s with Williams' announcement and the nascent work of the Birmingham Centre for Contemporary Cultural Studies. This approach tends to treat the Birmingham Centre as the major progenitor of a discipline which now penetrates the humanities and social sciences in all major universities across the globe. As we have seen, however, the study of culture and meaning-making processes stretches well beyond the Birmingham moment, engaging various forms of philosophy, textual studies, Marxism and social theory. The aim of this chapter is to explore the context in which British cultural studies evolves, and the ways in which the British approach constitutes a distinct analytical paradigm.

We begin with an examination of the intellectual and cultural sources of British cultural studies, and the ways in which the Birmingham Centre adapted and altered existing theoretical and methodological paradigms. Specifically, British cultural studies emerges through various lineages in literary studies, history, sociology and politics. It attempts to adapt existing analytical models for a more expansive study of 'culture'. The intellectual heritage of Romanticism, which had contributed to the development of the liberal arts and English literary studies, in particular, is reviewed by authors like Richard Hoggart, E.P. Thompson and Raymond Williams. This review leads to the re-focusing and hybridization of the Romantic approach to culture. While retaining an interest in the elevating potential of knowledge and learning, Hoggart, Thompson and Williams devote their intellectual energies to the study of industrial, working-class culture. Thus, while British Romanticism had focused on the transcendent possibilities of high art, Hoggart, Thompson and Williams become more interested in the meaning-making activities and texts of the working classes.

This move away from a strictly 'bourgeois' culture leads also to a broader study of 'popular' culture. Later members of the Birmingham Centre, Stuart Hall in particular, argue that the analysis of contemporary culture necessarily implicates the study of the popular media. Hall, adapting French language theory, provides a substantive theoretical framework for the development of appropriate methods of media analysis. Hall's work seeks to integrate the two distinct definitions of culture:

culture as 'way of life' and culture as meaning-making. The study of popular culture necessarily frees cultural studies from the limits of class-based analysis, allowing culture to operate at the level of textual consumption and a broadly based audience meaning-making. This approach has proven enormously influential and popular for anthropological/sociological approaches to culture, and in the evolution of media studies. The 'popular consumption' approach to cultural studies has, however, spawned further debates about the validity and necessity of cultural politics.

GENERAL INTRODUCTION

The development in the 1960s and 1970s of a distinctively British style of cultural studies can be traced through two significant and related tensions. First, British cultural studies, especially as it became articulated and practised at the Birmingham Centre for Contemporary Cultural Studies (BCCCS), sought to distinguish 'popular' culture as a mode of textual and everyday practice from 'mass' or 'consumerist' culture. The need for a distinction of this kind arose out of the British and European intellectual traditions which privileged high art over popular or low art. British and German Romanticism had exerted enormous influence over the development of educational and academic practices. In forging the humanities and liberal humanism, for example, the Romantic aesthetic had argued that civility and the elevation of consciousness were only possible through the experience of sophisticated forms of music, art and literature.

As we have also seen, the Hegelian lineage in Marxist aesthetics also looked to high art to provide liberation from oppression, ideology and intellectual confinement. British cultural studies, however, drawing on the broader lexicon of social history, anthropology and Chicago-style sociology, felt deeply disturbed by the elitism of the Romantic heritage. A study of culture needs to incorporate the widest possible field of symbolic activities; expunging the idea that social 'value' and political emancipation are the exclusive province of complex intellectual and aesthetic forms. As Jim McGuigan (1992) suggests, the formation of British cultural studies is necessarily an engagement with, if not a celebration of, popular or everyday culture. This notion of the popular directly challenges those critiques which identified popular art with 'low', 'mass', 'commercial' or 'consumerist' art. The replacement of these pejorative epithets with the notion of 'popular' was designed to remove the assumption underlying the high art–low art distinction.

The second tension which underpins the development of British cultural studies, in fact, emerges directly out of this challenge to the literary and critical heritage. The distinction between the Frankfurt School's pessimistic appraisal of mass-produced culture and other, more anthropological, notions of the 'people's art' created significant theoretical challenges for the practitioners of British cultural studies, most particularly in their desire to create a critical framework for the reading of texts and culture generally. Indeed, and as Graeme Turner (1996) has noted, the principal question for cultural studies theory and practice relates directly to the problem of freedom and agency. To what extent is an individual subjectivity free and capable of independent thought and action, and to what extent is s/he a predetermination of institutional and structural power? The various answers British cultural studies offers to this question are rooted in a diverse and often antagonistic history.

It is important to note at this stage that our emphasis on a national typology in this chapter – that is, British cultural studies – is only justifiable in terms of the very distinctive attitudes and attributes that developed around the work of Raymond Williams and the Birmingham Centre. Quite obviously, there were significant differences between individuals and collections of scholars within the broad span of British cultural studies. The Leicester Centre for Mass Communications Research, for example, adopted a distinctly American-style of communications research. Our aim here is not to camouflage these differences but rather to measure them against the significant contribution of Williams and the Birmingham Centre to the formation of a distinctive and nationally locatable style of cultural analysis. In fact, within the Birmingham group itself there were some notable differences and similarities, many of which will be discussed in detail later in the chapter. What is important to note is that the various members of the Birmingham group, along with its innumerable followers, shared important ideological and academic concerns. To this extent, we may justifiably refer to this collective as a 'school' (of thought), even though it does not present itself as a uniform or institutional 'School' as in the Frankfurt or Chicago Schools.

THE LITERARY AND ROMANTIC HERITAGE

The formation of British cultural studies is very often characterized in terms of rejection or closure. Raymond Williams undoubtedly saw his mission as revolutionary, marking a new territory for the analysis of texts and everyday practice. While Williams' account of the genesis of the new discipline remains essential reading, its overriding engagement with reformulated, critical Marxism tends to obscure the equally significant contributions of alternative intellectual traditions (see esp. Williams, 1981). In order to understand Williams' own position and contribution, and the evolution of a distinctly British cultural studies generally, we will need to look more closely at these traditions. In fact, the heritage of British cultural analysis reaches well back into the Enlightenment and owes much of its current momentum to the perspectives and challenges developed through Romanticism, liberal humanism and literature studies.

Humanism and Utility

As we discussed in Chapter 2, German philosophical idealism played a central role in the genesis of the social and cultural sciences, and in the political manifestos of Karl Marx and Friedrich Engels. British philosophy is generally seen to have been more pragmatic and less abstract than its German counterpart, seeking a more sustainable framework for the progress of humankind. Philosophers like Thomas Hobbes (*Leviathan*, 1651) and John Locke (*An Essay Concerning Human Understanding*, 1690), for example, sought to elucidate specific moral, epistemological and empirical precepts for the foundations of human improvement and the collective functioning of a state which was no longer the privileged dominion of warlords and aristocrats. Hobbes' theory of causality parallels the foundational processes of nature with the logical and deterministic framework of society and government. Hobbes' 'leviathan' is not a radical rendering of a democratic state, but a framework for the orderly transition to logically framed social and political relationships. Equally, Locke's notion of the *'tabula rasa'* – humans as blank pages upon which experience is written – focuses attention toward empiricism as the basis of knowledge; the collective of this knowledge produces the possibility of society and culture. Thus established, the British philosophical paradigm inclined later writers to an analysis of statehood that returned inevitably to the exposition of moral values and the liberation of humans from the degeneracy of their present conditions.

Adam Smith (1723–1790), David Hume (1711–1776) and Jeremy Bentham (1748–1832) each in his own way, contributed significantly to the espousal and enhancement of British philosophical liberalism during the later eighteenth and early nineteenth centuries. However, it was Bentham and his utilitarian disciples, James and John Stuart Mill (1806–1873), who most noticeably prepared the way for the emergence of what we might call British cultural Romanticism. Struggling to account for the opposing tendencies in nature toward creative order and destructive chaos, Bentham developed the principles of human usefulness or 'utility' which would liberate individuals from the unfortunate circumstances of this paradoxical nature. Bentham's attention to the legislative process and to the mechanistic logics of human reform, including the reform of the penal system, generated widespread approval from his middle-class contemporaries, most particularly in the wake of the chaotic events of the French Revolution (1789). This reaction against the 'natural' rights, as they were expressed by Rousseau and other revolutionaries, inclined the British population toward a more measured and thoughtful reform.

This graduated reformism combined three major elements: Adam Smith's commercial utopianism; individualism (the psychology of the individual); and the imperatives of a concentrated, collective existence.

Indeed, the psychological well-being of the individual British citizen appears to be a central concern for the utilitarian philosophers. The cataclysm and ultimate failure of the French Revolution, along with the devastating and dislocating effects of industrialization, had forced British intellectuals to consider carefully their agenda for reform and progress. This double-edge of modernization is expressed in William Blake's (1751–1827) famous poem 'London':

In every cry of every Man,

In every infant's cry of fear,

In every voice, in every ban,

The mind forg'd manacles I hear.

Freedom, according to Blake and other intellectuals of the nineteenth century, was severely threatened by the new machine culture. But with the spectre of the French Revolution lingering in their consciousness, middle-class intellectuals and reformers sought a more controlled and institutionally responsible pathway to freedom. John Stuart Mill's writings on representative government and utilitarianism espoused a kind of self-interested, almost hedonistic, underpinning for the formation of collective responsibility. Individuals seek to be happy, Mill declares, and if happiness is best served by co-operation, then the needs of the individual and the society are mutually achieved. Being useful within the collective is the greatest assurance an individual can have for pleasure and happiness: As Mill expresses it in *Utilitarianism* (1863): 'The creed which accepts as the foundation for morals, Utility, or the Greatest Happiness Principle, holds that actions are right in proportion as they tend to promote happiness, wrong as they tend to produce the reverse of happiness' (1971: 7). Morality and social values are co-extensive, so that an individual's improvement will necessarily constitute the progress of society. For Mill and the other utilitarians, the 'liberty' of the individual 'from the highest class of society down to the lowest' is the ultimate determinant of economic, moral and governmental progress.

Mill seeks to resolve the significant tensions that inform modernism, most particularly those that revolve around individualism and collective or social responsibility. The basic tenets of utilitarianism can be summarized as follows:

1   All citizens should be useful.
2   Usefulness is generated through increasing individuals' personal happiness. To be happy, a person must be useful.
3   Personal happiness is a form of self-interest. This self-interest is logical and reasonable.
4   Reason tells individual citizens that their happiness is a contingency of usefulness. Usefulness is only possible through collective harmony and social order. Logic leads the individual to prosper for him- or herself, but this prosperity will necessarily generate improvement for the general good of the nation.
5   Representative government and public education are facilities and outcomes of usefulness.
6   Personal enterprise and hard work will generate personal happiness and will benefit the state as a whole.
7   Moral and social order are necessarily interdependent.

Samuel Taylor Coleridge and British Romanticism

Mill is astute enough, however, to recognize that his writings on politics and morality are incomplete, and that innumerable tensions and contradictions will persist in a complex social formation. Thus, while he attempts to systematize the moral, social and political imperatives of individualism, British Romanticism attempts to articulate these complexities through a more intense and transcendental rendering of the individual's state of being. Thus, while Blake records the spiritual and literal evacuation of the English church, other nineteenth-century Romantic poets evoke the darkly menacing presence of social progress that is inevitably bound to the human condition. Their aesthetics are profoundly wedded to prayer and the hope of secular or liturgical transcendence: the liberation of the individual spirit through the generative power of essential nature.

Samuel Taylor Coleridge (1712–1834), in fact, speaks for many of the Romantic artists and poets in his essays on politics, aesthetics and imagination. Clearly influenced by Kant and Goethe, he sees the degeneration of nineteenth-century Britain as inevitably tied to the loss of provincial connection and the degradation of the human spirit. Imagination, he claims in *Biographia Literaria* (1817), is the centre of human sensibility: 'The primary Imagination I hold to be the living power and prime Agent of all human Perception, and as a repetition in the finite mind of the eternal act of creation in the infinite I AM' (1962: 246). Coleridge articulates the shock of modernist individualism: a sudden awareness that 'I am' a separate being in a social mass, and no longer a cohort in a local community or parish. As with many other Romantics, he seeks to reconcile this new self-awareness with a collective sensibility, either by humanism or by spiritualism. It is this 'I am' which constitutes the underlying and immutable current for Romanticism generally and the Romantic conception of culture in particular. Indeed, Coleridge and many other British essayists and poets of the nineteenth century appear to have absorbed the Kantian/German conception of individual and cultural elevation, proclaiming that the arts are most likely to regenerate the spiritual condition of the nation and its people. The arts, that is, drawing their inspiration from the beauties (and occasional terrors) of nature, could refine the mind and the spirit of the individual, and hence the social group as a whole.

Like Bentham, the Mills and Edmund Burke, however, Coleridge was not a radical so much as a liberal who believed that society could be degenerated by chaos, ignorance and social vulgarity. He also followed the classical German distinction between *Kultur*, which refers to hierarchies of achievement in the arts, literature and intellectual refinement, and *Zivilization*, which refers to the general body of a people's knowledge and everyday practices. As we have noted previously, this deployment of culture as 'high art' confines the notion of 'cultivation' to elite groups of intellectual leaders. Coleridge, however, like William Blake, is concerned for the spiritual well-being of all humankind, most particularly within the context of environmental, community and religious decline. He draws the parallel, therefore, between the cultivation of agriculture, which serves the interests of the individual farmer and the community, and 'spiritual cultivation' in the arts, which also serves the interests of the artists and the community. Spiritual cultivation, in fact, is a fundamentally 'inner' condition, contrasting with the outer or material state of human existence. While the inner and outer states are coterminous,

they are fixed in tension; the imagination dissolves, diffuses and dissipates the effects of the external world of mechanical progress which threatens to destroy the individual.

The dualism between subjective/inner and objective/outer human experience was, of course, established in Descartes' famous notion 'I think therefore I am' (*cogito ergo sum*), and further elaborated in Immanuel Kant's epistemology. The separation of subject and object is a central theme in modernist philosophy, art and poetry. The question of how the subject might know the world is answered in two quite distinct ways by modernism:

1 The inner and outer worlds are treated as distinct and separate entities. The objective world is measured and analysed through the application of scientific methods that are not impinged upon by human emotions and personal interests.
2 The object is merely a projection of the unique perception of the individual subject. The world, therefore, exists in terms of individual consciousness and individual subjectivity.

Philosophy from the eighteenth and nineteenth centuries sought to reconcile these two approaches to the problematic of reality and knowledge. Coleridge, in a truly Romantic gesture, argues that this conundrum can only be resolved by the imagination or 'culture' as cultivation. To this extent, the poem or literary essay has a unique status, being neither genuinely objective nor purely subjective. The poem, as the highest expression of the imagination, constitutes a mode of discourse which is neither idea nor material thing, but which is a resonance, a complete and unified expression, which spans the full breadth of the human condition.

In *On the Constitution of Church and State* (1830), Coleridge explains the need for social leadership for the spiritual and intellectual improvement and protection of the broader community. Intellectuals and artists, Coleridge declares, should assume the role once performed by the 'clerisy' or church leaders. This notion of a secular, intellectual leadership is also favoured by other British liberal Romantics like Thomas Carlyle and Matthew Arnold. Clearly, the idea may be understood as a challenge to the overwhelming impetus of capital and material expansionism, symptomatic of the increasing isolation of nineteenth-century artists and thinkers. However, we might also read this apologia for high art and the unique status of the artist and imagination as an articulation of modernism's more general intensification of the individual. Romanticism often immerses itself in nostalgia for a more provincial and communal experience, seeking its transcendence in nature or in the 'natural condition' of primitive or exotic lifestyles. This nostalgic communalism, however, contrasts with an equally formidable interest in individual innovation and personal achievement.

The Romantic tradition, in fact, places significant value on technical aesthetic inventiveness, originality of expression, the integration of exotic themes and techniques, the genius of the individual, and the transcendence of the individual imagination and soul. The communion of old and new, of object and subject, of perpetual desire and the breathlessly new, mark Romanticism as the abstract representation of the same sorts of technical and innovative forces that were driving capitalism itself. It is not surprising that the Romantic thinkers of the nineteenth century were politically liberal and sought a freedom that would generate greater pleasure, and at the heart of that pleasure was desire and self-gratification. Nor is it surprising that they were suspicious of the exclusiveness of aristocratic privilege, on the one side, and proletariat anarchy, on the other. Theirs was a confined, class-based pleasure which was built around an orderly and thoughtful exposition of self-worth. It was an ideology of self-interest and was deeply political.

Thomas Carlyle and Matthew Arnold

It is for this reason that the cultural writings of Coleridge, Carlyle and Arnold are steeped in ideological intent, an intent clearly reflected in the Romantics' writing on government and society. The social panacea imagined Thomas Carlyle (1795–1881) would install an 'heroic' order through which the 'masses' ('the great unwashed') would be led from their ignorance and squalor by a class of intellectuals and artists. These intellectual leaders would acknowledge the working classes' claims to freedom, without surrendering social order or civility to the commoners' propensity for moral degeneracy and chaos. Unlike Marx, therefore, Carlyle is not an apologist for working-class culture, though he recognizes its heroic potential. In fact, Carlyle is seeking to avoid the anarchy and dissolution which necessarily issues from a 'mechanical age' motivated only by money. If the working classes are not freed from their subjugation and humiliation, then they will surely turn mad:

When the thoughts of a people, in the great mass of it, have grown mad, the combined issue of that people's workings will be a madness, an incoherency, and ruin! ... A Reformed parliament, one would think, should inquire into popular discontents before they get the length of pikes and torches! ... The condition of the great body of people of a country, is condition of the country itself. (Carlyle, 1967: 167)

Matthew Arnold (1822–1888), who is often impugned as the principal apologist of culture as 'high art', conceives of something similar in his discussions in 'Equality' (1861), 'Democracy' (1978) and *Culture and Anarchy* (1919; orig. 1869). In the period of significant political reform (cf. 1832 and 1867 Reform Acts), Arnold characterized British social, political and cultural life as largely anarchic. Indeed, in 'Democracy' Arnold sees the nation as largely transitional, moving between the moribund and repressive inertia of the aristocracy and the new forces of democracy and popularization. However, this transition cannot be successfully accomplished without the reimposition of a social order built around intellectual refinement and individual and social drive to 'perfection'. Culture, as the expression of the best and most elevated of human expression, must necessarily guide the common people of a nation toward that greater condition. The task, therefore, is to facilitate the enhancement of the moral, social and political benefits of culture. Anticipating the significant claims of later discourse theory, though with a more hierarchical sense of the operations of language and art, Arnold identifies culture as the central force in all human enterprise:

But, finally perfection – as culture from a thorough disinterested study of human nature and human experience – learns to conceive it – is a harmonious expansion of *all* the powers which make the beauty and worth of human nature, and is not consistent with the overdevelopment of any one power at the expense of the rest. Here culture goes beyond religion. (1949: 477)

For Arnold, the great conflict of the future is less about population and industrialism, and more about this pursuit of perfection. Culture is the ultimate salvation – social,

economic and political. This form of cultural leadership, Arnold argues, must necessarily embrace the perfection of all citizenry, a perfection which is the true source of 'equality':

And now what has this condition of our middle and lower class to tell us about equality? How is it, must we not ask, how is it that, being without fearful troubles, having so many achievements to show and so much success, having as a nation a deep sense for conduct, having signal energy and honesty, having a splendid aristocracy, having an exceptionally large class of gentlemen, we are yet so little civilised? How is it that our middle and lower classes, in spite of the individuals among them who are raised by happy gifts of nature to a more humane life, in spite of the seriousness of the middle class, in spite of the honesty and power of true work … which are to be found in abundance throughout the lower, do yet present, as a whole, the [degenerative] characters which we have seen?

[I]t is easy to see that our shortcomings in civilization are due to our inequality; or in other words, that our great inequality of classes and property, which come to us from the Middle Ages, and which we retain because we have the religion of inequality, that this constitution of things, I say, has the natural and necessary, under present circumstances, effect of materialising our upper class, vulgarising our middle class and brutalising our lower class. And this is to fail in civilisation. (1949: 600–1)

Arnold, therefore, is seeking some resolution to the divisions that continue to beset and compromise social conditions. Not surprisingly, he sees the solution in elevated communicative forms which are ultimately to be found in the province of middle-class intellectualism. In fact, Arnold marks a new territory for the exploration and definition of culture; it is this space, this confluence of symbolic representation and everyday social practice, which is marked as the territory for speculative and theoretical investigation.

LITERATURE AND PUBLIC CULTURE

F.R. Leavis

Coleridge, Carlyle, Arnold and a number of other social reformers of the nineteenth century believed passionately in the value of education as the route to individual enlightenment and elevated culture (civilization). The realization of this prescience might seem to be evident at the beginning of the twentieth century when universal suffrage was being accompanied by the establishment of universal public education and programmes of mass literacy. Certainly, the arrival of Frank Leavis (1895–1978) and Queenie Leavis (1900–82) at Cambridge in the period following World War I is notable on two counts: first, it announces the entrance of a new social class, the lower middle classes (petite bourgeoisie), into the highest levels of British educational and intellectual life; and, secondly, it forecasts a significant change to the focus and curriculum of university study. The discipline of English literature was brought out of the margins and placed at the centre of the liberal arts education. The Leavises, along with a number of other young scholars of the time, brought to the humanities, and to British intellectual life generally, a fresh approach to social investigation, one which embedded social knowledge in moral and aesthetic elevation. As Arnold had insisted, humanism, liberalism and moral improvement were all facilities of culture and cultural knowledge: culture was necessarily a contingency of knowledge and the will to 'do good'.

This concept of culture, as we have seen, is confined to a narrow body of complex texts and representational forms. The meaning-making of groups other than those who were engaged in the production and consumption of these texts was simply not acknowledged (see Figure 4.1). The arrival of people from the lower middle classes into the university sector might seem to suggest a broadening of the concept. Critically, however, this broadening didn't lead to a more inclusive approach to the production of culture; it led to a more energetic and expansive distribution of those texts which the Leavises and other scholars regarded as virtuous and worthy. That is, culture was not to include the meaning-making of the lower classes, but the lower classes were to be 'included' in the spread of the highest values of culture. English literature was to be distributed to all social groups through a general, public education programme. The birthright of all Britons, Leavis insists, is this 'great tradition', a tradition whose fundamental morality must be made available for all to share and experience.

This moral vision may be understood in several ways:

1   It was a genuinely political tenet, supporting the precepts of liberal humanism. Leavisite Romanticism sought to resolve the ongoing problematic of alienation. Just as institutional democracy was designed to reconcile individual and collective interests, Romanticism and liberal humanism sought to elevate the individual from the immediate conditions of life, reconciling each member of the society with the needs, interests and demands of the whole community. A shared morality, a shared aesthetic, a supreme knowledge – all would bring people together in a community of reasoned and respectful interdependence.

2   The aesthetics were humanist and constituitive of social order. Like the empirical social sciences, the liberal arts were developed as a counterpoint to the genuine terrors of modern life. The

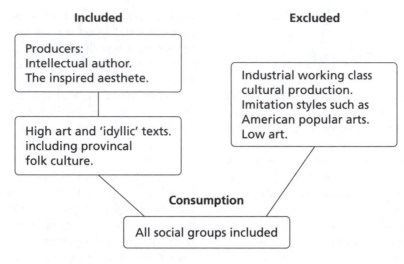

Included

Producers:
Intellectual author.
The inspired aesthete.

High art and 'idyllic' texts.
including provincal
folk culture.

Excluded

Industrial working class
cultural production.
Imitation styles such as
American popular arts.
Low art.

Consumption

All social groups included

Figure 4.1   Leavis's culture

Great War (1914–18) demonstrated for all the peoples of 'civilized' Europe that the advanced condition of their technology and lifestyles could turn vicious and bloody. The morality constituted in literature, and the pedagogical and critical processes which would elucidate artistic vision for the masses, would necessarily contribute to social order. The liberal arts would help us avoid the degeneracy and excesses that led to the devastation of war, poverty and social chaos.

3   The moral vision and the liberal arts contributed significantly to the ideology of nation and nationhood. Leavis's humanism and his notions of the 'great tradition' were tinged with a crippling and fearful xenophobia. Presented through the most utopian and heroic images of Britannia, the Leavisite construction of the artistic ideal was deeply vested in communal nationalism.

4   The terrors of modern life and the devastating effects of warfare had led to

a deepening mood of nihilism and despair, most especially in continental philosophy, where, of course, the effects of war had been most profound. Leavis's moral vision was seen as an antidote to capitulation and the relinquishement of religious faith.

In fact, Leavis's rendering of the 'great tradition' seeks to reconcile the substantive moral and existential tensions that had been narratized in the English novel and which were representations of the broader cultural dialectics of modernism. In this sense, his work represents a point of scholarly departure, bringing Romanticism into the mainstream of institutional education. However, it is also a harking to the past whereby the consummate threads of moral and spiritual idealism are theorized against the overwhelming pressure of philosophical and everyday negativism. In particular the events of the Great War and the continuing degenerations of industrialization had stimulated enormous fears and doubts amongst everyday people and scholars of the early twentieth century. The Existential philosophers – Kierkegaard, Heidegger, Nietzsche and Sartre – who sought to break with the Romantic idealist tradition were delivering messages of serious doubt. The absence of God and an ultimate moral referent had inspired thinkers like Søren Kierkegaard, for example, to distinguish between those people who could make some irrational and mystical 'leap of faith', and those, like himself, who could never find it in themselves to believe. Leavis and the other British literary scholars seem to have made that leap, despite the confronting and devastating experience of warfare and mechanical existence, despite the absence of God, and despite the overwhelming knowledge of death and meaninglessness as it was being explored by the artists and philosophers of the early twentieth century – including the novelists whom they studied and admired.

Undoubtedly, Leavis's leap of faith demonstrates a heavy investment in the method or 'science' of literary criticism, in the social benefits of liberal humanism, in the ultimate goodness of humanity, and in the possibility of spiritual transcendence. His methods were aimed at delivering a knowable and sharable truth about a text and the actions and morality of narratives and characters. But like Russian Formalists and Marxist critics, Leavis's 'truths' were clearly determined by the methods he employed; and these methods were determined by the moral and ideological context in which he was working. That is, Leavis tended to locate in his studies precisely the moral vision that he, himself, idealized. The institutional and historical context in which literary criticism was forged and practised was clearly informed by the whole tradition of utopian, liberalist Romanticism. In this sense, Leavis was far from radical. His interest in the working classes resonates with the suspicions and ideological timbre of his mentors, especially Arnold and Carlyle. In fact, Leavis rejects the notion of ideology and is deeply suspicious of the concept of class, preferring to concern himself with a moral confluence which ameliorates human difference by producing modes of social harmony and individual, ethical purification.

This 'communion' draws the working classes out of their distinct social hierarchy and articulates the purity of their individual souls as much as the nobility of their condition. Leavis lingers with awe in his discussion of Joseph Conrad's and D.H. Lawrence's descriptions of working men and women, returning frequently to what he regards as 'the inevitable creativeness of ordinary, everyday life'. Leavis delights in the fictional renderings of quotidian experiences. Lawrence's coal-miners, for example, are not members of an oppressed social group, but participants in a social mosaic which was meticulously and powerfully rendered for the emotional and moral betterment of the reader and the social formation at large. In fact, Leavis's method continually draws the text, the author and the reader into a contemplative and disarmingly tepid dialogue, one which seeks quite self-consciously to euphemize the world and its disjunctures through a celebratory nostalgia and the complicity of shared experience. This idealization of the everyday experience re-emerges through the work of more socially directed cultural studies, even though there are some significant challenges to its underlying assumptions.

Popular Culture and the Leavisite Legacy

While there can be no doubt that the Leavises and the body of scholars who followed them were politically moderate and that their new discipline of literary studies supported an intellectual utopia, it is inaccurate to characterize them as either quaint or wholly conservative. Very often, such characterizations have been made by recent scholars seeking to demarcate their own liberatory projects against an intellectual corpus which fails to appreciate the significance of popular culture (e.g., Docker, 1994: 20–32). Frank Leavis and others did, in fact, celebrate the sort of folk culture in which a number of later British cultural analysts locate their studies and utopian values. Moreover, Leavis's interest in texts and cultural formations, his bland optimism and the tepidity of his political humanism are sometimes repeated in postmodern cultural analysis. As we shall later see, particular zones of postmodernism (the aesthetics of Charles Jencks, for example) constitute a 'leap of faith', a belief in a humanist and bourgeois aesthetic, which would save humanity from the terrors of modernist expressionism, minimalism and existential nihilism.

Provincial Sentimentalism and Contemporary Tourism

Romanticism is often criticized for its sentimentalization of provincial lifestyles, and especially the folk culture of the rural poor. British Romantics such as Samuel Coleridge, Matthew Arnold and F.R. Leavis tended to valorize the English provincial worker as the essential English character. American, Canadian and Australian Romantic literature and film have also tended to valorize their pioneers and non-urban lifestyles as the quintessence of pure nationhood, the pioneering spirit and essential human virtue. Jean-Jacques Rousseau extended this sentimentalism to non-Western cultures, including tribal cultures. He spoke of 'the noble savage', that pure state of being which was uncorrupted by modernization and modern institutions. This strand of Romantic valorization continues today through various forms of celebratory consumerism. The noble savage motif, for example, has become a central part of Third World tourism. Tourist promotions frequently sell their product through images of 'natural' and 'primitive' lifestyles. The discourse of tourism abounds with essentialist and Romantic idealism. Artefacts, rituals, dance performances and agricultural lifestyles are imagined as 'authentic' or paradisaical. Whether it is Sri Lanka, Morocco or Jamaica, the discourse of Romantic elevation constructs an experience which is positioned as 'other' – as markedly different from the conditions of the modern world. Primitivism, that is, is re-imagined in terms of its purity. Leavis's nostalgia for a pure and authentic English experience parallels the world's yearning for a purity of pleasure, a paradise that could, temporarily at least, release us from the trials of modern life.

The Indonesian island of Bali, for example, is pre-figured in terms of what former Indian prime minister, Jawaharlal Nehru, referred to as the 'morning of the world', and what Indonesia's first president, Ahmed Sukarno, called the cradle of Hindu civilization. This 'island paradise', 'island of the gods', 'island of temples', was absorbed into the European Romantic lexicon by Dutch governors and painters. In more recent times, however, the island has become integrated into the mass tourism industry with visitors coming from all parts of the developed world. The Indonesian airways and tourism company, Garuda, describes the island in typically Romantic terms:

> Welcome to Bali and Indonesia known as the 'Island of the Gods'. Bali has unique and magical attraction. Mystery, romance and adventure, an unspoiled paradise with every imaginable facility and service you could desire.
> Enjoy Bali's warm and friendly people, the richly fascinating culture with majestic temples, colorful dances and religious festivals. (Garuda-Quantas, tourism brochure)

This familiar hyperbole, in attempting to marry the spiritual/innocent ('unspoiled paradise') with the vacational/commercial ('every imagined facility'), expresses precisely the development objective of the Indonesian government as well as the often unacknowledged fantasy of the First World tourist.

Having said this, however, we need also to concede that Leavis's vision of popular culture, like Arnold's and Carlyle's, is an atavistic imagining, a Romantic vision which projects an idyll of a hard-working, noble community rooted in substantial time and inviolable values. In *Culture and Environment* (1933), Leavis and Denys Thompson contrast the contemporary decline with the munificence of the past:

> What we have lost is the organic community with the living culture it embodied. Folk songs, folk dances. Cotswold cottages and handicraft products are signs and expressions of something more: an art of life, a way of living, ordered and patterned, involving social arts, codes of intercourse and a responsive adjustment, growing out of immemorial experience, to the natural environment and the rhythm of the year. (1977: 1–2)

Leavis' own Romantic and poetic demeanour, which in many respects constitutes a radical sensibility, inclines him against the rabid and aggressive mechanizations of modernist progress. He disavows the language and materialism of unbridled commerce and advertising. He repudiates the dissolution of community and socially bonded values. He abhors the ignorance and 'mob passions' that have led to mechanized social behaviours, social decline and warfare.

Queenie Leavis and American Movies

Queenie (Q.D.) Leavis presents an even more direct and hostile account of contemporary mass culture. Significantly, Queenie also distinguishes between a mass-produced entertainment and the finer qualities of English literature and the classical arts. Thus, in regretting the decline of cultural 'authority' in English society, Queenie impugns specifically the impact of Hollywood movies as 'masturbatory' and the popular press as intellectually regressive.

Significantly, the Leavises' arguments parallel the more strident criticisms of the Frankfurt School (see Chapter 3), who also believe that 'mass', mechanized culture, especially in its most delirious, American form, is responsible for the de-educating of the working classes. While many aspects of the arguments are different, the Leavisite legacy and the Frankfurt School critique share a certain pessimism, a fear that human society is disintegrating under the weight of mass-mediated messages and the dehumanizing effects of impersonal, mass urbanization. In both cases, too, the solution to this ignominy is to be found in the high arts: for the Leavisites, literature and the arts offer a transcendent personal and moral elevation; for Adorno and others of the Frankfurt School the high arts offer an escape from the oppression of ideological and material deprivation.

Mass Culture vs Popular/Folk Culture

We have seen that the Chicago School of sociological and cultural enquiry developed a more inclusive, pluralist and less fearful approach to everyday practices and culture (see Chapter 2). Indeed, the School sought to elucidate the matrices of social relationships, experiences and attitudes which contribute to the formation of culture. It should be remembered, however, that the Chicago School tended to adopt the methodologies and perspectives of journalism and anthropology, and that their work tended to examine and understand particular sub-sets of people: immigrant groups, urbanized neighbourhoods and ethnic sub-cultures. Neither their methodology nor their theoretical frames of reference inclined Chicago sociologists toward an examination of the social whole, the mass of people who might collectively be regarded as the society, nation or culture. When social science did turn its attention toward the conglomerates – as in the Payne Fund studies – it generally did so with some sense of misgiving. The primary questions for the Payne Fund researchers revolved around the impact of mass media messages on the well-being of individual citizens: for example, how were these messages affecting democratic sensibilities, moral perspectives or the mental health of children? Both the Chicago and the Payne studies were conceived from a liberalist and pluralist ideological perspective. Both sought to maintain and protect the individualist ethic, morality and democratic institutions. But both also wanted to contribute to the enhancement of the ideology of prosperity and freedom which was the persistent ideological framework around which pluralism was built. The rise of the mass media and profound suspicions about its messages may have constituted a threat to pluralism, which, in essence, was a finely balanced social compound which adhered a varied constituency to a homogenizing ethos of assimilated Americanism.

The ascendancy of Talcott Parsons, an immigrant intellectual who had seen the worst excesses of human divisiveness and disorder, might be explained partly in terms of this precarious compound, partly by the instabilities being generated by the Cold War. In either case, Parsons' devotion to social order and to the positivist rendering of complex social phenomena represents a broader commitment in American scholarship to the values of assimilated individualism. Parsons contributes to an American approach to popular culture which is both partial and suspicious, vacillating between complete fear and pragmatic recognition. There are, in fact, two significant omissions from American analysis of the popular media:

1 There is an absence of interest in the ideological and political dimensions of the popular media. While the Frankfurt School brought an interest in the mass media and ideology, their analysis, as we have seen in Chapter 3, was based on notions of social control and a pessimistic rendering of resistance. In many ways the

Frankfurt School echoed the sorts of suspicions that motivated the Payne Fund studies.

2 The radical potential of popular culture and the popular media doesn't appear in American sociology and cultural studies until at least the 1970s. Sociologists like Herbert Gans (1973) provide a critique of the mass culture–popular culture division. Others, like Alvin Gouldner (1976), explain how ideologies are multiplied through the rise of popular media technologies and texts; these multiple ideologies present opportunities for alternative social ideas and readings.

Herbert Gans was, in fact, one of the first American sociologists to critique the mass culture perspective. The notions of mass culture and culture industry were developed by the Frankfurt School to distinguish folk or popular art (art of the people) from mass-produced or commercial art (produced by industrialists for consumers). While folk art was positive and generative of positive and creative values, mass culture was formulaic, superficial, commercial, as well as morally, politically and artistically destructive. The Frankfurt School and the Leavisites both condemned mass-produced art, while celebrating folk or popular art. Gans, however, was alert to the fundamental contradictions of this distinction. He was also alert to inconclusive findings of a phalanx of media studies in the United States:

A ... far more serious theme of the mass culture critique accuses popular culture of producing harmful effects on the people who use it. A number of specific effects have been postulated: that popular culture is emotionally destructive because it provides spurious gratification and is brutalizing in its emphasis on violence and sex; that it is intellectually destructive because it offers meretricious and escapist content which inhibits people's ability to cope with reality; and that it is culturally destructive, impairing people's ability to partake of high culture. (Gans, 1973: 30)

Gans explains that there is no evidence to support the idea that the vast majority of Americans who are exposed to popular culture are 'atomized, narcotized, brutalized, escapist, or unable to cope with reality' (1973: 31). He goes on, in fact, to claim that the criticisms of both high and mass culture are delivered by those who have a vested interest in one dominion of expression over the other. Gans' apologia for popular culture disavows the distinction between mass, popular and high culture, claiming that there is a continuum and that all expressive forms are valid in themselves, and all should be available for sociological analysis.

Gans' relativism introduces a much broader scope for media and cultural analysis in America. However, this relativism also introduces new problems for media criticism, as it problematizes the whole notion of value. Gans' perspective provides for the popular media a new status and centrality in contemporary cultural analysis, as it dissolves the dialectic that has always positioned the popular media as an inferior expressive mode. British cultural studies, as it progressed during the twentieth century, was also forced to confront this problem. Birmingham-based British cultural studies sought, that is, to reconcile the conceptual division that had been established between mass and popular culture: first, by a general re-rendering of the dignity and social value of working-class community and history; secondly, by dissolving the elitism of Leavisite and Frankfurt School analytical paradigms; and, thirdly, by adopting modes of enquiry which had been developed in American sociology and various zones of social history, linguistics and anthropology.

Even so, the British/Birmingham approach could not accept entirely the relativism which Gans and others recommended. In particular, it wanted to maintain its allegiance to critical traditions, forestalling the embrace of American liberal pluralism. In order to maintain this critical distinction, British cultural studies established, or at least reconfirmed, another analytical dialectic: between cultural production and cultural consumption. At the level of consumption, British cultural studies dissolved the distinction between high, popular and folk art. What mattered to British cultural studies was the processes of meaning-making; these processes implicated media institutions and media consumers in a particular, culturally constituted communicative context. The challenge for British cultural studies, that is, was to build a new premise for critique and analysis without recourse to elitist perspectives, and simple conceptions of text, reader and culture.

CULTURALISM AND THE FORMATION OF A NEW CULTURAL STUDIES

While neither Raymond Williams nor E.P. Thompson was directly associated with the Birmingham Centre for Contemporary Cultural Studies, their work, along with various members of the Centre, is regarded as central to the formation of a substantially new form of cultural enquiry. According to Richard Johnson (1979), the second director of the Birmingham Centre, the concept of 'culturalism' most succinctly describes this new mode of cultural analysis. Initially applying the concept to the work of Williams, Thompson and Richard Hoggart, Johnson refers to a particular kind of theoretical coherence and mode of analysis which has since proved

enormously influential across the humanities and social sciences. Culturalism, in this sense, suggests that a social group's behavioural and social patterns can be revealed through the analysis of textual production and documented practices. For many analysts today, culturalism also implies a broader interest in questions of ideology and hegemony as they are articulated in popular culture. This mode of analysis is clearly manifest in the writings of the various members of the Birmingham Centre and those, like Williams and Thompson, who are engaged in their respective forms of culturalist exposition.

The Birmingham Centre: Brief Overview

Before looking at some of the most notable, individual contributors to the development of the Birmingham-style cultural research, it is worth examining briefly the genesis and development of the Birmingham Centre itself. The Birmingham Centre for Contemporary Cultural Studies grew out of a significant shift in the mood and direction of British social, aesthetic and cultural enquiry. While the Leavisite paradigm had remained largely ascendant during the early and middle years of the twentieth century, sociology, anthropology and historical studies were seeking new heuristic terrains, new ways of considering the relationships that defined human practices and meaning-making. In particular, scholars influenced by Marxism were seeking alternative perspectives on a post-World War II society that was racked by guilt, Cold War tensions, the nuclear arms race, and a profoundly vociferous conservatism which insisted that prosperity and social order were mutually dependent. Underlying this conservatism, however, were the stirrings of two significant social movements: the beginnings of youth culture in the developed world; and the ascent of the working classes into positions of cultural and social leadership.

Having never developed a strong class system, and being driven by a pluralist and liberalist ethos, American politics resisted the formation of a formidable industrial-based political party. However, in Britain and Europe, with their strong traditions of class polemics, critical theory and radical politics, the post-World War II period offered significant opportunities for social progress. Prosperity, conservatism, an expanding youth population (the baby-boomers), labour shortages, changes from manufacturing to service-based industries – all contributed to a vastly increased demand for education and educators. The influx of young teachers and academics brought new ideas which sought to resolve the social degeneracies that had led to World War II and the Cold War, and which now expressed themselves through a repressive regime of social conformity. These young educators influenced the rising generations, giving legitimacy to the new styles of music and cultural discourses as they questioned the validity of previous generations' social values and ideas. In Britain during the 1950s and 1960s, in particular, many of these new educators were drawn from the working classes. Their specific interrogation of prevailing social norms directed a new approach to the academy, critical thinking, and education generally.

Certainly in Britain there had existed in the earlier part of the century a persistent, though marginal, interest in the culture and heritage of the industrial working classes. While the Leavisite paradigm continued to exclude the cultural productions of those outside the intellectual elite, areas of community studies and community-based arts groups supported an interest in working-class practices and modes of expression as forms of folk culture. Thus, while particular zones of public and academic discourse were arguing that culture was largely an homogenized, centrist and bourgeois phenomenon, a minority of scholars were projecting a distinct social and cultural status for working people and their community. The Centre for Contemporary Cultural Studies was set up at the University of Birmingham in 1964 with Richard Hoggart as its first director. In many respects, the Centre functioned within the general context of interest in a more egalitarian approach to culture, its institutions and social practices. It became the nucleus for the burgeoning and maturing of that interest. From its beginnings, the Centre seemed to occupy a privileged position in researching and articulating contemporary, especially working-class, urban culture, with the majority of its work being dedicated to postgraduate studies and publications.

Significantly, the Birmingham Centre, most particularly under the influence of Raymond Williams and its second director, Stuart Hall, deviated from the American effects model of social enquiry. While the Leicester Centre for Mass Communications Research remained fixed in statistical and empirical methods, Birmingham aimed to explore culture and the media anthropologically and discursively – as lived experiences. The difference between the Leicester and Birmingham approaches is significant since the Leicester Centre had adopted the communications research model developed in America early in the twentieth century. The aim of this approach was largely scientific: researchers measured the cognitive and attitudinal effects that a media message would have on its recipients. The methods of measurement were scientific, disinterested and quantitative. The Birmingham Centre, however, treated the media as a fundamentally ideological and cultural phenomenon. Their meaning-making processes were essentially and inescapably problematic, rather than assumed, as in the theoretical premise of the Leicester approach. The interaction between audiences, texts, producers and culture was complex, and could only be elucidated through the application of discursive and ethnographic methods: that is, through interpretations, detailed language-based descriptions and detailed qualitative interviews and observations.

Through the work of Williams and Hall, in particular, the media were considered in terms of political processes and language systems. Drawing their influences from French language theory, as well as Marxist theory, the Birminghams regarded culture as a diffuse matrix of linguistic and ideological relationships. Text, textual meanings and culture functioned reciprocally, necessarily implicating social differentials of power and knowledge. Under Hall's directorship, in particular, the work of the Centre and its students explored an ever-widening corpus of cultural phenomena, applying an ever-widening set of methodologies. Dick Hebdige's anthropology on youth culture, David Morley's ethnographic work on television audiences, Angela McRobbie's engagement with feminism and culture – all contributed to the breadth of heuristic activities by which the Centre expanded its influence.

Richard Johnson replaced Stuart Hall in 1979 and took a more restrained approach to the diversifying field of the Centre's work. As an historian, Johnson was a little sceptical of some of the ethnographic work in which the Centre was engaged. Jorge Larrain replaced Johnson and oversaw its transformation into a standard university department, teaching undergraduate programmes and suffering from seriously reduced research funding. After the resignation of Larrain in 1991, the department has had a succession of heads including Michael Green, Ann Gray and Frank Webster. Prior to this conversion, the Centre never had more than three full-time staff at any one time yet managed to produce an extraordinary volume of work and publications.

Richard Hoggart: Working-Class Culture

One of the earliest analyses of British industrial working-class culture was carried out by Richard Hoggart. In *The Uses of Literacy* (1958), Hoggart explores the relationship between working-class culture and folk culture, and the 'imposed' and 'external' culture of mass-produced popular texts. Unlike Leavis, Hoggart is interested in the fabric of industrial and urbanized working-class experience; like Leavis, however, Hoggart maintains a deep suspicion of externally contrived cultural production, most especially as it floods into the creative quarters of the working-class community. Laing (1986) and Turner (1996) have suggested that Hoggart's own working-class background and his experiences in teaching literature to adults from his own social background helped maintain his interest in the conditions and culture of his class. While this is probably true, there is an ambivalence in Hoggart's work, a certain abstraction, which clearly demonstrates his uncertainties and subliminal doubts about the treasure of working-class culture. In many respects, this ambivalence is a symptom of the abstraction itself, the need to record the very immediacy and spontaneity of the cultural practices of the working-class community. But it also reflects a sense of alteration, of loss, the very thing which Hoggart regrets but of which he is necessarily a part.

The Working Classes and British Punk Music

In Chapter 1 we described some of the key characteristics of the concept of culture. As an 'inclusive' concept, 'culture' refers to a range of meaning-making processes and activities. An individual, therefore, might participate in a number of different cultures simultaneously: family, professional, national, technological, recreational, and so on. The British cultural studies group made some important discoveries in relation to this idea. Most specifically, they transformed Leavis's idea that culture was a set of complex texts; Richard Hoggart, Raymond Williams and E.P. Thompson, in particular, demonstrated that the industrial working class also constituted a culture with its own values, artefacts, rituals, texts and meaning-making processes. Thompson believed that culture was a relatively open concept as it was always subject to struggle and change. In many respects, however, Thompson's writings betray a genuine admiration and pride in the quality of the English working-class culture about which he was writing. Hoggart's *The Uses of Literacy* is quite explicit in its nostalgia for the cohesion and dignity of the pre-World War II working-class culture of England.

A number of commentators argue that today's postmodern world is dissolving the industrial sector of the economy, and thus the whole notion of an industrial working class is obsolete (Bell, 1973; Giddens, 1994; Poster, 1995). Even so, the resonance of industrial working-class history and culture remains a powerful presence in various zones of contemporary discourse and textualization. British punk music of the 1970s and 1980s, for example, articulated a strident and self-consciously offensive working-class identity. Bands like the Sex Pistols and the Blockheads represented a cultural positioning which, while engaging thoroughly in global media commerce, deliberately assaulted bourgeois taste, 'mainstream' popular musical styles and social hierarchy, particularly as it was represented in the heritage of the British aristocracy. Punk musicians challenged the increasing tendency in popular music toward high levels of production, commercial formulae, and what they regarded as an intellectual or virtuoso pretentiousness amongst certain musicians. The irony is, of course, that punk music itself quickly became part of the commercial music lexicon and is now filtered through various forms of independent styles such as American (Seattle) grunge.

The working-class motifs continue in British popular media, with punk music and working-class films experiencing a significant resurgence during the 1990s and 2000s. While Thompson's book on the English working class establishes a typically Marxist tension between the working classes and the bourgeoisie, this tension has largely dissolved in contemporary textualizations. The tension that is more often dramatized and represented in current music and film texts is between the imagined possibility of a working-class culture and its complete dissolution. Indeed, rather than offer a celebratory depiction of the working classes, films like *The Full Monty* offer a somewhat deflating nostalgia in which genuinely good people are seen as the victims of social progress and the dissolution of their class dignity. We are led to ask, therefore, is the resurgent interest in working-class industrial culture an exercise in nostalgia comparable to Leavis's invocation of a nineteenth-century provincial folk culture?

This transformation of city spaces has motivated film-makers and musicians to document an atrophying culture. Mike Leigh's *Secrets and Lies*, for example, addresses these questions through a general exploration of cultural dilution. The transformation of urban spaces is analogous to the cultural transformation of a particular working-class family. Leigh, however, is not nostalgic in his depiction of the family, presenting the raw and debilitating effects of class subjugation. In fact, *Secrets and Lies* dramatizes the tensions that persist within a transforming working-class culture: the limits of educational, vocational and material ambition are set against the dignity of individual and collective struggle. The 'secrets' are not just the personal histories of individual characters, but the failings of a class system which protected itself from the truth of its own savagery.

This nostalgia for the pre-World War II working-class culture, the culture of his childhood, tends to skew Hoggart's sensibilities. Indeed, his repudiation of popular culture – American popular music, jukeboxes, popular novels – refers both to the superficiality of the texts themselves and to the threat these texts pose to the maintenance of the class and its culture. That is, American jukebox culture constituted an allure, a distraction, for the youth who were to inherit the deep traditions of the industrial, urban working-class culture. While Hoggart believes the working-classes and their codes of practice and morality are sufficient to withstand the invasion, there remains a distinct sense of foreboding in his writing, a one which derives as much from his 'bourgeois' intellectual training as from a loyalty to his cultural heritage. Indeed, there exists in Hoggart's work a profound and occasionally puritanical suspicion of America and American popular culture, a fear of its superficial and sensual engagements, a fear of its glitter and surface glamour. Like the Leavises, Hoggart seeks a nobility that could be projected as a universal moral paradigm. His disappointment with contemporary youth and the mutating effects of introduced culture reflects a utopianism that spreads well beyond his repudiation of institutional power and obsessive consumerism.

Hoggart's contribution to the evolution of cultural theory is certainly significant. *The Uses of Literacy* helped to refocus interest in a 'bottom-up' conception of culture: culture that is segmentary, specific and deriving from the symbolic and everyday practices of lower-level community. However, like the Leavises and the Frankfurt School theorists, Hoggart was deeply suspicious of the imposed culture of mass-produced texts. He simply found the invasion of American, alien culture overbearing and necessarily attached to dubious relations of power and production. Even so, he was responsible for establishing the Birmingham Centre in 1964, after which (1968) he became Assistant Director-General of

UNESCO. He was never able to reconcile his anthropological interests in working-class culture with his distaste for what he regarded as 'phoney' American popular culture. To a degree, this ambivalence reflects not only his personal disjuncture but the absence of a theoretical framework which could allow the analyst to negotiate the very difficult path between understanding and sympathy. That is, Hoggart was not able to comprehend adequately the role of mass-produced culture in the lives of working-class people because he had no way of framing it critically. He saw the changes the invasion was making to the class structure of his youth, but he lacked the theoretical tools necessary to accommodate these changes. The only means of comprehending and analysing mass-produced culture were provided by Leavis and neo-Marxist works, on the one hand, and the sympathetic engagement with the texts by the working-class consumers themselves, on the other. In many respects, the history of British cultural studies after Hoggart is characterized by various attempts to negotiate this path. McGuigan (1992) argues that British cultural studies resolves the problem by wedding popular-folk culture to mass-produced culture. While this is true to an extent, McGuigan's conclusion that British cultural studies then attempts to imitate the focus of its analysis – i.e. populism – is far from accurate. As we shall see, the cultural theorists who follow Hoggart constructed extremely sophisticated strategies for elucidating and critiquing the production and consumption of media texts.

Raymond Williams: The Problem of Culture

Raymond Williams, the son of a Welsh collier, also taught in adult education in the post-World War II period and also sought to integrate the Leavisite methodology with a left-wing political perspective. Between 1946 and 1960 Williams' involvement with the adult education journal *Politics and Letters* demonstrates an increasingly sophisticated interest in the whole idea of culture. In many respects, *Culture and Society* (1958), one of the most important books in the development of British cultural studies, represents a flowering of this effort to understand the relationship between literature and politics. Williams employs the technique of close textual reading, but he is most concerned to illuminate the context within which the literary text functions. His notion of culture remains largely untheorized, but there is a strong sense in which the social and political processes which surround and inform the text are necessarily integrated into the meanings that the text offers.

Williams' account of the literary history of Britain is fundamentally liberated from the confinements of Romantic immanence and transcendence. Of course Leavis himself would acknowledge that an author works within a context, but for the Leavisite tradition the 'genius' of the author is always a contingency of moral and spiritual elevation. Society is filtered by the author's imagination so that the narrative of the novel or poem becomes ahistorical, a moral and spiritual exigency that denies the immediacies of historical context. Williams, therefore, also defies the direction of the American New Criticism, which attempted to revitalize Leavisite Romanticism by an even more extreme theorizing of the 'poem' as an inviolable and self-contained corpus of meaning – the thing Cleanth Brooks calls a 'well-wrought urn'. While American literary scholars like W.K. Ranson and Cleanth Brooks were seeking to liberate literature from the imperatives of social and political context in order to establish its uniqueness as human articulation, Williams was trying to fix the meaning-making process within the immediate social conditions of the contemporary context. A text, for Williams, was necessarily a contingency of social relationships, including relationships of power.

Of course, Marxist scholars like Georg Lukács had developed an alternative to the Leavisite position, though there is no real evidence that Williams had access to the critical Marxist perspective and only late in his career did he acknowledge directly his indebtedness to that creed. Moreover, Williams did not have available to him the increasingly sophisticated lexicon of French language theory; writings on complex language systems like semiotics and structuralism were not readily available in translation. Terry Eagleton (1978: 35–40) has argued that Williams' work, in fact, lacks a truly socialist perspective as it remains faithful to Leavisite notions of nostalgia and provincial Romanticism. While it is true that Williams fails to confront the issues of industrialism directly, it is also true that he conveys in his writings generally a desire for justice and social equality. Significantly, he remains caught between the notion of culture as an aesthetic category (literature specifically) and culture as a generative and ubiquitous set of everyday practices (the anthropological notion of 'way of life'). To this extent, *Culture and Society* does not quite resolve or abandon the Leavisite perspective, and we find the same ambiguities in his more elaborated attempt to define culture, *Keywords* (1976). Culture is 'one of the two or three most complicated words in the English language' (1976: 76), Williams tells us. But we are never able to escape the intransigence of a definition which is distinctly qualitative and entirely incorporative.

Williams' conclusion to the entry on culture reflects his contrary inclinations toward inclusiveness, on the one hand, and intellectual or social leadership, on the other:

It is significant that virtually all the hostility ... [to the notion of culture] has been connected with uses involving claims to superior knowledge (cf. the noun INTELLECTUAL), refinement and distinctions between 'high' art (culture) and popular art and entertainment. It thus records a real social history and a very difficult and confused phase of social and cultural development. It is interesting that the steadily extending social and anthropological use of culture and cultural ... has, except in certain areas (notably popular entertainment), either by-passed or effectively diminished the hostility and its associated unease and embarrassment. (1976: 82)

From *The Long Revolution* (1965) to *Culture* (1981), Williams demonstrates his desire to converge these definitions, identifying culture as the organization of complex relationships 'between elements in a whole way of life' (1965: 63). Popular arts remain regrettably poor quality, Williams maintains, but there is no special place for the 'arts' as a privileged and transcendent discourse, as Coleridge, Arnold and Leavis had claimed. Rather, Williams treats the arts as practice or 'elements' within the complex of the whole way of life. In *Culture* (also titled *The Sociology of Culture*), in particular, Williams seeks to elucidate a sociology which engages fully with the popular arts and the media. In the later works, especially, Williams is interested in the social conditions and social relationships that inform and surround the arts through the operation of ideology (Williams, 1981: 26–30) and institutions. He remains untouched, however, by the influences of French structuralism, and even in an important book like *Television, Technology and Cultural Form* (1974) there is a certain failure to appreciate the full implications of his analysis of contemporary popular media. For example, while Williams points to the unique conditions of television programming and institutions, and while he incisively attacks technological determinist and effects analysis of television, he remains distinctly suspicious of TV's intent and popularity.

Once again, we can see that Williams is sensitive to the institutional and ideological processes that contribute to the formation of texts and textual meanings. He is also aware that the meanings constituted in these texts are substantive and contribute themselves to the construction of culture as way of life. However, the resonances of his Leavisite training and his own preference for more complex artistic forms seem to limit his analyses, drawing him back into a more restrained account of the 'value' of TV texts in aesthetic and cultural terms. That is, Williams recognizes, that television is a major part of contemporary culture, but he retains his right to question its worth.

E.P. Thompson and Historical Cultural Studies

More so than Williams, who retained some residual affiliations with Leavisite textual values, E.P. Thompson's monumental study *The Making of the English Working Class* (1980) represents a substantiation of a critical link between cultural theory and politics. Like the French Annales school of historiography, Thompson sought to articulate the lives, as well as the social and political conditions, of the common people. Thompson's work, however, is not satisfied with a mere wresting of history from the control and interest of elite groups. Rather, he seeks to produce a history of the working class themselves, one which is experiential and vested in everyday practices and everyday culture. That is, Thompson's historiography avoids the sorts of sentimentalism and nostalgia that are evident in Leavis's provincialism, and which can be seen in traces in Hoggart's comparative study of pre and post-World War II working-class England.

Moreover, Thompson's project is not merely descriptive. Beginning from the perspective and experiences of the industrial working class in the period leading up to the 1830s, Thompson seeks to explain its condition and cultural formation in terms of the progress of capitalism. While he had resigned from the British Communist Party by the time of the book's publication, he demonstrates a significant allegiance to Marxist conceptions by which class is defined as 'a social and cultural formation arising from processes which can be studied as they work themselves out over a considerable period' (1980: 11). This 'making' of a class, Thompson explains, 'happens when some men, as a result of common experiences (inherited or shared), feel and articulate the identity of their interests as between themselves, and as against other men whose interests are different from (and usually opposed to) theirs' (Thompson, 1980: 8–9). This description engages an anthropological approach to human groups with Marxist precepts. It is comparable to the Chicago School approach to social mapping in that it seeks to explain processes and identity through complex associations and influences. It is unlike Chicago sociology in its focus on class and on the political context in which class is formed.

Thompson, thereby, diverges significantly from Williams' approach to culture, which focuses on the capacity of people to produce an organic, interactive and consensual whole. Thompson begins with notions of class and struggle, but insists that culture can never constitute a single way of life, only conflict between different ways of life. Clearly, his work is based around macro structures of class. However, the conflict model he applies to an analysis of culture informs much of the thinking about culture and cultural difference that has arisen in more recent years. Thompson's Marxism, nevertheless, treats the structure of class as a more or less homogeneous category, though, unlike Marx, he does not see this category as the outcome of the economic 'base'. That is, Thompson, along with Williams, rejects the base–super-structure model, insisting that economy and culture must necessarily interact to produce effects in identity, behaviour and belief. Also like Williams in *The Long Revolution*, Thompson rejects entirely the notion of class domination, postulating rather that power difference contributes to, rather than determines, the formation of class culture. The dignity and freedom of the working classes are as much self-determinations as acts of resistance. Thompson's picture of the working class is not of an oppressed and inert social forma-tion, but of a dynamic and complex mix-ture of oppression and agency. The working classes are not merely determined, but determining.

Thompson's major contribution to the development of cultural theory may be summarized in terms of his complete rejection of the Leavisite high art–low art dialectic. For Thompson, everything con-tributes to the formation and legitimation of culture. Notably, he seeks to explain the experience of being immersed in culture without direct reference to external deter-minations independent of the perceptions and experiences of the cultural group under focus. For Thompson, this means that the 'blind alleys' of history, those ele-ments which Michel Foucault later calls 'discontinuities', are necessarily integrated into the general cultural mosaic. Thompson, therefore, is not merely interested in his-torical causalities which lead one event or phenomenon into another; he is equally concerned with the details and immedia-cies which contribute to the mood and

appearance of a particular historical moment.

Thompson's approach sets him against other significant cultural theorists at the time. In particular, he became engaged in a significant debate during the 1970s over the relative value of what may be called cul-turalism and structuralism (see Thompson, 1976; Neale, 1987). Structuralism, as we have noted in our discussions on Durkheim (Chapter 2), Marx and Althusser (Chapter 3), concerns itself with those social struc-tures which bind and determine the major forms of a society and culture. While Durkheim is interested in legal and religious structures, Marx, of course, is primarily interested in the structure of class. Structural anthropologists such as Lévi-Strauss and Saussure (see Chapter 5), and neo-Marxists like Louis Althusser, are inter-ested in the structures of language – those macro formations which function to pro-duce major cultural and social adhesions. Structuralists tend to be more interested in these substantive forms rather than the infinite and constituitive details that make up the structure. Culturalism, as Richard Johnson (1979) defines it, concerns itself precisely with those details: local practices and symbolic microcosms in which everyday life is patterned and experienced. Once again, this divide represents a tension between collective patterns and microtic level details – the collective and the indivi-dual. Among numerous others, Thompson, Richard Johnson and Stuart Hall argued out the relative value of structuralist and cultur-alist propensities, with the most acid and passionate articulations appearing in the journal *History Workshop*. Johnson, who espoused the values of an Althusserian approach to cultural history over excessive humanism and localism, applied the critique of 'culturalism' against Thompson and others. Thompson rejected the nomencla-ture, criticizing the implied determinism of the structuralist approach. The notion of structure, Thompson claimed, inevitably lessened the power of working people to determine their own life experiences, culture and freedom. It limited descriptions and explanations of the world to structured causes.

Stuart Hall: The Transformation of Cultural Studies

Stuart Hall's personal struggle with Althusserian structuralism, and indeed the whole Marxist enterprise, in many respects parallels the Birmingham-based cultural theory's struggle to produce a productive theoretical framework for the analysis of popular culture. In his own account of this struggle, Hall contends that British cultural studies is necessarily implicated in the politics and postulates of Marxism; indeed that cultural studies exists 'within shouting distance of marxism, working on marxism, working against marxism, working with it, working to try to develop marxism' (1996: 265). For Hall, the theoretical interests of Marxism and cultural studies were never perfectly matched, most particularly because Marxism fails directly to address the key concerns of cultural studies: culture, ideology, language and the symbolic.

Thus, Birmingham cultural studies turned to the ideas of structural anthropology and Althusserianism to explain the problem of language and power: 'The power involved here is an ideological power; the power to signify events in a particular way' (Hall, 1982: 69). But for Hall, with his particular interest in popular media texts, the Althusser – cultural studies nexus remained problematic. Hall's own experiences as a West Indian immigrant might seem to have complicated his willingness to accept the structuralist explanations of power. That is, ethnicity seemed to add a further

dimension to the Althusserian notion of domination, which tends to locate power in the relatively closed categories of social class. Ethnicity, migration, social mobility and the shared product of popular culture seemed to create for Hall a more complex social scenario than could be explained by Althusser's notion of ideology. Unlike Hoggart, Williams and Thompson, Hall was not part of the British working-class heritage, and the inclination of Birmingham theory to aggregate the particulate experiences of so many people, communities, rituals and practices into the one, distinctly British, symbolic system seemed overly reductionist to him. If nothing else, it placed Hall himself on the outer of the theoretical and analytical activities of the Centre; it marginalized him as a social being.

In his account of the move from structuralist to Gramscian cultural analysis, Hall notes that Marxism and its derivatives remain decidedly 'Eurocentric' (1996: 269). In his co-authored book *Policing the Crisis: Mugging, the State and Law and Order* (Hall et al., 1978), his own ethnicity becomes foregrounded as he provides a view of culture which emphasizes localism and subversion, as well as active participation in the mediation of people's lives. While race has not been a central theme in Hall's writings, there can be little doubt that the absorptive interests of nation and national culture represented in the works of Hoggart and Thompson would be of less concern to him than interplays of ideology and power. While this is partly due to Hall's own fascination with theoretical problems, it is also a measure of his interests in the broader constitution of culture which is not vested in class and nation but which is engaged through much more expansive cultural and textual practices. This is not the pluralism of American communications research – Hall explicitly denounces pluralism as artificial

All practices mediated through
media texts

Dissolves high art – low art
dichotomy

Dissolves middle – working-class
dichotomy

Includes working-class
consumption

Includes creative consumption
practices of all social groups

Politics through all levels of
production and consumption

Politics through all social classes
and groups

Figure 4.2 Stuart Hall's culture

and assimilative – but rather it is an exploration of wider fields of oppression, privilege and resistance.

From Althusser to Gramsci   The need for a theoretical perspective which could accommodate social diversity, popular media, power and resistance led Hall away from Althusser toward Antonio Gramsci's notion of hegemony. Certainly, the 'turn to Gramsci', as Tony Bennett (1997) calls it, provides for Hall a more engaging and productive approach to the analysis of media texts. Gramsci's concept of the 'organic intellectual' (see Chapter 3) presents a critical space in which both free agency (the ability to act independently) and oppression can be seen to operate. Challenging Althusserianism, Hall notes that it is difficult 'to discern how anything but the

dominant ideology could ever be reproduced in discourse' (1982: 78). The Russian linguist Volosinov (sometimes identified with Bakhtin) provided the basis for a more thoroughgoing analysis of the 'struggle to signify':

> For if the social struggle in language could be conducted over the same sign, it followed that signs (and by a further extension, whole chains of signifiers and discourses) could not be assigned, in a determinate way, permanently to any one side in the struggle. (Hall, 1982: 79)

Antonio Gramsci's theories of hegemony and the organic intellectual, Hall contends, provide the facility for the construction of, and resistance to, power. When leadership must be negotiated across a whole range of 'organic' fields of interest, space is opened up for the everyday citizen to challenge, query and demand. Ideology, as Althusser imagines it, is a blanket effect; in Gramsci, however, individuals and groups might form pockets of resistance, creating their own symbolic nodes which challenge the imposition of external culture. The problem of social control is mediated, therefore, by the everyday practices and agency of smaller and 'less powerful' groups in the community. Leaders can only lead when they are sanctioned in respect of these smaller symbolic nodes. The 'struggle to signify' is not a uni-dimensional process, but an ongoing act of power, resistance and negotiation. This approach to power and symbolization allows Hall to maintain his adversarial politics without surrendering to the pessimism of Frankfurt-style social control theory. Hegemony and its functioning through the mass media necessarily open the culture to the possibilities of subversion, change and reform. In reviewing his adoption of Gramsci's theoretics, Hall acknowledges the theoretical 'conundrums' with which Gramsci was forced to work:

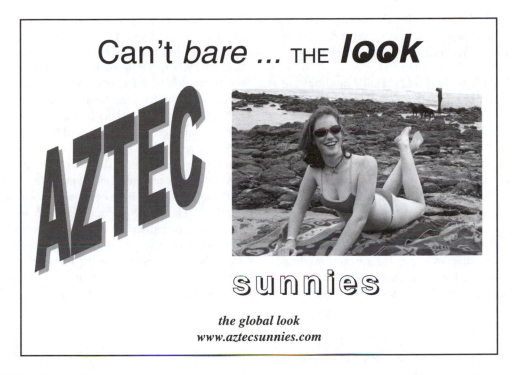

Plate 4.1   Aztec Sunnies ad.

[T]he things about the modern world which Gramsci discovered remained unresolved within the theoretical framework of grand theory – marxism – in which he continued to work. At a certain point, the question that I still wanted to address in short were still inaccessible to me except via a detour through Gramsci. Not because Gramsci resolved them but because he at least addressed many of them. (1996: 266–7)

The Gramscian notions of hegemony and the organic intellectual allowed Hall to examine media texts in terms of challenge and struggle, as much as domination. Moreover, it allowed him to admit into the nexus of his cultural analysis an approach to the media which was not restricted by the claims of class and structure (see Figure 4.3). Indeed, while other zones of cultural analysis were being influenced by the ideas of French poststructuralism and American postmodernism, Hall's own Gramscian theoretic was sufficiently positioned to admit a broader political field, including feminist, race-based and postcolonial analysis. Even so, Hall concedes that the admission of these wider politics into cultural studies strained the efficacy of the Birmingham Centre's theoretical conceits:

[A]ctually getting cultural studies to put on its own agenda the critical question of race, the politics of race, the resistance to racism, the critical question of cultural politics, was itself a profound theoretical struggle.... Again it was only accomplished as the result of a long and sometimes bitter – certainly bitterly contested – struggle against a resounding but unconscious silence. (1996: 270)

Hall also concedes, however, that these struggles were a necessary, and, we might add, paradoxical, process of change.

Encoding/decoding Hall's methods are as varied as his theoretical encounters. His approach to textual analysis, however, is clearly outlined in his essay 'Encoding/decoding' (1980). For Hall, a text is thoroughly embedded in its cultural context, which, in turn, is determined by relationships of power and hegemony. In many respects, Hall's approach to text and context resolves the dichotomy that developed in Birmingham studies between culturalism, as elucidation of particulate cultural details, and structuralism, an investigation of ideology and structures as sources of power (see Bennett, 1986). The encoding/decoding process is designed to supplant simple notions of authorship and interpretation. Essentially, various agencies contribute to the formation of a textual 'code': investors, media institutions, creative staff, and so on. Each is informed by particular cultural experiences, including various ideological perspectives and convictions about what would constitute a successful media product. Textual coding engages these aspects through a dynamic of meaning potentials known as signifiers. The text is a product, therefore, of individual, hegemonic and cultural ingredients. Texts carry a series of meaning possibilities whereby signifiers can be interpreted in a variety of ways. This potential for varied 'interpretation' is known as polysemy.

Coding and Representation

A text represents (re-presents) the world around us. It is not a mirror or identical reproduction of everyday reality, but creates a version or impression of that reality. In other words, texts mediate and in a sense create a new 'reality' out of the cultural resources of life. In a process he calls encoding, Stuart Hall (1980) argues that cultural resources are shaped into sharable textual codes (language systems); these textual codes are then decoded (or interpreted) by audiences. Through this representation of the world, text-makers and text-readers are able to share and create meanings for themselves and for one another. Ideology and hegemony play an important role in this encoding/decoding process since they enable members of a society and culture to locate specific meanings out of a given text's range of possible meanings. Dominant groups within a social formation are able to exert greater influence in what Hall calls the 'struggle to signify': that is, the battle over cultural resources which enables some individual and groups to have their own specific interests and needs satisfied.

One of the most common motifs in contemporary culture is the body of the thin, young woman. Text-producers deploy this motif or symbolic form for a range of libidinal, narrative and commercial purposes. Feminist cultural theorists like Angela McRobbie (1982) have argued that texts like that in Plate 4.1 'position' readers and therefore reinforce dominant ideologies of sexism and patriarchy. The ad tells teenage girls, for example, who they are and how they should act. Similarly, Laura Mulvey (1975) argues that the perpetual availability of women's bodies in contemporary visual culture satisfies the interests of the dominant gender, men. Naomi Wolf (1991) argues that the depiction of generally unattainable body shapes in advertising serves to discipline and control women. Real women are perpetually dissatisfied with their bodies and hence spend excessive energy and time on the project of thinning.

In all cases, this disproportionate representation of attractive young women distorts the actual conditions of everyday life. Stuart Hall's point is that the media create their own representational 'reality' which is formed through the interests of dominant groups, hegemony and ideology. The abundance of attractive, usually Anglo-Celtic, young women in the media is not an accident, but represents a very specific cultural predilection.

Decoding is a mirror process by which the audience or consumer is confronted with a series of meaning potentials in the text. These meaning potentials struggle for prominence, but audiences tend to aggregate around what is known as the dominant or preferred reading. Dominant readings are derived through hegemonic processes whereby audience members draw on their knowledge of culture, cultural values and cultural norms. Where the audience is more alike or homogeneous, the likelihood of a dominant reading is greater. Hall insists, however, that the decoding process is far from unilateral and variations in reading are always possible. Certain textual meanings – the value of capitalism, nation, individualism, for example – are repeated and presented so frequently and unreservedly that they appear as forms of ideology. Others are presented in more varied ways and may be subject to what Hall calls the 'struggle to signify'; these more contested areas of discourse can lead to more varied decodings. In either case, Hall recognizes that the mass media offer opportunities for the presentation of significant cultural values and ideologies which may reinforce the interests of dominant groups

(organic intellectuals, as Gramsci calls them). Equally, however, polysemy offers opportunities for challenge and varied decoding practices. Social challenge and social reform are possible through the fissures and imperfections of the encoding/decoding process. The task of the analyst is to illuminate the processes by which preferred or dominant readings are constructed; close textual analysis can illuminate particular assumptions and ideologies that are engaged in cultural representation.

Identity Politics In a number of important essays on globalism and identity written during the 1990s we can see once again Hall's own personal struggles with the atrophy of Marxism and Marxist solidarity. The well-canvassed fragmentation of the social and cultural landscape, accompanied by an equally fragmenting theoretical landscape, has led to further and more profound abandonments of the Marxist polemic. Indeed, while Hall is prepared to maintain his disavowal of psychoanalytic and poststructural theory that is not informed by political intent (see Hall, 1988, 1991a, 1991b), his more recent writings on identity appear to be seeking a more inclusive and flexible approach to the mutability of subjectivity and personal identity. The paradigm of political resistance is now a matter of diffusion and identity creation:

> The more social life becomes mediated by the social marketing of styles, places and images, by international travel and by globally networked media images and communications systems, the more identities become detached – disembedded – from specific times, places, histories, and traditions, and appear 'free-floating'. We are confronted by a range of different identities, each appealing to us, or rather to different parts of ourselves, from which it seems possible to choose. (Hall et al., 1992: 303)

While the postmodernists appear to welcome this new permutation of individual freedom, Hall's mood is a little more restrained, betraying an ambivalence which hearkens to his Marxist, reformist heritage.

OTHER MODES OF BRITISH CULTURAL STUDIES

There is no doubt that the Birmingham Centre for Contemporary Cultural Studies has exerted an influence over the development of cultural analysis which is significantly disproportionate to its actual size and membership. While the growth in cultural studies across the world cannot be attributed to the work of the Centre directly, there is no doubt that the writings of Hall and others have provided a valuable paradigm for others to follow. The Birminghams were particularly influential in drawing attention to French language theory, Gramscian hegemony and variants on the concept of ideology. In many ways, the Birminghams rearranged the relationship between popular media, Marxism and culture, providing the opportunity for

critical analysis that admitted substantial possibilities for liberation and agency. Writers like John Fiske and John Hartley, whose early work came out of the Polytechnic of Wales, draw heavily on the Birmingham paradigm in the formation of their own, rather more celebratory, account of popular culture.

John Fiske's Pleasure in the Text

While I will have more to say about the work of John Fiske in Chapter 8 on audiences and popular consumption, it is worth noting here that his interest in the concept of 'pleasure' contributes significantly to the broadening of the cultural studies lexicon. Fiske's early work is especially intrigued by the French structuralist theories of Claude Lévi-Strauss and Ferdinand de Saussure. Fiske follows Hall's approach to textual reading, presenting analyses which illuminate power relationships in the representation of blacks, trade unions and women. Fiske's interests, however, lead to a more complete entrancement with the writings of Roland Barthes, especially *The Pleasure of the Text* (1975). For Barthes, the interaction between a text and an audience necessarily produces particular pleasures; these pleasure are informed through a 'naturalizing' or 'doxifying' of often repeated narratives or stories. These doxa are so thoroughly embedded in the everyday experience of people that they become part of an everyday mythology. The analyst's task is to disclose these 'bourgeois norms' as cultural and therefore political rather than natural or necessary. There is an ambivalence in Barthes's work, however, a sense in which these narratives and mythologies may provide sensual pleasure as well as political repression. Fiske's adaptation of

Barthes serves merely to accentuate this ambivalence; popular culture, which the analyst should reveal as an inducement to blind mythologizing and dominant reading, becomes a pleasure which may stimulate bodily incandescence. These bodily responses, in turn, may constitute a resistance to the dominant ideology and mythology of rationalized, patriarchal capitalism. Fiske's writings, in fact, are replete with an acknowledgement of pleasure – not *of* the text but *in* the text. In this sense surfing might be a form of oppositional 'bliss' (Fiske et al., 1987); Madonna is a sexual liberationist (Fiske, 1987); and football, when viewed from the terraces, constitutes the strategic raiding of cultural meaning (Fiske, 1989b).

In Fiske's approach to popular texts we are returned to the problematic of cultural criticism. Stuart Hall had promoted a finely balanced critique of the media, combining the control theories of neo-Marxism with the liberationism of Gramsci's hegemony. Fiske, however, takes cultural studies a step further towards the surrender of its political credentials. In celebrating the liberational potential of popular texts, he is moving well outside the borders of the Marxist critical heritage. In fact, in adapting Barthes's critique of bourgeois French culture (*Mythologies*), Fiske et al.'s *Myths of Oz* (1987) seems to sacrifice the seriousness of Barthes's intent in order to emphasize the playfulness and humour that operate in culture-making (see Turner, 1991). This celebration of popular culture has been severely criticized by authors like Jim McGuigan (1992), who regards Fiske's work as capitulatory, superficial and populist. According to McGuigan, Fiske and others working in a postmodern cultural studies have become so entranced by the object of their study that they have come to imitate it.

John Hartley

John Hartley, whose formative and recent work also comes out of Wales, has applied a similar conception of pleasure in his analysis of contemporary newsmaking. For Hartley the key to understanding modernity and its interaction with contemporary news texts resides as much in the phenomenon of populism and sensational news reporting as it does with the high-minded idealism of liberal humanist journalism. Hartley, in fact, betrays his own postmodernist credentials as he seeks to reach beyond the Left–Right divide, which, he believes, limits our understanding of journalism and its rendering of contemporary culture. In particular, Hartley takes issue with cultural theorists like John Frow (see 1995), whom he regards as being constrained by outmoded theoretical and political traditions:

> In fact part of my purpose in this book is to go beyond binarized, adversarial criticism of the kind to which John Frow ... falls victim when he recognizes that journalists are part of the 'knowledge class', only to dismiss them wholesale (along with priests and teachers) on the grounds that their class function is simply to inculcate ruling class ideology. This is a standard leftist denunciation of journalism – especially popular (commercial) journalism. (Hartley, 1996: 26)

Hartley's enterprise, then, is to elucidate the ideological value of journalism without the constraint of traditional divisions of Left–Right politics and popular – serious journalism. His disavowal of Althusserian notions of class division and dominant ideology – whether or not they are fairly attributed to John Frow's work – treads a very fine line between critique and celebration. Like Fiske, Hartley's work is predicated on a precarious conception of pleasure and sensation; his avowal of popular news texts at times slips into an almost voyeuristic delight where the 'sexualized body' becomes the focus of an ambiguous, if not ambivalent, emancipatory politics – an agent for the ideology of democratization and social/cultural progress.

DISCUSSION: THE VALUE OF BRITISH CULTURAL THEORY

Graeme Turner has argued that cultural studies cannot easily be separated into specific fields of interest; nor is it a discrete constellation of disciplines: 'Cultural studies is an interdisciplinary field where certain concerns and methods have converged; the usefulness of this convergence is that it has enabled us to understand phenomena and relationships that were not accessible through the existing disciplines' (1996: 11). Cultural studies, however, is not just an interdisciplinary 'field', as Turner suggests. It is also a set of concepts and apprehensions which necessarily problematize the focus and methods of the traditional humanities and social sciences. Cultural studies, that is, raises the question of how reality is constituted. Its answer is that all reality is culture, since all reality is mediated by discourse and meaning-making processes. The traditional disciplines which have assumed their realities must choose either to ignore this knowledge or accommodate it through the transformation of their scholarship. If culture is always the starting place of reality, then literature, sociology, politics, history and anthropology must redefine themselves in terms of cultural analysis, or else surrender entirely to the new humanities, the new 'field' of study.

What distinguishes British cultural studies is that it was perhaps the first in the English-speaking world to address the problematic of meaning-making and the need to conceive more fully of the broad field of human experience known as culture. While the Birmingham Centre seems remarkably organic with the hindsight of history, as both Johnson and Hall record, there were many bitterly contested battles over methods, strategies, resources, theories and values. By the time the Centre was folded back into the academic mainstream during the 1980s, these wide-ranging programmes and strategies had been variously adopted by emerging cultural studies schools and traditional disciplines around the world. While it's true that many of the Birminghams' ideas on culture, power and language were being explored in various ways, the Centre (Stuart Hall in particular) provided an extremely systematic and coherent approach which synthesized many of these ideas into a workable programme.

This move from studies in class and ideology toward a text-based critique seems to have facilitated a more diffuse and less adversarial analytical paradigm. Through its further engagement with forms of ethnography, French poststructuralism and American postmodernism, British cultural studies is now barely distinguishable from cultural studies in Australia, Canada or the United States. In fact, while particular areas of communications and media sociology maintain an adherence to positivist principles, especially in the United States, the hybridizing of various areas of cultural studies through the English-speaking world has significantly transformed the demarcations which once separated the disciplines. For American sociology and communications studies, the Birmingham theoretics articulated in a formidable way many of the ideas that had been explored through Chicago sociology, phenomenology and symbolic interactionism. The elision of hardline Marxism in a generalized cultural critique seemed somehow to bring to American cultural analysis a vigour that was not threatening to the liberalist and pluralist ideals of its scholarship.

James Carey's *Communication as Culture* (1989), for example, represents a significant departure in American communication studies. Carey's analysis of communications technology brings British notions of culture into the foreground. Carey insists, in fact, that the symbolic and political dimensions of culture were as significant in the formation of 'America' as were economic and industrial processes. Similarly, Lawrence Grossberg's essay 'Birmingham in America' (1997: 1–32) explores the problematic of culture through an adoption of British cultural studies strategies. Grossberg's work has been heavily influenced by Birmingham writers like Dick Hebdige, who pioneered analysis of youth culture in the 1970s. Contemplating the various permutations of American youth and popular culture, Grossberg argues that culture cannot be parenthesized or reduced to concepts of social control:

> Cultural studies believes that culture matters and that it cannot simply be treated (dismissed) as the transparent – at least to the critic – public face of dominating and manipulative capitalists. Cultural studies emphasizes the complexity and contradictions, not only within culture, but in the relations between people, culture and power. (1997: 12)

This transatlantic adaptation of Birmingham-style cultural studies rejects the economic bottom-line as the determinant of cultural forms. Grossberg's cultural studies, while not a mainstream in American cultural sociology and communications studies, nevertheless constitutes a significant heuristic zone, one in which the problematics of power and popular culture are centralized. America's long-standing interest in popular culture is now reframed in terms of power and ideological formations.

Significantly, however, Birmingham-style cultural studies is being forced to accommodate the new theoretical inflexions of poststructuralism and postmodernism. While particular zones of cultural studies have tried to resist the effects of these inflexions, others have been much more absorptive. In the United States, in particular, the mutating aesthetics of postmodernism has found its way into various fields of cultural analysis. Grossberg himself struggles with the contending influences of postmodernism and the residual Gramscian politicism of Birmingham-style cultural studies. While the details of this tension are more clearly outlined in Chapter 8, there is certainly a crisis of emphasis in the minds of many cultural theorists: in crude terms, critics of postmodern cultural studies believe that it has surrendered excessively to the claims of consumer capitalism and has lost its capacity for social and cultural critique.

It may be, in fact, that the liberalist pluralist scholarly tradition in American cultural studies leads it more fully toward a postmodern, as opposed to a Birmingham, style of cultural studies. In this sense, the liberalism of the Chicago School, the localism of symbolic interactionism and the transcendentalism of phenomenology constitute forms of rehearsal for a more complete and indigenous analysis of American popular culture. In fact, Birmingham-style cultural studies has transmogrified into various forms of cultural politics, opening the way for the appropriation of popular culture by a more expansive and celebratory popular cultural studies. The residues of Gramscian analysis can be located in various universities around the world, but this is less typical than Hall and others would certainly have preferred. A crisis in cultural studies may be prevalent, as Grossberg (1997) laments, but in other respects we are witnessing a ferment of theoretical and methodological expansionism as the humanities and social sciences attempt to redefine themselves and their interests in terms of culture and mediation. Old methods and ideas are being welded to new. Various forms of scholarly hybridization are taking place. Conferences are replete with calls for a return to empiricism or political economy or the purity of Gramscian concepts. What is clear, however, is that the new disciplines can no longer function without recourse to significant debates about language and culture. Whether these debates encompass issues of power, ideology and emancipation is a function of emphasis and definition. Certainly, the British tradition of cultural studies has provided, above all else, a way of thinking about culture which makes such issues ineluctable.

Part Two

Cultural Locations

Part Contents

5

Language and Culture:

From Structuralism to Poststructuralism

Outline of the chapter

From the 1960s, cultural analysis became increasingly interested in the processes of meaning-making. The move from an interest in high art into a more integrated study of 'way of life' remained somewhat disjointed until the introduction of various forms of language theory. Stuart Hall was especially active in theorizing culture in terms of 'language' or 'discourse'. This interest in language as a cultural phenomenon parallels significant changes within philosophy generally and the philosophy of language in particular. While the Enlightenment had been interested primarily in the question of how individuals 'know' their world, a number of late nineteenth- and early twentieth-century philosophers began to change the focus of their enquiry: they began to ask, how is knowledge possible? The answers provided by philosophers like Friedrich Nietzsche, Bertrand Russell, Ludwig Wittgenstein and Charles Sanders Peirce treat language as the primary mediation between an individual and the real world. That is, we can 'know' nothing except through the mediation of language, and so language has to be the central focus of our studies of the world.

Initially, many of these studies treated language as a cohesive, ordered and operative system of meaning-making. 'Semiology', which developed during the middle years of the twentieth century, attempts to explain how all meaning-making is constituted through 'signs' and a 'sign system'. Ferdinand de Saussure argues that particular patterns or structures which support a given sign system are common to all meaning-making. Claude Lévi-Strauss argues that culture is informed by similar meaning-making processes and patterns. He calls these patterns 'myths': commonly repeated narratives which are designed to resolve underlying social tensions. Roland Barthes applies the notion of 'myths' to explain the domination of particular meaning-making patterns in contemporary French culture.

These 'structuralist' approaches seek to understand how meanings are possible and how universally repeated patterns facilitate meaning-making. More recent French language theorists have asked questions about the imprecise nature of language and meaning-making. This emphasis on the incompleteness of meaning-making, history and culture generally is central to the work of Jacques Derrida, Michel Foucault, Jacques Lacan and Gilles Deleuze and Félix Guattari. Poststructuralism, therefore, provides a theoretical basis for a broader questioning of meaning-making in contemporary culture, informing directly the deconstructive theoretics of particular areas of postmodernism. The work of Jean-François Lyotard constitutes a theoretical bridge between poststructuralism and postmodernism.

GENERAL INTRODUCTION

As we noted in the previous chapter, British cultural studies moved away from a Marxist-based analysis of working-class life into a broad field of study. Politics and everyday practice remained pivotal in cultural enquiry; however, writers like Raymond Williams and Stuart Hall focused on texts and the media in the formation of culture. Hall (1982), in particular, sought to free cultural and media analysis from the linear reductionism of the American effects tradition, on the one hand, and the materialist determinism of Marxism, on the other. Hall recognized that both the effects tradition and the Frankfurt School of neo-Marxism presented a limited vision of the relationship between culture, media institutions, texts and audiences. The effects model treated language as a given and the process of communication as a simple matter of message transmission. A message and its effect on an audience could be simply measured by the application of statistical methods. In the Frankfurt School model, messages were also conveyed but the intent was always and everywhere ideological. Adorno, Horkheimer and Marcuse believed, pessimistically, that the masses were passive and uni-dimensional victims of the overbearing power of state and media institutions. The material privation of the masses was legitimated through the ideology of mass-produced texts.

Hall understood that the relationship between texts, institutions and audiences could not be reduced to hierarchies of effect or ideology. He recognized that politics was a central and defining category in the study of culture and media, and that Althusser's account of ideology – the representational dimensions of power and imagination – presented significant opportunities for effective critique. The realization of this potential, however, would be possible only through the engagement of ideology with other significant categories such as Gramsci's hegemony and a more complex rendering of the processes of language and meaning construction. For Hall and many others working in the field, the most formidable explanation for the complexity of the text – institution – audience relationship was provided through forms of linguistics or, more particularly, 'semiotics'. The merging of French language theory with Birmingham-style cultural studies contributed significantly to the widening of the cultural studies project in Britain and elsewhere. Undoubtedly Hall's personal qualities and experiences provided an ideal conduit for the hybridization of Gramsci, Althusser, French semiology and class-based politics.

Even so, the ferment of interest in French language theory in the English-speaking world eventually reached well beyond the interests of Hall and the other Birminghams, most especially through the emergence of a *post*structuralist theoretic which invaded cultural studies from the 1980s onwards. In this chapter we will look at the lineage of French language theory from structuralism through to poststructuralism. Many scholars might object to this juxtaposition, arguing that the rupture between structuralism and poststructuralism constitutes a distinctive and categorical break. My own view is that the challenge presented by poststructuralism to structuralism, while significant and defining, does not erase the substantive issues, interests and themes which connect the two within the genealogy of contemporary cultural theory. Many of the debates within current-day cultural studies centre on the viability of poststructuralism for the analysis and comprehension of postmodern culture.

FOUNDATIONS: WITTGENSTEIN AND ALGEBRAIC LANGUAGE

Universal Language

As we have noted in previous chapters, modern scientific principles and methods were developed through the philosophical writings of people like René Descartes, John Locke and Immanuel Kant. Descartes, for example, explains that knowledge is only possible through the removal of doubt, and by the application of universal principles expressed through a universal language, the language of mathematics. The social sciences, developed during the nineteenth and early twentieth centuries, also adopted principles of reason and universalism. In particular, the 'science' of philology uses an hierarchical index to compare tribal and other ethnic languages with the 'standard' of the European languages. This mathematical index translated various language functions and codes into a quantity of value; this 'objective' index generally demonstrated beyond doubt that non-European languages were vastly inferior to European languages.

As Edward Said (1978) explains, this index is itself informed by modernist

ideologies which have very little relevance to the non-European languages being investigated. All language functions (vocabulary, syntax, tense, etc.) are fundamentally embedded in the needs and interests of a specific cultural context. These cross-ethnic comparisons, which remove a language from its context of operation and which claim to be objective and universal, are positioned, in fact, in terms of the interests of the researcher. In other words, the language under study is removed from its original context and re-contextualized in the culture of the researcher. The language is placed on a scale of performance according to the interests and needs of the researcher's culture; these standards are of course entirely different from those of the original culture. In fact, as Said points out, philology reconstructed the non-European languages according to what the philologist regarded as important or normal: that is, according to an ideology which privileged very specific standards of function and value.

Early Wittgenstein

As with the formation of communication studies in the United States and the deployment of the concept of culture in aesthetics, sociology and anthropology, the study of linguistics at the beginning of the twentieth century is characterized by a drive for objective and universal descriptions. The philosophies of language and the social science of linguistics, that is, sought to construct a universal index of comparison, one which could incorporate all languages without the 'disruptive' intercession of context. Thus, while philosophers like Friedrich Nietzsche were investigating the complexities of language and representation, others, like Charles Sanders (C.S.) Peirce, Gottlob Frege, Bertrand Russell and

Ludwig Wittgenstein (1889–1951), were seeking a final and encompassing explanation of language, one which would formulate an absolute definition for the communicative function of language.

Wittgenstein, in particular, follows the work of Frege in attempting to isolate language from its direct and necessary connection to the world of sense. Frege had explained that a concept bore no necessary relationship to the thing to which it referred: there is nothing in the word 'blue' which connects it to the colour of blueness, nothing about the word 'chair' which necessarily connects it to the thing upon which we sit. While Charles Sanders Peirce and others use this information to explore language operations in terms of psychological processes, Wittgenstein's earliest works attempt to explain the processes of language and meaning-making in terms of the essential 'structure' of atomic units of language. Wittgenstein's philosophical method is clearly associated with this fundamental precept: a precise and well-formed proposition (statement of an idea) could act as a lens to the external world. That is, the world-out-there could be rendered available for communication through the construction of propositions.

Wittgenstein shifts the emphasis of nineteenth-century epistemology, however, by focusing on the act of constructing propositions in language, rather than emphasizing the formation of knowledge in the mind of the subject. As we noted in earlier discussions, eighteenth- and nineteenth-century philosophy created a fundamental problem when it theorized a distinction between the subject (I, me) and the object (everything outside myself). The question of what is knowledge and how can it reconnect subject and object preoccupied philosophy from empiricism, idealism through to phenomenology. Wittgenstein, like Nietzsche, refocuses the problem by asking questions

about the nature of language and how language operates in relation to the subject and the object. Bertrand Russell, Wittgenstein's mentor, was also interested in this question; however, Russell directs his attention toward the nature and limits of the world-of-sense. Wittgenstein, on the other hand, is more interested in the nature and limits of language itself.

In the most widely invoked of his writings, *Tractatus Logico-Philosophicus* (1922), Wittgenstein addresses these problems in terms of understanding how language might function in order to best represent the external world. He argues, in fact, that the logical forms of language must necessarily operate to reproduce the logical forms of the 'lifeworld':

> In a proposition a situation is, as it were, constructed by way of experiment. ... One name stands for one thing, another for another thing, and they are combined with one another. In this way, the whole group – combined like a tableau vivant – presents like a state of affairs. (Wittgenstein, 1922: 4.031–4.0311)

Wittgenstein argues that propositions, as the logical representation of reality, must be limited by tautology at one extreme and contradiction at the other. In other words, a proposition in language may simply produce itself as a mere repetition where the repetition is redundant to any actual meaning; at the other extreme, the proposition in language may present itself as a contradiction where the meanings are cancelled out. A tautology in this sense would be: The red flower is red. A contradiction would be: The red flower is blue. Within those broad boundaries are 'truth functions', which are the 'forms' of elementary propositions.

What every picture, of whatever form, must have in common with reality in order to represent it at all – rightly or wrongly – is the logical form, that is, the form of reality. (Wittgenstein, 1922: 2.18)

Elementary propositions, therefore, are the simple, everyday propositions in language which enable us to communicate in accordance with our lifeworlds. 'Lifeworld', we recall, is a key concept in phenomenology. It is the idea that we live in a world of phenomena, and that we are connected to those phenomena by our consciousness or awareness. We are connected to others through our shared experience of consciousness. Wittgenstein has something similar in mind here, arguing that the lifeworld is constructed of logical 'forms' with which language connects. The elementary proposition 'I will give you a red rose' makes sense to us because it is part of the lifeworld. Such elementary propositions, which are representations of reality, cannot therefore include abstract or self-reflexive discourses such as ethics, values or the meaning of life. Wittgenstein's own *Tractatus*, which explains the operation of language, is therefore not an elementary discourse.

Later Wittgenstein

Not surprisingly, the *Tractatus* has been used in various zones of social science to substantiate positivist methodologies and the paradigm of logical or rational analysis. The problem, in fact, as Wittgenstein outlines in a later essay, 'Some remarks on logical form' (1929), is that different propositions may need to account for degrees rather than absolute conditions of distinction. In order to deal with this problem of relativity, Wittgenstein argues in the *Philosophical Remarks* that

just as the graduation marks are on *one* rod, the propositions corresponding to the graduation marks similarly belong together, and

we can't measure with one of them without simultaneously measuring with all the others – it isn't a proposition which I put against reality as a yardstick, it's a *system* of propositions. (1975: 110)

Wittgenstein, therefore, comes to realize that a proposition cannot of itself be absolute and unconditional – atomic – but must refer always to its system of significations – its context where different propositions must engage with and relate to one another. In other words, the proposition 'I will give you a red rose' can only make sense when the concept of 'red' or 'rose' is understood in terms of categories of distinction: what distinguishes red from blue, or a rose from a daffodil. The 'system' of language operation therefore becomes the significant unit, rather than the atom of a particular proposition. While, on the surface, this may seem an innocent enough realization, it effectively undermines the whole project of logical positivism and its claims to absolute knowledge. Wittgenstein goes on to renounce the whole enterprise of the *Tractatus*. In *Philosophical Grammar* he notes that the idea of bringing to light what was hidden in sentences through the application of logical propositions should largely be replaced by a philosophical analysis which merely elucidates 'ordinary language'.

At this point in his career, Wittgenstein moves far more closely toward a cultural activity. The idea that a common structure underlies all language – that of the logical representation of reality – was found to be utterly inadequate for a rendering of ordinary language practices. In fact, Wittgenstein insists that we should not assume that elements categorized under the same term necessarily have something in common. Rather, we should acknowledge that there is a whole matrix of relationships and assemblages that function through a range of relationships in language.

Wittgenstein deploys the analogy of game-playing (card games, board games, etc.) to illustrate the ways different relationships operate within the sphere of ordinary language use. This 'family of resemblances' indicates how language games are played through ordinary practice.

Significantly, Wittgenstein's use of the concept of language games remains somewhat inconsistent during the course of his writings. At times, it appears to emphasize the functioning of rules and the common grammar that brings meaning to a sharable condition. At other times, Wittgenstein appears to use the concept to emphasize the flexibility of these boundaries, emphasizing the relativity of language and meaning. In *Zettel (The Blue Book)* (1967), where the concept first appears, he uses it to refer to primitive forms of language which are much simpler and easier to understand than is the case with modern, ordinary language. At other times, he refers to specialized linguistic systems (or specific applicational contexts of ordinary language) as language games. Significantly, Jean-François Lyotard, one of the major theorists of postmodernism, adopts the concept for his study of contemporary culture. Lyotard is also a little inconsistent in his application of the term, but essentially he is attracted by the concept's confluence of unpredictability and formalism. A language game, that is, facilitates a free flow of action, motivations and outcomes within a context of rules. For both Wittgenstein and Lyotard, language games infers a mutable and restless activity of pleasure, meaning-making and uncertainty.

In either case, the value of the concept for Wittgenstein relates to the problem of meaning and the operation of meaning or sign systems. Wittgenstein's great contribution to the development of cultural theory and a specifically defined cultural theory of language centres on his understanding of the importance of context and the imprecise nature of it. The system of signs and the language games that render them meaningful are never free of their context; the rules, the games and the communication occur directly through the context of their activation. Freeing himself from an 'algebra' of language, Wittgenstein came to understand that language is never independent of its operational context.

THE ARRIVAL OF THE SIGN:
C.S. PEIRCE

The American philosopher and psycholinguist C.S. Peirce (1839–1914) is often identified as one of the major foundational theorists for the development of American symbolic interactionism and continental linguistics (see Peirce, 1958). Along with other linguists such as Ogden and Richards (1923), Peirce made a significant contribution to a form of language study which Ferdinand de Saussure was later to call semiology or the science of sign systems. According to Peirce, a sign is something which stands for something else in the mind of an individual. A sign may construct an 'equivalent sign' or a 'developed sign' in an individual's cognition. Peirce recognizes that the sign of an object will necessarily produce a further sign for the individual; he calls this the *interpretant* of the original sign. A sign is not just a public notice like 'Keep off the Grass' or 'Enter'; it is a symbol which signifies for the reader some form of meaning. A sign, therefore, might be smoke indicating fire, a word or a visual image. A red traffic light indicates stop; the word 'cat' refers to a fluffy creature with four legs and an appetite. The reason why signs can present meaning is because they belong to and operate within a system.

The significant part of Peirce's work is his acknowledgement that the sign functions in relation to the mind of the interpretant and the object, but cannot be equated to either. Significantly, the sign has meaning only in terms of the mind of the interpretant. The interconnection between the sign, the object and the interpretant determines the general processes of language systems. The red light of a traffic signal has meaning in the mind of the interpretant, then, because the interpretant is aware of the system of meanings: red, amber, green. The red light would have no meaning at all if it were not for this knowledge and the context or system in which the red light is operating. In another context a red light may have an entirely different meaning: to distinguish a massage parlour from an ordinary suburban household, for example. This same process applies to the sign system of language. The word 'water' of itself has a very limited scope of meaning. However, when placed in relation to other elements in the sign system, more substantial meaning is possible: 'The water is cold'; 'The water I am drinking is cold'; 'The water in which I am drowning is very cold and deep'. In each statement the meaning of the sign 'water' is quite different. Peirce was particularly interested in the psychological processes by which meanings are formed.

STRUCTURALIST LANGUAGE THEORY

Semiology: Ferdinand de Saussure

The Swiss linguist Ferdinand de Saussure (1859–1913) extends many of the arguments and interests of C.S. Peirce. Saussure's work proceeds from the basic premise that the relationship between symbols (signs) and the things to which they refer (referents) is arbitrary. Saussure's project, therefore, is to elucidate the operations of language, particularly through its relationship with culture. Like Marx, Durkheim and Weber, however, Saussure understands these operations in terms of major, determining forces and formations called structures. Less like the earlier social theorists and more like Wittgenstein and Peirce, however, Saussure sees language as the principal agent in the foundation and formation of these structures. According to Saussure, therefore, society, culture and meaning-making are contingencies of language and language structure. Language is conceived in terms of rational, totalistic and orderly frames which integrate the multitude of complex associations and relationships underscribing human experience. Saussure, again like the early Wittgenstein, offers us a science of language. This science provides universal explanations for the formation and operation of language across all cultures and contexts. Saussure's 'semiology' seeks to elucidate, that is, the principles underlying the formation of any language within its given context. While these contexts vary across culture, the principles which organize human languages do not.

For Saussure, therefore, the operations of language can only be understood in terms of the system of that given language. A system or set of structures will determine the discrete relationships between words and their formation into sentences (syntax). A word has no meaning except through its relationship to other words and hence its deployment within a system of words. In Saussure's terms, 'language has neither ideas nor sounds that exist before the linguistic system, but only conceptual and phonic differences that issue from the system' (1974: 120). A given culture will have a particular need to discriminate between two or more objects or experiences. Consider, for example, the rapid invention of new words in the current computer boom: bytes, webpages, URL, email, digitization, .com. The culture requires new ways of discriminating objects and experiences, so old words may also be reinscribed with new meanings (virus, crash, superhighway). Similarly, the Inuit people of North America (Eskimos) have a vast array of words that describe discrete differences in what the English language categorizes as 'snow' or 'white'. The culture and its needs determine the categorizes of meaning.

Saussure's interest in discrete differences and the systems within which these differences function informs his scientific account of semiology. Some writers like to distinguish between 'semiology', as the science of signs or language systems, and 'semiotics', as a form of cultural and textual analysis developed at the Birmingham Centre for Contemporary Cultural Studies (see Chapter 4). In either case the semiotics practised in the English-speaking world has been critically influenced by Saussure and his science of semiology. The difference between the two resides mainly in semiotics' less substantial adhesion to scientific principles, and its greater focus on particular forms of textual representation, most especially in film and television.

Saussure believes that semiology should concern itself with the current-day (synchronic) conditions of language and language use, rather than with its historical development (diachronic approach to structure). Accordingly, analysts may elucidate the structures of language in terms of *langue*, the overall system, and *parole*, the particular operations and selections which determine meaning in a given context. Specifically, Saussure claims that in order to construct meaning (*parole*) a language user will select words, syntactical forms, grammar, and so on, from all the possible operations and categories available within the system of a language (*langue*).

Comparing these operations to a game of chess (cf. Wittgenstein's language games), Saussure suggests that the homogeneity of the structure or system is what makes possible the heterogeneity of the individual actions and meaning-makings of the *parole*. The system is what holds the details together.

Recalling Peirce's conception of the sign, Saussure's science attempts to extend a theory of language to all meaning-making or sign systems. Saussure observes that the same principles of operation, discrete differences and similarities, and rules may be applied to all human communication. To explain this more clearly, he separates the sign into its two constituent parts thus:

$$\text{SIGN} = \frac{\text{signifer (material sign)}}{\text{signified (mental concept of sign)}}$$

Saussure argues that the signifier can be sounds, marks on a page, light, images, and so on, but the signifier has no inherent meaning. The mental picture or concept which is produced as a person interacts with the particular signifier is the fount of meaning. However, this interaction between the person and the sign (both the concept and the material signifier) only creates meaning when the sign is understood in relation to its *langue* or system. Like Wittgenstein and Peirce, Saussure insists that the mental concept and the material sign can only produce meaning when the sign is functioning in relation to its system. The red light is the signifier; the concept of stop is the signified; the system of traffic codes is the *langue*.

This means, of course, that a word and its assemblage in syntax must be constantly referred by the user to the *langue* from which the words and rules are drawn. The *langue*, as we have noted, is inevitably bound to the social and cultural context in which the language *parole* (specific utterance) is operating. Similarly, a photograph will have its material dimensions (signifiers), but this assemblage of colour tones, images, shapes and textures is meaningful only in terms of the contexts within which they function. This context will necessarily include the space or place within which the photograph appears: newspaper, art gallery, friend's photo album, the Internet. Both the photograph and the contexts will relate to further contexts in time, space and culture. The *signified* is produced through a complex interaction of these various levels of *parole* and *langue*: specific instance and containing context.

Structural Anthropology: Claude Lévi-Strauss

Beginning with a similar interest in language systems, the French anthropologist Claude Lévi-Strauss adapted Saussure's semiology for the analysis and elucidation of culture. In particular, Lévi-Strauss wanted to describe the unconscious frameworks or formations which bind and define so-called 'primitive' culture. His analysis explores a wide range of cultural practices, including language, rituals, modes of dress, art works, myth and language. As with Saussure, Lévi-Strauss sees these practices as expressive of the essential culture. Perhaps the most resonant and certainly most frequently visited dimension of Lévi-Strauss's work relates to his account of myth. Myth, however, should not be conceived in terms of 'untruth' or an unscientific account of spiritual reality. For Lévi-Strauss, in fact, myth functions like language whereby individual myths must rely on the whole system of myths in order to produce their meaning. The comprehensibility of these myths by members of the culture relies on the distinction and heterogeneity of the

individual narrative as it interacts with and draws from the system of myths which govern rules, operations and available interpretations or meaning-making. Like a single word, a single myth has very little meaning. Placed alongside the corpus of a culture's mythologies, the individual myth becomes meaningful.

Lévi-Strauss is particularly interested in the narrative shapings of the human mind and how the world is comprehended through those fundamental structures. Specifically, he believes that all myths share a common structure, one which divides the world into binary oppositions: good/bad, culture/nature, insider/outsider, male/female, material/spirit. One of the functions of myth, therefore, is to resolve these contradictions in narrative. Thus, while the story establishes fundamental tensions, it also provides the mechanisms for resolution, which, according to Lévi-Strauss, leaves the cultural participant in a kind of satisfied or cathartic condition. The narrative is satisfactorily resolved and the world is rendered comprehensible. Here is a myth borrowed from the Hall's Creek Aboriginal community in Western Australia (an echidna is a small spiky marsupial, a little like a hedgehog or porcupine).

In the dreaming there was once a large tree that grew in the middle of the desert and shaded the people from the scorching sun. The Dreaming people were all animals then. They hunted daily while Echidna stayed behind to care for the children. When the hunters returned home each night, they gave the tastiest morsels to the children, but poor Echidna only received the scraps. Echidna became very angry and shook the shade-tree. He shook it so hard, he tore it out of the ground, roots and all. With the tree on his back, Echidna ran off.

The other members of the tribe knew that they would perish without the shade-tree. They chased after Echidna, begging him to stop. But Echidna just kept on marching.

The others threw boomerangs at Echidna. Surely this would stop him! But no. A boomerang struck Echidna's feet and broke his toes. Still, though, Echidna shuffled onwards. Finally, in desperation, the others threw dangerous spears at Echidna. The spears buried into Echidna's body. He howled and dropped the tree.

Now the tree crashed to the ground and began rolling across the land. Over and over it rolled with the huge branches splintering and piercing the ground.

Echidna lay dying, and soon the other spirit animals felt sorry for him. Cockatoo flew over to him and asked where Echidna would like to be buried. 'Between the rocks', Echidna answered.

Today echidnas live in rocks hunting ants. Mostly only their quills are visible. Desert people keep cool under the small trees that have spawned from the branches of the shattered shade-tree. Where the shade-tree was taken from the ground a small lake has appeared. It is called Nongra.

This narrative might be read as a cosmological text explaining the current conditions of life and natural landforms. Lévi-Strauss's anthropology tells us, in fact, that the narrative is fundamentally sociocultural. Essentially, the story tells us about the problem of social organization, resource allocation, the limits of nature, and the contradictory character of crime and punishment. Echidna is marginalized by the group, forced to perform a social duty which has low social status and material rewards. His crime is to seek justice and fair treatment. But resources, especially in the desert, are scarce. He removes an important element in the resource economy. The culture recognizes that Echidna has a claim, but he is ostracized even further by attack. The insider/outsider, nature/human contradictions are played out and resolved through a process of integration. The crime is punished, but Echidna is

apotheosized nevertheless. His spirit is continuous and there is an ultimate serendipity in his perpetuity. The world is as it should be, though it has become so through tension, drama and pain. There is no ultimate and absolute death since the spirit of Echidna is perpetual. The natural world and the social world are therefore coterminous, but barely distinguishable in their interdependence. The knowledge of the natural is the knowledge of the human. The insider and the outsider become resolved.

Lévi-Strauss's analysis became particularly popular in contemporary film analysis during the 1970s and into the 1980s. Will Wright's *Sixguns and Society* (1975) applied Lévi-Strauss's analytical methods and principles to reveal the underlying structure of the Hollywood Western. For Wright, the Western is built around oppositional structures such as insider/outsider. Wright argues that, for all the specific variants and institutional forces that inform different Westerns, their fundamental oppositional structures create character and narrative types which are essential to the American consciousness. Thomas Schatz (1981) extends Lévi-Strauss's and Wright's perspectives by arguing that all commercial film-making is fundamentally a process of constructing contemporary myths. Schatz argues that the development of film genres during the twentieth century is a form of 'compulsion repetition' arising from collective responses to mass audience interests and tastes. As with more general semiotic adaptations of Lévi-Strauss's structural anthropology, Schatz's analysis claims that film-making divines the underlying social conditions and mythologies which constitute contemporary culture. Film and other texts are our window to ourselves.

EARLY ROLAND BARTHES AND THE SEMIOLOGICAL MOMENT

Myth and Ideology

Roland Barthes's work is often regarded as the cross-over between structuralism and poststructuralism. Certainly in his discussions of myth and his re-rendering of Saussure and Lévi-Strauss, Barthes seeks to elucidate contemporary French culture in terms of fundamental, mythic structures. His project, however, may be distinguished from those of Saussure and Lévi-Strauss in as much as he is far more concerned with the political dimensions of mythology, and the important problem of its taken-for-grantedness. In particular, Barthes seeks to elucidate the ideological foundations of contemporary myths, arguing that particular narratives are so frequently repeated in culture that they are essentialized or 'naturalized' as absolute and common-sense truth. In *Mythologies* (1973), *The Fashion System* (1983) and *Elements of Semiology* (1967), Barthes maintains an adherence to scientific semiological principles as he describes the complex chain of cultural operations that produce signification.

In a manner that anticipates his later works, Barthes emphasizes the *process* of signification, arguing that meanings continue to accumulate over signs through what he calls 'connotation'. That is, a sign might have its literal, primary or 'denotative' meaning, but through the operations of signification further layers of meaning are attached as connotations of the original. Words are literal, but their operation in context produces meanings that may be psychologically, emotionally or ideologically charged. The word 'black', for example, has a literal meaning, but further

meanings are connoted by the word's deployment in specific cultural, social and political contexts. These are what Barthes calls the secondary level of meaning. While these meanings may be unstable over time, at any given moment they will be attached to specific systems of social knowledge and socially constructed truths. When the word 'black' is attached to a person from a particular ethnic, racial and social background, it may be connoted in terms of crime, vilification, prejudice or hatred.

For Barthes, these accretions of meaning constitute cultural myths. These myths or 'second-order semiological systems' may also be understood as ideology: those prevailing ideas, narratives and representations which support dominant socio-cultural structures. For Barthes, contemporary cultural myths form a fabric of belief upon which politics are built. A number of critics have pointed out that Barthes doesn't fully distinguish between myth and ideology, claiming that the two concepts seem to be entirely interchangeable. He does, however, point to the polysemic nature of signs: that is, their capacity to carry alternative meanings. Let's consider again the word 'black' and its attachment to a human type. As we have noted, the word may be used in support of a dominant ideology, a set of 'myths' or narratives which identify whiteness as the norm or standard for the developed, advanced world. Whiteness is often attached to the notion of goodness, purity, clarity and enlightenment. Blackness, on the other hand, is often attached to the notion of darkness, salaciousness, poverty, marginalism, and so on. The white culture remains the dominant ideology or paradigm on TV and in contemporary films. Whiteness orders itself in terms of success, legitimacy and beauty.

The mythology of blackness may be understood in terms of the media's frequently repeated stories. News stories very often present blackness in terms of crime, sexuality or physical performance. In many respects, black is associated with a narrative of essential nature. Blackness appears in the sporting pages of the newspapers. In film blackness is related to street crime, or as the sacrificial partner of a (benevolent) white hero-cop. Blackness is often anti-authority, presented through narratives of bodily excess and a wildness resistant to bourgeois standards of normality. The exceptions to these narrative standards constitute, Barthes would claim, the polysemy of the concept. Popular music has been particularly robust in its challenges to the ideology and mythology surrounding blackness, though in all the media there are opportunities for repositioning the term's cultural connotations. Black people themselves have sought to redeem these connotations, rebuilding their own identity as black. 'Young, gifted and black', 'black power', 'black music', 'black style', 'black liberation' – all phrases designed to challenge the prevailing order.

Barthes claims, and this is a point which Stuart Hall and many others have appropriated in their development of British cultural studies, that this polysemy constitutes a 'struggle' for domination: the struggle to signify, as Hall himself puts it. The 'reading' or 'viewing' of a text by an audience is therefore historical and political. It is the task of the textualist to produce the second-order signification through an effective selection of signs; the reader draws on the same system of cultural and social knowledge in order to construct his or her own meanings from the text. The task of the analyst, however, is to de-naturalize or 'de-doxify', as Barthes puts it, the assumed naturalness of the second-order meanings, most especially as they inscribe dominant ideologies.

The Appeal of Structural Semiology

French semiology was attractive to anglophone literary and cultural studies for three quite related reasons:

1   It provided an important theoretical link between social practices and textual representations. Saussure, Lévi-Strauss and Barthes were able to demonstrate very forcefully that language and culture must necessarily interact with one another to produce reality. This means, of course, that an interest in texts and in culture were necessarily self-confirming. The analyst of language and texts was no longer an intuitive abstractionist, but could point very directly to the imperatives of social mediation. For Stuart Hall and other cultural analysts, the seminal work of Hoggart and Williams could now be validated through substantive theory. The popular media, the social practices of the working classes, indeed all non-mainstream or marginalized cultures could now be drawn into focus. This new heuristic enterprise would free texts from elitism and from the evaluative practices of Leavisite literary criticism.

2   High modernism maintains a privileged position for science and scientific discourse. Governments and government funding bodies, echoing the mythology of public interest, have certainly favoured discourses which pertain to scientism and a notion of provable outcomes. Abstract discourses, which rely on abstruse aesthetics or notions of a transcendent morality, are often viewed with suspicion. Semiology provided a concrete and clearly defined pathway for the analysis of texts and culture. That is, rather than being an esoteric

and 'indulgent' engagement with art and spirit, the new theories presented their knowledge as pragmatic, scientific and socially verifiable. Semiology provided a discourse which satisfied the utilitarian and progressivist ideology of official culture.

3 The third reason for semiology's attractiveness to English-speaking cultural studies is associated with the problematic of ideology. Early British cultural studies, in particular, maintained a vigorous interest in Marxist social critique. The dilemma for cultural studies is that the meaning-making processes which constitute culture are not evenly distributed. How then do we account for the greater capacity of some groups to exert disproportionate power over cultural meaning-making while acknowledging that everybody in a culture has some capacity to determine that culture? As noted in the previous chapter, Stuart Hall sought to reconcile the determinism of Louis Althusser's notion of a structural and dominant ideology with the possibilities of individual freedom and agency. Hall adapts Gramsci's 'hegemony' for the study of texts and culture.

Barthes' notions of myth, ideology and polysemy provide further opportunities for the resolution of the cultural studies dilemma. In fact, his greater interest in texts as opposed to linguistics has proved particularly appealing for a number of Anglophonic cultural analysts. John Fiske, for example, has been particularly attracted to Barthes's approach to textual and cultural analysis. Barthes' witty and at times disarmingly simple critique of bourgeois French culture has been imitated through a number of Fiske's writings (see Barthes, 1973; Fiske et al., 1987).

In America, where the popular media had been studied within the scope of contending paradigms, French structuralism made its first significant entrance through the peripheries of literary studies, anthropology and, circuitously, symbolic interaction and phenomenology. Jonathan Culler (1975) provided one of the earliest adaptations of structural language theory for the analysis of literature. Culler's approach directly challenged the paradigm of New Criticism which was emerging as the dominant force in American literary studies, replacing the moral pragmatism of the Leavisite approach. New Criticism treated the work of art as a self-contained and self-referential system of meanings. A 'poem' (the generic work of literature) could be analysed as an entity in itself, divorced both from the culture and experiences of the author, on the one hand, and from the reader, on the other. In a peculiar way, the act of aesthetic analysis was analogous to the act of scientific method: the phenomenon under investigation was to be divorced of all extraneous effects, all history, all culture. The author and authorial intent were entirely obliterated from critical practice; the analyst, therefore, was free to expose the 'truth' of the poem.

While Barthes' famous essay 'The death of the author' (in Barthes, 1977) might seem to subscribe to a New Criticism perspective, in fact Barthes was suggesting rather that the author is a mediation between socio-cultural context and the text itself. The author is removed from the high seat of modernism, that seat of individual genius which denies the contingencies of culture and mediation. Structuralism, as Culler points out, removes the text from the author and itself, opening its meanings to the dynamic imbrications of culture and context. In particular, the text is opened to the polysemy of multiple readings. Meanings are produced by readers who engage with the raw materials (discourses) of the text and remould them through the contexts in which their reading takes place. While Culler prefers Noam Chomsky's notion of reading competence and performance to Saussure's *langue* and *parole*, he nevertheless conceives of reading as an engagement with systems of social knowledge. Interpretation, therefore, is an exercise in determining the social rules that govern reading. Skilled readers can make sense of a text, invoking those rules and articulating the knowledge that is invisible in the text but implicit in the reader.

THE POSTSTRUCTURALIST CRITIQUE OF STRUCTURALISM

The most commonly noted problem with structuralism is also its strength. That is, structuralism, with its invocation of underlying grammar, structures, ideology and social knowledge, tends toward a social and theoretical universalism. In emphasizing shared social knowledge, structuralism tends always to seek a commonality, a shared objective space which crosses temporal, spatial and even cultural boundaries. Like Marxism and other forms of 'rationally' construed social knowledge, structuralism has sought to explain the world and human actions in terms of major, inclusive and universally applicable conditions. We can summarize structuralism's attempt to resolve this problem in the following terms:

1 Structuralism seeks to explain society and culture in terms of major structures which are common to all societies, cultures and languages. The particular is

drawn into, though never extinguished, by the universal.

2 An analysis may thus begin with a particular instance and context: for example, the exclusion of black people from news broadcasting on television in Jackson, Mississippi USA. Structuralism explains this example in relation to overall structures such as:

(a) dominant cultural myths;
(b) underlying pattern of ideology: shared values, beliefs, norms, symbols;
(c) forms of signification which are rooted in power structures in a society; and
(d) broad linguistic patterns which are common across time, space and culture.

The discrete differences between signs, which Saussure highlights and which constitute the operations of language, are subjugated, therefore, to broader structural categories. These categories are the *langue* or referential language system. According to structuralism, specific socio-cultural instances or contexts (*parole*) are inevitably referred back to the system of social knowledge. The *langue*, the underlying linguistic and social order, will therefore always predominate over the particular instance or *parole*.

It should not surprise us, then, that the scientific methods used to divine this underlying order are themselves constructed around an assumed objectivity and orderliness. Thomas Kuhn (1970) and, later, Jean-François Lyotard (1984) have argued that the whole of modernist scientific method is implicitly designed to articulate an order which is a predicate of itself: science, scientific methods and scientific principles are formed around orderly processes and are designed to uncover the underlying patterns of natural order. The social sciences conceive of society in a very similar way, applying very similar methods and principles. Structural linguistics, like social and critical structuralism, is built around a social scientific paradigm; the social knowledge it assumes is designed to prove the existence of social and cultural order. While this order may need to be re-formed or re-shaped, it nevertheless exists according to fundamental and underlying patterns. The objective of structuralist critique is to expose these patterns and bring to bear a new social order.

Poststructuralism, however, has suggested that this underlying linguistic order, the referential system, is conceived through certain leaps of faith which override the actual functioning of language and discourse. In particular, the stability of the relationship between the *parole* (instance of language use) and the *langue* (system) is achieved only through the parenthesis of history's vast array of details and the local conditions of culture. It is this problem of detail, change and instability which continually challenges the systems that structuralists claim are the foundations of signification and meaning. Poststructuralist theory, in general terms, sees the formations of stable and orderly systems – including the theories and methods of structuralist language analysis – as just another language gesture, just another *parole* or instance of language use. For poststructuralism, language is bound absolutely to its context of use, its moment of utterance, and all efforts to form language into orderly patterns, categories, systems or *langue* merely corrupt the context in which the discourse is operating. Order, that is, is imposed by the structuralist and is not a characteristic of language itself.

This problem has many sides to it. In particular, Saussure and other structuralists like to maintain the stability and unity of the sign, even though they have theoretically divided it into two not entirely connected parts: the signified and the signifier. Saussure suggests that the actual operations of language use incline signifiers toward their particular signifieds or concepts. Language-users need this secure attachment in order to make sense of one another. Poststructuralism, however, has emphasized the gaps and incompleteness in this process, suggesting that the signifier and signified are as arbitrary in their relationship as the sign and the thing to which it refers. The sign is not a unity of two fused parts, two sides of the one coin; rather, poststructuralism suggests that signifiers and signifieds are two operational layers which momentarily touch in an almost accidental intersection of highly unstable and temporary meaning. The emphasis, that is, is on the problem of meaning and not its systematic certainty.

While this problem is clearly evident in the translation of one language into another since there is often no equivalence in grammar and vocabulary, it is also a problem within the one language 'system'. The dictionary, for example, is generally regarded as the ultimate referent, the principal means by which a signified (word) is fixed to its signifier or meaning. However, when we look in the dictionary we'll often find a number of definitions for the same word. Each of these definitions is of course a signifier in its own right and impels the reader toward further signifiers and signifieds in order to locate meaning. Thus, the word 'stable' will be defined as: something persistent; unchanging; not unstable; secure; a place to house horses or other livestock; and so on. Each of these words will also be defined in the dictionary and in pursuit of meaning we can look them up only to find more words that need to be looked up – the trail is endless. Meaning is processed through a matrix of complex relationships which clearly challenge the unity of the signifier/signified. The operationalization of the signifier is possible, not in spite of these deferrals, but as a result of them. By placing the signifier into a language context, language-users problematize meaning in their attempts to create it. Meaning is never assured; it is merely sought as it is deferred.

This problematization of meaning is also profoundly related to the issues of ideology. Those areas of structuralism which contend a necessary relationship between language systems and ideology assume a certain stability in the sign and in the struggle to signify. While Hall and others in the Birmingham tradition acknowledge a degree of uncertainty in these struggles, their polemic relies on structural divisions by which power is fixed within particular social groups. Gramsci's negotiated hegemony and Barthes's notion of variant interpretations or polysemy are concepts that anglophone cultural structuralists developed and deployed as a way of evading Marx's more totalistic explanations of power and ideology. Even so, the British cultural studies lineage, with its particular interest in class, power divisions and language structure, retained an interest in ideology as the political manifestation of language war. And indeed, for those cultural theorists who remain interested in a reformist politics, the structuralist concept of ideology has proved extremely difficult to surrender (see Hall, 1991a, 1991b). The significant problem for structuralist cultural politics, however, is that polysemy doesn't begin and end with its own frame of interest. Ideology begins to fracture under the stress of multiple audiences and multiple interpretations; the instabilities of meaning run entirely through a reformist politics and its aspiration for a logics of change.

Structuralist and Poststructuralist Approaches to Culture

Structuralist and semiological language theory was adopted into the Birmingham Centre for Contemporary Cultural Studies during the 1960s and 1970s (see Chapter 4). The influence of writers like Saussure, Lévi-Strauss and Althusser has been enormous, most especially as cultural studies has expanded its interests from an analysis of class-based culture to the broader fields of ideology, popular media and representation. The penetration of poststructuralism, however, has been far more diffuse, though no less significant. Table 5.1 highlights some of the major differences in emphasis between a structuralist and poststructuralist style of cultural analysis. It is important to note that these differences are not entirely chronological, and that specific zones of contemporary cultural studies may prefer one style of analysis over another.

Table 5.1 *Structuralism and Poststructuralism*

Structuralist cultural studies	Poststructuralist cultural studies
Language systems	Language as diffuse
Signifer/signified	Slippery signifer, language wars
Way of life	Meaning-making
Class structures	Cultural communities
Ideology/hegemony	Everything as representation
Institutional and fixed power	Power as personal relationships
Structural resistance	Power at the level of the body
Democratic socialism	Democratic multiculturalism
Media institutions	Media-making

Stuart Hall and numerous others working in contemporary cultural politics continue to struggle with this problem. Hall (1991a) identifies culture as the radiation of media and its discourses within a broad global postmodernism. As he moves away from class and other levels of cultural localism, Hall conceives of a cultural whole in which power and structure are unevenly experienced and distributed. In order to critique the condition of contemporary culture, then, Hall must match these macro formations with macro challenges. Hegemony or negotiated leadership remains valid because it conceives of meaning-making in structural terms. Poststructuralism and the theoretical wing of postmodernism, however, challenge the Gramscian approach by limiting the scope and relevance of structure. Power and ideology, therefore, are conceived in vastly different terms, terms which for many working in the field constitute a reactionary politics and a capitulation to those powers which exert disproportionate influence within the culture.

THE LATER BARTHES

Barthes' earlier works are characterized by a certain ambivalence toward signification and meaning-making. While subscribing generally to the Saussurian paradigm which analyses systematically the structures and stability of language, Barthes was also interested in the processes of signification and the possibilities of polysemy or multiple interpretations of words. In *Elements of Semiology* (1967) the same glimpses of a poststructuralist awareness emerge from some otherwise standard structuralist precepts. In particular, while claiming that semiology could explain all the operations of language, Barthes comes to recognize that his own semiological discourse functions as a 'second-order' language which could be seen to substitute for the 'first-order' textual discourses under study. That is, for example, his analysis of Baudelaire, which produces a new 'version' of the original text, could be seen as a form of metalanguage which might now be placed in the position of Baudelaire's text, making it available for further analysis. Barthes recognizes that his own interpretive discourse had become a substitute for the original text and that this 'second-order' text might itself now be interpreted or analysed, setting forth an ongoing trail of replacement discourses. Thus, there emerges a whole series of metalanguages which inevitably replace the original Baudelaire text. All texts are equally fictional, therefore, and should not be read in terms of absolute truth or origin.

This realization marks a major departure from semiological scientism; it establishes a level of interest which is to blossom in Barthes's later writings. In his collected essays *Image–Music–Text* (1977), for example, Barthes announces quite clearly that the notion of authorial authority can no longer be assumed. In essays such as 'The photographic message', 'Writers and readers' and 'The death of the author', Barthes problematizes the relationship between the author, the text and the reader, noting in particular that a text should be understood as a 'multi-dimensional space in which a variety of writings, none of them original, blend and clash. The text is a tissue of quotations drawn from the innumerable centres of culture' (1977: 146). The semiological assumptions about stability and secure meaning-making are thereby surrendered as Barthes seeks more acute insights into the uncertainties of reader meaning-making and what he subsequently calls the pleasure of the text. The author's role in text construction is parenthesized, not simply in a gesture of isolating the text from intentional design, but as a more complete acknowledgement of the active engagement of audiences with the polysemic multidimensionality of discourse.

In *The Pleasure of the Text* (1975) Barthes seeks some further clarification of the reader's power to pursue his or her own capricious delights. Barthes notes that, in an engagement with the text, a reader is free to abandon the directives of the signifier in favour of his or her own cognitive and sensual responses. In other words, the polysemy or multiple interpretation which is available for a reader's cognitive engagement is also available for sensual or bodily response. Different readers will respond differently to the meanings and sensual pleasures which are generated from the signified. In many respects, Barthes is seeking an explanation for textual engagement and meaning-making that moves beyond his earlier interest in myth and binary resolutions. Even so, the notion of pleasure is founded upon two distinct dimensions of response: 'pleasure' and a more concentrated, more intense experience which he calls 'bliss' (*jouissance*). It is at the level of bliss that Barthes again approximates a poststructural positioning, if only because 'bliss' is characterized by an unstable, contradictory intensity which comes to defy the stable and secure conditions of language (mere pleasure).

Mere pleasure is typical of a 'join' or contact between two surfaces: garment on bare skin, or the reading act and the text. In the reading act, pleasure is likely to be engaged as the reader remains fixed and aware of the action of reading. If the reader skips pages, or reads particular realist discourses, the pleasure arises out of the contact or join that is facilitated in the act of signifier and signified. However, when the reader is engaged beyond awareness, then s/he is approaching the condition of bliss. These moments of complete aesthetic immersion render the reader oblivious to all external conditions and to the reading act itself. There arises now the possibility of an intensity of experiences which may do away with the join, do away with language itself, since the reader is now thoroughly engaged in his or her own bliss. Now the reader risks the collapse of cultural assumptions. Meaning is precarious; politics are precarious; culture and language are precarious. If the reader resists this ecstatic condition, however, the intensity might collapse into boredom.

Barthes's pleasure of the text, therefore, is an account of some more sublime, post- or pre-linguistic condition. His theories have proved particularly well suited to anglophone analysts who have been interested in the processes of textual reading and more particularly the pleasure-giving dimensions of textual consumption. That is, Barthes's later interest in pleasure has provided a theoretical framework for those cultural theorists, like John Fiske, Henry Jenkins and Richard Dyer, who have sought to celebrate in varying ways the significance of popular culture for the lives, pleasures and cultures of everyday consumers of the popular media. This style of cultural analysis, with its emphasis on multiple meanings and individuated pleasure, provides a significant theoretical bridge not only to poststructuralism, but also to the expanding territory of postmodern cultural studies.

The Difference Between Poststructuralism and Postmodernism

For many cultural commentators there is very little difference between poststructuralism and postmodernism. Both emphasize cultural diversity, the individual emancipation, the impossibility of an absolute truth, the unstable nature of history and a politics which is broad and inclusive and not restricted to issues of class or social order. Both, in fact, are critical of notions of structure. Both tend to be interested in the popular media, globalism and new expressive forms and identities.

However there are significant differences in the heritage and history of the two terms. Poststructuralism tends to rise through certain areas of French language theory. Its principal exponents are later Roland Barthes, Jacques Derrida, Jacques Lacan, Julia Kristeva, Michel Foucault, and Gilles Deleuze and Félix Guattari. For all their significant differences, these writers represent a radical break from the philosophical tradition which treated reality as a distinct, epistemological fact. Poststructuralism challenges us to think about the world in terms of language and mediation, the problematic of meaning and non-meaning, and the rupture of taken-for-granted and universal Truth. Poststructuralist writing is often difficult because it accepts the improbable nature of any logical order and claims to knowledge – including its own.

Postmodernism has two distinct sources. One of them is philosophical and derives from poststructuralism. The theoretical bridge between poststructuralism and postmodernism has been provided by Jean-François Lyotard, Jean Baudrillard and the American Marxist literary critic Fredric Jameson. The other source of postmodern theoretics comes through American aesthetics, where the term was conceived in order to describe a particular style of art and literature.

Postmodernism can sometimes be used to describe the historical phase that follows modernity (some time in the last thirty or so years). It has also become a popular way of describing the cultural 'condition' or ways of thinking that currently predominate. Theoretically, it is a very loose collection of ideas which has traces of poststructuralism, utopianism and celebratory popular culture.

Undoubtedly, Barthes's work moves toward the edges of a poststructuralist theoretic, yet his account of 'bliss' also carries an unmistakably Romantic resonance with it. In particular, there is a certain level of essentialism in his account of textual bliss, a sense in which the pre- or post-linguistic condition of bliss is analogous to the 'finer tone' referred to in John Keats' letters and poetry. This finer tone, Keats explains, is a kind of ecstasy where the sublime aesthetic washes over the poet in an ephemeral but unmistakable fusion of opposite intensities. Moreover, Barthes's turn toward Japanese art and culture in his later writings is reminiscent of the Romantic poets' interest in an Orient which transcends the lineality of decay and the oppositionalism that underpins European culture.

DECONSTRUCTION: JACQUES DERRIDA

Subject and Language

While Roland Barthes drifts unevenly between a structuralist and poststructuralist perspective, Jacques Derrida is unrelenting in his pursuit of the gaps and irregularities of language and meaning-making. From his earliest investigations of Husserl's phenomenology, Derrida has been suspicious of the project of structuralism and the idea that a fundamental 'grammar' underpins culture, language and the human mind. In particular, he challenges the notion of a sub-stratum or 'essence' which grounds, as it makes possible, a re-rendering of consciousness through highly abstracted theoretical or empirical methodologies. In his early discussions on discourse and structuralism in the human sciences (see 1970), Derrida argues that the human sciences, like the natural sciences, are engaged in an enterprise which would force the fluidity and imprecise nature of language into structures which effectively legitimate themselves as absolute and unassailable truths. These truths or true findings, Deririda maintains, are merely transgressions, denials of the natural operations of language. That is, language, according to Derrida, is not of itself constructed out of truths, essences or ultimate reference points – there is no origin that lies behind language. Rather, language is a restless an ever-moving mass of imprecise details, constantly seeking, but never quite achieving, some approximation of meaning.

Derrida refers to this meaning as a kind of 'presence': that is, he claims, people seek some confirmation of knowledge of themselves and their capacity to make sense of who they are in relation to others. Their *presence* in the world is substantiated, therefore, by the exchange of absolute meanings. We need to note here that Derrida is moving far beyond the epistemological problem of the subject–object split (see Chapter 2), which preoccupied philosophy and social science during the eighteenth and nineteenth centuries. The problem of language and the self (the subject in the lifeworld) overthrows epistemology as the major concern of philosophy and cultural theory during the twentieth century. The notion of a unified subject – that is, the unity of the 'me' or 'I' of the world – is generally assumed in pre-Freudian descriptions of the self. Western culture has produced a substantial vocabulary which describes this condition of fixity: origin, essence, consciousness, structure, centre, being, substance, truth.

Psychoanalytic theory, especially the adaptation of Freud by Jacques Lacan and Julia Kristeva, opens the way for theorizing the subject as 'unfixed'. Psychoanalysis also theorizes a more precarious and indeterminate relationship between subjects and the language which connects them. That is, the subject no longer exists as an absolute condition, a deeply rooted and basically unchangeable entity; the subject is dynamic, mutable, open and formed through various relationships and experiences, all constituted in language. Derrida, therefore, is highly dubious about the possibility that a subject 'originates' in some essential form. Rather, the subject exists as a contingency of language. The question of origin, therefore, is placed under erasure, as Derrida explains it.

This process is rather tricky. The concept of 'origin' continues to be claimed in language, but because language itself has no origin, 'origin' cannot be replaced or substituted. That is, Derrida's methods prevent him from critically obliterating the concept of 'origin' since that would require some substitution in language. Derrida's methods of analysis, therefore, do not seek to replace origins or centres but merely highlight the problems associated with false foundationalism. This is true not only for the concept of 'origin' but for any concept, any word. If he were to substitute the origin of the concept of 'origin' or any other word with another possibility, then he would be risking the re-establishment of a different origin for the one he has dismissed. Therefore, Derrida's analysis merely exposes the principles and processes which inform specific instances of language use without offering alternatives.

Derrida's strategy of critique, therefore is quite deliberately focused. He wants to remove the notion of essence, centre, presence or origin from all language acts. Language exists as a particulate and incomplete gesture which operates within a particular context and perpetually seeks, though never actually fixes on, meaning. Derrida therefore cannot substitute this dynamism with a fixed meaning alternative. He doesn't claim that we can think outside

or beyond a particular concept, for to do so would entrap us in the (false) gesture of origination. It is not what a concept can 'really' tell us, or what it really means, but rather what is missing (or absent) in the concept itself. For example, if we were to critique the concept of 'knowledge' as it was being used in a particular instance – by someone with whom we violently disagree, for example – we may wish to substitute this person's claim about knowledge with an accusation of 'ignorance'. In other words, we would seek to substitute the centre/presence of the concept 'knowledge' with the alternative concept 'ignorance'. Derrida, however, warns us against this sort of critical approach, which, he argues, merely transgresses the basic principles of language. Because language has no centre or origin and because our subjectivity is open and unfixed, our claim to truth is false, our substitution is misguided. All we can do, in fact, is *expose* the binary nature of this claim to meaning and truth (knowledge/ ignorance) without preferring one over the other – without, that is, restoring a centre to the status of fixed and absolute language presence. This method of 'deconstruction' is fundamental to our understanding of what Derrida calls 'writing'.

Deconstruction

Derrida's methods are established in his two early works *Of Grammatology* (1974) and *Writing and Difference* (1979). Essentially, his interest in language emerges through an initial analysis of the phenomenology of Edmund Husserl and the processes by which the Western philosophical tradition constitutes itself as paradigm knowledge. The methodology associated with Derrida's key concept 'deconstruction' has been adapted in a variety of ways by recent cultural analysis. Derrida himself uses the technique to illuminate the processes by which philosophy legitimates itself in language, most especially the language of writing. His method is similar to Barthes's 'de-doxification' in that it seeks to demonstrate how particular writing positions are constructed in meaning, even though those meanings must constantly elude definition. That is, Derrida explains throughout his work that philosophy has legitimated itself by its own constant self-reflexivity, one philosopher referring to his/her precedent. The meanings of the text are thereby constructed around these intertextual references.

Unlike the political intent of de-doxification, however, the primary task of deconstruction is to expose the principles and processes which construct language and history, especially as it is articulated in Western philosophy. To this end, Derrida accepts the general notion that European thought and language have been built around systems of opposition (good/bad, life/death, present/absent). These binary poles insist for their resolution on the domination of one over the other, a 'presence' which is facilitated by its opposite's 'absence'. Conventional 'critical' methods merely engage in shifts within the system, allowing for the predominance of one pole over another. As in the above example of knowledge/ignorance, this selection of one pole over the other merely shifts the centre and origin of the binary oppositions. We remain trapped within the system. Deconstruction, however, seeks to elucidate and therefore override the binary oppositions through a questioning of their legitimacy and a recognition that they are merely formations in language (writing especially). Deconstruction attacks the centre and the system not by attempting to replace it (for that would be yet another origin), but by elucidating it and its infinite deferrals of meaning – by removing the grounds upon which it is built.

Writing

Derrida, in fact, contrasts this oppositionalism in language with non-Western linguistic possibilities. He uses the notion of 'logocentricism' (*logos* = word) to illustrate how Western philosophy is structured through systems of opposition and logical inference. Thus, proposition A may be contrasted to proposition B but the inference of this *logos* is proposition C. It works like this:

Men grow beards. Women do not. I have a beard, therefore, I am probably a man.

This form of philosophical processing is built into the very foundations of our language. While this point was well established in the writings of Russell, Wittgenstein and Saussure, Derrida seeks a complete rupture of its value and values, a radical overthrow of the *logos* that is mobilized through a system of meaning-making. *Logos*, as Derrida reminds us, is the full attachment of logics with the origin of 'the word'. It is this word, most especially the spoken word ('phonocentrism'), which presents itself as the 'non-originary origin', that seeming absolute presence which is articulated in the Bible as the first of human presence: 'In the beginning was the Word.' Thus, 'the spoken word' presents itself as the centre and beginning point of our European culture; the word is the foundation upon which our civilization is constructed.

In *Of Grammatology* (1974) Derrida claims that, rather than the spoken word, it is writing which constitutes the articulation of the system of the sign. Writing (*écriture*), which forms itself in and around the presence of an imagined origin, substitutes for the possibilities of language. *Écriture* is able

to designate not only the physical gestures of literal pictographic or ideographic inscription, but also the totality of what makes it possible and also, beyond the signifying face, the signified face itself. And thus we say 'writing' for all that gives rise to an inscription in general. ... The entire field covered by the cybernetic *program* will be the field of writing. (Derrida, 1974: 9)

Language and writing, however, are never fully able to establish this origin and presence since they are always in a state of deferral: every word and every text can only be understood in terms of other words and other texts. Moreover, the meanings of words can never avert fundamental gaps, fissures and slippages which are always engaged through the processes of communication. To illustrate this point, Derrida invokes the concept of 'difference', which was so important in the structuralist account of language systems. Difference, for Derrida, cannot be simply equated with the discrete discriminations which fix a word to particular categories of meaning. That is, Saussure sought to understand the differences between words in terms of the system of differences which constitute a language: the difference in meaning which is constituted between the signifiers dog and cat, or dachshund and poodle, are provided by the system of signifiers.

Derrida, however, is interested in the differences between and within words which frustrate the formation of meaning and which disable the movement toward systematic categorization of things. He explains that difference can operate to confuse meanings and produce ambiguities; these ambiguities constantly propel language into receding dispersals of meaning. As is common with Derrida, he illustrates this problem through the concept under scrutiny. In French the pronunciation of the word difference could itself be written with an 'e', as it is, or with an 'a' to form 'différance' – a word that doesn't actually exist in the dictionary. In either case, the word would sound the same when spoken; only in writing would a difference be discernible. Derrida goes on to suggest that this dualism is contained further in the word's meanings, where the verb *différer* means both 'to differ' and 'to defer'. Derrida combines these literal meanings in order to construct the problematic of writing and 'difference'. To differ, Derrida explains, is a spatial concept by which a system places some semantic or categorial distance between one word and the next. To defer, however, is a temporal concept whereby the signifying system is in a state of perpetual delay of its meanings. In writing, these deferrals are constantly exposed whereas in speaking they are disguised within the general claim of presence. *Différance* is hidden, that is, because the spoken word seems to be constantly present in the presence of the speaker and the speaking. *Écriture* displays the signifiers in their raw, agitated and ever-referential (intertextual, deferred) condition.

Derrida suggests in *Writing and Difference* and *Of Grammatology* that writing has been generally regarded as an impure version of speech language. This 'violent hierarchy' constitutes a coupling of superior and inferior conditions or cases where speech is preferred to writing. Thus, in Derrida's reading of Rousseau, he sees Rousseau's privileging of (natural) speech over (dangerous) writing as a form of supplementarity. Rousseau sees writing as a supplement to speech, something which adds an inessential quality to the primary condition:

> Rousseau considers writing as a dangerous medium, a menacing aid, a critical response to a situation of distress. When Nature, as self-proximity, comes to be forbidden or interrupted, when speech fails to protect presence, writing becomes necessary. It must be *added* to the world urgently. ... Writing becomes dangerous from the

moment that representation claims to be presence and the sign of the thing. (Derrida, 1979: 144)

In French the word *suppléer* means both to supplement and to substitute. Derrida seeks to reverse the writing – speech hierarchy by identifying common characteristics and by arguing that privileging of any kind implicates the processes of supplement (and substitution). As with the interdependence of self and other as outlined in psychoanalytic theory, conceptual couplets like speech/writing, presence/absence, nature/civilization, necessarily engage each pole in the supplement and substitution of the alternative. In Derridean terms they are already always present in the other. Speech, therefore, is already always written, nature is already always present in civilization, and so on. Deconstruction takes place as the text dissolves the hierarchical structures which privilege one position or concept over another, when the supplementarity, that is, is lain to rest.

Derrida and Cultural Studies

It must be said, however, that deconstruction is simply the strategy of exposing these processes. Derrida's deconstruction is no longer analogous to Barthes's 'deconstruction' in that it cannot and will not offer an alternative. Since no alternative is possible, Derrida's work has limited political interests, most especially when compared with either Barthes or Michel Foucault. In fact, Derrida's position in cultural studies is politically ambiguous. Many critics have condemned his resistance to direct political and contemporary cultural engagement (see Dews, 1984; Poster, 1989), arguing that the elliptical nature of his analysis produces a witty but redundant form of rhetorical sophistry. This sophistry, because of its resistance to

real-world problems, contributes to the formation of a distracting and reactionary political field. Other cultural critics, however, have seen enormous potential in deconstruction for the location and exposure of the ideology which functions through language, most especially through forms of textual representation. In particular, cultural politics has used a 'deconstruction' method to illuminate the normative values that inform representations of gender, race, ethnicity and sexual orientation. This adaptation of the concept is well removed from Derrida's original deployment and in many respects is a hybrid of conventional critique, though with an added assumption about the inadequacies of pure structuralism.

This transformation of Derrida's ideas and methods for the analysis of popular culture is sometimes attached to notions of postmodernism. A good many of the discourses which celebrate postmodernism deploy various versions of Derrida's key concepts: deconstruction, difference and logocentricism. Most particularly, this form of postmodernism uses these concepts to position itself against the prevailing standards of modernism: postmodern analysis deconstructs the high arts, scientism, hierarchical homogeneity and logocentricism of modernism. However, these adaptations are not strictly within the field of Derrida's analysis. Christopher Norris (1987, 1990) has suggested, in fact, that Derrida's work sits comfortably within the heritage of Western philosophy as it employs standard practices of reason, critique and rhetoric. Norris contrasts Derrida's work with the openness and illogicality of postmodernism. Don Thade (1991) goes further, suggesting that Derrida's recent work on the white spaces and margins of a page of writing is largely encompassed within the frame of contemporary hermeneutical (interpretive) phenomenology. Thade places

Derrida beside interpretive phenomeno-logists like Paul Ricoeur (see Chapter 3), who shares an interest in the problematic of non-meaning and meaning. This positioning of Derrida, once again, returns his radical conceit, his deconstruction, to the more general and conservative realm of the philo-sophical tradition he seeks to overthrow.

These ambiguities in Derrida's critical reception are puzzling in some respects, but understandable in others. Derrida's reluctance to deal directly with real-world issues – with contemporary culture – creates an elusiveness about his work which funda-mentally confirms the precepts of his analysis. Language is an imperfect conduit or mediation that both binds and separates human subjects. Not surprisingly, the deconstruction method has been as popular with conservative critics as it has been with more reformatory interests. Derrida's great insight is that language processes and structures can be readily reversed. While Derrida advocates against using this rever-sal to re-originate or re-privilege particular perspectives, the temptation to do so seems irresistible to many critics. Indeed, even in producing this reversal, many critics have been subtly able to instate the condi-tions of the binary structure in order to serve the interests of conservatism: again this is understandable for an analytical strategy which insists we should elucidate, but not alter, the course of things.

In American literary studies the conserv-ative critic Paul de Man has adapted this solipsistic spirit for the deconstruction of the underlying principles of fictional prose and poetry. In reviewing the equally apoli-tical and liberalist critical strategies of Leavisism and New Criticism, a number of Yale English scholars sought to expand literary studies beyond the walls of limited interpretive models. New Criticism had provided useful strategies for the close reading of texts, and Leavisism remained popular with an older generation of scholars who unflinchingly defended their high arts against the encroaching interests of film, TV and popular music studies. Poststructuralism permitted these conservative dominions to open their doors to a little popular culture without surrendering the integrity and knowledge of complex interpretive tech-niques. In particular, Paul de Man and others in the Yale School embraced the Derridean methods for the analysis of liter-ature and popular texts.

De Man, in particular, applies decon-structive strategies for an analysis of Romantic poetry. He argues that Romantic poetry, which seeks to articulate epiphinal experiences beyond the limits of struc-tured language, is already predisposed to a poststructuralist analytical paradigm. In *Blindness and Insight* (1971) he suggests that the significant insights of literary criti-cism emerge from a paradigm which is at odds with the actual findings. That is, crit-ics like Lukács, Blanchot and Poulet analyse texts according to a particular critical theory or framework, but their insights seem to emerge in contradiction to that theory or framework. De Man suggests that these insights occur through an unconscious slide from one theoretical positioning to another. The insight-through-blindness is sustained because the critics impose a cer-tain meaning or unity on the text which is actually part of their own theoretical slide. Criticism, therefore, must be ignorant of its own insights.

Terry Eagleton (1984), who has moved from a pure to a postmodern Marxist perspective, has characterized de Man's work as both reactionary and ahistorical. Certainly de Man and others of the Yale School have used Derridean deconstruc-tion to create a new way of understanding criticism and critical appraisals, yet de Man's own close reading techniques resist any inclination to situate literature within a broader historical or cultural context. Like the Romantic poets he so admires, de Man also engages in a certain mysticism, a certain solipsistic and introspective aestheticism. This aestheticism re-intensifies the conditions of the literary text, placing it inevitably outside the influences and problematics of culture. The text remains privileged over and above politics and the conditions that had given it meaning. As with Romanticism, Leavisism and New Criticism, de Man's strategy places the text out of the reach of history. De Man deconstructs the literary criticism which rationalizes the text into what Barthes calls second-order meanings; de Man rejects the formation of these second-order interpretations, which distort the original text through the process of supplementarity. However, his own intuitive, ahistorical critical aestheticism appears to constitute an equally formidable, though less specific, form of supplementarity.

De Man's work, like the other Yale literary scholars of the time (e.g., Geoffrey Hartman and Harold Bloom), is significant for its attempt to consider texts in terms of dispersals of meaning rather than as unified, organic and complete systems of meaning. While Eagleton has characterized the Yale scholars as re-instituting forms of New Criticism, the poststructuralist techniques which they explore move well beyond the parameters of a self-referential system. The Yale scholars' version of deconstruction, at least, seeks an explanation for the elisions and gaps that incline meanings toward persistent deferrals and fragmentations. More recent literary scholarship has filtered Derrida's methods and precepts through a wider matrix of influences and interests, including British cultural studies, postmodernism and alternative forms of poststructuralism. The influence of Derrida in the development of cultural theory can't be denied; however,

the solipsism of his work, and his persistent elision of questions of politics and power, in many ways limit the value of his concepts for a general analysis of contemporary culture.

MICHEL FOUCAULT

Foucault's Poststructuralist Writing

Perhaps the most often cited and accessible of the French poststructuralists is Michel Foucault. Foucault's work is far less consistent than the writings of Derrida, and many critics have questioned the efficacy and exact character of his contribution to cultural studies and cultural history. In particular, a number of critics have suggested that his work is riddled with contradictions and ambivalence, suggesting variously that it might be characterized as existentialist, structuralist, poststructuralist, radical, reactionary, feminist and anti-feminist (see Hoy, 1986a, 1988; Arac, 1988; Rabinow, 1991; Hekman, 1996). In fact, Foucault's work is an exhilarating exploration of the possibilities of language, culture and power. This exploration seems necessarily to impel Foucault into forms of self-conflict and toward the limits of his own conceptualizations. Both within particular texts and across his career, his work is clearly pushing the boundaries of what might be said about human meaning-making within a context of complex associations of power and historical rupture. Indeed, while Derrida's great strength is the playful but unremitting consistency of his argument, Foucault's work is more agitated and dissatisfied, seeking to create the conditions of political, as well as intellectual, liberation.

Yet, as has been discovered by Barthes and numerous others seeking a cultural politics, liberation is seriously problematized when the central project excludes structure and materialism in favour of the uncertainties of language and culture. But this is precisely what Foucault came to argue. Liberation, Foucault contends in the post-structuralist phase of his work, is not a revolutionary Marxist enterprise, nor is it a matter of structuralist realignments of language. Rather, he insists, liberation is a process of identification, of exposing the frigidities in the relationship between language (discourse) and power. The liberation of the self is conceivable only in terms of its unfixing, its escape from social and historical inscriptions, and its engagement with its own potential to be anything other than what it is. In other words, Foucault seeks to free the individual self from totalizing discourses which falsify power and the subject. These totalizing discourses may be instituted through the state and its apparatuses of surveillance and discipline; they may also be produced by the pseudo-liberationism of Marxism, which fixes the self (the individual) in structures of class and revolution.

Foucault wanted to free the subject from the constraints of other people's and institutions' discourses. To this extent, he claims that his books are 'bombs for others to throw', and 'tools for the revolutionary demonstration of the established apparatus' (see Foucault, 1977a: 113–38). In his post-structuralist phase, that is, Foucault wanted to be sure that his liberational enterprise would not slide away into some other form of discursive hegemony where the intellectual would 'speak for others', leading them into the artifice of someone else's freedom. He criticizes Marx and others for falsely investing their own liberation in the conceptions of class warfare. The proletariat would not save the world; this was the duty of individuals, including individuals in the middle classes. Foucault did not wish to be accused of fixing other people's liberation within the walls of his own discourse:

What, do you think I would take so much trouble and so much pleasure in writing, do you think that I would keep so persistently to my task, if I were not preparing – with a rather sticky hand – a labyrinth in which I can venture, in which I can move my discourse, opening up underground passages, forcing it to go far from itself, finding overhangs that reduce and deform its itinerary, in which I can lose myself, and appear at last to eyes that I will never have to meet again. I am no doubt not the only one who writes in order to have no face. Do not ask who I am and do not ask me to remain the same. Leave it to our bureaucrats and our police to see that our papers are in order. (Foucault, 1972: 17)

Taken from his mid-career text *The Archaeology of Knowledge*, these comments indicate clearly that Foucault's thinking is diverging decidedly from a view of the author and the intellectual – indeed the self generally – as a fixed and immovable presence in the construction of text and discourse. As with Barthes's rejection of authorial authority, Lacan's unfixing of the self and Derrida's denial of origin, Foucault is requesting that any subject should be allowed to shift ground and become something other than what he or she is at any given moment of the present.

In fact, we can identify three distinct phases in Foucault's writing career, and *The Archaeology of Knowledge* marks a shift away from an earlier historicism which was grounded in existential variations of Marxist teleology (theory of ultimate causes). This, the second phase of Foucault's writing career, incorporates the following texts: *The Archaeology of Knowledge* (1972), *The Order of Things* (1974), *Discipline and Punish* (1977a) and *The History of Sexuality, Volume One* (1981). This poststructuralist phase of his career is characterized by the following:

1   Foucault rejects Marxist materialism. The disturbances that took place on the

streets of Paris during the 1968 student agitations left many left-leaning intellectuals disappointed and disillusioned. Foucault, along with other French poststructuralists, was already developing doubts about the structuralist approach to power and ideology, but the disturbances seem to have galvanized these thoughts into a clear rejection of Marxist precepts. In particular, Foucault rejects the Marxist explanation of history and the investment of revolutionary authority in structural revolution.

2 Foucault rejects notions of a unified subject, preferring instead a notion of the subject as an open and mutable site for the construction and exchange of discourse.

3 Foucault rejects biological or social determinist theories. In particular, he argues against the idea that the body is an outcome of biological imperatives. Rather, biology serves the interests of discourse, culture and history.

4 Foucault develops the notion of archaeology, then genealogy, to explain the operations of history. History is replete with imprecise and capricious details: elements, characters and issues which discontinue as often as they continue. This is not to say that Foucault does not uncover patterns and links in history; rather, like E.P. Thompson, he insists that history is not about the movement of large structures and significant historical events. It's about people and their relationships within a broad context of power and knowledge.

6 Power and knowledge are not embedded in social structure. Power is a process, a matter of exchange. Where there is power there is challenge. Power is unstable, processual and forever switching direction. People and structures do not possess power, they merely transmit it. Power is always experienced at the level of the individual subject's body, the local level, the level of 'microphysics'.

The Problem of Power

In fact, for Foucault's poststructuralism, power, knowledge and discourse are the central contingencies of history. Foucault's basic method is to examine an historical period which for him constitutes the building blocks of cultural modernism. That is, he examines particular phenomena (hospitals, mental institutions, prisons, sexual technologies) of the eighteenth and nineteenth centuries, using his historiography to shed a broader light on modern culture. He follows Nietzsche's strategy of compounding concepts which are so thoroughly embedded in one another as to make them entirely interdependent. Power/knowledge and discourse/power are mutually reflexive; culture is fundamentally constituted around these key compounds. At one point Foucault claims that everything is discourse and power is everywhere. According to Foucault, then, nothing in culture exists that is not mediated in some way by the meaning-making of discourse (language, images, etc.) and its corollary of power. This is not the same as Althusser's claim about the ubiquity of ideology, which is a mechanism of social control and domination (see Chapter 3). Foucault, rather, is suggesting that power exists at the level of everyday practice and everyday exchanges between subjects. Power is personal, immediate and unavoidable:

Foucault and the Power of the Particular

Foucault refers to the immediate and particular levels of power as its microphysics. He illustrates the operations of the microphysics of power in the historical development of prisons and modern sexuality. However, he is strangely reluctant to apply these precepts for an analysis of contemporary culture. Even so, we can observe the operations of the microphysics through an infinite range of personal interactions and experiences: for example, in the ways in which the medium of TV is consumed. A *macro*physics would emphasize the power of institutions to produce and distribute messages. A *micro*physics would be interested in the ways audience members interact with one another, with the medium and with TV texts. A range of complex interactions may take place over the selection of a TV programme. These negotiations may mobilize institutional power (justice, income, paternity), emotional power (tantrums, sulking, imploring) or sexual power (favours for favours, seduction). In an analysis of these relationships and discourses, power is treated as unstable and exchangeable. Thus, a victory in the negotiations over the TV programme may be 'hollow' and may result in various forms of loss: the victor may be treated by other members of the family as selfish, unreasonable or conniving. The victor, therefore, may ultimately surrender important dimensions of power in other contexts and conditions (e.g., seeking approval or affection). Power exists only in discourse and can therefore never be fixed in structures; power operates always at the level of the individual body.

[I]t is in discourse that power and knowledge are joined together. And for this very reason we must conceive of discourse as a series of discontinuous segments whose tactical function is neither uniform nor stable. To be more precise, we must not conceive of a world divided between accepted discourse and excluded discourse, or between the dominant discourse and the dominated one; but as a multiplicity of discursive elements that can come into play in various strategies. It is this distribution that we must reconstruct, with the things said and those concealed, the enunciations required and those forbidden, that it comprises; with the variants and different effects – according to who is speaking, his position of power, the institutional context in which he happens to be situated – that it implies; and with the shifts and revitalization of identical formulas for identical objectives that it also uses. (Foucault, 1981: 100)

Thus, in his analyses of sexuality (1981), prisons (1977a) and the social sciences (1974), Foucault demonstrates that power is never separable from the instance of its expression. Power and knowledge are inevitably identifiable with one another since each is productive of the other. It is not simply that knowledge produces power and works its way out from the centre as a universalizing and hegemonic exigency, but rather that power/knowledge exists at all points of the particular.

The Problem of Truth and Theory

Foucault attempts to go beyond the Enlightenment dialectic (power/powerlessness), leading him, as it leads Derrida and others, away from the very centralizing postulates of rational theory itself. It is on this point that liberational theorists like Edward Said and Stuart Hall have distanced themselves from Foucault's argument, arguing that Foucault never fully realizes the liberational potential of his claims. However, just as Gilles Deleuze insists that theory be 'partial and fragmentary … functional, disposable and unrenewable' (1977: 205), Foucault insists that authorial reason (logocentricism) should function to undermine its own discursive and self-validating power. Like Derrida, Foucault wants to resist the temptation to re-centre the language of argument or critique: he wants to leave theory to destabilize itself. If it were not to do so, then it would simply reproduce the sort of grand and encompassing claims that so severely impede Marxist writings.

In fact, as Foucault reminds us throughout this phase of his career, power can only be produced as a localized 'microphysics' (Foucault, 1977a), an outcome which produces and is produced by its own impulses away from the centre. Thus, 'truth', like 'power', can only ever be partial and incomplete, existing in the matter of human action and beyond the isolating closures of theory:

> [I]f it exists at all … truth is a thing of the world. It is produced only by virtue of multiple forms of constraint. And it produces regular effects of power. Each society has its own regime of truth, its own 'politics' of truth: that is, the type of discourse it accepts and makes function as true. (Foucault, 1980: 131)

Foucault's 'archaeological' method is designed to uncover historical discontinuities as much as continuities: that is, his history is one which is as interested in the particulates and details of history as much as those things which progress toward subsequent events and subjectivities. While some critics have been confused by this notion, essentially Foucault is trying to distinguish his own exposition of localized truths from the Marxist historiography which constantly seeks grand explanations of structures, causes and outcomes. In particular, his key texts *Discipline and Punish* (1977a) and *The History of Sexuality, Volume One* (1981) demonstrate the effectiveness of this strategy.

Discipline and Punish

Discipline and Punish maps the experiences of prisoners during the modern period, and, in particular, how these experiences are formed through their representation in discourse. Foucault attempts to maintain a liberationary intent in his account of the 'body' as it is inscribed by power relationships. Thus, his description of the change from torture to imprisonment in the eighteenth century interrogates the basic assumptions and 'discourses' of Marxism and liberal humanism. Marxism sees the change as an exercise in the division of labour: the capitalist classes seeking new ways of controlling the proletariat and exploiting their labour. Liberal humanism, especially as it is articulated in the utilitarian philosophies of Jeremy Bentham, conceives of the prison as a more humane and reformatory mechanism for the treatment of miscreants. Foucault, however, sees the prison as a means of constituting the self and the body. In particular, he is interested in describing the apparatuses by which the body is inscribed with power/discourse. The 'panopticon', a prison blueprint drafted by Jeremy Bentham himself, becomes the metaphor for Foucault's understanding of the relationship between the state and the individual. In a panopticon system the individual is always under the observation of the prison wardens; for Foucault, this system of continuous and ubiquitous surveillance is a reflection of the modernist predilection for power/discourse and the 'disciplining' of the citizenry. It is precisely the relationship which his discursive liberationism would seek to unfix.

More broadly, *Discipline and Punish* continues Foucault's interest in the modernist predisposition for drawing the world and individuals out of the immediacy of their experience and into the constructed world of language or discourse. This reconstitution of individuals and their subjectivity is clearly an exercise in the formation and re-formation of power relationships. Thus, at the time when British cultural studies is preoccupied with structural linguistics and 'the struggle to signify', Foucault is exploring how power is experienced at the level of the individual subject. In *The Order of Things* (1974) he had described the emergence of the social sciences in terms of this increasing need for the social organization of language, most particularly the need to fix individuals in social and psychological description. The social sciences, Foucault argued, were a means of placing the human experience into forms of knowledge that were not so much humanistic or liberational, but were rather constituitive and administrative; in a sense, human subjectivity was invented by the social sciences and rendered available for state administration. In *Discipline and Punish* Foucault also argues that the emergence of criminology is a discursive process aimed at administering and 'surveying' individual subjectivities and bodies in a collective and organizational stream. Moreover, the scientific discourses of criminology are inevitably woven into practices and technologies of power which undermine completely science's claim to be disinterested, objective or impartial.

The History of Sexuality

In *The History of Sexuality, Volume One* Foucault extends these arguments into the sexual and reproductive experiences of individual subjectivities and bodies. Again, he examines the discursive dimensions of sexuality in the modernist period. Foucault argues, against the claims of recent liberalists, that the eighteenth and nineteenth centuries were not periods of sexual repression so much as they were periods of sexual transformation. The immediacies and openness of sexual and reproductive experiences, Foucault contends, were transformed into various forms of discourse: religious, educational and social scientific. This transformation allows the experience of sexuality to be both stimulated and surveyed by the state. The contradictions, displeasures and pleasures that are associated with sex and sexuality are thereby engaged through new ways of speaking and writing about sex. On the one hand, sex is facilitated by its articulation in bio-medical and psychological discourses; but, on the other hand, the state, through census and educational processes, is able to observe the sexuality of its citizenry. Foucault suggests that these articulations are sexual experiences in much the same way as actual physical engagement is. There can be no sexuality, Foucault insists, without discourse.

Clearly, Foucault is arguing here that the biological and materialist interpretation of sexuality are misguided and that all reality is mediated through discourse and culture.

These arguments are most forcefully articulated in the *History of Sexuality, Volume One*, where he outlines his project as the exposition of these discourses, rather than the examination of actual practices. In the later volumes of the series, however, he retreats significantly from this position, marking a third and final shift in his theoretical positioning. In fact, the latter volumes of *The History* might be conceived as 'straight' histories, outlining practices and events without the problematization of their discourse. In the first volume of the series Foucault is interested in the disturbances and obsessions of middle-class sexuality, and his liberational intent seems to be invested in the potential of the discursive release of sexualized bodies: new ways of articulating and experiencing the individual's sexual subjectivity. However, he never completes this project, preferring, it would seem, to prepare the way for others to take more deliberate or active steps toward their own liberation.

Foucault and Cultural Politics

Edward Said (1986), among many others, has rebuked Foucault for this retreat. In particular, Said expresses his frustration with Foucault for not fully embracing the political corollary of his studies. Mark Poster (1989) has explained the retreat in terms of Foucault's own gay sexuality and the occlusion of his liberational designs. Certainly, Foucault's final major essay, which preceded his death from an AIDS-related condition, demonstrates a significant and somewhat puzzling attempt to reconcile his thinking and writing career with what he imagines to be his philosophical heritage. In 'What is Enlightenment?' (1984), Foucault places his work within the general project of the Enlightenment.

Jürgen Habermas, in particular, finds this reconciliation puzzling since Foucault's poststructuralism had been so antagonistic toward the structuralist, rationalist, materialist heritage which is generally associated with Enlightenment philosophy. Foucault's poststructuralist work would seem to question the very grounds upon which the Enlightenment liberational enterprise is founded. His emphasis on discourse and the instability of power/knowledge seems very clearly to repudiate any notion of social structure. Interestingly, however, many of the liberationists who have followed Foucault's work have tended to focus on the formation of power/discourse in particular zones of cultural and institutional interest. To this extent, Foucault's poststructuralism has provided some theoretical substance to a cultural politics which seeks to destabilize power/discourse formations that are centred on gender, ethnicity, imperialism and sexual preference. Foucault's poststructural writings, therefore, have proved enormously influential even though he found himself retreating form the whole project of discourse analysis at the end of his career.

PSYCHOANALYTIC THEORY: JACQUES LACAN

Western intellectual thought has explored the notion of subjectivity in various ways. The concepts of 'subjectivity', the 'subject', the 'self' and the 'ego' generally refer to the 'I' (me) of any particular human context. Descartes and Kant established a significant split in the way we conceive of this experience, distinguishing between the subject as internal and contained, and the object as all phenomena external to the subject. Descartes's famous 'I think, therefore I am' directs Kant's later epistemological (through knowledge) conception of an intrinsic conceptual framework by which the human subject is able to 'know' the external world of objects. Romantic philosophy and aesthetics project over Kantian epistemology a view of the subject as a profoundly mystical exigency. The 'I' of Romantic poetry, for example, frequently seeks to transcend the cloying and demeaning circumstances of the material world through a form of spiritual ascent, an apotheosis which liberates the self from oppression and degeneration. Phenomenology, most especially as it is represented in the work of Edmund Husserl and Martin Heidegger, also seeks to explain the 'reality' of the world – phenomena – through the direct experiences of the subject. Marxism and its various derivatives reject all notions of the subject which aren't fixed in material and economic conditions: for Marxism and other forms of structuralism the subject is fixed in its relationship to material, economy and social organizations.

Psychoanalytic theory, most particularly Jacques Lacan's poststructuralist adaptations of Sigmund Freud, seeks to examine in detail the relationship between the various 'I's of the world and their wider experience of language. Following Émile Benveniste's idea of subject positions, Lacan argues that the self exists only in relation to other subjects. This means that when I say, 'I am hungry' and the other person says, 'I will give you food', the two 'I's are functioning in a delicate and highly unstable relationship with one another. Each 'I' exists only at the moment of utterance; the receiver of the utterance is delicately poised to take up the subject position 'I' when it is his/her turn to speak. Psychoanalytic poststructuralism, therefore, seeks to understand the gaps and the instabilities that operate through, and mediate, these shifting subject positions.

Language is pivotal to the self's ability to locate an appropriate subject position, and Lacan's adaptation of Freud centres on the relationship between human experience of language (the conscious) and that dimension of human experience which pre-figures language (the unconscious).

This relationship between the conscious and unconscious dimensions of human experience is complex and often unstable. Lacan, again following Freud, distinguishes between various developmental stages in a person's life which place him or her in relation to language and levels of consciousness or adulthood. The unconscious, however, is never obliterated in this process; rather, it is subsumed beneath the surface of language and consciousness, ready to re-emerge through critical moments and experiences. A central motif in psychoanalytic writing, then, is the notion of 'lack', a form of loss which has various manifestations in human experience. In the three critical developmental phases outlined by Freud/Lacan – mirror, *fort–da* and Oedipal – the condition of lack constitutes a central and defining characteristic. As we progress through life, we are driven by the desire to recover this lack; as we look back, we idealize a condition of completeness or plenitude when we were one with the mother. This mythical phase of plenitude engages the self in a complete identification with the mother, and a complete union of subject and object. The recovery of this lack and lesion directs the three stages in the following ways:

1 Birth disrupts the union of the infant in the womb and now the infant must be satisfied with intermittent contact with the breast. This 'fragmentation' of the completeness of the union impels the infant toward a form of self-awareness. This 'mirror phase' occurs (around 6–19 months) as the child develops a

sense of self through self-observation in a real or imagined mirror. At this point too, Lacan/Freud introduces the notion of *misrecognition*, whereby the infant (mis)recognizes its self in the mirror which is not the actual self, but a representation of the actual self. In fact, this image gives the impression of a more unified and complete subject than the life-stage actually warrants. The mirror phase is characterized by the experience of the 'imaginary', which Lacan distinguishes from 'the symbolic'. Thus the child imagines its unity through a real or imagined mirror, failing to notice fully that this 'image' of the reflected self may not even be itself but may be another child which the infant confirms as itself. The imaginary continues even through the full formation of the ego (self) since the myth of the unified selfhood depends on the ability to identify with 'objects'.

2   This construction of self or ego also depends on the child's ability to distinguish between itself and objects. The father's prohibition marks the child's entrance into the 'symbolic' by which s/he learns to distinguish differences (right/wrong, male/female, son/father, present/absent, etc.). Thus, the *fort–da* (gone–here) game phase is really about identifying oppositions. The principal part of this game is the recognition that things are present and then they are absent; the child articulates this entry into language through this simple game of recognition.

Lacan, also following Freud here, makes particular note of the symbol of the penis (the 'phallus'). The penis is not merely a physiological apparatus, but is meaningful in many different ways. The symbolic penis or phallus can be projected in many ways and attached to many different symbolic contexts. For Lacan, the most important dimension of the symbolic penis is its capacity to unite meanings generally: the 'phallus' becomes the privileged signifier in Lacan's system, as it allows all other signifiers (material symbols) to make contact with their signifieds (concepts or meanings). (This relationship remains unstable, however, since the phallus is also constituted around the problem of 'lack' or absence which becomes intensified during the Oedipal stage.)

Thus, this entry into language intensifies the experience of 'lack' since we are able to articulate our needs and recognize the lack of satisfaction. Gesture, therefore, runs on a series of discourses and is necessarily implicated in language. As we have noted, the subject and subjectivity are themselves contingencies of language. There is no essential or 'pre-linguistic' self but merely an imaginary and its productive misrecognition. The subject shifts in relation to other subjects and their subject positions. The 'I' about which I speak in a sentence is never the same 'I' which is doing the talking. Thus, the unity of signifier and signified is constituted on an unstable premise. Language shifts and so do signifiers and subjects.

3   In the Oedipal stage the child subject achieves sexual maturity. Lacan's rewriting of the Oedipus complex treats the unconscious as though it were structured like a language. As we have seen, Saussure attempts to weld together the separate systems of signifiers and signifieds in order to unify the sign. According to poststructuralists, however, this adhesion fails because the two systems are subject to the incessant deferrals of meaning over time. As we have just noted, this problem is exacerbated when the subject is considered since the 'I' of any utterance is never a

complete fusion between the material sign and the conceptual meaning. Sexual maturity intensifies the subject's desire to recover his or her 'lack' through the reunification of self and language. Desire, in fact, represents the process of pursuit, whereby the subject seeks to fix the signifier to the signified: the 'other', the 'real', the moment of plenitude. In order to resolve this 'lack' the subject seeks to fix his or her body to the object of desire but is forever confronted with a further signifier in much the same way as the seeker of meaning is haunted by the forever receding possibilities of definition in a dictionary. One signifier is met with more and yet more signifiers.

Lacan's outline of these three stages is significant for our general understanding of poststructuralist notions of subjectivity. The subject's immersion in the symbolic (language, discourse) is never complete because neither the self nor the sign is unified. Even sexual desire, which might seem to override or escape language, is symbolic because the object of an individual's desire is always produced symbolically in language. When I desire a person I am seeking to reunify myself, to recover that loss which separated me from the completeness of gestation. My desire is therefore generated by a need to reunify signifier with signified, conscious with unconscious, self with other. My hope is that the person whom I desire and the act of sexual engagement will liberate me from language, but inevitably the person whom I desire will exist for me in language. My desire is bound by language.

Lacan's work has been highly influential in cultural studies, both for those working in a direct psychoanalytic line and for others applying a more generalized version of his key concepts. In feminist film studies Lacan's theories have influenced notions of visualization and 'the male gaze' (see Chapter 6). In postcolonial theory his notion of the 'other' (or 'otherness') has been variously interpreted and applied, most frequently to refer to the European construction of identity against the otherness of non-Europeans. In cultural politics more generally Lacan's theories about open subjectivity and the construction of identity have been particularly significant. This poststructuralist perspective of an unfixed self has also been adapted in various domains of postmodernism where individual pleasure and the liberatory potential of the self are broadly canvassed.

POLITICS AND DIFFERENCE: DELEUZE AND GUATTARI

Anti-Oedipus

The relationship between poststructuralism and cultural politics is highly problematic. As we shall see in later chapters, the primary criticisms of poststructuralism are generated through structuralist and related political perspectives. In many respects the perception of poststructuralism's political limitations has prompted a more strident postmodernist critique which seeks to transform poststructuralism's interest in language and authoritative discourse into a more radical and culturally oriented politics of difference. Indeed, while we have investigated the political interests of Michel Foucault, his work remains framed by a certain resistance to contemporary social and cultural critique; his books are 'bombs for others to throw', and his analysis is generally restricted to earlier periods of modern history. Equally, Jacques Derrida confines his interests to the textual and philosophical processes by which meanings are formed, deferred or dissolved. Although his key concepts of deconstruction and difference have been clearly appropriated for popular and political critique, Derrida himself remains politically elusive, if not inert.

Gilles Deleuze and Félix Guattari are perhaps more self-consciously political than either Foucault or Derrida, and in many respects their work represents an embryonic postmodern political critique. Deleuze was a radical philosopher, a sort of anti-philosopher, who sought to remove social and metaphysical thinking from the hierarchies of elite intellectualism and intellectual discourses. Guattari, on the other hand, was a practising, Lacanian-trained psychoanalyst who sought the overthrow of historical and hierarchical discourses by which the doctor–patient relationship was inscribed by savage divisions of power and knowledge. Both Deleuze and Guattari wanted to produce a form of political criticism which was liberated from the artifice of intellectual hegemony and Marxist structuralism, both of which fixed human groups within immutable and historically persistent divisions of power. To this extent, Deleuze and Guattari's early writings are devoted to a triad of tensions – Marxism, Nietzschean existentialism and Freudian psychoanalysis – which are explored in order to produce a more radical account of human desire and politics.

In *Anti-Oedipus* (1983), for example, Deleuze and Guattari examine human desire in terms of authoritarianism and the codes which construct it. Like Adorno, they are interested in the relationship between human desire and the ascent of authoritarian subjectivities (versions of the self) which lead in the most spectacular instance to the formation of totalitarianism. This condition, extending Nietzsche's extension of Marx's concept of 'alienation', is a manifestation of the pandemic desire for security, the need to be led, the need to be affirmed

and fixed in the leadership of others. Thus, Nietzsche's repudiation of the church in *Antichrist* is invoked by Deleuze and Guattari in order to repudiate the codes of conventional, Freudian psychoanalysis. From its inception, Deleuze and Guattari argue, psychoanalysis has constituted a kind of church with stipulated rules of order and behaviour. Its treatments, predicated upon the separation of power and the definition of neurosis, rely on a faithfulness which is unassailable and which divides humanity between the leader who treats and the herd which is to be treated. Subjectivity for the neurotic is self without distress, self without pain (Deleuze and Guattari, 1983: 428), a tranquillized position which faithfully restores the might of the herd.

Like R.D. Laing and other psychiatric practitioners who seek to free the individual from this pathologic definition of neurosis, Deleuze and Guattari pursue the possibilities of 'breakdowns' and 'breakthroughs' (original insights and experiences) as expressions of desire, intensity and what they refer to as the general flows of human experience. They describe their approach as 'schizoanalysis'. This method of engagement with the subject contrasts in every way with the pathological impetus of conventional, Freudian psychoanalysis, which, they argue, measures everything against divisions of Oedipal theory, 'castration' and neurosis. Schizoanalysis begins with the 'schizo', the individual's subjectivity and his/her breakdown and breakthrough – the 'schizophrenic out for a walk' is a better model than a neurotic lying on the analyst's couch.

The Oedipus complex, according to conventional Freudian theory, refers to the Greek story of Oedipus, who mistakenly kills his father, marries his mother and ascends to the throne. Freud adapts the story to explain a neurosis involving sexual disruption and neurosis. Deleuze and Guattari argue that this breakdown and the schizophrenia which is involved are not an illness at all, but a breakthrough, bringing particular insights, opportunities and pleasures to the problematic of open subjectivity. Deleuze and Guattari contrast the Oedipal discourses and territorialities of individual, family, church and state against the possibilities of deterritorializing experiences of desire and subjectivity that have not been confined by the codes of the Oedipus complex and neurosis – these are the free flows, the lines of escape which lead us elsewhere. Desire is not to be abjured or feared, but released for the greater purposes beyond restrictive and pathological codes:

> Desire then becomes the abject fear of lacking something. But it should be noted that this is not a phrase uttered by the poor or dispossessed. On the contrary, such people know that they are close to the grass, almost akin to it, and that desire needs very few things – not those leftovers that chance to come their way. (Deleuze and Guattari, 1983: 27)

Anti-Oedipus should not simply be read, however, as a retreat into hedonism and sensual pleasure, as escape from the authoritarian discourses of psychoanalysis and capitalism. In fact, Deleuze and Guattari seek a social and cultural critique which moves beyond Marxist structuralism, on the one hand, and bourgeois psychoanalysis, on the other. *Anti-Oedipus* is explicitly an optimistic text, Deleuze and Guattari explain, but this optimism is built around the dissolution of all authoritarian discourses. In many respects, the Marxist–Freudian opposition is neutralized by the book's discussion of Friedrich Nietzsche's account of alienation and desire. Most particularly in *On the Genealogy of Morals*, Nietzsche illuminates the relationships

between desire, will and the processes of capitalism. The history of humanity is identified as an alienating process toward 'becoming reactive'. Nietzsche's escape from reactivity through the assertion of an existential will provides for Deleuze and Guattari the possibility of a revolutionary subjectivity, a freedom which liberates desire rather than confines it in the terminal conditions of class warfare or Oedipal concessions.

A Thousand Plateaus

In *A Thousand Plateaus* (1987) Deleuze and Guattari extend the liberatory impulses of subjectivity into the realm of all language codes, including their own. Like Derrida, Deleuze and Guattari seek to neutralize their own textual predispositions to authority by offering a de-centred, non-originary structure to their book. To this extent, they suggest that the reader need not follow the hierarchies that are generally built into texts – linear processes which privilege particular orders, sequences, chapters or sentences. The book, therefore, might be read from any angle and at any beginning point which the reader desires. The book has no linearity, no beginning, middle or end, but is part of a free flow of discourses, each neutralizing the authority of the other. Like Barthes and Foucault, Deleuze and Guattari introduce *A Thousand Plateaus* through the denial of their own fixed identities and authorship, moving on, however, to renounce the presence of the book itself:

> A book has neither object nor subject; it is made of variously formed matters, and very different dates and speeds. To attribute this book to a subject is to overlook this working of matters and the exteriority of their relations. ... A book is an assemblage of this kind, and as such is unattributable. It is a multiplicity – but we

don't know yet what the multiple entails when it is no longer attributed, that is, after it has been elevated to the status of a substantive. (Deleuze and Guattari, 1987: 3–4)

Deleuze and Guattari imagine, then, a discourse that is unbordered and which flows with the associative alacrity of the memory or the unconscious. *A Thousand Plateaus* is an assemblage of thoughts, 'nomad thoughts', which are liberated from the strictures and structures of author and reader.

The notion of 'nomad thought' constitutes a central motif for *A Thousand Plateaus*, though Deleuze and Guattari are careful not to allow any notion to take on the solidity of a 'concept'. Concepts may be useful as 'the founding bricks of a courthouse', but Deleuze and Guattari are seeking a more unstable and ephemeral language form, one in which assemblages replace fixed, organic systems composed of discretely organized and hierarchical components. An assemblage of like matters, therefore, is not a fixed concept or category; it is always a heterogeneous and convenient arrangement. Thus, in analysing the world, Deleuze and Guattari insist on their own immersion and on the continuing possibilities of rearrangement, disassemblage and the integrity of components. The primary condition of nomad thought is affirmation, even when the focus of the thought is negative. An assemblage of like matters, therefore, is not a fixed concept or category; it is always a heterogeneous and convenient arrangement.

In the hands of Deleuze and Guattari, in particular, poststructuralism becomes a utopia which distinguishes itself from the alienation of Marx and the nihilism of Sartre. The enabling capacity of this affirmation is 'force': the ability to break the walls at any moment and move on to a new thought, a new condition. Force is to be distinguished from power which builds walls. Force facilitates the 'smooth space' by which thinking travels from point to point. Consequently, *A Thousand Plateaus* might be read as a forcefield of pleasures where thinking across the many expressive media – most notably in mathematics and music – carries the potential for creating smooth space and new ways of conceiving of things. The music of the text is specifically noted in terms of its potential for flow and exploration. In particular, the musical refrain, evident in infants' *fort–da*, ethnic music, mothers' ditties and Schubert's songs, facilitates the forever-becoming potentials of human identity:

It's not really known when music begins. The refrain is neither a means of preventing music, warding it off, or forgoing it. But music exists because the refrain exists also, because music takes up the refrain, lays hold of it as a content in a form of expression, because it forms a block with it in order to take it somewhere else. *The child's refrain, which is not music, forms a block with the becoming-child of music.* An assemblage of like matters, therefore, is not a fixed concept or category; it is always a heterogeneous and convenient arrangement. (Deleuze and Guattari, 1987: 300)

DISCUSSION: POSTSTRUCTURALISM AND STRUCTURE

A Thousand Plateaus is notable for its engagement of complex artistic forms with everyday experiences in human culture. Deleuze and Guattari are interested in how humans experience and make sense of their world and their culture. Deleuze, the philosopher, draws on his knowledge of the European intellectual tradition; Guattari, the militant psychotherapist, draws on his knowledge and critique of psychoanalysis. While each is critical of his respective training and traditions, the narrative movement of both *Anti-Oedipus* and *A Thousand Plateaus* is undoubtedly driven by an unacknowledged tension, as much as by the pair's collaborative confluence. Indeed, the notion of 'nomad thought' functions to neutralize these tensions. At a particular level, both books are actually affirmations of the power of complex knowledge and complex art. Guattari's militancy never really draws the intellectual intensity of the text back into the realm of everyday functionality.

The problem, in fact, is precisely as Deleuze and Guattari acknowledge in their account of the child's refrain. Music is forever becoming and there can be no final and marked territory. The de-territorialization of language, identity and human culture more generally is a process that requires 'lines' and 'blocks' – the structures of thought. Deleuze and Guattari retreat consistently from those de-territorializing territories, preferring, it would seem, the pleasures of their own immersion in complex thought, complex art, to an analysis that would necessarily alter this pleasure as it re-forms it in language. In separately authored essays on the potential of new communications technologies (Crary and Kwinter, 1992), Deleuze and Guattari evince this underlying divide: Deleuze remains fixed in a metaphysics which forever defers the question of culture, while Guattari becomes explicitly radical, seeming to surrender the poststructuralist precepts that had driven the earlier, co-authored texts.

In fact, the purity of a poststructuralist position is almost impossible to sustain since the act of forming thought in language necessarily re-originates a claim to truth and knowledge. Deleuze and Guattari seek to ameliorate the effect of authorship and authority by creating an 'open' text: open it anywhere and open the ideas to a free flow of associations. The concept of 'system' is replaced by 'assemblage', which is supposedly more limited and less self-assured. But even a commitment to ephemera seems a contradiction in terms. Peter Dews (1984) was one of the first critics to analyse this limitation in poststructuralism. According to Dews, poststructuralism's anti-theory and anti-authority is a fundamental contradiction since any utterance, any discourse, removes the reader from the concrete and everyday and places him or her in the realm of abstraction. The acts of writing and reading are designed as communicative processes engaging comprehension, interpretation, truth claims and knowledge. Foucault's anti-theory and his belief that truth can only ever be 'localized' (if it exists at all) seem to contravene the truth claims of his own text as well as the parameters of common sense. Why would Foucault write his books if they were not to be believed? Moreover, Foucault is opposed to conceptions of structure or fixed power, and yet his books are replete with references to the state and governmentality. Derrida cleverly withdraws his commentary from the very brink of 'originification', or truth claim. At any point, he is prepared to undermine his own propositions because they exist in language. For Derrida, this game of proposition and retreat sustains his texts and frees him from the necessity of confronting real-world issues and problems.

The difficulty for poststructuralism, in fact, leaps from its own theoretic: can we say anything at all that approximates the truth or which directs us to the world of real problems and issues? For cultural studies, the answer to this question is constantly deferred. Cultural studies accepts a level of relativism in order to perform its analyses of everyday meaning-making. The problem of non-meaning exists for cultural studies, but in general terms it constitutes a theoretical extravagance which cannot be allowed to distract excessively from the primary task of cultural elucidation. Cultural studies borrows heavily from the poststructuralist perspective on language and subjectivity. However, the relativism by which culture constitutes itself and the politics which continue to frustrate the distribution of meaning-making resources appear to motivate cultural studies out of this theoretical bind. Even so, the problem is only ever deferred and, as we shall see, both feminism and postmodernism are frequently drawn back to the issue in the formation of their own theories and analyses.

6

Feminism:

From Femininity to Fragmentation

Outline of the chapter

Feminism encompasses many different theoretical, political and academic traditions. At the centre of feminist concerns, however, is the liberation of women from oppressive social practices and ideologies. The tensions and contradictions which characterize modernism are evident in the development of a feminist politics and cultural perspective. The competitive character of capitalism, for example, provides both a source of oppression and the promise of liberation. The Suffragettes were forced to distinguish women's interests from the general ideology of liberalism and capitalist progressivism in order to create a political space for women's liberation. In the early twentieth century Virginia Woolf articulated the need for women to conceive of themselves as a distinct social and political category since liberal democracy of itself was not able to complete the project of women's emancipation.

The project of women's liberation, therefore, combined direct interests in institutional politics and policies with broader cultural interests. Woolf's analysis of textual meanings and practices of reading influenced mid-century feminists like Kate Millett and Simone de Beauvoir. Millett examined the representation of women in modern, male-authored literary texts, concluding that women's oppression was aggressively formed through the writings of people like D.H. Lawrence, Henry Miller and Norman Mailer amongst others. De Beauvoir, a Marxist feminist, argued that liberation would only be possible when the patriarchal and hierarchical ideologies of capitalism were completely overthrown.

While feminism has never been an entirely homogeneous or unitary perspective, its integration with various forms of poststructuralism and postmodernism has led to significant theoretical fragmentations. In particular, these more recent permutations of feminism have sought to liberate women's desire and identity from the prescriptions of authoritative discourse. Older and more structuralist versions of feminism constitute a form of authoritative discourse for many younger feminists. The feminism that operates within cultural studies seeks to explore the cultural condition of 'being female' in a wide variety of cultural contexts. Many of these explorations have precipitated a challenge to earlier assumptions about being female and the nature of oppression.

GENERAL INTRODUCTION

Modern feminism is often dated to the French Revolution; it is suggested that the social revolutionary Charles Fourier coined the term at the beginning of the nineteenth century. However, while once it may have been possible to define feminism quite precisely and unproblematically, recent developments in gender and feminist theory have brought about significant divergences and fragmentations. The basic aspiration of feminism may still be the liberation of women from gender-based oppression, but even here we are forced to consider seriously definitions of 'women', 'liberation' and 'oppression'. The influence of poststructuralism, postmodernism, psychoanalytic theory and new modes of political and cultural analysis has undermined several core assumptions of feminism, leading a number of key theorists to claim that feminism is itself ruptured and that the older interests should now be replaced by a more contemporary perspective – something which some commentators might refer to as cultural politics, new feminism or even postfeminism. In any case, these new debates in feminist theory are both ubiquitous and critically embedded in contemporary cultural theory.

Recent histories of the feminist movement have located women's liberational activities in terms of three distinct waves:

1 The first wave refers to the suffragette movement, which was seeking primarily to have women's political rights inscribed into the democratic process. The suffragette movement was part of a general middle-class agitation that began during the nineteenth century.

2 The second wave occurs from the 1960s, where specific legislative and social processes excluded women from full and equal participation in public life, work and culture. This phase of agitation begins as the 'women's liberation movement' and evolves into the common nomenclature of feminism.

3 The third wave refers to the current period. Women's rights are now enshrined in legislation, but the culture and its ideologies remain fundamentally 'patriarchal', sexist and prejudiced against women. Men and male interests still dominate the culture, and women have to confront implied limits on their social and economic progress.

While these broad temporal categories provide some useful insights into the feminist critique, the historicism of the approach also has a teleological (cause and effect) or deterministic connotation. In fact, feminism might better be understood as a cultural space which has enabled criticism to take place throughout human history. Indeed, the tension between males and females as broad social, cultural and biological categories has always been problematic. The three-wave theory tends to isolate this tension, presenting it, as with Marx's class warfare, in terms of an inevitable, modernist social progress. This progressivism appears to place feminism outside the general clamour of culture, as if feminism itself were a privileged perspective by which the progress of all culture might be revealed.

A cultural studies approach to feminism doesn't dispense with history but is more interested in the genealogy of branches, forces and elements which struggle to constitute themselves in culture. To this extent, Stuart Hall's description of discourse and culture in terms of the 'struggle to signify' (see Chapter 4) usefully illuminates the female experience. While it may be profoundly desired, there is nothing inevitable about the liberation of women, nor about the critique developed as feminism. Feminism, like the phenomena it examines, is a form of cultural discourse. Like Marxism, liberal democracy, postcolonialism or postmodern politics, feminism is embedded in culture and has had to work through a raft of incarnations, as well as internal and external disputes. This chapter examines feminism as a cultural positioning as well as a cultural politics. The aim is to move away from treating feminism teleologically, as an outline of ultimate causes; rather, the chapter wants to explore the disputes as much as the continuities which form feminism. For the purposes of this chapter, feminism is understood as the collection of ideas and practices which are centred on the liberation of women.

FEMINISM AND MODERNISM

Capitalism and Culture

Margaret Mead's anthropology, for all its deficiencies, has demonstrated clearly that the social categories 'man' and 'woman' are utterly unstable. In her broad survey of human cultures, Mead found no inevitable connection between particular social roles – child-rearing, nurturing, labouring, military service – and gender. In many cultures men are more nurturing than women, and in some cultures women are more aggressive and militaristic than men; very often there is a high degree of role interchangeability. Different cultures, that is, deal with the demands of economy, reproduction, sex and kinship in entirely different ways. It appears, however, that modernity, with its own particular economic and cultural requirements, has tended to resolve the complex of tensions and needs through a high degree of gender specialization.

Specifically, modernity's economic system, capitalism, is constructed around a fundamental contradiction: on the one hand, it requires a 'scarcity' of products and services in order to command a value; on the other hand, it requires access and 'demand' for these products and services. It works like this. A pair of shoes requires labour and materials in order to be produced; this is the product cost. If the shoes are needed (some cultures don't wear shoes), then there will be 'demand' for the product. If there is only one pair of shoes and many people want them, then there is 'scarcity' and the product will attract a higher value. But if the product is too expensive to make or the producer simply wants too much for them, then there is too much value attached to the shoes. The value becomes invaluable because nobody can afford them. Alternatively, if there are too many shoes, then they will attract less value because there is over-supply. And if the shoes are considered uncool, poorly designed or seem to transgress the ideology of the given culture of the time (e.g., in wartime all shoes should go to the soldiers for free), then the shoes will also fail to attract value. The problem for capitalism is how to mediate the opposite issues of too much supply and too much demand. Demand operates as a liberational and inclusive process which absorbs all members of the market into a shared pursuit of products and services; scarcity is a privileging or restricting process which is conducted through forms of social hierarchy, privilege and competition. This contradiction works itself out by finding the right balance of scarcity, value and access to the products.

This classical market theory only partly resolves the problem, however, since the market is never free of the incredible complexities of human culture. As well as the instability of demand generally, the hierarchical conditions of scarcity lead to various forms of institutional privilege. While everyone in the culture may want a pair of shoes, not everyone is privileged enough to be able to 'afford' them. Particular social groups may have the ability to limit their supply (willingness to pay high prices, social manipulation, legislative controls on supply, etc.), and they will do so if shoes are an important part of that group's self-definition (see Bourdieu, 1984): 'Only *we* wear shoes'. Favoured groups in a society, that is, are able to exert disproportionate influence over social and cultural processes, and hence they distort the supply–demand cycle. Marx simplifies this point in relation to two social classes: the bourgeoisie, who own capital and supply, and the proletariat, who own nothing but their labour. According to Marx, the proletariat's 'demand' is impotent because workers are excluded from the supply–demand cycle.

Capitalism, however, has proven a good deal more canny than Marx anticipated. To ensure its own survival, capitalism has redirected its operations through new and original ways of maintaining the contradiction between the hierarchical predisposition of 'supply' and the inclusiveness of demand. Over the past centuries, therefore, capitalism has widened its embrace, stimulating new fields of demand and new, increasingly specialized, strategies of production and consumption. Of course, capitalism has not operated independently of culture; quite the contrary. The three great pillars of cultural modernism – capitalist economics, humanism and democratic political institutions – have worked through various forms of co-operation and dispute in order to maintain the opposite trajectories of freedom and privilege. The complex codes that underwrite the modern era are best understood, therefore, as ideological battlegrounds where notions of equality of opportunity and equal rights clash persistently with new forms of privilege, cultural manipulation and oppression.

The Suffragettes

Gender, like class, has been a central category in the unfolding of these ideological and language wars. Marxist feminists argue that women's labour is exploited by capitalism, most particularly as women have been excluded from the ownership of capital and property. Whether or not this is the case, there is no doubt that the confinement of women to nurturing, domestic and sexual services is associated with a general exclusion from other, more prominent, cultural zones. In particular, women were far less prominent in public debate and political processes than were men during the reform period of the nineteenth century. The Suffragettes, a group of largely educated, middle-class women, sought to redress this situation, arguing specifically that political representation and the right to vote should be extended to their own class of women, if not to all citizens. While their aims were in one sense quite specific, there is no doubt that the Suffragettes were motivated by broader ideological concerns about the role and rights of women in a patriarchal culture. In particular, concerns over the legal rights of women in marriage and property were inscribed with a cultural politics that had emerged through the significant fictional writings of Jane Austen, the Brontë sisters and George Eliot.

While these texts represented many of the injustices and indignities that were being suffered by middle-class women during the nineteenth century, a more specific women's liberation was being articulated in British utilitarianism. Utilitarianism (see Chapter 4) was largely committed to the prevailing economic and social systems, though it sought a general improvement to the conditions of life through a strategic implementation of social and political reforms. In particular, the utilitarians believed that the general good of a society would be served by the enhancement of individuals' own 'usefulness' or utility. Public education, public works and eventually universal suffrage would enhance the pride and moral condition of individuals and the citizenry. If individuals could enhance their own usefulness and the conditions of their own personal morality, then there would be a general improvement to society at large. According to John Stuart Mill and Harriet Taylor Mill (1970), this principle of utility extended to women as well as men. Properly educated and informed in the ways of economics and business, women could contribute equally to the public good – including the political well-being of the nation. In achieving their own personal sense of utility, women could mobilize their own special faculties for the betterment of the nation as a whole. Moreover, according to Mill and Taylor Mill, if women are to be most responsible for the education of the young, then it would be far preferable that women themselves were well educated and capable of sharing their knowledge and abilities.

Women and the Clash of Ideologies

As we have noted, capitalism's opposite inclinations toward freedom and constraint operate through the cultural ascriptions and representations of women and their 'femininity'. Theories which emphasized social justice, equality and liberal humanism struggled constantly against deterministic theories which positioned people hierarchically. Darwin's notions of the evolution of species and 'survival of the fittest' were applied as ideological counterparts to competitive capitalism. These social Darwinist theories claimed basically that individuals and groups found themselves in a particular social 'station' or position because their personal, class-based or ethnic biologies determined their merit and hence their place on the hierarchy. This biological determinism was also associated with various forms of cultural determinism whereby an individual's level of civilization was also conditioned by his or her 'cultural' context. When Governor Arthur Phillip arrived in the New South Wales colonies in 1788, he was carrying instructions from the Secretary of State ordering him to 'civilize the savages'. Similarly, Matthew Arnold and Thomas Carlyle didn't blame the poor for being poor, but their own principles and assumptions about civilization and culture made them deeply suspicious of a universal suffrage which would include the uneducated and illiterate. These people were simply not sufficiently civilized to participate in government.

The same sorts of arguments, of course, were levelled against women. Femininity, as a cultural condition, was characterized in terms of women being 'fair', weak, emotional, natural, sexual, unreasonable, nurturing and domestic. In other words, the social role that women had been ascribed during the rise of modernity had become ideologically integrated into what Barthes would call the cultural mythology of the times. Women's biology and (lack of) civility inevitably positioned them on a lower social scale. As numerous feminist historians have explained, these ascriptions of character were produced through various representations and discourses; the cultural space that women occupied in the nineteenth century was justified in terms of biological deficiency and the determinism of 'nature'.

These discourses were challenged, of course, by the literary liberalism of the great British authors, most especially those female novelists who sought a more dignified public role for women. But even the liberal tradition was not a single and homogeneous set of arguments within which equality and universal suffrage were the central platforms. As we have noted, Arnold and Carlyle were distinctly unenthusiastic about universal suffrage, fearing that one-man-one-vote would open the way to the chaotic and illiberal excesses that followed the French Revolution. Moreover, the feminist liberalism articulated in the novels of Charlotte and Emily Brontë, Jane Austen and George Eliot was highly localized in terms of class and ethnicity. As many critics have pointed out, these novels pay little attention to the poverty of working-class women, and to the plight of the black people upon whose labour the British middle classes were building their wealth. These early feminist challenges to the masculine hegemony were highly particulated expressions of an educated, white, middle-class woman's experience.

The limits of inclusion and exclusion continue as a problematic for both feminism and liberal humanism today. Clearly, the humanism articulated by Austen, the Brontës and Eliot constitutes the fundamental ideal of modernism; this ideal, however, is constantly compromised by this paradox of exclusivity. Modernism, including feminism, is founded on values and ideologies which implicate the subjugation of excluded others: men and women of colour, slaves, felons, and the indigenous peoples of conquered nations. A spectacular example of this paradox can be seen in Australia, where Aboriginal women and men were excluded from a 'universal' suffrage until 1967. The federated nation of Australia was one of the first countries of the world to grant the vote to women and install universal suffrage. In such a politically progressive society it is difficult to understand how the indigenous people and their rights could have been bracketed for so long.

This is not to suggest that the women of the Suffragette movement were merely self-interested, nor even that black men were more socially and historically disadvantaged than middle-class, white women. It is merely to acknowledge that the social and cultural discourses that emerged through the period of modernism are complex, contentious and inconsistent. In fact, the problematic of these contending discourses was by no means resolved by the granting of universal suffrage and the inception of a universal public education system. Rather, the discourses of twentieth-century modernism appear to have produced quite distinct and possibly opposite effects for the cultural condition of women's lives. That is, women still seem to have been constrained from a broad participation in culture, especially in government and public decision-making. However, the role of women as consumers and as sexualized figures in the consumption process seems to have expanded considerably during the earlier years of the twentieth century. Once again, capitalist contradiction (scarcity and demand, privilege and freedom) appears to have been implicated in this cultural mutation.

Women and High Modernism

Kate Millett (1971: Ch. 4) claims that the period from 1930 through to the 1960s constitutes a general reversal of the sexual liberation of the previous century, which had culminated in the granting of universal suffrage. For Millett and other feminists of the 1960s and 1970s, this 'decline' of feminism represents a certain slackening of focus, a sense in which the war had probably already been won. The writings of Virginia Woolf and Simone de Beauvoir would represent the exception in Millett's exposition. Woolf's *A Room of One's Own*

(1978, orig. 1929) and de Beauvoir's *The Second Sex* (1972, orig. 1949) attempt to place women very directly within the matrices of cultural representation in language. Woolf, a member of the Bloomsbury group of literary critics, sought to reorder Matthew Arnold's aesthetic and social criticism through the development of a distinctively female literary voice.

Woolf's aesthetic and literary criticism has provided recent feminism with a framework for reading and writing, as well as a cultural perspective of what numerous commentators refer to as 'modernism' or 'high modernism'. We should note that this use of the concept of modernism is quite restrictive, referring to a narrow cluster of ideas and texts, mostly appearing between 1890 and 1930; this is a common categorization used in areas of literary and aesthetic history (see Wolff, 1990: 79). (Our own, much broader and more culturally oriented use of the concept refers to ideas and texts from the Enlightenment through to the present.) Woolf is highly regarded in terms of aesthetic modernism, most particularly because she polemicizes the social and material conditions within which art and literature are produced. The inventiveness of avant-garde literature and art, Woolf insists, necessarily implicates the issue of gender. Women, she urges, need to liberate themselves and their aesthetic from the constraints of the male 'sentence', both literally and metaphorically. Woolf uses Dorothy Richardson as an example of the expressive potential of all women writers:

> She has invented, or, if she has not invented, developed and applied to her own use, a sentence which we might call the psychological sentence of the feminine gender. It is of a more elastic fibre than the old, capable of stretching to the extreme, of suspending the frailest particles, or enveloping the vaguest shapes. (Woolf, 1979: 191)

Woolf claims, therefore, that women need to move beyond the sentences provided by men, adapt and extend the existing discourses in order freely and openly to articulate their own sense of the world. 'A room of one's own' becomes the cry for space, both intellectual and material – the minimum resource for the full participation of women in culture.

Simone de Beauvoir: French Marxist Feminism

Woolf's arguments maintain the logics of British liberalism and a humanism which now specifically includes women. While anglophone feminists of the 1960s and 1970s would return to this theme, Simone de Beauvoir's assault on patriarchal capitalism and the confinement of women's expression and cultural participation has a more radical edge to it. Unlike Woolf's extension of Matthew Arnold's literary humanism, de Beauvoir is influenced by Marxist and existential raillery against the standards and norms of bourgeois society. Indeed, while Woolf's discourses never threaten the formidable elitism of British 'high culture', de Beauvoir takes a more expansive view of social discourse and power. In particular, she establishes the important relationship between identity and gender, noting that the fundamental issue for a woman in defining herself is: 'I am a woman.' A man, de Beauvoir maintains, would never feel the need to begin with this fundamental, genderized statement of identity. Women's dispersal in history is always measured against the primary definer of masculinity; this dispersal has prevented women from developing a collective identity, as is the case with other oppressed groups. Women, therefore, are fixed in an asymmetrical relationship with men; he is the norm(al), the One, while she is the abnormal, the Other. Her identity is measured necessarily against what a man is. Her exclusion from public participation constantly and permanently confines her identity.

Clearly influenced by Marxist existentialism, de Beauvoir rails against the artifice of 'equality' which never fully extends to women, because the ideology of equality assumes the inferiority of women, creating belief in both men and women that this is the normal state of affairs. Women themselves, rather than sympathetic men, are best placed to comprehend the actual conditions of their own existence, and thereby create the conditions for genuine equality and liberation. De Beauvoir lays the blame for this co-operative oppression at the feet of patriarchal capitalism. Women become the construct of men and surrender their potential for freedom, through insidious processes of discourse and history. Femininity construes women as the pleasure and labour objects of men, as 'men compel her to assume the status of Other' (de Beauvoir, 1972: 29). The solution, de Beauvoir considers, is a form of socialism which radically alters the hierarchical predispositions of capitalism, preferring a human nexus which liberates women and men from the limitations and unfreedoms of patriarchy.

De Beauvoir's existential socialism bears the marks of her long-term friend and erstwhile lover Jean-Paul Sartre, who identified freedom as the major project of human existence. This more radical assault on the standards of bourgeois life, aesthetics and sexuality also challenges the fundamental links between liberal humanism and women's liberation. In a society where women were becoming increasingly embedded in capitalist consumerism, de Beauvoir's socialist feminism sought to unravel the capitalist commodification

process and the restrictions capitalism imposed on women's lives. Her desire to liberate femininity from the constraints of male proprietorialism and romantic idealism was to prove a major inspiration for the sexual liberationists of the 1960s and 1970s.

SEXUAL AND POLITICAL EMANCIPATION

The 1960s was a period of major political and cultural reawakening. During the postwar years and into the 1950s the world was gripped by the deep freeze of Soviet and capitalist polemics. America had reasserted itself as the major world military, economic and cultural power. Its solipsistic and jingoistic views became expressed in terrible forms of conservatism and internal repression. The so-called 'McCarthyism' of the 1950s led to deep internal rifts as the right of politics became increasingly paranoid, accusing America's own citizens of Soviet sympathy, sedition and treason. Communist sympathizers were spotted at all levels of American society. Bohemians, artists, intellectuals, actors, writers – indeed anyone who dared challenge the rigidities of authority and the overriding ideology of societal unity – were immediately suspected of anti-Americanism. Undoubtedly, the ferment of artistic, cultural and intellectual activities of the 1960s was a response to the suffocating conditions of the previous decade. The emergence of the teenager as a new, autonomous consumer, the arrival of the contraceptive pill, and the widening distribution of media technologies like TV – all added to a political ferment which included the revival and popularization of the women's liberation movement.

Sexual Politics

Kate Millett's *Sexual Politics* (1971) seeks to define contemporary politics in terms of two distinct social classes – not the proletariat and bourgeoisie, but men and women. While this definition might most obviously accord with a structuralist perspective of human society, Millett makes it clear that her politics functions very much through the levels of personal relationships. Sexual politics, even in the era of supposed political equality and equality of opportunity, works beyond the level of traditional Marxist definitions; patriarchy, Millett declares in a sustained and vitriolic critique, is an insidious undercurrent which barely admits the humanity, let alone the status and dignity, of women:

> The rationale which accompanies the imposition of male authority euphemistically referred to as 'the battle of the sexes' bears a certain resemblance to the formulas of nations at war where any heinousness is justified on the grounds that the enemy is either an inferior species or really not human at all. The patriarchal mentality has concocted a whole series of rationales about women which accomplish this purpose tolerably well. And these traditional beliefs still invade our consciousness. (Millett, 1971: 46)

While Millett's book lacks the theoretical density of Althusser's 'ideology', she is speaking here about a similar exigency: patriarchy is an economic and cultural system which forms around the subordination of a whole class of people, women. The major focus of *Sexual Politics* is the exposition of these negative stereotypes and images of women, the mechanisms which justify the control and oppression of the sexual Other. Millett makes clear that she is distinguishing between the biological condition of the female and the culturally constructed conditions of gender and femininity.

Accordingly, Millett's analysis of Henry Miller, D.H. Lawrence, Jean Genet and Norman Mailer elucidates a patriarchal intensity which constantly validates the perspective of the male as sexual activist and female as sexual focus. Like de Beauvoir and Germaine Greer, Millett sees the female experience of sex and sexuality as fundamentally constrained by the need to satisfy male's material and ideological interests. Thus, Norman Mailer's *The American Dream* is impugned as a murderous and sodomite attack upon women. Henry Miller's *Sexus* – 'she kneeled at my feet gobbling it' etc. – is regaled for its tone of 'one male relating an exploit to another'.

Defenders of the works of writers like Henry Miller and Jean Genet have suggested that Millett's reading is both too narrow and too literal. Miller's work was significant in as much as it brought the whole experience of sex and the problematic of idealized love into a new critical and aesthetic focus. Millett sees the surrealism and homosexuality of Jean Genet's *The Thief's Journal* only in terms of female subjugation and degradation. Millett, it is argued, tends to homogenize the complex associations and meanings offered in these works, reducing them to a monochrome of her own polemic. Indeed, just as critics had seen Georg Lukács's Marxist interpretations of particular novels as reductionist, Millett's reading of Mailer, Miller and Genet might seem to bracket out a broader potential for liberation and subversion. Certainly, this is the defence mounted by Mailer himself in *The Prisoners of Sex*, where he accuses Millett of deliberately altering the meanings of the texts she analyses to suit her political project. Mailer repudiates Millett's critique, arguing that she fails to acknowledge that a text may not simply mirror the sexist attitudes of its cultural context. Artists and writers, Mailer argues, create the conditions of experience which might challenge the assumptions of the exterior world – a male author does not necessarily reproduce nor confirm the ideology of the world from which he draws his discourse.

The Mailer–Millett debate, in fact, raises a significant issue for feminist strategies, one which is taken up more fully in post-structuralist and postmodernist accounts of feminist politics. That is, the text and its interpretations are fundamentally problematic. Millett's framework of reading provides particular insights into the culture, and cultural politics generally. Mailer argues that this framework is only one possible approach to the text, and a highly polemicized and inadequate one. According to Mailer, Millett and others, including Germaine Greer (*The Female Eunuch*), have *mis*interpreted the text, imposing meanings that are not necessarily the intention of the author nor the mirror of the culture. These sorts of debates persist, even through the application of more sophisticated semiotic techniques of reading.

The Male Gaze: Laura Mulvey

In her essay 'Visual pleasure and narrative cinema' (1975), Laura Mulvey attempts to integrate feminist precepts with Freud/Lacan's language-based psychoanalysis (see Chapter 5). In many respects, Mulvey's reading of popular cinema texts parallels the feminist textual studies of Angela McRobbie at the Birmingham Centre for Contemporary Cultural Studies. Mulvey seeks to understand the processes and power relationships in culture which consistently represent women (and men) in socially idealized roles, using sexually idealized imagery. In particular, Mulvey is interested in the relationship between the sexualized and stereotyped image of women as they are subjected to, and

produced out of, the focus of the male gaze and male desire. While Mulvey's gender distinction remains typically structuralist, the innovative application of psychoanalysis to explain the relationship between men and women in textual processes has proven enormously influential for feminist media studies, especially during the 1970s and 1980s. It is central, for example, in the formation of what Stuart Hall (1988) calls '*Screen* Theory', cinematic analysis formed in and through the journal *Screen*; it has also been prevalent in feminist analysis of television (Moores, 1993).

Mulvey's objective is consciously political, seeking to deconstruct the fundamental patriarchal conditions of 'phallocentrism': 'the paradox of phallocentrism in all its manifestations is that it depends on the image of the castrated woman to give order and meaning to its world' (Mulvey, 1975: 746). Phallocentrism is not merely the pre-eminence of the male sexual organ, but the symbolic and cultural pre-eminence of the gender male. Mulvey's analysis attempts to demonstrate how the ubiquity and centralization of the male gaze upon the female form is an outcome of significant psychological and therefore cultural processes. Cinema, for Mulvey, constitutes an 'advanced representation system' through which a range of pleasures may be derived. 'Scopophilia', for example, is a fundamental sexual drive, a form of voyeurism, which the conditions and text of cinema-viewing facilitate. Scopophilia, in fact, is a conscious and concentrated way of 'looking' which engenders feelings of lust and satisfaction that are not necessarily directed toward concupiscence; at its more extreme, scopophilia manifests itself as a kind of Peeping-Tom syndrome. The cinema, Mulvey argues, has consciously evolved a viewing context which promotes scopophilic pleasures, presenting 'a hermetically sealed world which unwinds magically, indifferent to the presence of the audience, producing for them a sense of separation, and playing on their voyeuristic phantasy' (Mulvey, 1975: 749). The darkness, beamed light and the dream-like qualities of the cinema create a mood of privacy and the illusion that the spectator is looking from a distance and looking alone.

The second major pleasure derived through cinema spectatorship derives from the complicated processes of narcissism (self-love) and identification. The identification of spectator with spectacle is a necessary part of self-definition. Mulvey parallels this process with Jacques Lacan's description of a child's mirror phase, where the child misrecognizes his/her 'reflected' image as more complete, powerful and perfect than is actually the case (see Chapter 5). Mulvey argues that this misrecognition occurs in cinematic identification. This matrix of recognition/misrecognition constitutes the significant articulation of the 'I' of the world, the viewer's fundamental experience of self:

> This is a moment when an older fascination with looking (at the mother's face for an obvious example) collides with the initial inklings of self-awareness. Hence it is the birth of the long love affair/despair between image and self-image which has found such intensity of expression in film and such joyous recognition in the cinema audience. (Mulvey, 1975: 749)

The dual move in cinema spectatorship leads the viewer to identify with the perfection of the screened image, creating a false sense of completeness, while at the same time drawing the viewer into the pre-recognition phase of the unconscious, that condition in which viewers forget time, place and their own self. As we have noted in various discussions, this condition is a form of unconscious textual immersion, comparable to Barthes's concept of textual bliss, and what Lacan describes as the phase of immersion in the identity of the mother prior to the recognition of 'lack' and entrance into the symbolic world of language.

Mulvey points out that these two pleasures are necessarily in tension: scopophilia is based on the separation of the spectator from the spectacle; narcissism is a function of the engagement of the spectator with the 'ego-ideal' (the image of a perfected self) represented in the spectacle. These contradictions, however, are resolved somewhat through the social functioning of cinema, a functioning which ascribes the role of spectator to men and spectacle to women. Hollywood cinema, in particular, actually systematizes these roles through highly efficient practices. Camera techniques reinforce modes of looking by drawing the eyes of the audience into the eyes of the male protagonist; the female star is eroticized by the male protagonist and hence by the male audience, reinforcing the disciplinary and controlling processes on the female body. Such pleasures, however, constitute a dominant patriarchal order which needs to be challenged in order to 'conceive a new language of desire' (Mulvey, 1975: 748).

While Mulvey's essay has been enormously influential in the development of a feminist media and cinema studies, more recent appraisals of audiences and visual pleasure have asked disarmingly simple questions about the essay's validity. In particular, the issue of the female gaze and eroticization of the male body has caused remarkable perturbations for Mulveyan analysis. That is, Mulvey's essay ideologically connects the repetition of female images types in cinema with broader social control mechanisms; is it then not possible that the repetition of male body images might provide symbolic material for sexual and ideological reversal? Just as the female body is repeated and centralized for spectatorship, the male body is clearly rendered for the fantasy and freedom of female spectatorship (see Williams, 1992; van Zoonen, 1994). Moreover, Mulvey's essay assumes a heterosexual engagement; it's becoming increasingly clear that gay, lesbian and bisexual spectatorship will appropriate 'straight' imagery for an adaptive homosexual pleasure (see, e.g., Cowie, 1984; Matthews, 1997).

Of course, these variations in spectatorship processes may reflect the realization of Mulvey's objective, which was to dismantle the patriarchal continuities of Hollywood cinema. Certainly, during the 1970s, the articulation of women's visual pleasure was considerably more constrained than is presently the case. Mulvey's own psychoanalytic schema, nevertheless, clearly restricts the acknowledgement of a varied visual erotica, maintaining, as it does, that the underlying structures of patriarchy determine male as normative and female as other. Mulvey's own experimental films (with Peter Wollen) represent a strident assault on patriarchal looking and the Hollywood template. But even these efforts have encountered criticism, as commentaries have accused Mulvey of elitism and inaccessibility. In the context of an increasing academic interest in the 'value' of popular arts and popular cinema, Mulvey's critique of Hollywood and TV imagery has been seen as limiting and limited, denying women's sexuality and capacity for erotic looking, rather than liberating it.

POSTSTRUCTURALISM AND FEMINISM

The theorists discussed above share a common belief that the two human genders, women and men, represent more or less distinctive social classes. Patriarchy is an historically constituted political, economic and cultural system which necessarily facilitates the domination of one group over the other. These two classes may not be the only significant structural divisions functioning within a society, but for many feminists they are the principal determinants of a person's life experiences – more so than social class, which may be abrogated or transcended by individual effort and the greater facilitation mechanisms of patriarchal social mobility. A woman may learn to speak, dress and act in ways that belie her social class, but she can never escape the inscriptions of her gender.

Clearly, this form of structuralist feminism tends to homogenize the experience and cultural constituency of the respective conditions of male and female. Both Millett's repudiation of patriarchal objectifications of women and Mulvey's psychoanalytic model of eroticization 'reduce' much of the complex interplay of identity, gender and culture to a simple ideological polemic. Poststructuralism, as we have noted in the previous chapter, questions the stability of signification processes, thereby casting doubt over the oppositions and fundamentalism of structuralist polemics. For feminism, this is particularly pertinent since the reformist agenda of first and second wave feminism relies so critically on the homogenized poles male and female and on the historically perpetuating *system* of patriarchy. Not surprisingly, many feminists reject poststructuralism's emphasis on language and the limits of structure, most particularly those feminists who have sought the democratic or revolutionary overthrow of structured male privilege.

Even so, particular zones of poststructuralism have presented themselves in terms of political objectives. Michel Foucault, for example, seeks to expose personal or microphysical dimensions of power, most particularly as it is experienced at the level of the individual body. Deleuze and Guattari seek to undermine normative discourses which treat human desire and psychology as pathology. In both cases, power is conceived as a formation in language and knowledge, as a matter of process and unstable exchange, rather than as a fixed and inherent facility of structure. For a feminist analysis, this means that the social and cultural construction of gender can no longer be conceived as a necessary outcome of social structures. The symbolic constitution of male and female is problematized as the categories themselves become contingencies of uneven and unstable language processes. Poststructuralist feminism, therefore, could no longer accept the feminist project which sought to overthrow the old structures of male–female and replace them with new ones. Rather, a poststructuralist feminism had to dissolve the fixed position of structure altogether and open the question of gender to a general deconstruction.

A poststructuralist feminism, that is, needs to focus on the personal and unstable dimensions of power without reducing the complexities of sexuality to essentialist or generic statements. This means that poststructuralist feminism could not make broad claims about the way 'men' look or the way particular representations gratify a patriarchal system. Poststructuralism attempts to dispense with the notion of 'system', as it dissolves generic and structuralist statements like 'women are nurturers'. Poststructuralism can go on to explore the possibilities of new language formations, but without certainty or stability. This emphasis on language games and the immediate and personal experiences of language disinclines poststructuralism from a direct assault on the structures of power. That is, power is analysed at the level of the personal, the individual body and

individual subjectivity. While structuralism seeks to replace iniquitous social structures with more just and compassionate structures, poststructuralism is more interested in elucidating power as it functions in personal relationships. Therefore, poststructuralism rejects Mulvey's approach to the gaze, arguing that the assumption of a structural difference in the way men and women 'look' is dubious. Nor, indeed, can poststructuralism accept the basic feminist precepts which might claim 'all men are sexist', or 'all men are rapists'. For poststructuralism, these statements are as unsustainable as 'all women are nurturers'.

Desire and Freedom: Julia Kristeva

Julia Kristeva, a French theorist, has attempted to produce a poststructuralist feminist theory based on Jacques Lacan's psychoanalytic model. Lacan's theories, of course, were adapted by Laura Mulvey's more structuralist analysis of cinema in order to explain the system of Hollywood movies in terms of distinct gendered differences. Kristeva (see 1980), however, sought to extend her analysis of texts and representation beyond the limits of 'system'. In particular, she wanted to develop Gail Rubin's theory of a sex–gender system, exploring the possibilities of subjectivity and desire without recourse to prescriptive differences between men and women. Kristeva uses Lacan's description of subject-splitting to emphasize the instability of knowledge and identity. Like Derrida, Kristeva challenges the 'logocentricism' of Western philosophy, arguing that the whole notion of a unified, knowing subject is fundamentally designed to exclude the possibilities of the 'subversive noise of pleasure'.

Desire, according to Kristeva, unfixes the subject, creating new possibilities for experiencing self and identity. In particular, poetic language demonstrates how 'new' discourses might penetrate the authority and standardization of familiar and constrained discourses and subject positions. Thus, unlike Mulvey's subject, who appears, in the end, to be a victim of the subject-making of systematic, male, authority discourses, Kristeva's subject is always in process and capable of choosing alternative subject positions. Kristeva's psychoanalytic model for a revolutionary feminism emphasizes continually the potential for the liberation of desire. The rhythm and sound of poetic language mimic the sense experiences of sexual engagement. Poetry liberates the individual from the unconscious. Only when these raw materials of sense – the semiotic – become regulated do they return to the conditions of logics, order, authority and fixity.

Other French Poststructuralist Feminists

Thus, while Mulvey appears to offer little escape from the socially contrived unconscious (other than perhaps her own unapproachable filmic texts), Kristeva seeks constantly an anarchical discourse for the liberation of women and men from the limitations of logocentricism and the authority of phallocentric 'symbolic' order. This revolution of language is closely linked to avant-garde artistic and literary expression and to the actual overthrow of political and legal processes which limit women's full participation in culture. Other French feminists (Chantal Chawaf, Xafière Gauthier, Luce Irigaray, Hélène Cixous) argue similarly that female sexuality is an immense and mysterious force for revolutionary reconstruction. Irigaray and

Cixous, for example, have each argued that women need to present the fundamental differences inscribed in their bodies and sexuality as formidable revolutionary tools.

In this sense, French poststructuralist feminism marks its distinction from earlier anglophone feminist writings which seek primarily to expose the material and symbolic deprivation of women's lives. For Kate Millett, the differences between males and females have been exaggerated as they have been inscribed by the systematic conditionings of patriarchal society; biology has been used in the rhetoric of control and subordination: 'weaker sex', 'irrational', 'emotional', 'nurturing', 'passive'. For French feminists like Irigaray and Cixous, however, these biological differences can be harnessed in the celebration and articulation of feminine power. Women, therefore, cannot be conceived as merely one thing, but are infinite and expanding. Rather than emphasizing the negative conditions of patriarchy, French poststructuralist feminists have tended to seek an articulation of new possibilities, new differences, new horizons.

In her co-authored essay 'The laugh of the Medusa', Cixous (with Clément) outlines a formidable and almost joyous account of female bodies and their articulation in text. While acknowledging the potentialities of female masculinity and male femininity, Cixous nevertheless insists that female writing is inevitably an expression of women's own distinctive corporeality: 'The difference becomes most clearly perceived on the level of *jouissance*, in as much as a woman's instinctual economy cannot be identified by a man or the masculine economy' (Cixous and Clément, 1986: 81). Thus, echoing Roland Barthes' notion of textual bliss, *jouissance*, Cixous is referring to some finer and more complete state of writing and reading. The nexus of text and body is a condition of cultural advance – that new and irretrievable expansion of the female experience.

The Problem of Representation

Clearly, Cixous', Irigaray's and Kristeva's approach to sexuality and text provokes further complexities for feminism and feminist thought. In particular, the desire to articulate the uniqueness of the female aesthetic and unconscious – the heightened and celebrated state of difference – risks a return to essentialism ('women are *essentially* like this'). That is, while opposing the possibilities of a biological essentialism which can be articulated as a reason for subjugation, the French poststructuralists seek another brand of essentialism which broadens rather than diminishes the horizons of female sexuality and subjectivity. In many respects, this theoretical complexity parallels broader difficulties within poststructuralism itself, most especially as it attempts to translate its notions of discourse and power into political strategy. Notions of language instability – the unfixing of signifiers from their signifieds – open the way for the removal of all forms of essentialism, fixed systems and categories, and structure. A feminism which seeks to restore the unique conditions of the 'female' tends to risk the subversion of its own theoretical premise.

As it merges with cultural studies, feminism has confronted the issue of how women are represented in texts, and how those texts function at a political level. A good deal of feminist cultural analysis has tried to reconcile the structuralist and poststructuralist approaches to the question of representation. In its efforts to present a genuinely political account of representation, feminist cultural studies has offered a range of arguments about the absence, presence and nature of these representational discourses. These arguments continue to inform and frustrate contemporary feminist textual analysis. They can be summarized as follows:

1a Women are historically absent/ excluded from public discourse because men have controlled the facilities of representation. This means that women (or 'non-idealized' images of women) are absent because men like to tell their own stories about their own interests and objects of desire. This classical feminist argument suggests that structural forces operate to exclude women from full participation. While recent textualizations are attempting to redress this historical exclusion, it is still obvious in the arts, politics, business and commerce.

1b Alternatively, women are actually present in public discourse but this presence is not acknowledged because women's discourses have been seen as 'inferior' to men's; men, in fact, control the mechanisms of acknowledgement. Women actually tell their own stories, but the texts are more locally distributed, more personal or not appealing to mass market and popular cultural consumption. The significance and value of these texts (novels, poems, conversations, short films, family photos, etc.) are not seen as important by hegemonic cultural discourses controlled by men. Women will not participate, for example, in the aggressive, adversarial political institutions that have been established by men; women's politics are more personal and quotidian, involving creative and community participation.

2 Men are not able to represent women accurately because they are not corporeally or experientially capable of knowing what it is to be a 'woman'.

This is the French poststructuralist feminist approach discussed above. Women and their experience of their lives and bodies are unique and can be only adequately represented by women themselves. The completion of women's liberation is only possible with the release and exploration of desire through the woman's own body and through artistic representation. Women are *essentially* different and must be given the means of expressing that difference.

3 As a corollary of (2), it must follow that men and women experience their lives differently. As only women can genuinely represent the female experience, women should be absent from representations by men and men should be absent from representations by women. This extreme poststructuralist perspective suggests, further, that each subject and subjective experience is unique, casting doubt on the whole enterprise of representation.

Foucault and Feminism

Attempts to overcome these difficulties have produced some interesting and diverse arguments both within and outside feminism. In particular, a number of feminists have applied Michel Foucault's conceptions of discourse/power for the broader analysis of representation and sexuality. Foucault's *History of Sexuality, Volume One* has provided feminists with a view of power which acknowledges the imperatives of representation (discourse) and the processes of control and liberation. Thus, while Marxist and liberal materialist visions of sexuality tend to seek liberation in the specific conditions of social revolution or legislation, Foucauldian liberation is premised on discursive and ideological transformation. As we noted in the previous chapter, however, Foucault presents his books as 'bombs for others to throw', a challenge which poststructuralist feminism applies to the analysis of the textual representation of women in a multitude of contemporary discourses. Foucault has pointed out that sexuality as a set of texts and practices (all discursive or carrying meaning) is fundamentally in dispute. Bodies as sets of discourse are never finalized, never complete, but always in a state of flux, always under siege, always a site of power and discursive contestation. Thus, the bourgeois sexuality of the nineteenth century was not repressed, as is so often reported. Rather, the discourse of sexuality was transformed into something new and different: medical, population, educational, social scientific and even confessional discourses all provided a conduit for sexual language and sexual expression. Thus, while the European *scientica sexualis* contrasts with the *ars erotica* of the East, there was nonetheless a discourse available for the constant pleasures, anxieties and disputes in power of modern, bourgeois sexuality.

Foucault's poststructuralist phase, thereby, provides a conception of subjectivity and identity which acknowledges the multiple levels of discourse and power. The subject, like discourse itself, is never complete but is always in a state of flux. In following Foucault, recent feminists (e.g., Sawicki, 1991) have left the question of biological difference entirely open, acknowledging further that gender is only one discursive inscription among others (such as class, ethnicity and sexual orientation). That is, feminism has tried to move away from conceptions of the feminine which re-essentialize the experience of women and which seek liberation through the elite or avant-garde arts. The eschewal of sexism, therefore, is not to be found in the unique (and generic) female experience nor in the aesthetics of an avant-garde poem or film. Rather, the liberation of women must be viewed as a more inclusive but personal and particular project, one which may engage with other aspects of an individual's identity and experience of the world. The liberation of women, to put it simply, is about the liberation of each woman as opposed to the collective class.

This quite radical move provides a certain freedom for Foucauldian feminism; Theresa de Lauretis, a poststructuralist feminist film theorist, conceives of identity, for example, in terms of a subjectivity which is

> constituted in language, to be sure, though not by sexual difference alone, but rather across language and cultural representations; a subject engendered in the experience of race and class, as well as sexual relations; a subject therefore not unified but rather multiple, and not so much divided but contradicted. (1987: 2)

Gender, in this sense, is conceived in terms of process and exchange rather than as a fixed condition. Foucauldian poststructuralism, therefore, declares that the subject is ultimately open. Foucauldian feminism slips away from the semiotic–symbolic dichotomy outlined by Julia Kristeva. Kristeva criticizes the symbolic as it relies on realistic or direct representations of the world in accordance with prevailing (patriarchal, post-Oedipal) ideological order. The eschewal of these authoritative discourses exists only in the pre-symbolic (pre-Oedipal, semiotic) dimensions of the unconscious/poetic. It should be remembered that the terms 'symbolic' and 'representation' are being used here to locate a particular set of popular texts (filmic, photographic, literary); these are distinguished from more complex and poetic, avant-garde textualizations which defy the symbolic because they produce a sort of 'new' or 'original' discourse which parallels the pre-linguistic demeanour of the unconscious (pre-linguistic, before the discovery of 'lack').

A Foucauldian approach tends to reject such distinctions, parcelling all forms of meaning-making (practices and texts) into the one category of 'discourse'. This is more than a semantic difference, however, since the Foucauldian approach would see all meaning-making as cultural contingencies and subject to the analytical strategies of deconstruction and discourse/power. Foucauldian feminism would claim, therefore, to present a broader strategy of sedition; this strategy seeks to undermine both the authoritative, realistic texts impugned by Kristeva and any other discourse (poetic, avant-garde or otherwise) which would fix the subject in a particular subject position, including positions based on the prescription of gender. Foucauldian subjectivity is always in process, always seeking that new and untraversed possibility. Both audience-based and postmodern feminisms have adapted this approach in order to explore a broader notion of gender and gendered identity. Unlike Kristeva's approach, therefore, a Foucauldian feminism would avoid the restoration of the 'unique' or 'essential' experience of being a woman; gender is opened to an infinite array of possibilities.

MAGAZINES AND CULTURAL FEMINISM

Foucauldian feminism provides a significant facility for those feminists interested in liberation and individual freedom. The move which takes gender issues away from notions of a fixed or essential identity and the determining conditions of gendered structure or class clearly releases the potential for individual agency and self-determination.

The limits of this approach, however, relate to a broader problematic in the relationship between poststructuralism and cultural politics: that is, can we have a politics which opposes oppression or injustice but which is not rooted in structure or structured ideology? Critics of the Foucauldian approach argue that the de-centered subject must ultimately be conceived in terms of language, and language must ultimately re-centre (re-originate, re-fix) its content as a claim to knowledge or truth. Foucault's particular deconstruction of gendered knowledge, it is argued, must inevitably constitute an alternative discourse, a new way of conceiving the subject, and thus of re-centring the subject. This alternative, revolutionary discourse will be centred or positioned somewhere: it can't exist in a vacuum.

These critics of Foucauldian feminism argue, further, that the emphasis on discourse inevitably limits the very real conditions of female poverty, disadvantage and underprivilege. The material world is necessarily parenthesized in Foucauldian analysis (Mitchell, 1984). Marxist and liberal humanist feminists retain their interest in what they see as the conditions of cultural and economic privations, pointing out, for example, that women on a global scale have incomes of less than half that of males. Postcolonial feminists point to the high mortality rates, debilitating poverty and excessive labourloads of women in the non-developed world; they also point to the continuing political and public exclusion of women, and to the oppressive legal conditions in nations which execute women for sexual infidelity or for being the victim of sexual assault. This material and physical oppression is measured through vigorous ideological processes which continue to represent women as socially and culturally abnormal.

Angela McRobbie and British Cultural Feminism

We have discussed in detail the development of a particular form of cultural studies at the Birmingham Centre for Contemporary Cultural Studies during the 1960s and 1970s (see Chapter 4). The Centre's emphasis on the material and ideological privileging of particular groups within a culture over the interests of others contributed significantly to the evolution of contemporary cultural analysis. As Stuart Hall (1996) has noted, the question of politics was never too far away in any of the work carried out at the Centre. Angela McRobbie, who was one of Hall's associates at Birmingham, brought a vigorous and determinedly feminist perspective to those politics, challenging the Centre's own dominant approaches of class, ideology and culturalism.

McRobbie's early work on gender and youth culture is framed around Althusserian ideology. In particular, McRobbie illustrates how text, audience and industry interact to produce specific significations and ideological effects. In her essay on the teen magazine *Jackie*, McRobbie (1982) defines the publisher, D.C. Thompson, in terms of a capitalist logics and anti-unionist politics. She argues that the producers of the magazine consciously seek to produce a social and cultural order 'in terms of femininity, leisure and consumption' (1982: 87). McRobbie follows Althusser's notion of Ideological State Apparatuses in pointing to the manufacture of images, discourses and ideas which lead young women to consent to the conditions of their oppression and control. That is, young women are 'disciplined' into a patriarchal way of thinking about themselves and their femininity through a repetitive exposure to idealized feminine forms.

Publishing houses, which have a particularly invisible but significant status within a culture, are able to exert excessive power within the 'struggle to signify', despite the uncanny capacity of youth to subvert imposed culture. McRobbie acknowledges the potential for internal disruption to the conditions of cultural hegemony (social and cultural leadership), though for young women this capacity is limited by their gender. That is, in the normal conditions of hegemony the followers are able to manoeuvre and 'negotiate' certain aspects of the leaders' control. Youth culture, as Dick Hebdige (1979) demonstrates, is particularly well versed in taking the artefacts of an imposed culture (the transistor radio, clothing and hair-styles, street corners, etc.), adding to them and making them part of their own cultural experience. However, the restricted access of girls to the public sphere limits their ability to reappropriate cultural products and hence disturb the predominant processes of control and consent. McRobbie argues, in fact, that girls' use of teenage magazines tends to take place within private spheres, and that cultural practices, which Gramsci believed would produce the conditions for negotiated domination, are never really available for them.

McRobbie uses standard semiotic analysis to demonstrate how particular images and motifs are repeated in order to produce gender-based stereotypes. Sex and love become the defining qualities of life. Boys are classed in terms of action and access; girls are blonde and sexy, brunette and unreliable, or plain and uninteresting. The major objective is to attract the interest, love and fidelity of a boy, and hence female relationships are defined in terms of competition and threat: 'The girl's life is defined in terms of emotions – jealously, possessiveness and devotion. Pervading the stories is a fundamental fear, fear of losing your boyfriend or never getting one' (McRobbie, 1982: 107). Overall, McRobbie's analysis treats *Jackie*, in her own words, as 'a massive ideological block in which readers were imprisoned' (1991: 141). Her later work on teen magazines, influenced by some revisionary analysis of audiences and texts, tends to admit a greater possibility for feminine subversion. In particular, McRobbie appears to have moved beyond dismissive accounts of women's magazines (cf. Jackson, 1996) which condemn them universally for their imposed and controlling images of female femininity.

Cultural Feminism and Postmodernism

McRobbie (1997) notes that poststructuralism and poststructuralist psychoanalysis have extended the boundaries of feminist analysis beyond the sort of 'austere' Althusserianism which had directed her own work on *Jackie*. According to McRobbie (see also Winship, 1987; Driscoll, 1995), poststructuralism opens up the question of meaning and identity for women, illustrating a more complex relationship between what is known and what might function at the level of the unconscious. Battles for meaning, power and identity rage across the broad gamut of discourses, including the discourses of commercial women's magazines, feminism and the private imaginings of the mind. In the progress of her work, McRobbie comes to question her earlier assumptions about girls' capacity to interpret and reject cultural texts and artefacts. She adopts a more Gramscian approach to feminism and to the ways in which discourses are evolved; she argues, in fact, that adolescent girls' identities are negotiated through these various discourses. Ultimately it is these battles and exchanges which lead McRobbie to acknowledge the possibility that there may be

> no truth of womanhood, just as there can be no single or true feminism. Power resides in the currents of meaning which condense at key cultural sites in society, including magazines. Hence one important task for feminism is to show how magazines compete to construct the subjectivities of millions of female readers by producing these great bundles of meanings on a weekly basis. So familiar are these that they enter our unconsciousnesses producing desires and pleasures even when consciously we might not want them to. (1997: 193)

This question of pleasure has become central to postmodern and audience-oriented cultural theory. McRobbie herself concedes that it is women's pleasures, filtered through the feminist critique, which ultimately disrupt the monochrome of ideological analysis. Feminists themselves experience a love–hate relationship with the popular texts they study, seduced perhaps by the feminine imagery and the romantic narrative of popular women's magazines.

This new or diversified brand of feminism facilitates a critical efficacy which brings feminism back into a more empathic relationship with women's (as opposed to 'feminist') culture. Feminists are now able to admit their own pleasures and anxieties into the broad lexicon of everyday women's experience, deconstructing the loftiness or superiority of their academic knowledge and facilitating a significant engagement with the broadly based political potentialities of popular culture. In this sense, McRobbie's recent studies have sought to explain the transformation of women's, especially young women's,

magazines and the reformulation of the notion of femininity. In particular, she notes in her analysis of the British magazine *More* that there has been a movement away from sexual restraint and the obsessive interest in *the* boyfriend toward images of sexuality and identity 'which break decisively with the conventions of feminine behaviour by representing girls as crudely lustful, desiring young women' (1997: 196). For McRobbie, this new identity marks a significant moment in which the relationship between feminism and femininity is loosened; the new teenage girl is free to seek her fun and pleasures, though ultimately, even in this liberated territory, the question of power and capitalist consumption remains problematic.

FEMINISM IN CONTEMPORARY POLITICS

McRobbie's account of current-day feminism demonstrates clearly that the field of gender critique is far from monodic and singularly motivated. During the 1980s and 1990s this greater interest in pleasure and identity, and the shifting nature of gender analysis continued to challenge the conventions of structuralist feminist analysis. Contemporaneously, women's liberation penetrated broad areas of popular, personal and governmental discourses, bringing significant changes to the way the culture conceived of and experienced gender. Even so, the liberation imagined by feminists like Simone de Beauvoir and Kate Millett has evolved and fragmented in ways which have produced often contradictory and unanticipated consequences. Perhaps the most notable manifestation of these unexpected consequences has been the appropriation of feminist ideologies and aspirations by conservative politics. In particular, the rise and dominance of Margaret Thatcher in British politics demonstrated the double-edge of feminism. Thatcher's austere contraction of public welfare, the arts, health, education and public transport, along with her vicious assault on labour organizations and the public service, marshalled a policy position which shattered the optimistic visions of 1970s political feminism. Thatcher's free-market philosophy exposed an unsettling dimension of feminism which demeaned weakness and vulnerability – especially in men – in favour of a performative competitiveness which hearkened to the deep values of British conservativism. The consequences for feminist philosophy can be summarized as follows:

1 Thatcherism shattered the traditional image of the 'female' as nurturer and carer, the keeper of community and personal welfare.
2 Thatcherism demonstrated that women could be just as vicious, imperious, chauvinistic and brutal as any man, shattering the stereotype of masculinity which had informed earlier feminist critique.
3 The unleashing of Thatcherist power illustrated that power was more than just a fixity of gender, but could easily be moved to the female. The essentialization of gender needed to be modified against other conditions of class, education, race, sexuality, nation.
4 Thatcherism raised the question of the purpose of liberation. If a woman were to accede to power and act so terribly against other women (and men), then what had feminism achieved?
5 A number of feminists explained Thatcherism as another manifestation of patriarchy, that Thatcher merely took on the characteristics of males in a male political context. If this were so,

then how could a feminine power be conceived as an alternative? And is feminine power to be conceived as some mysterious, ineffable and essential force?
6 The rise of a conservative feminism obliterated the putative disadvantages of gender, arguing that if an individual were good enough, he or she would necessarily succeed.

This conservative feminism has been particularly prominent in English-speaking nations with a Westminster system of government: Britain, Canada and New Zealand have all had conservative female prime ministers or opposition leaders. It may be that the absence of such significant female political leaders in the United States has contributed to a more assertive affirmative action legislation. It may also be that feminist politics in the United Kingdom has been mollified by the potency and austerity of Thatcherist feminism. In either case, feminism has been forced to confront a potential for deep, economic and social conservatism (see Heywood and Drake, 1997). Certainly some feminists dismiss Thatcherist feminism as either no feminism at all, or an inevitable part of female participation in public life. In the latter sense, feminists continue to impugn a social and political system which still limits female representation, arguing that parliament, congress and the presidential office will never be truly democratic until all forms of female experience are represented there. Only when women have an equal presence in government will the Suffragette project and democracy itself be fully realized.

As we have noted, a significant strand of feminist politics has been grounded in capitalist and bourgeois ideology. Utilitarian feminism embraces the opportunities of market-based economy, and certainly this brand of feminism is present in Thatcherist politics. It shouldn't surprise us, therefore, that one of the most prominent demonstrations of feminist political success has been associated with classical, free-market economics and the rights of the individual to succeed. The conservative political position which promotes individual progress as the root of social progress lies at the heart of Thatcherist feminism. It may be that the final lesson of Thatcherism is that the liberation of women is more likely to be accomplished through an aggressive individualism, rather than through an intricate rendering of collective, leftist agitation. That is, conservative individualism may well produce the reforms and successes sought by feminism.

Certainly, the successes of 'conservative' feminism, along with a general diversifying and modulating of the politics of the Left since the 1980s, has contributed to a significant fracturing of the feminist project. The increasing gap between rich and poor inside and between nations is facilitated by a brand of capitalism which is necessarily associated with free-market ideology. Conservative feminism has certainly played its part in this extension of hierarchical principles, urging a liberation of the (female) self which is bound by an ideology which celebrates personal gratification and the accumulation of personal wealth. Other feminists, however, remain less enthusiastic about this ideology, attaching their liberational feminism to the other reformist issues: social equity, social welfare, poverty, education, ethnicity, sexual orientation, environmentalism. In either case, it is clear that the older style of feminism, which was largely monophonic and which tended to locate the female experience as the 'victim' of history, has been transformed into a new and radically more diverse political movement.

FEMINIST CULTURAL POLITICS

Equal opportunity and affirmative action legislations have been enacted in most developed nations. The aim of this legislation is to reduce discrimination and promote greater access to public life by women and other disadvantaged groups. These types of legislation have been designed to draw women into the protection of the state. Yet again, however, many feminists argue that such laws contribute to the discourses of 'woman as victim': that is, such legislation promotes the idea that women are the victims of history and can't look after themselves. Conservative feminism sees these discourses as fundamentally offensive and unnecessary, but a number of more reformist feminists also see the construction of legislation as a discursive imposition which may impede rather than facilitate freedom. These cultural feminists, many influenced by poststructuralist theory, are broadly dissatisfied with the ideological and structural imperatives of liberal humanism, democratic institutions and the process of power delegation itself. Legislation, which is the classical modernist means of solving problems, tends to homogenize human experience, reducing liberational potential to a consolidated and inclusive discourse.

The alternative to the delegation of power and to legislative solutions would seek to keep power at the level of the individual. As mentioned in our discussions on Foucauldian feminism, this approach to power and to culture shifts the emphasis of liberation from the replacement of one fixed and structured discourse by another to the promotion of a personal experience of power. This personal experience of power is constituted through the formation of personal meaning-making (culture) and the formation of alternative identities. The emphasis on ever-accumulating legislations is replaced by a 'cultural politics' which has the experiences and interests of individual subjects and lower-level communities at its core. Cultural politics is characterized by:

(a)   an interest in everyday experiences and the means by which ordinary people create and fulfil their liberational potential;

(b)   an emphasis on texts, textual pleasure and textual representation, including popular texts and everyday cultural artefacts – this emphasis on everyday 'culture' engages liberation at the level of community; and

(c)   an emphasis on the liberational potential of 'difference' and 'heterogeneity'. True liberation is possible only through the acknowledgement and celebration of human diversity. According to these theories, the process of delegating power and producing legislation might be necessary in some ways, but the ultimate effect is to reduce diversity and the richness of human cultures.

The influence of (especially Foucauldian) poststructuralism is evident in these characteristics. What is also clear is that contemporary culture and the contemporary cultural experience of women cannot be explained purely in terms of older, structuralist feminist discourses. Even so, the formation of a feminist cultural politics, which examines culture in terms of a liberational project, encounters the same problems as does poststructuralist feminism. These problems attach to some fundamental questions: in a diversified feminist project, what is the female experience that needs liberating, where is oppression to be located, and is it possible to produce an alternative 'culture' that doesn't restore fundamental aspects of essentialism? That

is, can we have a distinct and unique female experience that is not attached to the broad and distinct categories of male and female?

These questions are further complicated as feminist cultural politics attempts to engage with the transforming, contemporary cultural condition. While these issues will be discussed in greater detail in our analysis of postmodernism, it's certainly clear that the liberational project of feminist cultural politics is struggling to find a firm perspective in a world that is becoming increasingly dominated by electronic communications and visual imagery, and where visceral pleasures are heightened through new modes of experiencing time, space, self and individual identity. Even so, feminist cultural politics is distinguished by its efforts to account for the female experience, especially the female experience of power, within this changing cultural context. A number of different types of feminist cultural politics have emerged in an attempt to account for the contemporary female experience. These feminisms can be categorized as adversarial or socialist feminism, postcolonial feminism, audience/postmodern feminism and celebratory postmodern feminism.

Adversarial and Socialist Feminism

The long tradition of Marxist feminism continues today with a number of feminists dismissing poststructuralist and postmodernist accounts of feminism as a form of capitulation. In a sense, this type of feminism, rooted in structuralist accounts of history and maintaining its assault on structured patriarchy, argues that the continued material and political privileging of males necessarily reduces the category of female to subordinate. Postmodernism, for these feminists, can never transcend the fundamental categories which keep men and women apart. The imagery of TV, film and popular journalism continues to confine the bodies and social conditions of women. Globally, women continue to bear the burden of excessive work and of reproduction. Women are far poorer than men and experience both institutional and social discrimination. Even though contemporary feminist analysis recognizes the importance of discourse and ideology in forming sexist attitudes and institutional controls, it is this material poverty which remains central to the socialist feminist project. The new conditions of the world merely serve to satisfy the material and cultural interests of patriarchy and men. Texts remain institutionally bound; ideology remains the force by which texts exert their control.

This type of feminism, most particularly as it has attached itself to other liberational ambitions such as lesbian separationism, remains determinedly adversarial. The notion of 'difference' becomes the rallying point whereby belief in matriarchy and hostility to patriarchy inclines its proponents to a non-consensual, at times aggressive, stance against the conditions and perpetrators of oppression. Sexuality, therefore, is a political weapon which needs to be used 'strategically'; difference is an essential and fundamental condition which necessarily assaults the idealized imagery, deceptive pleasures, sentimentalism and political relativism of particular versions of postmodern theory. At its most extreme, this form of feminism imagines a new space for the biological and discursive dissolution of men (see, e.g., Hart, 1994). Donna Haraway (1991), for example, anticipates the collapse of gender through the ascent of a cyborgian woman. Men, masculinity, patriarchy and capitalism will all implode through the evolutionary reign of the cyborg.

Postcolonial Feminism

Postcolonial feminism (see Spivak, 1987, 1992; Gunew, 1993; McClintock et al., 1997) has generally been influenced by Foucauldian and psychoanalytic theory. However, rather than filtering these theories into a new mode of pleasure and personal creativity, postcolonial feminism has seen the issue of representation as fundamentally political. Here, the notion of 'self' and 'other' becomes highly politicized; the white, colonizing male is seen as the dominant or normative self and the Oriental or colonized female is seen as alien and the object of sexual and material 'colonization'. Feminist postcolonialism adds the problematic of gender to the politics of national and ethnic liberationism. It applies poststructuralist accounts of subjectivity and language to its emancipatory project. The 'construction' of meaning through text is treated as entirely ideological: the white male colonizers legitimate their extra-territorial conquests through the formulations of textual legitimacy: the Orient is created as an exotic and wild territory which is available for the civilizing power of European, masculine rationalism.

As Edward Said (1978) has argued, the eroticization of the Orient necessarily creates a control relationship between the male colonizer and the feminized Orient. This eroticization is expressed through notions of the Orient as 'exotic', feminine, mysterious and unruly. The art and poetry of the colonizing nations of Europe are replete with images of bare-breasted women, sleek and feminine-looking males. This sexualization matches femininity with subordination. Postcolonial feminism seeks to 'deconstruct' the images of the non-West by interrogating the colonial and patriarchal systems which give them legitimacy. The concept of 'difference' (diversity, multiculturalism, etc.) becomes the political alternative to a deconstructed cultural imperialism.

Audience Postmodernism

As with postcolonialism, audience-based postmodernism incorporates a wide range of political and cultural commentary; however, feminism has been central to the interests and orientations of much audience-based cultural analysis. Janice Radway's *Reading the Romance* (1987) and Ien Ang's *Watching Dallas* (1985) mark a significant moment for feminist analysis. Whereas the work of Angela McRobbie and others had treated women as the 'victims' of textual meaning and ideology, Radway and Ang pioneered a perspective of female audiences as active choosers of texts and creators of textual meaning. The increasing sophistication of audience analysis has led a number of postmodern feminists to consider more positively the value of romantic imagery and its liberational potential. As with recent analysis of women's experience of popular magazines (e.g., Winship, 1987), the work of Radway and Ang treats personal pleasure and identity formation as positive forces in women's lives. There are a number of postmodern feminists, such as Meaghan Morris (1988), who celebrate the transformative power of particular popular cultural texts like *Thelma and Louise* and *Cagney and Lacey*. However, for Radway and Ang, the textual meanings identified by Morris and others are less important than the processes by which female readers and viewers engage with the text and participate in the formation of its meanings.

In this sense, soap operas and romances have as much liberational potential as have texts which consciously seek to overthrow the stereotypes of femininity. Ien Ang (1996), while acknowledging that the heroines of romantic fantasy are generally less independent and publicly powerful than the heroines of crime dramas, claims nevertheless to be as emotionally engaged by characters like Sue Ellen (*Dallas*) as by police heroines like Christine Cagney (*Cagney and Lacey*). She argues that the 'conventional' feminist criticism of characterizations such as Sue Ellen are fundamentally flawed:

> [T]his approach ... implies a rationalistic view of the relationship between the image and viewer (whereby it is assumed that the image is seen by the viewer as a more or less adequate model of reality); it can only account for the popularity of soap operas among women as something irrational. In other words, what the role/image approach tends to overlook is the large *emotional involvement* which is invested in identification with characters of popular fiction. (1996: 92)

Ang suggests, therefore, that neither the poetic avant-garde advocated by Julia Kristeva, nor the heroic transgressions of *Thelma and Louise*, guarantees liberation. Emotional engagement and the constitution of a female experience, according to Ang, are essential for the mobilization of a genuinely female liberation. Ang's argument revives the problem of whether the 'female' experience has been excluded from culture, or whether it has simply been unacknowledged. The female experience of everyday culture through everyday romance has surely been disregarded or denigrated in public or academic discourse, not the least by older forms of feminism itself.

Postfeminism?

A number of commentators claim that we are now entering a 'postfeminist' cultural phase. There are three major reasons for this transformation: first, so-called 'second wave' feminism has produced the desired effects of focusing attention on the oppression of women during the modern period; secondly, legislation protecting the economic and social rights of women has been established in the major developed nations of the world; and, thirdly, the fragmentation of the feminist project has led to serious questions about the validity of treating women as a single social category, supported by a single political vision.

In a sense, the move to a postfeminist perspective has been motivated by the success of feminism. It is really this last point that preoccupies current feminist thinking. However, the very serious divisions and disputes within the field of feminism have led a number of cultural commentators to query the validity of the whole notion of 'feminism'; a number of women interested in the female experience have questioned whether their particular reformist project and their own identity can be productively associated with the nomenclature of 'feminist'. Whether we use the notion of 'postfeminism' or not, the problematic of contemporary feminism may be summarized as follows:

1   The strict categories of 'male' and 'female' are based on biological differences and cultural ascriptions. The liberating of these social and cultural ascriptions has led to a far more mixed social scenario where the historically ascribed characteristics of femininity and masculinity may be attached to either gender. Contemporary men and women may be more or less nurturing, athletic, aggressive, sexually assertive, and so on. Feminism which essentializes femaleness but excludes qualities of traditional 'femininity' risks being authoritarian and prescriptive. That is, feminism may commit women to social ascriptions which they may not wish to employ in their subjectivities.

2   Men's own subjectivity may be prescribed by a feminism which is supposedly dedicated to liberation.

3   This greater mixing of gendered subjectivity has led to a range of revisions within feminism. One of the most important questions is: can 'men' be directly linked to 'patriarchy', and are men responsible for patriarchy? Many women interested in the liberation of women have come to dissociate 'particular' men from the sins of sexism and patriarchy. (In many respects, this question parallels the problematic of racism: can all whites be held responsible for racism?)

4   Can women still be treated as a distinct, homogeneous and unitary social category independent of race, ethnicity, sexual orientation, education levels, income, community and age? Can we assume in contemporary society that being female is necessarily a subjugant social position? Is this really plausible or valuable for a politics of reform?

5   Patriarchy and capitalist specialization had allocated the roles of carer, educator, nurturer and community-builder to women; these roles had been regarded as generally inferior to the tasks allocated to men. Rather than

seeking to elevate the value and social status of caring work, feminist advocacy has been largely devoted to increasing women's access to areas of economic and public activity. Women's successful penetration into these areas has further diminished the status and value of caring activities, leaving a good deal of 'community' work vacant or devolved to low-paid and low-skilled workers. A good deal of public discussion on family, nurture and community care centres on the general absence of appropriate resources and personnel to ensure the emotional and mental health of the community. Postfeminism is asking difficult questions about the efficacy of this general exodus by women and men from the responsibilities of care.

Celebratory Postmodernism

There is a further permutation of postmodernism which is positively affirmative and which seeks to extend the parameters of the poststructuralist theoretic beyond polemical politics. In many respects this form of celebratory postmodernism assumes that the great battles of feminism have been won and that feminism must now reinvent itself as a liberational and inclusive project which seeks new experiences, new subjectivities and new modes of pleasure. For some commentators, this new feminism constitutes a kind of postfeminism, a radical break with the austere and adversarial assault on systematic oppression. Meaghan Morris (1988, 1993), an advocate of popular culture, excludes any pre-postmodern (modern) discourses as fundamentally incapable of elucidating contemporary conditions. In this sense, Morris, like a number of other postmodernists, rejoices in cultural conditions which connect popular media texts with their consumers. New representations of women's experience, therefore, are to be found in the unfolding present; TV programmes like *Ally McBeal* and *Friends* articulate an experience of the feminine which liberates subjectivity from the phlegmatic ideologically driven concerns of structuralist, modernist discourses.

Clearly, this type of feminism is subject to the same criticisms as other forms of poststructuralism and postmodernism. That is, many commentators believe that postmodern feminism fails to address adequately the problems that continue to beset women and that the emphasis on pleasure risks political capitulation, market sovereignty, even the complete surrender of a feminist critical position. Here, the emphasis is not on men and women, but on social ascription and self-imposed sexual constraint. In many respects, this new feminism parallels much of the celebratory, affirmative advocacy of New Age cultural activity – that hybrid of Asian and European erotica, mysticism, technologies and alchemic practices (see Ross, 1991). In many New Age theories the environment, sexual liberation and female symbolism are centralized in a form of counter-culturalism. This cultural alchemy seeks to dissolve masculine adversarialism and logocentricism in a new form of celebratory utopian relativism. The New Age movement has sought to release both genders from fixed ascriptions and the limits of hierarchical knowledge.

DISCUSSION: THE IMAGING
OF THE FEMALE BODY

While a good deal of feminist analysis has focused on the material privations of women, it is possible that this form of discrimination is less conspicuous than the proliferation of women and women's bodies in the popular media. In a culture which is now dominated by visual imagery, the commodification of female sexuality has caused considerable consternation for many feminists. Naomi Wolf's widely read text *The Beauty Myth* argues, for example, that women's subjectivity has been crippled by a pervasive and pernicious patriarchal strategy of control and discipline. According to Wolf, legal and social liberation has not protected women against the 'beauty economy', which manacles women to impossible images, cosmetic products and modes of patriarchally imposed starvation diets and diseases:

> Beauty is a currency system like the gold standard. Like any economy, it is determined by politics, and in the modern age in the West it is the last, best belief system that keeps male dominance intact. In assigning value to women in a vertical hierarchy according to a culturally imposed physical standard, it is an expression of power relations in which women must unnaturally compete for resources that men have appropriated for themselves. (1991: 10)

Wolf's book, which has proven one of the highest grossing feminist texts of all times, simplifies and popularizes the work of earlier feminists such as Kate Millett and Laura Mulvey. The paradox of Wolf's work, however, is that it employs similar discursive strategies and themes to those used in the magazines she attacks. The emphasis on beauty might seem to play on the insecurities that are so replete within contemporary image-driven culture. Other than the obvious problem of sustaining a relatively simplistic, structuralist conspiracy theory, one of the major criticisms of Wolf's book relates to its reductive approach to gender. The rigid categorizations of men and women, control and submission, power and powerlessness reduce the world to an amazingly simple place – as if there were only one type of man and woman, and as if men were not themselves subject to the lure and oppressions of their own masculinity, including the condition of male beauty.

Even so, the question of subjectivity, and the relationship between subjectivity and the proliferation of images in contemporary culture, has become central for recent feminist analysis. One of the deficiencies of Wolf's approach to representation of women is her treatment of the female audiences as passive receivers, even dupes, of received messages. This 'active-sender', 'passive-receiver' model of communication has evolved through what is generally called the American effects tradition (see Chapter 2). The approach attempts to measure the impact of messages on the behaviour, attitudes and psychology of the individual receiver of institutionally driven messages.

Wolf's approach may also be regarded as a type of reformist liberal humanism; like other styles of liberal humanism, it is characterized by a belief that patriarchy is the dominant social system (ideology or structure) and that this system, along with certain aspects of capitalism, needs to be controlled by protective legislation. While Wolf is still very much enamoured of capitalism, her reading of the beauty industry parallels various forms of Marxist and structuralist analysis which ascribe significant power to texts and their capacity to deliver messages and influence audiences. More recent versions of feminist cultural analysis, as we have seen, question this power. These forms of feminism, influenced by poststructuralism and postmodernism, claim that women are more powerful, discriminating and able to determine their own lives and cultural meanings than is appreciated by Wolf and others like her.

These debates are crystalized in the extreme case of sexualized female representation: pornography. Earlier feminists, like Kate Millett, Laura Mulvey and Angela McRobbie, regarded the pornographic depiction of women as fundamentally demeaning and exploitative. However, postmodern feminism has taken a more 'tolerant' view, arguing that pornography is largely harmless and that the sexual depiction of women is not of itself politically problematic. In this sense, sexual imagery is regarded as potentially liberating, offering women (and men) opportunities for sexual display and sexual engagement which are actually released from patriarchal and puritanical restrictions on women's sexual enjoyment. Moreover, some feminists insist that the challenge for women is to be as sexual in as many different ways as possible, exploiting the new technologies as well as the desires of men and women to maximize cultural pleasure (see, e.g., Creed, 1997; Hardy, 1997).

In many respects, the issue of bodily pleasure represents the point of departure for new forms of feminism. Catherine Lumby (1997) suggests, for example, that sexuality marks a generational shift between so-called 'second wave' feminism and the rising group of younger women who have their own particular liberational needs and interests. Lumby equates the institutional power of older feminists with 'the enemy' since, like 'patriarchs, some senior feminists are inclined to think they represent, and speak for, women as a whole' (1997: 156). The celebration and exploration of new sexual imagery is most clearly evident in the analysis of rock and popular music, where Madonna, perhaps more than any other single female figure, has self-consciously 'explored' and displayed women's sexuality through the aesthetic of her music and visual imagery (see Fiske, 1989a). The Madonna image has been presented and used as a source of arousal, sexual pleasure and identity exploration.

Nevertheless, this character or image is yet another mediated construction which has been provided in capitalist exchange processes. The producer of the image – the woman behind the character – has been canny enough to both read and create cultural trends, drawing some peripheral or less overt sexual imagery into the mainstream of popular text consumption. The Madonna imagery, therefore, needs to be understood as a cultural conduit, drawing on and providing a discourse for particular sexual subjectivities; it also needs to be understood as an integrated player in the globalized, corporatized capitalist machinery. The debate for feminists centres on whether the Madonna imagery contributes to, or detracts from, the liberation of women and their sexuality from masculine libido and patriarchal economic control.

Madonna's mainstream and corporatized mediations nevertheless have stimulated further explorations of women's experience. This mainstreamed, commercial imagery contrasts, in many respects, with the more aggressively marginalized sexual imagery of other female rock musicians. As with broader debates surrounding the popular and the artistic in contemporary entertainment, many rock musicians find themselves contemplating the dilemma of personal, artistic control, on the one hand, and commercial imperatives, on the other. Popularity and the sale of CDs and concert tickets are the means by which most artists measure their success. However, there are a number of rock musicians who regard their creative activities as far more important than the aspiration of commercial success. The 'grrrl power' movement of the 1990s reflects the desires of a number of young women's bands to maintain the integrity of their creative and political activities and the presentation of themselves and their art through the media. In many respects, grrrl power sought to liberate the message and the messenger from the commercial control of record companies and media meaning-makers. As female musicians and performers became increasingly popular during the 1990s, a number of younger female musicians sought to pursue a more didactic and assertively feminist polemic in their music. Supported by the Feminist Majority Foundation, the US based riot grrrls set out to encourage audience members 'to educate themselves, speak out, register to vote, and learn what they can do to protect their right to abortion and birth control' (Cause sleeve notes). As the movement spread to the underground rock scene in the United Kingdom, the messages of power and independence were intensified, forming a consciousness which sought collectively to subvert the masculinities which dominated rock culture.

Clearly, the aim of grrrl power and the riot grrrls was to wrest the power of representation away from male or patriarchal control and place it in the hands of the performers. This collective consciousness and the ideal of female emancipation which informs it, however, have not been sacrosanct. As Marion Leonard (1997) has pointed out in her discussion of grrrl power, the movement was simply incapable of sealing itself from the imperatives of ideological and commercial challenge. Girrrl power becomes grrrl power in the hands of the marketing machinery and as the aspirations of self-representation become modulated through capitalism and the commercial ideology. A highly commercialized and marketable product group like the Spice Girls has been able to appropriate the concept of 'grrrl power' for the promotion and consumption of their own musical and image products. Feminism, like any other cultural formation, that is, may be transformed into commodity and dispersed as something predictable, mainstream and comfortable. For the celebrants of popular cultural texts, this form of feminism may represent, in fact, the cultural reality. Spice Girls feminism – ephemeral, attractively packaged and evasively defined – might prove to be the high point of social transformation. In any case, feminism has been enormously influential in achieving this transformation. Whether it is the pinnacle of its successes is yet to be determined.

7

Postmodernism and Beyond

Outline of the chapter

The postmodern is classified in many ways. Some theorists distinguish between 'postmodernity' (description of an historical phase) and 'postmodernism' (ways of thinking about and representing culture). More generally, the postmodern may be formed around aesthetic, deconstructionist, critical pessimistic and celebrational descriptions.

Postmodernism was first used as an aesthetic description to distinguish avant-garde literature and forms of pop art. Ihab Hassan argues that postmodern literature expresses the changing nature of contemporary life. He contrasts the heterogeneity and multiple ironies of postmodern literature with the logocentricism and hierarchical forms of modernist literature. Andreas Huyssen, among others, has broadened the avant-garde position in order to define new forms of cultural representation. For Huyssen, postmodernism is a mode of representing and theorizing the world which is more positive and creative than is the case with French poststructuralism. Huyssen combines an interest in aesthetics with a reading of the cultural circumstances in which the aesthetics operate. Daniel Bell suggests that these new social circumstances are more clearly enunciated through modes of thinking associated with science and the 'information age'. Jean-François Lyotard also conceives of the new cultural condition as being centred on ways of thinking about and representing the world. Like Bell and Huyssen, Lyotard believes that we are entering a new historical phase. However, unlike Huyssen, who regards poststructuralism as a modernist mode of analysis, and unlike Bell, who works primarily from a sociological perspective, Lyotard applies a deconstructionist method in order to illustrate the fallibilities of modernist ways of thinking. Lyotard, therefore, describes a dialectical relationship between modernist modes of thinking and representation and new forms of postmodernism. Fredric Jameson and Jean Baudrillard also apply deconstructionist methods, though their views of postmodern culture are somewhat more pessimistic than Lyotard's, and considerably more pessimistic than Huyssen's. Jameson sees postmodern culture as suffering from an historical amnesia: culture has forgotten its past and therefore has no reference for the construction of alternative social and political modes. During the course of his career, Jean Baudrillard has also surrendered his hope for an alternative social order, arguing that contemporary reality has become a hyperreality where meanings are absent and everything is an imitation of everything else. Charles Jencks, like Huyssen, presents a far more optimistic vision of contemporary culture and its future. Also like Huyssen, Jencks argues that the new aesthetics represents contemporary culture far more accurately and productively than does modernist aesthetics. Jencks' 'theory of the postmodern' becomes a 'postmodern theory' since it embraces fully the objects and sensibilities it analyses. There are a number of criticisms of postmodernism, most particularly of those forms of postmodernism which reduce and caricature elements of modernism.

GENERAL INTRODUCTION

Over the past two decades the concept of postmodernism has achieved remarkable currency in cultural and public discourse. It's now virtually impossible to speak of contemporary culture without recourse to this resilient and encompassing concept. Like 'culture' itself, in fact, postmodernism appears to have penetrated every level of academic discourse from the humanities and arts through to the social and natural sciences. The concept, however, remains highly disputed, its mixed history directing scholars and other commentators through a phalanx of cognitive, critical and aesthetic possibilities. In this chapter we will examine the concept of postmodernism in relation to these key cultural debates. However, before proceeding, it is worth clarifying a few significant definitional issues.

Postmodernity and Postmodernism

A number of commentators distinguish between postmodernity and postmodernism. Postmodernity represents an historical phase or period which is characterized by the presence of particular cultural elements. Postmodernity supersedes the previous historical period of modernity. Of course there are many elements of the previous period which continue, but as Fredric Jameson (1991) argues, the new elements are sufficiently prevalent to suggest that we have entered a new historical phase. Postmodernism refers more specifically to a way of thinking, articulating and symbolizing. In other words, postmodernism might refer more specifically to a cultural mode of thought which ultimately expresses itself in discourse (see Hutcheon, 1988; Connor, 1989).

The periodizing of cultural history allows us to conceive of social elements which constitute a distinctive chronological order; however, there is little agreement about the nature, definition or date of postmodernity. The concept of the 'modern', for example, is sometimes restricted to a period of art production between 1880 and 1940 (see Bradbury and McFarlane, 1978; Gilbert and Gubar, 1988). Jean-François Lyotard, in his famous work *The Postmodern Condition* (1984a), allows both cognitive (ways of thinking) analysis and historical description to merge somewhat, creating the distinct sense that the 'knowing' in postmodernism is fundamentally inscribed in the condition itself: being part of the historical times, we necessarily 'think' in accordance with conditions of the culture. Meaghan Morris (1993, also 1998) goes as far as to suggest that our capacity to elucidate contemporary (postmodern) culture is linked fundamentally to our adoption of contemporary cognitive modes: analysts retaining older theoretical and analytical frameworks simply cannot understand the contemporary condition.

Categorizing the Postmodern

This interconnectedness of the two concepts, postmodernism and postmodernity, has discouraged many commentators from bothering with a distinction. Even so, the problem of how to define the postmodern and what should be included under its heading remains highly contested in aesthetics, sociology and cultural studies. These disputes can be summarized in terms of the following questions:

1   What is it that constitutes postmodern modes of thinking and knowing?
2   What is it that constitutes postmodern modes of practice or action?
3   What can be called a postmodern artefact (product, commodity, thing)?
4   What constitutes 'representation' in postmodern culture? Is it only specific artworks (art, literature, architecture, film, etc.), or can the nomenclature of postmodern be applied to anything that exists as discourse or text (meaning-making process) within the culture?
5   What proportion of postmodern elements and processes in a culture might warrant its re-classification as the 'postmodern' epoch?
6   Can only a postmodern way of thinking (postmodern theory) adequately elucidate a postmodern culture? How can non-postmodern elements, processes and meanings be incorporated into a general theory of contemporary culture?

These questions have been addressed and answered in various ways by cultural analysts. In this chapter we will look at the ways in which the concept of 'postmodernism' has evolved and contributed to our broader understanding of contemporary culture. Specifically, we will explore the ways in which the concept has evolved through the development and integration of American aesthetics, social analysis, French poststructuralism and British cultural studies. Of particular interest are the ways in which the concept has been broadened and now applies across a wide field of disciplinary categories: aesthetic, social-historical, cognitive (way of thinking) and cultural (way of representing).

Within the general field of cultural theory and cultural studies this broadening of the analytical spectrum of the postmodern may itself be understood in terms of three formative categories; each of these categories contains elements of social, aesthetic and theoretical commentary. Our discussion, therefore, will lead us later in the chapter toward a more thorough understanding of these three approaches to the study of postmodernism:

1   *Deconstructionist postmodernism*. This approach derives directly from post-structural theory (see Chapter 5), and is generally associated with Jean-François Lyotard's essay *The Postmodern Condition* (1984a). Lyotard accepts that there is an emerging cultural condition which is antithetical in many ways to the modern condition. He uses his deconstructionist methodology to 'destabilize' various aspects of modernist systems and linguistic structures, and opens the way for new ways of thinking and representation (the postmodern condition). This deconstructionist methodology provides a facility for the development of a postmodern politics, one which seeks constantly to destabilize the authority and

privilege of inherited discourses (e.g., Eurocentricism, sexism). In many ways the deconstructionist critique becomes an end in itself.

2 *Pessimistic postmodernism*. Theorists espousing this position, including Daniel Bell (1973, 1976), Fredric Jameson (1991) and Jean Baudrillard (1983a, 1984a, 1995), acknowledge the arrival of the new historical phase, but are highly pessimistic about its implications. While these analysts might have a substantially different theoretical heritage, they share a gloomy view of contemporary culture. Bell regrets the surrender of shared values in American society. Jameson believes that the proliferation of televisual images is producing a cultural condition he calls 'historical amnesia'. Baudrillard believes that the same qualities are producing a hyperreality in which there can be no referent, no truth and no direct or materially oriented human experience.

3 *Avant-garde and celebratory postmodernism*. This category derives from aspects of avant-garde aesthetics, popular cultural studies and deconstructionism. Authors like Charles Jencks (1987a, 1987b, 1995) and John Fiske (1989a, 1989b; Fiske and Glynn, 1995) seek and celebrate heterogeneity, multiculturalism, new forms of subjectivity and identity, and new political and aesthetic styles in terms of the celebrated postmodern against the denigrated, superseded modern. Many of the representational forms and discourses that are critiqued by the pessimistic postmodernists are welcomed by the celebrationists. A number of these utopian and celebrational discourses move from being theories of the postmodern to become postmodern theories: they celebrate and apply frameworks which privilege certain cognitive and ideological modes

(e.g., anti-logic, untruth, instability, pastiche, multiple irony).

This chapter examines the derivations of the concept of postmodernism; it then moves toward an analysis of these principal forms of cultural postmodernism.

LITERARY AND AESTHETIC POSTMODERNISM

Postmodernism and the New York Avant-Garde

There is general agreement that the term 'postmodernism' was introduced by Frederico de Onis in the 1930s to describe some marginal reaction against the ascendant aesthetics of modernism (see Hassan, 1985). During the 1960s a loose collective of writers, musicians and artists adapted the term as a means of distinguishing their own avant-garde and rejectionist style of art from what has been referred to as the high modernism of the mid-century and post-World War II period. In particular, New York aesthetes and commentators like Susan Sontag, Ihab Hassan, John Cage, William Burroughs and Leslie Fiedler rejected the codes and status of institutionalized artistic forms.

William Burroughs, for example, sought to reinvigorate language and everyday experience through the exterior of human experience, rather than through the profound and intellectual mimesis of James Joyce or William Faulkner. Like Jack Kerouac and the Beat poets, Burroughs' language is experiential, liberated from the constraints of grammar and form. This paragraph from *Exterminator* represents the sort of muted and everyday epiphany that underscores the postmodern style proclaimed in Burroughs' writing:

You couldn't say exactly when it hit familiar and dreary as a cigarette butt ground out in cold scrambled eggs the toothpaste smears on a washstand glass why you were on the cops day like another just feeling a little worse than usual which is not unusual at all well an ugly thing broke out that day in the precinct this rookie cop had worked a drunk over and the young cop had a mad look in his eyes and he kept screaming. (1966: 162)

This sort of everyday apocalypse has often been associated with forms of popular pleasure and hedonism. Burroughs' engagement with street life and with the language of street talk brings high literature into contiguity with popular cinema. This is the surface texture of language rather than the profound inner expressionisms of the individual as it had been explored by William Faulkner and other modernists. Burroughs' postmodernism is an excursion which directly challenges the borders between language and image, vision and collapse, high art and popular discourse.

Susan Sontag (1966) seems to parallel the rising interest in popular culture in Britain in her repudiation of academic textual studies which emphasize elite artistic forms and the activity of 'interpretation'. She rails against the exclusion of popular art forms such as photography and film from the academic canon. The reinvigoration of culture and cultural activities, she argues, is only possible through the radical reformulation of what it is that constitutes art and legitimate artistic expression. Interpretation serves merely to gratify the interests of academic institutions and the interests of a bourgeois cognoscenti. In particular, Sontag rejects the processes of canonization by which the avant-gardism of modernist texts – the literature of Joyce, T.S. Eliot and William Faulkner – becomes stabilized by bourgeois academic discourses and institutions. What might have been a

radical transgression of artistic and cultural standards becomes stifled by institutional acceptance. 'Interpretation' is the act of normalizing texts; the radical elements of a text are transformed by forming them as palatable and recognizable tropes for consumption in schools and universities.

In *The Dismemberment of Orpheus: Towards a Postmodern Literature* (1982), Ihab Hassan attempts to explain the emergence of a literature which explicates, as it questions, its own literary and narrative techniques. This meta-fiction (see also Hutcheon, 1995) reworks a number of self-reflexive strategies that had been present in earlier literary forms, including Shakespearian and Jacobean dramas, and the eccentric tale-telling of Laurence Sterne (*Tristram Shandy*) and Henry Fielding (*Joseph Andrews* and *Tom Jones*). For Hassan, the most significant literature of the twentieth century reaches beyond the nihilism of high modernism; postmodernism is formed around a 'literature of silence' which succumbs to an Orphean dismemberment, but which nevertheless 'sings on a lyre without strings' (Hassan, 1982: xvii). Orpheus is the Greek poet/ musician who is slain and dismembered by the Maenads because they were jealous of his attention to young men. Orpheus and the dismembered head are cast into the river Hebrus, where the dead poet continues to sing and defy his death. For Hassan, the poetics of postmodernism defies the logical conclusions of modernism (i.e. that all is death, that God is absent, that the universe makes no sense). The voices go on, despite the implications of despair which a nihilistic modernism brings to cultural knowledge.

Hassan, however, is not speaking so much about a rupture or jettison of modernist sensibilities as about an intensification of modernism's absurdist heroics. Postmodernism, that is, is somehow coiled

Table 7.1   *Modern and Postmodern Literature*

Modernism	Postmodernism
Romanticism/symbolism	Pataphysics/Dadaism
Form	Antiform
Purpose	Play
Design	Chance
Hierarchy	Anarchy
Mastery/*logos*	Exhaustion/silence
Art object	Creative process
Synthesis	Antithesis
Preference	Absence
Centring	Dispersed
Root/depth	Rhyzome/surface
Origin/cause	Difference
Metaphysics	Irony
Determinacy	Indeterminacy

Source: Hassan, 1987: 267–8

into the imperatives of modernism, whereby the absurdism and alienation explored in the literature of William Burroughs represents another resonant tune, another silence, in the sexualized heroics of alienation. Madness, sexual ecstasy, the unstitching of form, the uneasy slippages of tragedy and comedy – all represent the extremes of modernism through the incarnation of postmodernism. In the 1982 edition of the book Hassan adds a 'Postface' which attempts to delineate the differences between the modern and the postmodern. Table 7.1 presents a summary of his distinctions.

Literary Postmodernism and Popular Culture

Significantly, Hassan's account of literary postmodernism relies on a rather separatist view of the expressive power of literature. Indeed, despite their attempts to integrate various literary genres, including the popular genre of mystery and detective novels,

into the lexicon of the postmodern, the aesthetic commentaries of the 1960s and early 1970s fixed their vision on avant-garde arts rather than on the mass-produced texts of popular culture. Popular culture was treated as a resource which the avant-garde could use for the construction of its own texts. Andy Warhol's texts, for example, mimicked popular iconography in the same way Burroughs' language imitated the openness of everyday street talk. This artistic 'egalitarianism' became a favoured trope for avant-garde postmodernism. Literary analysts like Ihab Hassan and Brian McHale, in fact, maintain an adherence to the Romantic idea that literature possesses a unique capacity for the articulation of culture beyond the confines of space and time. Brian McHale (1987), for example, sees the modernist literature of James Joyce, William Faulkner or even Franz Kafka as being fundamentally epistemological: the way human consciousness knows, understands or interprets the world. Postmodernism is more interested in what McHale calls an ontological (essential) rendering or construction of the world. That is, while McHale accepts that modernism is interested in the structures and processes involved in literary form, this interest is driven by a continuing desire to know the world from which the individual has become alienated. Postmodernism releases the world to the 'possibilities of impossibilities'; the individual capitulates to his or her alienation and explores the processes of construction and the multiplicity of form, rather than his or her own alienated state of mind. Postmodernism, therefore, is a building and working of textual styles – a 'carnivalesque' of styles, registers and possibilities which may be marked by joy as much as by terror. These cacophonies and heterologies nevertheless remain fixed in the stable progress of an organic literary history, a history which remains accessible to genealogy and comprehension. Thus, novels like Joseph Heller's *Catch-22*, Ralph Ellison's *Invisible Man* or Thomas Pynchon's *Gravity's Rainbow* should not be read as a protest against alienation so much as a recognition of absurd social and human conditions, and an attempt to endure them.

More recent commentators, such as Umberto Eco (1984), Linda Hutcheon (1988) and Jim Collins (1989), have extended McHale's definitions, insisting that postmodernism, in fact, deconstructs the boundaries that contain literary interaction. In particular, the boundaries between literature and other forms of discourse, including 'popular culture', are dissolved in favour of a more embracing and inclusive reading of media and mediation processes. While these analysts begin with an interest in literature and derive their analytical reference from the traditions of literary analysis, their work reflects a broader interest in the theories of structuralism and poststructuralism. Hutcheon, for example, diverges from the work of Hassan and McHale by suggesting, as with Roland Barthes, that the interplay of textual discourse is not an intensification of reality through the greater reality of human consciousness; literature is neither the 'mirror' of reality, nor a 'refraction' which exposes the deeper realities of life. Rather, Hutcheon's postmodernism refers to the interplay of continuous textualities in the world. There is no void separating text and reality since they are all part of the same discursive and mediatory processing. Everything is discourse and there is no special place for literature.

Hutcheon also deviates from earlier versions of postmodern aesthetics by raising directly the issue of power. However, he repudiates conventional notions of structured power and subversion, preferring a more Foucauldian and Barthesian description of unstable power relationships functioning always at the level of the personal and through discourse. Similarly, Jim Collins celebrates these more fragmentary and elusive 'discursive ideologies', arguing that their expression in literary and other popular forms have required a paradigm shift in the way cultural production should be analysed and understood: arguing against the homogenizing effects of neo-Marxist 'mass culture' theory, Collins celebrates the heterogeneous potentials of new modes of postmodern textualities which constitute an open culture, a culture of options and multiplicities:

The significance of the emerging school of cultural analysis comes from its recognition that all cultural production must be seen as a set of power relations that produce particular forms of subjectivity, but that the nature, function, and uses of mass culture can no longer be conceived in a monolithic manner. (1989: 16)

Postmodern Media Texts

There are many different ideas about what constitutes a postmodern media text. Some observers argue that films like Francis Ford Coppola's *Apocalypse Now* mark a significant move from a modern to a postmodern aesthetic style. The nihilism of modernism is replaced by uncertainty, a 'singing silence' as Ihab Hassan calls it. In Coppola's film there is a dualism or tension between, first, the possibilities of the complete vision ('the horror') as it was articulated in Joseph Conrad's novel *Heart of Darkness,* around which the film is based; and, secondly, an apocalyptic hedonism which is never complete but which becomes part of a spurious and absurd game of images and incompatible ideals. The 'smell of napalm in the morning', the pointless journey, the battle-ground surfing – all are part of the uneasy pleasure/terror of warfare and imperialism, and their atavistic aspirations.

Other commentators have seen the combination of textual elements in David Lynch's film *Blue Velvet* and TV series *Twin Peaks* as fundamentally post-modern. The emphasis here is less on the thematic content of the text and more on its formal organization of elements. These texts, and many others of the 1980s and 1990s, combine allusions to, and elements of, other texts and textual styles. This bricolage or pastiche formation seeks to create a sense of textual and cultural inclusiveness. Generally, the texts dissolve the distinction between high and popular art, creating new ways of 'being popular' and speaking through the everyday discourses of everyday audiences.

The appellation 'postmodern' has also been applied to 'cult' films like *Clerks,* which has been sometimes called a popular grunge movie: a transgressive text designed to destabilize institutional filmic and cultural norms. *Clerks* tells of the relationship and vocational problems of a young college dropout who now works in a convenience store and is caught between the loves of two women. The multiple ironies, crudity and basic carnality of the film betray a deep sense of loss and hopelessness. The dissolution of institutions and prescriptive relational forms creates new freedoms, subjectivities and terrains of pleasure. However, these pleasures are tinged with the persistent threat of loss and meaninglessness. This film is postmodern because it reflects faithfully the everyday experiences of everyday members of the postmodern tribe.

Postmodernist expressive forms – in Collins' terms, everything from literature, architecture and film to pornography – construct 'a vision of cultural production that is decentered without being anarchic, heterogeneous without being "democratic"' (1989: 26). Collins' version of postmodernism sifts various aspects of poststructuralist theory to produce a political postmodernism which rejects the centring and homogenizing impulses of modernist democracy. Postmodern cultural production

222

is always 'political' in that texts, Lacan (1977) explains, actively 'position' individuals in relation to one another. That is, the text and the reader/viewer interact in order to form meanings; these meanings are only possible because the reader/viewer shifts (positions) his or her perspective, identity and subjectivity in relation to the text.

Collins' work emerges out of that line of postmodernist aesthetics which challenges elite, bourgeois distinctions between high and popular art. As we noted, such precepts underscore the aesthetics and critical commentary of the 1960s American avant-garde. Andreas Huyssen has suggested, in fact, that the 'great divide' that separates high and popular art is mediated, if not dissolved, by the emergence of 'postmodernism'. For Huyssen, the postmodernism of the 1970s replaces an exhausted avant-garde aesthetics:

> By the 1970s that avantgardist postmodernism of the 1960s had in turn exhausted its potential, even though some of its manifestations continued well into the new decade. What was new in the 1970s was, on the one hand, the emergence of a culture of eclecticism, a largely affirmative postmodernism which had abandoned any claim to critique, transgression or negation; and, on the other hand, an alternative postmodernism in which resistance, critique and negation of the status quo were redefined in non-modernist and non-avantgardist terms, terms which match the political developments in contemporary culture more effectively than the older theories of modernism. (1986: 188)

This split which emerges in American postmodernism mirrors a similar division in British cultural studies between those who sought to extend poststructuralist analysis into forms of audience and youth culture studies, and those who wanted to pursue a more politically oriented neo-Gramscian approach to cultural politics.

For Huyssen, the political or critical postmodernism is most evident in the writings of women and minority groups, those who have done most to recover 'buried and mutilated traditions' (1986: 198).

Huyssen, nevertheless, rejects the idea that poststructuralism constitutes the critical or theoretical parallel of aesthetic postmodernism, most especially as the French theories have been adapted in the United States. His questioning of the poststructuralist contribution to critical thinking in the US, however, neglects seriously the catalysing effects of writers such as Lyotard, Deleuze and Guattari and Foucault. Indeed, since the early 1980s there has been a continuing integration, hybridization and multiplication of the various discourses of British cultural studies, French poststructuralism and American postmodernism such that the three fields of enquiry have at times become almost indistinguishable. In attempting to account for contemporary culture and what Lyotard (1984a) calls the 'postmodern condition', recent analysis has virtually dispensed with substantive lineages or disciplinary borders. The common interest in heterologies, sexualization, multiple discourses, multiculturalism, new political modalities and liberated subjectivities has drawn postmodernism into the widest possible arraign of applications.

Huyssen's attempt to quarantine American postmodernism from French poststructuralism has proven to be quite unsustainable. Indeed, one of the earliest proponents of British cultural studies, Dick Hebdige, notes that it is becoming more difficult 'to specify exactly what it is that "postmodernism" is supposed to refer to as the term gets stretched in all directions across different debates, different disciplinary and discursive boundaries, as different factions seek to make it their own'

(1988: 181). The American avant-gardist and aesthetic postmodernism with elements of French poststructuralism informs many of these disputes, most particularly as postmodernism extends to social and cultural theory.

DANIEL BELL: THE COMING OF POST-INDUSTRIAL SOCIETY

Daniel Bell's place in the canon of postmodernism is somewhat problematic. His sociological perspective is concerned with changes to the social structure, economy and 'occupational system' that America was undergoing during the post-war period. In both *The Coming of Post-Industrial Society* (1973) and *The Cultural Contradictions of Capitalism* (1976) he explains these changes in terms of fundamental reworkings of the relationship between science and technology, and what he sees as the increasing separation of economy, polity and culture. He is critical of the presciences and technological determinism of other social commentators like Alain Touraine (1971), who claimed that the new social patterns would be increasingly 'programmed' by the predominance of technocrats and their post-industrial technologies. Bell's predictions for the ensuing forty to fifty years argued that abstract thinking of pure science and scientific research would dominate the practical activities of technology. Post-industrial society would be different from the technocratic determinisms of industrial society, most especially as the abstract and objective knowledge of science began to infiltrate all levels of society.

There can be little doubt that Bell's understanding of theory and knowledge is both optimistic and naive. Nevertheless, his conception of a post-industrial society built around the ascendancy of (abstract) science over (practical) technology acknowledges significant changes to the mechanisms of capitalist economy; in particular, he recognizes that heavy industry was being gradually replaced by a wide range of service industries, including entertainment and information services. Bell retains a level of critique in his reading of contemporary society, arguing that many of the features and failings of industrialism persist into the new post-industrial conditions. However, unlike Marxist or Romantic/humanist critiques, his major criticisms of the new society derive from his Christian Protestantism and a belief that the social nexus of the American community was being profoundly disturbed by the new social forces. That is, the increasing separation of economy, government and culture is clearly the result of a flagging Protestant ethic and an alienating intelligentsia. Capitalist modernization processes, such as the availability of instant credit and the hedonism and self-interest it produces, can largely be blamed for the disintegrations of modern society.

Postmodernism, therefore, is the result of this assault on modernism, a permutation of previous trends rather than a radical or subversive break. Postmodernism, for Bell, represents this widening gap between the failings of technocratic instrumentality, on the one hand, and the emergence of a narcissistic and nihilistic literati, on the other. Bell bemoans the dissolution of the integrated whole, the single value system which maintains 'culture', character, structure and economy. Ironically, the hedonism inscribed in the promises of mass production and mass consumption produced a capitalist system which continues to feed on itself and its own fabric: 'The Protestant ethic had served to limit sumptuary (though not capital) accumulation. When the Protestant ethic was sundered from bourgeois society, only, the hedonism remained and the capitalist system lost its transcendental ethic' (Bell, 1976: 21). So for Bell the over-riding problem with modernism is one of spiritual crisis; postmodernism is merely the degenerative outcome of a disintegrating cultural sphere, a separationism which decries the founding unity of American Protestantism and capitalist democracy.

JEAN-FRANÇOIS LYOTARD

The Modern and the Postmodern in Lyotard's Writing

Daniel Bell's criticism of avant-garde postmodernism, with its emphasis on popular art and everyday consumption practices, parallels his broader concerns about the fragmentation of American society. While Bell himself doesn't directly identify the postmodern aesthetic with the condition of a postmodern culture or postmodern society, other commentators certainly do. Jean-François Lyotard, for example, shares Bell's suspicion of contemporary divisions between 'the technical intelligentsia who are committed to functional rationality … [and the] literary intellectuals who have become increasingly apocalyptic, hedonistic and nihilistic' (Lyotard, 1984a: 46). Like Bell, he is seeking an explanation for the current state of knowledge which engages with the tensions, continuities and discontinuities of an evolving historical epoch. Lyotard, however, defines these historical and social transformations in terms of what he calls the 'cultural condition'. For him, this general assemblage of elements – economic, political, intellectual, cognitive, artistic, industrial – marks a change from a modern to a postmodern condition. By comparison, Bell's historicism concentrates primarily on the mode of economy and the move from an industrial, technocratic society to a post-industrial society in which abstract scientific thinking is ascendant.

In fact, Lyotard never entirely resolves the relationship between modernism and postmodernism, as either an historical or a cognitive dialogue. As noted at the beginning of this chapter, Lyotard doesn't distinguish between postmodernism (cognitive system or way of thinking) and postmodernity (historical and cultural elements which define an epoch). For him the way of thinking about a culture and the various economic, social, political and discursive elements that comprise it are integrally, if not absolutely, linked. The modern and the postmodern, therefore, represent an interplay ('language games') of elements and discourses, with each cognitive system informing, as much as challenging, the other. For Lyotard, the modern and the postmodern are a mixture of historical and cognitive (knowledge-based) modes of reference; postmodernism is a 'gestant' form of modernism, a mutually dependent permutation. Much of the confusion surrounding Lyotard's work assumes that he is advocating the replacement of the modern by the postmodern, and that the two 'conditions' can be clearly marked in terms of rupture and separation. As we shall see, this is not generally the case, and in fact his engagement with the postmodern is rather ambivalent, reflecting a genuine desire for liberation without the complete surrender of modern modes of social or aesthetic critique.

Ihab Hassan (1987) argues that Lyotard was influenced by American avant-garde postmodernism, and that his extension of the term for social and historical criticism confuses the term by restoring it to a modernist framework. According to Hassan, Lyotard's use of the concept of postmodernism to describe the state of contemporary 'knowledge' is not a radical challenge to bourgeois aesthetic (and social) values.

Rather, Lyotard's criticism of modernism and modernity is framed in terms of modernism itself, its own principles and ways of thinking. Lyotard is not able to escape the modernist mode of thinking, Hassan argues, and merely corrupts the concept of 'postmodernism' by applying it as a general description of history and culture. Hassan, as we have noted above, prefers to restrict the concept to an aesthetic or cognitive category, rather than one which embraces all culture.

Gillian Rose (1988) claims something similar in her discussion of Lyotard's adaptation of the term from a style of art and architecture to a tool for social enquiry. According to Rose, the transmission of the term from literary and aesthetic criticism to social and philosophical analysis removes a good deal of its potency and precision. Lyotard himself, in fact, has elaborated his position on the relationship between aesthetics, philosophy and postmodernism, noting that postmodernism is 'undoubtedly part of the modern' (Lyotard, 1984b: 79). Equally, '[m]odernity is constitutionally and ceaselessly pregnant with its post-modernity' (Lyotard, 1991: 25). Thus, while most commentators read Lyotard's *The Postmodern Condition* (1984a) as a celebration of the arrival of the postmodern, across the breadth of his work there is a much clearer recognition of the interdependence of the modern and the postmodern. To a degree, Lyotard's own elaborations might seem to support Andreas Huyssen's claim that 'deconstructionist' or 'poststructuralist' postmodernism remains somewhat fixed in the parameters of modernist critiques of itself (Huyssen, 1986: 208–16); Huyssen, and others, however, fail to appreciate the efficacy of Lyotard's perspective for cultural and political analysis, most especially as it attempts to reach beyond the flagging limits of Huyssen's own literary postmodernism.

The Postmodern Condition

In fact, Lyotard's *The Postmodern Condition*, along with his contiguous essay, 'Answering the question: what is postmodernism?' (1984b), seeks to illuminate the present 'condition of knowledge in the most highly developed societies' (Lyotard, 1984a: xxiii). This condition of knowledge, culture and history is characterized in terms of transformation and 'crisis'. The source of this transformation is the fracturing of discourses and systems of knowledge that had informed the progress and ideology of what Lyotard defines as 'the modern'. While directing attention toward this dismantling of systems of knowing in literature, religion, Marxist politics and the arts, Lyotard is most concerned to demonstrate the dislocating effects of postmodernism on the truth claims of science. Modernist science, Lyotard explains, is constructed around a form of self-legitimizing narrative (metanarrative) which confirms its own validity through the imposition of its own self-justifying and self-reflecting standards of knowledge. Modern science, that is, proclaims its own value in its own terms; its truth is therefore a grand truth, a universal truth, which underscores the methods and belief system of the whole modernist culture. Thus, as with other commentaries on postmodernism, the definition of the postmodern is fundamentally embedded in the definition of the modern.

Lyotard's interrogation of modernist metanarratives clearly draws on his own disappointment with the imaginary potential of modernist discourses, especially in reformist politics and avant-garde aesthetics. Indeed, his discourse wavers between a description of social and cultural processes, and a form of cultural advocacy. In *The Postmodern Condition* he describes his methodology in terms of Wittgenstein's 'language games' (see Chapter 5): a remodelled analysis of discourse and the processes of meaning-making. Lyotard claims that his analysis of these language games provides a means of elucidating and deconstructing modernist metanarratives. This poststructuralist technique is designed to expose and ultimately dissolve the assumptions which support the 'truth' claims of modernism's grand explanations and theories: for example, Marxism, capitalism, and Enlightenment science. For Lyotard, however, these language games are like Stuart Hall's notion of 'the struggle to signify' (see Chapter 4): the games are formed around adversarial conditions by which one discourse will impose itself over another. In particular, Lyotard emphasizes the agonistic dimensions of language games; rules are produced by players in order that they may 'play' or 'fight', and thus engage in speech acts: 'Great joy is had in the endless invention of turns of phrase … [b]ut undoubtedly even this feeling depends on a feeling of success won at the expense of an adversary, and a formidable one: the accepted language, or connotation' (1984a: 10). Lyotard's method, in fact, establishes a tension between, first, the language 'agonisms', their productive pleasures and inclination to heterogeneous meaning-making (culture and imagination); and, secondly, those broader language 'moves' which produce conformity, homogeneity and metanarratives.

Lyotard clearly sees the new, post-industrial societies as facilitating new modes of heterogeneous language games. However,

the persistence of modern predispositions in science and technology threatens to refurbish 'systems' of knowledge and discourse which are fundamentally oppressive and self-legitimating. Lyotard's description turns again to advocacy as he seeks the invigoration of human imagination and the deconstruction of these knowledge systems:

> [F]unctions of regulation, and therefore reproduction, have been and will be further withdrawn from administrators and entrusted to machines. Increasingly, the central question is becoming who has access to the information these machines must have in storage to guarantee that the right decisions are made. Access to data is, and will continue to be, the prerogative of experts of all shapes. The ruling class is and will continue to be the class of decision makers. (1984a: 14)

Lyotard's political or ideological intent, therefore, is inscribed with this deep suspicion of systems of control – the discourses that constitute a privileged social status. However, while his advocacy creates a political space for deconstruction, this politics is construed in terms of thought and aesthetics, rather than direct action. Lyotard's alternative political discourse provides later postmodernists with a facility for further political exploration, although Lyotard himself rarely ventures beyond the realm of modernist political engagement: that is, he applies a modernist mode of deconstruction to expose the deficiencies of modernism.

Quantum Mechanics and Postmodern Science

A number of commentators, including Jean-François Lyotard and Charles Jencks, have argued that the new physical sciences are exposing the deeper dimensions and true character of 'nature'. Enlightenment science, borrowing from classical Greek mathematics, had believed that the universe functioned according to relatively straightforward laws of causality in three-dimensional space: the universe operated like a machine. The scientist's task was to uncover, define and prove these laws by the processes of objective observation. Albert Einstein's general theory of relativity, which identified time as the fourth dimension of space, required science to re-conceptualize the universe; however, scientific method remained largely unchanged.

The study of sub-atomic particles or 'quanta', however, has created significant problems for traditional scientific methods of observation. Quanta are the smallest particles of matter and hence constitute the fundamental building blocks of the universe. These particles, however, do not behave in ways that are familiar to naked-eye observation. Specifically, quanta may behave like a 'wave' sometimes, and like particles of matter at other times. That is, they may behave with quite incompatible properties and propensities. This incompatibility, however, is never simultaneous. Contradicting standard scientific procedure, these contradictory aspects of quanta will be observed in exactly the same experiment, but never at the same time. In fact, the act of observation appears to change the behaviour of quanta, raising critical questions about the value and validity of 'objective' observation itself.

For Lyotard and others, quantum physics can be understood as a postmodern science which fundamentally dissolves traditionally formed systems of knowledge. Postmodern physics, that is, opens the way to the imagination and the creative dimensions of knowledge. The metanarratives of Enlightenment (modern) science are shown to be based on false assumptions. Science is just another discourse, just another language game. Quantum mechanics provides material evidence of those games since, like language, it draws together the practical and technological facilities necessary for human survival with the ultimate mysteries of nature and the universe. As Paul Davies has explained, quantum theory integrates the broadest dimensions of human knowledge from Zen Buddhism to technologies such as the laser, the electron microscope, the transistor and the semiconductor (Davies, 1983: 100). For postmodernism, his integration and reconfiguration of various levels of reality confirms the underlying diversity of the universe and its delicate mediation of complexity and chaos (Jencks, 1995).

Lyotard's reading of contemporary physics – quantum, atomic and fractal theory – functions as both metaphor and panegyric for the dismantling of controlled systems. The new physics, Lyotard explains, disengages nature from modern scientific explanations. According to him, the relation between the scientist's statement and what nature says seems to be organized as a game without perfect information. But science itself needs to be foregrounded as a body of knowledge which legitimates itself as a primary discourse.

When we examine the current status of scientific knowledge – at a time when science seems more completely subordinated to the prevailing powers than ever before and, along with the new technologies, is in danger of becoming a major stake in their conflicts – the question of double legitimation, far from receding into the background, necessarily comes to the fore. For it appears in its most complete form, that of reversion, revealing that knowledge and power are simply two sides of the same question: Who decides what knowledge is? Who knows what needs to be decided? In the computer age the question is now more than ever a question of government (Lyotard, 1984a: 8–9).

The control of knowledge, indeed the very definition of what constitutes knowledge, is central to Lyotard's account. In particular, Lyotard appears to rejoice in the social and cultural potential of the new science, which can no longer 'measure' accurately. Lyotard demonstrates this point by referring to Jorge Luis Borges' story of the emperor who seeks to map exactly the dimensions of his entire empire. The only truly and absolutely accurate map of the empire turns out to be an exact replica in full dimension; the construction of the simulacra ultimately bankrupts the empire. Modern science is caught in precisely the same dilemma; modern science seeks to produce absolute knowledge, even though such knowledge is impossible. A fundamental contradiction necessarily subverts the entire enterprise of modernism and its discourses:

> This inconsistency explains the weakness in state and socioeconomic bureaucracies: they stifle the systems or subsystems they control and asphyxiate themselves in the process (negative feedback). ... Even if we accept that society is a system, complete control over it, which would necessitate an exact definition of its initial state, is impossible because no such definition could ever be effected. (Lyotard, 1984a: 55–6)

For Lyotard, the contradictions that beset the modern reveal themselves as opportunities

within postmodern discourse. There can be no simple disengagement. The postmodern condition reflects the dialogue taking place through these transitions.

'What is Postmodernism?'

Thus, Lyotard's suspicion of systems might seem to place his discourse clearly in the realm of postmodernism, though his suspicion of computers and the inevitable agglomeration of information 'bits' (see also Lyotard, 1991: esp. Ch. 2) distances him from other areas of postmodern utopianism (see Lewis, 1997a, 1998). Moreover, his interest in 'undecidables' in postmodern science propels him toward broader discussions of agonism in language games, those 'differends' or differences in perspective that defy mediation or resolution. Lyotard himself appears to be engaged with the *differend* of modernism and postmodernism, seeking a mediation which gives voice to the new modes of heterogeneity and the subversion of systems without the complete surrender of the modernist capacity for experimentation, reform and what he calls the sublime. In 'Answering the question: what is postmodernism?' (1984b) he explicates these problems through his criticism both of a consensual language system, proposed by Jürgen Habermas, and a postmodernism which fails fully to embrace the potentials of imagination, including experimentation. The postmodern aesthetic, Lyotard fears, threatens to do away with avant-garde experimentalism, which constituted the 'alternative' discourse within modernism: that is, which provided an escape from the more oppressive, authoritarian and systematizing inclinations of the modern.

Lyotard had already dismissed the philosophy of 'anything goes' (1984a: 76), but in the later essay he is quite specific in his repudiation of postmodern architecture which fails, in his view, to pursue the potentialities of an architectural avant-garde. At its most exhilarating, therefore, postmodernism is that part of modernism which is perpetually 'nascent'; not the conclusion of modernism, but its re-generator, its precipitant. This somewhat contradictory view of the relationship between the postmodern and the modern is expressed in Lyotard's account of the sublime:

> If it is true that modernity takes place in the withdrawal of the real and according to the sublime relation between the presentable and the conceivable, it is possible, within this relation, to distinguish two modes. ... The emphasis can be placed on the powerlessness of the faculty presentation, on the nostalgia for presence felt by the human subject, on the obscure and futile will which inhabits him in spite of everything. The emphasis can be placed, rather, on the power of the faculty to conceive, on its 'inhumanity' so to speak ... since it is not the business of our understanding whether or not human sensibility or imagination can match what it conceives. (1984b: 79–80)

Lyotard is suggesting that the modern evolves as a gap between what an individual can conceive or think about, and what can actually be presented as discourse. The art and literature of modernism represent this problem as a withdrawal from what might be regarded as 'realistic'. Picasso's paintings, T.S. Eliot's poetry and James Joyce's novels all are examples of how 'the real' is replaced by this gap. The despair or 'nihilism' (sense that there is no meaning in life) that is evident in much modernist aesthetics expresses this feeling of loss, the feeling that the real is no longer present. Lyotard claims, however, that there is another side to this withdrawal of the real. This 'second emphasis' is more optimistic since it allows us to reflect on this

withdrawal, this inhumanity. This is the point of the avant-garde.

When considered in terms of aesthetics, this definition allows modernism to be nostalgic for the thing it no longer can present, but only conceive. The art and literature of modernism are fundamentally fixed in the 'solace and pleasure' of form: that is, of the shape and structure of an artwork. Paradoxically, however, this solace and pleasure are also evident in the pain modernists experience as they realize that the form of an artwork has been depleted of content and meaning. A postmodern aesthetics, according to Lyotard, confronts the same modernist problematic though without the solace of good form and 'the consensus of a taste which would make it possible to share collectively the nostalgia for the unattainable' (1984b: 81). Postmodernism, according to Lyotard, finds itself with a stronger sense of the unpresentable since there can be no pre-established rules which might govern form or the artistic act itself. Rather, the rules are to be reinvented, or at least invented after the fact of the artwork existing. In other words, the work of art or literature comes into being as if it were an event, and as if there were no possibility for content or form. The rules are invented after the work appears and must be conceived *post facto*; the work of art's 'realization' (*mise en oeuvre*) always begins too soon. Postmodern has to be understood according to the paradox of the future (*post*) anterior (*modo*).

FREDRIC JAMESON

Lyotard's deconstructionist postmodernism has influenced many recent commentators, most especially those who have sought to expound a theory of general cultural evolution. The deconstructionist method, however, has been appended to quite varying appraisals of postmodern culture, some of which are highly pessimistic and critical, others of which are more welcoming and celebratory. Of this former group, Fredric Jameson and Jean Baudrillard, in particular, have treated the emergence a televisual, postmodern culture with deep suspicion. Both Jameson and Baudrillard form their critique of consumerism and televisual culture through a substantive and complex interweaving of structuralist and poststructuralist theoretics. In the end, however, the critique is pessimistic, offering very little relief or alternative to the ubiquity of the postmodern move.

The Political Unconscious

Like the British cultural theorists, Fredric Jameson adapted Louis Althusser's notion of dominant ideology in order to elucidate the underlying political and ideological patterns of cultural texts. In *The Political Unconscious* (1981), Jameson articulates for American readers many of the theoretical and critical arguments that had been well established in French semiology and British cultural studies. He seeks to revive American literary criticism by drawing it out of solipsism and bourgeois relativism. In particular, he regards the critical paradigm of New Criticism, which treats texts as entirely unique and organic utterances, as both atavistic and ideologically humanist. That is, he argues, criticism which refuses to acknowledge and analyse the social and ideological patterns which inform all literary texts necessarily endorses a reactionary and conservative political position. Jameson's own analysis welds Althusserian dialectical criticism with Lacanian/Freudian psychoanalysis in order to elucidate these patterns. According

to Jameson, ideologies are forms of containment which society uses to explain and reconcile 'History'. History itself functions as a form of self-validating repression. Literary texts offer solutions which are merely symptoms of the suppression of History.

Following Althusser, Jameson notes that the task of interpretation is to unmask the ideologies which function to create an illusion of textual unity:

> [T]he appropriate object of study emerges only when the appearance of formal unification is unmasked as a failure or an ideological mirage. The authentic function of the cultural text is then staged rather as an interference between levels, as a subversion of one level by another. ... The aim of a properly structured interpretation or exegesis thus becomes the explosion of the seemingly unified text into a host of clashing and contradictory elements. (Jameson, 1981: 56)

In other words, the text gives the appearance of unification; the task of the literary critic is to unravel the illusion to expose the competing elements and ideologies.

The distinguishing feature of *The Political Unconscious* is its combination of reformist politics (neo-Marxism) with structuralist and even poststructuralist analytical themes. In fact, Jameson acknowledges the powerful imperatives of contemporary culture and the problems of fragmentation and alienation. He attempts to absorb aspects of Deleuze and Guattari's *Anti-Oedipus*, which accepts the fragmentary nature of human existence but which refuses to countenance any form of reunification, including the act of interpretation. Jameson, however, while accepting the validity of this position, declares that all utterance, including interpretation, implicates a form of organizing and transcendent reunification: a restoration of text into a secondary shape of narrative or story-telling.

The critic's task, therefore, is to accept this restorative impulse, and to use ideological concepts and strategies in order to overcome (conservative/dominant) ideology. Althusserian criticism, adapted by Jameson, provides the vehicle for reconciling problematics of unity and fragmentation.

> I have found it possible without any great inconsistency to respect both the methodological imperative implicit in the concept of totality or totalization, and the quite different intention of a 'symptomal' analysis to discontinuities, rifts, actions at distance, within a merely apparently unified cultural text. (Jameson, 1981: 57)

Postmodernism and the Logics of Late Capitalism

As with the British literary critic Terry Eagleton, Jameson's efforts to reconcile the problematic of fragmentation and unity have drawn him to broader considerations of contemporary culture. In his essay 'Postmodernism and consumer culture' (1983), subsequently revised as 'Postmodernism, or the cultural logic of late capitalism' (1984), Jameson theorizes postmodernism in terms of an Althusserian model. Postmodernism is thus conceived as social fragmentation, a new historical phase in which the dominant ideology or 'cultural logic' is characterized by what Ernest Mandel calls late or multinational capitalism. This third-phase capitalism, following market and then monopoly capitalism, 'constitutes ... the purest form of capital into hitherto uncommodified areas' (Jameson, 1984: 78). As with Pierre Bourdieu's analysis of contemporary French culture, Jameson recognizes that this new capitalism is built upon 'symbolic exchange-value'. That is, once capitalism has satisfied basic needs (food, clothing, shelter), it must necessarily seek new phenomena to sell. Products and services, therefore, have a new value attached to them, a 'symbolic' value whereby the culture discriminates value according to status, fashion, prestige, and so on. For example, a pair of sunglasses bought from the Two Dollar Shop will perform the same function, but attract less value, than the 'name-brand' equivalent (Oakley, Arnette, Polaroid). In postmodern culture this symbolic value is produced through the 'ephemera' of televisual imagery and 'information' processes. In a sense, the symbol (name-brand, image-endorsing celebrity, etc.) becomes the commodity. These highly valued 'ephemera' underscore the fragmentation of a culture, which is being produced through increasingly large and globally oriented corporations.

Culture, therefore, is inescapably embedded in the processes of capital. For Jameson, the cultural dominant is fundamentally expressed through this proliferation of symbolic products and images. Not surprisingly, contemporary artists and writers have sought to articulate this new expressive verbiage, the popular symbols and texts which proliferate in postmodern culture:

> The postmodernisms have been fascinated precisely by this whole 'degraded' landscape of schlock and kitsch, of TV series and Readers' Digest culture, of advertising and motels, of the late show and the grade-B Hollywood film, of so-called paraliterature with its airport paperback categories of the gothic and the romance, the popular biography, the murder mystery, and science fiction or fantasy: materials they no longer 'quote' as a Joyce or a Mahler might have done, but incorporate into their very substance. (Jameson, 1984: 55)

Jameson thus acknowledges the power and ubiquity of new cultural forms and modes of expression. However, unlike postmodernists such as Charles Jencks, he maintains a level of distance and critique, arguing, for example, that postmodern architecture is merely an outward expression of modernist capitalism. Jameson's critique, therefore, is constructed, a little like Lyotard's, around a sense that certain elements in the new (postmodern) culture are politically, socially or even aesthetically bereft. Thus, the postmodern culture, as the embedded expression and logic of third-phase capitalism, is more than a mere style and more than the individual elements that constitute modes of popular expression. For Jameson, postmodernism is a 'periodizing concept'

> whose ultimate function is to correlate the emergence of new formal features in culture with the emergence of a new type of social life and a new economic order – what is often euphemistically called modernization, postindustrial or consumer society, the society of the media or the spectacle, or multinational capitalism. (Jameson, 1983: 113)

This cultural dominant is of course both implicitly and explicitly political. Even so, this new social order can't exclude alternative elements, oppositions and the cultural legacy of previous social constituencies; in keeping with Althusser and Raymond Williams, Jameson's theory of postmodernism provides space for contradictions and countervailing movements:

> The 1960s are in many ways the key transitional period, the period in which the new international order (neocolonialism, the Green Revolution, computerization and electronic information) is at one and the same time set in place and is swept and shaken by its own internal contradictions and by external resistance. (Jameson, 1983: 113)

While he is careful to avoid a determinist perspective, Jameson seeks to illuminate these contradictions in terms of the new social order's compression of time and space. To this extent, pastiche and 'schizophrenia'

become the principal markers of the new modes of cultural expression. Pastiche articulates in texts the sort of de-centred globalist capitalism which dominates the new economic and political order. Pastiche, being the combination of elements and styles into an assemblage of form, is distinguished from modernist parody: the deployment of specific tropes or styles in a text in order to mock them. Parody is used in modernist literature and film as a comic technique which substantiates the central aesthetic and moral perspective of the text; pastiche mimics styles and tropes in order to give the sense of dispersal and multiple dialogues or perspectives.

In broader cultural and political terms, pastiche becomes the articulation of the unleashing of the individual and individual subjectivity. According to Jameson and many others, modernism is marked by a substantial cultural investment in the individual subject. The highly stylized and unique author is the cultural articulation of these earlier periods of capitalism. The dissolution of the unique and unifying authorial voice and its replacement by assemblages of ephemeral elements and voices indicates a broader shift in cultural conceptions of subjectivity itself. Postmodern pastiche, therefore, represents a dissolving of bourgeois subjectivity, as much as the end of individualized imagination and aesthetic invention. The models of Proust, Picasso and T.S. Eliot 'do not work anymore ... since nobody has that kind of unique private world and style to express' (Jameson, 1983: 115). Jameson struggles to disguise his ambivalence about these changes, noting again that pastiche, as a series of de-centred imitations of style, produces the fundamental effects of dislocation:

> [I]n a world in which stylistic innovation is no longer possible, all that is left is to imitate dead styles, to speak through the

masks and with the voices of the styles in the imaginary museum. But this means that contemporary or postmodernist art is going to be about art itself in a new kind of way; even more, it means that one of its essential messages will involve the necessary failure of art and the aesthetic, the failure of the new, the imprisonment of the past. (1983: 115–16)

Enthusiasts of contemporary popular culture (cf. Chambers, 1988; Grossberg et al., 1988; McRobbie, 1994) often identify Jameson's collapse of high art into the amorphousness of 'mass' cultural production as a revivification of the Frankfurt School critique (see Chapter 4). Yet Jameson's position is somewhat more subtle, even ambivalent, as it seeks to illuminate a new social order in terms of fragmentations rather than simple social control. Jameson's unease with the new social order and with capitalist consumption and production practices arises not so much out of a desire to reinstate homogenizing modes of centred culture, but out of a disappointment with its alternative. That is, for Jameson the postmodern solution to modernist social and political oppression is fundamentally deficient.

To this extent, the 'nostalgia film' (e.g., *Back to the Future*, *Blue Velvet*, *Angel Heart*) is a spectral imitation of a lost time. Postmodernism regresses, in Jameson's view, not by producing historical drama, but by creating as new and with an overload of sentimentality a time when desire was pure and privileged. This commercial reproduction compares with postmodern architecture, which Jameson views with equal suspicion, an architecture which parades its pastiche of elements in a thorough and unremitting bonding of commerce and capitalist hegemony. This perpetuation of the past in the present

dislocates time, producing the effect of unreality or schizophrenia. The history of aesthetic style replaces real history and temporal continuities break down. Historical amnesia thus intensifies time as an internal experience, rendering it more vivid and more dislocating, creating moods that glow 'with hallucinatory energy'. This new culture, then, is both morally and imaginatively bereft. The deep seriousness and utopian imagery of modernist thought are dislodged by a radiating triviality, a superficiality which constantly eludes critical analysis and political hope.

Certainly, Jameson's disappointment with postmodernism is more acutely expressed in the later essay, 'Postmodernism, or the cultural logic of late capitalism', where he seems to despair of the possibility of ever fully grasping the political and epistemological implications of this new (dis)order. For Jameson, the spatial and temporal co-ordinates that provide for us a sense of our world have been swept over by the new cultural conditions. Jameson's great contribution to discussions on cultural postmodernism (see also Jameson, 1998) rests in his transferral of various aspects of structuralist and poststructuralist theoretics. Like Lyotard, Jameson draws poststructuralism away from its somewhat solipsistic interrogation of modernist texts to focus on the problematic of contemporary culture. The gloom that occasionally descends over his analysis, and which is especially evident in the cultural logics essay, is not just a residue of Marxist structuralist pessimism. He seeks genuinely to understand the new culture and appreciate its potential for liberation. Unfortunately, he is forced to concede that the postmodern presents a set of problems which are at least as intimidating as the modernist ideologies its seeks to replace.

JEAN BAUDRILLARD

Criticisms of Jameson's perspective have tended to be situated within the broad corpus of postmodern and popular consumerism theories. In particular, critics have argued that his critique is written from the position of a high modern neo-Marxist. According to these criticisms, his residual Althusserian structuralism confounds his attempts to embrace fully the political and aesthetic projects of postmodernism. Jean Baudrillard's writings on postmodern culture have also been attacked for being excessively pessimistic and for their barely acknowledged undercurrent of modernist (especially Marxist) nostalgia. His analysis of postmodernism, however, is less easy to situate than the analysis of either Lyotard or Jameson. The main reason for this is that Baudrillard has assumed the position of the postmodern poet; his own writings have taken on a discursive tenor which seems to mimic the phenomena he is discussing. Some critics, such as Christopher Norris (1990), have found his style of analysis frustrating, illogical and deliberately obscurist; others have rejected it as gloomy or even nihilistic. In either case, Baudrillard's recent writings centralize the media and media images as the defining force in cultural analysis. In fact, media imagery, Baudrillard claims, creates the discourses upon which the culture – or the phantom of the culture – is formed. Baudrillard's own apocalyptic and hedonistic discourse betrays a particularly elusive ambivalence, an ambivalence which, in its own way, has proven remarkably penetrative, alluring and controversial.

Baudrillard's analysis of postmodern culture combines elements of technological determinism, pessimism, bewilderment and wonder in a discourse that often evades substantive critical analysis. In fact, one of the most distinctive features of his cultural theory is its self-reflexive engagement with the postmodern funhouse of meaning, meaning gaps and multiple ironies (see Kellner, 1989; Norris, 1990).

Early Writings

Baudrillard's earliest writings, *The System of Objects* (1996, orig. 1968) and *The Consumer Society* (1998, orig. 1970), adapt Marxist analysis of economic production for the study of the processes and effects of capitalist consumption. Baudrillard's application of semiology (the study of signs, see Chapter 5) for an understanding of how consumer culture functions stimulated his broader interest in communication processes. Signs themselves, Baudrillard explains, attach themselves to consumer products; these products become identified with the signs which carry them, and consumer behaviour becomes largely classifiable according to its relationship with coded products. Meanings are transferred to the consumer through the act of consumption.

In *For a Critique of the Political Economy of the Sign* (1981, orig. 1972) Baudrillard begins to question the structuralist strategy both in his own analysis and in the semiology of Saussure (see Chapter 5). Retaining an interest in Marxist critique, Baudrillard applies a vaguely poststructuralist or deconstructivist analysis of the two halves of the sign: the signifier (physical symbol) and the signified (the mental concept). Saussure had pointed out that the relationship between sign and its referent (the thing to which it refers) was arbitrary, and that meaning only occurs when the sign is functioning in relation to other signs. Meaning, that is, is created through the interaction of various signs, not because there is a 'meaningful' relationship between the sign and its referent: the word 'dog' has meaning because we know that 'dog' is defined as 'a hairy, canine creature with four legs and a tail', not because the word has an intrinsic relationship to the creature itself. The sign is therefore a contingency of particular categories of signs within a context of their use. Baudrillard argues that political economy (Marx's description of capitalism) functions in a similar way: a commodity may be divided into its two operational parts: exchange-value (price) and use-value (the actual use and 'meaning' of the commodity). In fact, Baudrillard tells us, the price or exchange-value obscures the utility of the product, just as the symbol obscures the meaning of a sign. Baudrillard uses this critique to examine the historical functioning of capitalism, deconstructing its obscure operations to reveal its underlying mode of signification.

The End of Marxism

In *The Mirror of Production* (1975) and *Symbolic Exchange and Death* (1993, orig. 1976) Baudrillard breaks entirely with political economy and structuralism, marking a broader interest in the territories of proliferating communication, images and information. These books also announce the beginnings of Baudrillard's epiphanic and hyperbolic style, where the thought of a new social epoch becomes an opportunity for prophetic vision. In a later text, *The Ecstasy of Communication*, Baudrillard expresses his bleak vision in terms of an end to all meaning:

> The end of labour. The end of production. The end of political economy. The end of the dialectic signifier/signified which permitted the accumulation of knowledge and of managing the linear syntagm of cumulative discourse. The end simultaneously of

the dialectic of exchange value/use value, the only one to make possible capital accumulation and social production. The end of the linear dimension of discourse. The end of the linear dimensions of merchandise. The end of the classic era of the sign. (Baudrillard, 1988: 127–8)

These conclusions are fundamentally social, brought about by the unfixing of symbols and signs from familiar, historically determined references. For Baudrillard, this new epoch is dramatically symbolized by the arrival of new temporal and spatial conditions, a highly mediated reality or 'hyperreality' which renders all former social theories and accounts obsolete.

In arriving at this conclusion, however, Baudrillard seeks to understand its implications. The new mediated reality is double-edged, bringing together the ecstatic possibilities of unrestrained communication and the inevitability of loss and alienation. Thus, while other postmodernists rejoice in the ascendancy of mediated and prolific popular culture, Baudrillard's apocalypse is both hedonistic and anxious. The proliferation of signs and information in the media challenges the possibility of meaning, imploding the media themselves into a fluid and indistinct series of simulations: 'Information devours its own contents; it devours communication and the social' (Baudrillard, 1983a: 100). In essence, Baudrillard is erasing the message and its content from primacy in the communications process, emphasizing instead the importance of the conduit or carriage of these messages. However, the medium which carries the message is also less significant than the sheer volume of communication itself. McLuhan's centralization of the medium ('the medium is the message'), which Baudrillard had earlier rejected as technological determinism, is rejected a second time because the medium can no longer mediate messages at all; it can no longer carry the information about 'the real':

> Strictly speaking this is what implosion signifies: the absorption of one pole into another, the short-circuit between poles of every differential system of meaning, the effacement of terms and distinct oppositions and thus that of the medium and the real.... This critical – but original – situation must be thought through to the very end; it is the only one we are left with. It is useless to dream of a revolution through content or through form, since the medium and the real are now in a single nebulous state whose truth is undecipherable. (Baudrillard, 1983a: 102–3)

Simulacra, Seduction and Hyperreality

Thus, while structuralist and poststructuralist theories might concede a place for 'reality', even though it may be highly mediated and barely relevant, Baudrillard extends Umberto Eco's notion of hyperreality, arguing that all is simulation – the imitation of an imitation. This proliferation of 'simulacra' renders the real inert, dispenses with the representational imaginary, and entirely obliterates the need for empirical theories of knowledge:

> No more mirror of being and appearances of the real and its concept. No more imaginary co-extensivity; rather, generic miniaturization is the dimension of the real. The real is produced from miniaturized units, from matrices, memory banks, and command models – and from these it can be reproduced an infinite number of times. It no longer has to be rational, since it no longer has to be measured against some ideal or negative instance. It is nothing more than operational. In fact, since it is no longer enveloped by an imaginary, it is no longer real at all. It is a hyperreal, the product of an irradiating synthesis of combinatory models in a hyperspace without atmosphere. (Baudrillard, 1984b: 254)

The other side of this bleak vision, of course, is the recognition that the conditions of hyperreality are perpetually stimulating. A person can no longer be conceived in terms of a rational relationship with the external, objective world. A subject is a communicating process, constantly aroused through the unceasing flow of images, source-less and destination-less simulations. In *Seduction* (1990, orig. 1979) Baudrillard prefigures later readings of the free-flow of arousal and simulacra, arguing that 'seduction' is the most appropriate mode of human interaction, replacing intersubjective or objective modes of 'truth' which would penetrate beyond the surface play of sense and stimulation. But this seduction, which is a perpetual play at the surface of all communication, including sexuality, can no longer facilitate the types of 'carnality' which once functioned to inform and challenge the rationality of modern social practices. The modern subject maintained a private space where the tensions between rationality, sexual ecstasy and sexual repression could be played out. In hyperreality there is no private space, no depth; sexuality and communication must constantly and relentlessly be experienced at the surface: 'Unlike this organic, visceral, carnal promiscuity, the promiscuity that reigns over the communication networks is one of superficial saturation, of an incessant solicitation, of an extermination of intestinal and protective spaces' (Baudrillard, 1983b: 131). This 'ecstasy of communication' defines for Baudrillard the fundamental conditions of culture. The obsessive sexual imagery deployed in all communicative modes explicates sexuality and constantly stimulates a desire that cannot possibly be satisfied, nor indeed is it meant to be satisfied. While Baudrillard's earlier writings on commodity and symbolic exchange emphasized the (capitalist) functionality of these proliferations, the later writings have emphasized the boundless waste that now accompanies sexual desire.

In *Forget Foucault* (1987) Baudrillard contrasts his own theories on communication and sexuality with those of Michel Foucault. Baudrillard's wish to think through the implications of poststructuralism 'to the very end' lead him to a condemnation of Foucault's account of sexuality and power. Baudrillard argues, in fact, that Foucault's centralization of desire largely extinguishes it in much the same way as 'Marxism put an end to the class struggle, because it hypostatizes them and buries them in their theoretical project' (1987: 13). Significantly, Baudrillard dismisses Foucault's political interests, suggesting that 'power' ultimately unravels itself in direct proportion to its self-assertion. Baudrillard's politics therefore are fundamentally dismissive of activism since activism itself depends upon content. If there is no content, only stimulation and simulation, then power itself is a baseless imitation: neither a fixity of structure, as in the Marxist imagining, nor a process of exchange, as in the Foucauldian schema.

> What Foucault does not see is that power is never there and that its institution … is only a simulation of perspective – it is no more reality than economic accumulation – and what a tremendous trap that is. … There is something in power that resists as well, and we see no difference between those who enforce it and those who submit to it; this distinction has become meaningless, not because the roles are interchangeable, but because power is in its form reversible; because on one side and the other something holds out against the unilateral exercise and the infinite expansion of power. … This resistance is not a 'desire'; it is what causes power to come undone. (Baudrillard, 1987: 42)

For Baudrillard there can be no hierarchy of ordered positions, nor battles between differently situated and empowered groups. Power is always and forever played out in the simulations of hyperreality. For this reason, he can claim in all seriousness that the Gulf War did not take place (Baudrillard, 1995), not only because the images were a manipulation of coded interests, but because there were no actual adversaries, no real challenges, no essential disputes in power: 'This war is an asexual surgical war, a matter of war processing in which the enemy only appears as a computerized target, just as sexual partners only appear as code-names on the screen of Minitel Rose' (Baudrillard, 1995: 62). In other words, the passion and bodily sensations that might accompany a real war, in Baudrillard's view, were entirely missing from the screen- and information-based war that was simulated as the Gulf War. Just like a TV soap opera or the Olympic Games, the Gulf War was a production event, something lacking the sex and carnality of previous times, a dissolving event that had already finished before it had begun, an exercise in global entertainment.

Baudrillard's current writing continues this theme of proliferation and waste. We have become so implicated in this production of information and imagery, so completely embedded in the imagery itself, that we can no longer expect anything productive or useful to be achieved. In fact, the images are already waste before they appear. Humans themselves are waste before they have done anything useful:

> The worst of it is that, in the course of this universal recycling of waste, which has become our historic task, the human race is beginning to produce itself as waste-product, to carry out this work of waste disposal on itself. What is worse is not that we are submerged by the waste-products of industrial and urban concentration, but that we ourselves are transformed into residues. (Baudrillard, 1994: 78)

Baudrillard's postmodernity offers little political or cultural relief from this pessimistic vision. Indeed, while we may find ourselves wallowing in the delights of Baudrillard's own linguistic and theoretic excesses, being 'seduced' by the imagery and decadent sexual allusions, we are never allowed to release ourselves from the sense that the present and culture itself have already disappeared into the waste of history. For Baudrillard, the generation of waste by humans has ultimately constructed us as imagery and residue, prior to the operations of any productive value.

As noted earlier, Baudrillard's work has been severely criticized by other postmodern theorists for its pessimism and deterministic political vision. Of course, Baudrillard would himself explain his work in terms of the shattering of conventional social theory and social critique. Very simply, he is not interested in maintaining a critical trajectory which, for all intents and purposes, was designed for a previous historical epoch and which failed to deliver fundamental social reform anyway. Even so, his complete erasure of familiar discursive strategies and the common discipline of logical analysis or measured argument may be regarded, on the one hand, as original and exhilarating, but, on the other, as confusing and pointless. His method, that is, might seem to be faithful to the thing it claims to analyse: meaningless hyperreality, lack of content, lack of sequential order. The question that is often asked of Baudrillard, however, is not merely one of usefulness or comprehensibility so much as: does his writing genuinely lack content, as he might claim, or is he pretending that his own text has meaning when nothing much else does? In fact, Baudrillard never escapes these contradictions, and at times defends them as a virtue in his work.

POSTMODERN ARCHITECTURE

Up to this point, we have discussed three, more or less distinct categories of postmodernism:

1 *Avant-garde postmodernism*. This attaches the concept to a particular style of aesthetics.
2 *Deconstructionist postmodernism* (Lyotard). This combines a more general discussion of aesthetics and representation with a discussion of 'knowledge' and history. These poststructuralist-inspired theories have influenced other forms of postmodernism, most especially those that see 'postmodernism' as a general cultural and social description.
3 *Pessimistic critical postmodernism* (Jameson and Baudrillard). This views postmodern culture with deep suspicion.

To this list we need to add a fourth category:

4 *Celebratory postmodernism*. This group theorizes postmodernism in a far more welcoming and celebratory manner than the deconstructionists and critical pessimists. In fact, it combines elements of deconstruction theory with an interest in the stylistics of avant-garde postmodernism. In many respects, Andreas Huyssen's book *After the Great Divide* (1986) represents an attempt to reach beyond the early avant-gardist postmodernism by relinquishing its residues of modernist negativism or nihilism in favour of an aesthetics which could incorporate popular creativity and a more egalitarian spirit. For Huyssen, the postmodern sensibility is different from avant-gardism and from that modernism which is constantly in revolt against itself: postmodernism 'raises the question of

cultural tradition and conservation in the most fundamental way as an aesthetic and political issue' (Huyssen, 1986: 216). This fourth group, therefore, is interested in themes of pleasure, multiple discourses, individualism and the emancipation of subjectivity. (Particular fields of celebrationism are also interested in consumerism; this issue will be taken up more fully in the next chapter.)

Art, Architecture and History

The art historian Charles Jencks has transformed the concept of postmodernism from its avant-garde roots and applied it in a more general taxonomy of architectural and aesthetic style. Jencks' major contribution to the development of the concept rests largely in his notion of 'double-coding'. By this, Jencks suggests that postmodern artistic and intellectual modes are dialogic, drawing together various 'voices' or components into the one text and allowing them to speak without resolution. In other words, a postmodern form of expression does not try to obliterate or replace one voice with another (as modernism would do), but facilitates an ongoing dialogue between various parts. In his earliest writings on postmodernism, Jencks applies the notion of double-coding to refer specifically to the interrelationship between modernism and postmodernism, an idea he maintains throughout his work. In architecture he claims that double-coding could be understood as

> the combination of modern techniques with something else (usually traditional building) in order for architecture to communicate with the public and a concerned minority, usually other architects. The point of this double-coding was itself double. Modern architecture had failed to remain credible partly because it did not

communicate effectively with its ultimate users ... and partly because it did not maintain effective links with the city and history ... To simplify, double-coding means elite/popular, accommodating/ subversive and new/old. (1986: 29–30)

Jencks' categorization of architecture applies across a whole range of expressive and social processes, even though 'postmodern movements vary in each cultural form' (1986: 29). His further subdivision of postmodern art and architecture (see also Jencks, 1987a) emphasizes the capacity of postmodernism to restore aesthetics to a human scale for human pleasures. In particular, the postmodern style of new or neo-classicism celebrates the human form, liberating it from nihilism, expressionism and the abstract or geometric rationality of modernist art styles. This revivification of the recognizable, sensual and pleasurable dimensions of the human form re-places art into the context of everyday practices – even as these representations of the human form are 'double-coded' and pluralized in the expanding embrace of postmodern aesthetics. Postmodernism, therefore, includes all expressive modes, allowing the interaction of popular culture with the intensity and complexity of profound thought. In Jencks' terms, postmodernism is everything that can be articulated, imagined and enjoyed in human terms.

To this extent, Jencks also sees postmodernism as a periodizing concept. Art and especially architecture, which is the most highly corporatized, physically extant and expressive form in contemporary culture, are indicators of broader social and historical trends. Jencks (1987) outlines thirty-two characteristics or 'variables' which constitute the defining assemblage of postmodern aesthetics – these include ideological, stylistic and design qualities. While these variables are common to many definitions of postmodernism and embrace such things as humour, pastiche and language play, Jencks' later definitions tend to celebrate postmodernity against the limits of modernity.

Considered in these terms, Jencks defines the world as a distinct advance on previous epochs. This new world is a multinational constituency which is ordered through its major cities: New York, London, Paris, Tokyo, Hong Kong, Singapore and Frankfurt. The 'radical eclecticism' and humanly scaled architecture of these cities draws together the broad span of human cultures and human history, allowing them to exist in a heterogeneous harmony of parts. Nothing is subsumed by the homogenizing force of cultural imperialism; the multiplication of ideologies and bourgeois pleasures facilitates the capitalist desire for difference and change. These new cities and the postmodern context through which they function are predicates of pleasure and function. Beauty and joy are reintroduced to the increasingly human spaces. The old, grey and falsely egalitarian monoliths of the 'modern' city are being replaced by consumerized funhouses, open and eclectic settings where people of all types might congregate, converse, do business and enjoy the allusions and interplay of cultures, spaces and time. Postmodern architecture, according to Jencks, 'calls up the memories of a culture to which we were connected, and by respecting these associations, by giving them the honour of transformation, it manages to have a dimensionality greater than the present' (1987a: 8). This new world is inclusive and de-centred, offering immense possibilities, in Jencks' mind, for a post-cultural eclecticism which would liberate all humanity from the intensity, limits and dangers of modernist national allegiance. These new transnational experiences are being accompanied by a move to economic and industrial

reformation: post-heavy industry, post-Fordist mass production, and an information age which offers small-scale economies, flexible work and business operations, new pleasures and new expressive modes.

Like many other postmodern utopians, Jencks tends continually to parenthesize the more negative implications of his vision, while simultaneously caricaturing modernism and its failings. This optimism underscores virtually all of his writing, and we are left with a sense that anything that is good must be postmodern, and anything that is bad must be modern.

While Jencks himself leaves a space in postmodernism for modernist perspectives, he constantly presents the two in polemical terms. According to Jencks, the contradictions which had plagued and critically limited the modern vision have been overcome through postmodernism's greater emphasis on the individual and personal pleasure. Jencks' radical eclecticism, which functions at a human scale of experience and perspective, provides new opportunities for enhanced, complex lifestyles. Capitalism can now be harnessed and re-shaped through these lifestyles, creating more choice and an even greater potential for aesthetic experimentation, social diversity, inclusiveness and sensate gratifications. Capitalism is no longer a master, but a servant of choice and of a pluralized society. Public and private interests are no longer in conflict since the ascendant self will always find a place, a niche, in the ever broadening eclecticism of the global postmodern.

Postmodern Nature

Jencks' theory of postmodern satisfaction reaches its zenith in *The Architecture of the Jumping Universe* (1995), where

Plate 7.1   Terry Batt, *The Dada Cowboy Rides Again* (173 x 274 cm).
Postmodern art is characterized by qualities of pastiche, irony and the motifs of
popular culture. Terry Batt's painting harks back to the New York avant-garde of
the 1960s, though the wit and interplay of cultural elements reflect the postmodern eclecticism celebrated by Jencks and other more recent postmodernists.

postmodernism and its aesthetic forms are validated in terms of a theory of nature. As with Andrew Ross's *Strange Weather* (1991) and Jean-François Lyotard's *The Postmodern Condition* (1984a), Jencks develops a social and cultural theory which derives in part from a reading of contemporary science, most particularly the so-called 'new physics'. Postmodernism generally, and postmodern architecture in particular, is explained in terms of theories of 'complexity' and a 'purposeful' universe. Thus, the universe is not interested in the petty human squabbles which characterize modernity; it

> is always seeking out the tenuous position of maximum choice, maximum computability, where almost any outcome might occur. Creativity is balanced at this knife-edge between predictability and randomness. A completely ordered or completely chaotic system is not very valuable because it cannot evolve very far; it cannot improve or progress. By contrast, a system pushed far-from-equilibrium to the boundary between order and chaos – to that crucial phase transition – is rich in possibilities. (Jencks, 1995: 85)

These progressive or transitional phases represent evolutionary 'leaps' or 'jumps' where a plateau of increasing complexity in the universe and nature is replaced by a rapid advance. The history of the universe can be chronicled in terms of these varying phases: stable or plateau periods; periods of modestly increasing complexity; and leaps in which stability is replaced by this knife-edge of chaos and order. For Jencks, the progress of natural evolution and ultimately human history can be chronicled in much the same way. The present postmodern phase is a transition; its complex associations integrate potential chaos (drastic decline in biological diversity, human population explosion, greenhouse effect, the depletion of the ozone layer, etc.) with new forms of order (radical eclecticism, fractal theory, global village, etc.). The outcome is a more complex and more beautiful (human) condition, a postmodern culture. These complexities can be represented architecturally, which for Jencks is their ultimate truth. The system, which is the architectural design, might thus incorporate references to chaos and order, ecological conditions and natural processes. That is to say, a truly postmodern architecture will appear more like the self-repairing system of a living organism than a nineteenth-century machine. The new architecture may in fact replicate the complex processing of computer systems, or a cybernetic which, 'with its changing software as the driving force, is losing its mechanical nature. In ten years' time the word and concept of 'machine' will be self-contradictory because it will have become creative, anticipatory, non-routine – that is non-mechanical' (Jencks, 1995: 160).

So for Jencks, postmodernism promises all. Organic architecture will be integrated with 'smart' machinery (computers) which are no longer constrained by their mechanistic ancestry. This self-organizing cultural system is both a part of, and a representation of, a self-organizing universe. Following theorists like Paul Davies (1987), who also argues that the universe is evolving in accordance with a particular organizational 'blue-print', Jencks' vision is decidedly progressivist, if not precipitative and teleological:

> We are driven from behind by destructive universal forces, and pulled from in front by positive ones. It is to these second, optimistic cosmogenic forces that we, and the many living things and characters who resist entropy, owe our existence. To them, this friendly polemic is dedicated. (Jencks, 1995: 16)

Jencks' 'friendly polemic' argues that the ecological and social traumas being experienced in contemporary culture are to be expected during a time of rupture and transition. What's more important is that nature must run the fine edge between chaos and higher levels of order so as to advance the condition of complexity. Architectural and social forms, therefore, must mimic this natural complexity – fractals, quanta, wave theory – in order to realize fully the promise of postmodernism.

HABERMAS AND THE PROBLEM OF POSTMODERN POLITICS

The notion of a postmodern politics is highly debated within social and cultural theory. As we have indicated, there are three distinct groups of theorists of the postmodern: avant-gardists, deconstructionists and celebrationists. At this point in our discussion, we might add a fourth group, which would peripherally include Daniel Bell, but which is grounded more fully in a form of materialist and structuralist critique of both the theoretical and cultural dimensions of postmodernism. This group would include Marxists, liberal humanists and liberal phenomenologists. In many respects, the principal question informing this group's critique of postmodernism refers quite directly to the possibility of a postmodern politics. In fact, these theorists argue that postmodernism is both theoretically and culturally conservative. Their reasons for arguing this are threefold:

1 Celebrational and deconstructionist postmodernisms tend to limit their theory in order to reject universal principles of reform. A sense of principled social justice, liberation and reform can never reach to all people in all situations. Universal principles like human rights, social equity, freedom of speech, freedom of assembly, freedom from poverty, are all too broad and too sweeping for celebrational and deconstructionist postmodernists. Postmodern emphasis on 'difference' risks a complete surrender of universal principles of liberation.

2 The emphasis on discourse or language tends to neglect questions of 'real power' and real material deprivation. Questions of poverty and privilege which are determined by formidable social power can never be tackled by postmodernism. As Charles Jencks has argued, these are the questions of another time. The interests of the bourgeoisie of the developed world are more focused on aesthetic and personal pleasure.

3 The emphasis of celebrational postmodernists on popular culture and consumerist practices tends to legitimate capitalist processes, consumerism and forms of social and cultural hierarchy.

Among this group are theorists like Peter Dews (1984), David Harvey (1989) and Jürgen Habermas (1981, 1983, 1984b). For these commentators, the celebration of a new epoch called 'postmodernity' or 'postmodernism' is premature. Habermas (1983), in particular, has impugned the whole notion of a postmodern condition, arguing that modernism is a political and theoretical project which remains fundamentally 'incomplete'.

Habermas is himself a complex and interesting theorist who sits somewhat outside the canon of postmodern theory (see Chapter 3), even though his work from the 1980s shares a significant interest in the social and cultural dimensions of language. His earliest work, in fact, engages with major debates on sociological theory and the methods of people like Talcott Parsons and Max Weber. However, when he turns his attention toward the rising influence of French poststructuralism, Lyotard and Foucault in particular, his response is strangely hostile. In many ways, Habermas's debates with Lyotard and Foucault reflect a professional competitiveness, since both sides were seeking to extend cultural and reformist thinking beyond the boundaries of Enlightenment reason and Marxist ideology. Habermas wanted to complete the project of the Enlightenment (or 'modernity') by focusing on the problematic of language and inter-subject communication (intersubjectivity); this interest in intersubjectivity contrasts with the interests of other phenomenologists who are more preoccupied with the 'consciousness' of individual subjects. To develop this reformist analysis of intersubjective communication, Habermas deliberately avoids the sort of pessimism which, in his view, prevented groups like the Frankfurt School from offering a genuine escape from social control and oppression:

> The project of modernity formulated in the eighteenth century by the philosophers of the Enlightenment consisted in their efforts to develop objective science, universal morality and law, and autonomous art according to their inner logic. At the same time, this project intended to release the cognitive potentials of each of these

domains from their esoteric forms. The Enlightenment philosophers wanted to utilize this accumulation of specialized culture for the enrichment of everyday life – that is to say, for the rational organization of everyday social life. (Habermas, 1983: 9)

The Ideal Speech Situation

In his most detailed and extended work on the political and social dimensions of language, *The Theory of Communicative Action* (1984a, 1987a), Habermas explains his dissatisfaction with Enlightenment reason in terms of its concentration on epistemology or knowledge. To this extent, he seeks to expound a theory of social reform based on communication and action, rather than on the overthrow and replacement of the structure or the 'system'. Habermas is influenced by the work of Max Weber (see Chapter 2), who distinguishes between instrumental rationality and communicative rationality. Instrumental rationality refers to those practices which are formed through institutions and bureaucracies of state and economy, and which constitute the foundations of social stability. Communicative rationality refers to those everyday practices of everyday people (the lifeworld) which function to socialize people, facilitating a sense of order, social knowledge and cultural reproduction. In communicative action individual 'actors' are able to assert themselves and their knowledge, bringing their private 'truth claims' into a public space.

Communicative rationality, thereby, allows individual actors to present their own personal truths and measure them against the truths of other individuals; this process contributes to the formation of a general, social and consensual truth. This mutual construction of truth becomes culture, and in what Habermas refers to as 'the ideal speech situation' the various

truth claims are rationally engaged with and resolved. While this public forum constitutes an idealized or utopianized version of human communicative action, it provides Habermas with a focus for the completion of the modernist project – a space in which politics may be respectfully played out and differences acknowledged and resolved. In this ideal speech situation, communicative rationality overrides the centralizing and excessively bureacratic controls of instrumental rationality.

Habermas's theory functions as a general elevation of democratic ideals and the significance of public participation and public policy-making. Habermas argues, in fact, that a fully functioning modern, democratic society would draw together its various spheres of activity through the genuine activism of its citizenry. Again, Habermas follows Weber's description of modernization as the separation of art, science and morality into distinct spheres. Modernization can only be completed when each of the spheres is optimized through communicative action and through the confluence of their ideals. That is, the ideals promised in each of the spheres of art, science and morality will only be fulfilled when they are transferred back to the realm of individuals, their communicative actions and their lifeworlds. Emancipation becomes the perfection of these public speech conditions; rationality and society are reintegrated through the experience of publicly fostered consensus.

When the system intrudes on the lifeworld of actors – and this is the deficiency of modernity which must be overcome – pathologies are produced. In an increasingly technical society, where the state continually imposes itself on the ideal speech situation, the instrumental rationality produces hierarchical effects on communicative exchange. The imperative toward consensus is replaced by communicative rupture as one party tries to overthrow the interests of the other through an instrument of force. Habermas argues, in fact, that the poststructuralist and postmodernist critique of reason is therefore appropriate only in terms of this instrumental rationality, and cannot be used against communicative action. Communicative action, in Habermas's view, facilitates the free flow of individuals and groups through rational and rationalized discourse. A postmodern precept which demands the deconstruction of state apparatuses and the abandonment of hierarchical discourses is provided for in the conception of the ideal speech situation and the intersubjectivity of individual lifeworlds. French poststructuralism and postmodern theoretics, Habermas argues, serve only to mystify modernism's fundamental critique of itself, complicating the project with a fundamental surrender of its positive political aspirations or modernism (see Habermas, 1981, 1983). In other words, Habermas finds some value in the postmodern/poststructuralist critique of state apparatuses and ideologies, but postmodernism/poststructuralism's refusal to offer an alternative politics simply denies the force of modernism's reformist project, its efforts to complete itself.

Much of the debate about the differences and respective value of Habermas and deconstructionist postmodernism centres on the question of truth and science. While Habermas argues that the ideal speech situation of communicative rationality is free of hierarchical distinctions and dominative structural ideologies, Jean-François Lyotard thinks the opposite. According to Lyotard (1984b), Habermas reconstructs the conditions of universal and systematic domination, both in his privileging of scientific discourse and truth validity claims, and in the obliteration of difference through the imagining of 'consensus' resolution. Lyotard's thesis welcomes that part of postmodern culture which allows

differences (*les differends*) to assert themselves beyond the homogenizing impulses of scientism, universal values and consensual law. Any rationality which finds itself restoring truth claims and the methodological impositions of science is not to be trusted.

DISCUSSION: POLITICAL POSTMODERNISM

Habermas's dispute with poststructuralism/postmodernism rests in the fact that modernist rationality suffers not from an excess of logic, as Derrida claims, but rather from a deficiency. In Habermas's view, modernist rationalism never fulfilled its promise as society remains beset by irrational processes, practices and modes of organization. The ideal speech situation, by which all citizens participate in the processes of constructive, consensual and reasoned decision-making, is the ultimate aim of liberal democratic history. Habermas thus reconfirms the democratic ideal as a participative process, reducing state management to the servant, rather than the master, of public consensus. Habermas's maintenance of a collective or universal solution to the problem of politics has failed to find favour with those postmodernists entranced with the idea of difference. For Habermas, however, a politics that does not reconnect individuals to their public sphere, and which does not ground its theory in universal principles and pragmatics, is no politics at all. Fredric Jameson's and Jean Baudrillard's pessimistic account of consumer culture would seem already to have surrendered the possibility of a reformist, consensual postmodern politics.

This view, of course, is not universally held by theorists of the postmodern. In the following chapters we'll look more closely at various permutations of contemporary cultural politics, but what is certainly clear since the later 1980s is that the whole field of cultural analysis and its relationship with reformist politics has diverged significantly and now incorporates many fields of social and theoretical analysis. The sorts of problems confronted by Lyotard, Jameson, Habermas and others in the 1980s have become central to the cultural studies project. Thus, pragmatist philosophers like Richard Rorty (1984) have attempted to reconcile the poststructuralist theoretic with Habermasian reformism, suggesting that the ungrounded nature of language still allows us to reform particular problems in concrete instances. John Docker (1995) has suggested that in a postmodern political pantheon, working-class reformism must stand alongside other liberatory claims: feminism, postcolonialism, multiculturalism, gay politics, and so on. This dissolution of the centrist notion of class warfare, Mark Poster (1989, 1995) insists, actually facilitates a broader and more inclusive political landscape, one which honestly represents the breadth of human and societal aspirations. Linda Hutcheon (1988), recalling Charles Jencks' view of postmodern art and architecture as a new form of political aesthetics, establishes for many literary critics a postmodern political method which treats 'representation' as the locus of radicalism. Hutcheon disagrees with those critics who regard postmodern aesthetics as fundamentally apolitical 'because of its narcissistic and ironic appropriation of existing images' (1988: 3). Her own analysis seeks to demonstrate that images and stories of postmodern representations

> are anything but natural, however 'aestheticized' they may appear to be in their parodic self-reflexivity. While the postmodern has no effective theory of agency that enables a move into political action, it does

work to turn its inevitable ideological grounding into a site of de-naturalizing critique. To adapt Barthes' general notion of the 'doxa' as public opinion of the 'Voice of Nature', postmodernism works to 'de-doxify' our cultural representations and their undeniable political import. (1988: 3)

Borrowing from the deconstructive methods which seek to illuminate the false groundings of discourse, Hutcheon insists that the postmodern aesthetic (and by extension the postmodern critic) is political in as much as it challenges the taken-for-grantedness of the dominant culture's social behaviours, attitudes, mores and 'aesthetics'. Postmodern aesthetics and poststructuralist deconstruction work to de-doxify dominant forms (see Chapter 5).

Hutcheon's methodology runs parallel to critical developments in a wide range of cultural and social analysis since the 1980s. The capacity to redefine politics beyond the needs of class warfare, homogenizing democratic liberalism and the imperatives of social/political action (or agency), has been often sourced to the later writings of Michel Foucault (see Chapter 5). As we have seen, Foucault claims that his books are 'bombs for others to throw', and 'tools for the revolutionary demonstration of the established apparatus' (see Foucault, 1977b: 113–38). He provides an ideal foundation for a postmodern politics which is experiential and cultural rather than fundamentalist and directive. In particular, his deconstruction of prisons, mental institutions and finally human sexuality provides for postmodernism a template of methodologies which legitimate the interests, aesthetics and anxieties of the bourgeoisie. His reformism, therefore, is constituted through personal interactions and is not founded on a vicarious and untenable working-class revolution. He resists extravagant and curative claims for social ills; rather, human experience becomes available for a raft of resistances and politically validated pleasures. Foucault's personal life – his homosexuality and tragic death from an AIDS–related illness seems to substantiate the liberation of a profoundly personal deconstruction of power, a martyrdom that requires neither heroics nor revolution.

The politics of postmodernism, then, attach themselves to a range of theoretical and perspectival lines. The avant-gardism of the American 1960s integrates with French deconstructionism and older forms of textual analysis, most especially those associated with New Criticism and close textual reading. British cultural studies, which had also adapted close textual reading techniques, provides for more recent cultural politics a 'de-doxifying' strategy: that is, a technique which exposes underlying patterns of textual ideology and hegemony. Hutcheon herself cites the structuralist/semiotic analyses of the working class, women and blacks that had been carried out at the Birmingham Centre for Contemporary Cultural Studies. This analytical paradigm, she claims, provided a useful resource for the elaboration and development of a postmodern analysis of aesthetic representation. Hutcheon invokes Raymond Williams' work in her transatlantic re-rendering of the cultural studies project. Indeed, other North Americans, such as Lawrence Grossberg (see Grossberg et al., 1988), have usefully realigned the Birmingham Centre's structuralist analysis with French poststructuralism and American postmodern aesthetics.

This move to a postmodern cultural politics, however, is entirely mixed, with some advocates maintaining a desire for agency along with a postmodernist celebration of diversity. This move is particularly strong amongst postcolonial theorists, many of whom apply deconstructionist techniques while maintaining an interest in essential political agency and ethnically based liberation. Edward Said (1993), for example, deploys a deconstruction technique to attack the cultural hegemony of the European literary canon and contemporary American foreign policy – most especially as it applies to the Middle East (see Chapter 10). Thus, while he acknowledges his indebtedness to Foucault's analytical paradigm, he criticizes the French theorist's passivity and unwillingness to follow through on the discoveries he makes (Said, 1986). Other postcolonial theorists, such as Arjun Appadurai (1990, 1996), argue that the global postmodern provides opportunities for diversification, new forms of subjectivity and identity, and new forms of liberational cultural hybridity. According to Appadurai, the whole enterprise of globalization is about the forming and re-forming of what he calls 'the cultural' – that never completed and perpetually restless process of discursive contests, conjunctions and disjunctures.

Many other postmodern cultural analysts also believe that personal identity and personal pleasures are the centre of cultural resistance. In this sense, sexuality and popular texts (music, TV and film especially) constitute a form of bodily resistance to rational instrumentalities. Sex, sense and the stimulation of bodily responses facilitate an even broader political lexicon, one in which Foucault's conception of the microphysics of power is extended into the corpus of an intensified individualism. Concepts like 'self', 'subject' and 'identity' become codes for the surface play of discourses; this type of surface level liberation replaces the modernist obsession with the deeper dimensions of individual and transcendent consciousness. Where modernism regarded liberation as the possibility of a collective consciousness or personal acts of will or spirituality, postmodernism is more concerned with play and pleasure. In these terms, the task of a postmodern politics is to create the circumstances in which this play and identity exploration can take place without the extraneous restrictions of collective norms and imposed notions of social order. Postmodernism, therefore, is a free space in which individual beings can deconstruct the artifice of authority without the need to replace it.

In fact, this is perhaps the most radical of postmodern cultural claims: that there can be no hierarchy of value beyond the pleasures, interests and gratifications of the individual. Of course 'the individual' has always been present in capitalism and cultural modernism, but this form of celebratory postmodernism appears to relinquish entirely the reconciling imperatives of the collective, the social. Postmodernism of this kind claims that there are no collective interests except in as much as they arise out of the randomness of difference, hybridity and individual subjectivities. Postmodern politics de-doxifies the normative standards that culture imposes, and then releases the individual to the free-for-all of the struggle to signify. This means, of course, that no text, discourse, perspective or individual should be superior to another. We cannot refer to the great works of art, literature or music because these works are just another entry in the lexicon of human history. Culture as way of life liberates each subject position from the standards of accepted social value. Shakespeare's tragedies, therefore, are neither better nor worse than Muriel Unknown's website or George Unknown's conversation in the local bar. Postmodern politics is a pluralized egalitarianism, a cultural site in which all voices carry equal validity and value. In later chapters we will examine how this politics is played out in contemporary culture.

8

Popular Consumption and Media Audiences

Outline of the chapter

This chapter examines audiences in terms of mediation processes, everyday practices and relationships. There are various ways of conceptualizing the audience, and various ways of interrogating and 'measuring' them. As we indicated in Chapter 1, however, audiences are an active part of the meaning-making process. In contemporary cultural studies the audience has become more than just a group of people watching a television programme or passively receiving a media message. Audiences interact with texts, text producers and culture in order to engage with, create and disseminate meanings (see Figure 1.1, p. 5 above). All points of the mediation triad operate as contingencies of all other points; each point interacts with all other points and with the culture that contains them. This mediation process, therefore, functions within a context of existing meanings, though it is also active in the dynamic which stimulates the construction and dissemination of new meanings.

  Particular areas of cultural theory regard audiences as 'text consumers'. This approach to audiences and audience practices has two related dimensions:

1 It refers to the economic practice of 'buying' and 'consuming' media texts. This may include the purchase of a media technology and the complicit consumption of advertising (as with 'free-to-air' radio and TV texts); it may also include the purchase of an admission ticket, say to the cinema, or the purchase of a media product such as a newspaper, CD or magazine.
2 It also refers more generally to the production and consumption of meanings that are attached to all capitalist products. In this sense, all capitalist products have meanings or 'symbolic value' attached to them. All products are consumable 'texts'; a clothing style, a Cadillac and a suburban address all say things about the people who consume and display them. The consumption of media texts is only one example of this cultural spectrum. While it is common to refer to mass-produced and commercial media texts as elements of 'popular culture', particular theorists argue that everything in the capitalist economy is part of the range of popular cultural consumption. Therefore, the everyday practices of ordinary people are part of popular culture.

The analysis of audiences as 'consumers' in this broader capitalist cultural context can be located in Pierre Bourdieu's work on symbolic exchange and taste. Bourdieu applies an empirical method to the study of cultural consumption. He examines the way different consumers (audiences) discriminate between different media texts according to their socially formed notions of 'taste'. Michel de Certeau argues that ordinary people can use their consumption practices to destabilize capitalist processes. John Fiske adapts these ideas, claiming that the consumption of popular media texts is inherently transgressive. According to Fiske, popular media consumption and other everyday practices disrupt the hegemony and patriarchal rationalities of capitalism.

Ien Ang, Janice Radway and Henry Jenkins all apply a similar theoretical framework to their study of the creative and transgressive consumption of media texts. These theories are often supplemented through the application of a celebrational postmodernism.

GENERAL INTRODUCTION

The history of culture demonstrates that new elements don't necessarily obliterate existing ones. Even if we accept Fredric Jameson's claim that present culture is sufficiently different from previous times to warrant a new name (postmodern, post-industrial, information age, etc.), older elements continue to operate within the 'new' culture. There are closures or discontinuities, certainly, but there are also adaptations, continuities, reincarnations and evolutions. Culture is a mixture of old, new and adapted elements. The computer has not replaced the television, which has not replaced the radio, print or interpersonal communication. Similarly, the various tracts and discourses that comprised modernist culture are not necessarily extinguished in the current cultural conditions, but may exist contiguously with the new discourses. Various practices and ideologies persist, integrating and reworking themselves into ever-mutating contexts. In particular, the tension between individual freedoms and needs and collective (social or structural) freedoms and needs continues within the various frames of contemporary cultural discourse.

As we have seen, a good deal of modernist cultural and social theory sought to overcome these tensions through the formation of universal 'narratives' or 'grand theories' which would cover all humanity in all circumstances. Marxism, utilitarian capitalism, liberal democracy, socialism – all are designed to produce a balanced relationship between individual and social structure with varying degrees of emphasis for one or the other. Capitalism is not 'economy' separable from culture, but is deeply embedded in ideologies and meaning-making processes (symbolic exchange). To this extent, all capitalist products are 'texts' as they involve the exchange of meanings (use, value, social status, group identity, etc.); media texts are a particular category of capitalist products. In reading this chapter, we need to be clear on the following points:

1   All capitalist products have meanings attached to them.

2 Therefore, all capitalist products may be regarded as 'texts' which can be 'read', 'used', 'shared' and 'interpreted'.
3 Media texts are, of course, texts and capitalist products.
4 Audiences therefore may be understood as 'consumers' of media products; consumers may be treated as 'audiences' who read and interpret a whole range of capitalist products, including 'the media'.
5 We may usefully engage both media and forms of economic theory in order to investigate the audience.

Our reading of the audience and consumption practices must, therefore, account for the underlying patterns of contemporary capitalism. Capitalism conducts itself through substantive ideological cultural patterns, which are themselves constructed around the individual–collective tension. Capitalism necessarily implicates collective processes in production and consumption (markets), though these 'co-operative' capitalist structures are formed through hierarchies of reward and social advantage. Collectivism, that is, is a fundamental part of capitalism, but, unlike other forms of social organization, capitalist collectivism is constructed around quite fierce forms of competition and individual privilege: this collective–individual tension is the fundamental contradiction of capitalism. Adam Smith's classical text *The Wealth of Nations* (1776) outlines the basics of 'self-interest' and 'natural liberty' as the foundation of modern capitalism. The utilitarian ethic postulated by Jeremy Bentham and James and John Stuart Mill explains that liberal democracy and economic well-being are merely social expressions of the same deepseated individualism: to be happy, one must be useful, and to be useful, one must necessarily contribute to the overall social and economic well-being of the nation. The ideology that allows the destitution of some and the affluence of others is both a 'natural' and social outcome of the imperatives of liberty.

Postmodern cultural theory addresses this problem of contradictory capitalism and liberal democracy by generally deconstructing it. That is, postmodern cultural theorists argue that structuralist solutions to the collective–individual bind, and to the problematic of freedom generally, are fundamentally flawed. In fact, celebrational and deconstructionist postmodernists seek to avoid the question altogether, claiming that the modernist contradiction of the collective–individual is fundamentally irresolvable and therefore atavistic. Moving into a new cultural condition, postmodernists argue that we need to think new thoughts in order to avoid old problems. In particular, the Marxist emphasis on reforming the collective formations such as class structure and production arrangements (the mode of production, capital and labour) misunderstands the value of individual freedom, and especially the freedoms attached to individual consumption. According to some postmodernist thinkers, the pleasures that issue from choice, consumption and from the everyday practices of everyday people are never quite understood by Marxists and other structuralist reformers. Individuals (individual agents, subjects) are not merely the dupes of structures and dominant ideologies, but are capable of actively constructing themselves, their identities, and their fields of pleasure through the practices of everyday media consumption and interaction.

The problematic of capitalist culture lies at the heart of these discussions. The shift in interest from structures and commodity production to an interest in individual subjectivity and commodity consumption has paralleled shifts in consumer capitalism itself. Theorists like Daniel Bell, Fredric Jameson and Pierre Bourdieu argue that capitalism has shifted from the production of goods and services meeting particular survival needs toward the production and consumption of 'symbolic value'. That is, having met basic needs, capitalism now seeks to construct new needs for 'symbolic' consumption – fashion, style, and images are attached to products in order to make them attractive, meaningful and valuable to consumers. Simultaneously, popular entertainment, information and the proliferation of texts and visual imagery have become the conduit for much of what consumer culture regards as valuable, pleasurable and important. While we have touched on a number of these issues already, this chapter examines more directly theories that have developed around popular consumption practices. In particular, we will examine the development of media consumption theories, some of which attach to postmodernist cultural analysis, while others append to the variety of readings of the notion of 'audience'.

PASSIVE AUDIENCE MODELS

As we noted in our study of British cultural studies (Chapter 4), the Birmingham Centre for Contemporary Cultural Studies divorces itself quite dramatically from psychological analyses of media and culture. Stuart Hall (1982), in particular, challenges the assumption that media messages can be mathematically measured without recourse to politics and culture. These differences between American and European conceptions of media texts and audiences are as much rooted in forms of national culture and history as they are in academic tradition. Specifically, the absence of a strong and representative working-class politics and the presence of a more intense ideology of individualism seem to have predisposed American research toward the effect of texts on the psychology of particular audience members. The Payne Fund studies (1933), which were designed primarily to examine the impact of the new medium of film on the lives, attitudes and behaviours of young people, established a research paradigm which persists today.

The Payne Fund studies were significant in that they found that the relationship between texts and audiences is a good deal more complicated than had previously been assumed. The exposure of an audience to particular textual messages did not directly determine particular and predictable changes in behaviour or attitudes. Specifically, it was found that exposure to violence or sexually explicit material does not create murderers or sexual licentiousness. Nor is it possible to assume that advertising creates demand and political propaganda brainwashes electorates. Information about the world, morality, behaviours and ideologies are assembled through more longitudinal exposure to mass media texts and interactions with community and 'significant others'. As the various Payne Fund studies discovered, media texts were assumed to have much more power than could be proven through the application of their particular psychological and statistical techniques.

The development of communications research in the United States has attempted increasingly to identify the complex sets of relationships that exist between media, text, social system and audiences. Much of this work, however, has had difficulty relinquishing the early belief in the power of the mass media to exert significant influence over vulnerable audiences.

Transmission Models

These models, in fact, underscored a good deal of the thinking that surrounded early broadcast regulation in the English-speaking world. Britain provided a model for Canada, Australia and New Zealand, where broadcasting was regarded with profound suspicion. Part of this suspicion, of course, derives from the fact that radio had itself evolved rapidly during World War 1. Its transference from a point-to-point medium to a broadcast medium stimulated the interests of governments, who immediately identified its potential for the broad delivery of political messages. The propaganda minister of Hitler's Third Reich, Joseph Goebbels, provided the citizens of Germany with radios and placed radio loudspeakers on every corner. However, this extraordinary power for public institutions to infiltrate the private sphere of the home – to beat the tribal drum, as Marshal McLuhan calls it – also constituted a potential weapon for those who would infect the mind of the citizenry with seditious or disloyal messages. In recognizing the significant potential of the radio for propaganda, the American philanthropist Edward A. Filene established the Institute for Propaganda Analysis in 1937, which was designed to teach people how to resist propaganda messages.

Britain's response to the same trepidations was to establish an 'independent' public broadcasting system, funded by the government. Australia and Canada created a dual system of government and private participation. This solution provided some insurance against excessive government control and influence, particularly if the government was unreliable or of a politically unsound character. This was a typical modernist answer to the problematic of private and social interests. It was thought that a dual broadcasting system would provide 'checks and balances', giving the widest possible access and representation to the public voice. The government broadcasters in Britain, Canada, Australia and New Zealand were designed to produce objective, social accounts, while the private sector would play out private interests. In the United States the role of social advocacy and objectivity was entrusted to the private sector entirely; community broadcasters would fill any gaps. In either case, regulations controlling radio, television and later computer networked communication have all tended to treat audiences as passive receivers of information and vulnerable to the processes of persuasion.

Radical reformist and Marxist theories have also tended to treat audiences as relatively passive message receivers. The Frankfurt School writers, who fled Hitler's Germany in the 1930s and established their research centre in New York, despaired of the German people's vulnerability to brutal despotism. Equally, though, they despaired of the excesses of consumerism and popular culture, which, for Theodor Adorno in particular, reduce the audience 'mind' to a form of slavish obedience. The standardization of popular music, for example, rendered the listener inert, incapable of discrimination or aesthetic transcendence:

> Standardization of song hits keeps the customer in line by doing their listening for them, as it were. Pseudo-individualization, for its part, keeps them in line by making them forget that what they listen to is already listened to for them, or 'pre-digested'. (Adorno, 1994: 208)

Adorno believes that the new media technologies reduce people's lives to highly scheduled and over-determined patterns. This instrumental rationality becomes the fundamental ideological system, which is reproduced over and over again until it is entirely naturalized as ideology. Technology,

9/11 Media War and the Audience as Public

One of the most notable features of the 9/11 and Afghan war is the relatively high level of public support for the US government and its policies. For transmission and Marxist theories of social control this apparent public support for the US-led 'war on terror' is clearly related to the power of the media to deliver effective messages. Susan Carruthers (2000) argues, in fact, that the confluence of state policy, public consent and the media appears to have become a pre-condition of contemporary military engagement. The state's meticulous management of information and the media during the Gulf War (Taylor, 1992) is being reproduced in the 9/11 and Afghan war in order to ensure public support. Noam Chomsky suggests that the media complicitly surrenders its critical function during times of crisis so as to support national stability and security:

> It is entirely typical for the major media, and the intellectual classes generally, to line up in support of power in a time of crisis and try to mobilize the population for the same cause. That was true, with almost hysterical intensity, at the times of the bombing of Serbia. The Gulf War was not at all unusual. (Chomsky, 2001: 30)

This view is corroborated by Young and Jesser who argue that 'opinion polls have shown overwhelming popular support for constraints on the media during recent limited conflicts' (1997: 11). The surging popularity of President Bush and the oft-cited 80 per cent public support for US reprisal policies might seem further to substantiate this 'consensus' of media, state and public. Eric Luow, following a social control model of audience analysis, suggests that the compliance of the public is effected through a state sponsored PR-ization of war and the co-option of the media (2001: 180). In this model, audiences and their 'public opinion' can be directly influenced, even molded, through carefully managed information and misinformation programmes. In this sense, a government derives its mandate by 'creating' public opinion and then appearing to serve it through policy formulation and action.

This view of audiences as susceptible to the controls of powerful organizations has been challenged by many cultural commentators. In particular, it is argued that audiences and their 'opinions' are far more diverse and volatile than the control theorists appreciate. Thus, while numerous polls have reported extremely high levels of public support for President Bush and other incumbent state officials during the period of the 9/11 and Afghan crisis, this support is extremely volatile and precariously constituted. As much as anything else, this volatility issues from the very character and constituency of 'the public' which, after all, is a broad assemblage of individuals, perspectives, agonisms and community interests. The convocation of this public and its opinion merely parenthesizes the complexity of its elements by casting them through a precarious, media-generated discourse of unity. Moreover, it is argued, the social knowledge that is formed through the media is of itself ephemeral and fluid; according to Baudrillard, the predominantly sensate, emotional and imagistic character of televisual media information predisposes its audiences to change rather than to fixity and logical judgement. State and military managers of information are condemned, therefore, to ongoing battles with their audiences over the meaning and value of war and the policies of the state.

media technology in particular, exerts excessive control over the everyday experiences of ordinary citizens, but there are no opportunities to resist and challenge this rationality because the audience's minds are so enmeshed in the content (and ideology) of the media they watch.

This technological determinist perspective is also invoked by theorists of postmodern culture. Jean Baudrillard, most specifically, conceives of contemporary culture in terms of the consumption of mediated imagery. Audiences are dutifully positioned by the unceasing flood of sensate images and 'simulacra' (imitations of imitations). The Baudrillard world is one in which reality has been replaced by hyperreality; audiences are bound to the culture by the media's perpetual arousals, by the stimulation of an unsatisfiable desire. For Baudrillard the text and the audience are seen to merge in a flurry of empty and titillating images. The new media experiences ultimately erase the distinctiveness of subjectivity as the private and public spheres merely obliterate one another:

The one is no longer a spectacle, the other no longer a secret. Their distinctive opposition, the clear difference of an exterior and interior exactly described the domestic *scene* of objects, with its rules of play and limits, and the sovereignty of symbolic space which was also that of the subject. Now this opposition is effaced in a sort of *obscenity* where the most intimate processes of our life become the virtual feeding ground of the media. (Baudrillard, 1983b: 130)

THE USES AND GRATIFICATIONS MODEL

A more complex audience schema has evolved which is generally known as the 'uses and gratifications model'. Fundamentally, the model switches interest from media institutions and messages to the ways in which audiences use and derive gratification from media messages. While this switch from negative effects to positive uses is generally attributed to the work of James Lull, the beginnings of a uses model can be identified, in fact, in Elihu Katz's (1959) rebuttal of claims that the whole field of communication research was fundamentally dead. Katz pointed out that much communications research up until this point had examined the effects of mass communications persuasion campaigns, asking the question 'What do the mass media do to people?' Having accepted that such research proved very little, Katz recommends that communications research should ask a new question: 'What do people do with the mass media?' Katz's survey of a range of media research findings demonstrated that audiences derive 'pleasure' and respond in active ways to the mass media. Assumptions about the passivity and vulnerability of audiences neglect important dimensions of audience research.

Subsequent work in the area attempted to connect effects with uses and gratification. However, the work of James

Lull introduced important methodologies which drew uses and gratifications research away from a strictly psychological model toward a more ethnographic model. Lull's essay 'The social uses of television' (1980) published the findings of a three-year project in which his team observed the TV viewing practices of over two hundred households in California and Wisconsin. The observation team became 'participant observers' in the household, eating dinner with the families, doing chores, participating in group entertainment and watching TV. Lull argues that the presence of the observer eventually became less exceptional and barely disrupted the families' normal domestic activities. Lull's work is clearly linked with the phenomenological school of sociology, which had achieved some significance in the United States from the 1970s. While the method had been used in a wide range of sociological enquiries (mostly to do with 'deviant' and sub-culture activities), this was the first time a genuinely ethnographic technique had been applied in American media analysis. As we shall see below, this application of an anthropological 'ethnography' brought Lull's sociology of the media quite close to the incipient ethnographies that were being conducted at the Birmingham Centre for Contemporary Cultural Studies, most particularly through the work of David Morley.

Lull divided the uses of the TV into two general categories: structural and relational. Structural use refers to the TV as an 'environmental resource' which can be drawn upon at various times to achieve various ends. As a background facility, the TV provides companionship for the accomplishment of household duties. At any given time, however, the TV may be foregrounded when users are engaged by particular informational or entertainment messages, or when the user simply needs a break from routine. The relational use of TV refers to the means by which the TV is deployed in interpersonal relationships within the household. For example, Lull is particularly interested in the way the TV might be used as a point of contact between household members, drawing them together for discussion, negotiation and analysis of particular programmes. As well as this 'affiliation', the TV may be used for 'avoidance' by creating space between different household members.

In fact, the great majority of Lull's essay is concerned with the interpersonal dimensions of TV use. His own links with cognitive enquiry and the academic context in which his research was conducted clearly influenced his interests and focus. The 'uses and gratifications model' as it evolved in the US maintains a strong connection with psychological processes and the relationship between the media and individuals. Unlike European media analysis with its interest in ideology, hierarchical social discriminations and social groups, the 'uses and gratifications' approach tends to be concerned with personal psychology and interpersonal relationships generally. As we shall see later in the chapter, however, the engagement of audience studies with consumer practices and pleasures has produced interesting parallels between this psychological approach and more recent postmodern versions of audience analysis.

SCREEN THEORY

The move toward a postmodern audience theory, however, has been filtered through the heritage of European structuralism and poststructuralism. The translation into English of a largely French structuralist approach to language theory can be traced to a number of British media and cinema analysts working in the 1970s. In particular, the journal *Screen* provided a forum for the exploration of new approaches to the audience and the audience experience of cinema texts. Two of the journal's significant contributors, Colin MacCabe and Stephen Heath, took a particular interest in French structuralist and psychoanalytic theory. Heath and MacCabe constructed a theory of film analysis which integrated Jacques Lacan's notion of 'the gaze' as a cinematic experience with Louis Althusser's concept of dominant ideology. While the relationship between reader and text had been problematized in literary studies through phenomenology and poststructuralism (see Bleitch, 1978; Iser, 1978; Tompkins, 1980), cinema studies was drawn more fully into the cultural studies perspective through a particular interest in the act of watching images and connecting those images with the audience's whole sense of self.

Althusser, we recall (see Chapter 3), had argued that key institutions (family, school, mass media) create the ideological conditions necessary for the maintenance of privilege and authority. The oppression of particular groups is achieved through the engagement of these groups and the imagined conditions of their oppression, more than through direct force or coercive deterrence. Althusser's notion of Ideological State Apparatuses provided a new tool for cultural critics who wanted to expose the nexus between text, audience and the cultural/political contexts in which interpretation takes place. According to the *Screen* theorists, the particular circumstances of cinema exhibition and consumption predispose the medium to a psychoanalytic study which would enable the relationship between audiences, film texts and ideology to be exposed. That is, the dream-like experience of watching fragmented images of flickering light in a dark, social, yet intensely personal space was analogous to those zones of the deeper psyche that psychoanalysis seeks to reveal. The audience, then, is understood as a subject/spectator who experiences the world and culture in a deeply personal way, but who remains connected by these experiences to the world at large. This relationship, however, is not fixed and unitary, as classical, humanist Marxism might claim. And, indeed, Althusser's (1984) own reading of Freud and Lacan had convinced him that all individuals are fluid and open, rather than 'centred' and permanent; the subject's relationship with culture and ideology, therefore, is changeable and inevitably problematic.

Of course, ideology (the dominant beliefs and imaginings within a culture) tries constantly to fix individual subjects in the hierarchy of capitalist relationships. Once we have moved from the pre-linguistic state of our identification with the mother into what Lacan calls the 'symbolic order', we become vulnerable to ideology. The way we make sense of things, interpret texts and make meaning is contingent upon how we are positioned in the culture. We rely on the existing pool of knowledge and meanings (symbols), most of which are supplied by those pre-existing institutions, the Ideological State Apparatuses. In this way, ideology and social order sustain themselves. It is only the imperfectness of the relationship between subjects and texts which permits mutation and change. Lacan explains that, in fact, our belief that we are fixed and that we exist in some permanent and inevitable relationship with the outside world comes about through 'misrecognition'. As we noted in our discussion on Lacan (Chapter 5), misrecognition refers to the mirror phase of subject development where the child misrecognizes its reflection as its true self. This misrecognition continues throughout life as the illusion of a fixed self. The misrecognition is repeated every time an individual says 'I' or addresses others as 'you'. In fact, Lacan explains, individuals are 'positioned' by their experiences in discourse. That is, the subject exists only in relation to interaction with the outside world as it is represented in discourse (language, texts, speech, imagery, etc).

According to the *Screen* theorists, then, the questions for the study of cinema are: what is the subject, where is the subject and how does the subject exist in relation to the text? Recalling Bertolt Brecht's condemnation of realist literature, MacCabe (1974), for example, criticizes Hollywood realist cinema for 'positioning' the spectator/subject as though he or she were experiencing 'real life' in the text. The classic Hollywood film feigns transparency, creating an illusion for the spectator that what is being displayed can be believed because it is a natural and realistic representation of life. The spectator thus misrecognizes the image as real while at the same time experiencing the perspective or gaze of the camera as actually his or her own. When the image is displayed it is as though the spectator were looking directly from within the fictional construction, projecting him- or herself into the action as the camera eye becomes the spectator's own eye. In contrast, the work of Brecht and the film director Sergei Eisenstein foregrounds the artifice and machinery of art production and constantly turns the camera or textual gaze back on the audience, thus potentially eliding realism and its ideological imperatives.

When Laura Mulvey (1975) published her famous essay on the male gaze (see Chapter 6), she was inscribing the Althusserian/Lacanian position with a feminist polemic. Mulvey's critique challenges spectator positionings which are achieved through the repetition of particular sexist, fictional motifs. We might consider, for example, a film like *Jerry Maguire*, a seemingly innocuous representation of the real life of American sport. On the surface, the film appears to critique the obsessive and mercenary nature of sport. Jerry's professional success appears to confirm the validity of business ethics, loyalty, persistence, familial ideals and the triumph of talent over racial and class discrimination. A *Screen*-style analysis, however, would point out that the film merely confirms the ideology of capitalist utilitarianism, American nationalism and sexist, patriarchal values. The audience is 'positioned' into a state of belief where Jerry's personal struggles and ultimate triumph are ideologically naturalized. As spectators, we project to Jerry, accepting his perspective of sport, romance and duty. Jerry's discovery that 'passion must accompany duty' provides a solution to the contradictions that beset our own lives, our own struggles, our own dissatisfactions. Jerry's triumph becomes a reconciliation in which we can all share and with which we can all fix ourselves and our identities.

As with MacCabe and Heath, Mulvey sought to liberate audiences through the elucidation of invisible discursive strategies. Radical feminist depictions of women's experience, ones which shatter the assumptions of patriarchy, would further enhance the liberatory potential of avant-garde modernist cinema. However, while the work of the *Screen* theorists proved appealing to many reformist thinkers during the 1970s, the emphasis on avant-garde radicalism failed to excite other theorists, who imagined a more inclusive and participatory emancipation. The avant-garde in Britain and Europe provided useful material for the refurbishment of cultural and textual studies. However, avant-garde art was often regarded as elitist and bourgeois by many commentators, including Stuart Hall (see 1980, 1988). In the Lacan/Althusser approach, Hall argues, the subject's capacity for liberation is always limited by the position offered by the text. The subject, that is, remains walled within the text and its ideology; the subject remains fixed by the text and has only a minimal role in his or her own liberation.

HEGEMONY AND ENCODING/DECODING

This reading of the subject has proven somewhat problematic for Althusserian and Lacanian analysis generally. Hall's own approach, representing the broader interests of the Birmingham Centre for Contemporary Cultural Studies, opens the text and the audience to a more Gramscian style of negotiated hegemony. That is, meaning and power are formed through a complex set of relationships between the text, audiences, production processes and culture. According to Hall, Antonio Gramsci's concept of hegemony permits greater freedom and agency for subjects to challenge ideological and structural restrictions. The Birmingham Centre under Hall's leadership rejected the idea of an avant-garde-led revolution, preferring instead to focus on the tensions that exist within the relationship of text and audience. As we noted in Chapter 4, Hall's highly influential essay 'Encoding/Decoding' (1980) integrates a semiotic and sociological analysis which finely balances structural notions of influence and control with the possibility of individual agency and meaning-making. Particular readers construct particular meanings out of particular texts; however, this freedom to construct meaning is always a contingency of the pre-eminent ideological and semiological system. According to Hall, culture is formed and shaped into codes (signs, symbols, images, language, etc.) by text producers. This selection and shaping process is both a conscious and unconscious attempt by producers to create 'meaning-full' texts which will be attractive and comprehensible to the consumer. The consumer draws on the same body of culturally available meanings, signs and ideology to interpret or 'decode' the messages presented in the text.

Hall's encoding/decoding paradigm, thereby, provides a compelling reason for studying popular texts, especially TV texts. Dominant meanings are necessarily implicated in dominant ideology, though, again, Hall prefers Gramsci's notion of hegemony to Althusser's (supposedly) more restrictive notion of ideology. For Hall, the encoding/decoding nexus is never perfectly engaged and so the capacity for ideology to control individual agents and oppressed social groups is always limited. Somehow or other, individual text audiences can reposition themselves against the dominant semiological and ideological order. Unlike the passive receiver theories, which fix the reader's position or which assume the inevitability of message transmission, encoding/decoding concedes that the engagement of audience–text–culture is never complete and is always subject to interpretive and experiential variabilities – a contingency of tensions as much as collective or structural consensus.

The concept of 'polysemy' – the potential of signs to carry multiple meanings – illustrates for Hall the imperfect connection between signs and their meanings. However, just as signs may be variously connected to culture, so individual audience members and groups may variously draw on the raw materials of culture in order to make sense of those signs. Hall (1982) argues that audiences produce multiple accentualities or emphases when interacting with texts. For Hall and other members of the Birmingham Centre, the source of these multiple accentualites or variant perspectives is to be found largely in an individual or group's social class or economic circumstances. As the Birminghams' work in encoding/decoding progresses, however, this source of variation becomes more widely considered. Later work at the Centre concentrates on gender, ethnicity, age-group, employment status, sexuality, and so on.

While Hall's work generally, and the encoding/decoding paradigm in particular, has proven tremendously influential, a number of commentators have expressed dissatisfaction with its heuristic outcomes. Hall leaves unanswered, for example, the problematic of the audience itself. In fact, Hall's own work and the work of many of his colleagues and students tends to 'assume' the audience, preferring to concentrate on the nature of a text's ideological and semiotic constituency. The Hall method, that is, retreats from direct analysis of audiences, tending to assume responses rather than directly interrogate them. David Morley, one of Hall's students at Birmingham, identifies this elision as a fundamental flaw in Hall's Gramscian theoretics. In order to overcome the elision, two distinct branches of audience analysis have developed in recent cultural studies: one emphasizing the empirical and anthropological dimensions of audiences and audience meaning-making; the other merging with notions of media consumption and theories of postmodernism.

QUANTITATIVE AND QUALITATIVE APPROACHES TO AUDIENCE RESEARCH

While still a student at the Birmingham Centre, David Morley (1980b) had critiqued *Screen* theory for its treatment of audiences as being merely 'positioned' by text. Morley's quite seminal work on audiences integrated the Birmingham Centre's

increasing interest in empiricism with the encoding/decoding model. Empiricism, we might recall, is the methodology which emphasizes the accurate recording of experience. The Enlightenment mathematicians and scientists pioneered the method of empirical analysis for the study of the physical sciences, while Durkheim and Weber successfully adapted it for the investigation of society. Generally speaking, empirical methods may be divided into two broad fields, quantitative and qualitative:

1 Quantitative research seeks statistical descriptions of social and cultural phenomena. It generally adds things up and tries to identify how often a particular event may occur. In audience research, for example, statistics provide information about how many people are watching a TV programme at any one time (ratings), and what sort of social groups are watching (demographics). Psychological social science has often attempted to explain changes in behaviour and attitudes when audiences are exposed to certain media stimuli. Very often, quantitative methods seek correlations between 'variables' (events, characteristics, attitudes, etc.). For example, quantitative research might try to find out whether there is a relationship between attitudes to domestic violence and particular television viewing habits. The research method uses broad-based surveys, sales numbers, website hits, ratings, statistical computer packages and laboratory experiments; the aim is to produce objective and predictable accounts of social phenomena.

2 Qualitative research tends rather to seek more detail about fewer events or elements. It seeks to uncover, in particular, the intricate details of people's everyday lives, including the complex of attitudes, behaviours, relationships and

meaning-making within the specific conditions of their culture. Qualitative techniques have their origins, in fact, in a range of disciplines, including journalism, history and ultimately anthropology. In fact, a qualitative approach to empirical data collection proved an ideal heuristic tool for those researchers seeking to describe highly localized experiences of people living in tribal or village-style cultures. Sociology's adoption of qualitative techniques in the 1960s and 1970s (see Berger, 1967) represents a significant shift in thinking about society itself: society could now be considered and recorded as a series of sub-cultures and social groupings rather than just a single formation that could be statistically explained.

While there is considerable dispute in the social sciences about the status, scientific validity and heuristic value of the respective methods, qualitative research is proving attractive to those audience researchers who seek to explain reading/viewing practices in terms of everyday life and cultures. There are a number of qualitative research techniques, including the following:

1 *Focus groups*. Here the researcher engages a number of people in a relatively unstructured and conversational discussion of a particular phenomenon. This sort of research is being done increasingly by marketers who want to gain more information about how particular samples of audience groups might feel about a TV programme, an advertising campaign or a celebrity's hairdo. Focus groups are also being used for market testing new (Hollywood) films. Audiences express their approval or disapproval of particular events in films, especially climaxes.

2 *Open-ended interviews*. These tend to be used to elicit detailed information from respondents. Unlike simple tick-the-box-and-add-it-up surveys, open-ended interviews tend to be very discursive and produce huge amounts of data.

The anthropological method of describing everyday practices and everyday life in these localized communities is generally referred to as ethnography. These 'human graphs' attempt to record particular human experiences in context. In fact, the context of action is as important as the action itself, so ethnographers tend to apply detailed recording methods. Some researchers become part of the group they are observing (participant observation), while others attempt to maintain an 'objective' distance from the group and employ technologies like video cameras, computer data casting and audio recorders. Again, there is dispute about whether or not the qualitative research methods that have been adopted by audience researchers can be genuinely called 'ethnographic' (see Nightingale, 1989). For a number of researchers coming out of the Birmingham Centre in the 1970s, ethnography provided a mechanism for analysing the 'decoding' part of the encoding/decoding process. Dissatisfied with the quantitative and effects traditions prevailing in American communications schools, researchers like David Morley and Roger Silverstone embraced the idea of a discursive, anthropological study of audiences which acknowledges the significance of the cultural context of text reading and text consumption. Unlike the uses and gratifications research being conducted in the US by James Lull and others, however, the Birmingham audience research was very much embedded in questions of power and ideology. While qualitative research uses a range of methods, ethnographic audience research tends to examine audience activities within the normal context of their viewing. An ethnographic study, therefore, would tend to record people's activities within the home, where people normally watch TV. The domestic context of TV watching is an essential feature of the process of audiences' meaning-making.

DAVID MORLEY

The Nationwide Audience

David Morley's (1980a) early study of the British TV, magazine-style, current affairs programme, *Nationwide* marks a significant moment in the development of cultural studies. While American cultural analysis had been influenced by anthropologists like Clifford Geertz and the various permutations of phenomenological sociology, British cultural studies had tended to merge its literary and sociological lineages through the development of a more speculative, textual method. That is, because of their strong interest in questions of ideology and a general belief that all discourse is politically positioned, the British cultural theorists had tended to defer significant questions about science and scientific methods. Even the 'scientism' of Saussure's semiology and Lévi-Strauss's structural anthropology becomes mollified in the translation to British cultural studies. The British practitioners of semiotics were less interested in presenting a scientific edifice and more interested in presenting the processes of textual coding in terms of hegemonic and ideological forces.

As we have noted, the Birmingham methodology tended to concentrate on the text, elucidating its meanings through speculations about how an audience might engage with its discourses, and the dominant ideologies and hegemonic conditions of a culture. Stuart Hall's notion of 'preferred reading' suggests that audiences will select a particular meaning from a text, depending on their social position and the ways in which they relate to the culture. All texts are 'polysemic' (having multiple meaning potentials), so audience members are able to select a 'dominant reading' position in accordance with prevailing cultural norms, standards and ideologies. Polysemy, however, also facilitates forms of 'negotiated' reading, whereby audience members can *actively* engage with the text's meaning potentials to create a more individualized or divergent reading space. As we shall see later in the chapter, these divergent spaces may actually challenge or transgress the authority of the dominant reading.

Once again, we have the emergence of a substantive difference in emphasis between the various members of British cultural studies. The *Screen* theorists had argued that the text 'positioned' its readers: that is, the text told them how it should be read and from what perspective. Hall offered a more active role for the audience in the processes of meaning-making. Morley's work, however, forced the Birmingham group to acknowledge the significance of a new way of understanding and analysing audiences. Rather than simply make assumptions or speculations about an audience, Morley argued that analysis should present 'empirical', scientifically derived data. This was not a capitulation to positivist social science, but an embrace of the more qualitative methods of anthropology. Meanings were formed out of the relationship between audiences, texts and cultural contexts, but audiences were to be the central focus of research.

The first stage of the *Nationwide* project examined the news text and offered speculations or hypotheses about the ideological conditions in which the text would be read. According to the research, *Nationwide* was a common-sense, regionally based interpretation of the main news events of the day. It was designed to speak to, and from, the common person. It also aimed to acknowledge the diversity of Britain, giving a voice to the interests of various social sub-groups. Morley's qualitative analysis sought to uncover the degree to which actual social subjects accepted or rejected *Nationwide's* reading of the news. Video recordings of the programme were shown to twenty-nine socially located groups comprising either managers, students, trade unionists or apprentices. Morley's research team found significant variations in groups' attitudes toward the programme's style and its readings of particular events. Bank managers, for example, rejected the programme's style as merely entertainment but endorsed its ideological readings, even when they opposed their own. Trade unionists endorsed the style, but rejected the ideology. One group of black students didn't reject the programme's preferred reading of events, but chose not to 'read' the programme at all. Indeed, the strongest conclusion that was drawn from this seminal work was that there is no clear or direct relationship between socio-economic group and a preferred reading of a text. Morley argued that the various social groups draw on much more complex resources when reading a text than had been assumed. Indeed, the reading patterns that were identifiable linked together various cultural traditions, political allegiances and institutional/professional discourses – black youth culture, Labour Party politics, Marxism, professionalism, bourgeois educational perspectives, and so on, could all be invoked in the course of reading a text.

Family Television Consumption

During the latter half of the twentieth century, the disciplines of sociology and psychology were developing increasingly sophisticated theoretical frameworks for the investigation of society and the individual. The divide between an objectivist view of social phenomena (employing quantitative methods) and one which sought to illuminate intricate details of subjective life (employing qualitative methods) created significant tensions within particular fields of social enquiry. For cultural studies and cultural theory, however, no such tensions existed since the whole *raison d'être* for cultural studies emerged through its rejection of the objectivist, positivist perspective. Culture and politics were entirely embedded in one another; analysis could not be objective in the extreme Cartesian sense, nor could it be apolitical. Cultural studies began with a deep suspicion of science, grand truths and universal explanations. From its emergence as a distinct discipline it was deeply committed to the possibilities of difference and the social margins. Nevertheless, the significant relationship between culture and the contemporary media necessarily admitted debates about the validity of particular types of audience analysis. David Morley was convinced – along with a number of others in the Birmingham Centre – that the best way of accessing audiences was through the deployment of empirical methods.

This sort of empiricism, however, is generally claimed to be distinct from the heavily statistical, positivist social scientific methodology, largely because it emphasizes language, narrative and difference.

Morley's experience with the *Nationwide* project demonstrated that the patterns of audience reading were even more diverse and complicated than he had originally anticipated. This discovery encouraged Morley, no doubt, to investigate an even more highly localized cultural zone, the family. At the same time, he came to reject the encoding/decoding model, which concentrates on issues of power, ideology and preferred reading. In a postscript to the *Nationwide* project, in fact, he admits a level of uncertainty about the whole notion of 'preferred reading', suggesting that it is probably no more than 'the reading the analyst is predicting that most members of the audience will produce' (1980b: 6). In centralizing the audience, Morley had come to believe that a more generalized investigative model would be required if the full implications and details of audience practices and readings were to be elucidated. In this sense, his work brings him closer to the sort of anthropological models that had been developing through subjectivist and phenomenological sociology practised in the United States.

In fact, this problematization of the text and the preferred or dominant reading concept was taking place in wider fields of cultural analysis, most especially as poststructuralism was being integrated into theories of consumption and postmodern theory. Barthes, Derrida and Foucault had all deconstructed the notion of the original work of art and the 'authority' of the author; poststructuralism had claimed, in fact, that all discourse was formed in relation to all other discourses and no text could claim to be unique and meaningful in its own right. Morley's *Nationwide* research had convinced him of the validity of these claims, most particularly as the polysemy of texts seemed not to surrender to the structuralist imperatives of homogenizing and dominant ideology. That is, his research seemed to validate the poststructuralist belief that there are as many gaps in meaning-making processes as there are confluences. In *Family Television* (1986) Morley ceases to interrogate the ways texts and readers interact to produce meaning in relation to dominant ideologies. Rather, his research focuses on the way individual family members interact, struggle and create meaning for themselves in relation to other family members. While *Family Television* retains some interest in issues of power, this approach to power is more consistent with Foucault's notion of microphysics or personal power: between men and women, parents and offspring, and siblings. To this extent, the 'content' or texts of the TV medium become less important than the technology or medium itself, since what matters most in the relationships within the family is the symbolic value of the medium in terms of its consumption, rather than the specific readings of specific texts. The important questions for Morley include the following:

1   How do individual family members use the television?

2   Who controls the television and in what circumstances?

3   What do people do when the television is switched on?

4   In what ways does the television confirm the various relationships, including the power relationships, within the family?

Morley and others who have followed the empirical cultural studies model have attempted to graph the culture of television viewing. As the most prominent domestic communications technology, one which constitutes the central entertainment and informational mode, TV occupies an extremely significant cultural space. As with early radio and the rising use of the Internet, television conflates the public and private spheres. Morley's recent work continues to graph the ways in which domestic technologies are constituted through this highly localized culture of the family:

> Broadcasting (along with other domestic technologies of communication) has, therefore, to be understood as enmeshed within the internal dynamics of the organization of domestic space, primarily with reference to gender relations. However, our interest lies in formulating an analytical framework which goes beyond the question of the internal relations of the domestic sphere to include the shifting relations between this domestic or private sphere and the public sphere by which it is framed. From this perspective we see that not only has the development of communications technology been affected by the pre-existing organization of domestic space but that broadcasting, for example, can be seen to have played a significant part in rewriting the relations between the domestic and public spheres – for instance, by increasing the attractiveness of the home as a site of leisure. (Morley and Silverstone, 1990: 38)

Morley's interest in the symbolic dimensions of communications technology parallels the work of James Carey (1989) in the United States. While Carey's methodology is distinctly historical and discursive, there is no doubt that both researchers acknowledge Marshall McLuhan's claim that the 'medium is the message', and that the interaction between a technology and the context of its consumption necessarily and significantly contributes to the shaping of culture. Moreover, Morley's empirical methods have proven highly influential for those researchers who have actively engaged with issues of communications and cultural policy. Governments across the developed world have been more inclined to heed the advice of (and fund) cultural research that is framed in empirical or scientific terms. Morley's insistence that cultural studies research should be empirically based has provided a valuable paradigm for researchers since the 1990s who have sought to examine broadcasting and broadcasting policy.

FROM READERS TO CONSUMERS

The theories and analytical models we have examined so far have all sought to explain the meaning-making process in terms of the relationship between text, audience, text producers and the social-economic-cultural context in which the relationship functions. It's important to remember that these discussions actually conceive of the text and the audience in very particular ways. That is, the audience is not just an assemblage of 'real' people reading a newspaper or watching a TV programme. An 'audience' is a concept which operates in a particular discursive framework. We can categorize these various approaches according to their specific conceptual emphasis:

1 The Effects researchers and Frankfurt Marxists emphasize the power of the text to transmit its meanings. In most cases they are concerned with the negative effects of media texts on the audience.
2 The 'uses and gratifications model' also measures media effects on audiences, but looks more to 'positive' effects. The model emphasizes personal gratification; the text is a vehicle to personal, active engagement.
3 *Screen* theory is interested in the power of the text to 'position' an audience.
4 Hall's encoding/decoding model attempts to reverse some of the negativity of

the Frankfurt School without surrendering entirely the political dimensions of the text, audiences and culture. Hall's model attempts to balance active audience engagement with a text's political power.

5 Morley and other ethnographic audience researchers seek to illuminate the ways in which audiences actively create meaning. In Morley's work, however, the text again is reduced to the status of 'vehicle' or 'facility'.

Morley and Silverstone's work, in fact, moves from a conception of the audience as 'readers' to a more integrated conception of audiences as 'consumers'. These notions of text consumption and audience consumers are themselves quite varied, and different authors mean different things by their application. Some treatments, for example, are quite industry-specific. TV executives treat their audiences as 'consumers' of media products; they also treat audiences as products which can be sold to advertisers. That is, executives sell their 'ratings' (percentage of TV households watching a particular programme) to those people who want to promote their own commercial interests.

Audiences are also referred to as 'consumers' in broader academic terms. In particular, analysts interested in the operation of the text–audience relationship as it operates in a broad governmental and regulatory context often conceive of the audience as 'consumers' of product. Some theorists like to distinguish this approach to the media as a 'materialist' analysis, distancing it from the analysis of the audience as a concept operating in discourse. This approach would see itself as investigating the 'real' conditions of media operations and textual consumption, emphasizing, for example, the ways in which particular texts are facilitated and formed through the presence or absence of specific government controls and legislations. In fact, many of the theories we have analysed above have a 'governmental' dimension to their analysis. The greatest problem with the materialist notion of the audience is its failure to recognize that the audience is always and inevitably a concept formed in discourse: even their own notion of audience as consumer is no more than a particular version of the audience – certainly valid, but never alone.

The other use of the concept of audience consumption is one that has become quite significant in cultural studies, most especially through the context of the cultural postmodern. We will now look at the evolution of this application of the concept of the audience as consumer in some detail.

PIERRE BOURDIEU AND SYMBOLIC CONSUMPTION

David Morley's shift from an investigation of the text–reader relationship to a focus on media consumption reflects wider moves within the field of cultural analysis. In particular, the problematization of the text and textual meanings produced through phenomenology, on the one hand, and poststructuralism, on the other, has led to some significant rethinking of the status of the text and how it functions in relation to the everyday practices of everyday people. Certainly, the general principle that different people interpret texts differently has led particular theorists to ask questions about how texts and their medium can be related to the broader culture. Significantly, attention has been focused on the value of text as part of the culture of consumer capitalism. The French sociologist Pierre Bourdieu was one of the earliest theorists to examine the question of symbolic consumption, outlining in particular the ways in which consumption, as an everyday practice, is implicated in ideology and capitalist hierarchies. That is, Bourdieu sought to explain how capitalism and its forms of discrimination and social hierarchy sustain themselves through the everyday practice of consumption, rather than through the processes of production and labour.

In *Distinction: A Social Critique of the Judgement of Taste* (1984) Bourdieu articulates, in a distinctly sociological framework, many of the ideas that had been infiltrating British cultural theory. In particular, he demonstrates that the idea of 'taste' – the 'innate' power of consumers to discriminate qualitatively between products – is fallacious. According to Bourdieu, the 'tasteful' selection and consumption of products is used as a social insignia for the privileging of particular individuals and groups. The selection of a product and the display of its value necessarily implicates consumption in the symbolic positioning of people and their everyday lifestyle and practices. Bourdieu argues, however, that symbolic consumption doesn't merely reflect a person's social position, but actively and actually generates it. That is, everyday players are not socially positioned through their variant levels of education, income and occupation; their position in the mode of production and labour. Nor are they merely the victims of ideology and the limiting effects of symbolic information. They are also, Bourdieu argues, constructions of particular consumption practices, practices which produce and reproduce their position in the social hierarchy. Accordingly, the less privileged groups in the community are ideologically infected by 'lack of taste'; however, the choices they make as consumers serve to construct their social roles and reproduce their lack of privilege.

For example, the consumption (and style of consumption) of different types of alcohol reinforces the social position of the consumer. A man in a suit may sip wine at an expensive restaurant or may choose boutique beers at a comfortable bar. By contrast, an unskilled labourer might drink considerable amounts of mass-produced beer in a public bar or pool room. The respective consumption practices reinforce the social position of the consumers, functioning as symbolic indicators of occupation, education and income levels.

In many respects, Bourdieu's empirical work illuminates similar cultural territory to that which Roland Barthes was investigating in *Mythologies* (1973). However, while Barthes was examining the ideological and mythological dimensions of French suburban life, Bourdieu wanted to know how suburban life reproduced itself in terms of actual consumption practices. To a degree, that is, Bourdieu's empiricism begins where Barthes concludes, seeking explanations for the taken-for-grantedness (doxa) of everyday suburban life. Bourdieu's empirical work in *Distinction* consisted of a questionnaire survey of around 1200 respondents, covering a broad sample of occupations and social 'classes'. His analysis linked consumption with social class, noting, for example, that there were strong correlations between social status and such things as housing styles, musical tastes and food preferences (1984: 1). However, 'taste' in Bourdieu's terms refers as much to 'distaste' or disgust as it does to positive preference (1984: 56). In either case, Bourdieu's principal interest is in the systematic accumulation of symbolic power through the act of consumption. This structuralist conception of everyday practice had been discussed in earlier works such as *Outline of a Theory of Practice* (1977), where Bourdieu explains the significant notion of 'symbolic capital' (see esp. 1977: 70). Symbolic capital, however, is more than just a differentiation of incomes or the power of discretionary spending. It is more than just an outline of dominant and subordinate social players. In fact, symbolic value, as we have suggested, attaches to notions of cultural distinction and necessarily produces a cultural economy in which 'taste' becomes the fundamental currency. In this sense, two groups may have the same income, but one has superior knowledge and intellectual or aesthetic discretion. Within the middle classes this discretion might distinguish the vulgar, tasteless *nouveau riche* from the well-educated and highly informed professional.

Again, a simple example might explain this difference in symbolic hierarchies. Bourdieu points to the differences between people of taste and the more vulgar groups who have achieved some level of wealth through a trade or manual labour. Quality or fashionable furnishings in the home, the engagement with classical rather than popular music, speech intonations, and clothes – all may be deployed as symbols of superior taste. Even within youth culture, where income and occupation should barely be relevant, there are the same sorts of discriminatory dynamics. Brand-name clothing, for example, might distinguish the cool or fashionable from the uncool. Schools, which institutionally position young people according to age or academic performance, are replete with sub-cultural hierarchies, all of which are distinguished by symbolic value. Preferences for particular musical or clothing styles distinguish insiders from outsiders; the power elites within the student community are identified as much by symbolic taste as by academic, athletic or sexual performance.

MICHEL DE CERTEAU

Bourdieu's work has proven highly influential for those areas of cultural studies preferring a sociological framework for their analysis (see Featherstone, 1991). However, Bourdieu, like Louis Althusser, has been accused of a kind of intellectual conservatism, despite his desire to present a case for radical social realignment (see Jenkins, 1992; Moores, 1993). Specifically, his empirical structuralist approach tends to reinforce the structures he would subvert by limiting the opportunities for agency and transcendence. Social actors seem to be so completely embedded in their symbolic and cultural conditioning ('habitus') that there appears to be little possibility of subverting the social standards of taste; as with Althusser, Bourdieu offers little space for emancipation.

Michel de Certeau is one of the most significant French cultural theorists to critique and expose these limits. His two major texts, *The Writing of History* (1988) and *The Practice of Everyday Life* (1984), use a psychoanalytic model to develop a liberational space for ordinary people and their everyday practices. Significantly, de Certeau (1984: 45–60) expresses some dissatisfaction with Bourdieu's structuralist polemic. Yet, his dissatisfaction also extends to Michel Foucault's poststructuralism; de Certeau feels exasperated by Foucault's reluctance to provide political solutions for those people whose liberation he claims to encourage. According to de Certeau, Foucault's description of the apparatuses of power neglects those operations which are not 'privileged' by the writings of history, but which are active in innumerable ways in the technological machineries about which Foucault writes: 'These techniques which are also operational, but initially deprived of what gives the others their force, are the "tactics" which I have suggested might furnish a formal index of the ordinary practices of consumption' (de Certeau, 1984: 49). People act within the corporate or state apparatuses and their technologies; Foucault fails to give adequate recognition to these actions. Just as Said (1986) has expressed his disappointment with Foucault's ultimate political inertia, de Certeau rejects Foucault's disinclination to examine thoroughly that 'power' Foucault himself detects in the operations of everyday procedures.

As Frow (1991) has pointed out, de Certeau's writing has focused on popular culture as a set of practices, rather than a set of texts. The sustaining argument of *The Writing of History* centres on the parallel projects of historiography and rhetorical (literary) analysis. According to de Certeau, historiography and literary rhetoric treat 'understanding' as the effects of representation; in other words, a culture may be analysed and explained through the elucidation of textual representations, through the symbolic force of language and writing. In contrast to this approach, the Lacanian derived notion of the *real* – that unbordered realm of space and time that cannot be mediated or marked by language – provides for de Certeau a compelling alternative to the 'reality' composed through systems of knowledge such as historical or literary writing. The real, that is, exists at the margins of these systems, a matter of sensory apprehension and the unconscious 'other' in the dominion of objects (see de Certeau, 1988, esp. Chs 2, 5, 6, 8). Lacan, we recall, identifies a pre-linguistic experience in childhood. At its most perfect, this unconscious, pre-linguistic experience exists when the child is part of the mother; when the child is introduced to the world of language and knowledge, he or she becomes aware of his or her separation from that perfect state. The unconscious, therefore, is the ultimate, the 'real' and must be distinguished from the 'reality' of symbolization, representation and language. In other words, the 'real' is the realm of pre-language, of sensory responses to objects, nature, action and practices that are not invaded by knowledge; 'reality' is the realm of knowledge, thought and language.

The writing of history, therefore, invades the spaces of the real by forcing it out of the unconscious and into the rationalized world of knowledge. While culture imposes itself on the real (nature), it is only through the rifts and gaps in this writing system – zones which knowledge can't rationalize – that the true unconscious and otherness of history is revealed. Historiography will assert itself and its rationalist discourse as a will to truth; but the discourse itself betrays its otherness through a paradoxical veracity, a set of details and meanings that defy the imposed order of writing. Thus, history will write about the French Revolution and inevitably the narrative of the event will force the infinite details of people's lives at the time into a systematic discourse. This discourse will transform or 'reduce' the infinity of details to documents of causes, politics, leaders and results. However, the 'other' dimension to this period of the past will defy rationalization. It is the way people will go about their lives amidst the turmoil of the event. Will wash, talk, eat and sleep. Will seek to protect themselves from disease or pain. Will reproduce and care for their children. The writing of history misses these minutiae, since they slip through the ambit of language and writing to exist merely as practices and actions in everyday life. These everyday sensate experiences which motivate and delight us become the unwritten 'other' of history.

In *The Practice of Everyday Life* we can see that de Certeau's interest in the otherness of power (which Foucault neglects) derives from these same precepts. However, here his desire to foreground the lived experiences of ordinary people is more intensely politicized in a contemporary context. The historical 'otherness' of everyday practice is centred, revealed and valorized as a form of 'continuous present'. The alternative 'structures' of power are thus to be apprehended in the *practices* of the everyday raiders of culture within the dominion of the 'real'. 'Writing', with its textualized 'reality', is once again revealed as an ordered and bordered system of knowledge; de Certeau unravels the presence of writing in order to expose its unconscious subjectivity. The everyday practitioners, with their propensity for 'tactical' raidings of objects and meanings, become the heroic 'anti-heroes' of de Certeau's popular culture – the culture of the people and their everyday practices.

Yet these heroes are not the oppressed proletariat of the Marxist mode of production, nor the *extra*-men (or superman) of Nietzschean philosophy, nor the liberated utilitarian entrepreneurs of market-based capitalist economics – all of whom are fixed in structuralist conceptions of culture and 'reality'. De Certeau's heroes are ordinary people, liberated by their capacity to act, to feel, to 'practise' at the level of the pre-symbolic, pre-linguistic real of the everyday. The official culture becomes pre-eminent through the evolution of writing:

> But all through this evolution, the idea of producing a society by a 'scriptural' system has continued to have as its corollary the conviction that although the public is more or less resistant, it is molded by (verbal or iconic) writing, that it becomes similar to what it receives, and that it is *imprinted* by and like the text which is imposed on it.
>
> This text was formerly found at school. Today, the text is society itself. It takes urbanistic, industrial, commercial, or televised form. But the mutation that caused the transition from educational archaeology to the technocracy of the media did not touch the assumption that consumption is essentially passive. (de Certeau, 1984: 167)

Text, then, can be identified as a set of machineries, technologies or apparatuses – including televised media – which may be equated with society itself. Text is therefore to be distinguished from the operations or practices which defy their internal logics. The non-text, we might assume, slips out of its discursive boundaries *as operation*, resisting the solidifying impulse of textuality, and eluding the compromising order of society.

Resistance to this official, textual culture, thus, becomes the territory of the real, the unconscious, the pre-linguistic practices of everyday life. De Certeau argues that in work and leisure everyday practitioners are engaged in the operations of 'making do' – they must take what the society and culture offer and create 'transverse' spaces which become the 'play in the machine', the source of an individual's power and freedom. De Certeau distinguishes between 'strategies' and 'tactics', both of which produce this effect of disrupting or altering the processes of contemporary capitalist culture (de Certeau, 1984: 29–30). Strategies constitute a level of apparent conformity to the conditions offered by social circumstances; tactics are the 'invisible' activities or operations which everyday practitioners employ within the framework of these circumstances. In this sense a North African emigrant may choose (strategically) to live in Paris and take a job in a factory which enables him and his family to survive with a reasonable degree of comfort and security. However, within this general strategy, the immigrant may 'find ways of using (tactically) the constraining order of the place' (de Certeau, 1984: 30) in order to further advantage his life circumstances. De Certeau refers to the notion of *la perruque* or 'wearing the wig'. These are the disguises that are used by everyday practitioners in order to create the illusion of conformity; behind or within this apparent conformity they are creating a space for their freedom. The worker, therefore, may use his or her time to pilfer, send personal emails, run a football betting competition, speak about television programmes, arrange social engagements – all on the company's time and money. But these creative spaces are not simply defined by the workplace; they are created in the home and in the general activities of consumption and 'making do':

> Without leaving the place where he has no choice but to live and where it lays down its law for him, he establishes within it a degree of *plurality* and creativity. By an act of being in between, he draws unexpected results from his situation. (de Certeau, 1984: 30)

For de Certeau there are three significant characteristics of this resistance:

1   It exists at the level of the unconscious (what Lacan calls the real) and is therefore outside the realm of consciousness, language and inherited culture. Resistance or subversion is not achieved through the instructional content of a text, nor by its special aesthetic qualities, as theorists like Julia Kristeva, Bertolt Brecht or the American postmodernists might claim. Resistance exists outside the text altogether, except in as much as the tactical raiders of everyday life make the text, or any other cultural activity, object or artefact, 'their own'.

2   It functions as operations (or actions) at the level of everyday life and is not predetermined by structure or ideology, which are societal and therefore textual. Where an everyday person becomes subversive of rationalized order is where he or she functions against the flow of discourse. Practitioners do not think their liberation; they merely experience it through their everyday activities.

3   It operates necessarily through consumption and consumption practices. These are 'tactical' since they are used by everyday people to maximize their own pleasures and life satisfactions. The everyday raiders act in their own interests without recourse to grand narratives, reformist ideology or direct challenge to authority. Their self-interest is sufficient motivation to disturb the rationalizing effects of social conformity.

The 'Weak' and the 'Strong'

De Certeau's notion of popular consumption practices has proven extremely attractive to those celebrational postmodernists who have sought to raise consumption to a higher theoretical and political plane (see Fiske, 1989a, 1989b; Featherstone, 1991; Featherstone et al., 1991; Jenkins, 1992; Marshall, 1997). Applying his theoretical density for a reading of popular culture, John Fiske, in particular, rejoices in those practices of consumption, which provide for all social groups the opportunity to create meanings and community outside the structures established by the 'official' culture. Fiske and others tend to parenthesize some of the more difficult aspects of de Certeau's theory, including his psychoanalytical ideas on 'writing' and 'the real'. Popular cultural analysis tends, for example, to collapse the distinction between 'writing' and 'practice' into a general theory of transgression which incorporates all forms of textualization and everyday practice. What matters for popular cultural theorists like John Fiske is that all texts (all culture) are available for consumption (using, reading, viewing, listening). The texts provided by capitalist culture are strategically adopted and tactically raided for the personal, transgressive pleasures of the consumer/everyday practitioner.

In this sense, de Certeau and Fiske break significantly with Bourdieu's conception of symbolic value. They reject the idea that taste merely reflects and determines social hierarchy, arguing that Bourdieu seriously misunderstands the power of social groups to form meanings and constitute themselves culturally. De Certeau specifically rejects the idea that the lower classes are 'weak' and vulnerable to the structuralized and controlling powers of the 'strong' and their socially determined privileges and tastes. According to de Certeau, 'the weak' use their consumption tactically to over-throw the putative power of 'the strong', who are fixed and restrained by the ratio-nalized order of language and history. In fact, the 'strong' are weak because they have no idea that they are being duped. The 'weak' wear disguises or 'wigs' (*les per-ruques*) by which they hide their tactical raidings. As Fiske takes up this idea, he argues that the strong (corporate powers) are vulnerable to these selective practices of the 'weak' (everyday consumers) since it is the consumers who decide what will and won't succeed commercially. The 'weak' select products from the vast array of overly structured and overly invested materials and services on offer. The weak are nimble, deft and creative, while the strong are tor-pid, culturally and intellectually obese, and fixed in overly rationalized systems of struc-ture. By far the greater majority of all prod-ucts remain unsold and it is the 'strong' who are left to puzzle over their failure, second-guessing the shifting interests, tastes and sensibilities of the 'weak'.

Fiske argues, in fact, that the 'strong' must anxiously and despairingly wait upon the choices of the 'weak'. The 'weak' form fashion and taste. Their popular consump-tion liberates them from expectation and the hierarchy of overbloated and competi-tive superiority. The 'weak' transform pro-ducts, practices and places and make them their own. Old people use shopping malls to save money on heating and cooling; young people transform street corners into social totems. They raid the second-hand stores, remove labels from expensive items and sew them on to cheaper imitations. They wait for the post-Christmas sales. They tear at the knees of blue jeans and transform

them into symbols of a new community. They remove the wheels from roller skates and drill them onto plywood boards. The 'weak', that is, overthrow the reality bondage of the 'strong' through their own (unconsciously) 'tactical' consumption and meaning-making at the level of the *real*.

JOHN FISKE: POPULAR CONSUMPTION

John Fiske's celebration of popular culture began during the 1980s when he appended many of the precepts of the Birmingham Centre for Contemporary Cultural Studies to the theories of Bakhtin, de Saussure and Barthes; in the later 1980s and 1990s he further elaborated his analysis of popular culture through the work of de Certeau and celebrational postmodernism. Through-out his work, Fiske has been intrigued with the idea of (bodily) pleasure as the source of popular resistance. Like other English-speaking theorists working in the field (see Hebdige, 1979; Dyer, 1985; Frow, 1991; Jenkins, 1992; Hartley, 1996; Marshall, 1997) his work combines an interest in text with an analysis of audience or reception practices. However, it has continually sought to reconcile the text–audience divide through speculative readings about how a particular audience might respond to a given text. While these speculations were built around notions of preferred reading (encoding/decoding) in his earlier writing, Fiske has later adapted Barthes's notions of pleasure and bliss to develop a politics of audience pleasure.

It is through the reworking of textual polysemy or multiple meanings that audi-ences are able to experience a pleasure that frees them from the instrumental rationalities and order of patriarchal capi-talism. In this way, Fiske clearly moves from investigation to celebration of popular culture, where the 'popular' is conceived as necessarily political and transgressive, and necessarily implicates the bodily pleasures of readers, viewers and users. Texts which are 'popular' or 'of the people' carry far greater potential for bodily liberation than do the putative high arts, which are always constrained by abstruse, overly rationalized and inaccessible discourses. However, Fiske's work, for all its inconsistencies, is not merely populist or opportunistic, as Jim McGuigan (1992) and others have claimed. A text, which may be anything from a beach to a football match to a television soap opera, becomes liberatory when it engages the viewer/consumer in particular subject 'positions' and practices. Fiske feels genuinely that these engagements constitute the best hope contemporary culture can offer for the liberation of individuals and communities.

The Carnivalesque

Clearly, Fiske attaches meanings to the activity of consumption which are distinct from classical Marxist or radical environmentalism, both of which identify consumption with social control, and social and environmental damage. Fiske's work, in fact, follows the lead of Mikhail Bakhtin (Valentin Volosinov), who reversed various aspects of classical Marxism to produce his theory of the carnivalesque. The carnival of the Middle Ages, Bakhtin explains, removes hierarchy and law in what appears to be a sensate, almost Dionysiac, disordering of social norms.

> The laws, prohibitions, and restrictions that determine the structure of ordinary, that is noncarnival, life are suspended during carnival: what is suspended first of all is hierarchical structure and all the forms of terror, reverence, piety, and

etiquette connected with it – that is, everything resulting from socio-hierarchical inequality or any other form of inequality among people (including age). All *distance* between people is suspended, and a special carnival category goes into effect: *free and familiar contact between people*. (Bakhtin, 1984: 122–3)

Clearly, Bakhtin is idealizing a social reversal which dissolves identity, rules and bodily and social distance. As with the early English festival 'Twelfth Night' or the contemporary Mardi Gras of Sydney and Rio de Janeiro, Bakhtin's carnivalesque is a time when sensual experience overtakes logical order; the carnival culture, which privileges laughter, parody, disorder, sexuality, abundance and transparency, overrides official culture, which prefers intellect, order, governance, opacity, stasis and control. Politically, however, the carnival was not merely a temporary negation of the official order, but carried the promise of a better world, a utopia, which could release the common person from the drudgery of his or her obedient and fixed conditions.

Fiske identifies the carnivalesque with the liberationism of popular TV (1987, 1989a). According to Fiske, TV's engagement with excesses of bodily display, grotesqueness, degradation and spectacle identifies the medium as a carnival of carnality and sentimentalism. TV watching thus becomes a source of freedom and reversal, a site in which everyday viewers can relieve themselves of order, obedience and capitalist-directed tedium. We must remember, however, that this television viewing and indeed all the popular practices identified by Fiske and others operate at the level of the unconscious. Consumption is not a deliberately seductive act, but is rather an outcome of self-interest and the maximization of personal pleasure.

The Beach, Pleasure and Popular Culture

In fact, Fiske's work leaves the question of pleasure open. While insisting that culture is at its very core contradictory, Fiske nevertheless seeks resolution in the political exigencies of the body. His own (non-empirical) ethnology of TV watching and other everyday cultural practices relies on a patchwork of theoretical positions, all of which locate resistance in sensate experience. Even so, Fiske would insist that this theoretical assemblage is not a derivative of ontology or Romantic transcendentalism; it is purely experiential and without recourse to deeper spiritual or emotional conditions. Thus, his resistance is a loosely theorized and loosely ideological polemic. If we consider the example of the beach, we can see how his textual and representational analysis engages with his reading of everyday people and their unconscious, oppositional practices.

Fiske has moved from universities in Wales, through Australia and now the United States. His stay in Australia led him to consider the beach in relation to popular practices and consumption, most particularly through a reading of Lévi-Strauss, de Certeau, and Barthes's *Mythologies* and *The Pleasure of the Text*. Fiske would want to disestablish political elitism by constructing a politics of everyday practice that extends beyond hedonism or the conventions of British utilitarianism. In the realm of the popular, Fiske tells us (1989a, 1989b), everyday practices constitute a direct challenge to the impositions of patriarchal capitalism; the body and the sensory (nature) are welded in opposition against the reasoned hegemonies of domination (civilization). This loose alliance of theoretical postulates allows Fiske to construct 'beachgoers' as unselfconscious raiders of meaning. In their everyday practices on their everyday sites, the beachgoers become actors in the realm of the popular. They challenge, as they confront, the discursive and structural fabrications imposed by the 'strong', destabilizing them through the very act of their beachgoing pleasure. For Fiske, therefore, the beach must be understood as a battleground, a site replete with semiotic divisions, meanings and ideological tension:

> [D]ifferent people use the beach differently, that is, they find different meanings in it, but there is a core of meanings which all users, from respectable suburban family to long-haired, dropout surfer, share to a greater or lesser degree. The beach is an anomalous category between land and sea that is neither one nor the other but has characteristics of both. This means that it has simply too much meaning, an excess of meaning potential, that derives from its status as anomalous. (1989a: 43)

The beach's anomalousness, Fiske goes on to explain, can be treated politically and in accordance with structuralist precepts. There are spheres of ideological tension where either civilization (the esplanade, the lawned picnic areas, the council signs) or nature (the surf) may predominate. The sand and shallows are sites of struggle where cultivated humans will divest themselves of social status and power (clothes, status symbols, regulation) to play amid the (tempered) perils and pleasures of nature. But it is the 'surfie', Fiske concludes, who takes the greatest risks and derives the greatest pleasures beyond the polemicizing of signification:

> The wave is the text of bliss to the surfie, escape from the signified, potential reentry into nature, constantly shifting, needing retreading for each loss of subjectivity. It contradicts, defines, momentarily the ideological subjectivity through which discourses exert their control. (1989a: 76)

'Bliss', of course, is the most extreme of Barthesian pleasures. This politics of pleasure, which so interests Fiske and others concerned with 'resistant' textual practices, is posited as a possible escape from, or alternative to, the Althusserian dominant ideology – experiences like the 'un-signified' wave might constitute, therefore, 'our only way of situating social change within the domain of the popular' (1989a: 76).

Fiske is somewhat less enthusiastic about the wave as it is textualized – i.e. discursively reconstituted – in the 'surfie journal' (also Fiske et al., 1987: 67–70). The subversive potential of surfing (body, nature, desire, alternative language) can be easily neutralized, Fiske regrets, through its conscription into standard modes of social and cultural experience. Sex confounds the radicalism of surfing as the male surfer inscribes his discourse with patriarchal conceits: 'The surfie's sexuality is one of blatant male chauvinism. … And the women consent willingly to this male hegemony, not only in sexual activity but also in surfing' (1989a: 73–4). Females, that is, are represented in the 'surfing literature' as passive and generally subordinate adjuncts to male power; the female becomes an analogue to surfing 'ecstasy', a beach-based distraction from it, or the representative of normalized and official domestic culture. For Fiske this treatment of the female in the surfie journal is necessarily associated with the culturalization of the surf (nature) through the normative processes of land-based society (patriarchal capitalism). The radical potential returns only when the surf is removed from the city and its discursive and ideological structures.

Problems in Fiske's Approach

There is an ambiguity in Fiske's work here, one that is common to a good deal of contemporary cultural analysis concerned with the relationship between text and reader/audience. Throughout this chapter we have argued that meaning is formed out of the text–reader relationship, and that different theorists have emphasized either the power of the text to transmit (impose) meanings, or the power of the audience to create meanings. In British cultural studies, in particular, this nexus is further complicated by the desire of theorists to present a critical and political perspective of the operations of culture. Using his Gramscian model, Stuart Hall sees a confluence of hegemonic conditions operating through media institutions, the text, the audience and the cultural context. In other words, there is a sometimes delicate, sometimes robust, shifting and negotiating of power and meanings which tend to settle into a relatively stable hierarchy of order. Change is possible, but so is power and structure. For de Certeau, the relationship is tilted toward the consumer/audience and practices rather than text. The weakness of this position is that it constitutes power as an unconscious operation; text and textual content, including radical content, are largely irrelevant to freedom and the formation of culture.

Fiske, however, wants it both ways. While he is attracted by de Certeau's notion of everyday practice (textual reading and consumption), he wants to retain some level of ideological power for the text itself. De Certeau insists that the popular is operational and can only exist in the realm of pre-discursive practice; for Fiske, the radical potential of the popular moves rather uncomfortably between operation and text. This softening of the divide between text and audience/consumer leads Fiske into some awkward theoretical moments. For example, his reference above to the 'surfie journal' makes clear that texts may themselves contain dubious ideological 'content', even though a text should only operate in relation to the perspective and subjectivity of the consumer and his/her everyday practices. Fiske struggles to convince us that these meanings can only operate in reference to cultural and subjective context, but there is no doubt that his main interest here is in the text itself and its representations of the female. Content and perspective are restored to the text, rather than existing merely in relation to the reader.

Similarly, Fiske finds it difficult to explain how a popular text, such as a football match, might be more or less radical depending on the *perspective* of the viewer/consumer. The football match, unlike the surfie journal, has no content of itself, but will become ideological in relation to the spectator. But it is not the spectator's personal politics which counts; it is the position from which he or she views the match that determines whether or not the perspective is popular and therefore transgressive. In Fiske's example the spectator becomes popular/ transgressive only when s/he is watching from the terraces. The spectator cannot be popular/ transgressive when s/he is watching the match from a corporate superbox. Fiske moves away from de Certeau's underlying claim that any everyday practitioner can be a tactical raider as long as s/he is operating at the level of the unconscious. Fiske's division appears to restore modernist hierarchies based on class or income. This opacity inclines the argument toward a neo-structuralist position where the world can be divided very clearly into dominant and subordinate social groups.

Indeed, while Fiske's arguments may be a little more sophisticated than this, there is no doubt that he never quite manages to forge a convincing theoretical framework for his popular politics. The assemblage of structuralist, de Certeauian and postmodernist perspectives never adequately accounts for the meaning-making and political dimensions of text–audience

interaction. For Fiske, in fact, and this is a point developed further by John Hartley (1987), the audience is probably an elusive concept, another discursive contingency or text which should be read, interpreted and constituted in relation to broader cultural imperatives. That is, the audience may be 'assumed' and interpreted like any other text without recourse to ethnographic or other forms of empirical research. For Fiske, applying a rather loose reading of de Certeau's radical psychoanalysis, the audience and their popular readings can be interpreted for us and presented in terms of a political radicalism that satisfies Fiske's own polemical project. The beach is a site of pleasure for Fiske, but he never quite produces a theory of text consumption which allows that pleasure to be political.

Race, Gender and Postmodernism

In his analysis of race and gender representations in the US media, Fiske (1996) seeks to elaborate his interests in 'dominant' discourses through an analysis of public, personal and mediated politics. While he remains interested in popular texts and sensate audience responses, he moves away from simple engagements of pleasure to ask more probing questions about the nature of sensate responses in relation to 'sensational' news stories and narratives. Avoiding complex theoretical frameworks, *Media Matters* attempts to resolve many of the tensions besieging contemporary cultural studies through the textual analysis of significant political events and their representation in the media. In particular, Fiske attempts to elucidate the often bewildering mix of cultural ideologies, contradictions and tensions, citing such events as the Rodney King beating, the O.J. Simpson trial and the Clarence Thomas sexual harassment case. This elucidation of contemporary American culture draws on liberatory and oppressive discourses which, according to Fiske, constitute the formation of cultural identity in 'actual' and mediated life; for Fiske, however, there is no difference since everything is text and everything needs to be read. The changes in political relationships during the 1990s can only be accessed through careful reading of the media:

> A change in the structure of feeling involves a change in the proportion of ingredients that constitute the cultural mix, a change in which of the currents come to the surface and which are submerged. But not all currents change. In the politics of age, gender and sexuality we can trace visible changes: the election put more women into Washington than ever before, Bill Clinton has put a slew of women and non-Caucasians into powerful positions, and the White House staff is younger and more ethnically diverse than previously. ... The White House and Washington, however, are not the only sites of cultural and political activity, and in many ways are unlike others. A change in administration is abrupt, complete and visible. No other change is. Most other cultural currents are much muddier. (1996: 13)

For Fiske, these 'muddier' changes are the ones which occur at the personal, interactive and mediated levels of human culture. These are things that can be elucidated through the analysis of media text, the pleasures of which are as confused as the events that excite them. Fiske's study attempts to come to terms with the flux of a postmodern culture where blacks can hold prominent positions but where the resonances of older ideologies still haunt their lives and subjectivity. In many respects, Fiske's work on culture illustrates the deficiencies of the concept of dominant ideology, though, as with his earlier works, he is never able to escape his structuralist methodologies and perspectives. Fiske remains trapped in the structuralist–poststructuralist,

modern–postmodern nexus where meanings float uncertainly between text and audience.

IEN ANG: WOMEN, WATCHING AND LIBERATION

Watching Dallas

As we saw in the discussion on feminism (Chapter 6), the liberation of women has been theorized in a wide variety of ways, raising significant questions about the nature of women's subjectivities, subject positions and identity. We have seen, for example, that the representation of women and women's bodies has been widely critiqued in feminist and *Screen*-based psychoanalytic theory. However, more recent feminist studies have seen the critique of the 'male gaze' and the ideological effects of structural patriarchy as limiting the possibilities of liberation and the female experience generally. The representation of women and the experience of female audiences is a good deal more diverse and facilitatory than is acknowledged by these earlier forms of feminist analysis. As an example, Angela McRobbie's career study of teenage women's magazines shifts from a structuralist repudiation of stereotyped representations (1982) toward a more audience-based analysis of the ways in which these magazines and their discourses are consumed and deployed for pleasure and the formation of identity (1991).

Similarly, Ien Ang's (1985, orig. 1982 in Dutch) analysis of the American soap opera *Dallas* represents a significant shift in the way feminism considers the text–audience relationship. While earlier feminists and social control theorists condemned soap operas for their restrictive and stereotypical presentation of women and women's lives, Ang's *Watching Dallas* emphasizes the creative, liberatory and meaning-making potential of text consumption. One of the most interesting features of Ang's book is its attempt not merely to elucidate a conception of the audience as active meaning-makers, but also to elucidate that meaning-making in terms of diversity and personal agency. That is, Ang wanted to understand how Dutch audiences responded to, interacted with and constructed meanings from this very popular American soap opera. Ang's point of departure was her own contradictory experiences with a TV programme which she found intriguing, stimulating and appealing, on the one hand, yet ideologically offensive, on the other. Ang confesses that she enjoys soaps for their romantic intrigue, opulence and glamour, but recognizes that they clearly contravene her rationalized ideological sensibilities. That is, her own ambivalence becomes a tacit acknowledgement of the capacity of television programmes to position readings both between various audience members as well as within the one subject reader:

> [M]y own ambivalent relation to *Dallas* will also have its repercussions. This ambivalence is on the one hand connected with my identity as an intellectual and a feminist, and on the other hand with the fact that I have always particularly liked watching soap operas like *Dallas*. At one time I really belonged to the category of devoted *Dallas* fans. (1985: 12)

Central to Ang's research, then, is the question of personal pleasure. Ang seeks to understand how she and others derive pleasure from watching television, 'without having to pass judgement on whether *Dallas* is good or bad, from a political, social or academic view' (1985: 12). In other words, Ang is attempting to weld a cultural politics out of the popular cultural model being forged in British cultural studies and American postmodernism. Her aim is not to jettison politics from cultural and textual analysis, but to foreground the experience of the audience, most particularly the audience experiences of pleasure.

Ang's empirical methodology has been widely condemned for its untidiness and lack of genuine rigour. Ang placed an ad in a leading Netherlands women's magazine which read: 'I like watching the TV serial *Dallas* but often get odd reactions to it. Would anyone like to write and tell me why you like watching it too, or dislike it? I should like to assimilate these reactions into my university thesis' (1985: 10). This 'volunteer sample' provided the data for the development of a general theory of TV watching based around the generalized notion of pleasure. Thus, while theorists like John Fiske were adapting de Certeau's notion of 'making do' and strategic consumption, Ang was seeking an exposition of pleasure as the central and moulding derivative of constituted female identity. Women and women's pleasure could no longer be parenthesized or treated as an 'effect' of ideologically formulated social control.

The challenge for theorists of audience pleasure is to maintain a political focus without denying the validity of personal pleasure and the variability of textually constituted subject positions. Ang's solution to this problem in *Watching Dallas* is to provide a particular framework for the audience responses, explaining them in terms of a feminist semiotic. That is, she reads the relationship between various characters in terms of a feminist framework and then matches that interpretation against the pleasures and responses of text readers. Ang ultimately finds this question unresolvable since 'the project of feminism ... is impelled by an angry rejection of the existing social order as essentially unpleasurable, and by a projection of pleasure into a (mythical) ideal future' (1985: 133). But even for feminists, Ang suggests, there is a need for fantasy and pleasure, and the soap opera, with its 'tragic structure of feeling' and inescapable, seemingly interminable, hopelessness, seems strangely befitting of a female sensibility.

Ang's *Watching Dallas*, therefore, differs from John Fiske's approach to audiences in two fundamental ways:

1 Ang attempts to combine an interest in text and ideology with a more direct interest in audiences. Fiske also wants to understand the ideological context of a text but prefers to speculate about how an audience constructs meanings in relation to the text. Fiske retains an interest in preferred or dominant readings, while Ang uses an empirical investigation to find out more exactly what audiences are thinking and how they are making meanings.
2 This empirical investigation leads Ang to question her speculations about the relationship between texts, ideology and audiences. While David Morley virtually surrenders his interest in the text-ideology relationship, Ang is left to ask questions about it, and Fiske holds tight to it.

Living Room Wars

Ang's later solutions to this problem seek to reinvestigate audience pleasures or consumption against the context of cultural and media institutions. In *Living Room Wars* (1996) Ang combines her earlier interest in the interpretive processes of audiences with broader concerns about institutional and cultural contexts. Following similar studies by, for example, Roger Silverstone (1990), David Morley (1986, 1992) and Charlotte Brunsdon (1981), Ang entirely dispenses with any notion of the audience as passive. Rather, she insists,

it is the actual nature of active audience meaning-making that has become the central 'problematic' for contemporary audience research. In particular, meaning-making needs to be considered in terms of the three way relationship audience–text–context. Audiences, therefore, are positioned in their readings not only by the text and its 'codes' (the encoding/decoding model), but also by institutions, politics and a whole range of complex and interacting socio-cultural elements:

> [I]t is in this context that the practices of active meaning making in the process of media consumption – as part of creating a 'lifestyle' for oneself – need to be understood. I want to suggest that the significance of the new audience studies should not be sought in their deconstruction of the idea of the 'passive audience' ... but in their exploration of how people live within an increasingly media saturated culture in which they *have* to be active (as choosers and readers, pleasure seekers and interpreters). (1996: 12)

This postmodern consumer culture impels audiences to become more astute choosers and users, as they navigate their way toward a valid and valuable lifestyle.

As with Lyotard, Ang uses the concept of postmodernism as a cognitive and socio-cultural category. As a cognitive or epistemological category, postmodernism problematizes the whole notion of the audience and meaning-making. While Ang's earlier studies on *Dallas* may have presented some challenges to the notion of 'audience' as a fixed and categorical description, *Living Room Wars* comes to explain in postmodernist terms that the audience can never be a complete or unified description. In deconstructing the concept, Ang comes to acknowledge that the meanings created by audiences are far less precise and far more mutable than is generally assumed. Postmodern theoretics confirm for her a sense that the audience is always shifting away from fixed positions and descriptions, and that the text–context–audience relationship is never settled long enough to produce anything other than ephemeral descriptions.

Equally, as an historical or cultural category, the postmodern 'condition' is seen as replete with consumable and proliferating images as well as some fundamental changes to television and audience consumption practices. Television, like so many other media, institutional and cultural phenomena, has undergone significant changes since the 1980s, changes which reflect and constitute broader transformations in capitalist society:

> [T]elevision itself has undergone massive postmodernization – manifested in a complex range of developments, such as pluralization, diversification, commercialization, commodification, internationalization, decentralization. ... This transformation of television points to the central 'mover' of postmodern culture: an increasingly global, transnational, postindustrial, postFordist capitalism, with its vociferous appetite to turn culture into an endlessly multiplying occasion for capital accumulation. (1996: 3)

Ang's interest in audiences, therefore, turns toward the central issue of cultural consumption and the construction of meaning through engagements with lifestyle and pleasure. Like Fiske and others, however, Ang seeks some space for the critique and deconstruction of these processes without denying the value of pleasure and the dignity and freedom that (potentially at least) are derived through everyday practices. Her attention once again returns to women's social status and the liberational facility of 'women's' television. The fairly loosely constituted empirical methods deployed in *Watching Dallas* (1985) are not repeated, though Ang maintains that her work is fundamentally 'empirical'. This empiricism, however, presents itself as a theoretical rather than a practical claim in *Living Room Wars*, where she speculates about audiences, contexts and texts rather than engaging in scientifically formulated ethnographic research. In fact, Ang's explanation of the relationship between postmodernism and empiricism reflects a fairly strained attempt to deny the particulations of postmodernism and its deep suspicions of any claim to empirical fact. Ang suggests, for example, that 'it is an empirical fact' that different sections of an audience relate differently to particular TV programmes; this postmodern empiricism clearly transgresses Lyotard's (1984a) belief that the postmodern necessarily relinquishes any claim to 'facts', universal truths or objective scientism. Ang would have us believe that her speculative writing constitutes empiricism whereby looking at TV experiences and practices 'provides us with an excellent inroad into what it means, concretely and empirically, to live in a culture which can be described as "postmodern"' (Ang, 1996: 2). In order to construct this putative empiricism, however, Ang is forced here to parenthesize postmodernism as a way of thinking that denies such empiricism as a unifying and homogenizing description. While beginning with a claim that audiences are virtually 'unknowable', in as much as they are perpetually shifting in their interactions with text and culture, Ang nevertheless wants to bring herself and her own readers into a more fixed realm of 'empirical' knowledge.

WOMEN AND ROMANTIC COMMUNITIES

Ien Ang's attempt to elevate her writing through the invocation of empiricism reflects several concerns:

1 It demonstrates Ang's own dissatisfaction with pure speculation which is rooted in textual and philosophical studies. There needs to be a greater effort, she argues, to strengthen the sociological claims of cultural enquiry.

2 It indicates that Ang is seeking to lever open the private lives and practices of everyday people, making them available to broader fields of knowledge.

3 It reflects an effort to overcome the theoretical inadequacies of postmodernism, most especially through an attempted reconciliation between the historical/cultural application of the concept and its use as a mode of thinking.

4 It demonstrates that Ang is seeking an empirical description of text–context–audience as a means of reconciling the further problematic of postmodernism: the tensions between social control and individual agency. That is, as in *Watching Dallas* (1985) and *Desperately Seeking the Audience* (1990), Ang puzzles over the ways in which social organizations and institutions ideologically and discursively manipulate the thinking, actions and identity of individuals, most particularly through TV texts and cultural contexts. But she also acknowledges that these texts and contexts bring immense pleasure with them and that these pleasures are a source of individual and collective freedom.

Other cultural investigators confronted the same problem during the 1980s and 1990s, most especially in their studies of the audience–text relationship. Some, such as Janice Radway, Richard Dyer and Jackie Stacey, have been particularly interested in the construction of women's pleasures and identity through fantasy and romantic imagery. Radway's (1987) famous study of romance readers in the American township of Smithton represents a significant movement in American sociology toward a cultural studies perspective. Radway herself claims never to have heard of cultural studies when she completed her research, though the analysis parallels much of the interest and work being conducted in Europe and Britain under the cultural studies banner. Radway's research involved a community of women who patronized Dorothy Evans' bookshop, famous for its romance listings and Dot's own romantic eruditions. The research consisted of face-to-face interviews, small group discussions and questionnaires – a far more meticulous and carefully managed piece of qualitative research than was conducted by Ien Ang.

A Question of Popularity

Theorists of popular culture have varying views on what constitutes 'the popular'. The popular is conceived sometimes as a set of commercially successful texts (popular with audiences), sometimes as a set of practices which emerges through the appropriations and interests of 'the community' (cf. 'folk culture'), and sometimes as a 'political perspective' which also emerges from the position of the community and which usually involves conditions of pleasure and bodily sensation.

From an industry perspective, popularity is simply the process of attracting audiences. In order to gauge the success of texts, executives employ some quite simple measurement devices. These can be listed as follows:

1 Circulation figures for newspapers and magazines. Sales figures for other print publications such as books.

2 Diary records for radio. Research companies are employed to distribute diaries to a given number of listeners. 'Ratings' are measured according to the recorded listening behaviours of a given sample of radio listeners.

3 TV 'people meters'. These are computerized recording systems. Members of a given sample of TV viewers press a button on the recording box whenever they enter a room with a TV switched on. The programme and length of viewing time are recorded. The information is transmitted directly to a source computer and the 'ratings' are calculated (usually every fifteen minutes). For TV, ratings usually refer to the percentage of TV households with at least one TV switched on to a particular programme at a particular time. A figure of 20.1 for *Friends* would suggest that 20.1 per cent of TV households would be watching *Friends* at this particular time. This figure *is not* the percentage of total households with a TV switched on at that particular time – it is a percentage of *all* TV households, whether or not the television is switched on or not.

4 Feedback lines, letters and emails. Radio stations, in particular, generate programming data from their own surveys of their own actual listeners. This form of 'market research' provides 'qualitative' information about the tastes and interests of actual consumers of the product.

5 Website visits or 'hits'. These measure the number of visits made to a particular website. The figure can identify these numbers over any given time period. While this provides a measure of the popularity of a given site, it is also used as a complementary measure of popularity for other media programmes. For example, producers of public broadcast programmes often supplement their programmes with on-line chats and records of programme content. The website hits indicate the relative audience interest in particular programmes.

For private commercial media companies, the popularity of a programme is a commodity which can be sold to advertisers. The more popular the programme, especially with particular age-groups with high consumption demands (18–45 years), the higher the price of advertising time. For high investment media such as film and television, programme producers often market test a product before full commission or release. In the United States this practice of pre-testing major cinema products is almost an art-form. Audiences watch a film, or various versions of a film, holding an interest measurement device called a 'worm'. Approval and disapproval are mapped and the film-makers use this information to create the most acceptable version of the film before it is released. Little wonder that so many American films construct (salvage) a happy and well-resolved ending out of their drama.

Along with the institutional and marketing processes which had contributed to the popularity of the genre, the primary focus of Radway's research was the ways in which female audiences within this symbolic community used the texts to constitute themselves, their relationships and their own lives. Most of the readers were married with children, and Radway found that the practices of textual selection and discrimination constituted a significant dimension of social pleasure and freedom. Thus, as de Certeau and Fiske had argued, the practice of textual shopping (cultural consumption) constitutes a significant form of identity creation and personal liberation. Through her investigations, Radway found that the women were searching for an ideal romance, rather than an ideal male protagonist. The ideal romance is one in which intelligent, sensitive and independent women work through threat and cruelty to be overwhelmed by the love of an intelligent man, who in turn must be transformed by the emotional competency of the woman. As Radway explains, her research found that a popular romance is one which is not so much about discovering the ideal life-partner, but is a 'ritual wish to be cared for, loved, and validated in a particular way' (1987: 83). This nurturing male mythology harkens back to a deeper, psychological fantasy about the time when the reader was the focus of an intensely individualized nurturing experience – the experience of her own nurtured childhood. Romance and the hero–heroine relationship, Radway argues, draw the reader back to her own nurtured inner-self, creating a deep sense of security and care; this fantasy reflects across the role of carer which the reader herself is expected to perform for others, as wife and mother.

This process of identification with the hero-heroine relationship illustrates for Radway two significant cultural processes in the act of romance reading. First, it shows that the women's pleasures in reading reach beyond the institutional and commercial processes which provide the text. The institutions derive only financial returns, while the women readers derive significant emotional and psychological gratifications which they themselves select and control. Secondly, as these pleasures extend beyond the text, Radway acknowledges that it is the process of reading itself which empowers the women and enhances their sense of individual and collective identity. Once again, we find that the power of the text to transfer and impose particular ideologies, including patriarchal ideologies, needs to be measured against the liberatory dimensions of creative cultural consumption and meaning-making. Women use the romance text as a subtle resistance, a way of creating space, of challenging the mundane repetitiveness of their daily lives. The romance, in this sense, becomes a space where women can escape the surveillance of men and the continuities and limits of their social and familial roles.

Richard Dyer (1985) argues similarly that women use the cinema and romantic Hollywood films for the construction of a utopia in which their own lives are radically enhanced through the process of identification. The screen experience for women is conceived in terms of 'heavenly bodies': the textual formation of women's idealized selves, a space where women can experience the freedom to imagine. Along with other film analysts, such as Jackie Stacey, Dyer explores a notion of celebrity and the self-projections that women make through cinema fantasy. Celebrity provides a site of interaction and identity-building for women, a place where they can think and experience life outside the cloisters of their own everyday rhythms and restrictions. Stacey's (1994) empirical investigations of women's enjoyment of cinema demonstrates, moreover, that the actual context of the cinema adds to the sense of utopia. Stacey notes, in particular, that the furnishings, luxuriousness and sense of shared experience or community are key elements in women's enjoyment of cinema.

FANS AND POSTMODERN COMMUNITY

Women romance readers, however, are not the only group who may constitute a particular textual sub-culture. As we noted earlier, the work of Roger Silverstone (1997) and David Morley (1986, 1992) has concentrated on the deployment of specific media (especially TV) within the domestic cultural context. As we know, the concept of culture or sub-culture may be defined in terms of particular social formations at a range of levels – everything from a family, neighbourhood, ethnic group, nation or globe may be defined in terms of culture. A number of cultural analysts have sought to explain culture in terms of the consumption of particular texts and textual groupings. Dick Hebdige (1979) was among the first cultural studies academics to apply this sort of anthropological framework to the study of the assemblage of people he refers to as 'youth'. While 'youth' may be a category of age, youth culture, in Hebdige's terms, is framed significantly around clothing style, practices, rituals and musical texts. For Hebdige, youth sub-culture constitutes a significant challenge to inherited social values and lifestyles. Like Michel de Certeau, Hebdige applies Lévi-Strauss's concept of 'bricolage' to describe the ways in which sub-cultures borrow from existing or conventional culture to form new cultural elements. For Hebdige, youth culture constitutes a bricolage of elements which

ultimately combine to form a distinctive and transgressive 'sub-culture'.

Thus, 1960s youth culture in Britain was formed through the cultural propinquities and bricolage of urban black migrant culture, the popularization of American black culture and the incorporative commodifications of middle-class white culture. The sub-cultures constituted themselves through a 'style' which might have had little to do with the cultural source but which was 'enabled' through appropriation. In this sense, the mod movements of the 1960s, which formed around the music and style of bands like The Beatles, came to disguise many of their original cultural influences. The Beatles' music and appearance were influenced by black American rhythm and blues, though these roots become obscured somewhat in the development of the new sounds and presentational styles. The Beatles made palatable for white middle-class audiences the sub-culture of former slaves, ultimately creating a new liberatory space for further cultural experimentation and hybridization. For The Beatles and the youth culture which came to surround them, this hybri-dization later incorporated the musical sounds, religion and cultural narcoses of India.

Hebdige explains the creative and liberatory formation of such sub-cultures in terms of broader historical and social phenomena. The formation of youth culture, therefore, needs to be understood in terms of structural changes as well as community-level experiences. In particular, the experimentations and adaptability of British youth culture during the 1960s can be explained in part by accelerated migration into Britain from Jamaica and elsewhere, and the associated 'decline of empire'. In many respects, Hebdige's work lays the foundation for wider cultural analysis of youth culture (see Redhead et al., 1997; Skelton and Valentine, 1998; MacDonald, 2001). The work of Lawrence Grossberg in the United States and Simon Frith in Britain centralizes rock music as a cultural and political formation. Frith, in particular, argues that earlier (modernist) paradigms of musical analysis fail dismally to account for the 'popularity' and importance of rock music in contemporary culture. The commodification of music and musical forms has facilitated the ongoing and restless shifts in identity formation which surround the highly particularized pleasures of listening to rock music. Taste not only determines the formation of an individual and group's identity, but it actually calibrates that identity against broader cultural formations, expectations and norms. The way someone 'is' seems closely associated with the type of music he or she chooses. In this sense, the 'meaning' of a musical text is thoroughly bound to the listener and the context of listening:

> To grasp the meaning of a piece of music is to hear something not simply present to the ear. It is to understand a musical culture, to have a 'scheme of interpretation'. For sounds to be music we need to know how to hear them: we need 'knowledge' not just of musical forms but also of rules of behaviour in musical settings. (Frith, 1996: 249–50)

Henry Jenkins (1992) applies the same understanding of the community of meaning to his analysis of the fans of the long-running TV and film series *Star Trek*. Like John Fiske, Jenkins adapts Michel de Certeau's notion of strategic raiding to explain the way fans 'poach' the meanings of a corporatist, mass-distributed text like *Star Trek*. For Jenkins, 'the fan' constitutes a particular social and cultural category; a fan doesn't merely watch a text but uses it as a central symbol, a way of bringing order, meaning and community to his or her everyday experiences. The text is 'poached' because fans do much more than treat the text as a distraction or escape from everyday experiences. The text helps the fan actually construct those experiences. Jenkins (1992: 277–81) outlines the complexity and diversity of fandom as a sub-cultural community, according to five general levels of activity:

1 Fans are distinguished by their capacity for cultural proximity and critical distance. Fans scrutinize texts multiple times and with considerable expertise; fans discuss, debate and create meaning from texts through enunciative as well as experiential practices.

2 Fans' expertise engages particular kinds of interpretive and critical practices. Fans insist on consistency of detail across a programme and between programmes. Part of 'becoming a fan' involves the learning of the fan community's particular mode of reading, and the dominant meanings that generally issue through community expectation. Fan criticism often involves filling in the gaps, overcoming inconsistency and rendering the text amenable to the community's preferred reading. That is, the fans 'supplement' the text in order to make it fit with the fan group's preferred way of understanding and relating to the text.

3 Fan expertise also involves consumer activism. Fans lobby TV networks and their advertisers when they feel a series is in jeopardy or when they disagree with a programming decision. They also express their dissatisfaction with any changes to the text, its characters, plot or orientation.

4 Fandom engages with particular forms of cultural production, and aesthetic traditions and practices. 'Fan artists, writers, videomakers and musicians create works that speak to the special

interest of the fan community' (Jenkins, 1992: 279). This appropriation and bricolage process draws from commercially available materials in order to produce a highly specific, sub-cultural style which identifies the community members with their group. Again echoing de Certeau, Jenkins claims that this sort of appropriation challenges the corporatist power of institutions which claim to have copyright control over popular media narratives. The art is made for a general sharing, and not for profit – it becomes the basis for a genuine folk culture.

5　Fandom functions as an alternative cultural community, one that is not predisposed to mainstream social and commercial practices. The utopianism of the *Star Trek* text is transferred, Jenkins argues, into an alternative discourse to mainstream culture. Fandom, that is, offers an alternative reality 'whose values may be more humane and democratic than those held by mundane society' (Jenkins, 1992: 280). For Jenkins, this alternative offers fans options for dealing with the real-world issues of conflict, alienation and despair.

Jenkins, like Dyer, Stacey and Fiske on occasions, tends to utopianize his cultural consumers, projecting for them an identity which evades the homogenizing order of official culture. The carnivalesque celebrated by Mikhail Bakhtin is absorbed into a theory of bodily conviction, a delight in the capacity of ordinary people to make their lives less ordinary. In a sense, this is the fundamental contradiction of Jenkins' analysis: in celebrating the everyday practices of ordinary people, he treats these textual poachers as postmodern heroes, lower-level groups who are able to liberate themselves from the status of their ordinariness to become part of a pre-eminent cultural form – the popular

text. The difficulty remains, of course, that the problematic of ordinariness is a statement of desire that would overcome banality, that would invest itself in fame, glamour, social prominence and adventure which their own lives so clearly lack. While Jenkins insists that this desire to overcome lack is both justifiable and positive, it might as easily be conceived as a form of personal and cultural pathology. The idealizing of this desire never quite escapes Baudrillard's dread that the simulacra that drive contemporary media culture, including media consumption, are entirely vacuous, pointless, an endless stream of stimulation, a desire that has no end.

DISCUSSION: PROBLEMS WITH POPULAR POLITICS

From the 1980s and 1990s cultural theory and cultural studies have engaged more fully with questions of popular cultural consumption, most particularly through the auspices of postmodernism. This evolving field of enquiry has led to some significant theoretical problems, most particularly as cultural analysis attempts to re-constitute its political and reformist projects. The centralization of 'pleasure' and 'everyday practices' opens the way for a politics of individual agency. Popular culture, therefore, becomes a site for liberation through desire. As Lawrence Grossberg has put it, 'Opposition may be constituted by living, even momentarily, within alternative practices, structures, and spaces' (1988: 169). These alternative spaces are provided through choice and the continuing diversifications that postmodern consumer culture provides. De Certeau's arguments, which have their roots in Bakhtin and others, seek a space in which the overwhelming ubiquity of capitalist structures is neutralized and sent into retreat, a space where capitalism becomes the servant of the strategic raiders, and where the promise of postmodernism can be fully realized. This promise – choice, diversity, multiculturalism, individualism, sexual liberationism, self-constituting identity – becomes the basis for contemporary culture and contemporary cultural politics.

Recent political theory has moved quite markedly from a strictly structuralist analysis of politics toward a politics which acknowledges the significance of culture, identity and the personal or 'visceral' dimensions of democracy and political expression. Writers like David Held (1987, 1992), Ernesto Laclau (Laclau and Mouffe, 1985; Laclau, 1996) and Anthony Giddens (1994) have attempted to construct a democratic cultural politics which liberates reformism from a Marxist 'grand narrative' and universalism, on the one hand, and from institutionalized liberal-democratic relativism on the other. Giddens, in particular, expounds a reform theory which would extend the possibilities of democracy and culture beyond what he regards as the stasis and interdependency of Left and Right politics; however, he would also want to conceive of a politics which is not reduced to the kind of convergent, centralist and economic-rationalist relativism which now predominates in Western liberal democracies. Giddens' alternative is a personal politics which restores power to the microphysics of everyday human experience.

Jürgen Habermas (1984a, 1987b, 1989) has also attempted to reconcile the various dimensions of popular culture and political reformism. Habermas's point of departure, however, is markedly different from the poststructuralists, psychoanalytical theorists and postmodernists. For him, the public sphere exists as a transformative space where democracy is removed from the control of the state and restored to the

level of public participation. Communication becomes the central focus of democracy, as the 'populace' take control of politicaldiscourse in order to create the ideal speech situation – that utopian 'space' where all views are discussed in public and disagreements are resolved through informed and rational debate. Habermas describes the development of modernity in terms of the separation of the state (and its discourses) from the private individual. The state reproduces itself in terms of ideology (false consciousness), public intervention and control of the individual. The separation of the individual from state-sponsored ideology leads inevitably to the dimunition of private and public freedom:

> If ideologies are not only manifestations of the socially necessary consciousness in its essential falsity, if there is an aspect to them that can lay claim to truth inasmuch as it transcends the status quo in utopian fashion, even if only for the purposes of justification, then ideology only exists from this moment on. (Habermas, 1989: 88)

Modernity, thus, becomes the unfinished project (Habermas, 1983), the project that will return politics to the public sphere and where governmentality and democracy are refurbished as participative domains of communicative action. This communicative action centralizes individual agency and the capacity of citizens to express and construct their own truths within the bounds of a regulated and secure lifestyle.

Notions of pleasure are not excluded from Habermas's theory, though he would reject its centralization in the organization of social and cultural life; reason and social order are the preconditions of individual pleasure at whatever level it is experienced. Jim McGuigan (1992) makes a similar point in his critique of popular cultural studies. McGuigan argues that the whole project of cultural studies and cultural theory has fallen into crisis because writers like John Fiske and Henry Jenkins have seriously overstated the political and subversive potential of popular culture. This excessive celebration of popular culture and the transgressive potential of pleasure and textual (symbolic) consumption, McGuigan claims, comes about because the finely balanced tensions that exist in Gramsci's theory of hegemony have been tipped in favour of individual choice and agency. Gramsci, we recall from Chapter 3, argues that hegemony (social 'leadership' by organic intellectuals) is actually 'negotiated' by the dominant and subordinated groups in a culture. Leaders in all fields maintain their privilege by adjusting their power to the needs and interests of subjugant groups and individuals. Subordinates feel some measure of engagement with and commitment to the social arrangements to which they themselves have contributed.

According to McGuigan, recent cultural studies, most especially through the analysis of youth culture and popular television, have tended to override important aspects of the political economy of cultural production:

> The uncritical endorsement of popular taste, from an entirely hermeneutic perspective, is curiously consistent with economic liberalism's concept of 'consumer sovereignty', the weaknesses of which are particularly manifest in the debate concerning broadcast policy conducted in Britain since the 1980s. ... An adequate account of contemporary popular culture demands analysis of public communication, institutional power and, in a materialist perspective, socio-economic relations. (1992: 6)

Questions of policy, institutional power, ethics and production, in fact, have been marginalized in theoretical debates and textual studies since the 1980s and 1990s. However, these questions persist and

particular areas of cultural analysis, including audience, ethnology and 'materialist' sociological studies, have returned in various ways to questions of government and institutional processes. McGuigan's reference to broadcast policy and the movement in the English-speaking world toward more general laissez-faire social and economic policy (economic rationalism, market sovereignty) has proven significant.

As we noted above, this movement represents a reorientation of left–right political divisions toward the centre. Globalism, corporatism, competition policy, savage reductions in public services and public employment, and the deregulation of labour, industry, the media and markets – all are symptoms of an ascendant ideology. The problems with balance of trade and enormous debt that had crippled the economies of Britain, Australia, New Zealand and Canada during the 1980s served to fuel the rhetoric of classical economics or 'economic rationalism'. As media industries became over-priced and relatively underperforming, they liquidated and dramatically cut costs; deregulation was a way of both subduing costs and increasing tradability. Government broadcasters were savaged while cable, satellite, video and interactive digital media expanded exponentially. The classical economic theory of consumer sovereignty placed individual choice at the centre of consumer capitalism. Cultural studies, whatever its motivations, became implicated in the ever-expanding embrace of privatization and commercialization. For McGuigan, the popularity of the media, especially youth media, was seen to infect the academy with its own market sovereignty and populist discourse. To be popular, that is, became an economic imperative for an academy besieged by the demands of economic rationalization.

Beyond McGuigan's general condemnation, however, significant theoretical problems continue to beset popular cultural studies. While the vocabulary of the debate has shifted from 'hegemony' to 'postmodernism', the question of structural controls against individual agency remains. That is, the 'powerful text–active audience' tension remains largely unresolved. Numerous theorists, including Ien Ang (1996), have despaired of ever clearly identifying 'the audience'; Ang, in particular, has presaged a move toward a more direct analysis of the specific industrial, commercial and regulatory context in which the text–audience relationship operates. Feminists like Angela McRobbie suggest even further that the irresolvability of this tension threatens the very basis of her political project. Women are socialized and 'controlled' by a textualized structural patriarchy; however, it is possible that the pleasures that are creatively extracted from these texts by women may constitute a resource for personal liberation. In order to mediate this conundrum, McRobbie (1994) recommends the restoration of a neo-Gramscian approach to media and culture, reformulating the analysis of consumption in terms of the context of production. By treating texts as 'reproductions', McRobbie claims, we will be able to understand the institutional practices which give them form. McRobbie seeks a return to ethnography which would illuminate institutional and audience practices.

Tony Wilson (1993, 1995) attempts to mediate deconstructionist theory with a fully theorized empirical analysis of audiences. Postmodernism, Wilson considers, is a theory of difference and diversity, a political paradigm which treats audiences and textual reading as necessarily subversive of homogenizing structural intent. In poststructuralist terms, the audience cannot be 'known' as a group of living breathing human beings, but must be regarded as another discourse and as ultimately 'unknowable' (Hartley, 1992: 110). Wilson (also Jacka, 1994), however, argues that these discourses are built around the experiences of real people and are therefore available to knowledge. The link between audience as discourse and the empirical rendering of those discourses can be found in the philosophy of phenomenology and hermeneutics. Put simply, audiences and their interpretation of texts take place within a certain cultural context, a certain system of knowledge or 'consciousness'. Of course audiences are written and spoken about and are therefore discourses; but they are also people who engage with and reproduce their own forms of discourse. The methods of social science – observation, discussion and interview – give the researcher access to these audience discourses. An audience can be therefore 'known' empirically.

Wilson deploys the theoretical frame of phenomenology in order to access the 'everyday' or 'ordinary' lifeworld of television viewers. Following in the traditions developed through Husserl, Weber and Habermas, he seeks to resolve the problematic of subject and object, whereby the individual's 'cognitive horizon' unifies familiar and unfamiliar objects into an organic and comprehensible reality:

> Horizons are frameworks of cognitive knowledge underlying perceptual experience, allowing aspects of that experience to be recognized and identified as types already encountered. Our concept of circularity, this cognitive horizon, both from and with which we interpret the world, allows us to anticipate that half-experienced circles will turn out to be round and to recognize them as familiar when they do. Our horizons of understanding the people around us permit differences to be perceived between human beings and animals, to anticipate and recognize their distinct activities. These frameworks operate as the fundamental basis of expectations about how things will be in the future. (Wilson, 1993: 17)

The phenomenological approach to audiences, then, follows a Kantian precept of pre-existing or essential reality, the source of which unifies subjects and objects. Wilson wants to understand the convergence and divergence of audience perceptions; the concept of horizon neatly represents a perceptual space which nonetheless can be confirmed as a reality. The cognitive horizon of the audience allows for variance in perception while inclining toward a dominant or common reading reality; for Wilson, 'reading' is always and everywhere a 'fusion of horizons' drawing upon, and producing, differences (Wilson, 1993, 1995).

Not surprisingly, Wilson invokes the authority of the phenomenological hermeneutics (interpretive theory) of Paul Ricoeur (see Chapter 3). For Wilson, as for Ricoeur, the convergence/divergence of subject perception challenges structuralist precepts about language and subjectivity. In particular, Ricoeur rejects the substitution of the subject by the dominance of social (or linguistic) structure. In this sense, Riceour's 'new hermeneutics' appears to parallel poststructuralist arguments about the relativity of language and the primacy of the subject in forming reality through interactions with language. Don Thade (1991) argues, in fact, that the deconstructionist method of poststructuralism, Jacques Derrida in particular, clearly parallels the hermeneutical method of Paul Ricoeur. Thade refers specifically to Derrida's shift in reading emphasis from the immediacy of its content centre to the 'edges'. Derrida's focus on margins, borders, signatures, titles, borders, divisions – that is, everything which constitutes background to the text content – is similar to Ricoeur's focus on the linguistic consciousness. Thade argues that Derrida's strategy is fundamentally phenomenological since reader perception and interpretation necessarily implicates the background in the 'field of perceptivability' (1991: 132).

This phenomenological strategy de-centres focal perceptions in order to address the taken-for-grantedness of fringe elements.

Ricoeur himself has opposed poststructuralism for its 'internalism', rejecting the incapacity of Derrida, in particular, to bring the reading act into the lifeworld of narrative and meaning-making subjects. Even so, there is a sense in which the 'cognitive horizon' of phenomenology parallels the interminable play of language where meaning becomes a kind of shadow presence for Derrida and his followers. Vincent Descombes (1980: 136–45) reminds us, in fact, that Derrida's initial writing on Husserl resolves itself into a deconstructive method which nevertheless constitutes an extension and radicalization of the phenomenology he critiques. For Descombes, the whole poststructuralist enterprise is born out of an attempt to extend and radicalize phenomenology, an attempt to understand more thoroughly the act of communication, its facilitations and failings.

Of course the major difference between phenomenology and poststructuralist theory centres on the former's attachment to a transcendental or pre-existing reality. Phenomenology, at least in the hands of Husserl and the new hermeneutics, seeks to identify the possibilities of meaning over the difficulties of variant perspectives. Poststructuralism is more concerned with the impossibilities of meaning, the gaps and limits of language. For phenomenology, the subject seeks to confirm the lifeworld reality of the cognitive horizon; the deconstructionist seeks to explode its illusion. The challenge for postmodern theoretics is to overcome the illusion and the limits of meaning without recourse to a transcendent or pre-existing 'reality' or 'consciousness'. In this sense, postmodernism's emphasis on otherness, difference, identity and consumerist pleasure seeks to hold the subject within the borders of everyday life, while maintaining the possibility of liberation. This liberation is not transcendent, however, nor does it rely on the possibilities of some extra-dimensional consciousness or reality. In a simple materialist sense, what we can experience directly and immediately, the release of bodily experience, has become the centre of much postmodern liberationism.

Postmodern Audiences and the End of Politics?

These various approaches to the audience have tried in their respective ways to explain the complex processes of meaning formation. The Gramscian approach, critical theory and various permutations of interpretive hermeneutics have all sought to resolve the tension between notions of the text as powerful ideology and the creative meaning-making of audiences. They have also tried to integrate some of the important insights of poststructuralism into a theory which maintains some level of materialist interest: that is, they have attempted to combine an interest in discourse with a sense in which the audience is comprised of real people with real sufferings, interests and vulnerabilities. These critical approaches attempt to mediate the text–audience tension within a distinctly political framework. The greater problem for critical analysis is associated with the problematics of audience/consumer pleasure. For critical theory, 'pleasure' can only be conceived in terms of the relief of suffering and oppression. For postmodernism, however, pleasure is not merely the end of political enterprise, but the means and very centre of political engagement. To this extent, the question of whether the audience is comprised of real people or not is entirely irrelevant; the audience is merely an 'engagement', an immersion of imaginations and discourses, which are ultimately constituted through pleasure. 'Meaning' is not something that can be located in an heuristic examination of either text, audience, or both: it is a sensibility which facilitates ongoing discursive imaginings and gratifications.

Andy Warhol wanted to articulate the pleasures of life as they are experienced at the surface and through the proliferation of consumerist images and products. As this theme is taken up by postmodernism and its centralization of the audience/consumer, particular theoretical problems emerge. The theoretical danger for postmodernism is twofold:

1 It threatens to collapse into an irreversible relativism which perpetually separates individuals from one another. If postmodernism is true to its heterogeneity, then it can be little more than a form of indulgent and relativist hedonism. In supporting a consumer sovereignty ethos, postmodernism claims that everything is acceptable if it brings pleasure to the individual. In this sense, postmodernism and popular consumerist theoretics can have little to say about the suffering of others.

2 It threatens to present its politics as a grounded and privileged theory of utility: that is, one in which pleasure, difference, creative consumerism, individualism and audience creativity become the 'essence' of a generalized politics of liberation. Postmodern discourse might actually transgress the imperatives of deconstruction by claiming to be true, absolute, centred and 'essentially' significant. It may return to the conditions of knowledge; it may claim a special insight, a ground which might deny its fundamental constituitivity. That is, rather than the world being mediated by language or discourse, the

danger is that the discourse may present itself as the reality.

In this sense, de Certeau's own consumer raiders are suspect since their political reversal is entirely without content or consciousness, being constituted by a popular consumerism and self-interest that pre-exists language. De Certeau's raiders, that is, are the product of psychoanalysis – the pre-conscious, pre-linguistic other of history. However, the subconscious and the everyday become essentialized themselves when they are presented in political terms: this special realm of the subconscious defies language and the reality it creates. This pre-linguistic realm, the unconscious, therefore, appears a little like phenomenology's special realm of consciousness. Of course the two are deliberately opposed by Lacan and de Certeau, but they are similar in as much as they both provide for the unique possibilities of human liberation. De Certeau's unconscious – mysterious and devoid of content – is nevertheless a resource for freedom which is fundamental to the human condition – something which is greater, it seems, that language itself and which appears to parallel the special transcendence of Romantic aesthetics and philosophy.

While de Certeau and his followers would clearly reject any suggestion that they are returning to a kind of phenomenological or Romantic essentialism, there are clear parallels between the everyday and the lifeworld. The writings of Fiske, Jenkins and others have tended to position everyday reality and popular culture above critique. This optimism is infectious but limiting. Indeed, while the notion of pleasure is significant for an understanding of culture and meaning-making, it has been seriously undertheorized. What is needed in cultural analysis is a more complete rendering of the concept, one which is less reliant on the merely superficial expositions of 'bodily pleasure', and which re-examines these sensibilities through a broader lexicon: happiness, satisfaction, neutralization of displeasure, release, joy, bliss, gratification, and so on.

Not surprisingly, cultural studies and cultural theory have moved somewhat beyond simple celebrationism and are concerning themselves more fully with issues of the human presence in contemporary culture, most especially through the formation of 'identity' or personal subjectivity. In the following chapters we will examine the problematics of contemporary cultural politics, most specifically in reference to key themes: the body, globalism and new communications technologies.

9

The Body

Outline of the chapter

The body emerges as a principal focus and theme for contemporary cultural analysis. The body has been theorized in various ways throughout the period of modernity: Enlightenment philosophical dualism, for example, privileges the mind over the body; Marx theorizes the body as an economic condition; humanism presents the body in terms of happiness and economic utility; science conceives of the body as a biological system; social science conceives of the body as a social unit in a social system; Michel Foucault presents the body in terms of 'discourse' – as a set of inscribed and negotiable meanings.

More broadly, poststructuralist and postmodernist theories identify human sexuality as a central theme in cultural analysis of the body. These insights have influenced recent developments in feminist theory. The release of women's 'bodies' through various forms of sexual performance may be understood as an extension of patriarchal discursive modes, or as the liberation of new female subjectivities. Postmodern and other forms of contemporary cultural analysis raise further questions about the ascription of gender and sexual orientation. The release of new sexual modes facilitates the broadening of choice in relationships and lifestyles.

This political interrogation of social and cultural discourses about the body also raises questions concerning health, beauty and ageing. Cultural assumptions about 'muscularity' and athletic performance, for example, are also being deconstructed, raising questions about the nature of femininity and masculinity. The commodified sporting body, like the sexual body, has become centralized as a form of cultural spectacle. This spectacularization of the adversarial body has further intensified the social experience of masculinity. Cultural politics provides alternative discourses for the study and understanding of males and masculinity.

GENERAL INTRODUCTION

The body has always been a significant presence in anthropological and aesthetic studies. Classical sociology, however, has tended to view the body as a functioning unit which contributes to specific social outcomes. From the 1960s various forms of cultural politics have sought to understand the effects of social processes and power on the individual and individual body. Feminism, in particular, focused attention on the negative effects of social inscriptions on the body: the ways in which a society constructs meanings around the biological conditions of gender in order to discipline and control the body. Poststructuralism and postmodernism have provided a more theoretically substantive framework for analysing the relationship between subjectivity, language (discourse, symbolization) and the body. According to poststructuralists like Foucault and Deleuze and Guattari, bodily sensations like pleasure and anxiety are inextricably linked to the formation of subjects in language. The liberation of individual subjects, therefore, is a contingency of the body as much as it is an articulation of identity formed in language. If an individual subject is to be free, then the body must be mobilized through the cultural expression of difference and pleasure.

The emergence of a cultural theory of the body has been associated with broader historical trends, such as the following:

1 *The intensification of individualism.* As noted in Chapter 7, postmodern culture has extended the modernist ideology of individualism, seeking its solutions to the complex of social claims through a rejection of collective action in favour of individual pleasures and liberation.

2 *The increasing sexualization of culture, including the ever-proliferating discourses of sex and sexuality.* Contemporary culture has become increasingly saturated with discourses on sex and the possibilities of new forms of sexual identity, sexual relationships and modes of pleasure.

3 *The increasing deployment of the body as spectacle and commodity.* During the twentieth century the rise of advertising was coupled with a rise in the deployment of the body as visual spectacle and commodity. This 'symbolic exchange of the body' has often compressed the bodily spectacle with products (like cars, clothing, toothpaste, etc.) or entertainment services (sport, television programmes, etc.).

4 *The paradoxical imaging of idealized youthful bodies against the problematic of bodily flaws, disease, obesity, ageing and death.* Sensate bodies are imperfect, they decay and suffer damage. Contemporary culture has obscured or deflected the negative effects of biology through its proliferation of bodily perfections and projections of pleasure. However, these bodily failings continue at the level of the non-televisual, beneath the surface of culture, an absent presence, as Derrida puts it.

Thus, in a culture where images are persistently foregrounded and where desire, consumption and bodily beauty are primary indicators of human value, the body assumes a cultural significance far beyond its biological foundations. The body, that is, becomes a cultural site in which its many competing discourses subsume, though never entirely escape from, its biological, quotidian or mortal limits.

This chapter examines the body as a cultural site. This is not to deny the existence of a biological or sensate condition for the body; rather, it is to place that biology alongside the discourses which produce sensations. Very simply, bodies are biology, they emit and receive sensations; these biological actions, however, are elicited through culture – stimulated, experienced, understood, made meaningful through culture. Hair grows, but immediately it is subject to the actions of culture – shaved, coloured, combed according to cultural interests. The food we eat and how we eat it, the way we experience sex and sexuality, our shelters, our relationships, our definition and responses to beauty, our desires and needs – all are subject to culture. Equally, however, culture is a contingency of the presence of the body; subjectivity, identity, politics, discourse are formed through the presence of human bodies. Our aim in this chapter, therefore, is to examine the body as a confluence of sensate and cultural processes, recognizing that the mediated and biological bodies are necessarily and interdependently linked, the two sides of the one coin.

THE DUALISM OF MIND AND BODY

The Classical Body

It is important to remember that ordered, rational or logical thought was theorized, but not invented, by Enlightenment philosophy. As the German philosopher Friedrich Nietzsche points out, the broad spans of history, including classical Greek and Roman history, have tended to divide human experience between the forms of rational thought celebrated by the Enlightenment and more sensory experiences. At times, Nietzsche explains, these separate domains have worked harmoniously together, as in the formation of sophisticated art and architecture; at other times they are in tension. The ancient Greek philosopher Plato (427–347 BC) identified this duality as the principal problematic, for example, in the formation of human civilization, most particularly in the formation of a rational and orderly republic. Plato argues that the body and the sensate need to be disciplined by the higher values of the mind, the soul and the highest form of knowledge, Wisdom. In fact, Plato sees the physical world as a denigrated form of what he calls the Idea. This metaphysical

explanation of the universe is reproduced in his understanding of the human experience. For Plato, the mind (soul, reason), while it is the prisoner of the body, must necessarily rule sensory or appetitive desire. Personal harmony, like the harmony of the state, is only possible if physical and potentially chaotic urges of the body are governed by reason.

It is for this reason that Plato thought it sensible (though not entirely desirable) to exclude the poet from his ideal republic, since poets are the agents of a formless and miraculous aesthetic which defies rational order. In his aesthetic writings, Aristotle (384–322 BC) is rather more forgiving, although he insists that playwrights should never leave the audience in a state of agitated emotions. For Aristotle, artists have a social duty to return audiences to a calm and enlightened (cathartic) state of mind following the subliminal arousals of the tragic fall. For this reason, Aristotle prefers the tragedies of Sophocles, which produce a sublime moral effect, rather than those of Euripides, in which the 'catharsis' (literally purgation of the bowel) is never complete. In fact, the dramatic tension of Euripides' *The Bacchae* quite consciously deploys the mind–body dichotomy, contending that the sensory and experiential dimensions of the human condition are just as important for moral order and justice as is rational authority. In *The Birth of Tragedy* (1956, orig. 1872) Nietzsche argues that Euripides' play presents a fundamental tension which comes to dominate Greek and ultimately modern human life: on the one side there is the Apollonian (the god of light, Apollo) vision, which constitutes enlightened, rational morality, the arts of literature, sculpture and philosophy; on the other, there is the Dionysian vision (of the trans-sexual god of music, dance and alcoholic swoon, Bacchus/Dionysius), representing sensory desire, bodily ecstasy and illusion.

The Greek and Roman pantheon attempts to symbolize these variant dimensions of human experience. However, in both Greek and Roman culture the reduction of this diverse family of gods into a more monolithic and inclusive godhead represents an attempt by the culture, or at least its hegemonic governors, to reconcile the contradictions. This reduction of the symbolic cosmos can be read semiotically as a drawing down of the complex range of human discourses, political and ethical claims, into a new form of homogenizing order. The reduction of many gods into one – including the collapsing of the Apollonian and Bacchanalian divide – represents an attempt to reconcile differences through the institution of an integrated and monolithic authority. Plato himself may have been premature in praising the value of an homogenizing, rational authority – this is certainly one reason for his execution for heresy. Undoubtedly, however, Plato's prescience was founded around a formidable conviction that a single god would constitute a single authority, an orderly cosmic governance which would draw together the diverse needs, desires and sensibilities which might threaten the integrative purity of his republic.

The conversion of the Roman Empire to Christianity might therefore be read, at least in part, as a movement toward a more centralizing and resolute philosophical order. The process of conversion, however, is somewhat more paradoxical. Numerous commentators suggest that the conversion can be explained in terms of Christianity's propensity for social consolation: that it is a religion for the subjugated and downtrodden, since it offers everyone grace whatever their hardships, low status and sufferings in mortal life. It has also been suggested that the religion's popularity amongst women contributed specifically to its broader infiltrations in the community (see Stark, 1996). Women's particular oppression sought the compensation of a single loving deity, a godhead who would substitute for the oppressive and patriarchal relationships to which women were subject during the period of the Roman ascendancy. In other words, the horrors of bodily discipline and controls that were culturally constituted during the Roman Empire were challenged by a political theology which separated the spirit from the instrumental rationality of Roman authority. Community politics promised grace and transcendence for all; official culture demeaned and reduced women, indeed all subjugant groups, to variant forms of bodily bondage.

The implosion of the Roman Empire might be explained, partly, through a politics of bodily release from the rationalizing order of Rome. Paradoxically, however, the institutionalization of the community religion brought into being another ideology, another system of rational order, which would convey the same tensions of body and reason into the modern period.

Enlightenment: Bodies in Motion

Numerous histories of the Enlightenment (seventeenth and eighteenth century Europe) tend to credit the great theoretical split between mind and body to the French mathematician/philosopher René Descartes (1596–1650; see Chapter 2). Descartes' famous aphorism *cogito ergo sum* (I think therefore I am) refers generally to the assumption that existence or bodily presence is really a condition of rational thought and the quality of doubt. The Cartesian method, which has influenced the formation and methodology of all modern science and rational thought, insists that all proof requires complete doubt. That is, the truth can only be revealed when it is not assumed or 'given'. Doubt must precede truth. Existence is only possible when it can be proven, and 'proof' necessarily requires the exertion of rational thought. Descartes, therefore, establishes the superiority of the mind over the body by insisting that only knowledge can produce the proof of matter, reality and the sensory experience of the body. Descartes, along with many other Enlightenment scientific philosophers, separates the material world of objects, including the object of the body, from the mind, which has its own metaphysical connections to the spirit, the soul and God. The body is 'nature', while the mind and God are the controllers and creators of nature.

In many respects, this dualism of body and mind (soul, consciousness) informs a good deal of Enlightenment epistemology. John Locke's (1632–1704) famous notion of the human mind being a *tabula rasa*, the blank sheet upon which experience is written, parallels Christian notions of innocence, the Fall and redemption. The child's soul is pure but temptation ultimately seduces him or her into evil; Christian faith redeems the evil for the granting of eternal grace. Enlightenment dualism, which separates the mind and body, locates its own forms of moral and social redemption in the mind against the amoebic responsiveness and potentially chaotic impulses of the body. In this sense, Thomas Hobbes (1588–1679) equates the elevation of the human mind with the elevation of human morality and the collective ordering of rational government and the rational state. Isaac Newton (1642–1727), who theorized that the universe is governed by rational and discernible laws, believes similarly that all natural objects can be reduced to the operation of bodies in motion. The orderly conduct of human affairs is no exception; society is an assembly of bodies in motion and all governments and citizens need to do

is to ensure that these operations are governed by rational and sensible laws. Newton's description of the 'clockwork' or mechanistic universe becomes analogous to humans and human bodies. That is, the body and its various parts operate, like a machine, to achieve certain effects; the system is the greater formation of the individual parts. Human bodies are conceived, therefore, as biological and operational machines which simply need to reproduce the orderliness that God has created in nature.

Aristotle, Spinoza, Kant and Essential Nature

Other philosophical and aesthetic lineages have sought to overcome the mind–body dichotomy through an exploration of the underlying or essential qualities inherent in nature and natural objects. That is, nature is not merely the material condition of objects, but also the abstract qualities (the mysteries) which create and sustain them. God is the most commonly invoked abstraction underpinning nature or the universe. However, these 'essences' are also part of the human condition; philosophy variously defines the abstract human essence as consciousness, the mind, reason or the soul. Aristotle, for example, conceives of human essence in terms of the rational mind, since what is peculiar to 'man' is the life of the rational elements. Significantly, Aristotle also identifies essences in terms of potential and actuality. That is, the abstract state of 'coming-to-be' indicates how any being or natural object is in transition: it will become something else, even as it is currently not that thing in actuality. A child, therefore, is not merely a child, but a coming-to-be adult. The essence of the child is its potential as well as its current condition. While these changes originate in the child itself, other changes (running, fighting, gesture) may originate outside the individual organism.

Baruch (Benedict) Spinoza (1632–77) takes a particular interest in Aristotle's theories, most particularly as they relate to the problematic of the mind–body dialectic and the question of individual agency or freedom. Spinoza argues that a being is free when it acts in relation to the 'necessity' of its own nature without reference to others (1989, orig. 1675). Something is free, according to Spinoza, when it is the source of its own existence and is the sole determinant or source of its actions. This means that no existent (existing being), other than God, is truly free, according to Spinoza, since only God exists by His own laws and necessity. Human will, like all other aspects of finite nature, cannot be called a 'free cause' (action caused by free will) but is rather an outcome of necessity. Spinoza, however, conceives of this infinite free being not in terms of self-consciousness or will, but rather in terms of a 'God' of substance. Clearly, this substance is not matter but an assembly of 'attributes', each one of which expresses 'eternal and infinite essences'. This eternal substance consists, that is, of nothing external to itself; it is the cause of all finite things but it is not a self-conscious subject.

The mind and body in Spinoza's schema are therefore attributes connected to the same substance – two dimensions of a common articulation, two sides of the same coin. An act of will (mind, thought) and the movement of the body (extension) are not distinct realms of the human condition, as Descartes might claim. They are, rather, 'attributes' whose infinite dimensions are linked to the one irreducible and absolute God of substance. It is precisely on this point that Spinoza's work might be distinguished from Aristotle and Romantic philosophers like Immanuel Kant (1724–1804; see

Chapter 2). Kant sees little value in an essentialism (ontology) which has no place for individual subjectivity and the possibility of a subject's personal freedom. Thus, while Spinoza conceives of freedom in terms of the absolute essence of one's existence, Kant attributes it to a rational, self-conscious subject who, potentially at least, might act in accordance with his or her own will. Kant agrees that finite nature is not self-determining and causal. However, unlike Spinoza, he argues that human reason is not clearly part of this finitude, and is capable of initiating a new causal series – or, at least, causality through freedom is not entirely incompatible with nature.

Thus, like Aristotle, Kant sees reason as the quality which sets humans apart from all other nature. Freedom and the act of will cannot be predicated on emotions or whimsy, but can only be constituted through reason. Action, required by a 'natural' or social law that is determined by *reason*, is free because it is self-determined – determined, that is, by the principle of rationality which is the essence of human nature. If it is rational, then it is freely determined (an exercise of free will) since it accords with this essential human quality. Kant goes so far as to suggest that being free is tantamount to acting under the idea of freedom, or at least that it is the consciousness of freedom we have in being conscious of obligation that shows freedom to be more than just a theoretical possibility. By way of example, a person who is hungry might be tempted to steal an apple from a fruit cart. The person may choose not to steal the apple because: (a) it is unlawful to steal other people's property; and (b) it would be unfair to steal from someone who is carrying out his own business of survival and who has done no harm to the potential thief. The potential thief remains hungry, but is free because: (a) he didn't transgress the law and is therefore acting in accordance with his own essential nature for orderliness and law; (b) he is able to acknowledge the rights and freedoms of others; and (c) he has been able to assert his choice knowing that he has a choice.

The Romantic poets – Goethe, Samuel Coleridge and Matthew Arnold in particular – sought a similar union of reason and bodily action through the power of what Coleridge calls the 'imagination'. As with classical aesthetics, Coleridge (1772–1834) seeks to harmonize the contending realms of reason and sensory experience through the perfection of art. In particular, the British Romantics sought some amelioration or response to the bodily and spiritual degradations that were accompanying industrialization and mass urbanization. For Coleridge, the terrors of modern life could only be relieved through the transcendence of the human spirit. This transcendence could not be achieved through religious, poetic or sensory experiences that were not predicated on the workings of the human mind generally and human reason in particular. The imagination, therefore, is not mere 'fancy' but is profoundly fashioned through the harmonious convergence of all human faculties. In *Aids to Reflection* (1825) Coleridge argues that morality, virtue and freedom are all contingencies of the highest aspirations of the mind and cannot be reduced to what might be simply defined as sensibility or the sensory:

> [W]here virtue is, sensibility is the ornament and becoming attire of virtue. On certain occasions it might almost be said to *become* virtue. But sensibility and all the amiable qualities may likewise become, and too often *have* become, the partners of vice and the instrument of seduction. (1962: 453)

Bodily senses, that is, may serve the interests of good or evil, according to Coleridge.

Only human reason and the moral management of the senses ensure the elevation of the human spirit.

In fact, the social commentary of many of the Romantics, Matthew Arnold most notoriously, betrays a form of social elitism which is more suspicious of the bodily excesses of the industrial poor, than of their own social group. Neither Coleridge nor Arnold, of course, speaks for all Romantic perspectives, and certainly there are those Romantics, William Blake among them, who seem far less anxious about bodily or carnal ecstasies. Blake's naturism, Coleridge's opium smoking and Oriental naturalism, Lord Byron's sexual exploits, all represent forms of bodily ecstasy which betray the contradictions of Romantic epistemology and social theory. These contradictions expose the limits of Cartesian and Romantic conceptions of the mind–body dichotomy, a dichotomy which extends into the problematic of liberal humanism and capitalism more generally.

MODERNISM AND THE BODY

In summary, modernism tends to treat the body and mind as distinct, ontological categories, even when it devotes itself to their reconciliation. The modernist conception of the body can be located in four general areas of discourse:

1 *The economic body*. Marx complains that the capitalist system conceives of working-class bodies as mechanical units in the mode of production. Capitalism treats both the labour and the body as property, like other material objects. While slavery is the most extreme manifestation of this condition, the various Masters and Servants Acts which defined labour and industrial

relations during the eighteenth and nineteenth centuries legally bound workers to their bosses. Workers were forced to pay fees if ever they wished to leave their place of employment: that is, they had to buy their freedom. The owners of capital treated the bodies and labour of workers as they would treat any other productive machinery.

2   *The humanist body*. Utilitarianism and liberal democracy sought to ameliorate the excesses of capitalist rationality through a social programme based on individual pleasure, Romantic transcendence and modes of personal improvement. The utilitarianism of Jeremy Bentham and James and John Stuart Mill seeks to reconcile bodily pleasures with reasoned social improvement. Individuals will be motivated by self-interest and personal happiness; they will recognize that personal and social improvement is the most reasonable and logical way of achieving this happiness. Utilitarianism expected that being useful to a society would necessarily implicate personal pleasure. Personal self-interest and personal pleasure, therefore, become the motivation for general social improvement. A democratic state must necessarily issue from self-interest. It is always better to live in a rational state governed by principles of orderly conduct than it is to live in chaos. Public education, manhood suffrage and liberty were the necessary outcomes of personal pleasure and utility. The body and the mind would seem to operate harmoniously, as the mind came to accomplish the self-interests of the body.

3   *The biological body*. Philosophers and scientists like Descartes and Isaac Newton established the fundamental principles for studying the laws of the physical universe (physics). The work

of Émile Remarque and Charles Darwin extended these principles to the fields of biology and evolution. Darwin's *On the Origin of Species* (1859) provides a foundation for understanding biological systems. Bodies, in this sense, are treated as orderly and self-determining organisms which are comprised of functioning parts. The development and increasing complexity of the system are constituted out of a fundamental, rational principle: evolution.

When translated into human terms, Darwin's concept of 'survival of the fittest' became an equally forceful principle for the organization of human civilizations. Humans could be treated as competing organisms; human societies could be treated as competing civilizations. These competitive systems underpin the advance of human civilizations whereby superior biological and social groups would necessarily rule over and perhaps eradicate inferior groups. In this sense, Thomas Malthus's theory of population argues that survival imperatives place pressure on groups to spread and conquer new territories and peoples. This biological imperative provides a moral authority for imperialism and the competitive hierarchies of capitalism generally. That is, biology presents itself as the objective and scientific validation of bodily imperatives. In fact, the discourse of biology and evolution functions as part of the ideology and self-legitimation of capitalism and capitalist economics.

4   *The sociological body*. From its beginnings in the work of Durkheim and Weber, sociology has tended to accept the Cartesian dichotomy of mind–body, focusing interest on the mind as the primary definer of humans as social beings. To this extent, classical sociology has tended to treat the body as an outcome

of the mind; the body's actions are therefore measured as units in a mathematical system of descriptions. That is, bodily actions indicate the more important operations of the mind. This objectification of the body and its positioning within a system tends to replicate the reification of modernist science. Marx's interest in the deployment of bodies in capitalism, Weber's interest in the rationalization of the body and in styles of life and status, and Durkheim's interest in symbolism lay the foundations for more substantive analyses of the body which sociology develops during the twentieth century.

THE BODY AS DISCOURSE

The proliferation of signs, images and simulacra accompanying the rise of the mass media has forced theory to re-conceptualize the body and its relationship to culture. The body, in fact, has been at the centre of cultural theory's interrogation of mechanical, humanist and other systems-based theories which are grounded in the primacy of biology and material reality. In moving away from the universal explanations and 'grand narratives' of culture, contemporary cultural analysis has become more concerned with discourse and the processes of meaning-making. The body, therefore, is being conceived in terms of being inscribed, constituted or rendered meaningful in representation and culture. According to poststructuralist and postmodern theories, the body needs to be 'read' in terms of symbolic processes; this reading gives us insight not into what is real, but rather into what is cultural: that is, in terms of what is meaningful for the culture in which the body is deployed. A body, in this sense, may be read in what is

conventionally understood to be a 'text' (film, magazine, advertisement, TV programme). But the body may also be read *as* a text in and of itself. It is inscribed with meaning through all aspects of everyday life; through modes of dress and undress, through relationships, through work, through engagement with other discourses. In other words, the body *is* the text.

Sociologists like Bryan Turner (1992) and Chris Shilling (1993) have sought to develop a generalist analysis of the body, one which treats the body as material, functional, sensory and symbolic. Poststructuralist, postmodernist and social constructionists, however, have tended to emphasize the discursive and cultural dimensions of the body. Following earlier studies by Georges Bataille, Michel Foucault's studies on prisons (1977a) and sexuality (1981) have presented a direct challenge to modern biological notions of the body, most particularly as they are transformed into forms of social theory. In *The History of Sexuality, Volume One*, for example, Foucault makes clear that discourse always precedes biology. The biology of the body, that is, provides the raw material for sexuality, but it is only in culture and the mediation of discourse that sexuality can actually exist. Sex is not a natural urge so much as a carefully coded discourse, or series of discourses, which social groups deploy in order to have sexuality. Foucault's theories directly challenge the notion that sex is the great taboo of modernism. According to Foucault, religion, the social and medical sciences, families and educational institutions talk about sex in order to control it; sexual discourse, however, will also incite and facilitate modes of sexual experience:

From the singular imperialism that compels everyone to transform their sexuality into a perpetual discourse, to the manifold mechanisms which, in the areas of economy, pedagogy, medicine, and justice, incite, extract, distribute, and institutionalize the sexual discourses, an immense verbosity is what our civilization has required and organized. Surely no other type of society has ever accumulated – and in such a relatively short span of time – a similar quantity of discourses concerned with sex. (1981: 33)

Foucault's history of these discourses analyses the body in terms of relationships and processes of power. As with his studies on the medicalized, imprisoned and social scientific body, Foucault's study of sexuality is concerned with the body as a site of power. It is at the level of the body, Foucault insists, that power is experienced, exchanged and reformed. This power discourse, and the knowledge that it carries, is necessarily imprecise and personal, a matter of exchange and doubt, rather than structure and historical subjugation:

[I]t is in discourse that power and knowledge are joined together. And for this very reason we must conceive of discourse as a series of discontinuous segments whose tactical function is neither uniform nor stable. To be more precise, we must not conceive of a world divided between accepted discourse and excluded discourse, or between the dominant discourse and the dominated one; but as a multiplicity of discursive elements that can come into play in various strategies. It is this distribution that we must reconstruct, with the things said and those concealed, the enunciations required and those forbidden, that it comprises; with the variants and different effects – according to who is speaking, his position of power, the institutional context in which he happens to be situated – that it implies; and with the shifts and revitalization of identical formulas for identical objectives that it also uses. (1981: 100)

Power as it is experienced in this sexual 'microphysics' may may be usefully engaged for the enhancement of individuals' pleasures.

The Biological Imperative Argument

While *The History of Sexuality* is concerned primarily with the ways in which culture constitutes sexuality and inscribes the body with meaning, this phase of Foucault's work directly challenges biological approaches to the body generally. In fact, Foucault's work on the discursive constitution of the body parallels other approaches to the body which some sociologists refer to as constructionist: the notion that human experience is fundamentally constructed in language or discourse, and that subjects are constructed by culture. Most sociology, and indeed most social science and cultural theory, is more or less constructionist. At its most extreme, however, a constructionist approach would deny any role at all for biology, suggesting that all reality is mediated and therefore constructed by culture. All human problems are to be found in culture and society, as indeed are all solutions to those problems.

The constructionist argument, in fact, is most hostile to the 'biological imperative' arguments which suggest that human behaviours are fundamentally rooted in our biology, including our evolutionary or genetic history. Liberal reformism, Marxism and feminism have all had to confront these arguments whereby biology is invoked as an explanation for, especially hierarchical, patterns of human behaviour: humans are 'naturally' aggressive, discriminatory, self-interested, competitive, and so on; males and male sexuality are naturally predatory, visual, promiscuous, assertive. According to the biological imperative argument, these survival instincts are so completely patterned into our genes or hormones or psychology that we can only modify them at the margins rather than alter them in any essential way. The biological imperative argument suggests, in fact, that attempts to alter these essential patterns generally lead to some form of mental, emotional or psychological illness, a pathology which fundamentally disrupts not just the minds of individuals but ultimately the social order and the social condition. This nature or nurture argument persists in extremely sophisticated terms today with many reformist cultural theorists seeking to emancipate human subjectivity from the 'tyranny' of what they see as biology's false ideology and false knowledge.

SEX AND SEXUALITY

Feminism and New Sexuality

As may already be clear, a good deal of the recent analysis of the body in contemporary culture is centred on sex and sexuality. Feminism, in particular, has helped to reshape our thinking about the body, personal relationships and the conditions of power. However, as we discussed in Chapter 6, feminism itself has been substantially critiqued in contemporary cultural theory, most especially feminism which invests its politics in a structuralist classification of gender. This critique suggests that the older styles of structuralist feminism (Marxist and liberalist) tend to reduce all males to a particular political, cultural and sexual taxonomy; it also claims that liberation for all women can be reduced to a simple set of prescriptions. More recent feminist theory, influenced by Foucault and postmodern theoretics, has abandoned many of these assumptions, accepting the notion that emancipation is associated with a more fluid and unspecified subjectivity, one which resists the reduction of 'men' and 'women' to any form of assumed sexuality, subjectivity or political preconditions.

There is no doubt, however, that the political and sexual iconoclasm of feminism has contributed in significant ways to contemporary culture. Women's sexuality, which the feminists of the sixties sought desperately to liberate from patriarchal constraints, is now a fundamental exigency of contemporary culture. This release of the female body and female sexuality has not necessarily satisfied the higher ideals of structuralist feminism. Women have been released to greater levels of educational, professional business and public participation; however, women's sexuality has also been rendered available for appropriation by capitalist commodification, including the commodification of media imagery. The spectacle of (especially young) female bodies and sexuality has become so prolific as to appear normative, the standard by which all sexuality is to be known, stimulated and mobilized. If, as Foucault suggests, sexuality is primarily an operation of discourse, then the discourse of young women's bodies has become contemporary culture's primary sexuality. The great anxiety of contemporary feminism centres on the question of whether or not this primacy is liberational or another permutation of patriarchal control.

Of course, particular dimensions of feminist analysis would derive significant satisfaction from the emancipation of women's sexuality from the oppressions of sexual conservatism which limits women to domestic or maternal roles and which treats them as the sexual objects of male desire. Certainly, many feminists from the sixties sought a sexuality for women which would be assertive, uninhibited, freely expressed and lustful: that is, a sexuality which allowed females the same sexual privileges as culture accords to men. However, something of a divide has developed between these liberational forms and the sensibilities of younger feminists who feel entirely comfortable with a sexuality that is embedded in commodification and consumerist imagery. Certainly feminists like Germaine Greer and Naomi Wolf have expressed misgivings about a liberation which leaves women sexually complete but emotionally vacant. Greer, in particular, has asked quite directly whether her own project of sexual liberation has not been appropriated by a new kind of cultural superficiality, one which celebrates sex for its own sake but which leaves the questions of relationships and emotional satisfaction largely incomplete.

This new debate of liberationism stimulates particular hostility in younger feminists who suspect older feminists of retreat or a clear misunderstanding of the younger women's project. The centredness of pleasure, through both direct sexual experience or the act of consumption, has clearly become a fundamental theoretical impasse for contemporary feminism. The presence of the female body and female sexuality in popular culture has left a number of, especially older, feminists worried that liberation has become appropriated by the capitalist machinery, and that women are becoming more incarcerated by the modelling and presence of idealized and unattainable pleasures.

The Spectacle of the Body

Linda Williams (1989) in her study of film pornography expresses this feminist anxiety as a debate between feminists who fear the objectification of women's bodies in text, and those who are opposed to censorship. This latter group, Williams contends, remain concerned about certain depictions of women, but see the control of imagery and expression as fundamentally pernicious: 'These women are interested in ... defending the expression of sexual differences and in opposing the hierarchicalization of some sexualities as better, or more normal, than others' (1989: 23). This liberationism, however, is tested when Williams considers hard-core pornography: on the one hand, hard-core might be conceived as a matter of the free expression of a variant female sexuality; on the other hand, it might represent a form of sexual exploitation. Thus, Williams' ambivalent acknowledgement of these varied sexualities and modes of stimulating pleasure betrays a deep fear that hard-core pornography constitutes political and social harm for women.

Williams recognizes that pornography may be used and interpreted differently by different audiences, and that the issue of 'power' has become problematized in readings of the relationship between a text and an audience. However, neither of these revelations is sufficient in themselves to convince her that the genre is worthwhile, either aesthetically or politically. In film, unlike literature, the complete exposure of the female body implicates not just the imagining of an author and an audience, but the actual presentation of actual women in imaginary forms. The question of liberation and the visualization of the female body remain problematic in Williams' studies:

> But seeing everything – especially seeing the truth of sex – proves a more difficult project than one might think, especially in the case of women's bodies, whose truths are most at stake. ... [T]he visual terms of the cinema do not allow the female protagonists of hard-core films to authenticate their pleasure. This may be one reason why the confessing jewels in the filmic case are male, rather than female, genitals. (1989: 32)

In male-oriented pornography the film is climaxed by the 'money-shot', or male ejaculation, rather than in the presentation of female ecstasy, which remains a mere stepping stone. Williams' repudiation of hard-core pornography remains problematic since it is based on the uncertainty of presentational forms. That is, she rejects the idea that hard-core pornography can't be categorised and therefore can't be treated. She also rejects the idea that if it is sexual and pleasurable, then it is necessarily acceptable. Rather, she seeks to understand the problematic of a liberational sexuality which is based on the ultimate resolution of male climax. For Williams' feminism, it is this final gesture that reduces the hard-core to a politically unacceptable genre.

In his account of the development of anti-pornography politics, Laurence O'Toole argues that an uncomfortable alliance has developed between conservative moralists and particular zones of feminism:

> Although the feminist anti-pornographers may lack the social and political power of the moralitarians, over time their arguments have achieved a considerable cultural sway, with a profound influence upon the language of censorship, which finds anti-porn feminist terms such as 'objectifying', 'dehumanizing' and 'degrading' tripping off the tongue of patriarchs and old-style moral guardians. Feminist anti-porners have contributed, not only a new semantic vigour to the culture of censorship in Britain and the U.S., but also a fresh impetus for a level of policing of visual material that would be considered extreme if ventured by the moralitarians. (O'Toole, 1998: 28)

O'Toole contends that pornography is fundamentally indefinable, except in terms of the discourse of censorship. In other words, only the condition of control and exclusion – the things that others don't want displayed – can consistently define what is pornographic and what is not. For anti-porn feminists, including Linda Williams, this control should be levelled against the visualization of the female form for the satisfaction of the male gaze and male sexuality.

The problem with this approach has been outlined in more general terms in our discussion on feminism (Chapter 6). However, for contemporary feminism, which has the female form at the centre of its interests, there are significant difficulties in sustaining this position:

1 Subjectivity and sexuality become prescriptions of an all-knowing, structuralist authority. Only certain content, subjectivities and viewing positions are permitted. This 'authority' has been challenged from both inside and outside feminism.

2 Anti-porn feminism has trouble defining the exact nature of this permissible sexuality. The same explicit sexual content may be permissible in certain textual contexts, but not in others. When women produce explicit sexual depictions it may be considered 'erotica'; when men produce the same content it risks being damned as 'pornography'.

3 Perhaps the most difficult issue to deal with is the issue of reception. Heterosexual women, gay women and various permutations of loving couples may use the 'pornographic' text to intensify their sexual experiences. The text which is pornographic for heterosexual male onanism may be legitimate for the exploration of female sexuality. The text will be the same, but the audience response will define the status and politics of the text.

Some commentators (including D.H. Lawrence, Susan Sontag and Michel Foucault) have attempted to distinguish between pornography and erotica in more general ways. Such arguments, however, often invoke broader cultural prejudices which locate erotica in complex, high art and pornography in the pedestrian world of mass consumerism or unenlightened voyeurism. Erotica may be intellectually or aesthetically elevated, located in the female perspective or in bourgeois culture; pornography has often been located in male sexuality, working-class culture and mass consumerism. To exemplify this point, we might compare the French film *Romance* (1999), written and directed by Catherine Breillat, with the 1980s American porn film *Deep Throat*, starring Linda Lovelace. Both films present the sexual odyssey of a female protagonist, and both depict sexually explicit content, including intercourse, oral sex, male and female genitalia and actual male ejaculation. *Romance* is generally conceived and consumed as an arthouse movie; *Deep Throat* was produced purely for the pornography market, though in many ways it entered a more general cultural vernacular as a playful and absurd reflection on contemporary sexuality. Fierce battles were fought to protect *Romance* from being banned or censored in various parts of the world. In most cases the defence of the film was built around its artistic merit. *Deep Throat*, on the other hand, became a rallying point for anti-porn feminists, who believed that the depictions in the film debased women and were fundamentally dehumanizing. For a brief time, Linda Lovelace herself became the heroine of the anti-pornography movement in the United States. The bourgeois liberationism and intellectual elevations which protected *Romance* were not available for *Deep Throat*.

Table-top and other Erotic Dancers

Some recent writings have attempted to reach beyond these elitist conceptions as much as they have sought to dissolve the sort of feminist anxieties expressed by Williams and others. In particular, theories based on new subjectivities and the power associated with bodily pleasure have extended into ever-broadening areas of cultural activity and textualization. Arguments which locate emancipation in the consumption of popular music or popular television texts are being applied to the texts and consumers of sexually explicit erotica. John Fiske (1989a) describes the self-presentation of managed nudity by women on the beach as a form of auto-eroticism. Fiske's arguments, drawn from de Certeau's notion of corporate raiding and Bakthin's theories on the transgressive nature of everyday folk culture, liberate individuals from the control of powerful institutions. Bodily pleasure becomes the central and unconscious ambit of emancipation and opposition. This focus on the auto-erotica of personal sexual display underpins similar cultural studies analyses of dance.

McRobbie et al. (1989, 1994) have pointed to the dearth of studies on dance. Anthropological studies have identified dance as a significant ritualist practice for story-telling and for kinship and fertility activities. In particular, traditional cultures have used dance as a conduit of social and cosmological knowledge, as well as more sensate practices of sexual display and courtship. Dance, in fact, constitutes a language or discourse which is transferred ritually through generations and which constitutes a significant thread for the ongoing identity and self-definition of community and culture. Through emigration, globalization and diaspora – the postmodernization of culture – specific ethnic groups have attempted to sustain elements of this traditional identity through the re-constitution of dance and dance practices. For example, in the city of Freetown in Sierra Leone, Temne peoples have formed voluntary associations called 'dancing compins'. The ostensible function of these associations is to perform music and dance for significant cultural events: weddings, visits of important people, and fund-raising. Most members of the dancing compins have migrated to the city from rural areas and each of the compins is formed around particular regional derivations. While the dancing compins were clearly formed to re-constitute traditional cultural identity, they were also used for community lobbying and for the ascension of political leaders. Dance, that is, became implicated in the maintenance of social and cultural rituals and the formation of modern politics in Sierra Leone.

McRobbie et al. (1989) has suggested that for contemporary culture dance has become gender-specialized and that the social rituals and practices associated with dance have become associated primarily with femininity. There are a whole string of literary, cinematic and sociological accounts which show how men have seen dance as an unfortunate prerequisite to courtship (McRobbie, 1989: 143). While clearly this situation has changed over the past two decades, McRobbie et al's point is certainly valid for a good proportion of the twentieth century, during which gender specialization appears to have reached its zenith. We may suggest a number of reasons for this change:

1   *Instrumental rationality*. Modernity has tended to locate masculinity in capitalist processes of work and reason. Dance, as a sensate and 'naturalistic' activity, has become increasingly associated with femininity.
2   *The regression of leisure*. The notion of 'work' and economy have become privileged over leisure and pleasure. The male body has been integrated into the ideology of productivity. Dance has been seen as a leisured triviality, something which is more suited to the feminine.
3   *The dissolution of community*. Ritualized practices associated with community

have been dissolved through capitalist modernism. The dissolution of community has also involved the surrender of participatory dance narratives and knowledge. Even the residue of courtship practices have proved uncomfortable for masculinity.

4   *The isolation of women*. Dance remains popular for women where modernity excludes them from significant public participation and cultural prominence. The intensification of the feminine as carer, nurturer and home-maker limits opportunities for sexual expression and play. Dance, in this sense, provides an opportunity for activity and free expression of sensate experiences within the constraints of prescribed social roles.
5   *The intensification of the female body as spectacle*. Modernism is also characterized by the intensification of the female body in an infinite array of media texts. Dance legitimates the female body as spectacle, for both the male and female gaze.

Recent decades have seen a considerable re-shifting of this separation, especially amongst younger men and women. It is no longer considered effeminate or 'gay' for young men and boys to dance by themselves or together. Indeed, the 'mosh pit' – the congregation of dancers – has become a place of masculine competitiveness and at times aggression.

Despite these changes, however, the spectacle of a dancing female body remains a central trope in contemporary culture. Bourgeois culture has developed highly skilled and specialized forms of dance which continue to tell stories and explore ideas. Undoubtedly, the presentation of women on stage implicates the possibility of sexual display for the visual and vicarious satisfactions of the viewers. However, while bourgeois culture moved tentatively through its anxieties over the presentation of female bodies and female sexuality, justifying it through claims of erudition and aesthetics, proletariat culture seems a little less abashed. Burlesque and carnival culture in Europe and America frequently flouted obscenity laws as performers experimented with various forms of nudity and erotic dance. Lucinda Jarrett argues that the emergence of striptease in twentieth-century Europe is replete with the same cultural discourses and anxieties that are evident in pornography debates:

> The separation of the formal from the informal arts has led to the 20th-century opposition of art and pornography. Erotica sits ambiguously between these two poles on a slide rule where the marker is the censor, positioned by the moral values of a social context. (1997: 3)

Jarrett's primary interest, however, is not the problematic of censorship or the ambivalences of social values. Rather, she explores the activity of stripping in terms of the performers themselves, how the dancers conceive of their art: 'Female strippers are strong women proud of an expressive sexuality which is not easily contained by the formalism of classical dance' (1997: 4). Jarrett repudiates the pornographer's camera, which reifies the performer and the performance, criminalizing and exhausting its power. Jarrett argues forcefully that striptease is the erotic art of the people and that the history of erotic dancing is very much embedded in connections between 'sexually powerful women' and a culture's desire or libido. Jarrett's thesis moves well beyond the timidity of feminist anti-pornography arguments, claiming that strippers are sexual artists, heroines acting on behalf of all people's liberation.

Jean Baudrillard argues similarly that striptease constitutes a fundamental sexual reality whereby the dancer removes her clothes and puts on her meanings. This carnality contrasts, in Baudrillard's view, with the simulacra of contemporary sexual imaging where the naked female form has become a mimicry or echo of genuine sexuality. The nude female body is, of course, present in advertising, television, cinema and video production, but striptease engages live bodies in ways which are designed to challenge as they interact with the live bodies and living sexuality of the audience. Of course both the live and the televisual bodies are constituitive of fantasy and sexual imagining, but the live body engages much more fully with the cultivation of these imaginings. For Baudrillard, the visceral body, in fact, disappears with the televisualization; the fantasy loses its force and presence.

To this extent, striptease is a more direct and fleshly discourse than other forms of sexualized nudity. In fact, the most recent permutation of striptease, table-top and lap dancing, deliberately exploits the interactive potential of live performance, reducing the psychological and spatial distance between performer and audience in order to produce a more intimate and complete imaginative union. An intimacy is created by a performance which is often one-to-one and which, in many cases, involves conversation, proximity and eye-to-eye contact. In some venues there are also opportunities for the dancer to touch the client/audience, but this is highly specified and discretionary. In peep-shows, however, venues are organized so that audience members can self-stimulate. Touch becomes implicated in striptease through the direct engagement of the viewer on the performing body. As Jarrett argues, the fundamental element of this sexual congress is always the sexual power of the stripper. Erika Longley (1997) confirms this view in her autobiographical account of the peep-show dancers of the Lusty Lady in Seattle.

Longley records her first encounter with the eyes of a patron, and her own transformation from vulnerability to sexual power. According to Longley, her work as a stripper liberated her sexuality as it challenged the underlying limits that ideology and morality place on cultural expression.

The proliferation of table-top and peep-show venues across the major cities of the world reflects a broadening of sexual discourses. Table-top, in particular, constitutes a form of gentrification of striptease as it locates erotic dance in more middle-class consumption contexts; women and couples are also more commonly attracted to these venues than previously. The proliferation of the naked female form has become so significant that it may provide a facility and stimulus for all sexuality – not just the sexuality of heterosexual (patriarchal) males. Table-top dancing blurs the boundaries between performance and prostitution (though venues and dancers would reject this claim). The intimacy that the performance engages is more analogous to intimate contact than the more vicarious representations of the electronic media. The popularity of the live performance might partly be explained by the general trend in contemporary culture toward a more open and prolific sexuality, and a more transient sexual experience. This sexuality is one which:

(a) permits an intimacy that is not bound by commitment, permanence or ongoing responsibility;

(b) acknowledges the unparalleled ascendancy of consumerism in human relationships;

(c) avoids the problematic of love but which acknowledges the extravagant beauty of youthful femininity;

(d) permits a sexual polygamy, a desire, that is never quite consummated and never quite fulfilled; and

(e) avoids the problematic of sexually transmitted diseases such as AIDS through the vicarious experience of multiple sexual partners.

Other Sexualities: The Gay and Lesbian Mardi Gras

Structuralist politics has traditionally located sexually explicit performances like striptease in a patriarchal capitalist frame. However, worker and professional organizations defend the sex industry on the grounds of freedom of choice and personal sexual expression. Industry bodies like the Eros Foundation argue that the stereotype of the oppressed and victimized sex worker is fallacious, and denigrates the value and validity of pleasure in human experience. If we are to apply Foucault's notion of power as unstable and exchangeable in human relations, then the relationship between viewer and viewed, especially in the table-top context, becomes highly problematic. At various points in the interaction power is difficult to locate as the pleasure itself becomes destabilized through sexual and commercial gratifications. Of course the dancer may have a higher income than her patron, but she is still subject to a range of demeaning social attitudes. Even so, the youth, beauty, vigour and athleticism of the performer may place her 'condition' above that of the overweight, salacious viewer. In either case, the subjectivities that are engaged in the interaction are restless and mutable; neither viewer nor viewed can settle in a position, but will move through a whole range of subject perspectives involving a broad span of personal, ideological and political imaginings. The free-wheeling sexuality is never closed, never complete. The participants move on through other realms and relationships.

The text of dance and sexual performance is, of course, available for varied interpretation and gratifications. Moreover, the imagining of the text, its authorship, can never be authenticated. That is to say, while the text may be generally intended as a heterosexual performance, performers and viewers may apply their own sexual imaginings and preferences to the narrative. It is not surprising, in fact, that gays and lesbians, bisexuals and transgenders apply and construct sexual texts for their own pleasures and gratifications, against the specifications or intentions of the original text. In particular, notionally 'straight' texts like the TV series *Xena: Warrior Princess* have been appropriated by alternative sexualities. For *Xena*, the interaction between lesbian viewers and text producers has actually shifted the text to enhance its sexual ambiguity. Other texts and venues have moved in the opposite direction, from the social and sexual margins to a more general frame of sexual reference: the most spectacular example of this is the Sydney Gay and Lesbian Mardi Gras.

The Sydney Mardi Gras emerged as a political protest in June 1978 when about a thousand gay libbers marched down Oxford Street in Sydney singing 'out of the bars and into the streets'. From that protest a significant festival developed which reached beyond the social margins and into the view of the mainstream. The festival developed an international reputation, attracted private and government sponsorship and now engages over half a million participants and watchers. From the mid-1990s the ABC, Australia's major public broadcaster, brought the spectacle into the homes of between one and a half and two million viewers. The stars of *Xena* offered specialist comments for a recent broadcast. Little doubt, the spectacle and broadcast elicited some substantial level of voyeuristic curiosity from the 'straight' community; even so, it may also have enhanced the sexual vocabulary of mainstream viewers. The outcomes of the Mardi Gras and its broadcast may be summarized in the following terms:

1. The Mardi Gras has become a significant vehicle for celebrating gay, lesbian and cross-gender lifestyles.
2. It has facilitated the broadcast of new forms of sexual adventurism and subjectivities.
3. It has raised significant issues in the realm of personal politics.
4. It has raised the profile of issues such as homophobia and AIDS within the broader community (see Bersani, 1995).

The text of the Mardi Gras has met with familiar objections from conservative elements in the broader culture. Some church leaders and politicians saw the festival and its broadcast as a threat to mainstream values and sexualities; the tabloid newspapers feigned outrage, but boosted sales through the publication of provocative and revealing photos of the participants. More compelling objections, however, have come from within the gay and lesbian communities themselves. A number of commentators, for example, express the fear that the 'mainstreaming' of the Mardi Gras may weaken the integrity of gay and lesbian lifestyles and politics through an excessive contiguity with heterosexual voyeurism, and the reduction of the Mardi Gras text to a heterosexual spectacle. As Gavin Harris puts it: '[T]here were some who suspected that Sydney had begun to neutralise the parade's marginality and to tame its disrespect, that the parade's subversions and parodies, its naughty imitations of the heterosexual matrix could now be billed as safe tourist fare' (1995: 20). The fear that the integrity of the culture and its politics might be compromised by commodification is, of course, common to many realms of subversive or alternative cultures. Undoubtedly, the Mardi Gras has become Sydney's single, most commercially successful tourist event, attracting gays and lesbians from many parts of the world and drawing nearly half a million people into the streets. Local, state and federal governments have joyfully embraced the tinkling of the tourist cash register and the well-managed, well-behaved addition to the events calendar.

The commodification of transgression has become a major part of contemporary capitalist culture. As in Bakhtin's discussion of the carnivalesque, the question arises as to whether transgression can even exist when its space is provided by the hegemony it would seek to usurp. The temporary relief from power that the carnival provides may be seen as an hegemonic trick, a means of maintaining control through the release of resentment. The rulers allow a day of pleasure, but when it is over things must return to normal. If the Mardi Gras' popularity in mainstream culture merely serves to confirm the normality of heterosexuality hegemony and the aberrance of homosexuality, then the gay mission is itself problematized. The night of bodily revels may simply serve the interests of capitalism, on the one hand, and sexual hierarchy, on the other. As with the aberrances and transgressions of contemporary rock music, the freedom may simply be a façade for a more permanent and unrelenting conformity.

Good and Bad Sexualities

Part of the complaint registered by gay groups about the Sydney Mardi Gras relies on some conventional assumptions about the nature of gay and straight sexualities. While theories of pathology and genetic essence continue to be offered as explanations for gay sexual orientations (people are simply 'born' gay), discourse theories have offered an alternative perspective: that is, sexuality is far more open and fluid than previous ontologies have acknowledged. An individual subject might experience sex in an infinite variety of ways with members of either gender. The preference is constituted through the same conductors as tastes or preferences for any cultural product or experience. In other words, any individual can 'choose' his or her sexual orientation as they would choose an identity or a pair of shoes or a particular musical form; we might choose same-sex or opposite-sex partners in circumstances that may be experimental, occasional or ongoing.

This opening of sexuality to broader fields of experience and alternative pleasures reaches far beyond the kinds of normative conditions of the romantic ideal: a life-time partner of the opposite sex with whom one will have children and exclusive sex. Even so, this ideal remains remarkably resilient in constituting developed world relationships and for the management of fertility and reproduction. In contemporary culture the ideal has had to adjust to the potency of sexual liberationism, the proliferation of sexual imagery, the awareness of sexual alternatives and the saturation of sexual imaginings and arousals that are not constituted through the experiences of everyday domestic life. The ideal persists in mediated forms, of course, and a plethora of institutional structures have been formed and re-formed in order to support its reincarnations. However, it has had to make significant adjustments in order to sustain itself: serial monogamy and the free sexual phase of youth have replaced the ideal of restraint and pre-marital celibacy; no-fault divorce has eased the burden of unhappy marriage; relationship counselling and psychological services have become the modern confessionals designed to expiate the guilt associated with marriage dissolution or sexual imagining. This 'renovated' ideal has itself become part of the normative construction of 'good' or appropriate sexuality.

Even so, this good sexuality burdens young women's bodies with enormous cultural responsibility. Sexual innocence and sexual experience are converged in the young woman's body as she becomes the legitimate conduit for generalized sexual arousal. The ubiquity of the image is partnered by a cultural intrigue and responsibility which asks young women to be sexually adventurous, sexually giving, but through the paradoxical maintenance of their youthful 'unknowing'. The need for constant arousal and constant change, the seeking of new sexual territories, is attached to the symbol of the young female body. Her sexuality is good sexuality provided it holds true to the ultimate ideal of maturity and the immersion in a mature, maternal relationship. The popularity of TV programmes like *Friends* is due, at least in part, to the deployment of youthful female beauty and the constant possibility of sexual engagement. Female sexuality at least matches the male sexuality as normative, whereas in earlier permutations of the genre – programmes like *Dobie Gillis* and *Happy Days* – the world was viewed through the normative expectations of males. The liberation of young women has been accompanied by a more literal sexual expectation which becomes available, of course, for commodification.

Young women, therefore, are permitted to fantasize about and even experience same-sex relationships. The 1990s produced a new kind of adjustment to the ideal: the transient experimentation of same-sex encounters by (basically heterosexual) young women. Televisual and magazine discourses provide the vocabulary and grammar of these acceptable sexualities.

The ideal of good sex, however, is clearly limited and certain sexualities remain outside the borders. The rules of good and bad sexuality may be summarized as follows:

1 Beauty and health are central to the myth and only occasionally are we witness to sexuality that may take place with diseased or disabled bodies.

2 Sex is rarely featured or expected between people of vastly different cultural, class, racial or ethnic backgrounds. Where these differences are presented, they are mollified by a certain type of bourgeois romanticism. The difference becomes an exhilarating part of the relationship. TV producers of programmes like *Ally McBeal*, *Two Guys and a Pizza Shop*, *Sex in the City* and *Friends* are careful not to overstretch their audiences' expectations and imaginings. Where sex takes place between a black and white American, for example, it becomes a distinct feature of the narrative, and not just an incidental norm. Once it has done its work, the element quickly disappears from view. Equally, there are very few tramps or unemployed criminals presented in these programmes, and fewer still who have sex with the stars.

3 Sex is confined in age. Paedophilia and 'child abuse' have emerged as significant issues in contemporary culture. However, sexual contact between people of vastly different ages, whether as minors or adults, is treated with deep suspicion. The marriage of film-maker Woody Allen to his step-daughter has proved an uncomfortable issue – an example of a tainted and inappropriate deployment of the body.

4 Allen's romance with and marriage to his step-daughter raises further questions about the legitimacy of incestuous relationships. This taboo persists

in contemporary culture, despite attempts in art-house movies like *Lone Star* to raise the issue for public consideration.

5   There is the perpetual question of polygamy. The ideal seems to have adapted comfortably to the notion of sequential sexual partners, and can even endure a little transient multiple-partner experimentation. These experiments, however, are supposed to fail, and as we have seen in a film like *Two Girls and a Guy*, the ideal must ultimately resolve itself in the normative formation of 'a couple'. Long-term polygamous relationships, as they are practised in many cultures, create significant anxieties for cultures rooted in Judaeo-Christian traditions. It seems that a dishonest or phantasmagoric monogamy is preferable to a polygamy which transgresses particular normative (Christian) values and feminist stereotypes of patriarchal control.

6   Sex that involves violence, coercion or animals is treated with deep contempt by cultural commentary. Yet even when these elements are converted to imagination and become part of an entirely different discourse – as, for example, in Peter Shaffer's play *Equus* – the ideal is rendered silent.

7   Finally, the double code of sex/power in the workplace has produced a new anxiety, most particularly as the workplace has become a central sexual site in contemporary culture. Feminism has problematized sex between work colleagues because of the danger of differential power and exploitation. While this fear has been largely associated with women's subjugant positions in the workplace, the film *Disclosure* explores the problem for male subordinates as well.

Sexual Futures

Most predictions about the future identify specific elements or trends in contemporary culture and project them forward. This 'logical extension' approach to the future tends inevitably to reduce the complexities of cultural phenomena to a number of highly selective elements. Most often, the elements are chosen according to the futurist's own ideological and psychological predisposition. In *The Transformation of Intimacy*, (1992) Anthony Giddens, for example, anticipates some significant changes to human sexual relationships, arguing that the deconstruction of formal and institutional notions of marriage will enhance relational potential. According to Giddens, traditional, institutional relationships encourage forms of emotional and financial dependency; the liberation of human subjects from dependence will promote independence and the capacity for informed choice. Relationships will need to be constantly negotiated and renegotiated, creating the conditions for enhanced intimacy as partners consciously construct their relationship rather than assume its perpetuity.

In *Sex in the Future* (1999) biologist Robin Baker draws rather different conclusions. According to Baker, the problem with human relationships is that they have tended to override fundamental biological and evolutionary urges. Baker draws on anthropological as well as biological evidence to prove that humans are basically motivated by sexual urges which would have them 'go at it like rabbits', if it weren't for the limits imposed, especially on women, by reproductive and nurturing responsibilities. IVF technology and the ascendant ideology of individualism will continue to liberate women from these responsibilities, creating more opportunity for self-gratifying sexual and emotional relationships. It is not intimacy so much as pleasure, polygamy and independence which will characterize future sex, according to Baker. The family will become a playground for the individual rather than a security blanket for the unit. It can be expected that monogamy and serial monogamy will be replaced by a more comfortable arrangement of multiple partnerships. In this sense, we might expect simultaneously to have a live-in partner, a parenting partner, a same-sex partner, a gamete (or reproduction) partner, and so on. Families will be conceived aspatially, as being distributed across quite wide areas and through quite diverse circumstances and contexts. Jealousy will have no place in these relationships because this negative emotion was largely associated with male paternity – that biological imperative which males experienced as a protective instinct over offspring. With IVF reproduction men too would be released from the onerousness of paternal possessions, an emotion which vicariously spread to the control of women.

In many respects, Baker's vision of the future of sex accords with a good deal of the cyborg and posthuman theoretics which are gaining popularity in the study of technology and culture (see Chapter 11). What is clear, however, is that Baker conceives of a future which is thoroughly preoccupied with the delimiting of sex and sexuality: sex and sexual pleasure will cast off reproduction to become the undisputed centre of contemporary culture. For Baker, this means that our humanity is completed by the clinical facility of technology. Our ancient bodily urges are finally able to consummate themselves through the liberation of technology:

> Who can deny that the human sexual repertoire, from its most basic to its most subtle, is anything other than ancient – etched into our bodies by millennia of natural selection...?

I will argue that modern technology has the potential to do more than put an end to infertility. In the process, it can also tip balances and correct ancient inequalities. The result will be the creation of a more evenhanded and certainly much more varied sexual arena than has ever existed in the past. At the same time, for good or for bad, it will free much more time for men – and probably women – to concentrate on things other than reproduction. (Baker, 1999: 1–2)

Loving Bodies?

Through these new fluidities, of course, the idea of gender becomes far less relevant. Men and women might experience desire for one another in ways which are not constrained by social norms and the ascription of attraction to the 'opposite' sex. Most sexual futurists welcome this new sexual fluidity, though few have attempted to engage with the problematic of love and its role within the sexual future. Indeed, the problematic of love seems very much to have slipped away from the vast corpus of sociological discourses, even though it remains central to everyday experiences and contemplations, and even though it is a central discourse in popular TV, cinema and musical texts. As Margareta Bertilsson (1991) points out, the concept of love has been presented primarily in terms of functionalist perspectives in social research: that is, love is seen as serving particular social needs rather than as constituting a fundamental, valid or valuable human emotion in its own sphere. A functionalist approach to love, therefore, might treat the 'energy' of love as a mechanism for reproduction or, re-focused, as a energizing mechanism for the steering of the social system as a whole (Bertilsson, 1991: 297). Psychology has, of course, attempted to construct a discourse of love which classifies and rationalizes its emotional and cognitive dimensions. This approach is designed, very often, to treat love as a kind of pathology, a condition that might be defined and diagnosed in order to reorder behaviours and relationships.

Cultural studies, even through its aesthetic lineage, has a limited capacity for dealing with the concept of love. In fact, the problematic of social disconnectedness, which may be associated with the dissolution of community and the intensification of individualism, is rarely, if ever, discussed in terms of the notion of love or loving bodies. Rather, the cultural studies paradigm moves uneasily through more reductive concepts like 'relationship' and 'sexuality', which are more closely linked to the ideology of liberation and individualism. Even so, the concept of love appears remarkably resilient in popular discourse, its romantic mysteriousness defying the assaults of politicism, rationalism, commodification and deconstruction. Love, that is, sits as an isolated, even atavistic, concept which the various discourses on relationships, power and sexuality seem unable to incorporate.

BEAUTIFUL AND HEALTHY BODIES

Structuralist Precepts

A good deal of feminist analysis of the body has centred on questions of representation. In particular, feminists have been highly critical of advertising and other popular textualizations which constantly repeat particular images of svelte, youthful, thin, female bodies. These images are not only 'normative' or normalized as a cultural standard, they become 'mythic': an ideal toward which all women must aspire in order to complete their own identity as women. Men's institutional power enables them to construct this beauty ideal; they are the gazers and the owners of the mechanisms of gazing. In her account of this patriarchal process, Naomi Wolf (1991) points out that the most common depiction of the body ideal has changed from a buxom size 12–14 represented in the Marilyn Monroe figure of the 1950s to a tall, thin 6–8 in current imagery. Wolf argues that this shrinking of the female body ideal, at a time when men and women are actually getting larger, represents an attempt to keep women thin, undernourished, pre-pubescent and under control.

While the broad strokes of Wolf's analysis have been severely criticized, there is little doubt that women's bodies have been iconographed as a sexual and commodificational focus for the culture at large. Feminist analysis argues that eating disorders such as bulimia and anorexia are directly related to unrealizable, media-constituted body ideals: young women deliberately starve themselves in order to suit the ideal. Paradoxically, this pandemic of body dissatisfaction is occurring as fast-food diets and declining physical activity are predisposing bodies to increased levels of obesity. Patricia Vertinsky (1998) points out, in fact, that women across all age levels in the developed world are almost half as active as men, despite the clear health benefits associated with exercise.

Susan Sontag (1978) argues that the media fascination with youthful beauty carries a reciprocal social interest in the condition of ageing, constructing it as a 'problem' if not a pathology. According to Sontag, it is this horror of the ageing female body in particular which constitutes a dominant ideology in the understanding and reading of femininity. Because of the cultural intensification and prolific mediation of the young, healthy female body, female ageing is more terrible and more frightening than male ageing. Female ageing represents the fundamental loss of vitality and sexual potency, the fundamental loss of 'life'. Vertinsky goes further to argue that this horror is part of young girls' initiation into puberty; despite the great achievements of the women's movement, young girls are socialized into the culture of body-hating (Vertinsky, 1998: 87). However, according to Vetinosky and numerous other feminist commentators, even physical fitness – the leaner, fitter body – is subject to the controlling manipulations of patriarchal commodification:

> Through its immense popularity, aerobics has been linked to a changing aesthetic of the female form. ... This transformed body is a fit body, and a healthy body (in stark contrast to the anorexic – a body that is fundamentally unhealthy, too far in excess of dominant standards of acceptable femininity). While this is not to deny that aerobics can serve as a vehicle of enjoyment, sociability, energy and opportunities for self-care, it embodies the complex use of power over women's bodies in a sophisticated consumer society. (Vertinsky, 1998: 89)

Whether fit, anorexic or overweight, aged or youthful, the female body is vulnerable to the controlling power of patriarchal and consumerist structures. This form of feminist analysis, however, struggles to find an escape from such powers. The beauty and health of the female body, it seems, is perpetually doomed to serve the interests of the male gaze, male sexuality and commerce.

Beauty and Labour

All cultures seem to have ordained a particular value for beauty and health, although the definition of beauty and its status against other social values are highly variable. The prominence of beauty and health in our culture can only partly be explained by feminist structural analysis. We can identify, even within European cultural history, variations, for example, in the approbation of skin colour. Fair skin once meant wealth and leisure, significant aspects of commodifiable beauty. From the 1960s, however, skin tanning represented a healthy body which was sufficiently leisured to permit sunbathing or a beach-based lifestyle. With the public awareness of the dangers of sunburn and skin cancer, sun tans are no longer broadly acknowledged as indicators of health and well-being. Similarly, the extreme female thinness which became ascendant during the 1980s and 1990s seems to be at odds with other significant feminine idealizations – in particular the intensification of breasts as sexual and cultural icons. That is, while the fashion industry persistently deployed the sylph-like bodies of young women, creating an imagery of perpetual pubescence or even trans-genderism, other areas of the media were increasingly exposing and deploying breasts as dominant sexual symbols. Topless bathing, increasingly explicit nudity in films, and the explosion of the silicon breast implant industry – all indicated a more intense experience of feminine sexuality which in many ways transgresses the beauty myth of waif-like thinness.

Of course, this intensification of visual sexuality, especially youthful sexuality, has been accompanied by massive acceleration in beauty and youth-restoring products and services. Jean Baudrillard explains these developments in terms of the increasing visualization of contemporary culture, and the need for a generalized, commodity-driven state of arousal. The broad distribution of electronic media and mediated imagery has been accompanied historically by significant changes in the way capitalism functions. The shift from manufacturing to service economies, most particularly media-based services, has changed the way bodies are deployed in labour. Baudrillard (1981) himself acknowledges these changes, arguing that modern capitalism shifts the focus of labour from goods production to sign production. In an increasingly visual culture, it is not surprising that the exchange-value of the human body has shifted from action and thought to appearance. The value of what a subject can do (or produce) has become less important than what a subject can represent. In the symbolic exchange of beauty, therefore, the face has become centralized over the action of muscle and mind.

Complaints about the increasing superficiality of culture, the proliferation of ephemera, the increasing disconnectedness of human relationships, and so on, are directly linked to the ascendancy of this new exchange-value. The spectacle of the human form, especially the female face, provides an exchange currency. Youth equates to freshness and newness. In a culture that has so thoroughly surrendered its (modernist) imagination of deep time and chronology, where the perpetuity of newness is so highly valued, it is not surprising that youth has become such a major commercial resource. In postmodern culture, where all temporal and spatial themes are laminated into ever-self-constructing versions of the new and the present, youth is a self-feeding mechanism which must necessarily reinvent itself with each moment. Deep thought or 'knowledge' is slipping behind the visual as a commodifiable entity. And while we might speak blithely about the 'information age', it is clear that this information is not dominated by new forms of knowledge but is rather constituted out of imaged ephemera which must constantly be refreshed and reinscribed with a smiling, youthful demeanour. This constant reconstruction or re-origination of the new and its promise of popular 'success' inevitably subjugates the value of concentrated knowledge. Even, for example, a new cultural

facility like the Internet only become 'popular' when it became visual and available for sexual engagement. As a knowledge technology the Internet was restricted to the interests of warlords and academics. Its integration with visual culture and sexual imagining brought the Net out of the unknown and into the practices of everyday users for everyday information. Once again, the human form, especially the female form, has become the dominant iconography of the Net.

Ageing and Pathology

While other cultures might respect and value the sagacity or wisdom associated with ageing, the postmodern intensification of youth and youthful appearance inevitably creates significant anxieties around ageing, disease and degeneration. Sontag and other feminists have highlighted this problematic in association with women's ageing, but the decline of bodily prowess creates significant anxieties for both genders. In fact, postmodern conceptions of cultural time as the 'ever-present' and the ever-unfolding 'new' create significant problems for cultural subjects. Subjects may wish to obey this cultural norm and be forever youthful and progressive, but the simple fact is that bodies decline and age. In broader, demographic terms, in fact, developed cultures are becoming far less youthful as a social group; the baby-boom of the post-World War II period is well past its peak and total populations in the developed world are rapidly ageing.

At a personal level, Meyrowitz (1986) claims that this mismatch between ageing and ever-presence is associated primarily with new discursive challenges to the modernist chronologizing of the life course. Human imagining of life has changed radically, according to Meyrowitz, as children are behaving more like adults and adults more like children. There is an increasing continuity in modes of dress, cultural tastes and self-presentation as the ageing populations attempt to maintain the culture of youth against the biological necessity of decline and death. This temporal compression is clearly associated with postmodernization and the impact of televisual culture.

Contemporary culture's de-ritualization of life stages is part of a similar temporal realignment. Emphasis on youth and youthful perpetuity has challenged the cultural values and social rewards associated with ageing. Indeed, the presentation of idealized body types, which is so hotly condemned in much feminist analysis, operates as an obscurification of these chronologized life phases. Youthful energy, sexual arousal and the pleasures of adventure are provided as resources for the extension of the 'mid-life'. Advertising and televisual imagery guide their adult consumers through lifestyle experiences which are only vicariously associated with chronological age; comfort and luxury are constituted as a discernment of taste, rather than a condition of bodily degeneration. Ageing, that is, becomes camouflaged through the discourses of target marketing. It is not decay, wisdom or a senior social status that draws a consumer to a product; it is bodily vitality, arousal and youthful perpetuity which enables an identity to defy its biological decline.

Featherstone and Hepworth (1991) agree that this notion of mid-life, the period between youthful adult and old age, has been reconstructed in the past few decades. However, they go on to suggest that along with the openness and increased flexibility of this reconstituted mid-life is a discourse of 'crisis' (1991: 384). In terms of televisual iconography, this crisis

becomes another available resource by which subjects define themselves and adjudge their experience of relationships, health and sexuality. We have made reference to the explosion in anti-ageing products and services, relationship and psychological counselling services, and the vast array of lifestyle products designed to complete the identity that has been constituted through the mid-life. It seems, however, that mid-life becomes a point of awareness, a moment in which the perpetuity of arousal spoken about by Baudrillard may come home to roost. That is to say, the unceasing return of that arousal may lead in mid-life to an awareness of the impossibility of satisfaction. The paradoxical mingling of biology and discourse, in fact, may create the sort of fractures in subject identity which produce the sense of crisis. The mid-life crisis is the 'normal' outcome of realization: the impossibility of sexual or financial satisfaction, and the impossibility of immortality.

David Clarke (1993) suggests that the construction of marital sexual problems is linked to this normalization process. That is, the psychological, medical and pathological discourses which support the notion of 'crisis' in a relationship are built around notions of normality and abnormality. While constituting a more open approach to chronology, notions of mid-life have merely shifted 'well-being' and health problems away from ageing and toward other constituted forms of normality. Sexuality and sexual variation are barely countenanced in the construction of human sexual pathologies, Clarke argues. While some of these common sexual pathologies are identifiably physiological, many are also defined in terms of a psychological or relational 'illness'. For women, the most common problems are lack of sexual desire and failure to reach orgasm; for men the most common pathologies are erectile and ejaculant dysfunction.

For Clarke, however, it is the particular social arrangement which constitutes sexuality – marriage – which first harbours and constitutes the 'crisis'. The problematic of sex within marriage is concentrated through notions of sexual normality and the idealized marital body. The creation of relational or sexual disorders out of this normative approach, and therapies designed to cure it, deflects attention away from the relational formation itself and the broader question of sexuality. In other words, Clarke claims, the problems of the body are formed out of what is considered 'normal' in a socially and culturally sanctioned relationship. Crisis is produced because subjects' bodies are simply not able to cope with the emotional and psychological burden of these normative expectations.

THE SPECTACLE OF MUSCULAR BODIES

While discourses on sexuality and the youthful female body have tended to dominate cultural analyses of the body, more recent studies are considering alternative presentations, including the spectacle of muscularity and maleness. Indeed, through the progress of cultural theory, a greater interest in diversity and alternative ideologies has shifted some of the interest in the body away from feminist analysis of dominant ideologies and representations. As we have noted, the prevalence of the young female body in the media, and in culture more broadly, has tended to obscure the increasing heterology of sexualities and other everyday bodily experiences. For example, recent studies on the female body have examined female muscularity

as a reconfiguration of traditional female stereotypes. These analyses, either consciously or indirectly, reflect on the whole notion of body construction, body action and ascriptions of gender. The muscularity of women reflects on, for example, the constructive nature of body idealizations, including the discourses of masculinity. Leslie Heywood deconstructs masculinity through a carefully charted analysis of (female) bodybuilding in American popular culture:

> Perhaps more obviously than any other contemporary phenomenon, bodybuilding relies on a radical notion of plasticity while that plasticity paradoxically functions to bolster the most fixed, traditional masculine norms. More than any other sport, it draws attention to the fact that masculinity is a masquerade rather than an unquestionable essence. ... If display places one on the side of the spectacle in the sense of film theory, and the spectacle is the position of the feminine, then bodybuilding for all its hypermasculine posturing visibly marks masculinity as both posture and literal physical construction. By definition, bodybuilding is a spectacle which performs the masculine. ... Perched precariously on the balancing point between the slavish enactment of masculinity and its denaturalization and thereby deconstruction, bodybuilding is the fortification which will destroy the fortress. (1998: 65)

Bodybuilding acts in similar ways to the plasticity of cosmetic prosthetics. Strangely, the enhancement of female muscularity extends the potential of the femininity and the female form while simultaneously exposing the artificiality of the masculine. Muscles can be constructed like silicon breasts; anything is possible in the cultural construction of discourse.

While most feminists have been concerned to critique socially inscribed images of femininity, Heywood's deconstruction is designed to liberate women from the discursive and ideological limits imposed by the concept of masculinity. Heywood suggests that the extreme of bodybuilding actually constitutes a form of 'feminine spectacle' and thus self-parody. Of course, this problematic of gender ascription and identity construction applies equally to males. In particular, the low-fat, highly muscled body type is critically implicated in the formation of an idealized masculinity as it is culturally imagined and experienced by men. While Heywood considers 'masculinity' to be liberatory for women, it is being seen by various commentators (see Messner and Sabo, 1990; Buchbinder, 1998) as constraining and troubling for men. The ideal of the muscular body and the social significance attributed to size (phallic and body mass) may be constituted in similar ways as female beauty or the presentation of breasts.

As Murray Drummond (1998a, 1998b) has argued in his analysis of male body idealizations, bodies are of critical significance for the construction of male identity. While this identity has always been built around forms of bodily action, more recent displays of muscularity as spectacle in televisual culture are leading to similar pressures and dissatisfactions for men as are being experienced by women. Drummond (1998b) argues that body dissatisfaction is increasing among (especially younger) men. Susan Paxton (1998) agrees, claiming that at least 10 per cent of patients presenting with anorexia are now male and the figures for bulimia are virtually the same for men and women. Cornell (1990) argues that the desire of men to be big and muscular is not necessarily to enhance their pre-existing masculinity, but in order to match standards of social norms and to be simply acknowledged as male. This aspiration has proved particularly acute for gay men.

COMMODIFICATION AND SPORT

When associated with other cultural hierarchies such as race and class, the problematic of masculinity is even further intensified. Undoubtedly sport and games were once deployed in culture as forms of recreation and play. At its more functionalist levels, however, sport provided the sort of physical training necessary for labour, economy and military deployment. In more developed cultures sport was also used as a form of social differentiation, often confirming the social distance not only between performers but also between performers and spectators (see Bourdieu, 1991). The codification of sport, which took place in the late part of the nineteenth century and primarily in Britain, also provided an ideological currency for the maintenance and administration of nation, nationalism and empire. The British game of cricket provided a facility for the promotion and maintenance of imperial ideology and the hegemony of the British Empire. The potency of masculinity manifest in male sporting prowess became a useful vehicle in the public demonstration of national values and national potency. In the 1936 Berlin Olympic Games, Adolf Hitler presented the virility and machismo of the Fatherland through the performances of his German Aryan athletes. Cold War tensions between the United States and the USSR were articulated in a nuclear arms race, battles over space, and a brutish Olympic competitiveness which culminated in reciprocal boycotts of the other's hosted Games.

The Televisual Sporting Body

The evolution of television, satellite and digital technology has enabled immediate, global telecast of sporting events. In fact, along with the sexuality of young women, the greatest area of image proliferation has been in men's sport. The active male body as spectacle, therefore, has become engaged in new forms of televisual economy. Scarcity and capitalist value have found a new source of commodification, new forms of labour. The transfer of amateur or recreational sport into a highly valued commodity has brought new definitions to the nature and activity of sport. Bodies, male bodies in particular, have become defined in terms of excellence in action, a capacity to function at extreme levels of performance. Thus, the muscularity associated with industrial labour has been transformed into a muscularity of display. The product of the display is arousal that has no palpable resolution, no product, other than visual and visceral stimulation. Men are excited by the narrative of a sporting event, but the arousal can never be completed or satisfied. Like sexual arousal, like the commodity of the youthful female face, the sports body is a form of constituted symbolic value, an ephemeron, a discourse which can never be concluded because it never actually does anything except act out a narrative which will be perpetually emerging through the carnival of play and display.

The rise of the cult of the celebrity sports star produces new modes of subjectivity or self-presentation which are available for commodity consumption and the formation of celebrity community. As with movie stars or television celebrities, the sports celebrity has become a means of marketing the sport, the constituted individual, and the promise of identity for the consumer. Audiences (see Chapter 8) or 'spectators' are now able to constitute their own communities built around teams and individual performers. Whereas once these communities may have been located in villages and urban neighbourhoods, the transferral of sport into a TV commodity facilitates much broader engagements. The Chicago Bulls may now have followers in all parts of the United States as well as in Buenos Aires, Vancouver, Berlin or Christchurch. Manchester United is no longer located in the urban centre but is a spectator commodity available for community formation and consumption all over the globe. The sports stars of athletics or tennis are no longer confined to their home nation, but are available for spectacle and consumption in 'imagined' transnational communities that are linked not even by language, but through the televisual image and the merchandising magic that surrounds them.

Hierarchies and Winning Ways

The televisualization and globalization of sport have created a huge economy that is sustained less by the constitution of team, but more by the symbology of success. While numerous football followers invest themselves in the iconography of 'team' or 'club', the sustaining interest in that collective is the ideology of winning. Of course, this winning, or winning potential, is the ideological basis of capitalist economics. The joys and delights of winning, or imagining victory, are the sustaining power of loyalty and identity constitution. The self-projection of success – the same self-projection that operates in the broader capitalist economy – maintains the hapless football supporter through the often excessive tribulations of loss. Were it not for the glamourous elations of (imagined) success, then the capitalist dream would undoubtedly grind to a halt. Sport has become the natural bedfellow of an ideology which obscures the inevitability of dissatisfaction through a promise of achievement and victory.

Professional football competition is, perhaps, the most spectacular example of commercial manipulation. Football is played for TV, and the controllers of the sport in most parts of the world are manipulating the game to suit advertisement intervals and the spectacle of speed and action. Amidst the imagining of team loyalty, the promise of success is nearly always invested in individuals. Individual team members or stars are heavily marketed; sponsorship and membership, along with game attendance and TV rights, are lured through the presentation and potential of the 'latest young recruit', the new coach, the return of a star. Men, in particular, pay for the drama of sport, for the visceral excitement of its unfolding and for the athleticism of its action; but above all they pay for the imagining of success, an imagining in which they can participate and with which they can identify.

Not surprisingly, the often grotesque sums of money paid to sports celebrities and the manna maniacal prospecting for new recruits and stars provide significant opportunities for social mobility. African American and other coloured men in the United States experience low levels of education and opportunities for professional careers. As Blount and Cunningham (1996) have pointed out, the subjectivity of black men in dominant white culture has been substantially constructed through physical action and physical prowess. The complex representation of black men, most particularly in sport, constitutes a certain anxiety for the dominant culture, a certain 'antagonistic co-operation' (Blount and Cunningham, 1996: xi) whereby blackness and body become a reluctantly privileged cultural category which is built around a peculiar dialogue of fear and admiration. The popularity of boxing, especially amongst men, is necessarily linked to the colosseum mentality of discharging lesser minds and greater bodies into 'mortal' combat. The success of the Sylvester Stallone *Rocky* films, meanwhile,

may be partly understood as the reassertion of white supremacy, where Rocky/Stallone represents the 'great white hope' for white masculinity.

Sport, that is, has come to be associated with particular ideologies of race and gender. Boxing, as perhaps the most brutal and confrontational of all sports, is conceived fundamentally as masculine, and generally a sport of the lowest socio-economic groups. Other Olympic sports, such as synchronized swimming, are sneered at by many men because of their putative femininity. The radical overhaul of gender ascription, however, has led to much broader transferrals in bodily deployment and social conceptions. Thus, while heterosexual beauty remains highly appealing for marketing and news copy, alternative sexualities and body constructions for women and men have become increasingly evident in sports communities. Perhaps the most radical of these new bodily forms is associated with the technology of performance-enhancing drugs, especially anabolic steroids (male hormones) and growth hormones.

Sport and Bodily Enhancements

Steroids and growth hormones are used for power sports – sprinting, short distance cycling, jumping, lifting and throwing events – in order to increase muscle mass and training effects. These power events generally rely on sudden explosions of energy and muscular exertion. The Cold War tensions between the United States and the USSR and its allies (1945–89) encouraged the development of a wide range of chemical and mechanical sporting technologies. Concentrated male hormones were first used by East German female sprinters at the Helsinki Games. Along with increased muscle mass, the steroids also produce significant bodily side-effects.

For women, these could include increasing male characteristics such as facial hair, deepened voice, breast shrinkage, plus labial and clitoral development with significantly increased libido. Ironically, the increased muscle size and density for men is often accompanied by testicular shrinkage as the function of the testes is supplemented by an external agent. In both genders significant health risks have been reported, including loss of bone density as well as cardiovascular, respiratory and general heart problems. Deaths have been recorded, and there is some suspicion that the premature death of Florence Griffith-Joiner, the women's 100 metres world record holder, was associated with steroid taking.

For cultural analysis these bodily modifications are indicative of the openness of the body system and its vulnerability to cultural invasion. In everyday practice the deployment of steroids has been constituted around physical display and the problematic of gender ascriptions. While sports celebrities might use the steroids to enhance the possibility of success, non-elite sportspeople are are using steroids increasingly to enhance the look of their body mass. Steroid taking is popular amongst bodybuilders, including communities of gay men. It may be that the conception of beauty and sexual attractiveness which dominates heterosexual culture has its own equivalent in gay communities. The youthful, sporting, masculine body which is so ubiquitously imaged in contemporary culture may well have been adapted into areas of gay sexuality where the discourse of masculinity is intensified as a new beauty myth.

MASCULINITIES

There is no doubt that feminism has dominated discussions of the body, most particularly the sexualized or gendered body, since the 1960s. The preoccupation with women and women's bodies has tended to frame masculinity and male bodies in terms of patriarchy and the politics of sexism. In many respects, males have been seen as the perpetrators of women's subjugation, the cause of social misery and underprivilege. Where males have accepted these critiques, they have tended to cast themselves in the shame of their masculinity, rendering themselves and their bodies invisible as they seek to support feminist politics and the redress of gender discrimination. More recently, however, cultural analysis has become more interested in the formation of gender and the issue of masculinity in its own right. Men, in particular, have become more actively engaged in the study of culture and the discursive formation of masculine identity and gender politics.

In this sense, the rise of the so-called 'men's movement' in gender-based analysis of discourse and culture can be explained in the following terms:

1   A revision of structuralist approaches to gender (and class), and a reciprocal increase in analysis based on discourse and representation. The influence of Michel Foucault, in particular, encouraged many feminists to examine the concept of gender and the relationship between men and women in more expansive ways. Such analysis acknowledges the precarious nature of a reality that is mediated by discourse and which is constituted through an enormous variety of human characteristics and traits. Feminism revised its view that all women could be homogenized and categorized as a single social class; if women's identities were to be liberated, then differences between women must be recognized and encouraged. The notion, therefore, that all men

constituted a single, homogeneous social class, which was responsible for patriarchy, had to be questioned. Equally, the relationship between men and women could not always be epitomized in terms of the ideology of patriarchy as relationships between these two broad and diverse groups were constituted through a complex imbrication of discourses and localized truths.

2 These heterologies were also filtered through Foucault's theory of power. Rather than power being fixed in structures of class or gender, Foucault conceived of it as a process, an unstable exchange of positions and discourses. In particular, Foucault's notion of the 'microphysics of power' (Foucault, 1977a) was contentious for many feminists, who returned to statistical summaries of social differentiation to justify their outrage against the structured inequality and oppression of women by men. However, as Foucault and neo-Foucauldian feminists have explained, these statistics might actually camouflage important aspects of social and cultural life, which include the social limits placed on men as much as on women. The Foucauldian approach to power, in fact, facilitates greater agency for women and for men to overcome these limits, and for the construction of new relationships and new discourses based on equality and partnership.

3 This desire to improve personal relationships through the reformulation of gender ascriptions and gender-based discourses, including the discourses of power, has been influenced by the interests and approaches of the rising generation of mothers. These new-generation mothers are seeking enhanced intimacies and friendships with sons and male partners without recourse to 'hardline' assaults on men and masculinity. These relational aspirations are ocurring where the notion of gender equality is a given, rather than a radical reformulation. Women want better men, and it may be that the liberation of men may be the best way of achieving that end. Moreover, the reformulation of women's subjectivities has necessarily stimulated changes for men and their relationships. The difficulties and pleasures associated with these changes have forced many men to ask questions about their own identities and the cultural meaning of their own bodies – their role in work, military activities, sports, and so on.

4 Poststructuralism, postmodernism and discourse theory have all contributed to the broadening of the cultural politics agenda. In particular, the raising of the issue of sexuality and identity has facilitated greater interest in ethnicity, race and postcolonialism. These politics have been welded to issues of women's rights and gender; however, once problematized, the questions of gender and its relationship to other forms of cultural politics necessarily implicates the condition of men and their masculinity. Thus, the social, economic and health condition of many indigenous peoples of the world will inevitably involve gender-specific issues: the reproductivity of women, for example, and alcoholism and violence among men. This re-focusing or broadening of the cultural politics agenda demonstrates that men, as well as women, continue to suffer significant privation and oppression.

6 This has been particularly pertinent in issues of sexuality, where gay men have felt excluded from the feminist agenda. That is, while accepting the potency of feminist approaches to questions of sexuality and gender, gay men's groups have at times felt that their particular

questions about masculinity, identity and sexuality have been ignored in the cultural politics of feminism.

7   The fracturing of the feminist intellectual hegemony in the 1990s has paradoxically opened a space for greater masculine self-reflection. As feminists have begun to deconstruct their feminist heritage, a number of men have found the space to consider the negative dimensions of masculinity: the problematics of their relationships with other men, including their fathers; aggression; violence; muscularity; unattainable social expectations; the denial of nurturing; and so on.

Clearly, and as Homi Bhabha (1994) reminds us, masculinity should not be fixed to the condition of the biologically gendered male body as opposition to the biologically gendered female body. Of course notions of femininity are often associated with female bodies, and masculinity is associated with male bodies. However, our analysis of the body has demonstrated how these cultural ascriptions may be inverted or destabilized by transgressive bodily practices and the processes of deconstruction. Within this general frame it is clear that the notions of masculinity and masculine identity are formed around a broad range of subject positions and discourses. Masculinity, that is, must be read as text or a set of competing discourses; inevitably these discourses engage with questions of patriarchy, privilege and power that are so often associated with the concept of male.

Anxiety and Power

A good deal of the recent discussion on masculinity has, in fact, applied a fairly familiar feminist mode of analysis, most particularly in relation to forms of social expectation and the representation of male body ideals. Just as women experience a range of psychological and emotional dissonances through not being able to meet unrealistic body ideals, so men experience dissonance in not approximating their own muscular and powerful ideal. The privileges and power which patriarchy accords to masculinity may also function to produce men's sense of inadequacy and humiliation when they fail to exploit this cultural and political privilege fully. As David Buchbinder has put it, the key to men's social performance is the recognition of this privilege of masculinity:

> The process of recognition begins with the body: for what all boys and men apparently have in common, transcending differences of race, culture and class, traversing the distinctions of occupation, and crossing the limits even of time and history, is of course the penis. (1998: 29)

As we have noted, this (minor) biological difference is constituted symbolically in discourse; the penis, the phallus, is not just a biological organ, it is the representative of an expansive history of power and control. As Judith Butler (1995) explains, gender itself is more than merely constructed, it is actually 'performed'; the complex meanings associated with gender are therefore rendered as operations in behaviour, choice and representation. Men perform their masculinity as the ongoing and constantly reforming process of patriarchy. The anxieties of men are embedded, therefore, in their social responsibilities as much as in their personal self-image. The system, with all its privileges and pleasures, is founded on masculinity: to fail one's own masculinity is to fail the system.

This fear of inadequacy or failure in men has often been vested in physical and sexual performance. Pathologies like impotence are the most commonly reported sexual problem for men. The ceaseless threat of attack by other males and the need to protect sexual and genetic territory create profound, if subterranean, fears for men. Comparative demographies show that at any age level men suffer much higher rates of death and bodily harm than do women. Young men are the most assaulted and murdered group in the community; they are more likely to die or be seriously injured in motor accidents than are women; they are about five times more likely to commit suicide; and they have much higher rates of disease. While the reasons for these significantly greater rates of bodily damage amongst men are varied and complex, there can be little doubt that the imperative to perform, including acts of violence and self-violence, remains remarkably resilient, even in a broader culture in which women and femininities have changed so markedly.

Masculininist analysis of this kind is designed to liberate men from the bondage of patriarchal ideologies. Many feminists and cultural commentators, however, have been hostile to the male movement, arguing that the whole notion of male 'victimism' is an offence to the project of female emancipation. George Yodice (1995) points out, for example, that a number of men may be taking up the victim position in order to rearticulate and reconstruct contemporary discourses, including liberatory discourses. Yodice points to a number of examples of males appropriating feminist discourses in order to reposition their 'hegemony'. Citing Antonio Gramsci's notion of hegemony as a form of negotiated leadership, he explains that men may simply be maintaining their domination through an interaction with feminist discourse. If males are also 'victims' of patriarchal systems, and masculinity is the outcome of that oppressive representational code, then they are justified in (re)claiming a liberated social prominence.

In other words, that part of the men's movement which articulates men's cultural and social experiences in terms of an oppressive patriarchy may be surreptitiously reconstructing their dominance: 'Women have it bad, but so do men; we're all victims together so let's not point the finger at men.'

New Sexism

In her book *The Hearts of Men* (1995) Barbara Ehrenreich claims that the decline of patriarchy, as much as anything else, has been brought about through women's greater participation in the post-Fordist, global economy. This greater participation in the masculine culture of business and economy has been reciprocated in men's greater participation in the feminine culture of nurturing, domesticity and consumerism. Ehrenreich distinguishes between what she calls the 'decline of patriarchy' and the continuation of sexism and misogyny. Patriarchy, as it was originally conceived, refers to the privileging and power of men through the institution of the family. The decline of the position of patriarch – provider, leader and protector of the family – has led to formidable social changes in masculine values. The evidence of these changes, according to Ehrenreich, can be seen in the reluctance of men to marry, the increasing age of marrying men, the reduction in family, the disinclination of men to 'support' women and to compromise their standard of living during childrearing, and the defaulting of men on child maintenance payments. The sort of 'chivalric' or protective values which sustained patriarchy have been clearly diminished by the deconstruction of the patriarch.

This decline in patriarchy is not, however, attributable to women's liberation, since women clearly remain victims of forms of social and political privation. From the perspective of men, according to Ehrenreich, the decline in patriarchy has been associated with:

(a) men's own retreat from responsibility and the onerousness of protecting and keeping company with women;

(b) the reduction in men's wages, which has relieved men of the responsibility of sole financial provider; and

(c) men's greater immersion in the culture of femininity, which has encouraged a greater embrace of consumerism and consumer practices which could only be compromised by the sharing of income.

We might add to Ehrenreich's list by pointing to the increasing representations of males in feminine sexual culture through the increasing deployment of male body in sexually oriented advertising. These images often depict males in formerly female poses of heavy-lidded seduction; their bodies are hairless, and their pectoral muscles are often fetishized, maximizing their analogy to female breasts.

While Ehrenreich can feel no nostalgia for patriarchy, its decline has exposed women to the more fiercely sexist, competitive and violent aspects of masculine culture. Men's refusal to take care of women, emotionally or physically, is often justified in terms of women's liberation: that women are now free to do as they please so they can bear the brunt of what that means. In many respects, the recent writings by Germaine Greer and Naomi Wolf have expressed a certain regret that women's sexual liberation and the increasing propensity for multiple sexual partners has actually brought women into a more masculine sexual culture. For Ehrenreich, however, it is the violence and abuse which is so common in masculine culture that is the primary problem for contemporary women's liberation. While once women were accorded some level of protection against this abuse, they are now encouraged to participate in it as a matter of 'liberation'. The decline of patriarchy promises new horizons of freedom:

> But the other potential future created by the decline of patriarchy is not so promising. It involves a further descent into the barbarism of male violence. As men continue to turn away from being protectors of women and become increasingly *predators* of women, women will continue to 'masculinize' themselves, if only for purposes of self-defence. (Ehrenreich, 1995: 290)

Young Men and Macho Rock

A good deal of gender analysis tends to rely on Althusserian forms of dominant ideology theory. That is, there is a tendency to view men and women as distinct ideologically formed, and oppositional, entities. Even when the analysis is seeking to demonstrate a redrawing of the ideological boundaries, as with Ehrenreich, there is a tendency to restore oppositional structures in order to produce general statements about the respective gender. Within the broad fields of these gender typologies there exists, of course, substantial variation, not only between individuals, but also between different assemblages of individuals, and within individuals themselves. One person might carry around significant ambivalences and opposite attitudes and propensities. A given individual male or female might productively participate in various aspects of what Ehrenreich calls masculine or feminine culture. Depending on the nature of particular relationships and friendship patterns, a particular individual may be more or less promiscuous, abusive, sexist or protective.

Pumping Up

The predisposition of rock music to push the boundaries of social norms, authority and 'good taste' continues today. Among the targets of musical assault, especially by male musicians, have been the ideological standards of conventional feminism. Popular bands like The Prodigy, No FX and The Bloodhound Gang have all released songs that have a distinctly ironical disrespect for the prohibitions of feminist authority and conservative puritanism. The following are excerpts from the bands' lyrics:

> Smack my bitch up,
> Smack my bitch up,
> Smack my bitch up –
> Change my picture.
> > The Prodigy, 'Smack My Bitch Up'

> I like to jerk off with my left hand.
> Together on the sand,
> We walked hand in hand,
> On the beach front,
> She tightly held my hand.
> I had my thumb in her stubble.
> Country music on the radio,
> So I turned it on,
> We walked down to the water
> As I fucked her grandma's daughter.
> OH what a hole, oh what a hole, oh what a hole.
> > No FX, 'Together on the Sand'

> The lap dance is so much better when the stripper is crying,
> The lap dance is so much better when the stripper is crying,
> Well I find it's quite a thrill
> When she rides me against her will,
> The lap dance is so much better when the stripper is crying.
> > The Bloodhound Gang, 'The Lap Dance Is So Much Better'

While each of these songs is forged through a complex of uncertain ironies and textual positions, there remains a sense in which the sexual liberation which has enabled their expression is shaded by the perpetual threat of an invigorated and rebounding misogyny. The point is, we can never be sure which position the song is actually representing: liberation or a reconstituted masculine sexism.

Plate 9.1 Cyborg sexuality. The performance artist Stelarc has produced a number of cyborg apparatuses. In this performance Stelarc's body interacts with a bionic limb and a networked computer. The computer and the electro-chemical activities of Stelarc's body create various sensate, electronic and audio stimulations. Musical sounds and a 'dance performance' are generated through this cyborgian interaction. Stelarc is featured in this photograph with model Belinda Rikard Bell.

In assemblages of these ambiguous subjectivities, certain gender patterns are emerging. New forms of sexism appear as a discursive trend in popular music. The trend toward increasing female sexual liberationism in the 1980s, most popularly evinced in artists like Madonna, has appropriated the discursive ground of sexist masculinity. While a good deal of feminist commentary has welcomed the expressive lust of artists like Madonna,

the absorption of the territory by women and the presentation of men as sexual objects appears to have contributed to a resurgence of sexist discourse by men since the 1990s. While explicit and sexist male lyrics survived in the margins of heavy metal and hip-hop during the 1980s, their return to the mainstream is indicative of a more aggressive masculine sexism. Although a degree of this resurgent sexism may simply be a playful avatar, a response to women's chiding, there is in various musical texts a more vigorous and redolent anger, a resentment toward women that is complex, if not disturbing.

DISCUSSION: POSTHUMAN BODIES

As elaborated in our discussion of new technologies (Chapter 11), there has been a great surge in interest in the notion of posthuman bodies, most particularly those of the technology–human hybrid, the cyborg. Cultural theorists like Donna Haraway have conceived of the cyborg as a utopian ideal through which humans will evolve a more egalitarian and inclusive consciousness; the body of the cyborg will be liberated from the limiting physiognomy of race, age, gender and sexual orientation. The notion of posthumanism is also discussed by less extravagant commentators who point to the incorporation of various technologies into human morphology as evidence of an advanced human condition. Such enhancements would include spectacles, hearing aids, wheelchairs and prosthetics (breast implants, skeletal plates, pins and joint replacements). For many theorists of the posthuman condition, digital technology, more so than mechanical and electrical analogue technologies, mimics and enhances the very essence of our humanity: our neurological (brain and nerve) system.

Perhaps the most complex of these technological supplements, one most clearly heralding changes to our humanity, is the bionic ear. The bionic ear is a replacement for the complex system of aural neuro-receptors that have been damaged or diseased. However, rather than acting as an analogue amplification of sounds, the bionic ear actually receives external stimulus (sound), which it then re-transmits to the brain. These electromagnetic stimuli must then be unscrambled and reconstituted as meaningful sounds. The sounds that a bionic ear is hearing and transmitting, in fact, are entirely different from those of a 'normal' ear; the bionic-eared human is receiving different sounds which constitute a different world experience, a different language, a different interpretational field. The bionic ear, which is a form of smart technology, may herald the sort of hybrid humanity that Haraway and others anticipate, most especially when combined with various forms of genetically engineered or cloned human organic material.

Posthuman discourse, however, also incorporates those theories which are antagonistic toward the ideology of humanism. A number of critics, especially working through radical, feminist and 'queer' liberationism, have taken a strident anti-humanist approach to the body and the ideological humanism which houses it. Judith Halberstam and Ira Livingston argue that these forms of radical posthuman bodies 'thrive in subcultures without culture' (1995: 4). What is meant here is that culture is a dominant 'imaginary' or ideology which subsumes diversity and difference. Humanism, with its ideology of inclusiveness and uniform liberationism, actually violates the forming of human meanings, closing itself and its borders around the notion of 'culture'. 'Culture' is complete and marked at the borders; 'subculture' reopens the possibilities of an ongoing exploration of subjectivity, community and meaning-making. Posthumanism allows subcultures to experience their difference without recourse to dominant cultural terms. In other words, the bodily forms of the sub-culture remain emancipated when they are different, uncommodified and unexploited for general perception and consumption. The posthuman body is entirely liberational as it shows the significance of the family as a patriarchal, sexual and reproductive unit. This system, which specifies 'who can fuck what and how' (Halberstan and Livingston, 1995: 11), is replaced by a heterogeneous assemblage of choosing people, a sexuality that resists gender distinctions and a reproductivity which liberates women from the onus of biological replenishment.

Michel Foucault, of course, had imagined a time when reproduction and sexuality would be entirely divorced, and the possibilities of surrogate motherhood and male pregnancy would become desirable reproductive options (Foucault, 1981: 105). This drawing from the posthuman margins might ultimately obliterate the final, biological hierarchy in gender relations. Radical posthumanism, therefore, seeks to present human bodies as the means of liberation and not its expressive limits. Masculinity and femininity would be entirely merged, reconstituting bodily variations as another opportunity in the heterology of bodily pleasures and bodily postures.

Supporters of these radical conceits are careful to insist that the liberation they envisage will always resist homogenization, that the plurality of the body is never threatened by the 'assemblage' of cultural normalism; the posthuman body cannot ossify as an essential and monadic entity. Posthumanism, that is, is conceived as an heterological phenomenon, an ephemeron which is neither atomic and infinitely unmediated, nor concrete and immovable. The heterogeneity is assured. Even so, and this remains a problem for most postmodern utopianism, the radical conceit is built around the same sort of hostilities that parade men and masculinity as the ultimate terror. Posthumanism seeks to obliterate all traces of a masculinity which is conceived as the ultimate enemy of liberation. The merging of gender is not the hybridization of particular human variations, but an assimilation of only those (feminine) characteristics which are sustaining and generative. The gender pool is thus reduced as posthumanism cannot accept those characteristics which do not fit the political formula. While claiming that posthumanism is decidedly marginal and sub-cultural, posthumanists nevertheless prescribe a social condition which excludes a variety of masculine and feminine discourses and experiences. The passion of the reform leaves little space for alternatives to the prescribed political order.

Posthumanism of this kind overlooks the generative and positive dimensions of masculinities. Indeed, the literature on bodies has tended to treat masculinity generally as negative. Indeed, maleness and male bodies are by and large ignored unless they are operating at the margins and can be easily typified as non-white, non-straight. In fact, masculinities are as broad and varied as femininities. Even the categories of distinction which currently operate are many and varied and the investment of males and females with the broad sweep of the oppositional typologies is already quite inappropriate. The literature fails to deal adequately with the complex associations which constitute differences and similarities between gender, nor does it adequately deal with the

struggles which can produce joyful and generative moments. The pandemic of dissatisfaction which unquestionably plagues us can only partly be explained by the limiting effects of gendered bodily experiences. Our bodies return us pleasure and pain. Our loves and distresses, our consonances and dissonances are not to be resolved in a posthuman idealization.

Liberated Bodies

Barbara Ehrenreich is one of the few commentators to suggest that there may have been something vaguely good about patriarchy; she hastens to add, however, that this positive value is massively outweighed by the harm patriarchy has done to women and women's lives. In fact, the concept of 'patriarchy' has been used by most gender critics as the representative of all things evil: as representing a universal and systematic set of mechanisms, ideologies and structures designed to advantage males over females. Even those feminists influenced by poststructuralism and postmodernism have tended to apply the concept of patriarchy as an analogue of modernism: as an homogeneous discourse which is antithetical to the diversity and difference which their own liberational feminism represents. If, as has been suggested throughout this book, modernism is not as homogeneous as postmodernists would like to claim, but is better understood as a series of open and competing discourses, then 'patriarchy' is also problematized. Patriarchy, that is, might need to be understood not as a single block of integrated modes of action and ideology, but as a broad cluster of contradictory, antagonistic and competing discourses.

In this sense, patriarchy is not a system except in as much as gender critics construct it as a system (or structure). The set of ideas and representations which constitute gender (femininity and masculinity) from the period of modernity and into the present are themselves formed around various discursive contradictions involving economy, reproduction, sex and pleasure, biology, and a broad assemblage of competing claims to power. The hierarchical frameworks of capitalism, its contradictory impulses of scarcity and access, its grotesque embellishments of individual characteristics and life advantages along with their manifestation in reward and privation – all inform the relational nature of gender and sexuality. Masculinity is formed out of protectiveness, sacrifice, responsibility, care and love, as much as it is formed out of control, discipline, misogyny and surveillance. The continued presence of negative, damaging and oppressive discourses in contemporary culture is not the residue of a fracturing patriarchy. They are rather part of the ongoing problematic of exertions of power within discourses that are legitimated by competitiveness, self-interest and hierarchy. Love–lust, desire–disappointment, self–other, connection–disconnection, individual–community, body–technology, agonism–consensus, youth–age, life–death – these are the *differends*, the undecidables, which necessarily invade our desires for pleasure and liberation. The resolving of these polemics seems to motivate the corpus of contemporary analyses of body, gender and culture. However, in the absence of a complete and inclusive theory of resolution, these polemics will necessarily frustrate liberational designs, leaving us to hope for, though perhaps never experience, a freedom that is not contingent or partial. As humans, or even posthumans, at this moment in our history, this frustration may simply represent the extent and limits of our imagination.

10

Postmodern Spaces:

Local and Global Identities

Outline of the chapter

Globalization is defined in many ways. For some commentators it refers to an integrated cultural and economic system; for others it defines a set of processes which is increasing the levels and volumes of global interaction. In adopting the latter position, we can locate the operation of these processes throughout the period of modernity. Since World War II there has been an intensification of globalization processes, most particularly through the proliferation of mediated information and imagery.

Some theorists believe that globalization is a highly uneven set of processes. In particular, postcolonial theorists argue that the patterns of historical colonization continue today: while direct administration of territories has dissolved, first world nations continue to exert an 'imperialist' control over the economies and cultures of formerly colonized peoples. Various utopian theories, such as 'multiculturalism', have attempted to neutralize these historical inequities. Even so, major debates on globalization have circulated around two key questions: Is globalization perpetuating historical inequities? Is globalization drawing different cultures into an homogenized system which is directed by particularly powerful economic and cultural elites?

Some recent analyses of globalization have attempted to get beyond these questions, pointing out that culture is more than just a fixture of 'nation'. Postmodern theories, in particular, claim that the role and function of nation and national culture are collapsing under the weight of transcultural communication. The consumption, appropriation and 'reinvention' of cultural artefacts necessarily hybridizes culture. This hybridization is a two-way process: the dominant and subordinant cultures are changing each other, re-mixing their differences. These hybridizations are evident in the formation of 'postmodern' cities and their architecture.

Postmodern geographies are also enabling new forms of identity formation. A good deal of recent discussion on globalization is investigating the formation of hybridized identities and their political potential.

GENERAL INTRODUCTION

The concept of globalization has proved remarkably problematic, eliciting both positive and negative judgements. Indeed, there are a range of definitions of 'globalization'; these might be summarized as follows:

1 It is a process which draws different nations and cultures into greater communication and interaction.
2 It is a process which is associated with the formation of a 'world system' in which economy, communications, culture and politics are integrated into a substantial transnational order. This definition is close to what Marshall McLuhan calls 'the global village'. Different peoples, nations and cultures interact and hybridize to form a new world culture.
3 It is a process which is associated with 'modernization' and 'Westernization', where different peoples, nations and cultures are being homogenized as they adopt Western culture, economic standards and lifestyles. Western (especially American) media provide the resources for the other nations of the world to copy.
4 It is a process by which different cultures, peoples and nations become increasingly engaged with one another, but where this contiguity provides space for enhanced, rather than diminished, localism, heterogeneity and cultural difference.

While we will explore these contending definitions in considerable detail in this chapter, it is the first and most neutral perspective which will provide the basis for our general critique of globalization.

LOCATING GLOBALIZATION

Much of the analysis of globalization tends to date the phenomenon from the post-World War II period; however, transnational interaction extends to the earliest periods of human migration. In fact, it appears that the major land masses of Africa, Europe, Asia and Australia had been settled by at least 70,000 years ago. Significant patterns of territorial control were accompanied by equally significant inter-territorial trade and cultural exchange. In Australia, for example, it appears that tribal 'nations' had developed sophisticated and extensive international trade routes as well as highly regulated and ritualized international forums for the settlement of disputes and for the exchange of natural and cultural resources (Flood, 1989, 1990). Very often these meetings were scheduled annually or biennially and they involved sports and entertainment as well as serious discussions over territory, resources and kinship. By the time of European incursion from 1788, Australian Aborigines were trading with off-shore groups such as the Indonesian Macassins and various island societies from the Pacific.

The sophistication of these international arrangements represents a response to the overriding problem of all social groups: how to deal with outsiders. The pattern of peaceful exchange of cultural and economic resources may well camouflage historical complexities that would include warfare and detente, intermarriage, cultural shifts, migration, invasion, periods of affluence and periods of significant instability. Australian Aboriginal cultures constitute the most continuous of all human cultures, saved perhaps from more radical mutation by interglacial seas and a hostile desert environment which sheltered the local cultures from excessive external interest – at least until the late eighteenth century. Even so, like all other cultures, the indigenous cultures of Australia were forced to accommodate periods of new migration which brought with it new people and new cultural elements. How the existing groups managed these incursions is impossible to know, but we can assume that the relative sparsity of settlement and abundance of resources allowed for a relatively harmonious hybridization. By the time of European invasion, there appeared to be substantially little friction between existing territories and groups. In fact, it appears that the morphology of modern Australian Aborigines was a clear hybridization of the two major migration groups, suggesting an intermarriage and intermingling of the gracile and robust migrant types.

The formation of agricultural and urban societies appears to have placed far more pressure on resources and territory. While nomadic hunter-gatherer lifestyles allowed human groups a reasonable amount of flexibility in dealing with the effects of natural disaster, agricultural communities were far more fixed to the conditions of their settled environment. Militarism and territorial expansionism provided a means of ameliorating this vulnerability. Communities developed warrior factions which could appropriate external territories and protect against incursion. This pattern of colonization, which produced the classical empires of Persia, Greece and Rome, provided a template for modern capitalist societies. The formation of 'nation' in Europe was fundamentally linked to the formation of 'empire'. European nations, that is, deployed their military, administrative and technological resources to appropriate the territories of vulnerable peoples. Modern globalization, in fact, begins with this form of territorialization – the ideologies which legitimated economic expansionism,

nationalism and imperialism became the standardized discourse of global economic and cultural integration. At least until World War II this discourse of imperial globalization was regarded by European governments as a legitimate expression of superiority – of survival of the fittest and strongest.

In contemporary debates, 'globalization' is regarded by some critics as a continuation of this imperialist ideology. Other commentators view it as a more neutral, even evolutionary, process which is drawing the peoples of the world into greater economic, political and cultural propinquity. In either case, contemporary globalization integrates earlier social patterns, practices, processes and ideologies with new forms of cultural exchange. Most significant among these new forms of exchange are those media and new communications technologies which allow for what Anthony Giddens calls 'action at a distance' (1990: 19). These new media and technologies in themselves, however, cannot explain the increasing intensity of global cultural contiguity and exchange. The contemporary global panorama might best be understood as a series of discursive assemblages formed around the imperatives of economy, media, politics and what I would call 'bionomy'. It is the totality of these overlapping discursive forms that constitutes the best definition of globalization.

1   *Economy*. Capitalism is built around the imperative of competition, economic growth and the expansion of markets. As noted above, early capitalism was able to exploit cheap labour and resources in order to produce goods; the need continually to expand markets led capitalists to trade these goods internationally. The growth imperative led to the development of large, multinational corporations. These corporations, which are no longer bound by national borders, continue to

seek the cheapest labour and the most profitable markets. In postmodern economies, symbols, images and information have become principal exchange products – along with natural resources, manufactured goods and services (including labour). This global exchange of resources, goods, services and symbols has now become a canon for national governments, corporations and economic theorists. In terms of national sovereignty and national culture, the two most problematic exchange commodities are among the most abstract: first, the exchange of national cultures and identities through creative products and tourism; and, secondly the exchange of national currencies and finances.

2 *Media.* From the emergence of telegraphy in the nineteenth century, communication has been liberated from the constraints of space and time. Broadcast media, telecommunications, satellite technology and networked computer communication have facilitated the expansion in global cultural consciousness – the instantaneous exposure of local cultural groups to an infinite array of different cultural sites and possibilities. The flooding of global marketplaces with information and imagery has altered the cultural horizons and knowledge of all people with access to the media.

3 *Politics and ideology.* These exposures inevitably affect the formation of cultural politics, including the global distribution of ideologies. Just as print facilitated the broadening of ideologies of conformity and sedition, electronic media and the increasing propinquities of culture have enabled the expansion of dominant and oppositional ideologies, expanding discursive tensions throughout the world. While these ideologies may be formalized or institutionalized, most often they are produced in relation to various forms of media text. For example, the interaction between local discursive forms, ideas and values and global texts such as Hollywood blockbuster movies stimulates new discursive and ideological tensions.

4 *Global institutions.* The formation of distinctly globalist ideologies such as capitalism, democracy and progress has been accompanied by attempts to form global organizations which may support or challenge these dominant belief and political discourses. Institutions such as the World Trade Organization, the United Nations, the World Court, the Olympic Federation and UNESCO are constructed around forms of dominant order. The International Red Cross and Care are formed as antitheses to military solutions. Greenpeace and international terrorist/freedom fighter organizations are designed to challenge global hegemony. Within this broad global framework there exist innumerable local politics which are more modest in their aspirations and designs.

5 *Bionomy.* Human beings are among the most recent living organisms to inhabit the biosphere of Earth. Having distributed themselves across the globe in a relatively short period, humans have only very recently produced major disruptions to the natural ecology. In fact, the disruption and damage of the past fifty years is far more significant than for the previous two million years of human presence in the biosphere. Global economy and the proliferation of the human species are collapsing distinct natural ecosystems into a hybrid form. This hybridized, global environment is producing the greatest species extinction since the comet catastrophe which blackened the planet and obliterated 100 million years of dinosaur domination.

While a good deal of globalist discourse celebrates this new mixing of cultures and peoples, bionomic globalization is producing substantive changes to the biosphere itself. The increasing size and density of human population, along with grotesquely differentiated levels of resource consumption, represents the major feature of bionomic globalization. Human subjectivity and identity, the most personal dimensions of culture, are being radically transformed by the propinquities of other human subjectivities and bodies. Humans are on the move: at any one time there are as many as 100 million people preparing to move between national territories, at least 5–10 million of whom have no official documentation. As resources become more scarce, as wars, famines and natural disasters become more frequent, as the poorer localities of the world become more restless, and refugee camps swell, the flow of human migrations across the globe will surge to a torrent. Along with increasing business travel and tourism activities in the developed world, these vast movements of human beings will continue to alter irrevocably older biospheric forms, creating hybrid agricultural patterns, salination and expanding deserts, deforestation, polluted and touristized coastlines, and ever-broadening, continually denuded fields of urban landscape.

For cultural analysis and cultural politics these bionomic changes are matters of dispute and discursive/ideological contestation – they are not merely biological or geographical gestures. Thus, while we have located globalization in a set of postmodern processes and discourses, our task is to elucidate these processes and discourses through the application of particular theoretical and analytical frames of reference.

CULTURE AND HISTORICAL IMPERIALISM

Postcolonial Theory

World War II may be regarded as the second round of the Great War, but it is nevertheless distinguished by one important difference. During World War II, the American public only acceded to involvement when it had been convinced that the colonialist and expansionist ideology of Germany and Japan could be adequately countered by a legitimate oppositional ideology. The American citizenry's extreme reluctance to participate in a war that involved no direct threat to America's sovereignty or home territories was based in part on a general belief that European international politics was built around outmoded forms of colonialism. Even when the Japanese bombed Pearl Harbor in 1941, significant portions of the American public remained suspicious of any form of colonialist and extra-territorial expansionism.

American propaganda argued that the Japanese incursions in the Pacific and South-East Asia were illegitimate because they were a transgression of sovereignty and freedom. The American government was only able to enter the war by assuring its people that the key principle for which they were fighting – defence against aggressive territorialism – would ultimately apply to the colonialist nations of Europe. The colonialism of Britain, Holland and France was just as insidious as the territorialism of Japan and Germany. In the aftermath of the war, it was virtually impossible for any of the governments of the Allied world to justify their own continued colonialism; in the years immediately following the Allied victory, most colonial territories were (more or less) voluntarily surrendered.

This is not to say that the release of territories was smooth or bloodless. Nationalist movements within the colonized states had been active throughout the century and the weaknesses of the colonial administration during and after the war provided significant opportunities for activism. Thus, whether by force or grace, the de-colonizing experience has proved complex and profoundly problematic for the peoples and cultures of the postcolonized world. One of the most significant of these problems is the relationship between the former colonizers and their former subjects. As Homi Bhabha (1990) has pointed out, the nub of this relationship is a form of mutual dependence and antagonism, a form of identity production which never allows the formerly colonized people to be entirely free of their colonial masters and colonial past. Bhabha's point can be elaborated in three ways:

1 The actual construction of the new territory, the new nation, is produced by the colonizer's politics and cartography. The distribution of territories across Indochina, South-East Asia and Africa was facilitated by the interests and international relations of European nations. Cartographers simply drew lines around the map and distributed the territories according to the interests and claims of disputing colonial nations. The 'nationalism' of the colonized peoples is formed, therefore, out of the political pragmatism of the colonial administrators.

2 The whole notion of nation and national culture is a product of the colonizers' own cultural consciousness. Nation, that is, as a form of 'imagined community' (Anderson, 1991), is constructed out of the very fabric of European culture and has little to do with the indigenous people and culture that have been colonized.

3 This national consciousness, in fact, is produced locally through the formation of culture and identity. The intense interactions between colonizer and colonized produce a new subjectivity for the colonized person. He or she will think in terms of 'nation', and will locate that sensibility in cultural elements that are highlighted by colonization. For example, the nation of India must be constructed out of the territories and interests of vastly different groups. This blending consciousness must reconstruct the differences in an intensely contiguous symbolic form. Thus, the Indian national flag juxtaposes the orange of Hindu, the green of Islam and the traditional wheel symbol of Buddhism. The new subjectivity of nation is supposed to harmonize the elements.

One of the major resonances of the colonial period is the rise of a form of reformist cultural politics which seeks to liberate previously colonized peoples from the aftermath of ideological, cultural and economic domination. In fact, different groups who were the victims of colonization have experienced the residues of oppression in different ways. According to postcolonial reformist theory, however, all diasporic peoples have their humiliation, privation and oppression in common; this shared experience unites postcolonial people whether they are descendants of African slaves (e.g., black Americans), minority tribal cultures (e.g., Canadian Cree) or majority agrarian cultures (e.g., Indonesians). In this sense, postcolonial theory borrows from psychoanalytic and poststructuralist theory to explain the sense of these peoples being something 'other' than what a culture deems as normal, powerful or the standard. Most particularly, postcolonized peoples of colour are defined as 'the other' or as 'different' in relation to the normative condition of 'whiteness', especially male whiteness. The challenge for postcolonial and cultural politics is to reconfigure the world in terms of a multicultural norm, where being 'different' is a condition of pride and normality, as well as a rallying point for political action. In particular, it is the liberation from externally imposed identities which, for postcolonial theorists, offers the greatest possibilities for the completion of de-colonization.

Edward Said: Orientalism

Edward Said has attempted to explain the postcolonial experience in terms of discursive hegemony in the formerly colonizing world. Said uses Michel Foucault's genealogical methodology (see Chapter 5) to elucidate the mechanisms by which the 'West' defines itself against the otherness of the 'East'. Said's genealogy, however, seeks a political explanation for the subjugation of the colonized world, most particularly in terms of material and discursive privation. Just as Stuart Hall's encoding/decoding theory had been deployed for the elucidation of ideology and hegemony within developed world textualities, Said's genealogy seeks to elucidate the power/knowledge discourses which inform the West's conceptions of itself in relation to the non-West. In narratizing the 'Orient', Said argues, the Western text is fundamentally telling its own story about its own superior condition. Moreover, for Said, all discourses are political or ideological, and there can be no simple separation of the past from the present. The present condition draws its relevance and form from the past: 'Past and present inform each other; each implies the other, and in the totally ideal sense, ... each co-exists with the other' (Said, 1993: 2).

In *Orientalism* (1978) Said establishes the grounds for analysing the West's discursive construction of itself in relation to the Orient. The central issue for Said relates to the means by which realities are mediated linguistically, and the ways hegemonies and dominant ideologies are imposed:

> My contention is that without examining Orientalism as a discourse one cannot possibly understand the enormously systematic discipline by which European culture was able to manage – and even produce – the Orient politically, sociologically, militarily, ideologically, scientifically, and imaginatively during the post-Enlightenment period. Moreover, so authoritative a position did Orientalism have that I believe no one writing, thinking, or acting on the Orient could do so without taking account of the limitations on thought and action imposed by Orientalism. (1978: 3)

Orientalism, in other words, is the ideologically informed system which presents the non-West as the other, the 'Orient'; in the Orientalist system it is the deficiencies of this otherness which renders it (legitimately) available for Western discipline and control.

While Said insists that the voice of Orientalism does not speak for the whole of the Orient, he makes clear that Orientalism itself represents a network 'inevitably brought to bear on (and therefore always involved in) any occasion when that peculiar entity "the Orient" is in question' (Said, 1978: 3). Said's project, therefore, is to elucidate the sources and fallibilities of Orientalism in Enlightenment scholarship. In political terms, Said seeks to deconstruct the linguistic formations themselves in order to expose their critical and ideological foundations and the ways they have continued to influence contemporary thought. Orientalism is not merely the linguistic facility deployed by colonial administration, but a product of the knowledge system of imperialism and power. Both the knowledge system and its equivalent material system functioned to control the colonized people, as well as justify this control in the minds of the imperial subjects – at home and in the colonies.

It is this theme which is more fully elaborated in Said's more recent work *Culture and Imperialism*, where Said suggests that 'the enterprise of empire depends on the idea of having an empire … and all kinds of preparations are made for it within a culture; then in turn imperialism acquires a kind of coherence, a set of experiences and a presence of ruler and ruled alike within the culture' (1993: 10). Indeed, as a Palestinian-Egyptian, born in Jerusalem and now living and working in the United States, Said is particularly sensitive to the hegemonic impositions of imperial Enlightenment discourse over the Middle East, and his own scholarship is very much influenced by what Foucault succinctly calls 'the history of the present': that is, the processes by which the world becomes modern. Most particularly, Said is concerned to demonstrate how the discursive formations of power/knowledge become identified with the material oppression of the Middle East by contemporary Western powers, especially the United States. Thus, in outlining the general scholarly project of *Orientalism*, Said insists that,

> Positively, I do believe – and in my other work have tried to show – that enough is being done today in the human sciences to provide the contemporary scholar with insights, methods, and ideas that could dispense with racial, ideological, and imperialist stereotypes of the sort provided during its historical ascendancy by Orientalism. … If the knowledge of Orientalism has any meaning, it is in being a reminder of the seductive degradation of knowledge, of any knowledge, anywhere, at any time. Now perhaps more than before. (1978: 328)

Said, while applauding what he describes as Foucault's 'imagination of power', nevertheless laments his 'profoundly pessimistic' view of modern society, a view circumscribed by 'a singular lack of interest in the force of effective resistance to it, in choosing particular sites of intensity, choices which … always exist and are often successful in impeding, if not actually stopping, the progress of tyrannical power' (1986: 151). Thus, while Said's own work on writing and discourse is clearly influenced by French poststructuralism, he finds ultimately that Foucault's microphysics does not satisfy the demands of contemporary liberation, being no more than an 'imagination' of a power that seems 'irresistible and unopposable', and which fails to condemn the banality and irresponsibility of corporate managers by its own elimination 'of classical ideas about ruling classes and dominant interests' (1986: 152).

A vocal critic of the US involvement in the Gulf War (1990–1) and US Middle East policies more generally, Said seeks a political solution to the hegemonies which continue to subjugate people of difference, people of the non-developed anglophone world. In *Culture and Imperialism*, Said insists on actual solutions to the propagation of imagined identities and cultures:

> For the purpose of this book I have maintained a focus on actual contests over land and the land's people. What I have tried to do is a kind of geographical inquiry into historical experiences, and I have kept in mind the idea that the earth is in effect one world in which empty, virtually uninhabited spaces do not exist (1993: 6).

Most particularly, Said has been interested in the means by which the First World has been able to appropriate and administer the vast territories of the world, including Middle Asia. To this extent, he distinguishes between 'colonialism', the conquest and administration of external territories, and 'imperialism', the ongoing and cultural dimensions of identity projection and control:

> '[I]mperialism' means the practice, the theory, and the attitudes of a dominating metropolitan centre ruling a distant territory; 'colonialism', which is almost always a consequence of imperialism, is the implanting of settlements on distant territory. ... In our time, colonialism has ended; imperialism, as we shall see, lingers where it has always been, in a kind of general cultural space, as well as in specific political, ideological, economic, and social practices. (1993: 8)

In this sense, imperialism works with racism to form imaginings and practices which pervade the modern and postmodern consciousness. Critics disagree about the extent of racist imagining, and while various legislative and institutional regulations have been instigated in order to ameliorate their effects, there can be little doubt that the sense of insider–outsider imagining continues to pervade culture (see also Castells, 1997). In his most recent book, an autobiography entitled *Out of Place* (1999), Said assaults directly the problematic of racism in contemporary American culture, most particularly as it is manifest in anti-Islamic and anti-Arabic media representation and government policy. After living and working for forty years in New York, Said expresses his own sense of alienation in a culture which constantly parades the ethos of pluralism and freedom, but which maintains deep suspicions of its own internal constituency, its own people who live precariously on the edge of different worlds and different ideologies.

Imperialism, Language War and Terrorism

As we have noted during the course of this book, culture is formed through various levels of communicative imagining and discursive struggle. At their most spectacular and intense, these 'struggles to signify' may be characterized as language wars. The assaults on the New York World Trade Center and the Pentagon can be understood as part of an ongoing process of imperialist engagement and language war. Innumerable commentators have found their explanation for the atrocity in terms of a discourse of 'terrorism'. In the immediate aftermath of the tragedy, the focus of public, media and state attention was directed toward the identification and punishment of the terrorist perpetrators. Identification in this sense refers to both the nomination of the perpetrator (Osama Bin Laden) and the ascription of characteristics and meanings. This process of identity ascription, as the cultural studies community understands very well, is a form of what Lacan calls a 'double entry matrix': that is, the identity of the ascriber is reflected against and dependent upon the identity of the ascribee (and vice versa). It is not at all surprising, therefore, that each side of the language polemic refers to the other as 'demonic', while identifying themselves as innocent, heroic and victim. For the US officials, the perpetrators are evil terrorists; for the 'perpetrators' and their sympathizers, the Americans are oppressors, imperialists and faithless materialists.

Clearly, these language wars are associated more broadly with a long history of territorialism, colonialism, suffering, and cycles of retribution. What is equally significant for cultural studies, however, is the semiotic context in which the American state authorities are seeking to resolve and conclude this particular manifestation of the ongoing agonism they are calling the 'war against terrorism'. As much as this war is shaped through the horror of death, it is also being conducted through an engagement of the contending discourses of imperialism and liberation. President George Bush's invocation of the Dead or Alive posters of the American Wild West betrays powerful moral and ideological rectitude, a sense in which the war is a simple polemic of good and evil, Goodies and Baddies. That Bush was 'shocked' by the idea that any group or nation could 'hate the United States' so deeply also reflects the depths of American self-belief, intellectual solipsism and political insularity. As Edward Herman has argued in an Internet discussion of the war, American officials appear to have little understanding of their nation's own culpability and responsibility for the New York and Pentagon assaults; American attacks on the Sudan, continuing sanctions against Iraq, neglect of the Palestinian question, and a host of CIA incursions in other parts of the Middle East are all implicated in the US's self-legitimating global hegemony and in the loathings that domination incites in others.

The deep offence and shock experienced by George Bush and many other American citizens are amplified because of the symbolic force of the assaults. The World Trade Center, of course, was part of that pervasive imaginary of free market individualism and success in a land of bounteous wealth. Built by the Rockefeller dynasty and opened in 1972, the twin towers assumed a preeminent cultural status after the initial bombing in 1993. This earlier assault inscribed the building with an heroic demeanour; the World Trade Center defied the forces of darkness which would seek to destroy international commerce and the ethos of freedom, progress and prosperity. In effect, this attempt to damage the building and the 'American way of life' that it represented served actually to enhance the Center's iconic value. For others in the global community, however, the building

had clearly remained a symbol of tyranny and imperial domination. As much as the New Yorkers celebrated the building's durability and heroic defiance, the warriors of particular political factions in the Middle East saw it as a legitimate target in the war of global language. For these people, Bin Laden amongst them, the New York World Trade Center represented the symbolic heart of all that was evil in American cultural politics.

Thus, while America has sought to liberate the world from direct colonial administration, its global primacy renders its symbols and cultural products available for the appropriations and interests of others. The World Trade Center did not belong to America alone, but was part of an transnational cultural ambit – the field of vision of all peoples affected by America's global presence. This is not merely a feature of foreign policy or economic domination, but it is the seeping and flowing of America's cultural ubiquity. It is precisely this point which Jean Baudrillard (1995) is making when he claims that the 'Gulf War did not take place'. For Baudrillard the Gulf War was a foregone conclusion, an event that had been entirely and already conducted through the media. Much the same thing can be said of the so-called war against terrorism where the world media's persistent replaying of the aircraft striking the Trade Center towers and the subsequent inferno was strangely resonant of an imaginary already created by 'Hollywood' culture. That is, the ongoing language wars had already been engaged through American films and TV products. The heroic conquest of good over evil and the salvation of the American way of life had already been inscribed into the horrors of the twin towers assaults. In this sense, too, the American reprisal attacks on Afghanistan were scripted into the language war long before any decision was made by the American authorities.

MULTICULTURALISM

While Said and others regard contemporary culture as inevitably imperialist and racist, other critics draw hope from the reformulation of cultural heterogeneity. One of the effects of colonialism has been the integration of formerly colonized peoples into the ethnic mix of the First World. The once normative, in some cases exclusivist, status of homogeneous white culture within developed nations has been radically altered by migration during the past fifty years. The absorption of these various peoples into a pre-existing national-cultural formation, most especially those from non-European cultures, has required a substantial shift in ideological and discursive frames. While numerous critics, including Edward Said, have seen this integration process as largely imperfect, others have used a range of regulatory and institutional processes to promote new forms of national and cultural imagining. Multiculturalism has been promoted in several countries as a means of imagining nation and national culture which is liberated from race-based identity. In fact, multiculturalism attempts to create a postmodernist ethos which forms a cultural assemblage around the notion of 'unity in diversity', a sense in which the various peoples and cultures which may constitute a national imaginary are free to experience their diversity without surrendering the validity of the whole state. This form of multicultural democracy idealizes difference by promoting a healthy interactive tolerance; the nation is no longer a contingency of racial or racio-cultural superiority, but is a formation which acknowledges the great diversity in human groups and the advantages of harmonious interaction and co-operative, creative organizational processes.

Multiculturalism has been offered as a solution to the bionomic hybridities and propinquities of globalization. It is significantly different from the liberalist pluralism which had functioned as a cultural and social norm in the United States. According to multicultural theory, pluralism is a form of false harmony which in fact subsumes the diversity and dignity of migrating groups beneath the ethos of 'assimilation'. In the United States cultural difference was obliterated or significantly subjugated by an obedience to American capitalist/utilitarian principles and the grandeur of the American Dream of individual, material prosperity. American jingoism, that is, subsumed all other ideologies and discourses beneath the privilege of belonging to 'the greatest nation on Earth'. The continuation of Orientalist discourses, American imperialism and neo-racism betrays the deficiencies of pluralism. Multiculturalism, which liberates individuals and groups from the extremes of homogenized and collective identities, produces a more open and respectful acceptance of cultural difference, both within and necessarily outside the borders of nation.

The Image and Multiculturalism

For Mark Poster, multiculturalism promotes an ideology of ethnic and cultural mixing both within and outside the borders of the nation-state (1995: 40–2). Poster argues that the poststructuralist/postmodernist project of cultural heterogenization, the dissolution of Western *logos* and ethno-centrism, and the approbation of multiple linguistic forms are parallel with multiculturalist ambitions of dissolving geographic, cultural and ethnic borders. The new communications technologies are central for reordering and reconstituting subjectivities and cultural space. Poster recognizes that some political multiculturalists would privilege Third World or minority group subjectivities, thus risking the return of postcolonial political essentialism; such a restoration, however, would inevitably transgress the potentialities of poststructuralist theoretics, and more particularly the opportunities presented by the new media:

> In this case, multiculturalism is a process of subject constitution, not an affirmation of an essence. As the second media age unfolds and permeates everyday practice, one political issue will be the construction of new combinations of technology with multiple genders and ethnicities. These technocultures will hopefully be no return to essence, no new foundationalism or essentialism, but a coming to terms with the process of identity constitution and doing so in ways that struggle against restrictions of systematic inequalities, hierarchies and asymmetries. (1995: 42)

The diffusion of developed national cultures into more heterogeneous forms has prompted critics like Anthony Giddens (1990, 1994) to suggest that globalized multiculturalism represents the implosion of the whole idea of Europe and the 'nation' itself. Stuart Hall (1991a, 1991b) argues similarly that the migratory movement from the ex-colonial peripheries to the old centre of Britain is deconstructing the whole systematized identity of Britain and the notion of 'being British'. The change from an older form of imperializing globalization to a reciprocal and diversifying flow of global interconnectedness is eroding the very substance of the nation-state. But it is capitalism itself, Hall argues, which is transmogrifying the experience of citizenry and national identity as it seeks new and ever-expanding resources and imaginings for its own commodification. Global commodity culture, with its emphasis on the ephemera of the 'image', seeks out new forms of representation and pleasure. It is the 'image', Hall explains, which

'crosses and re-crosses linguistic frontiers much more rapidly and more easily, and which speaks across languages in a much more immediate way ... [and which] cannot be limited any longer by national boundaries' (1991a: 27).

Multiculturalism and Postmodern Consumption

The break-up of older forms of racial and cultural homogeneity through mass cultural consumption is, in fact, a response to the ongoing imperative of capital to expand. Hall contends further that in its advanced forms, capitalism transforms conceptions of mass production/consumption into more particularized fields of reference; utility allows capital to be more specific and more targeted. Identity-specific products, lifestyle and niche marketing techniques are wedded to what Hall calls 'just-in-time' advertising to produce a frenetic but ever-fragmenting capital sophistication. While Hall concedes that images of the all-encompassing, all-powerful, predominantly masculine elite still persist, these are being subsumed by newer images involving 'leading-edge lifestyles' which provide ever-diversifying cuisines, clothes and decoration choices, transcultural entertainments, and an infinite array of aesthetic and intellectual possibilities. This is a radically contracted cultural space:

> In one trip around the world, in one weekend, you can see every wonder of the ancient world. You take it in as you go by, all in one, living with difference, wondering at pluralism, this concentrated corporate, over-corporate, over-integrated, over-concentrated, over-condensed form of economic power which lives culturally through difference, and which is constantly teasing itself with the pleasures of the transgressive Other. (Hall, 1991a: 31)

The globalizing world is constructed, therefore, out of increasing communicative and bodily proximity. However, while multiculturalism may have achieved a level of official public and governmental sanction in contemporary societies, Hall and others suspect this discourse of being informed by less noble intentions and derivations. While reformists like Mark Poster have taken up the discourse as a rallying point, a means of defining social change, Hall and others argue that the reformism of multiculturalism constitutes a thin veil across the ongoing crisis of capital, the crisis which unceasingly seeks new opportunities, new symbols and meanings for commodification and consumption.

Like Stuart Hall, David Harvey (1989) suggests that the postmodern idealizes multiculturalism as it privileges the notion of 'difference'. This putative postmodern cultural diversity may in fact be obscuring the reiteration of old hierarchical forms of discrimination. Multiculturalism, which is built around superficial experiences of popular consumption, or an 'international cuisine', as Hall describes it, may be substituting real Difference for a modulated, commodified and palatable 'difference'. It is perhaps for this reason that the ideologies of racism and imperialism are able to survive even in the midst of significant articulations of tolerance, equal opportunity and affirmative action (see Wijeyesinghe and Jackson, 2001). Otherness, that is, produces a forceful rendering of pleasure in postmodern culture so long as it remains fixed in the scheme of the First World order of taste and consumability. One of the great debates in 'globalization' is whether the new diversities are diverse at all, or merely a show of diversity. The imaging of cultural difference through world music or international cuisines might simply be a distraction, a pluralism existing within the much more substantial borders of First World capitalism.

GLOBAL IMPERIALISM

The arguments here are complex. Some theorists claim that multiculturalism is a formidable reconstruction of cultural pluralism; it is an ideal toward which all cultures should aspire. This multiculturalism will deconstruct national borders and release local cultures from the homogenizing effects of nationalism. The opposite argument suggests that these pluralized differences are minor, and capitalism is merely homogenizing significant Differences, transforming them into minor (pluralized) differences suitable for consumption. A little difference is pleasurable; a lot of difference is threatening.

A further debate surrounds the question of the notion of cultural imperialism. This argument extends postcolonial theory, most particularly as it is expressed through writers like Edward Said (see above). Said and others claim that the commodification of culture is largely an exercise in continuing First World (especially American) cultural hegemony. Internationalization and global economy are necessarily absorbing the world into a system where dominant forces will eradicate challenge and the interests of 'local' culture, including national interests. While there may be some intermingling of cultures through the absorption of non-white, non-Euro/American cultural elements, the traffic has been largely one-way. That is, First World cultures import some minor cultural elements in order to dilute and commodify them; by and large, however, America is a net exporter of products, images and culture, flooding the rest of the world with its particular values, ideas and discourses. While the English-speaking world has been the most vulnerable to American cultural exports, American popular texts are a significant presence in most locales across the globe.

Proponents of this argument tend to regard the commodification of culture as largely insidious. The absorption of international cultural elements from the peripheries into the dominant, First World culture is simply another form of cultural entropy and loss of difference. Vietnam, Korea, Jamaica, Mexico, Indonesia, Angola – all become available for the pleasures of First World consumption. In the opposite direction, the world as a market becomes more available to the cultural producers of the First World. Of course the incorporation of global cultures and peoples into the 'market' parameters of First World cultural producers parallels the broader embrace of the world into the Euro-American-dominated capitalist system. Disneyland, *Titanic*, *Friends* and *Baywatch* are as internationally significant as Microsoft, McDonald's, Coca-Cola and Ford.

Global and Local Media

At its most pessimistic, this global domination argument points to the omnipresence of First World multinational corporations, which seem to have made their way into every part of the world, absorbing the peoples and transforming their economies, politics and ultimately their cultures. This argument points to this omnipresence as fuelling cultural imperialism, and Westernization, or, more particularly, Americanization. In Canada, for example, there are at least ten times as many American as Canadian films released in any one year; gross earnings of American films are on average ten times higher than the lower budget, limited-release Canadian films. Even the United Kingdom, which has seen something of a revival in its film industry in the last decade, struggles to dent the dominance of the American film industry. Moreover, the capacity of American

economies of scale to produce large volumes of TV text at low profit margins enables the US to saturate overseas, especially English-speaking, markets with its product. It is significantly cheaper for television suppliers in Canada, Australasia or even the United Kingdom to import cheap US programming than to invest in local product. In Canada, in particular, the open-trade policy with the US has allowed a flood of American product on to the cable networks. Local television production in Australia is seriously dwarfed by the weight and volume of American and to a lesser degree British TV product, even though local TV tends to rate quite well.

There has been little serious challenge to the dominance of American cultural products in the marketplace. An advertising company survey conducted in 1996 asked 20,000 respondents in nineteen different countries about the TV programmes they preferred. Over 41 per cent found US programmes to be excellent or very good, nearly twice the level of the nearest rival (Tomkins, 1996). In 1995 the US experienced a $6.3 billion trade surplus in cultural products. In Third World and small English-speaking nations like Canada, Australia and New Zealand the percentage trade imbalance is even higher. The domination of the US has historical roots, certainly, but there is also a persistent effort on the part of these advantaged corporations to control the complete stream of production, distribution and retail. Moreover, competitive advantage and economies of scale have allowed US cultural corporations to invest heavily in high-budget productions which continually find favour with global markets. In 1996, *Variety* magazine analysed the most popular films for the previous year, concluding that by far the most profitable movies were those that had budgets of over $60 million (Maltsby, 1996).

Americanization in these instances might seem inevitable. Fears about the dominance of American cultural exports, in fact, significantly delayed the establishment of the General Agreement on Tariffs and Trade (GATT), a largely First World initiative designed to facilitate greater free trade across the globe. The Agreement, which has now been signed and evolved into the World Trade Organization (WTO), seeks to eradicate the policies of national governments which 'protect' the local economy from external, international competition. The increased volume in trade is supposed to remove impediments to free trade, increasing the efficiency of local industry, enhancing the export orientation of local industry, and enhancing the wealth production and national economies of participants. France, in particular, saw cultural production as a special case since it directly contributed to local/national identity, aesthetics and cultural autonomy. This was not mere jingoism, but a genuine fear that American cultural products would infiltrate and alter the consciousness and dignity of French national culture.

The implications of GATT and the WTO are far-reaching. The removal of protectionist policies has exposed local cultures and consumers to increasing volumes of overseas text, but more importantly it has changed the orientation of local cultural production. The United Kingdom, Canada, Australia and New Zealand, for example, have refocused local film and TV production toward a more international market. While this point is still highly debated, there is no doubt that the majority of filmmakers in Australia and Canada are seeking to create films that can be understood and appreciated by American audiences. The Australian film *Babe*, for example, was created with American dictions, vocabulary and spoken accents, a not unsurprising extension of the commercial strategies of many recent Australian films. Similarly, the British film revival has been driven by a desire to exploit particular aspects of British culture which may facilitate an entrance into niche and popular American markets. Local cultural interests and needs might be served by such strategies, since the flow of American cultural product has entirely changed local cultures anyway. The question being asked is whether or not a local culture, distinct from American culture, can exist at all.

Graeme Turner (1994, 1997) has suggested that this rearticulation of national culture has substantially altered the mode and strategy of cultural analysis itself. The internationalization of book publishing has substantially diminished the space available for cultural and historical analysis focused around nation. For Turner, this new cultural studies will necessarily privilege particular texts and modes of analysis that are not contingent upon issues of nation or national significance. That is, cultural studies will be predisposed toward the analysis of Disneyland over local spaces and images, *ER* over local TV programmes. Inevitably, also, cultural analysis will shift its attention to those fields of theory and enquiry which are internationalist and de-contextualized, at least in terms of nation. A cultural politics which is not constructed through these de-contextualized and 'multicultural' theoretics becomes less visible and therefore less available as a challenge to cultural imperialism. The academy, like the arts, is forced to accommodate the interests and claims of global economy and global culture.

INTERNATIONALISM

The alternative to the cultural imperialist argument rests on an assumption of cultural de-centring. Arjun Appadurai suggests that the whole notion of dominant culture is outmoded, an excessive simplification of complex processes of hybridization, appropriation and reappropriation:

> The new global economy has to be understood as a complex, overlapping, disjunctive order, which cannot any longer be understood in terms of existing center–periphery models (even those that might account for multiple centers and peripheries). Nor is it susceptible to simple models of push and pull (in terms of migration theories), or of surpluses and deficits (as in traditional models of balance of trade), or of consumers and producers (as in most neo-Marxist theories of development). (1990: 296)

Appadurai attempts to move the argument beyond the simple definitions of power and imperialism forged by Said and other post-colonialists, suggesting, in fact, that new forms of international connectedness reduce the potency and validity of theories based on ideology and differentials of power.

Ien Ang and Jon Stratton (1996) have suggested that the discipline of cultural studies needs to be more sensitive to this realignment of national relationships. Thus, the redemptive rewriting of history which is the postcolonialist project should give way to a recognition that the world has moved on. Postcolonialism, that is, falls into the category of resistance, which relies too heavily on notions of localism – including national, ethnic or regional localism – as the fount of structural opposition. For Ang and Stratton, however, Asia is no longer a fabrication of Western imagination and Western power, but is a fully functioning partner in cultural and economic interactions:

> If Asia must no longer be thought of as Other, this is not just because of the moral/ideological liability of the discourse of Orientalism, but because the region that has come to be called Asia has become an inherent part of, and force in, the contemporary global condition. (1996: 20)

At a rather more theoretical level, analysts who have been influenced by poststructuralism and psychoanalysis have suggested that postcolonialism tends to reduce complex interactions between cultures and cultural identities to a simple polemic of dominant and subordinate. Homi Bhabha (1987, 1990) argues that an extraordinary interdependence is established between self and other through discourse: this interaction necessarily destabilizes absolute differences in power, opening the individual's identity and subjectivity to the influence of otherness. Put simply, Bhabha is suggesting that, whenever two people of a different culture interact, they will necessarily be changed by the interaction since both parties are dependent on it for meaningful communication. This means, of course, that the experience of cultural interaction more broadly, including the consumption and 'use' of cultural texts, implicates change for both parties: the message sender and the message receiver.

> It is only by understanding the ambivalence and the antagonism of the 'desire of the Other' that we can avoid the increasingly facile adoption of the notion of homogenized 'Other', for a celebratory, oppositional politics of 'margins' or 'minorities'. (Bhabha, 1987: 7)

This politics of the margins, according to Bhabha, is that form of postcolonialism which centres the dominated subject as the hero of resistance. In fact, Bhabha explains, both sides of the colonialist divide must necessarily shift their worlds in order to make sense of the other, in order to make meaningful contact. To this extent, the mixing of cultures leads to a revitalization of old meanings and old values – difference is created in a new and more interdependent context.

Gayatri Spivak (1988, 1992) argues that the creation of a subaltern (subordinate) relationship with dominant cultural powers tends effectively to reinforce the hierarchical nature of that relationship. The dependency trap tends to re-create the subordinate status in the minds of non-Europeans, thus defeating the project of emancipation. In other words, the agency and liberatory potential of the postcolonized subject is diminished as the subject conceives of himself or herself as being 'trapped' as the victim of imperialist structures. An heroic resistance is imagined but can never be fulfilled because the subject continues to be a subordinate, even in his or her own imagination. This argument of course, parallels, postmodernist repudiations of Marxist typologies, which tend to locate power in immovable structures rather than in mutable relationships or interactions.

John Docker (1994, 1995) has recognized the weaknesses of a postcolonial theoretic which attempts to fix power relationships in time and space. He points out that the whole enterprise of postcolonialism is problematic as it collapses into one category an extraordinarily diverse range of peoples, cultures and histories. Postcolonialism includes, for example, the de-colonizing experiences of the United States and Australia as much as Angola and Bangladesh – all countries which had to free themselves from European imperial control. A postcolonial analysis, therefore, is both totalizing and linear, reproducing the ideology of social and cultural 'progressivism' which draws all its subjects into a trajectory of civilization; while this trajectory for colonialism is based on notions of imperial evolution, the postcolonial project draws all diasporic people into a trajectory of collective 'liberation'. For Docker, the heroization of liberated diasporic peoples fails to appreciate the complex interactions and social fluidities which have come to produce contemporary culture. Docker is particularly critical of the essentialization

of diasporic peoples, migrants and indigenous peoples as a single liberational category. Just as Marxism invests its liberational hopes in the category of the proletariat, Docker complains that new liberationists are investing a general politics in an invented category of diaspora and difference. Resistance politics, Docker concludes, 'must be understood in terms of local situations and local tactics, as well as the imperatives of global capitalism' (Docker, 1997: 71).

John Tomlinson has objected similarly to the Westernization/homogenization/cultural imperialism triad of arguments, suggesting that the global scene is far more complex than this one-way process would seem to appreciate. The whole notion that non-European cultures are so easily appropriated into the cultural empire of the West merely reinforces the status and power of the West (Tomlinson, 1999; also Hannerz, 1991). Tomlinson suggests that the preoccupation with the presence of Western cultural elements in the non-West – fast foods, rock music, popular films – tends to distract analysis from the interests of other cultures and their peoples. The most serious deficiency of the homogenization argument, however, is its failure to appreciate the nature of culture itself and the ways in which different 'cultures' interact: 'Movement between cultural/geographical areas always involves translation, mutation, and adaptation as the 'receiving culture' brings its own cultural resources to bear in dialectical fashion upon cultural imports' (Tomlinson, 1997: 169). This process has been variously described as indigenization, cultural mutation, appropriation and hybridization. Fundamentally, however, it suggests that the importation of cultural elements will always produce changes to those elements. As it falls into the mix of the importing culture, it will be adapted, used and interpreted according to the local tastes and interests. Moreover, and as we have touched upon above, this process is two-way since the interaction with non-Western cultures will also produce effects of change and adaptation from the non-West to the West. We have seen, for example, the rapid uptake in the past two or three decades of Buddhism and other non-Christian creeds, most particularly by educated younger generations. This challenge to the orthodoxy which informs the West's basic belief system indicates that more than international cuisines are evolving through the integration of different cultural experiences within and outside the West.

Dependence, Independence, Interdependence

We might at this point summarize the basic arguments surrounding globalization theory:

1 The postcolonialist argument suggests that the new world order is built around the continued material and discursive domination of the formerly colonized peoples of the world. A system of cultural imperialism operates to maintain the privileges of Western economies and cultures.

2 Alternative arguments suggest that liberation is possible because the West and the non-West are mixing and interacting far more than ever before.

3 As an extension to the previous argument, some critics suggest that, in fact, 'the West' and the 'non-West' are collapsing categories. The new interdependence of cultures necessarily deconstructs these old structures.

4 As an extension to (3), it is also suggested that the whole idea of nation is imploding because of these greater, postmodern propinquities. The suggestion

here is that we do not necessarily have a 'world system', but a series of interacting operational zones: economy, communications/media, migrations, and so on.

5 At the level of cultural consumption this interdependence does away with old ideas about difference based around nation or ethnicity. Difference and heterogeneity are produced through greater cultural sharing. The interaction of cultural elements produces new ideas, cultural products and cultural symbols. This is the politics of postmodern hybridization. In this sense, the categories of West and non-West are entirely outmoded.

Before examining postmodern global consumerism, we should add a footnote to this progress of arguments. In many respects, the various arguments surrounding globalization are constructed around different approaches to the dependence–independence opposition. Postcolonial politics attacks ongoing imperialist discourses as they construct a dependency relationship between the subordinate non-West and the dominant West. In this sense, postcolonialism seeks to liberate previously colonized peoples from this dependency, so that they can be independent. Spivak, Bhabha and others who reject this approach argue that postcolonialism simply maintains this dualism of dependence and independence, seeking merely to tip the scales in favour of the postcolonized subject. In this sense, they argue that there is a greater interdependence between West and non-West subjectivities than the cultural imperialist argument appreciates.

This desire to break the dependent–independent opposition is very much a poststructuralist, deconstructionalist strategy. Both Spivak and Bhabha are clearly influenced by the work of Jacques Lacan and Jacques Derrida (see Chapter 5). While interdependence is clearly operating in the world, the notion nevertheless seems inevitably to camouflage the significant discursive and material hierarchies which capitalism imposes on various individuals and human groups. The problem is that interdependence can operate simultaneously with dependence in a context of relative advantages and privileges. The problem, as we will confront it through the remainder of this chapter, is how we can adduce a globalist politics which does not restore the dependence–independence opposition but which recognizes that the world is formed through the unequal distribution of its resources, rewards and pleasures.

POPULAR CONSUMPTION

The hybridization argument is reinforced in cultural theory by postmodernist and audience-oriented theories (see Chapter 8). The coupling of postmodernism with an interest in the ways different audiences use and 'consume' cultural texts has directed globalization theory to a broader analysis of the way texts are distributed across the globe. We saw earlier that the great majority of film and TV texts which are consumed in the English-speaking world are sourced in the United States – or at least they are produced by corporations which are listed on the American Stock Exchange. Increasingly, the head offices of these corporations are based in New York or in other capital cities around the globe. The Hollywood system that was established at the beginning of the twentieth century and which facilitated the mass production of cinema texts has largely dissolved with production and editing processes taking place in various locales across the globe. The

blockbuster *Star Wars* films shifted production from the United States to Britain and now to Australia, chasing the highest quality labour and production facilities at the cheapest possible price. Similarly, the popular TV series *The X-Files* was shot in Vancouver, where labour and set costs were much cheaper than in the United States. *Xena* and *Hercules* were shot in New Zealand, where the native-born New Zealand actors perform with broad American accents.

Even the art-house films of British filmmaker Peter Greenaway are supported by Japanese investment, with most postproduction in his latest films being conducted in the sophisticated digital studios of Tokyo. This 'hybridization' of cultural texts is evident in the increasing number of co-productions, translations and mixed-language releases. In the music industry, which has tended to be the most free-market and deregulated of cultural industries, texts demonstrate a dynamism which eludes simple cultural typologies. Indeed, while rock music is clearly a hybrid form deriving from African American folk music, it has moved restlessly between corporate formulation and grass-roots reformulation. Certainly, the major multinationals (Warner, Sony, EMI, Bertelsmann) treat rock texts like any other product and continue to assert their dominance over product, artist and market; however, this dominance seems precarious if only because musical texts and tastes perpetually shift, with particular zones of taste constantly eluding the control of the major corporations. The contemporary musical text, that is, constantly hybridizes, evading attempts to homogenize or Americanize its soul.

One good example of this is the attempt by MTV to impose its predominantly American textual format on Asia. MTV found that it had to modify the programming to incorporate local music and languages in order to attract audiences. This hybridized format of MTV and the Hong Kong-based satellite station Star TV provides a resource which can be adapted and transformed according to local cultural interests. In India, for example, the US text/celebrity Madonna has been thoroughly appropriated, with many Madonna look-alikes strutting the pop music stage, the most successful being the somewhat modulated, blondified sex-symbol Alishi. As Gregory Lee (1995) has pointed out, however, the youth of the People's Republic of China are still fixated by the original Madonna, who provides both an example of US cultural hegemony and a liberational focus against the alternative hegemony of the Chinese Communist Party. In either case, the text itself becomes a vehicle for local cultural expression. Imported texts, that is, become available for appropriation by the local culture, providing a resource for experimentation, new subjectivities and new cultural elements.

This textual hybridization is one of the most significant buffers to homogenization and imperialization claims. Popular music, in fact, has a chameleon core which prevents it from being fixed and standardized. Rap music, which began as the specific articulations of poor black youths in the West Indies and New York's South Bronx, became anthemized as an international black music – not bordered by what might constitute official American cultural export, but as a transnational art form which crosses and re-crosses what has been called the Black Atlantic. Indeed, this composite of cultural differences enables the appropriation of specific elements in order to re-create them as unique articulation. The rise of Aboriginal rock music in Australia and the international success of bands like Yothu Yindi demonstrates how this composite may include a remarkable diversity of elements. In the case of Yothu Yindi, the music incorporates specific arrangements of indigenous dialect and musical intonations (see Davies, 1993). The band's music, however, engages with both the global dance scene and African American protest music; the key to the band's international success, that is, is their combination of popular sounds with political Blackness. The final text signifies a unique cultural experience. Neither the culture nor the text is fixed and frozen, but both extend themselves through new imaginings – and new modes of cross-cultural commodification.

Of course there are those critics of popular music – indeed all popular art forms – who revile these hybrid sounds for their lack of authenticity. This argument echoes Theodor Adorno's (1994) Marxist lament, which sees popular music as an essentially formulaic and commercial platform for the sale of familiar, already digested musical sounds. Beyond Adorno's lament, however, complaints about commercial music's lack of originality or authenticity resonate through all fields of musical taste; enthusiasts of classical, jazz, blues, techno or hip-hop music all seem to assume that their own particular preferences can be justified in terms of originality and essence. The use by Yothu Yindi of the traditional Aboriginal wind instrument, the didgeridoo, for rock and roll music might seem to justify these concerns. However, the notion of 'authenticity' is problematized when we realise that the instrument itself was appropriated from Indonesia (Macassins) by Australian Aborigines between three and four hundred years ago. Of all the art forms, music seems the least resistant to exchange, appropriation and reinvention.

Hybrid TV

Herman and McChesney (1999) have pointed out that the medium of television has become increasingly exposed to internationalization trends, most recently through trade deregulation, satellite technology, digitization and the anticipated convergences with computer-based networking systems. The most obvious effects of this changing context will be a proliferation of product and increased commercial competition. As with all other production and service providers, local broadcast suppliers are having to confront these competitive conditions and re-orient their production accordingly. For some production houses, this has meant the creation of product that can be sold internationally. TV soap operas, for example, are often configured for maximum marketability – cultural specificity thus becomes marketable when it is formulated in an internationally digestable manner. British TV sells working-class nostalgia, Australia sells beaches, Canada sells snow.

The increasing globalization and commercialization of TV will also have a serious impact on public broadcasting services, especially in those English-speaking countries that have had a long tradition of publicly funded broadcast. Deregulation and (neo-classical) economic rationalism policies are continually dragging funds out of the public networks, leaving them to drastically reduce labour and production activities. Increasing competition from international suppliers and texts is also fragmenting traditional audiences and creating new imperatives for audience appeal. Combined with a declining role in the cultural production of national interests and national identity (see Chapter 11), the public broadcasters are struggling to redefine their position in the media marketplace and the cultural imaginary. Thus, while the British Broadcasting Corporation (BBC) has taken up the challenge of becoming an international player, the less well capitalized public corporations of

New Zealand, Australia and Canada are becoming shadow players in an increasingly dense media globalscape. Herman and McChesney (1999) anticipate, in fact, that public and commercial broadcasters will find it increasingly difficult to compete in a marketplace which requires increasing levels of sophistication and investment. Pay-to-view television, with its highly specialized channels and genres, will permit increasing diversification of choice, but these choices will operate within a specific range. That is, there will be less likelihood that generalized, free-to-air providers will be able to do much more than offer very conservative, low-budget programming. The establishment costs of digital satellite are so great that it is unlikely that the smaller commercial or public TV providers will be able to compete with the controllers of the new distribution networks. As Herman and McChesney claim, the programming of free-to-air providers is likely to become narrower and more conservative as the big players do battle over the digital airwaves.

Global Audiences

Hybrid TV therefore depends on the mechanisms available for appropriation and reconstruction of imported texts. Simon During (1999) distinguishes between the global popular and cultural globalization. The global popular represents those self-consciously formulaic media texts which are designed to capture world markets; cultural globalization is a multi-flowing process which may produce hybridities and enhanced localism. Cultural globalization, in fact, leads to some mysterious outcomes:

[H]ow do we account, for example, for the fact that the world's largest producer of *telenovelas* Protele has been successful in the French and Swiss markets (as well as in Mexico, Turkey, South Korea, and Russia)

but a relative failure elsewhere in Europe? How do we account for the way Bombay movies are popular in Greece but not elsewhere in Europe? To begin to understand these cases we need site-specific histories. In another mode of cultural globalization, a self-conscious commitment to the global can provide an impetus and marketing platform for new cross-culturally hybridized genres, particularly 'world music'. But such genres are not genuinely popular in many, if any, local markets. (During, 1999: 212)

By 'popular', During means specifically a high level of commercial consumption. He goes on to contrast this rather mysterious, even whimsical, consumption pattern with the mass consumption patterns of Arnold Schwarzenegger films, which were universally popular during the 1980s, in both the global and local dominions.

The limitations of During's approach become obvious as we consider the ways in which audiences actually use texts, and in the limited definition During applies to the concept of 'popular'. At the level of consumption and everyday practice, in fact, the distinction between the global popular and cultural globalization becomes unnecessary, since audiences choose their texts according to a complex of local and global cultural factors (see Chapter 8); whether a text is 'popular' or 'unpopular' (narrowcast), it constitutes a cultural resource which is available for any form of consumption by any consuming group or market. Substantial empirical work has demonstrated that audiences may take any form of text and convert it according to their own interests and cultural needs. A popular text, as During defines it here, is simply an available cultural resource; its derivation has little relevance except as the user/reader attaches meaning to that source. Any text may be appropriated, its meanings converted and reconstructed; any text, that is, may be hybridized for the enhancement of cultural localism. Textual meanings are constructed only in relation to the interests, needs and cultural contexts of audiences. During's emphasis on the text tends to parenthesize somewhat the intricacies of personal and community variations. The whole idea of homogeneity is therefore difficult to sustain.

James Lull (1995) has outlined some significant examples of the way global texts are being read and used by divergent global audiences. Here are some of his examples:

1   Jamaican reggae music played by Bob Marley, Peter Tosh and Black Uhuru pulsates at high volume in clothing boutiques located in the *medinas* (people's markets) of Fez, Morocco.
2   More than 400 million people worldwide, including countries like Russia, Tunisia, Zimbabwe and Switzerland, regularly watch TV soap operas that originate in Spanish-language nations.
3   German pop music bands travel to the United States, where they perform solely for Vietnamese-American immigrants, who use the music to unite their communities (1995: 145).

In Lull's terms, these are examples of the ways in which the world is comprised of 'new territories of meaning' which constitute alternatives to the traditional national territories. Audiences, it appears, are less interested in the national or cultural source of a text, and more interested in its capacity for cultural intersection. Like food, media texts are becoming a resource for the hybridizing tastes of an increasingly cosmopolitan local consumption.

GLOBAL SPACES

Discussions about globalism tend to centre on a recurring problem of localism and local identity. Commentary during the 1990s onward has tended to recognize that globalization implicates the creation of new cultural elements, discourses and spaces, but the actual nature and definition of what constitutes 'the local' is rarely specified; rather, 'the local' is presented merely in terms of its alternative: the global. What is clearer, however, is that the parameters and substance of 'nation' are seriously challenged by the globalizing process. The 'imagined community' of the nation, which, according to Benedict Anderson (1991) was constructed in relation to the rise of print technologies, urbanization, industrialism and imperialist economies, is being dissolved through new forms of imagining. Certainly the nation continues in many of its traditional forms and discourses, but the new globalizing economic, media and bionomic conditions of contemporary culture are changing the ways we conceive of our nation and ourselves. Moreover, the physical landscape of the Earth is being radically altered as it is enveloped in the intricate webs of globalization. In the midst of significant species extinction, surviving plants and animals are being increasingly distributed beyond the borders of their old ecologies. Cities and agricultural landforms are now constituting highly assimilative and repetitive spatial patterns across the globe. The formerly distinct disciplines of urban studies, architecture and geography are converging with cultural theory in order to explain these new spatial experiences.

Postmodern Architectures

Neo-Marxist and other more strident commentaries on global space (e.g. postcolonialism, feminism) have tended to divide the world between the centre and the periphery. The centre marks the territory of the developed world, especially developed cities; the periphery or margins tend to be located in non-developed, especially agrarian, regions. These modernist forms of critique remain fixed in notions of spatial distribution, function and materialism. Postmodernism, on the other hand, appears more interested in the aesthetic and representational dimensions of space. For postmodernism the question of distribution and models of centre–periphery are no longer relevant as the world's geographies converge into a shared space of 'the imaginary'.

Charles Jencks argues that the new globalized world is propelling architecture and urban space into a new and more optimistic phase of cultural evolution. Jencks' notion of postmodernism (see Chapter 7) converges historicism and aesthetics; postmodernism is the age of humanly scaled pleasures and the liberation from modernism's stifling pessimism, orthodoxy and prescriptions of universal order. In this globalized space the imaged and constructed environment is shifted out of the suffocating uniformity of modernist functionality. Architectural space is released, that is, from the hierarchies that position and separate humans, and then attempt to overcome the separation through an artificial unity. For Jencks, modern spatial design is typified by the formalism of nineteenth-century public building with its grand entrances and oversized monuments. These self-conscious hierarchies are replaced in the post-World War II period by grey functionalism – those rectangular concrete boxes which are self-consciously egalitarian and hideously unappealing.

Jencks celebrates a postmodern liberation from modernism's functional certitude; this new language of postmodernism, a new 'double-coding' of time and space, frees the past from itself. This emancipation facilitates the development of new forms of space which become a celebration of 'lateral' rather than 'lineal' time. Thus, the quality of pastiche (juxtaposition of diverse historical or cultural elements) that characterizes postmodern designs constitutes a new 'classicism' by which a building can again be 'beautiful' as much as functional (Jencks, 1987a, 1987b). This quality of pastiche is visible in a number of postmodern designs: Ralph Erskine's housing renewal project (Jencks, 1987b: 104–5); James Stirling's extension of the Tate Gallery in London (Jencks, 1987a: 288 *et passim*); and Kurokawa's Daimaru shopping complex in Melbourne, Australia (see Lewis, 1997b). This new spatial aesthetic, which celebrates time by lateral reference and propinquity, is very much in keeping with the political and ethnic diversifications now characterizing global cultural interactions. The new space, that is, resists reduction and lineality by allowing competing voices across time, geography and culture to engage in each other's pleasures and problematics.

Kenneth Frampton's (1985) theory of critical regionalism is also designed to evade the universal grammar of modernist architecture by which cultural and representational space is characterized as (modernist) sameness and the uncritical replication of building types. For Frampton, the distinguishing characteristic of postmodern architecture is its ability to reconstruct traditional regional values and ethnic designs through new technologies. Not only can a building function as a living museum, it enhances and preserves cultural difference within the urban landscape of postmodern fusion. Thus the language of a particular region is fused with the language of postmodernism to produce unique and beautiful architectural types. Difference, geography and tradition will always be heard in this dual coding of old and new; the logocentricism, capitalist metropolitanism, functionalism and monophonic voice of modernism that had dominated the world throughout the period of

Enlightenment imperialism is consequently banished, though not forgotten, since it too is a voice of history. In this way, Charles Jencks contends, the new architectural style of postmodernism produces a new ideology which can be understood as speaking to the 'elite' and the 'man in the street'; this is the necessary ideology of postmodern democracy since both 'groups, often opposed and often using different codes of perception, have to be satisfied' (Jencks, 1987b: 8). This ideology of a fused particularity is most poetically described by Frampton as an architecture of resistance by which a more complete range of symbolic senses will interact with the 'meanings' of a building:

> the intensity of light, darkness, heat and cold; the feeling of humidity; the almost palpable presence of masonry as the body senses its own confinement; the momentum of an induced gait and the relative inertia of the body as it traverses the floor; the echoing resonance of our own footfall. (1985: 28)

Jencks' periodizing of postmodernism leads him to suggest further that these architectural forms are associated with the new pastiche of the city and the postmodern globe. Nation and the separationism and alienation of modernism are being displaced by a world system in which the major cities are no longer confined to national functionalism, but are integrated into widening cultural and global relationships. Tokyo, Paris, London, Mexico City, New York, Rio de Janeiro – these are now global cities connected by significant economic, aesthetic, social and cultural matrices which enclose the whole of the world.

The Architecture of the Jumping Universe

Spatial and architectural formations are for Jencks theoretical as much as aesthetic representations. Architectural and artistic 'double-coding' is the capacity to say two potentially opposite things at once, including statements about time and space. Postmodernism is an idea which articulates the 'differences' of history or place in terms of an ever-present and a unity of knowledge. This harmony in difference (difference in harmony) constitutes the major ideal for postmodern idealism, its liberatory dimensions. Thus, while the architecture and art of modernism were constructed around functionalist and mechanistic theories of the universe, postmodernism aesthetics will formulate its technologies around a purer understanding of nature and cosmic principles. The Enlightenment laid the foundations for these new understandings, but through the discoveries of the 'new physics' – post-Euclidian geometry, relativity, quantum theory, fractals and chaos theory – we now need a new way of representing the essential nature of Nature.

Thus, in a subsequent development of the original double-coding theory, Jencks suggests that the new architectural horizon should emulate the increasing complexity of the universe. Jencks' adaptation of complexity and chaos theories for cultural and aesthetic analysis claims that nature evolves through a fine balancing of order and disorder. Increasing complexity within nature leads to the potential for complete randomness and breakdown. The same is true of social and cultural history. Late modernist painting, for example, is typified by profound complexity which risks a slide into randomness and chaotic expressions of emptiness, meaninglessness and disorder. The paintings of Jackson Pollock become increasingly random; the complexity of James Joyce's *Ulysses* dissolves into the incomprehensibility of *Finnegan's Wake*. Thus, just as the universe proceeds from the simple to the complex, art and social

organizations advance through increasing complexity – however, 'the reverse of complexity is not just simplicity but also entropy' (Jencks, 1995: 37): closed systems of any type must necessarily move from complexity to chaos and the expiration of energy, and ultimately death. A jumping universe, however, is an open system where development and disorder advance (and retreat) interdependently and with the ultimate, if mysterious, capacity for self-organization. The universe jumps in two ways:

1 Through evolutionary 'leaps' where there is a developmental convergence as the potential for chaos is mobilized toward greater complexity: the Big Bang, the solidification of planetary gases, the formation of air and water on Earth, the emergence of cellular life forms, the evolution of dinosaurs, the evolution of humans. According to Jencks, we are due for another spectacular jump as we produce forms of computer-based technology which will vastly outstretch the mechanistic technologies of preceding epochs; these machines will be self-replicating, self-organizing and much closer to the natural systems of organic nature. Between these leaps, of course, there have been numerous contractions where cosmic elements fall away into disorderly conditions: the cataclysm which brought the almost immediate extinction of dinosaurs is analogous to the current mass extinctions being precipitated by human activities. For Jencks, this contemporary threat to the condition of all life is directly related to the advanced state of human imagining, technologies and social life. Existence, that is, proceeds at the knife-edge of devastating chaos and generative progress.

2 The universe also jumps through the behaviour of its smallest and most

Plate 10.1 Storey Hall is a refurbished section of RMIT University in Melbourne, Australia. The developers have transformed the nineteenth-century office building into a cavernous art and exhibition hall which integrates crystals and other organic forms into its edifice. Clearly, the architects have tried to move away from Euclidean geometry in order to approximate the complex forms of nature.

fundamental particulates. According to Jencks and his theoretical mentors, the 'complexitists', the universe is structured around sub-atomic particles – quantum electrons – which display the same complex association of order and disorder which is evident throughout nature, including the 'nature' of human beings. The most basic characteristic of human knowledge is contradiction; we carry with us perpetual struggles

between different attitudes, emotions and behaviours.

More generally, Jencks explains the connection between the behaviour of sub-atomic particles and human thought:

> Some physicists believe, moreover, that thought is basically a wave phenomenon. This is intuitively obvious; after all, an idea weighs nothing, is contained all over the brain, is stretched out like a wave, can travel near the speed of light, and is changeable like an ocean wave. Quantum waves also have, like thoughts, paradoxical properties: unlike particles or objects, they can tunnel through walls – a miracle that happens in every television set.... Quantum waves can add up, cancel, go through each other, and be in several places at once. (1995: 40)

Jencks goes on to explain that the modernist notion of mechanistic order, where the universe is defined and explained in terms of linear processes and laws, provides only a superficial, even partial, vision of nature. The self-organizing systems which have evolved are themselves the outcome of complex and paradoxical quantum associations:

> [A] basic truth of quantum physics has been that the atom is itself an ecological entity with internal properties of organization. The electron, orbiting the nucleus as both wave and particle, jumps from quantum level to level, giving off, or taking on, energy. Its behaviour is partly self-determined and partly indeterminate. The electron cloud is said to 'choose' certain aspects of its activity just as we 'choose' whether to observe its position or momentum, particle or wave aspect. Its freedoms and our freedoms are circumscribed, but we both exhibit a degree of self-determinism and interaction. (1995: 162)

Quantum and complexity theories thus become paradigmatic for Jencks. Architecture, art and urban planning are available for complex associations of determination and self-determinism – neither is complete and entirely independent of the other. Buildings, cities and social life across the globe exhibit the same contradictions and paradoxes, and it is the challenge of postmodern thinking to arrange these cultural forms in order to maximize their complexity and potential for human pleasure. In this sense, postmodernism is embedding us more deeply into the true essences, the true characteristics, of nature. Jencks summarizes as follows these principles for a new architecture which draws all of humanity into a postmodern urban web that is no longer separated from nature, but which is an intrinsic part of it:

1 Buildings should be designed and constructed in relation to nature and natural languages, including atomic and sub-atomic forms, twists, folds and waves, cyborgs, crystals and bones.
2 Buildings should represent the basic cosmological truth, including self-organization to higher (and lower) levels.
3 Building design should be constituted through organizational depth, multivalence, complexity and the edge of chaos.
4 Architecture should celebrate diversity, variety and bottom-up participatory systems which maximize difference.
5 Diversity can be supported by techniques such as collage, radical eclecticism, and superposition. This enables architecture, drawn from different historical phases and through different ethnicities and human interests, to co-exist in an inclusive, pluralist system of design.
6 Architecture should acknowledge the context of the contemporary culture and its agenda, including questions of ecology and political pluralism.
7 It should have a double-coding of these concerns with aesthetic and conceptual codes.

8 Architecture must look to science, especially contemporary science, for its closures of the Cosmic Code. In order to go beyond immediate concerns and fashions, architecture must look to wider fields of knowledge and understanding.

Postmodern Geographies and Thirdspace

Jencks' architectural postmodernism has been severely criticized for its celebratory and unproblematic approach to the social and political arrangement of space. His polemical utopianism has failed to impress those (especially neo-Marxist) analysts who maintain a deep suspicion of postmodern theorisations.

Howard Caygill (1990), for example, rejects all notions of a postmodern spatial democracy, arguing that this postmodernism remains critically, politically and aesthetically bound to the elitism and uneven spatial distributions of the modernism it purports to replace. Indeed, Caygill uses Theodor Adorno's model of irresolution to demonstrate the incapacity of postmodernism to resolve its contradictory parts. Adorno's work would deny the inclination of postmodern theory to resolve the Enlightenment dualities – universal/particular, past/present, rich/poor – through the processes of representation. Caygill sees the postmodern aesthetic as an unconvincing ideology which forces the alternatives into a dissonant aesthetic partnership: 'Current postmodern theory and practices succumb to the desire to reconcile the two spheres by resolving their contradictions through the erasure of differences between the profession and the public, and within the public itself' (1990: 285). Thus for Caygill and others working from the neo-Marxist critique, the aestheticization and pluralization of space remain fixed by capitalist processes which cannot diminish the pervasive unevenness of spatial and resource distribution. Globalism and the new capitalist utility would merely illuminate the shifting focus of this unevenness across the world, without clear reference to the powerful forces that control and manipulate our constructed environment.

Thirdspace and the Olympic Games

The Olympic Games have become one of the most prominent and widely telecast of all global spectacles. Of course, the 'Games' are conducted in a physical space: arenas, swimming pools, football fields, boxing rings, and so on. However, the Olympics are also very much a part of international televisual culture, and are conducted through 'language games' or the imagined spaces of discourse. Politics, economy and power are all mobilized through these discourses.

The final of the men's 100 metres may be watched simultaneously by more than a billion people worldwide. A Thirdspace analysis would see the event as a form of colonisation: the athletes become the representatives of the territorial and commercial interests of their home nation. The spectacle of the event, that is, engages with the historical inequities upon which capitalist competition is founded:

1   For virtually the whole of the twentieth century the finalists in the 100 metres event were the descendants of African slaves, whether they were representing Britain, Canada or the US.
2   First World nations use their successful athletes as demonstrable evidence of national virtue and virility. This success acts as a warning to those external powers. It also acts as a source of national cohesion and national consciousness.
3   Successful athletes generate income and economic activity which also benefit the home territory. Poorer nations have neither the money (public or private) nor the technology which will produce high-level athletic performances. The 100 metres final represents the unevenness of wealth distribution across the globe.
4   The glamour of the spectacle also disguises the corruption and cheating which are rampant in the Olympic movement.

A celebrational postmodernist analysis would see the representational dimensions of the Games in a rather more positive light. The community of viewers who would come to the final are deriving their own pleasures from the spectacle. Perfected human bodies, enhanced by technology and the spirit of competition, come together to form the utopia of gamesmanship. Being 'black' is no longer a point of threat, but a source of celebration. The Olympics are a space where all countries can come together to celebrate their shared humanity.

Thirdspace analysis combines these two perspectives in order to identify and critique the representational and material dimensions of space. For Thirdspace the Olympics are a set of contesting discourses which culminate in the control and distribution of space. The ideal of the Olympics and their experiential unevenness must necessarily clash. However, it is not enough to point to these clashes; genuine solutions must be found and presented. Regulations and ethics must protect against corruption. Poorer nations must have wealth distributed in their favour. African Americans must do as Tommy Smith and Don Carlos did at the Mexico Olympics (1968): they must articulate the politics of their condition and express their anger to the world.

Edward Soja (1989, 1996) attempts to overcome the divide between modernist and postmodernist conceptions of space through a reworking of Henri Lefebvre's (e.g., 1991, 1992) theories of Thirdspace, 'the trialectics of spatiality'. According to Lefebvre, the logics of modernism had always reduced space to a material and physical condition, or a representational phenomenon of the mind; Thirdspace liberates spatiality from the constraining reductivism of this dialectic. Soja identifies the defining qualities of Thirdspace as

a knowable and unknowable, real and imagined lifeworld of experiences, emotions, events and political choices that is existentially shaped by the generative and problematic interplay between centers and peripheries, the abstract and concrete, the impassioned spaces of the conceptual and the lived, marked out materially and metaphorically in spatial praxis, the transformation of (spatial) knowledge into (spatial) action in a field of unevenly developed (spatial) power. (1996: 31)

Lefebvre's notion of a ubiquitous power, like Foucault's, is appealing to Soja as it liberates the concept of power from fixed structures like class and distribution of property. Again like Foucault, Lefebvre identifies significant divisions in social power but they are elusive and mutating, occurring at the level of relationships and in discourse – at the very centre of Being. This phenomenological definition distinguishes Lefebvre from those Marxists who can only define space in terms of structure (material or ideological), and from those postmodernists who can only define space in terms of representation. Even so, Lefebvre's particular brand of nomadic and complex Marxism, while liberating his analysis from simple definitions of centre and periphery (power and powerlessness), nevertheless returns to residual forms of binary oppositionalism. Thus, while moving away from the simpler alternatives of centre–periphery in his definition of global space, Lefebvre reconstructs notions of mind–body, man–woman, West–non-West in his critique of space.

Lefebvre's analysis seeks a geography which emancipates individuals from the homogenizing, fragmenting and hierarchically organized regimes of power which are at the heart of capitalist arrangements of space. *Le droit à la ville*, the right to the city, was a concept developed by Lefebvre to announce the new aspiration of reformist politics, the right to be different. This struggle was to be experienced at all levels of the life-world: the body and sexuality, household designs, architecture, urban planning and monumental design, neighbourhoods, cities and the global development. These struggles for difference were conceived in contexts of centred and marginal space which was both material and metaphoric. Unlike the post-modernists who have invested much of their liberational faith in deepening individualism, Lefebvre seeks to reinvigorate collective resistance, the Thirdspace of political choice. Thus, social relations are not inci-dentally spatial, as many Marxists might conceive, but fundamentally spatial: there are no aspatial social processes, according to Lefebvre, no ways in which the relationships of power can be conceived without the inscription of real and imagined space.

> Thinking trialectically is a necessary part of understanding Thirdspace as a limitless com-position of lifeworlds that are radically open and openly radicalizable; that are all inclusive and transdisciplinary in scope yet politically focused and susceptible to strategic choice; that are never completely knowable but whose knowledge none the less guides our search for emancipatory change and freedom from domination. (Soja, 1996: 70)

The concept of Thirdspace, then, provides a tool for the comprehension of global arrangements of space, including aspects of development, social relations within space and the construction, aesthetics and repre-sentational forms of our cities. For Soja, Thirdspace provides a valuable strategic tool for the reading of cityscapes that are now postmodern and constituted around complex simulations and media.

Postmodern Playgrounds

The postmodern city has now been transformed into an integrated space of shopping, display and functional and communicative ecstasy. Edward Soja, in fact, borrows directly from Jean Baudrillard's account of the 'ecstasy of communication' (1983b, 1988, see Chapter 7) to describe contemporary Los Angeles. In a contem-porary, media-centric city like Los Angeles, the old divisions of space and spatial iden-tity are continually transformed by new simulations of space: compressions which re-create formerly separate dominions and histories into a replica, a reproduction or simulation of what might (or might not) have been. As Baudrillard has pointed out, these are forms of simulation, imitations of imitations, which have no origin and no observable context other than the here and the now:

> This ecstatic disappearance permeates everyday life, enabling the hyperreal to increasingly influence not only what we wear and what we eat and how we choose to entertain ourselves, but also where and how we choose to live, who and what we vote for, how government is run, and also how we might be agitated to take more direct political action not just against the precession of simulacra but *within* it as well. (Soja, 1995: 278)

In other words, the world of simulacra becomes unavoidable. For postmodern architects, these simulacra constitute addi-tional resources for the design and con-struction of our material and iconic environment. However, the same buildings in which Charles Jencks rejoices become the source of discomfort for a critical post-modernism which seeks a deeper explana-tion of social and political relationships and which is distressed by the obscuration of history.

These design strategies are justifiable, according to the celebrational postmodern-ists, because all history is invented and all space is representational. Even so, we can see the problematic returning, even as

Plate 10.2

Plate 10.4   **Plate 10.3**

Plates 10.2–10.4   The postmodernization of space. Plate 10.2 features a real-estate sale on the small Indonesian island of Nusa Lembongan. The thatched hut is situated in a fishing village which overlooks a spectacular coral reef. The pressure of global tourism is already being experienced on the island, with the international hotel corporation Hyatt establishing a major resort a few kilometres from the hut. Plate 10.3 features the postmodernization of a nineteenth century industrial zone. The Shot Tower, which produced lead shot for artillery and kerosene lamps, has been incorporated into the Daimaru shopping complex in Melbourne, Australia. Plate 10.4 features the refurbished harbour in Montreal, Canada. Museums, restaurants and various forms of public recreational space have replaced the factories, warehouses and brothels which once dominated the harbour landscape.

Thirdspace, in the contemporary transformations of older industrial architecture and urban spaces that were constructed around nineteenth-century trade and manufacturing. The reinscription of such sites as museums, theme parks, recreational and cuisinal zones affirms a world of happy-endings and postmodern pleasures, but it marginalizes particular living and dead social groups. Specifically, the stories of dead workers, those who populated the former industrial spaces, are generally obliterated or obscured

by the refurbishments and the sanitization of the old, industrial shells.

This postmodernization has taken place in the former industrial zones which once bordered the northern end of Melbourne, Australia's principal manufacturing city. For over a century, one particular building in the former industrial zone, the Walter Coop Shot Tower, has been the subject of enormous debates and contesting cultural discourses. During the latter part of the nineteenth century, the Walter Coop constructed a lead shot factory, the most notable feature of which was the 152-foot Romanesque tower. The Shot Tower technology was effective but farcically primitive. Molten lead was dropped from the top of the tower; the descent cooled the material into spherical lead 'shot', which was then sorted and sold for artillery and kerosene lamps, among other uses. The enterprise continued through four generations of the Coop family until 1961, when, finally, even Australia's generous manufacturing protection policies could not save it from the challenge of more efficient and technologically advanced manufacturing techniques being used in other parts of the world. The Australian National Trust legislation became the new protector, however, and the site was saved from obliteration and redevelopment by a nostalgia which in a postcolonial nationalist discourse identified the structure with some of the great monuments of the world: the Statue of Liberty, the Eiffel Tower, Big Ben.

Even so, there seemed little interest in developing the building, and while the city continued to grow and the inner-city industrialism continued to atrophy, the old Tower's 'symbolic', rather than material, value was itself being challenged by the vigorous pragmatism of the 1980s. Discussions over the building's historic and cultural-visual value for the Melbourne streetscape began to change character. The influence of economic rationalism and globalist postmodernism began to challenge some of the established assumptions of historical-national value. While several redevelopment schemes had been mooted, they all collapsed at the door of the conserved Walter Coop complex. Finally, the giant Japanese consortium Kumagaigumi resolved the thirty years of temporal inertia by incorporating the old tower into its redevelopment plan. The acceptance of the project, which incorporated the Shot

Tower into a huge shopping complex and office tower, not only marked the complete re-configuration of the northern city streetscape, it also symbolized a more general abdication in the reign of cultural modernism.

According to the conceptual designer of the Daimaru, Kisho Kurokawa, the integration of the Shot Tower into the glass cone of the Daimaru shopping complex draws together diffuse spatial and cultural elements. The people who inhabit the building are perpetually exposed to a chaotic dialogue which confronts their assumptions about space and the world at large: 'The chaotic dimensions of people distinguishes them from machines and this is what architecture for the 21st century ought to express' (Kurokawa, cited in Childs, 1991: 5). According to Kurokawa, the Daimaru design principles supersede the domination of people and their vitality which are inherent in the ordered public design of cities like The Hague, Vancouver or Washington DC. The Daimaru is a 'commercial entertainment space, so I need a surprise. It's a surprise box' (cited in Childs, 1991: 5). Like Charles Jencks and numerous other postmodern enthusiasts, Kurokawa makes grand claims about the power of his aesthetic to produce pleasures that occur at the level of the human. According to Kurokawa, his critics remain trapped in an ideological system which is always overriding the human and which inevitably produces and reproduces modes of order, dominance and displeasure.

The Daimaru building, in fact, represents another 'happy ending'. The thirty years of historical, political, commercial and cultural dissonance are finally brought together within the totemic space of postmodernism. The past can exist in a context of financial imperative. The awkward and disjunctive ghost of Australian industrialism becomes iconographed as nostalgia, a quaint and curious relic which engages the pleasures and interests of the postmodern tribe. Now the Shot Tower becomes a comedy, a linguistic interplay where the oppositions of chaos and complexity, pleasure and displeasure, old and new, are resolved in ironical dispositions. The Daimaru dwarfs the old Shot Tower, incorporating its history into video screens, walking tours and a giant waist clock which plays 'Waltzing Matilda' on the chime of every hour. The tower itself is draped in a huge red SALE sign. On the hour the shoppers stare skyward, but they are not looking at the tower; they are standing in absorbed attention at the robotic pioneers who step from the corners of the giant waist clock while it plays the 'Matilda' anthem.

The past, that is, is woven interminably into the present. But it is not a past that the ghosts of the Walter Coop would recognize. Rather, it is a past that has been sanitized, standardized and re-rendered for contemporary tastes – literally and metaphorically. This new past is not merely a playground of historical references; it's a history built around untruths and the obscuration of past lives and past terrors. The ghosts cry out but the contemporary story-tellers and their play are impenetrable; they continue to varnish the disease, filth and degradation of 'other' lives, condemning them to anonymity while glorifying the memories of great (men) in new modes of pleasure and info-tainment. It may be, as Alan Bryman (1995) says of Disneyland, that it is the present that is obscured by this perpetual re-rendering of the past. In fact, the present may no longer be present at all but may be rendered absent by the fabrication of an idealized history. This obscuration excludes pain and the politics of struggle, so that contemporary problems 'are not real problems at all, or ones which, with our current know-how … can easily be overcome' (Bryman, 1995: 127).

Thus, the transformation of global city spaces – ports, warehouses, working-class residences – is fashioned out of this broader transformation of global capitalism and global culture. These transformations produce particular effects, depending on the site, history and design objectives of the redevelopment. For example:

1 The redevelopment of the Thames docklands in London has replaced one hierarchical system with another. From being a site which represented the poverty of wharf labourers, imprisoned underclass felons and the imperial gateway, it has now become an exclusive residential and entertainment zone. Only the best-paid postmodern professional could contemplate the mortgage of a docklands residence.

2 EuroDisney, the expansion of Disneyland into the most chic of cities, Paris, represents the integration of Europe into the ecstasy of popular American culture. This transformation is ambiguous as it adjusts for a more distinctly European style of spectacularization and entertainment. (For example, the drinking of wine, common in EuroDisney, is strictly forbidden in Disneyland.) The presence of EuroDisney on the borders of Paris replaces the sense of siege which has preoccupied Paris during the period of modernity. EuroDisney now sits on the outskirts of Paris as once the German troops had done. The 'threat' posed by EuroDisney, however, is one of the complete transformation of the integrity and aloofness of Parisian culture. The changes to the Paris skyline that have also taken place over the past two decades represent, further, this conceptual re-imagining of Paris.

3 The Tokyoization of Honolulu. One of the most significant changes to world

culture and global space since the 1970s has been the success and expansion of Japanese economy and culture. As Japan has become the world's second largest economy, its rapid accumulation of capital has brought further pressure to spend and participate in global consumption, including tourist consumption. Japanese corporations and private citizens seemed suddenly to appear in world tourist and real-estate markets. Japanese investors bought prize land in the coastal and tourist zones of west coast North America, Hawaii and Australia. Even with the current ebb of the Japanese economy, the impact of Tokyo culture and money is evident in the street signs, tourism facilities and cuisines of these coastal zones.

The notion of Thirdspace devised by Henri Lefebvre and Edward Soja would suggest that these playhouses are forms of complicated ideology. We can see how powerful groups in a society might advantage themselves and their interests by constituting the world as happy ending, as simulacra without source or conclusion. However, at the level of popular culture it is also clear that the tribe of postmodernist consumers derives genuine gratification from the spaces and the delights of design. The homogenizing effects of repeated design and corporate hegemony are balanced, therefore, by the sorts of complicated erasures, uses and re-configurations that building-users bring to the spaces. The playground is insidious, deft and deceitful. The postmodern tribe may be blind to particular effects and determinations of power, but the principles of post-modern consumerism permit a level of freedom for the users of these playgrounds which is denied them by modernist precepts. Gastronomy, Disney pastiche, beach-going and shopping – these are the new treasures of a postmodern, global space.

UNEVEN GLOBAL DISTRIBUTIONS

Even so, the new postmodern space is fundamentally uneven in its distribution of pleasure. Appadurai (1990) has argued that we can no longer think in terms of centre and periphery models; Lefebvre/Soja argue that centre and peripheries exist in multiple and mutating forms, some of which are characterized through the formation of space as representation and material. The concept of Thirdspace, in fact, allows us to think of space in terms of material and symbolic differentiations, while allowing for the possibility of 'meaninglessness', of space which is transformed into an absent core of simulacra. Certainly, the pleasures brought by consumerist postmodernism are not evenly distributed across the globe. The new forms of flexible accumulation of capital and the liberalization of international trade and finance are not an even bounty: wealthy countries and the majority of their citizens continue to do better, while the poorest countries continue to struggle under the burden of debt and devastating deficits in balance of trade. Even within developed nations the economic distance between the wealthiest and poorest people in the community is extending; social substrata are deepening as unemployment rates remain high and liberalized industrial relations laws weaken the bargaining power of ordinary wage-and salary-earners. Even in the United States, which, at the time of writing, has an extremely low unemployment rate by international standards, the image of economic success camouflages the continuation of severe poverty among many groups, including indigenous peoples, African Americans, single mothers and Hispanic immigrants. For all its enormous wealth, America has a huge proportion of underprivileged people who exist as a criminal underclass and who aren't registered in income or employment statistics.

Globalized Finance

Since the 1970s and 1980s one of the most traded commodities around the globe has been finance, the purest form of capital. The current fashion of deregulating international currency trade has allowed individual nations to participate more fully in various forms of product exchange; however, computer linking and deregulation have also allowed currency traders to speculate on minor variations in currency value, buying and selling national currencies on minor trends to reap enormous profits. At times these minor variations are purely speculative, based on the economic performances of particular national economies, or major enterprises within those nations. The international price of agricultural or mineral products (known specifically as 'commodities') can cause major declines in the tradability and value of a nation's currency. While a decline in a major agricultural trading commodity may not upset the currency value of a large, developed economy which may have many export industries, for a Third World economy which may export only a few agricultural products, the decline can be catastrophic. International financiers sell off that nation's currency, reducing its tradable value. The net effect of such a sell-off is to reduce that nation's capacity to buy materials from overseas (its currency is worth less) and its capacity to repay international debt (it has less income and its currency is worth less). The reduction in viability of debt repayment puts further pressure on the currency, making an already difficult economic situation much worse.

Currency trading, in fact, is one of the more insidious and mysterious global capitalist activities. An equally serious problem for Third World economies and peoples, however, is the modernization process itself. Economies being drawn into the international capitalist network are only able to do so through a radical restructure of their own internal economic, spatial, social and cultural arrangements. While colonialism undoubtedly set the trajectory of change in motion, the globalization of economies from the 1970s has accelerated these changes, bringing an enormous burden of debt as nations struggle to participate in the global capitalist circuitry. Of course there have been some notable successes where modernization and globalization have rapidly expanded economic production in countries like Taiwan, Singapore, South Korea and the Philippines. However, as Neil Smith (1997) points out, the poorest nations of the world have merely been caught up in capitalization, most frequently as sources of cheap labour and as a vacuum receptor for the excessive accumulations of capital in the developed world. David Harvey (1989) makes this point in his discussion of postmodernity. The successes of capital accumulation in the developed world lead necessarily to the need for its redirection. Small, vulnerable economies become sites for the deposition of excess capital: tourism, development investment, loans. Of course these economic changes are accompanied by significant political and cultural incursions which in effect alter the social and cultural fabric of globalizing agricultural economies. Dislocation and social upheaval in poorer countries have been well documented, but in fact the incursions of globalized economy and internal restructure are also having devastating ecological effects. Seas, forests and formerly fertile lands are being turned to waste by the exploitative activities of multinational corporations. Great rivers are turning to sewers. As Neil Smith says, the integration of poorer nations into the global web is generally accomplished to maximize benefits for the investor without any great regard for the smaller economy:

> In retrospect, we can see that the Sahel famine and the chronic famines in Ethiopia and Sudan lasting through the 1980s as announcing the beginnings of a new episode in the history of sub-Saharan Africa. The brutal ghettoization of sub-Saharan Africa in the global economy has many sides. It has been marked by the production and maintenance of extreme scarcities; sometimes vicious social struggles over access to place and power; the rigid crystallization of ethnic, class and regional identities; repressive and often corrupt postcolonial governments built on the exploitation of scarcity and backed by military power; and serious warfare in virtually every state in the last two decades. (1997: 179)

Debt

The sub-Saharan experience of the past two decades is perhaps the most spectacular example of problems of global economic integration and development. Yet, even the so-called 'tiger economies' of South-East Asia and parts of Latin America have experienced significant problems since the financial crises of the mid-1990s. These crises have been explained away by neo-classical economists of the West as part of the internal failings of a national economy which is not lean and efficient and which squanders borrowed money on non-productive activities like health and education. These neo-classical principles also underpin the policies of the international money lenders who provide funds to governments but who expect a significant profit for their financial support. As the crisis deepened, however, the major international lending organizations – the International Monetary Fund (IMF), the World Bank and the Asian Development Bank – became actively involved in the policies and spending activities of national economies like Indonesia, Thailand and Mexico. To remain solvent, that is, these independent nations were forced to surrender significant aspects of their independence and sovereignty: they had to cut back on education, health and welfare spending, open their borders to overseas investment and imports, reduce all forms of trade barriers, and allow foreigners to buy their resources, including significant natural and cultural resources. This monetary crisis, which saw the value of the Indonesian rupiah, for example, decline by 2000 per cent against the US dollar, resulted in serious shortages, increased famines and destabilized the political conditions of the state (not necessarily a bad thing). It also led to the surrender of policies and legislation that had tried to protect Sumatran forests against excessive foreign exploitation and ecological devastation.

Much of the postmodern celebration of diversity is attached to the dissolution of national borders. Postmodernism, however, has not accounted fully for the dismantling of national borders where these form a protective layer against excessive exploitation and hegemonic control. In *Stop: Think* (1999) Paul Hellyer traces the rapid expansion in international indebtedness, especially by Third World nations, arising from the 1981 global recession. According to Hellyer, the participation of Third World and smaller economies in the trading and financial activities of large, multinational institutions like the World Bank has been bought at the cost of national sovereignty and economic independence. Third World economies borrow money and transform their economies through developmental programmes and the sale of national assets to international interests. The sense of prosperity that may appear during periods of economic growth quickly disappears during recession. The escalation of interest rates combined with declines in exports critically wounds the economies of dependent nations, causing savage unemployment, bankruptcies and the hollowing out of national assets and economic activity. Governments have no option but to turn further toward the international begging bowl. The entity of nation and national interests are fundamentally eroded by this uneven relationship. The protective barriers of nationhood – including education, health and welfare – are cut away by dependency. Postmodernism may bring a few tourists to the impoverished Third World, it may bring a few clothing factories, but it rarely brings comfort and dignity.

NEW IDENTITIES

While we can talk quite expansively about trends and processes of globalization, international media and the compressions of time and space, the outcome of these processes is experienced most immediately at the level of the individual subject. Postmodern cultural theory has been most acute in its analysis of the subject (self) and the fragmentation of modernist conceptions of a unified subjectivity. This so-called 'crisis of identity' refers, in fact, to the localization of globalist processes and their manifestation in a reconstituted, fragmented, postmodern subject identity. Stuart Hall (1991b) suggests that discussion on identity needs to free itself from the structured opposition of the global and the local. The 'global postmodern', as Hall describes it, is a fluid and open space where identity is no longer considered an ongoing, essential and integrated self. The subject, that is, is opened by new discourses of change, freedom, interaction, instability,

process and language. The self in contemporary cultural discourse is not a single thing at all, but is an open 'system' subject to change, choice, personal motivation, desire, freedom and an infinite raft of interactions and redirections. The unfixing of culture and the de-bordering of nations have opened the way for new formulations of the self and the 'identity' which constitutes the self.

The point here is that the self – an individual human being and his/her experience of life – has not been the same throughout history. The notion of 'who I am' is only conceivable in relation to other humans and the culture within which the individual functions. Members of oral, tribal cultures, for example, conceived of themselves as 'extempore', beings mysteriously connected to animals, objects and spirit beings. Space consisted of interior and exterior forms – familial and tribal totems marked the territory of the inside and the outside, the knowable and unknowable; memory and time were conceivable only in terms of a non-sequential living memory. The self must surely have existed, but it was very clearly linked to a tribal consciousness, a pre-eminent collectivity.

Modernism, of course, re-created the subject-self in terms of the subject–object split. René Descartes explained reality (and subjectivity) in terms of knowledge. Technology facilitates a sequential memory, a perpetuity that celebrates both social hierarchy and an intensification of self. As we have noted elsewhere, the urbanization and increasing size and density of social organization through the course of modernity lead to a reciprocal intensification of the individual (see Chapter 2). The fluidity of the relationship between the individual and the collective that marks much tribal culture evolves into a more rigid and categorical differentiation. The scientism and objectification of philosophical thought seem merely to have ossified the individual, reinscribing Christian articulations of the essential soul with an equally essentialist discourse of the self. The pressures of perpetual change, the rise of media and consumerism, and the emergence of psychological discourses in the social sciences, and existential philosophy and aesthetics during the early twentieth century led finally to major revisions of the self and the politics of subjectivity. What it is to be human and the response to the 'who am I' question changed markedly in the post-World War II period. Cultural studies and cultural theory have placed identity at the centre of cultural politics.

Identity and Democratic Politics

The political project of modernism, from democratic liberalism and Marxism through to fascism, has sought to reconcile the radical separation of the individual subject from his or her social environment. While the reformism is expressed and practized in very different ways, this common thread characterizes and motivates modern political theory and action. Even the very divergent political poles of communism and fascism have at their centre the desire to restore an alienated individual with a more healthy and vibrant social constituency. Marx's solution to the evil of this individual – social dualism is to take the individual through a transient proletarian consciousness to a utopia of egalitarian and collectively functioning individualism. Freedom is maintained by mutual regard and a openly embraced social consciousness. The fascism of Benito Mussolini perverts Nietzsche's notion of a super-individual and centralizes the will of the individual over the inevitable weaknesses of lesser beings. Social harmony is achieved when the power of the individual is constituted

as the ultimate utility for the benefit of the social whole.

Liberal democracy is a good deal more subtle, seeking an institutional solution to the problem of variant interests and needs. Indeed, the fundamental principles of democracy seek to reconcile differences between individuals through a process of delegation which resists the ossification of dictatorial hierarchies, thus maintaining a precarious balance between subject and object, individual and collectivity, hierarchy and equality. These principles, though often inconsistent and contradictory, remain forceful as they contribute to the formation of contemporary ideologies of individualism and individualistic democracy. If we examine the core of these principles, we can see that their discursive deployment *as ideology* in contemporary culture is motivated by a desire for the reconciliation of the individual/collective problematic:

1 The gratification of the individual's needs and pleasures will produce its own social equilibrium. Capitalism, pragmatism and self-interest (pleasure and utility) lie at the centre of this ideology.

2 An individual's freedom is guaranteed within the social setting where the best and most able have the opportunity to succeed, prosper and lead. This leadership will be limited by the interests, tastes and freedoms of others who will exercise their own choice and seek to achieve their own potential, while recognizing that the more worthy person will do better. Political, economic and social institutions are forms of leadership which are the outward and symbolic manifestation of rational human action. Weber's writings on capitalism appear to promote these views; the recent revival of neo-liberalism (neo-utilitarianism, economic rationalism)

appears to be informed by this ideology of freedom.

3 Individual freedom is possible within the scope of collective gratification. This is the traditional left-wing (cf. Fabian) perspective, which emphasizes care, justice, community and collective responsibility. The individual will prosper when society is compassionate, informed, civilized and 'responsible'. While this principle appears somewhat atrophied in current discourses on freedom, it is far from moribund and is often invoked in discussions on health care, indigenous peoples' affairs and environmental issues. It also remains potent in community-level political agitation, and will appear, though somewhat paradoxically, in the discourses of sectionalized conservative interests (e.g., rural, small business, arts and nationalist lobby groups).

While varying in emphasis and direction somewhat, these elements contribute to the overall construction of freedom, social progress and social order. The ideology of democratic individualism, thus, is fundamentally formed around the binary opposition of individual and collectivity.

For democratic politics, then, the individual is conceived in terms of citizenship, the mutual obligation of state and subject. Nineteenth-century liberal democratic theory is founded on notions of essential goodness. The health of the state and democratic institutions depends, therefore, on an informed and committed citizenry grounded by knowledge and a commitment to the state and national sovereignty. Clearly, the notions of citizenship and identity that are fixed by the relationship between individual and state are challenged by the processes of fragmentation and global postmodernization. Critics have come to realize that the pluralist state and its ideologies of citizenship and democracy can no longer be assumed. The fundamental principles of state-derived freedom and democratic protection of rights is challenged in the same way the status of 'the nation' or the 'nation-state' is challenged. Moreover, the (imperfect) reconciliation between individual and collective interests which provides the ideological fabric for the modern state is no longer sustainable; the individual subject can no longer be defined purely in terms of his or her relationship with the state.

Political Postmodernism and Cultural Identity

At the beginning of this chapter we discussed the various dimensions of globalization, noting in particular that individuals and social groups are continually exposed to new forms of cultural, ideological, symbolic and bionomic propinquity. The physical borders that once separated human groups have been deconstructed by the flow of people, images, ideas and money across the globe. Inevitably, the notion of democracy and citizenship has been besieged, leading to new forms of relationships in which the mutual responsibility of state and citizen must operate in a context of multitudinous relations, responsibilities and practices of freedom and power. Decisions made in New York, Berlin, Tokyo or The Hague might clearly affect the life experiences and everyday practices of people in any community in any part of the world. Postmodern theory, therefore, has attempted to extend democratic principles by replacing the notion of an overriding social structure with a theory of society as a multiple-forming assemblage of social differences. Social order, that is, becomes the contingency of various social and cultural constituencies; individualism is enhanced and even intensified as it generates greater independence and regard for variations in interest, belief and heritage. The state and the individual are, in fact, mutually de-centred through a greater celebration of choice, agency and individual creativity. Most critically for postmodern thought, the individual now has the opportunity to create his or her own identity in whatever manner is considered desirable.

In fact, the great difficulty of modernist politics, especially the institutionalized forms of democratic liberalism, has been the constant move toward the centre. The need for reconciliation and forms of publicly sanctioned hegemony, even consensus, draws combative discourses toward an intensifying political middle ground. This political middle ground replaces old arguments about the fundamental character of capitalism with a general and homogenizing consensual order in which dispute is banished to the margins. In most developed nations of the world there is little parliamentary debate about the efficacy and validity of free-market economics. In such a bland and consensual political order, identity constructed around reformist and radical politics is equally constricted. That is, a radical or reformist identity is rarely constituted around the rejectionist, working-class politics of the Left. The parliaments and governmentalities of the developed world provide little space for alternative political subjectivities since the dominant discourse is largely about degrees of economic deregulation. Reformist subjectivities, therefore, tend to operate outside the dominant discourses of parliament, congress and executive government. New political identities are being formed around the subjectivities of women, indigenous peoples, radical environmentalists, ethnic minorities, migrants, gays or other specific characteristics and interests. While all these 'movements' have found their way into mainstream democratic institutions, various factions have consciously sought to resist institutional participation in an attempt, among other things, to maintain a more clearly definable, activist identity.

Postmodernization in politics and identity constitution has also become engaged in consumer practices and notions of everyday life. As Michel de Certeau and others have argued (see Chapter 8), everyday life and the practices of freedom are fundamentally embedded in objects and pleasures. The ability to choose products has always underpinned capitalist ideology and utilitarian political philosophy. However, the enhancement of use-value by symbolic-value has contributed to the exponential expansion in the amount of choice available to consumers. This proliferation of signs, as Baudrillard describes it, constantly stimulates desire and the promise of pleasure. Identity can now be attached to this infinite array of symbolic ephemera. This 'consumer sovereignty' may be replacing other forms of bordered, symbolic and physical spatial sovereignty, including the constituency of nation. In other words, our identity constructed out of the sovereignty of nation may be supplemented, if not substituted, by an identity constituted out of the sovereignty of consumption. The physical and symbolic space of nation is replaced by the physical and symbolic value of consumable products. When this product is an image only, as in a media image, then the sovereignty becomes almost entirely abstract.

Different cultural products are offered to consumers, including tourism experiences, Internet activities and images, television programmes, popular music and imagery. An individual consumer may now create his or her identity through attachment to these broadly available and ever-proliferating products and experiences. The fluidity and accessibility of capitalist products make them available as raw materials for the construction of new and ever-replenishing identities. *Who I am* may now be answered by *what I listen to*, or *how I dress* or *what I might eat*. The fixities of racial, national-cultural or religious identities can now be enhanced or entirely replaced by infinitely rearrangable ensembles of meaning. An identity thus becomes something that can be manipulated and shifted according to fashion, desire, context or impulse. An identity is something which can be mobilized and manipulated according to present needs, contexts and symbolic interactions. A subject need not feel confined. Just as there are infinite choices in a capitalist economy, so there are infinite opportunities for identity creation.

Tourism and the Resistant Identity

Marginal identities, therefore, carry the possibility of transgression and avant-garde aestheticism. As Stuart Hall (1991b) has pointed out, old ethnicities which might once have been the rallying point for political resistance have by and large succumbed to the ongoing and all-encompassing sweep of capitalist commodification. Hall's reference to the international cuisine suggests that ethnicity itself can be reproduced for the pleasures and gratifications of the mainstream culture. With the possible exception of Islamic cultures in the Middle East, most nations of the world have now capitulated to the capitalist cultural standard, their cultural specificity becoming available for consumption as tourism, curio, international art forms and decorative styles. The categories of Western and Oriental culture which were developed for the project of European imperialism are now reconstituted as saleable typologies; 'Eastern' arts are integrated into the consumer predisposition of First World

nations. Every major city of the world has a Chinatown, a Latin quarter, an Afghani or Indian restaurant. In every major city we can buy Indonesian batik, Buddhist carvings, Bronx-style homi pants, Indian classical music, Korean television sets and U2 CDs.

Resistance to the hierarchical and homogenizing order of capitalist politics can no longer be essentialized as a resistant identity, but must be delivered from within the grand sweep itself. Marxist resistance models have been deconstructed as countries like China, Vietnam and now even Cuba have embarked on modernization and capitalization programmes which offer their cultures for sale and consumption. The idea of localism is therefore problematized: the local can no longer be conceived as an articulation of class, ethnicity or spatially defined community. As Mike Featherstone (1996) has pointed out, globalization and postmodernization processes have removed the time-space stability which had produced the imaginings of 'locality' and a locally constituted community. The 'authenticity' of a local culture is fundamentally challenged by the commodification process, most particularly as processes like tourism re-render local artefacts and ceremonies for the palatability of visitor consumers. The international marketplace, therefore, can consume and reproduce images that become 'mainstreamed' for tourism and the effervescence of 'something new', something 'different'. While this tourism invasion has taken place in most parts of the world, it is about to get underway in the formerly pariah nation of Cuba, where the communist leader Fidel Castro is already iconographed for international consumption.

The Indonesian island of Bali provides an interesting example of how a culture can be imagined for international tourism consumption. Bali has a strident history of resistance to imperial appropriation (Vickers, 1990), but when it finally succumbed to Dutch colonisation it immediately became available for European aesthetic and tourist imagining. A journey to the 'Far East' might now include a stay in the tropical paradise of Bali, a remote Hindu enclave in the midst of an Islamic Dutch East Indies. During the 1920s and 1930s the Dutch, realizing the great tourist potential of Bali, began to promote the island and its culture to those European, American and even Australian tourists who may have been lured by the 'mysteries of the Orient' more commonly associated with India and particular regions of Japan and China.

Yet the lure of the island also worked for painters like Walter Spies, intellectuals like Miguel Covarubias, and later anthropologists like Margaret Mead and Clifford Geertz. While the work of these early visitors has been important in dignifying the culture as a source of knowledge and aesthetic/spiritual pleasure, more sensual and immediately accessible images have been produced by writers like Aldous Huxley, who uses Bali as the basis for his utopian novel *Island*. Recent painters like Donald Friend use the tropical motifs to glorify the island's (especially homophilic) sensual beauty. Hollywood films like *Road to Bali* (1952) apply the exotica of a tropical paradise in order to intensify the romance narrative and the sensual pleasures of a distant location. Following the ousting of the Dutch after World War II, Bali's significance, for both international tourism and aesthetic/intellectual appreciation, has been augmented rather than diminished. Sukarno, whose own intellect embraced the European and Asian heritage, regarded Bali as the museum of ancient Indonesian culture. And Nehru, in accompanying the revolutionary president to the island, echoed these sentiments when he described the island as 'the morning of the world'.

The island's dramatic development during the New Order period has, in typically pragmatic terms, expanded the tourist trade to nearly 400,000 visitors a year.

The success of Bali as a tourist destination has been bought, of course, at a high price. This 'Island of the Gods' has been forced to accommodate massive spatial and cultural restructure. The 'authentic' cultural experience is now queried consistently as high-rise hotels, recreational and commercial facilities, and a cosmopolitan dining cuisine has wiped away the old rice paddies and villages which once surrounded Denpasar and Kuta Beach. Religious pageants, dances and rituals can now be viewed nightly at the big hotels or on call for a small price. Up-tempo and melodified versions of traditional gamelan are available in any of the multitude of stores that now pulse out pirated European and American pop music CDs. Batik painting is now presented in motifs of European imaginings of a tropical paradise, a noble peasant, a topless beach-goer. The surf industry is thriving. Jakartan businessmen have bought up huge tracts of land and are developing commercial sites at a breathtaking pace. Inevitably, the visitor to Bali will ask: where is the 'authentic' culture? It is certainly not in the oil paintings sold in the art centre of Ubud; these painting styles and techniques were copied from the Europeans in the 1920s. It is not in the casual sexual encounters which have been so idealized by European visitors but which are now part of the Indonesian prostitution trade. It is not in the temples, which have become commodified and which are daily trampled by the tourist groups bussed in from the big hotels. Authenticity, that is, has been absorbed as a commodity for imagining and consumption.

Transgression based on local identity, therefore, is a matter of the struggle to signify or 'language wars'. While clearly these wars are fought for the gratifications of reward and social resource, they are also fought over the value of identity and the control of discourse. Appadurai (1990), Featherstone (1996) and many others have seen that globalization cannot be simply measured in terms of simple binaries: homogenization/heterogenization, global/local, universal/particular. Rather, globalization and postmodernization have deepened the problematic of these language wars, obscuring the borders which previously divided groups, identities and ideologies. Authenticity in culture has never been more elusive. The borders that once divided cultures are fundamentally challenged by these new language disputes and these new ways of imagining. Just as individual identities have become unfixed and fluid, so constituitive cultures are mixed and open. While writers like Donald Horne (1993) may seek to distinguish between a cultural traveller and an unthinking or exploitative tourist, the distinction collapses in the final effect: whether intelligent or bombastic, the tourist is the harbinger of fundamental cultural dislocations and the imperative of a new form of cultural commodification. The resistant identity is just one other identity in the general flux of reproduction, representation and cultural imagining. Resistance slips away when even the imagery of Fidel Castro can be sold as a tourist T-shirt which mimics ideological isolation, iconoclasm and anti-imperialist, anti-American resistance.

DISCUSSION: CULTURAL POLITICS AND IDENTITY

Enthusiasm for globalization processes might generally be summarized in two ways. First, there are those hegemonic capitalist discourses which treat globalization as another advance in the inevitable progress of capitalism. People and cultures may have to adjust, certainly, but the benefits far outweigh the problems. We need only note the differences between nineteenth-century living standards and those of the advanced world today. Sooner or later the benefits of capitalism will flow to the poorest peoples of the world; they too will reap the harvest of the new global order. Undoubtedly economic globalist discourses have become an orthodoxy. The General Agreement on Tariffs and Trade, the World Trade Organization and the various regional free-trade zones are all directed toward a nirvana of economic growth, productive diversity and the broadest possible distribution of wealth across the globe. Nations may surrender a little sovereignty and cultural specificity, but these are incidental to the greater good to be delivered by a global economic system.

The second corpus of discourses which support globalization processes are more directly cultural and are generally attached to notions of postmodernism, or, in Stuart Hall's terms, the global postmodern. As noted above, postmodern globalism tends to celebrate the new possibilities of cultural difference and the liberation of individual subjects. While the body of texts and theories associated with this position vary in focus or emphasis, the common thread in their arguments suggests that cultural and subject de-centring permits new choices and new possibilities for the creation of identity, the enhancement of individual choice and greater possibilities for gratification and pleasure. Those postmodern theorists interested in a political reading of culture go on to suggest that these subjective possibilities are of themselves conducive to a transgressive perspective. New identities and new, creative modes of consumption and self-expression constitute a politics of personal potential, a transgressive politics which is not bound by structure, collectivity or institutional paradigms and perspectives. Ethnicity, sexuality and identity are opened for play and interaction. The new technologies and the widening distribution of ideas and imagery facilitate the continual broadening of choice and opportunities for new modes of expression, including the deployment of texts for the creation of virtual communities and a boundless communicative ecstasy.

These two perspectives tend to parenthesize many of the problems associated with globalization. As with most utopianism, there is a danger that the optimism might merely deflect attention from fundamental deficiencies. Most particularly, globalization implicates the dissolution of national imaginaries. Clearly the whole notion of nation has been problematic, indeed utterly devastating, for many of the peoples of the world. Imperialism, war, class, gender and racial exploitation have all been implicated in the imagining of nation. Yet nation has also been engaged in significant political and cultural discourses aimed at protecting and liberating individuals and social groups. We have pointed to the contradictions which inform the underlying principles of democracy and liberal humanism. Responsible government, economy and national development, individual rights, representation, universal suffrage, industrial legislation, equal opportunity legislation and social welfare – all have been the province of the nation-state. The problematic of nation is even more acute in those postcolonial territories where nation and national consciousness were mobilized against the oppression of alien control. For many of the peoples of the postcolonized world the ideology of nationalism provided a rallying point and discourse for their liberational aspirations.

In a globalized context, where multinational corporations and hegemonic nations and cultures dominate and disrupt the sovereignty of smaller locales, positive as well as negative aspects of nation are being surrendered. Increasingly, health, welfare and education policies are being sacrificed in order to satisfy the interests of international hegemonies. National policies on employment, industry, asset and resource protection are being compromised by demands for lower government spending, lower tariffs and the free flow of finance. Allegiance to free-market orthodoxies and American cultural knowledge dissuades smaller governments from playing a more active role in economy. Such participation might lead to 'market distortions', or, worse, a transgression of the free-trade canon. Government privatization (sell-off) of public utilities and assets, plus the general down-sizing of public services, have radically altered the status and value of citizenship. Citizens can no longer rely on the public welfare system for health, education and aged care, but must now 'fend for themselves'. Citizens can no longer vote for economic policies but must now stand aside as the great corporations and governments of the world make decisions that affect the welfare of all people. If institutional democracy and freedom are to advance in the global postmodern, then the American government and the presidents of corporations like Microsoft and General Electric would probably need to be directly elected by all citizens of the world. This, however, seems unlikely.

Postmodern theories have substantially changed the spaces available for transgressive and resistant political action. As the individual has become further intensified in postmodern thought, the 'collective' and collective responsibility have become demonized as a cultural or political category. The global postmodern, that is, seeks to resolve the modernist individual–collective binary by rejecting collectivity in favour of an ascendant and unrestrained individualism. However, as numerous critiques of postmodernism have pointed out (see

Lewis, 1994, 1998), this celebration of individualism and difference becomes a new form of essentialization, even universalism. Difference, that is, becomes a referent category by which all human and cultural interactions might be understood and judged. The gratification of international cuisine or the originality of a tribal artefact or the authentic back-packer experience of Nepalese culture is little compensation to the three billion people of the globe who remain undernourished and incapable of such aesthetic ecstasies.

Globalization is inevitably political. Local resistance is as much a matter of the imaginary as is any other category of spatial or temporal experience. There is little doubt, however, that the proliferation of images and global simulacra, as Baudrillard describes it, might provide the raw materials for its own resistance. Certainly, this is the view of popular transgressionists like John Fiske, who, in following Michel de Certeau, suggests that everyday life constitutes its own radical potential. That is, the strategic raiders of meaning will unconsciously and necessarily disrupt the sovereignty of powers which would impose their meanings upon them (see Chapter 7). This ultimate postmodern optimism does away with activism or the political consciousness that emerges through textual content, and replaces it with a hedonism which is self-directed and necessarily opposed to the instrumental logics of social order. New identities will necessarily issue from the interaction between text and everyday player. According to this perspective, it is only these new and self-creating identities which can resist the marshalling order of capitalist hierarchies. Freedom exists only at the level of the unconscious living (and consuming) of everyday life.

In an increasingly globalized order, such theories of a highly localized imaginary are intensely appealing. The everyday raider lives out his or her life beyond the clutches of rationalist, progressivist, centralist, homogeneous ideologies. The raider is able to choose between all these wonderful products and images, and yet s/he can never become victim to that choice. The text is thus emptied of content as it is rendered up to the free-flowing subject. The subject re-fills the text and reiterates his or her freedom in so doing. Yet as numerous critics have suggested, this emptying of content also renders the text available for iniquitous and oppressive discourses. The language wars that are fought over the empty text might lead to as much terror as pleasure, or a combination of both. The 'floating' text becomes available for cruel and oppressive discourse, choice and action. Of course, the postmodern analyst might not be able to resist interlocution at this point: the analyst may tell us what the text actually means or might reassure us with a reminder that the text exists only at the level of the imaginary. In either case, the postmodern essentialization of difference is found wanting. Social difference cannot insure against a difference which is despotic or anti-semitic, since even fascism is a form of social difference.

Cultural propinquity, that is, cannot protect human groups and individuals from terror, disease and conflict. The essentialization of difference or multiculturalism cannot guarantee racial harmony. Culture remains highly unstable and the drawing of the world into greater contiguity will necessarily expose the limits of these essentialisms. A form of collective responsibility needs to accompany the celebration of difference if the benefits of globalization are to be maximized and more widely distributed. The notion of globalization as inevitable and good, in fact, needs to be measured against the hegemony, privileges and iniquities that are accompanying its uncertain cultural embrace.

11

The Culture of New Communications Technology

Outline of the chapter

Approaches to technology can be broadly categorized as dystopian or utopian. Generally speaking, however, a positive technological progressivism has constituted a significant ideology during the course of modernity. Very often this progressivism has expressed itself as a form of 'technological determinism': the idea that the mere existence of a particular technology produces revolutionary and predictable historical effects. We need to reject this approach in order to analyse the ways in which culture, history and technology interact.

Oral or non-writing cultures are characterized by a fluid approach to time and space. The introduction of writing and print facilitates new ways of recording and plotting time and space, most particularly through the formation of lineal memory or chronology. Print, in particular, facilitates the broad distribution of information, knowledge and ideologies. Electrical, broadcast and digital media have disrupted notions of lineal time, and provided the basis for new ways of conceiving space. New communications technologies provide a resource for the development of 'post-modern' conceptions of the human culture.

Many critics argue that the new technologies provide opportunities for improved living experiences, including the enhancement of democracy. Utopian, postmodern computer politics claims, for example, that networked computers provide increased opportunities for community and public participation in public decision-making. Some enthusiasts suggest that hypertext writing is essentially more democratic than older broadcast and print styles of communication. Many proclaim the arrival of a democratic and egalitarian 'virtual community'. Others celebrate the formation of transgressive, hacking (sub-)cultures and the technologically enhanced experiences of cyber-sex. Writers like Donna Haraway imagine a future presided over by 'cyborgs': the evolutionary hybrid of human bio-logy and digital technology. All of these celebrational movements need to be examined critically.

GENERAL INTRODUCTION

As we have noted many times in this book, language and discourse are central to the formation of culture. Contemporary cultural theory focuses on the ways in which culture and meaning-making are constituted through the operations of language. Nineteenth-century preoccupations with knowledge and reality are replaced in cultural analysis by an interrogation of how knowledge is formed in discourse. Contemporary culture, of course, has expanded exponentially the means by which discourse is created and conveyed. Electronic and digital media have broadened human discursive processes well beyond the facilities of interpersonal (aural/oral, gesture, graphics) and print technologies. These new technologies, however, are not just the tools or machinery employed by communications media and industry; they are profoundly embedded in culture, its ideologies, discourses and meaning-making processes. In many respects a medium is distinguished by its principal technology (TV, radio, computer networked communication), and this technology is constituted in culture through its own particular sets of disputes, values and meanings.

Humans have always used technology, of course, in order to enhance 'natural' abilities in the facilitation of economy, communication, bodily performances and pleasures, relationships and social organization. Romantic aesthetics and philosophy, however, conceived of technology and culture as fundamentally opposed. Responding to the hideous social and environmental conditions being produced by industrialization, the Romantics sought to blame industrial technology for the degradation of the human mind and spirit (see Chapter 2). 'Culture', therefore, was defined as a sublime and spiritually exaltant release from the instrumental horrors of technological industrialism.

This theme persists into the twentieth century, with particular social groups (e.g., the 1960s hippie movement) and intellectuals (Bell, 1973; Postman, 1993) questioning the social, moral and cultural value of technological progressivism and its de-humanizing effects. Once again, technology is regarded as something outside culture, where culture is the sublime of spiritual, intellectual and aesthetic transcendence.

Needless to say, however, these dystopian views of technology seem to have made little dent in the propitious and seemingly relentless force of technological progressivism. Even when it is questioned or challenged, even when it is positioned within its cultural context, technology appears to have asserted itself as a dominant idea, ideal or ideology which is associated with conceptions of individual lifestyle, social improvement, economic growth and historical progress. In the cultural analysis of technology this ideology has been characterized in its more extreme forms as a type of technological determinism: the idea that a technology exists and will necessarily produce certain historical effects. Technological determinism generally operates like this:

1   The cultural analyst looks back at history and identifies a particular new technology.
2   A causal link is established between the technology and new social trends or events. A causal link is established between the technology and the social effects. The cultural and historical trend which brought the technology into use are generally ignored.
3   The analyst claims that the technology caused or determined the effect, parenthesizing or ignoring all other associations or causations.
4   The analyst often looks forward (optimistically), using a 'new' technology to predict new trends.

A technological determinist perspective often surveys social and cultural history, using 'technology' as the primary definer of the particular epoch (periodization). For the study of communications technology, a determinist perspective marks the history of the world in terms of 'communications revolutions': periods that are marked and determined by the emergence of a particular communications technology. Contemporary technological periodizations, therefore, would treat history as a progress towards the current, superior technological culture. More than this, however, a technological determinist perspective also tends to be 'futurist', using the emergence of digital and computer networked communications to anticipate future social and cultural trends. For futurist technological determinists, the new computer technologies will not only transform communications, their revolutionary effects will reach across all areas of human life. Not surprisingly, this sense of an improving historical condition also affects the technological determinists' perspective of the future: undoubtedly the progress offered by these new technologies will bring us a future that is inevitably better than the past.

Marshall McLuhan's notorious 'global village' is one of the more spectacular examples of technological determinist futurism (see 1964, 1969); McLuhan predicted that the broad distribution of TV technology would compress the world into a positively homogenized global space. The current culture of networked computer technology is being represented in similar terms with futurists anticipating such things as the end of the office, networked cities, the eradication of pollution, virtual communities and the obliteration of human conflict. Our aim in this chapter is to explore the cultural conditions that constitute these new communications technologies without recourse to a determinist

perspective. While we are, of course, centralizing communications technologies, we are interested primarily in the cultural operations and meanings that flow through and around these technologies. To this extent, we are particularly interested in the ideological and discursive disputes which are associated with new communications technology.

COMMUNICATION AND TECHNOLOGY

The deployment of communications technology as a periodizing definer needs some closer attention. In particular, the problem with using technology in this way is that it may neglect or parenthesize the significant context in which the social and cultural transformations operate. That is, technologies exist because they are needed, have value or meaning for a given culture. While the culture continues to have a need for the technology, it will continue to have meaning; technological determinism tends to treat the arrival of the new technology as something 'revolutionary' and outside the interests and demands of the people who draw it from historical obscurity. Many inventions and technologies exist through historical developments, but it is only those which the culture needs or demands which become popularized and useful. Equally, the emphasis on 'the new' might also obscure the fact that particular technologies are remarkably longevous, their use-value being obscured by the dramatic and transformative emergence of a new technology. The facility or technology of oral language, for example, has been operational for around 100,000 years; amid the excitement of the new communications technologies, this old form continues to be a major part of the human communications retinue.

To this extent, the following survey of communicative cultures needs to be understood as a series of overlapping and open assemblages, rather than as a set of closed historical categories. As Carolyn Marvin has noted in her deconstruction of the notion of communications revolutions, *When Old Technologies Were New* (1988), new technologies were nearly always constructed out of a complex set of cultural processes, including the slow and evolving confluence of social need and available apparatus. The survey that follows is meant to de-emphasize the notion of revolution by returning the communications technology to the context which produced this correlation of need and availability. At any particular historical moment there will be many cultures and many forms and levels of cultural experience; culture is never one thing, but is a series of overlapping, sometimes disjunctive, meaning formations. Our survey of communicative cultures, therefore, is merely locating culture around a particular meaning formation: communications technology. We should not, therefore, assume that this particular cultural formation represents an epitome for all the elements that constitute a particular historical epoch. We are not defining the epoch, but locating our interests in the particular cultural formation of the 'pre-eminent' communications technology, and examining how this formation relates to other cultural elements. We should also remember that a particular technology, as noted above, may continue after its predominance has subsided or been mollified by the presence of new cultural elements or technologies.

Oral Culture

Periodization analysis has tended to treat orality as a closed cultural system, beginning somewhere between 60,000 and 100,000 years ago and ending with the arrival of writing (4000 BC) or movable print (Europe, between 1451–3). The anthropologist Eric Michaels (1985) has demonstrated, however, that periodization overlooks the continuities of oral culture, and the ways in which new cultural technologies, forms and facilities may simply be overlaid onto pre-existing processes and experiences. In this sense, oral culture may be characterized by the pre-eminence of orality, though this fundamental language technology may have been supplemented by graphic and artistic forms, dance, music, rituals and other meaning codes like smoke signals. In any case, the beginnings of the technology of language remain elusive since spoken language leaves no residue, no artefacts for archaeological investigation. Certainly, the complex system of communication called language is associated with the migration of humans across the globe and the imperatives of new forms of economy, environmental adjustments and social organization. Oral language seems necessary for such complex social and economic activities, including the movement and settlement of people in the Americas and through South-East Asia to Australia. Recent evidence is suggesting that these migrations took place perhaps as long ago as 100,000 years before the present (BP). Clearly, these long, migratory journeys required sophisticated forms of communication and organization: the cultural need precedes the facility.

The characteristics of oral culture may be summarized as follows:

1   Oral language is fixed in time and space. Because it can't be recorded and exists only for the duration of vocal sounds, oral information is ephemeral and relies on human memory for its durability.

2   The number of people involved in any given communication process is limited

by the range of the spoken voice. In direct, non-transmitted orality, the human voice becomes the range limit, and so the presence of the human body is critical to communication.

3   In oral cultures the communicator is immediately connected to the world around him/her: symbol and referent are engaged in a very close relationship. For example, the language use of the American Hopi Indians compels the speaker to consider his or her own concrete observations. For the successful transfer of information, the speaker must continually refer to the actual, physical space in which the communication is taking place. Past, present and future cannot be distinguished in abstraction as with English; the speaker must refer to a particular spatial element in order to make the information understood.

4   Information must be connected with immediacy and relies on ritualized practices of memory. Information is closely connected to 'narrative' or forms of story-telling. Social laws, therefore, are 'recorded' and communicated in repetitive practices like dance and ceremony. These practices cover birth, initiation, kinship, territory, death, hunting and gathering practices, resource distribution, fertility and sexuality.

5   Memory is imperfect and distorts information: knowledge is difficult to accumulate so only a limited corpus of knowledge can be transmitted generationally. Very often, the prized facility of memory provides a particularly high status for those with the longest memories, the elders. Elders pass their knowledge on to younger members of the tribe.

6   Rituals, totems, symbols and art are used to supplement limited knowledge, and the limits of human memory and

body. The oldest human art forms consist of simple cave engravings produced by Australian Aborigines about 40,000 years ago. More recent tribal cultures produce elaborate forms of art, including cave paintings, engravings, wood carvings and stone monuments.

7   History (all-time) is revivified and restored with every utterance. History lives in the present context or life-world. That is, there is a sense of the perpetual in the immediacy of oral culture and oral language. Since the memory does not work like lineal time or a chronology, the past seems to be forever preserved in a present utterance. The language use of oral cultures seems to compress time into an ever-unfolding now.

8   Therefore, lived experience embodies all history, reinterpreted and refashioned to make sense of present events, social practices, relationships, and so on. For example, in Nigeria kinship obligations are rooted in a past that extends some sixty years before dropping away into mythological time. This temporal compression is produced simply out of the life-span of a living memory. The human mind flows boundlessly between present events, memory and imagination. Mythological time and present time merge through the facility of human recall.

    For Australian Aborigines, knowledge of time extends only as far as the Dreaming, which is the time that surrounds the immediacy of living memory or life-span. Yet the Dreaming is also 'ever-present' in the spirit of all things: rocks, topography, the weather and animals are all imbued with the spirit of the Dreaming. Human ancestry, therefore, exists in the 'present' and present experiences of all animate and inanimate objects; while memory can only be specified through the memory of the oldest living person in the group, all-memory persists in the environment.

9 Mythology thus surrounds the immediacies of time as now. Mythology becomes the conduit to human perpetuity.

While orality has been subjugated by the ideological force of writing and print culture, it has remained a significant part of human connectedness over the past millennia. The arrival of electrical communication has not just facilitated a 'secondary orality', as McLuhan calls it; rather, orality has been a continuous presence in human communications. Postmodernism, with its emphasis on de-centralization, imagery and the compression of time, has in many respects reinvigorated this underlying orality. The communalism of decorative art, the intensification of time and immediacy as 'all-time', the experience of ephemera and the pleasures of the communicable bodily presence – all are shared by orality and postmodernism.

Writing and Print Culture

The introduction of writing in the cultures of Sumer (4000 BC), Egypt (3000 BC) and Greece (1000 BC) is undoubtedly associated with significant changes to economy, lifestyle and forms of social organization, including relationships of power. The settled communities along the Euphrates and Nile rivers employed economic and social strategies which were markedly different from those used by oral, nomadic hunter-gatherer communities. In agricultural communities territory becomes a more fixed resource, leading to changes in self-conception and notions of the cosmos. In a sense, settlement and writing are implicated in various forms of social differentiation and therefore ideology. Writing was an elite activity from its very beginnings, a tool for the control and management of resources – including property, products and human resources. Writing was also a tool for the production of political identity and the justification of privilege. It is not a question of whether the pen or the sword is mightier: it is rather a question of controlling them both.

Literacy, that is, is implicated in power and its transmutation during the period to modernity and beyond. What is interesting about the settlement process and the establishment of feudalistic social systems is that writing remained very much an exclusive practice. However, as the administration and economy of these systems became larger and more complex, the field of power began to extend and literacy served as a source and prize for those who would challenge the status quo. The administration of a complex feudal system facilitated the spread of the technology of writing, allowing alternative ideologies to challenge the dominant order. Manuscript books facilitated new forms of supplementary and sharable memory that were not confined by time and space. While the principal communicative form remained oral, the book became a new resource for exploring ideas and thoughts, some of which had been regarded as seditious. The flexibility of authorship – each scribe or copier might add or extract details of a book – permitted a certain anonymity and uncertainty. It was not until the introduction of movable typeface and large-scale printing machines that mass literacy was possible.

Again, there is the temptation to assume that the introduction of the Gutenberg printing press (first book published around 1451–3) led to specific cultural effects. This is not the case. Movable print had been used in China some time around AD 600 but was not applied in Europe until social and cultural forces had combined to construct a need. This need was associated with the development of a new and increasingly powerful group of merchants and traders, and the continuing complexity of social, economic and political administration. What is clear, however, is that mass printing facilitated the spread of literacy and with it ideology and ideas. While clearly this took some centuries to accomplish, print culture might be characterized in the following terms:

1 *Economy*. The printed, vernacular Bible was the first mass-produced capitalist product. Books, therefore, were both products and conduits of new ideas and ideologies. The vernacular Bible, in particular, was a clear challenge to the exclusivity of Latin scholarship and the power of Roman Catholicism. A vernacular Bible cracked the closed system of knowledge control which only Latin readers and writers could previously access. The printed book, therefore, becomes the ensign for a rising middle class (and bourgeois capitalism) as they access and create new forms of knowledge.

2 *Authorship*. This provides a new way of defining the individual and the ideology of individualism. The Copyright Act (England 1709) announces a significant change to the way society conceives of itself and its relationship to the individual. Previously, authorship was a highly mutable and generally collective concept: as soon as it appeared, a text could be appropriated, changed, copied and used by anyone with access to the material. The notion of authorship, however, comes to represent one of the key problematics of modern society, the division between the individual and the social whole. The public and the private, personal and governmental, individual rights and collective responsibilities are radically separated by modernism. Authorship represents the mind of the individual (intellectual property) within the context of complex interconnections in modern capitalist culture. Just as 'democracy' represents an effort to reunite politically these divisions, the notion of the author is presented as an aesthetic and intellectual resolution to social schizophrenia. The author, that is, becomes the idiosyncratic 'super-human' whose special attributes will articulate and overcome the opposite intensities of our modern individualism: freedom and alienation.

3 *Reason and individualism*. The existence of print further advances the concept of the rational self and composition of orderly text (and social order). Text objectifies the human mind, placing complex processes and ideas into an accessible, literate system. The high status of reason is clearly inscribed in the form and structure of a written text.

4 *The public–private divide*. Rational government becomes the nexus between public duties and private freedom. The written text facilitates the formation of democratic government and the integration of a new and inclusive social order. Written text facilitates the recording and rational distribution of government dicta, administration processes and laws.

5 *Durability*. This is further advanced in print. Concepts of history and time are reformulated; perpetuity becomes invested in the creative act, rationalized through written language. The past may be reconstructed and analysed in its own terms. The liberal humanist education is thus founded on the notion of durable and worthwhile knowledge and a

chronological, systematized presentation of the past. This chronology, of course, privileges particular events, characters and systems of causality.

6 *Privilege and standardization*. The division of knowledge carries particular difficulties for modernism. Just as mythology was employed in tribal cultures in order to overcome contradictions, print culture employed education processes to inculcate particular ideologies which justified social division and privilege. Equally, the existence of mass-produced text also encourages certain standardization in language. The arrival of the first printing press in Kent led to a standardization of a previously heterogeneous English. The Kentian dialect thus became the standard written English because it was the first English to be broadly distributed in print.

7 *Dominant ideologies*. Benedict Anderson (1991) argues that the spread of mass literacy through print facilitated the development and standardization of forms of nationalism. Not only were modes of administration and the formation of an ideology of citizenship made possible by mass literacy and mass education, the emotional sensibilities of nationalism were also rendered possible through available text. Nation, thus, became the 'imagined' community of modern social agents. Their community could no longer be seen directly but had to be experienced through the imagination. Imperialism and colonialism were necessary corollaries of this imagined community. Ideologies relating to capitalist processes, social hierarchy, sexuality and sexual norms, the family and religiosity were also distributed through the mass-produced text.

8 *Alternative ideologies*. As Alvin Gouldner (1976) has pointed out, mass-produced information such as the newspaper also facilitated the spread of alternative ideologies. Undoubtedly, print facilitated specific kinds of imagination and allegiance, certain pre-eminent ideologies, but it also facilitated opposition and sedition, pleasure and aesthetic transcendence. The text, that is, becomes the source of escape and transgression, as well as obedience.

Telegraphy

Walter Benjamin's famous essay 'The work of art in the age of mechanical reproduction' (1977, orig.) refers to a significant shift in modern understanding of art and popular culture. According to Benjamin, the capacity of film art to be copied and to be watched simultaneously by innumerable audiences significantly alters the cultural status of art and its author. Benjamin's essay acknowledges that the notions of authenticity and privilege have been significantly deconstructed by the application of electricity and mechanical processes. The broadcasting of images and information could no longer be confined by the limits of space and time. In fact, the processes of mechanical and electrical reproduction had begun well before the ascent of Hollywood cinema. As James Carey has explained, 'the innovation of the telegraph can stand metaphorically for all the innovations that ushered in the modern phase of history and determined, even to this day, the major lines of development of American communications' (1989: 203). For Carey, the most 'obvious and innocent' fact about the significance of the telegraph is that it enabled for the first time the separation of communications from the spatial limits of transportation. The application of electricity to communications allowed human contact to be constituted directly and immediately beyond the constraints of time over space.

Telegraphy, in fact, heralds the beginnings of both telecommunications, including networked computer communications systems like the Internet, and the electrical broadcast media: radio, film and television. Henry Morse's codification of electrical current into a binary system of dots and dashes (1838, Morse Code) not only facilitated the reunification of the United States after the Civil War (1861–2), but also produced significant effects in networking global communications. As with newsprint, however, this networking of communications produced contradictory effects through opportunities for greater homogenization and diversification of knowledge, identity, ideology and culture. Most obviously, the telegraph further enhanced the administrative powers of the state, and the processing of national and international trade. It contributed to the creation of the first great industrial monopoly, Western Union, and facilitated the consolidation and networking of major news services. In colonial outposts, the laying of the Atlantic and Pacific cables in the latter part of the nineteenth century produced two quite distinctly homogenizing effects:

1   The relative cheapness of newsprint had facilitated the proliferation of newspapers (and ideologies) during the nineteenth century. However, for English-speaking colonies like Canada, New Zealand and Australia, the provision of local news could not fully ameliorate the tyranny of distance and the profound sense of cultural isolation. News from London or New York might take as long as nine months to be received and reprinted. The arrival of international cable news allowed immediate contact with the outside world for the first time. The growing trend toward a diversity of news styles and content in the colonies was quite suddenly shattered by the provision of news from the centres of global knowledge and culture. Local news was forced to the margins as the important information from Europe and America was centralized.

2   The great expense of telegraphed information from overseas led to the syndication of news product. The major newspapers in the English-speaking colonies pooled their resources and shared information. Smaller papers couldn't afford the cabled news. They went broke or were bought up. After the arrival of telegraphy, the number of news sources in Australia and Canada, for example, was dramatically reduced and the conditions were prepared for the development of major news conglomerates. Into the twentieth century, the larger news corporations were able to take advantage of their competitive position and form even larger and more powerful news information centres. These centres thus homogenized news stories as they contributed to the hegemony of cultural imperialism.

For non-English-speaking colonies, the arrival of telegraphy created conditions for the greater assertion of centralized, colonial control. Distance had insulated the colonies from excessive interference from the colonial centres; however, telegraphy was used to strengthen the cultural and political impact of imperialism and the construction of colonized identities and cultural landscapes. Locally stationed colonial administrators were now subject to constant surveillance and the imposition of the urban centre's interests.

James Carey (1989) has argued that telegraphy, in fact, underscores the production of particular forms of ideology and consciousness. In particular, the costing of telegraphy by the word encouraged the development of a 'parsimonious' or 'minimalist' writing style. News stories which were dispatched on the telegraph discarded all redundancies, including complex ideas, language tropes and excessively descriptive phrases. The writing style of authors like Ernest Hemingway became a paradigm for all correspondents using the telegraph lines. More than this, however, the speed and volume of telegraphic information produced new forms of social and commercial organization which stripped the language of its personality, forming processes and protocols which were essentially impersonal, commercial and rule-driven. Communications theory, law, ethics, religion, and 'common sense' produced the necessary structures for impersonal communication, leading to new forms of consciousness and the naturalization of relations through etiquette. Much the same might be said of the introduction of email, which is going through a similar transformation and production of new knowledge and etiquettes. Like emailers, telegraph users had to develop a re-conceptualized time and space, and their own sense of locally constituted identity.

As Carey points out, however, the production of a communications system through the conduit of 'electricity' seemed to bring together, for the American mind at least, the divergent poles of modernism and modernization. That is, electricity and electrical communication brought into a more contiguous relationship capitalist materialism and the 'spirit' or ethos of individualism and individual transcendence. America's parallel histories of frontier materialist secularism, on the one hand, and religious emancipation, on the other, seem to achieve some level of confluence in the commercial and 'ethereal' qualities of electricity. The miracle of electrical energy could be deployed for the greater commercial power of individuals and the nation;

electrical communications would bring the American community together, but in a decidedly commercial context.

Broadcast Culture

This same messianic aura was deployed in the transformation of telegraphy into a point-to-point radio system, and ultimately to broadcast radio. This transformation was led initially by amateur enthusiasts, though World War I alerted governments and military officials to the importance of two-way field communications and the potential of a broadcast system. The original telegraphy acts in Britain, Australasia, Canada and the US were extended to include the word 'voice'. With the invention of the thermonic valve, which facilitated voice amplification, broadcast radio transmission fell immediately under the control of centralized governmental powers. Raymond Williams (see 1968, 1974) has suggested a number of reasons for the developing interest in radio broadcasting:

1   Accelerating social and geographic mobility in the early years of the twentieth century led to an increased potential for alienation and isolation. Combined with the increasing insecurities associated with international relations and internal economic stress, the potential for dislocation and the fracturing of community sharpened demand for a nodal and unifying discourse. Radio's human quality (the human voice) brought an immediacy and 'personality' to the imagined community of nation.

2   The social intensification of the small family home and independent dwelling space created a content of reception. Urbanization and the fracturing of old communities were accompanied by the

rise of the family as a social and economic unit. The family home became a source of consumption and private pleasure; radio facilitated governmental and commercial penetration into the private sphere.

3   Industrialists themselves may have understood the potential for profit. The radio, that is, constituted a commodity in itself, but more importantly offered the facility for advertising other products directly into the home. The radio, therefore, was heavily marketed as a consumer commodity.

We might also add a fourth reason to Williams' list. That is, governments themselves had identified the potential of the radio medium for gaining direct access to the minds and actions of their citizenry. While people had felt the need to be connected with each other in a mass society, governments would identify the potential of the radio for control, regimentation and propaganda. Certainly, the tight scheduling of radio programmes (including regimes of morning exercise and ablution) indicates a certain homogenizing intention in radio culture. Theodor Adorno and Max Horkheimer (1972) make the point that radio and later TV broadcasting were designed to control citizens through a certain instrumental rationality: that is, the technology and its content constituted forms of controlling ideology. Certainly, the Nazi propaganda minister, Joseph Goebbels, made sure that every citizen in Germany had access to a radio so that he or she could hear the word of the Führer directly and immediately.

The 'miracle' of radio, as it was promoted during the 1920s and 1930s, brought the sound of human voices into the the everyday lives of ordinary people. Marshall McLuhan's characterization of radio as 'the tribal drum' and the 'hottest'

of all media indicates the substantial appeal of a medium which amplified the human voice, bringing music, news and information directly and immediately into the private sphere of the home. The discourse of radio changed dramatically during this period, transforming the apparatus from a piece of tinkerer's technology into a fashionable and highly desirable domestic commodity. In fact, the introduction of the radio as domestic furniture marked the beginnings of commodity sexualization. Elegant and attractive young women were deployed in advertising to construct this confluence of sexual appeal and progressive media consumption. The radio became sexualized as women's bodies became the convergent public–private figures of domestic consumption. Advertising also promoted the new technology as in terms of its putative magical powers: the marriage of sound waves, sex and electricity was said to cure cancer and facilitate communication with the dead.

The arrival of TV might have spelled the death of radio, and, again, commercial, governmental and other discourses introduced the new media in revolutionary terms. McLuhan's famous 'global village' comment described a world in which TV became the information staple for all the world's citizens. Radio, however, like the technologies of orality, writing and print, maintained itself through a redefinition of role and cultural function. In particular, the application of transistor technology and the miniature battery permitted a new mobility. The radio voice changed from one of authority to one of youthful transgression. Rock and roll music and the emergence of youth culture during the 1950s and 1960s created a demand for new forms of commodification, leisure and communicative pleasure. As youth sought a space beyond the surveillance of senior generations and within the community of their peers, the transistor radio became adopted into a new cultural formation. The continuous music format, Top 40, and advertising directed specifically toward youth markets, all came to characterize new social and cultural practices. The TV displaced the radio from its central domestic location, but the radio lived on in youth parties, cars and other forms of mobile social practice.

ERIC MICHAELS: TECHNOLOGY AND CULTURAL DISSONANCE

Public Broadcasting and Diversity

One of the key debates in contemporary broadcasting relates to the ongoing viability and relevance of publicly funded broadcasting services. While the US established a privately funded broadcast system very early in the twentieth century, the United Kingdom established a purely publicly-funded system, and Australia, New Zealand and Canada developed a dual broadcasting system: private and publicly funded. These publicly funded broadcast systems, in most cases, had developed charters which insisted on their separation from direct government control. The aim of this 'hands-off' approach to public broadcasting was to facilitate the production of objective information which would serve the interests of the nation, national culture and national democratic institutions. In many respects, the public broadcasters in both radio and television have sought to serve the wider interests of good governance outside the specific interests of a particular, party-based government of the day. In this sense, public broadcasting has been built into the architecture of the modern democratic state, feeding quality information to the citizenry and supporting the highest ideals of public information and the formation of broadly based national interests. In postcolonized territories like Australia and Canada, these interests are also tinged with a form of national identity-building and protection, maintaining and supporting a national culture which is deluged with the interests and imagery of the United States and Great Britain.

Against this ideal, however, public broadcasters have not always managed to avoid government interference (see Scammell, 1989). Conservative governments, in particular, have often had a troubled relationship with publicly funded journalists and fictionalists who may be highly critical of the government's economic and social agenda. The 'national interest', that is, has often become a point of significant debate when journalists challenge conservative ideologies. Not surprisingly the assault by conservative governments on public enterprises during the last decades of the twentieth century led to a substantial contraction in funding allocations to the public broadcasters. What is a little more surprising, however, is the position of postmodern media theorists who are also opposed to the funding of public broadcasting. These postmodernists argue that public broadcasters in Britain (BBC), Canada (CBC) and Australia (ABC) assume a privileged social position which homogenizes national interests as an anglophone, middle-class and masculine perspective. Public broadcasters, that is, reduce the diversity of a nation to a nodal, encompassing and centralizing voice. Objective information, according to the postmodernists, is a ruse, a camouflage for a highly particular and elitist reading of culture and nation.

A new and unusual allegiance has developed, therefore, between the commercial de-regulators and the postmodernists, both of whom reject the model of privileged public broadcasting as an anathema to diversity and free expression. However, while commercial interests may see the public broadcaster as a waste of money or antithetical to free-market government policies, the postmodernist perspective tends rather to oppose the perceived elitism of the public broadcaster, preferring a form of diversified, multicultural and multi-interested narrowcasting. If public money is to be spent, the postmodernists argue, then it ought to be spent on a wide field of narrow interests, rather than on an homogenizing and artificial national public broadcaster.

Eric Michaels and Community TV

Clearly, this debate between forms of public, private and community media transmission relates to broader questions about the relevance and nature of the putative global village. Eric Michaels was an American anthropologist who studied the media experiences of Australian Aborigines. Michaels' work illustrates how the impact of broadcasting and the arrival of new media in a globalizing context produces significant cultural tensions and transformations. In a sense, his work functions as a cultural microcosm, drawing into focus various dimensions of media and technological culture. Michaels himself rejects vehemently McLuhan's periodization approach to the media, insisting that the relativism and transitional nature of culture indicates a more dynamic and fluid relationship between various cultural and technological experiences.

This transculturalism 'constructs' technologies and their meanings through the everyday discourses and practices of ordinary people. Michaels investigated the impact of new media technologies on the Warlpiri people, an isolated community in the Central Desert of Australia. These

people, who have survived a traumatic hundred-year history of European contact, continue significant cultural practices, including traditional forms of hunting and gathering, forms of social organization, lores and religious activities. The group has rejected continuous attempts to impose literate technologies and practices, most particularly through missionaries in the early part of the twentieth century and later the imposition of European schooling (Michaels, 1985, 1986, 1994). Having resisted literate culture, however, the Warlpiri became exposed to Hollywood video recordings in the early 1980s and then television broadcasting via the new Australian satellite system AUSSAT from the mid-1980s. Michaels explains how the fundamentally oral culture engaged with and adapted the new electronic culture brought into their lives by the spreading effects of global postmodernism.

We have available to us a raft of theories which might explain the ways the Warlpiri people interacted with and made meanings out of Hollywood texts like *Rambo*: polysemy, phenomenology, poststructuralism. What is clear, however, is that the Warlpiri concerned themselves with issues relevant to their own cultural interests and practices. The dominant reading, therefore, was constituted from issues of tribal and familial connection, rather than matters of national interest, Hollywood heroism and modernist imagining of the super-human. For the Warlpiri the key questions surrounded the disconnecting of relationships: Who is caring for the sister? What effect is this death having on the family? Michaels' analysis of textual reception clearly implicates aspects of audience/reception theory as it has been developed through the work of Ien Ang, David Morley and others (see Chapter 8). Michaels' ethnography, however, is as much concerned with the damaging effects of these new technologies at the level of reception and the means by which the Warlpiri reconstruct the technology to enhance their cultural interests.

This dual interest is illustrated in Michaels' report to the Australian government on the impact of the TV satellite AUSSAT. *The Aboriginal Invention of Television* (1986) contrasts TV knowledge and information with Aboriginal knowledge. Specifically, TV's ubiquity, availability and broad distribution contrast with Aboriginal knowledge, which is constituted through restricted social access, organizational divisions of status, role and authority. Aboriginal knowledge, that is, is highly localized and constitutes the underlying fabric of social relationships. Michaels summarizes the impact of the AUSSAT imagery and information in the following terms:

1   *Usurping the prerogative of senior people in the group.* Like most other oral communities, the Warlpiri 'store' information in the memories of privileged, senior individuals or 'elders'. The infinitely accessible information that is mediated outside an individual significantly undermines the position of senior men and women, leading necessarily to an unravelling of the general social fabric.

2   *Challenge to the localism of knowledge which is the basis of autonomy of the symbolic exchange system.* Aborigines wish to use the new media to record traditional cultural content, but when the information is broadcast it loses its autonomy and integrity. Its wide dissemination compromises the important value of the content in the information exchange system. As with other oral cultures, Warlpiri knowledge is embedded in the immediate context of telling. The removal of the context alters radically the meaning and value of the content.

3   *Challenges to the integrity and authority of the Dreaming.* The principal source of cultural knowledge is the Dreaming. For example, Warlpiri people are worried that romantic love, which underscores Hollywood narrative, will invade Dreaming rituals and kinship rites, disturbing laws on preferential marriage and prohibitions of incest.

4   *Violation of mortuary rites.* There is also concern that video recordings might transgress laws prohibiting the exhibition of the name, images and property of deceased people. While seeking to use videos for cultural preservation, the Warlpiri confront the inevitable problem of displaying the deceased (Michaels, 1994: 1 32).

The negative impact of AUSSAT and video recorders threatened serious violation of Warlpiri cultural integrity. And yet, as Michaels notes, the new technologies also offered possibilities for the culture's preservation and maintenance. At the production level, that is, the Warlpiri were able to extend the technology to suit their particular cultural interests, confirming the view of a number of Third World and indigenous peoples ethnographers that 'electronic media have proved remarkably attractive and accessible to such people where often print and literacy have not' (Michaels, 1994: 82 1). Michaels argues, in fact, that the sort of periodizing which places technologies and technological culture in a lineal sequence fails entirely to grasp the complex associations that exist between communicative experiences:

Aborigines and other 'developing' people do not conform to this sequence, and produce some very different media histories. For philosophers and historians such as Ong, Innins or even Lévi-Strauss, who posit special equivalences between oral and electronic society, these ethnographic cases ought to prove especially revealing. (1994: 82 2)

The Eurocentricism and logocentricism which privilege writing and reason and which invest themselves in an ideology of technological progressivism treat the present as an historical pinnacle toward which all previous history leads. Michaels argues that the adoption of the new technology by the Warlpiri entirely deconstructs such a notion, illustrating rather that culture is necessarily transitory and technology is merely a servant of that fluidity.

Micheals explains the Aboriginal adoption of television in the Western Desert in terms of the Warlpiri's attempts to overcome the negative effects of social and cultural transition. Thus, while the Warlpiri and other Aboriginal groups had resisted a hundred years of literate invasion, the adoption of electronic media constitutes an actual (re)invention of this more appropriate technology. It is not, as McLuhan and other technological determinists suggest, that the existence of a technology necessarily produces particular effects; rather, the technology is adapted according to the interests and needs of the community. It is re-made, re-shaped and re-configured with meaning and value by the users. Michaels' ethnographic investigations demonstrate how Aboriginal groups are able to produce and broadcast television programming which supports and enhances Aboriginal culture, language and cultural identity.

Michaels' ethnography also confirms the idea that the technology produces its own regime of meaning; the medium deployed in the telling of the story demonstrably affects the nature of the text. Even so, the texts produced by the Warlpiri were not mimics of Hollywood textual forms, but maintained significant characteristics drawn from traditional Warlpiri stories

and story-telling. The Warlpiri texts, for example, told stories in a hybridized documentary form which tended to deny the European fact–fiction dichotomy. Michaels speculates that Warlpiri TV texts will need to learn the whole notion of 'fiction' since traditional Warlpiri genres – sacred, hunting and monster stories – are fixed by belief. When the belief declines, the notion of fiction will be installed.

We might summarize the importance of Michaels' and other anthropological studies of the impact of new technologies on traditional societies in the following terms:

1   Technological determinist approaches which describe history in terms of the development of new technologies are First World-centric and fundamentally flawed. Different people adopt new technologies at different times and in different ways.

2   This periodizing is particularly problematic for those non-literate societies which skip historical literacy and adopt image-based technologies.

3   For various ethnically constituted cultural groups, community broadcasting offers much more than centralized and publicly funded broadcasting systems. Community broadcast allows the community to speak for itself, construct its own agenda, programming, celebrity and identity. Community broadcast contributes significantly to the preservation and reconstitution of local culture.

4   Therefore, the introduction of modern media technologies can have positive as well as negative effects. These effects relate directly to questions of global homogenization and diversification (see Chapter 10). Local cultures are changed by the presence of external media technologies and discourses, but the interaction between traditional and

external cultural elements tends to produce new, hybrid cultural forms.

ELECTRONIC DEMOCRACY

Modern Technology and Politics

One of the most notable features of electrical and broadcast media is their capacity to reach large numbers of people. As we have seen, the 'media effects' theories assume that the transmission of a message will necessarily produce particular effects on the attitudes, emotions and behaviours of particular audience members (see Chapters 2 and 8). These effects may work for evil (corruption of children, social and political domination, brain-washing, etc.), or for good (overcoming alienation, public education, informing electorates, etc). Among many others, Eric Michaels' work shows the limitations of these theories, not only in the ways audiences receive and interpret texts, but also in terms of the production and distribution of texts. In this sense, national broadcasters tend to produce texts that will have the widest possible appeal; community broadcasters like the Warlpiri produce local or narrowcast texts. Michaels, along with numerous other communications activists, argues that government policies which privilege national broadcasters over community broadcasters compromise the capacity of democratic and cultural politics to advance minority cultures and interests.

In fact, Michaels' work points to wider problems in the relationship between communications technology and democracy. As we have noted, the confluence of various social factors – urbanism, industrialism, rationalism and the spread of print technology – provided the underpinnings for liberal humanist democracy. Modern societies, in fact, attempt to resolve fundamental conflicts between individual and collective interests through the formation of democratic institutions; these institutions apply strategies of resolution, including the delegation of power by citizens to the state and the reciprocal return of that power through processes of governmental 'responsibility'. This 'rational system' of government was rendered possible by the recording and reasoning facility of print. Printed material not only facilitated legal and constitutional processes (law), its orderly and lineal arrangements of information also provided the ideal facility for rational and reasoned thinking. As the foundation of modern liberalism, John Locke's *Two Treatises of Government* (1651) insists that human freedom is a contingency of individual and governmental reason – each is the product of the other.

Through the progress of modernism, the media, most particularly the newspaper, became the 'fourth estate'. That is, along with government, the church and legal institutions, the news media came to represent an independent pillar in the structure of the modern democratic state. In this ideal sense, the news media supposedly informed the citizenry, providing objectively gathered and presented information necessary for debate within the public sphere. The arrival of telegraphy, as we have noted, served to reinforce the reach, speed and volumes of information for public dissemination. John Hartley (1996) argues that the self-proclaimed impartiality, rationalism and objectivity of modern news media are both exaggerated and illusory. Hartley claims, in fact, that all discourses are politically and ideologically 'positioned'. Moreover, the mass literacy so keenly sought by social and political reformers of the nineteenth century has been deployed as much for popular and sensate consumption as for the interests of political activism or rational public debate. According to Hartley, journalism, as the primary literate practice of modernity, combines intellectual and sensational experiences:

> Journalism is *the* sense-making practice of modernity (the condition) and popularizer of modernism (the ideology); it is a product and promoter of modern life. ... So much a feature of modernity is journalism that it is easy to describe each in terms of the other – both journalism and modernity are products of European (and Euro-sourced) societies over the last three or four centuries; both are associated with the development of exploration, scientific thought, industrialization, political emancipation and imperial expansion. Both promote notions of freedom, progress and universal enlightenment, and are associated with the breaking down of traditional knowledges and hierarchies, and their replacement with abstract bonds of virtual communities linked by their media. (1996: 33)

For Hartley, newsmaking is embedded in all the major and minor events, institutions and personal experiences which constitute modern life – including issues of sexuality and desire.

Televisual Politics

This dimension of modernism, however, extends well beyond literate culture and newsprint. Indeed, the sensate experiences which Hartley associates with the popular news media are clearly implicated in the development of aural and televisual broadcast media. Indeed, the move from written-language information to electronic media, as Michaels explains, re-enlivens the immediacies and sensory experiences that had typified oral culture. The mediation of politics through televisual representation, in particular, inscribes democracy with a new kind of cultural presence and

personality. The rigidity of institutionalized political and legal processes is compressed as human imagery. Politics becomes the 'face of politics'; official records and political forums become iconographed in the televisualized personality of the politician. Democracy thus becomes mediated not so much through delegation or representative government as in televisual campaigns, doorstop interviews, 'grabs' and news values which favour action over detail, personalities over policy, conflict over consideration.

In televisual politics the multiple and opposing claims which democratic institutions seek to accommodate, if not reconcile, in policy become highly visible. The craft of the contemporary politician is to navigate the complex of claims and discourses while maintaining a semblance of integration, consistency and honesty. Thus, language games played out in televisual politics might be better characterized as persuasion games. Politicians are trained to avoid direct answers to media questions when these might alienate particular members of the electorate. Politicians use the media, in fact, to repeat simple and generally non-specific policy positions. The media audience is available for persuasion; the televisual politician seeks to inculcate party views through various forms of personality and narrative construction. The politician uses the media to tell his or her story through various forms of narrative story-telling. To this extent, televisual politicians assume the proportion of a particular kind of media celebrity, one who operates in a highly fluid relationship with the truth.

This unhinging of the truth has become a significant feature of contemporary institutional politics. A belief that truth can be located and distributed is one of the informing principles of modern journalism and, in turn, modern democratic institutions. However, while it may be quite feasible to present a version of the truth in quite simple terms – yesterday the politician said this – it is much more difficult to locate truth in complex issues involving variant social needs. Not only do politicians tell lies quite directly, but they also hedge or obscure the truth in order to satisfy variant and opposite social interests. The availability of guns in the US, for example, may be valuable for certain interest groups, such as gun manufacturers, farmers or gangsters. But when we are told that the policy of gun availability is necessary for the protection of American 'freedom', the truth of that claim becomes far more dubious.

Marxism, poststructuralism, postmodernism and cultural studies theory have all told us that 'truth' is generally constructed out of particular social interests; the broad social acceptance of that truth is a contingency of the truth-tellers' social power. Televisual politics in contemporary culture is clearly a game of persuasion where the various interests, including the interests of dominant groups and ideologies, are played out. As previously noted, Jean Baudrillard's book *The Gulf War Did Not Take Place* (1995) illustrates how contemporary broadcast media engage in the persuasion game to produce the effects of truth. According to Baudrillard, the Gulf War was not a war about oil resources and sovereignty. It was not even a war in which the American military and political elite were seeking to discipline the non-Western world. Rather, this was a war constructed out of the emptiness of the news media, a publicity campaign which had neither source nor objective. For Baudrillard, the Gulf War was effectively a language war, another simulacrum, an impersonation of a war, a ghost that produced no effect. This is not a claim that 'truth is the first casualty of war' – where propaganda distorts the truth in order to control the citizenry. Baudrillard is claiming that the new media

have no truth to offer and that the world is merely replete with vacuous truth claims and counter-claims:

> Electronic war no longer has any political objective strictly speaking: it functions as a preventative electroshock against any future conflict. Just as in modern communication there is no longer any interlocutor, so in this electronic war there is no longer any enemy, there is only a refractory element which must be neutralized and consensualized. This is what the Americans seek to do, these missionary people bearing electroshocks which will shepherd everybody towards democracy. (1995: 84)

This publicity campaign war, then, draws the whole of humanity toward a lowest common denominator, the denominator of a democracy that is fundamentally emptied of content. And as far as Baudrillard is concerned, this publicity campaign which constitutes modern electronic media undoubtedly implicates us all in its phantasmagoria (1995: 64).

Not all commentary on electronic media is as pessimistic and deterministic as Baudrillard's account. In fact, there are some commentators who suggest that the new broadcast media provide greater access and accountability in the relationship between politicians and the electorate. The new visibility of politicians since the advent of TV has certainly intensified the relationship between public and private life. Even so, the culture of the personality politician has intensified the notion of leadership and the iconography of the individual. This personality politics and the centralization of the leader is manifest in US presidential-style campaigns and Westminster campaigns where prime minister and opposition leader have taken on presidential proportions for the media. In a sense, the election campaigns have been constructed in parallel ways to TV popularity quests; celebrity politicians are presented in carefully managed profiles as much through personality magazines as the nightly news. The development of the primaries system of selecting American presidential candidates seems to have extended the process of election campaigns, providing highly valuable copy for the sale of newspapers and advertising space on television.

This commodification of political celebrity is clearly associated with broader cultural interests in stardom and celebrity. The election of Ronald Reagan, a B-grade Hollywood actor, to the presidency in the United States symbolizes the confluence, especially in America, of political power and entertainment celebrity. It is sometimes argued that the absence in American cultural and political history of an aristocratic ruling class provided an ideal context for the ascent of entertainment celebrities. This putative egalitarianism draws political power from the people, and allows personality and individualism a freer range than was possible in the aristocratic legacies of Europe. America, in this sense, may have been waiting for its Hollywood star system and a president who could fulfil both political and celebrity roles.

DIGITAL DEMOCRACY

Over the past two decades the broadcast media have begun to surrender some of their homogeneity and nodalism. As mentioned earlier, satellite TV and the introduction of cable media services are facilitating the emergence of new, more specialized or narrowcast forms of media dissemination. Thus, while much of this increase has merely replicated existing texts and media models, some genuine variations have occurred, especially through community broadcasting. Greater variation, more precise textual targeting and the emergence of ethnic and community

broadcasting have, in fact, presented an interesting challenge for political theorists. Some would argue that these variabilities produce fracturing effects on the state and the unity promised by democratic institutions. Those commentators who maintain a faith in the efficacy of integrated social structures and the notion of delegated power and responsible government sometimes accuse media fragmentation of undermining the unifying force of the nation-state and its principles of 'shared values' and truth. This traditional, democratic model acknowledges the importance of variant voices, but insists on the pre-eminence of a shared consciousness, a national culture and a government which can resolve significant differences through the construction of consensus rule.

Other theorists have claimed that the fragmentation of the media is vastly overdue and that the new postmodern, information-based state is a more equitable and genuine political formation, one that respects and encourages the needs and interests of individuals and minority communities. The valorization of individualism and media diversity parallels broader theoretical interests in difference and otherness – the postmodern cultural politics which celebrates the margins (see Chapters 7 and 10). Networked computer communication which draws together a range of media and communicative functions has been particularly welcomed by commentators interested in cultural fragmentation and media diversity (see Pollock and Smith, 1999; Walch, 1999). A cultural politics which emphasizes the liberational dimensions of democracy has formed around interactive media systems. The flexibility of these systems can be summarized in the following terms:

1   Computer networked communication (CNC) may be broadcast, allowing

users to present information across vast global territories.

2 CNC may also facilitate highly targeted information transmission. Information may be directed at individuals, communities or interest groups. As with the more broadcast functions, these narrow-casts are not contained by space and time.

3 CNC is highly interactive and, compared with other forms of broadcasting, is inexpensive and accessible.

Thus, the new medium of interactive computer communication enables users to produce, distribute and consume information and entertainment texts through the complete range of communicative casting.

Nicholas Negroponte (1995) claims that the new media will thoroughly transform social, cultural and political processes. Economies in the 'information age' will be based upon the exchange of weightless information 'bits', rather than manufactured products of matter and atoms. Industrialism, with its large-scale factories and ports and its manufacturing of waste products, will be replaced by speed-of-light, non-polluting informate economies. Digitized information will thus supersede the cumbersome and wasteful forms of atomic information delivery, including the most outmoded media of all: newspapers, magazines and books. With its great advantages of flexibility, error correction and data compression, digitized information and delivery offer enormous possibilities for social and economic reformation: 'Wholly new content will emerge from being digital, as well as new players, new economic models, and a likely cottage industry of information and entertainment' (Negroponte, 1995: 18). Being digital, then, will most certainly release the everyday citizen from the clutches of large media corporations; in an age of optimism, Negroponte assures us, the negative consequences of computerization will be subsumed by its potential for liberation, social harmony and individual expression:

> The harmonizing effect of being digital is already apparent as previously partitioned disciplines and enterprises find themselves collaborating, not competing. A previously missing common language emerges, allowing people to understand across boundaries. ... But more than anything, my optimism comes from the empowering nature of being digital. The access, the mobility and the ability to effect change are what will make the future so different from the present. (1995: 230)

Negroponte's vision of a complete and sharable global language seems finally to have fulfilled Descartes's Enlightenment dream of a universal language. While Descartes imagined that language would have been mathematics, for Negroponte it is an ideal of digital information and its universal attachment to capitalist economics and liberal humanist institutions. A new democracy will be activated through 'all information for all people at all times'. Negroponte and numerous others identify the new facility as empowering, realizing the elusive democratic ideal of an informed public (cf Barney, 2000; Slavin, 2000).

POSTMODERN COMPUTER POLITICS

Numerous writers have discussed the political potential of the new computer networked communication systems. While some, like Negroponte, have emphasized the capacity of the networked computer to support institutional democracy, a number of 'postmodern'-influenced writers have spoken more generally about the computer's liberational potential. This section summarizes the major features of these arguments.

Hypertext Writing

Generally speaking, 'hypertext' refers to computer-based writing, though a number of commentators restrict the term to networked communication such as email, chat-rooms, bulletin boards and Internet pages. The imperative to 'be digital' is drawing together the full range of public and academic discourses, 'forcing a radical realignment of the alphabetic and graphic components of ordinary textual communication' (Lanham, 1993: 3). Thus the hypertext (see Landow, 1992; Snyder, 1996), or 'hypermedia', in McLuhan's terms, is seen to revolutionize writing, extend human experience and consciousness beyond the ossification of author-centred, lineal and fixed text: 'an electronic text only exists in the act of reading – in the interaction between the reader and textual structure, ... the writing space' (Boller, 1992: 20; see also Boller, 1993). The writing space, that is, becomes the field for the player of these new language games. According to hypertext enthusiasts like Ilana Snyder (1996), Richard Lanham (1993) and Mark Poster (1995), the qualities of this new hypertext space are intrinsically more democratic and liberational than older forms of print and script writing:

1 Hypertext is infinitely erasable and therefore it is not fixed in rigid forms and structures. For paper writing, especially formally published writing, the text remains as an archive, fixed in a stable relationship between author and reader. Hypertext is less easy to control and possess because it is necessarily ephemeral. The writer has more flexibility and creativity as hypertext facilitates a more adventurous and less inhibiting writing space. The concept of writing errors disappears.

2 The capacity of computers to correct grammar and spelling is far more user-friendly than printed writing. Hypertext permits greater access to people with lower education and language writing skills. Writing becomes less elitist and more available to all levels of literacy. It also facilitates language use by those of non-English-speaking backgrounds, thus supporting a multiculturalism as it abrogates the privileging of native English-speakers.

3 Email writing has helped transform organizational structures, facilitating contact across hierarchical borders. Like telegraphy, email reduces the status and status etiquette of the communicators. Email is a less formal and more open writing space which also facilitates wide-reaching communication between people and without the limits of bodily presence.

4 Hypertext writing is inexpensive compared with older forms of writing production. It facilitates 'desktop' publishing, which provides much wider access to creative and expressive activities. Expensive printing processes can now be by-passed and levels of specialization and training are no longer at issue.

5 The Internet provides an extremely accessible and inexpensive facility for distribution of ideas and creative activities. Whereas artists and writers would once have had to rely on expensive infrastructures and the gate-keeping processes of publishers, distributors and retailers, they can now use the Internet for global distribution and contact.

6 Hypertext also facilitates the dissolution of expressive categorizations, especially between alphabetic writing, graphics, video and animation. Especially when published on the Internet, these expressive modes can be comfortably

combined. Hypertext, therefore, doesn't privilege writing over imagery, but enables a free flow of textual experiences. Thus the Enlightenment privileging of *logos* (the word) and reason is fundamentally undermined.

7   Hypertext, therefore, restores the experiential immediacies of oral cultures. The author is no longer the privileged 'authority' of the text since the Internet dissolves many of the distinguishing and fixed characteristics of print culture. In particular, the Internet text is interactive and infinitely reproducible. Readers can take a text and make it their own. Texts are fully interactive, conducive to an unending chain of creativity. Individuals are constituted by the text in a community of knowledge and creativity without the solidifications of copyright and the authority of the author.

8   Internet writing also challenges logocentric structures or narratives which form hierarchies of reading and writing. Webpages are not written in lineal sequences but operate as mimesis, imitations of the mind. Just as the human mind links various zones of knowledge, memory and imagination, hypertext forms links between various sites or zones of knowledge. These hyperlinks are formed through association rather than lineal sequence. Readers access information as it suits their own interest, rather than through the logical and pre-arranged order imposed by the author. Linking, therefore, is a more democratic pattern, one which allows the free flow of ideas and sensibilities. Sensation, impulse, emotions and imagery are no longer subsumed beneath the authority of logic and pre-determined order.

In summary, then, hypertext writing is regarded by its enthusiasts as intrinsically liberational, most particularly as it appears to overcome many of the limitations and privileges of modernist print culture. It allows for a more flexible, de-centred and accessible creativity which dissolves privileged hierarchies of knowledge. Computer networked communication would thus be a personalized media form where information is released from the control of knowledge and 'knowers' (Numberg, 1996).

Virtual Geography/ Virtual Community

In our discussions on postmodernism it was noted that the theorization of contemporary culture often focuses on the compression of time and space. Major theorists such as Lyotard, Baudrillard and Jameson have all seen the acceleration of time and the overcoming of spatial or geographic separation as fundamentally problematic. However, while satellite and cable technologies have enhanced the 'televisual' congregation of previously distinct peoples and cultures into an ever-intensifying global web, these connections have been unevenly distributed and unevenly experienced. As many commentators have noted, Marshall McLuhan's 'global village' metaphor is troublesome because it fails to acknowledge the extreme differences in power and wealth that determine relationships within the village. The colonialism and imperialism that motivated modern globalism produced savage and long-lasting effects on the cultures of conquered peoples. Just as industrialism had fractured communities in the advanced world, so imperial conquest decimated tribal and agricultural communities in the non-West. McLuhan's TV village was thought to salve community and social dislocations through the mediated unification of world cultures.

These broadcast technologies, however, have tended to maintain dominant discourses of nation and imperial control. Edward Soja in *Postmodern Geographies* (1989) has noted that the reformulation of national, geographic boundaries has largely been accomplished through various forms of cultural and economic imperialism. David Harvey (1989) has made clear that multinational corporations are not so much global citizens as global raiders and rulers. The crossing of national borders by international information and entertainment corporations has not been arbitrary, but is rather a First World strategic incursion aimed at increasing market share, profit and cultural dominance. That is, broadcast media are clearly nodalized, formed around privileged economic, military and cultural zones.

Mark Poster (1995) has claimed, however, that we are moving into a more evenly distributed and less nodally controlled media epoch. In this 'second media age' the networked computer provides the ideal infrastructure for a deconstruction of centralized broadcast media. In a prescience reminiscent of Marshall McLuhan and other futurists, Poster claims that advanced technological societies are on the precipice of a cultural, social and political revolution, analogous to the emergence of an urban merchant culture in the midst of feudal society. The de-centredness of the Internet communication system necessarily produces a radical shift in the subject position of the user. A new, postmodern, informational democracy, Poster argues, is facilitated by this shifting subjectivity.

Individual users are able to connect with one another in original and necessarily de-centred forms of communication. The second media age moves the relationship between text and user into a new field of responsiveness that is no longer a predicate of differential power, wealth and infrastructure control. Thus, the 'electronic geography' of the Internet produces a

belonging and an identity position which only last as long as the user's connection to the Net. The ephemeral nature of this connection and this 'virtual geography', that is, necessarily releases the user from a fixed and stable identity or subject position. The user is now much more free as s/he moves between spaces, communities and identities. The subject no longer has to be a citizen of a nation which implicates him or her in the nation's rigid and homogeneous value system and fixed identity. The Internet geography defines the consciousness of the linked, postmodern user in a much more flexible and open manner. As a decentralized and egalitarian space, this Internet consciousness necessarily implicates a democratic and liberational subject position. This new consciousness is particularly acute as the Internet is no space at all; rather, it is an ephemeron, an abstract and invisible 'condition' which only exists in terms of the experience and connectedness of the individual user. There can be no question of control of the space, therefore, because the electronic geography is never anything more than the creation and experience of the individual user.

According to Poster, then, this new virtual geography constitutes a zone of democracy because it implicates new forms of communicative relations which are not based upon possession and differentials of power. In his book *Virtual Community* (1993), Howard Rheingold tests these theories through direct communications experience. Rheingold, an early user of networked computer communication, explains how he has formed substantial social and political relationships through the Internet. These 'virtual communities' are not constructed through spatial proximity, but are constituted through the congregation of personal interests, values and cultural predispositions. The community was formed by people who shared certain attitudes and interests, and then committed themselves to the formation of a relational space. For Rheingold, the Internet provides the ideal facility for restructuring social relationships and community, but in ways that are radically new and superior to the arbitrariness of geographic propinquity. The new community is devoid of class, gender or racial discriminations since they are essentially 'disembodied', predicates of a shared ideal, and a desire for social improvement and social empowerment. Writing from the perspective of a Californian idealism which has also produced the hippie and counterculture movements of the 1960s, Rheingold presents this new community as a political utopia. That is, the politics of the virtual community are constituted around the sheer pleasures of connection in the free space of the Internet:

> I suspect that one of the reasons for this phenomenon is the hunger for community that grows in the breasts of people around the world as more and more informal public spaces disappear from our real lives. I also suspect that these new media attract colonies of enthusiasts because CMC [Computer Mediated Communication] enables people to do things with each other in new ways, and to do altogether new kinds of things – just as telegraphy, telephone and television did. (Rheingold, 1993: 6)

What matters to Rheingold is the community-level culture which has appropriated the Internet from the control of the US defence forces and the academy. Thus the hobbyists who connected their computers to telephone lines during the 1980s established a pattern of free engagement, where the site of the Net became available for the people to use freely and without structured impositions and regulations. Charles Ess (1994) extends this notion of a community politics to argue that the Internet now constitutes that free public

sphere in which Jürgen Habermas's 'ideal speech situation' (see Chapter 7) could be realized: the Internet, that is, would become a space for democratic engagement and the production of rational and consensual communicative action. Democracy would thus return to its ideals of logical resolution, as it discarded the fixities and hegemony of institutional structure. Barney (2000) on the other hand, remains deeply suspicious of the extravagant claims of the new digital democracy.

Virtual Reality and Brain Machines: Liberation of the Mind

Subjectivity and identity have become central themes in cultural studies and cultural theory, including discussions on new technology. During the late 1980s and early 1990s a good deal of discussion about the liberational effects of computers centred on the notion of virtual reality. While some commentators use this concept quite broadly to include any levels of graphic computer simulation of experiential reality, others use the concept to refer specifically to particular simulation apparatuses which are worn directly over the body. The virtual reality suit, including helmet and gloves, completely surrounds the user in aural, visual and tactile simulations. For a number of its proponents the simulation experience represented a transcendent reality, one which could draw the user into new levels of consciousness. New Age philosophy, for example, with its emphasis on individual liberationism, ancient and Asian spiritualism, and a strange combination of alchemy and technology, has identified virtual reality as a significant pathway to expanded consciousness.

As Andrew Ross points out in his book on contemporary scientific culture, *Strange Weather* (1991), the New Age movement often presents these expanded horizons of consciousness through a theoretical confluence of scientism, technological progressivism and evangelism. The New Age theory of the 'holographic' mind, for example, draws together the operations of three distinct intellectual traditions:

1 Quantum (sub-atomic) particles constitute the smallest units and hence the building blocks of the universe.
2 Zen Buddhism constitutes the philosophy which reconciles the particulates and the complete form or structure of the universe.
3 Technology extends human capacity so that our understanding of quanta and Buddhism are formulated in consciousness. The holographic brain machine allows us to conceive of the universe in terms of its particulates and its whole. While this sort of virtual consciousness had been developed for use in the entertainment industry, Ross assures us that brain expansion remains the real aim of the machine.

Thus, a virtual reality machine like the holograph carries the potential to transform all human knowledge:

All these machines are designed to balance the left and the right side in holistic synchrony. In altered states of consciousness, brain waves become slower and deeper, moving from beta in normal waking life, to alpha, to theta, reaching delta wave levels in deep sleep. The operating hunch of these technologies is that the process of causation can be reversed; by first changing the brainwave frequency, one can induce altered states of consciousness. (Ross, 1991: 31)

The *Lawnmower Man* novels and films have explored this notion of expanded consciousness specifically in relation to virtual learning and virtual sexuality. As it has been adapted, VR has had to overcome problems of vertigo and nausea, though it has found some level of application in military, commercial and entertainment areas.

Virtual Identity

While Ross claims that these new forms of utopianism constitute a genuine political exigency, writers like Mark Poster argue that the Internet itself offers the greatest potential for the construction of new forms of identity and subjectivity which in themselves are politically transgressive. New identities and new subject positions, that is, are produced through the new context of Internet communication. Not only does the Internet facilitate community connection between marginalized peoples such as minority ethnic groups, gays, political lobby groups (feminists, environmentalists, etc.), it also allows for a more creative use of the space. Donna Haraway (1991, 1997) makes this point when she argues that the 'disembodiment' of Internet users liberates them from bodily, cultural ascriptions. That is, the user is free to create his or her own bodily conditions when interacting through email or chat groups; users are able to divest themselves of the norms and ideologies which are inscribed on their bodies by mainstream culture. The limits of sexuality, gender, ethnicity, age, appearance and disabilities lose their relevance for the Internet user. The egalitarian space of the Internet enables, therefore, a liberation of the body and a new regime of creative interaction that is abstract and eternally flexible. This abstract and self-ascribing body provides the foundation for the complete liberation of a subjectivity which can now invent and reinvent itself with unhindered creativity.

The Cyborg Manifesto

A cyborg is a cybernetic organism, a hybrid of machine and organism, a creature of social reality as well as a creature of fiction. Social reality is lived social relations, our most important political construction, a world-changing fiction. The international women's movements have constructed 'women's experience', as well as uncovered or discovered this crucial collective object. This experience is a fiction and fact of the most crucial, political kind. Liberation rests on the construction of the consciousness, the imaginative apprehension, of oppression, and so of possibility. The cyborg is a matter of fiction and lived experience that changes what counts as women's experience in the late twentieth century. This is a struggle over life and death, but the boundary between science fiction and social reality is an optical illusion.

Contemporary science fiction is full of cyborgs – creatures simultaneously animal and machine, who populate worlds ambiguously natural and crafted. Modern medicine is also full of cyborgs, of couplings between organism and machine, each conceived as coded devices, in an intimacy and with a power that was not generated in the history of sexuality. Cyborg 'sex' restores some of the lovely replicative baroque of ferns and invertebrates (such nice organic prophylactics against heterosexism). Cyborg replication is uncoupled from organic reproduction. Modern production seems like a dream of cyborg colonization work, a dream that makes the nightmare of Taylorism seem idyllic. And modern war is a cyborg orgy, coded by C3I, command-control-communication-intelligence, an $84 billion item in 1984's US defence budget. I am making an argument for the cyborg as a fiction mapping our social and bodily reality and as an imaginative resource suggesting some very fruitful couplings. Michael Foucault's biopolitics is a flaccid premonition of cyborg politics, a very open field.

By the late twentieth century, our time, a mythic time, we are all chimeras, theorized and fabricated hybrids of machine and organism; in short, we are cyborgs. The cyborg is our ontology; it gives us our politics. The cyborg is a condensed image of both imagination and material reality, the two joined centres structuring any possibility of historical transformation. In the traditions of 'Western' science and politics – the tradition of racist, male-dominant capitalism; the tradition of progress; the tradition of the appropriation of nature as resource for the productions of culture; the tradition of reproduction of the self from the reflections of the other – the relation between organism and machine has been a border war. The stakes in the border war have been the territories of production, reproduction, and imagination. This chapter is an argument for pleasure in the confusion of boundaries and for responsibility in their construction. It is also an effort to contribute to socialist-feminist culture and theory in a postmodernist, non-naturalist mode and in the utopian tradition of imagining a world without gender, which is perhaps a world without genesis, but maybe also a world without end. The cyborg incarnation is outside salvation history. Nor does it mark time on an oedipal calendar, attempting to heal the terrible cleavages of gender in an oral symbiotic utopia or post-oedipal apocalypse. As Zoe Sofoulis argues in her unpublished manuscript on Jacques Lacan, Melanie Klein, and nuclear culture, Lacklein, the most terrible and perhaps the most promising monsters in cyborg worlds are embodied in non-oedipal narratives with a different logic of repression, which we need to understand for our survival.

The cyborg is a creature in a post-gender world; it has no truck with bisexuality, pre-oedipal symbiosis, unalienated labour, or other seductions to organic wholeness through a final appropriation of all the powers of the parts into a higher unity. In a sense, the cyborg has no origin story in the Western sense – a 'final' irony since the cyborg is also the awful apocalyptic telos of the 'West's' escalating dominations of abstract individuation, an ultimate self untied at last from all dependency, a man in space. An origin story in the 'Western', humanist sense depends on the myth of original unity, fullness, bliss and terror, represented by the phallic mother from whom all humans must separate, the task of individual development and of history, the twin potent myths inscribed most powerfully for us in psychoanalysis and Marxism. Hilary Klein has argued that both Marxism and psychoanalysis, in their concepts of labour and of individuation and gender formation, depend on the plot of original unity out of which difference must be produced and enlisted in a drama of escalating domination of woman/nature. The cyborg skips the step of original unity, of identification with nature in the Western sense. This is its illegitimate promise that might lead to subversion of its teleology as star wars. (from *The Cyborg Manifesto* posted on the World Wide Web by Donna Haraway)

This new liberated subjectivity forms the basis of Donna Haraway's more radical conception of the technological body. In her 'Cyborg manifesto', published on the Internet in the late 1980s and reproduced in *Simians, Cyborgs and Women* (1991), Haraway argues the case for a utopian politics where human biology is radically enhanced by its integration with technology. This 'evolutionary' overhaul and hybridization of *Homo sapiens* would necessarily outmode hierarchical differentiations that have been historically inscribed on human biology: gender, ethnicity, health and class. While this is an 'ironic dream', Haraway's manifesto quite seriously seeks a politics in which the cyborg woman transforms social relations, 'our most important political construction'. Haraway's hybrid body, then, is transgender and ageless. As a utopian fiction, the cyborg transcends the limits of human biology and the social inscriptions of modernism:

The cyborg is resolutely committed to partiality, irony, intimacy, and perversity. It is oppositional, utopian, and completely without innocence. No longer structured by the polarity of public and private, the cyborg defines a technological polis, based partly on a revolution of social relations in the *oikos*, the household. Nature and culture are reworked; the one can no longer be the resource for appropriation or incorporation by the other. The relationships for forming wholes from parts, including those for forming polarity and hierarchical domination, are at issue in the cyborg world. (Haraway, 1991: 151)

Félix Guattari (1992) has argued similarly that the new computerized technologies reverse modernism's tendency toward machine or industrial-controlled subjectivity. These 'pseudo-stabilities' are discarded in favour of a genuine integration of machine and subjectivity: 'The machine is placed under the control of subjectivity – not a reterritorialized human subjectivity, but a new kind of machine subjectivity' (Guattari, 1992: 29). These integrated path/voices produce a polyphony of articulations which may now link into massive data banks and forms of artificial intelligence. The new, liberated subjectivities, therefore, are immensely more powerful than the nodalized media and telecommunications systems that have produced them, because they are more than merely human, and more than merely machinery. Radical politics, therefore, are conceived in terms of an evolutionary escape from the confining borders of the human body and the social limits that have been built around them.

HACKERS, CRACKERS AND CYBERPUNKS

While some writers (e.g., Rheingold, 1993) have seen cultural politics of the Internet as a primarily grass-roots or community-building domain, others have rejoiced in the Internet's propensity for deconstructing stable social formations. Some commentators, in particular, doubt the viability of any form of community in a cultural setting that facilitates dispersal and fragmentation (Nancy, 1991). These varying approaches to the value and viability of 'community', however, rarely provide clear definitions of what does or does not constitute a community. For some commentators, the concept may be restricted to geographically constituted groups within which there are direct, personal relationships; others define the concept far more expansively where 'the community' is the general citizenry of a nation-state. There may be a work community, a football community, an arts community, a virtual community. Community, like 'culture', therefore, is a variable concept which may be constituted and understood through a range of different levels.

To this extent, the whole of the Internet may be conceived as a series of overlapping and disjunctive communities and cultures. Cyberpunk culture, for example, represents a particular kind of Internet use, which is constituted through distinct social practices, identity formation and meaning-making. Unlike the generalized politics and virtual community that Howard Rheingold celebrates, the cyberpunks are more actively transgressive, seeking to destabilize the mainstream users and usages of computer technology. In many respects, cyberpunk culture operates from the margins, appropriating the tools and apparatuses of conventional capitalist culture in order to disrupt it. The cyberpunks take the products of capitalist culture, computers, and invert them through an engagement with various forms of game-playing.

The notion of cyberpunk as a transgressive computer activity evolves through a range of creative and artistic media, including punk rock and science fiction. From the 1970s and through various permutations and incarnations punk rock might generally be understood as an 'everyday' or basic art form which uses available and inexpensive sounds, products and technologies. William Gibson's science fiction novel *Neuromancer* (1984) has often been cited as the seminal cyberpunk text as it introduces the anti-hero cracker as the rogue consciousness of a dystopian near future. For cyberpunk culture this anti-heroics represents a form of social challenge, not through the overthrow of one corrupt system by another but through a kind of language warfare: a playful, partial and disrespectful assault on the great powers that create 'the game' and its rules. Put simply, the cyberpunks want to disrupt the world of mainstream computer use simply because it would impose itself upon them.

While both 'crackers' and 'hackers' seek to invade and destabilize computer networked systems, crackers are the freedom-fighters and hackers are the mischief-makers. This rather awkward distinction reflects a broader social and artistic tension which problematizes the whole activity of invasion and destabilization. As we have noted, particular theorists see networked computer communication as a facility for extending existing, institutionally derived democratic processes. This 'system' of course is also available for the forces of conformity and oppression. Depending on the perspective, then, a hacker/cracker might be regarded as a destroyer of democracy or the particulate who challenges oppressive systems; much of the dramatic action in recent science and futuristic fiction is mobilized through this tension – when is a hacker a cracker, and at what point does a computer system become a threat?

This is certainly the principal question that underlies films such as *Blade Runner* and *The Matrix*, both of which hark back to an older and remarkably enduring technology myth, that of Frankenstein. Mary Shelley's well-known romantic novel draws into tension the classically modernist desire for human transcendence in the face of nihilism and despair. Dr Frankenstein's beautiful dream becomes monstrous as it seeks to destroy the life that created its own wonderful and terrible being. We might interpret this thematic in terms of modernism's desire to achieve spiritual transcendence while recognizing its impossibility; we might also see this transcendence as a defiance of the instrumental horrors of modern industrial life and its technologies. Our splendid and exaltant technology, which is designed to enhance our being, fails and returns to destroy us.

In contemporary cyberpunk the same problematic arises as the splendid utopian ideal of networked society turns to oppression and illusion. Postmodernism transmogrifies the rattling despair of romantic technophobia, creating out of its ashes a barely convincing anti-hero who has no choice but to fight on against the absurdity of overriding, cybernetic social systems. The Replicant in *Blade Runner* return to destroy the informate corporatist plutocrats who have created their brief and splendid lives; it takes a rogue cyborg and a grounded, punkish anti-hero to defeat the Replicans and protect a system they despise. Similarly, the transmogrified, hacker-cyborgs of *The Matrix* emerge from the sewers to defeat the informate magicians of an illusory cybernetic society. In both cases, it is our essential humanity, plain, pedestrian and unremarkable, that is liberated from the infinite power of technology. In fact, neither the liberation nor the residues of human morphology and culture seem barely worth the effort: the catharsis provided by the film producers is hardly convincing.

Viruses

Of course the hacker heroes of cyberpunk movies are idealized versions of our everyday mischief-makers. Questions of security in networked computer communication systems run in both directions:

1 Hacking may be regarded as an invasion of personal freedom and privacy. Individuals may wish to protect their privacy from all forms of institutional, governmental, commercial and criminal invasion. The hacker disrupts the private space and lives of individuals who seek only to be left to carry out their work and participate in networked activities without fear of external irruption. The institutional protection of democracy may also be seriously disturbed by hacking activities.
2 Hacking may disrupt the institutional processes which assemble, survey and manipulate the private sphere. In this sense, hacking becomes a liberatory activity as is often portrayed in the hero movies of cyberpunk.

Hacking basically allows individuals to penetrate networked informate and communication systems for a range of inimical or benign purposes.

Perhaps the most pernicious and damaging invasion is carried out by computer viruses. The whole notion of virus suggests an infection within the system. Thus, while hackers deliberately penetrate secured computer systems by manipulating or cracking security codes, viruses penetrate systems by attaching themselves to 'legitimate' system operations. For example, the Melissa virus (1999) distributed itself across the globe by invading normal email systems. Melissa (a set of coded instructions like all other software) specifically targeted Microsoft products, disabling communication by replicating itself over the email software fifty times whenever the receiver unwittingly opened the message attachment. What's particularly interesting about the Melissa virus (see Walch, 1999; Best and Lewis, 2000) is that it actually assaulted the system by mimicking it. That is, by accelerating the communications processes and clogging their channels, Melissa merely did what the system does normally but under the pressures of intensification. Moreover, the virus itself was initially released through the alt.sex newsgroup, as unwitting participants in the global sex talk took the virus away, corrupted their systems and sent it on to their own online community. Supposedly named after a topless dancer in Florida, the Melissa virus therefore represented a consolidation of popular, computer and sexual cultures, incorporating the computer winky smile, the popular TV icon Bart Simpson, an attached list of pornographic sites, and an insatiable appetite for self-reproduction.

In this light, the virus maker might also be regarded as a corporate raider, a mild-mannered transgressive who uses his (sometimes her) time to disrupt the functioning of 'the system'. As a carnivalesque, the virus plays games with the legitimacy of instrumental rationality, ordered systems that deny the caprice and pleasure of play and sexual display. Undoubtedly, the creator of Melissa was displaying himself sexually, though it is difficult to know whether his disruptions are political or simply delinquent. In postmodern or de Certeauian terms, what matters is not what motivated the creator, but rather the 'tactical' effects of disruption.

Culture Jamming

Another area of transgressive computer sub-culture is known as culture jamming. Culture jamming is a conscious and politically motivated disruption of networked computer communication through the strategic, but generally not illegal, clogging of communication systems. While viruses actually invade systems, culture jamming uses entirely legal mechanisms for delivering political messages. One of the most common jamming strategies involves flooding the email channels of a politician or corporate office with protest messages. Interest groups and individuals simultaneously send messages into the receiver's mailbox and clog it with their particular point of view. Culture jamming approximates forms of expressive anarchy through the formation of various websites and more co-ordinated forms of global protest. In this sense, the culture jammers function more like international graffiti artists, creating spaces for parody, trickery and the reflexive practice of turning systematized facilities around on themselves in order to disrupt their instrumental operations. Like the appropriations of pop art, culture jammers use the Internet to appropriate official religious, governmental or commercial advertorial discourses. As the creator of the ABRUPT website, Daniel Moran, explains:

> There's an element of it that's purely fun and humorous. At the same time I'd like to think that in the right context, if these images that have been re-appropriated or whatever you want to call it, someone looks at them long enough to realize that something's not right. And if things like this are done enough and if people are made to see things like this a few times and they start to think, you know, maybe they've been too trusting of the imagery that they receive on a regular basis, and perhaps it will make one or two people even a little more critical of the information that they're swimming in all the time. (cited in *Background Briefing*, 1999)

Moran's global culture jamming is an informational protest about information. While it uses the tools and techniques provided by informate culture, jamming seeks to disrupt the even and unremitting orthodoxies of this new form of discursive deluge. In a sense, it takes up the protest of critics like Jean Baudrillard and actively seeks to reverse the imperatives of the information society. In particular, however, the culture jammers seek to disrupt the commodification and centralization of information. Protests such as International Buy Nothing Day have been organized through a culture jamming bulletin board, one of an increasing number of bulletin board communities whose interests merge around a general contempt for cultural gluttony, commodification and the loss of discursive control.

Bulletin boards such as RtMark and CRITICAL MASS, for example, specifically target corporate power for its organic and flexibly invasive demeanour. Another board, ELECTRONIC CIVIL DISOBEDIENCE, functions like an electronic sit-in, crowding corporate and governmental websites and email systems with protest messages. Five electronic artists created the FLOODNET site, which constituted a means of surrounding hegemonic electronic sites in order to disrupt their operations. When FLOODNET electronically bombed the Frankfurt Stock Exchange and the Mexican president's website, the American Pentagon returned fire, attempting to hack into and close off the FLOODNET server. Further battles with the Mexican government led to what was effectively a 'browser war' where each side was attempting to close down the other's web browser. The significant thing about culture jamming is the differences in scale and resources. An electronic terrorism which is built around humour, play and mimicry, and which is constituted around little more than the publishing of political resistance movements, represents a significant challenge to the hegemony of contemporary global power. In this sense, the culture jammers are seeking to do little more than expose this hegemony and deconstruct the cultural assumptions upon which it is constructed.

CYBER-SEX AND ELECTRONIC EROS

While minority interests and large corporations fight for control of the electronic pathways, it seems that most people are using the Internet for far more personal pleasures. While there are a range of estimates, it seems that the greatest proportion of website visits by men are to pornography sites. It is also clear that the most profitable Internet commercial sites are porn-based. Conventional feminist critique suggests that the populating of the Internet with male-oriented pornography represents a simple extension of existing cultural norms. Others have commented that the Internet pleasure sites represent a respite from the rational instrumentalities of institutional life. The Net, therefore, is 'erotic' because it is new, private, interactive and liberated from the hierarchies of nodal media and the social conformities which constantly restrain human pleasure; the new media enhance sexuality and erotica, providing a new facility for the stimulation of desire and sexual ecstasy (see Spender, 1995; van Zoonen, 1994; Turkle, 1999; Barney, 2000; Slavin, 2000).

In this latter sense, new communications technology becomes available for the sort of transgender and trans-sexual orientation which Donna Haraway seeks in her cyborg manifesto. The new technologies facilitate a broadening of sexual identity and subjectivity. While conventional feminist theory assumes pornography, for example, is constructed around broad ascriptions of gender (males gazing on women), more recent discussions have opened the possibility of mixed gazing and the pleasure of display. According to Laurence O'Toole (1998), the pornography experience is shifting from a restricted category of heterosexual men to an ever-broadening field of users: gay men, heterosexual, bisexual and lesbian women, fetishists, sex therapists, the disabled, the elderly, and so on. New communications technologies like the Internet provide the ideal facility for these interactions and for the ferment of new ideas on sexuality:

> The feelings and ideas behind such developments continue to thrive on web sites and newsgroups. People are speaking about porn as they've never done before ... . Likes and dislikes, cravings and disgruntlements. The posters and operators of the alt.sex groups treat porn as a legitimate product, not something to be ashamed about, but something to be critically evaluated. It would be nice to think that the views of the users could influence the style of the commercial, hard-core product. A new connectivity could find porn becoming more responsive to what users favour. (O'Toole, 1998: 285)

In this sense, cyberspace becomes a non-regulated arena for the exploration of fantasies and the forbidden, for both the consumption and production of sexual imagery. The facility of low-cost media production in the new technologies has permitted, in fact, the broader creation and dissemination of non-commercial imagery, a good deal of which is posted by couples and individuals. Newsgroups and amateur sex sites represent a volunteering of sexual imagery and a forum for sexual play and identity bending. These non-commercial home pages are used by women to present themselves in various modes of sexual display, effectively challenging the ideal typologies or stereotyped bodies which are created and controlled by professional site producers. Thus, while some feminists might criticize the sexualization of women when it is controlled by patriarchal systems, the amateur or 'home girl' nude sites allow women of all body types to publicly display their bodies in ways which provide personal as well as shared pleasures (see Kerby, 1997). This form of self-presentation and identity manipulation problematizes structuralist precepts on power and power relations, most especially in terms of definitions of victim and oppression. The use of the Net for the personal pleasures of display enables a liberational agency which places the gazed-upon body in an uncertain relationship with the gazer.

Email Romance

A number of theorists of postmodernism have suggested that the intense sexualization of culture is associated with the proliferation of mediated sexual imagery. Jean Baudrillard (1988), for example, believes that this proliferation has degraded erotica, producing a condition of perpetual arousal that has no source and no focus. Kroker and Kroker have suggested that the current digital age is 'typified by a relentless effort on the part of the virtual class to force a wholesale abandonment of the body, to dump sensuous experience into the trashbin, substituting instead a disembodied world of empty data flows' (1996: 3). Thus, while some critics welcome the virtualization of the body as a means to sexual and identity liberation, others believe it to be an exercise in superficiality which debases sexuality and limits liberation. In either case, there has certainly been a proliferation of explicit sexual imagery and sexual discourse in contemporary European and anglophone culture during the past two to three decades, and the Internet has provided another facility for those discourses.

Even so, sexualization has not dissolved nor excluded the discourses of romantic love. Amidst the flurry and lustful urgency of popular music, videos, films and TV programmes, romance and the possibilities of substantial, intimate connections remain substantially present – almost as though it were the final, imaginary vestige in the tidal wave of sexual exploration and experience. Indeed, with divorce rates running at over fifty per cent and increasing numbers of people choosing serial monogamy, same-sex relationships and sole-occupancy lifestyles, romantic intimacy appears a strangely atavistic yet potent part of contemporary cultural imagining. Adamse and Motta have suggested that romance is one of the most intimate of human connections, and that the 'Internet is a medium that can pique one's romantic interest in combination with a heightened sense of human curiosity' (1996: 108).

Online chat-room and email romances are clearly connected with broader cultural norms, values and practices, though they have also evolved a number of quite specific qualities. In particular, the anonymity and 'disembodiment' of the communicating individuals seem to facilitate a freer engagement with fantasy and dalliance. The exploration of one's own and the other person's mind, experiences and emotions is liberated from the drive to meet, or even be truthful. This anonymity allows for a freer flourishing of an idealized experience. Like fiction, though with the hauntingly exciting possibility of meeting and consummating the dalliance, email romance draws together fantasy and self-projection; the romancers can choose at any point to withdraw, create or re-create the romance (and their own character) in any way they choose.

A number of online romance analysts, in fact, regard this anonymity as the fundamental precipitant of the romance, permitting a kind of flirtatiousness that face-to-face and even phone communication couldn't allow. Thus, professional and work-related email communications become a space for romantic and sexual dalliances. The instrumentalities and rationalism of work, as illustrated in the film *You've Got Mail* (1999), are challenged, as they are eroticized, by the reconnection of people through the corporation's email system. As we have discussed, modernization has always implicated the threat of alienation and the dissolution of community. One function of interpersonal communications systems (telegraphy, telephony and now computer mediated systems) has been to ameliorate the negative effects of separation and 'social massification'. While it presents itself as a rationalizing mode of information transfer, corporate email systems provide a de Certeauian space (see Chapter 8) for the conduct of love and romance; work becomes a site for bodily pleasure as well as rationalized obedience.

In fact, there are those theorists who argue that the Internet itself brings particular qualities to human interaction. Adamse and Motta suggest that 'the Internet is a medium which often encourages users to open up and become more personally involved than they might in a real-life setting. Sharing of intimate thoughts and feelings is commonplace. Individuals lower defences quickly because they feel safe and less vulnerable in cyberspace' (1996: 105). The qualities of newness, anonymity, privacy and intimacy, however, become the life-line of the romance; they precipitate, sustain and then depend upon it. Reports on the outcomes of email romances are varied. Sometimes they are consummated online with specific sexual engagements, actions and emotions being posted in real time. Sometimes the consummation exhausts the relationship; sometimes it leads to the imperatives of actual meeting. Sometimes the romance disappears along with the imagined personae of the romancers. The anonymity, of course, permits chicanery and false identities, with many reports of men taking the identity of women and vice-versa. Some of the romances on same-sex datelines have provided a forum for the fantasies of 'heterosexuals'. In fact, most online romances fizzle without a trace. When couples actually do meet, it seems that the fantasies and intimacy that have sustained the romance are immediately surrendered; most romances end quickly. But not all. A graduate student from Australia embarked on an email romance with an unknown Microsoft employee from the States. They fell in love virtually, then actually; they are now married and living with their new baby in Los Angeles. (see Elizabeth Reid Steere's webpage, at http://alt.net/~alvlevi/).

DISCUSSION: DIGITOPIA

The possibilities for a globalized, interactive medium like the Internet are immense. However, the imagined utopia (digitopia) of the Net needs to be measured against some significant problems, most of which reconnect computer networked communication with the culture within which it operates. Utopianism of any kind requires a radical, if paradoxical, amplification and simplification of the complex processes that constitute the past, present and future. As we have noted in previous discussions, celebratory postmodernism's vision of the past synthesizes many of the complexities and contradictions of modernism in order to reject it. Digital utopianism also repudiates modernism and its tendency towards universalism, humanism and homogeneity. As we have suggested earlier, however, these repudiations tend to overstate modernism's uniformity: 'the modern' is not one thing at all but a series of complicated associations and claims, frayed and discordant elements which are never quite resolved, never quite complete.

Jürgen Habermas (1983) argues, in fact, that modernity is not yet finished, and that its solutions to the problems it raises constitute an 'incomplete project'. In this sense, the move to a postmodernism, a post-industrial or information society, even a digitopia, seems unable to escape many of the continuing contradictions of the modern. In particular, postmodernism seems thoroughly embedded in the modernist ideologies of progress and progressive individualism. This progressivism informs both the imperatives of capitalist expansionism and the discourses which provide meaning for technological culture. In fact, the ideology of progress underpins the utopianism of technological determinism and the utopian futurism which is built around networked digital communications.

Mark Dery (1996 see also Coyne, 1999) has argued that much of the futurism of the US west coast is a resonance of the counterculture movement of the 1960s. The counterculture was constructed out of the romanticism that ebbs and flows throughout modernity, challenging the deterministic and dehumanizing effects of industrialism, competitive capitalism and the ideologies of unceasing technological progressivism. While the counterculture was largely a middle-class phenomenon, attempting once more to overcome the alienating effects of industrialism and mass urbanization, its utopianism was built around notions of personal liberation and the rebuilding of a loving and caring community. That is, the counterculture was a contradictory response to those elements of capitalism which were themselves contradictory: the espousal of an individualist ethos within a context of social disconnectedness. Postmodern digitopianism carries a very similar contradiction: collective improvement and the reconnection of community are achieved through a more intense liberation of the individual. In a digitopian liberation the individual is more intensely centralized in a phantasmagoria of computer networks; these networks, which have no actual geography or fixed position, constitute the miracle of an ordered and progressive society.

Dery's critique, however, is quite acute, accusing the cyber enthusiasts of a brutal insincerity which can treat the bombing and slaughter of the Gulf War, for example, as yet another 'special effect':

> Naive, self-serving pronouncements such as these are commonplaces amongst cyberians. Their siren song of nineties technophilia and sixties transcendentalism seduces the public imagination with the promise of an end of the century *deus ex machina* at a time when realistic solutions are urgently needed. The cyberians' otherworldly trapdoor assumes various guises, among them the writing of the human race into a collective consciousness, the techno-pagan ability to dream up 'designer reality' through a judicious application of the knowledge that 'we have chosen our reality arbitrarily' and the 'chaos attractor at the end of time'. (1996: 49)

Dery's complaint, in fact, echoes numerous other criticisms of postmodern and digitopian idealism: the concern that this extravagant enthusiasm for technology and individualized transcendence defers or entirely banishes questions of ideology, social damage and the negative effects of contemporary economy and politics.

The discourses against which Dery rails are built around a utopian ideology of technological progressivism – a deterministic perspective which constantly reassures us that all will be well provided we maintain our faith in the future. This future is no longer an element of time, or chronology, but rather a matter of economic imperative. That is, capitalism can no longer sustain itself on the satisfaction of basic needs – clothing, food, shelter – but relies on the continual expansion of symbolic consumption within a hierarchical system of differential rewards; work and economy are motivated by the need to own symbols and symbolic pleasures which determine an individual's position on the social scales. This economy of signs requires an equally forceful economy of change or progress in order to sustain the motivation and the vitality of the system.

Of course, symbolic value has always been a part of modern capitalism; however, this abstract dimension of economy has been centralized in contemporary culture. Thus, while service industries replaced manufacturing and agriculture as the mainstay of economic activity during the twentieth century, the introduction of electronic communication systems, especially TV and computer networks, is re-configuring these services in terms of information and imagery. This re-configuration is producing a number of effects:

1   The increasing abstractness of contemporary economy is being accompanied by increasing uncertainty, mutability, evanescence and cultural precariousness. While numerous critics have pointed to this precariousness as a sign of capitalist limits (e.g., Lash and Urry, 1987; Harvey, 1989; Dery, 1996), the digitopians welcome the change, suggesting that an economy based on information implicates a freer and cleaner physical and social environment.

2   Modernism has always used information as a commodity. Copyright, patent, contract and commercial confidentiality laws protect information against commercial appropriation. Social elites protect their privilege through restrictive social rituals and knowledge (from etiquette to rules of grammar). Ideologies which protect privilege are replete within a culture. The modern education system, while claiming to be free and open, uses restricted bodies of knowledge which disadvantage particular social groups while privileging others. The competitive structure of modern education systems ensures that this privilege is maintained across generations.

The use of information as a commercial product in the post-industrial, information age appears to reinforce these restrictive and hierarchical practices and systems.

Information Economy

Free access to information has been one of the pillars of modern democratic politics; a free public education system was designed to produce an informed electorate. Modern capitalism, however, has also deployed knowledge and information as a resource for maintaining privilege and social advantage, and as a direct commodity (newspapers, books, etc). Thus, on the one hand, the whole political fabric of modernity relies on both information access and information restriction: information as a social resource and information as a commodity. Postmodern digital culture has intensified this contradiction through the facility of the Internet. The language war between free access and commodification is manifest in the current history of the Net; where once the facility was appropriated from the US military by academics and students who wanted to share information and ideas, the past few years has seen the mass invasion of commercial interests. Indeed, the ideal of free exchange and open, global communication appears to be seriously threatened by the (inevitable?) incursion of capitalist interests.

The Internet battleground reflects broader tensions in contemporary culture. A digitopian ideal operates, for example, in the labour economy, where various futurists see the commodification of information as a positive development. In its ideal, futuristic form, these speculations suggest that work in the new economy will be conducted through small, flexible organizations. These organizations will be supported by highly trained professionals whose workplaces could be located anywhere in the world. Such organizations will be light, low-polluting and democratic. There will be no rigid organizational structures with heavily normed and formalized organizational hierarchies. Women, non-whites and the disabled will all be free to participate as independent and creative individuals. Their offices will be their homes; their work schedules will be their own. This informate or 'cyborg' work will eradicate expensive, stressful and environmentally harmful commuting. It will lower stress and be more productive because the new independent and democratic stricture of organizations will eradicate unproductive manoeuvring and politicking within the workplace. A worker's labour will be his/her own. Robotics and contract flexibility will reduce the total need for (especially unskilled) labour, creating circumstances for increased leisure and pleasure for the whole society. The multimillion-dollar search-engine business Yahoo! is a clear example of this flat structure; the founder and managing director of Yahoo! has a contract clause which allows him to wear jeans and be bare-foot in the workplace, reflecting a direct symbolic challenge to the older, hierarchical workplace system.

Some of these assumptions, however, are proving highly dubious. Indeed, while the new information technologies have facilitated a wide-scale downsizing of the labour force in large organizations, the remaining work-force has been required to do increasingly more work. The labour economy is being divided into the overworked and the underworked. As executive salaries increase exponentially, the poorest members of the social formation are becoming less able to participate in the information economy. Workers are becoming increasingly insecure and increasingly burdened by the competitive demands of flexibility and down-sizing. As Tom Forester (1992) has pointed out, most of the predictions about the electronic future are proving apocryphal: more paper is consumed than ever before; people are still commuting to major urban centres; work-time for the employed has increased enormously; and robotics has pretty much plateaued.

Boring, repetitive and low-paid forms of labour persist in the informate economy since computers and robotics have not evolved sufficiently to input their own data. And while there has been an emergence of small, information-based companies over the past decade, these companies pale against the enormousness of the world's largest corporation, Microsoft. Microsoft's multinational, integrative structure has allowed it to capture an enormous share of the world's software market, producing monopolistic effects that are built on earlier industrial models. The 1999 US Supreme Court ruling against Microsoft's monopolistic practices barely indicates the power of an economic megalith whose finances are greater than half the world's national economies. Moreover, the zealotry of computer discourse has led to an absurdly inflated value being placed on the smaller information companies, most of which never return a profit but are valued at multiple millions of dollars on the US stock market.

We have suggested throughout this book that capitalism is driven by the fundamental paradox of scarcity and value: products must be scarce enough to attract value, but not so scarce as to limit access. Information has always functioned within the grip of this contradiction. William Bogard has pointed to the other great paradox of capitalism: the limits of labour. Capitalism requires labour in order to produce products, but it would prefer its eradication since labour is a *cost* which impinges on profit. In Marxist terms, capitalism recognizes the need to annihilate labour but always defers this annihilation since labour is still required to produce and create sufficient purchasing power to consume the products. The strategy for capitalism, then, is to defer annihilation by a general exploitation of labour – keeping it cheap and under control. According to Bogard, cyborg work constitutes the 'last, best solution for Capital to the problem of fatal dependence' (1996: 98). Capitalism, that is, transforms labour into something which is neither dead nor alive but which is merely 'virtual'. The increasing abstractness of capital also works its magic on labour:

> Capital in one sense no longer exploits labor at all, because *real* labor, i.e. labor corresponding to any coherent finality – to utility, to meaningful time or sense of place, to value itself – is dead or at least disappearing as a distinct, discernible form; it is mixing and bleeding into everything else, and what remains after this infusion is only a simulation of labor, a 'puppet-reference' to its former utility, which serves only to postpone its disappearance altogether. (Bogard, 1996: 100)

Darin Barney (2000) endorses this view, arguing that capitalism is actually de-skilling the labour force in order to reduce workers' social and economic power. A de-skilled cyborg worker is vulnerable to the problems of unemployment, underemployment and the vicissitudes of a low social status.

Surveillance

Bogard, in fact, follows Baudrillard's notion of simulation, arguing that cyborg work is merely a ghost produced out of the virtualizations of information. And since information is little more than an 'index of itself', its own record of itself, the act of producing information becomes something utterly embedded in the abstraction – producer and product become almost indistinguishable. This mutual dependence and embeddedness raises another problem for capitalism, according to Bogard, where the 'appearance' of producing and 'actually' producing can never be delineated. Workplaces, therefore, become realms of game-playing where the owners of capital are constantly trying to catch out their workers in traps of surveillance. Cyborg work is itself engaged in information indexing or self-organizing surveillance; to be a cyborg worker is to engage in surveillance. Put simply, workers attempt to evade surveillance while being thoroughly entrapped in its processes and production at a local and societal level. This means that a worker whose tasks involve some level of surveillance (indexing, statistical management) of others may well be using his or her worktime to email friends and lovers, do personal Internet searches, bet online or peruse pornography sites. Simultaneously, of course, they themselves are being indexed, examined and watched over by employers and security agents.

David Lyon (1994, 1999) suggests that employment, security, marketing and policing surveillance constitute the major threat to freedom in a networked information culture. According to both Lyon and Bogard, these forms of surveillance have at least two distinct dimensions. First, they are attached to the global network of communication systems, facilitating quite easy access and sharing of information between agencies. Secondly, these systems operate at both a macro and a micro level. Bogard's point that workplaces are in themselves surveillance systems suggests that colleague workers, as well as webmasters and bosses, can have access at any time to private email transactions, electronic files or the Internet activities of any particular employee. Part of the problem, of course, is that electronic activities tend to leave what are called 'crumbs' (of 'cookies') or electronic residues which can be easily traced or observed. These crumbs, which carry the details of a site visitor, facilitate surveillance within organizations, but they also become valuable information for commercial and government agencies. Even though most developed nations have privacy legislation, electronic residues become transactable commodities; marketing agencies pay considerable sums for the access to information which allows them to target their products to the unsuspecting network user. Internet Profiles (I/PRO) indicate how often a particular website is visited by a user; Netscape and Yahoo! are among the most prominent clients of I/PRO.

For many users this incursion into their privacy is more a nuisance than a threat to their freedom or privacy. What is more problematic and controversial, however, is the efforts by governments to control various aspects of the Internet, including the control of its coding system. In an attempt to standardize Internet security systems, the US government attempted to introduce a uniform encryption code in 1994. The government assured users that their privacy would not be encroached except in cases of national security. Where the US national security was threatened, that is, government agencies like the FBI or CIA would be able to 'listen in', in much the same way as they can do on the networked phone system. The debate surrounding encryption continues without resolution, partly because the Internet culture has always conceived of itself as beyond regulation and governmental incursion. In Australia the government has attempted to regulate the production and distribution of pornography and other socially threatening material on the Web. This decision to regulate the Internet and apprehend the producers and distributors of pornography came about as a matter of political expediency; the government required support for taxation reform and enlisted the vote of an independent senator who was crusading for the control of sexually explicit pornography. The regulation permits the surveillance of Internet service providers who may be allowing users to post pornography on the Web.

Access and Liberation

When nearly half the world's six billion people don't have access to a telephone, it's difficult to take seriously the utopianism of cyberians. The information superhighway is more a digital divide separating the information-rich from the information-poor. Even in the elite club of the developed world the digital divide separates individuals and groups according to gender, age, educational levels, income and ethnicity. Of course the borders are not complete and the hope of universal access and participation persists. In fact, the liberatory ideal that transformed the culture of the Internet from its military beginnings has never been realized. The recent invasion of the Internet by commercial and surveillance interests is serving to undermine further the often epiphanal, revolutionary and utopian discourses which have accompanied the arrival of this new communications technology. But this should not surprise us. The arrival of all new communications technologies seems to have followed a very similar pattern.

Even so, the networking of computers does present significant opportunities for cultural enhancement and the radicalization of politics. This promise can only be fulfilled when the computer is placed squarely within the context of its cultural value and its cultural use. As a communications medium which facilitates community creativity and exchange, the networked computer may in fact allow us genuinely to exploit the possibilities of a radical democracy and a cultural expression which is both challenging and formidable, a democracy which is less reliant on structures and delegation and which implicates personal pleasures as well as collective responsibility. The most important thing about the new technology is its anarchic potential: that is, its potential to resist regulation as it facilitates the broadest range of human ideas and expressions. What is needed is a thoroughly engaged language war in which the everyday user challenges the impositions of external order and externally constituted meanings. Corporatism, state control, exclusionism and surveillance must be resisted if free expression is to thrive. As noted elsewhere (Lewis, 1998), the Internet and its descendants need to allow discourses of hate and inhumanity to be heard and do battle with other modes of human imagining. But above all, the Internet must be as inexpensive as possible in order to provide the broadest access. More so than broadcast media or the telephone, the Internet should become the central technology for distribution by international aid organizations. After security, food, clothing and shelter, the Internet becomes a facility for cultural enrichment and the dissemination of knowledge. For all that is wrong with networked computer communication, its potential for the dissemination of culture is unparalleled.

12

Culture and Government:

Constructing the Future

Outline of the chapter

Cultural studies and cultural theory are necessarily engaged in issues of identity politics and democracy. Identity, diversity and modes of governance are central to our understanding of future culture. Contemporary cultural analysis is attempting to overcome the deficiencies of modernist democracy in order to predict and prescribe a future culture. This analysis of culture, politics and governmentalism may be divided into four groups:

1 *Cultural studies: ideology and poststructuralism.* Much of the work of the Birmingham Centre for Contemporary Cultural Studies (see Chapter 4) applied notions of ideology and hegemony in order to expose the ways in which culture is manipulated and controlled. More recently, this approach has revitalized Gramscian notions of hegemony, applying them to the study of identity, difference and cultural diversity. Laclau and Mouffe's (1985) radical democracy seeks to extend the emancipation offered by modernist democratic theory.
2 *The cultural policy and cultural governmentality.* This approach is built around a revitalization of liberal humanism. It often combines Jürgen Habermas's notion of the public sphere, intersubjectivity and the ideal speech situation with Michel Foucault's theories on governance. According to this approach, cultural studies should dedicate itself to the formation of good public policy, most especially in relation to the media.
3 *Posthumanism and radical separationism.* This approach begins with a poststructuralist and deconstructionist approach to culture, arguing that only radical separation and an aggressive, adversarial politics can provide genuine emancipation for individuals and oppressed minorities. Democracy is only possible through an intensification of difference and radical identity.
4 *Postmodern celebrational futurism.* This form of futurism also emphasizes the capacity of individual subjects and their 'difference' to promote

emancipation. Here, however, the utopianism is generated through capitalist consumption, technology, progressivism and bodily-sensate pleasure. The celebration of cultural and subject diversity is mollified through a broader embrace of liberal humanist principles and the homogenising effects of capitalist economics.

'Transculturalism' represents an alternative to these four approaches to cultural politics and the cultural future. Transculturalism accepts the inevitability of the tension between collective and individual interests. It also accepts the dynamic and indeterminate nature of cultural formations. It seeks to move beyond notions of a singular or unitary culture, speaking always in terms of cultures and diverse formations of power. Transculturalism engages with meaning-making and politics at a range of levels, including the possibilities of a new democracy.

GENERAL INTRODUCTION: FUTURE CULTURE AND THE DEMOCRATIC IMAGINATION

Cultural theory has become increasingly engaged in discussions about the future, most particularly in terms of how the future will be shaped and formed by the exertion of a politics of reform. Many of these discussions return, almost inevitably it would seem, to the problematic of personal independence or freedom within a context of social and cultural connection. That is, cultural theory and cultural studies continue to seek new emancipations within the field of future culture. Of course, societies have always been more or less 'networked', that is, connected through complex cultural codes: meanings, discourses, ideologies, values, laws, practices, rituals and texts. The problem for any social formation, however, is the maintenance of these connecting codes across the broad span of distinctive cultural experiences. As we have noted consistently throughout this book, culture operates through a broad range of experiences, some of which are conjunctive or co-extensive, others that are entirely disjunctive or antithetical. The great project of modernism has been to integrate these differences through the formation of unifying cultural codes: capitalism, nationalism, technological progressivism and of course democracy.

Thus, the modernist adaptation of classical democracy represents a genuine attempt to construct an inclusive cultural code which would reconcile if not harmonize these heterogeneous cultural elements. Democracy became the ideological framework for restoring individual interests and needs to the broader imperatives of mass society and the nation-state. The constitution of a representative and responsible government was a major advance for a progressivist politics which sought genuinely to enhance the power of the individual through an institutionalized liberal humanist ethos. In this sense, democracy became institutionalized in two distinct ways:

1   Through representation, where the rights and interests of the individual were 'delegated' to the state. This delegation was necessary, it would seem, in a complex, mass society that couldn't pause in order to consult with its citizenry. The authority of the state therefore was a symbolic power only as it

represented the interests of the civic community.

2   Through participation, where the citizenry is informed and politically active. In this 'public sphere' individuals are defined in terms of their rights and dignity, a dignity returned to them by the power of the state. Citizens, in this sense, participate in electoral processes, lobbying, petition, committees, education, public debate and persuasion, media activism and lawful protest.

The deficiencies of the system, however, may be summarized in the following terms:

1   Democratic institutions have tended to produce an excessive reliance on the processes of representation and governance. Too often 'citizenship' has become a limiting experience where state protection forms the cognitive and emotional horizon for social members, creating an excessive reliance on the state, regulation and state authority.

2   The ideals of democracy have never been able to overcome (and have in fact often been complicit with) the contradictory effects of capitalism: competitiveness, inequality, exclusionism, imperialism, excessive nationalism.

3   The formation of 'law' disproportionately increments the power of the state over the individual and smaller collectives of individuals (community). 'Law', as it is formed through the top-down process of government, reinforces the power and the rights of the state over the individual.

4   All of the above contribute to the limitation of public participation in 'democracy'. Of course the democratic ideal encourages public information and political activism, but the authority of the state and its ideologies contribute to a deep sense of political alienation

and powerlessness. The low electoral participation in the United States is a clear symptom of this alienation.

5   The authority of government, therefore, tends to seek proficiencies in control and action. Protests involving government policy are barely tolerated. The history of democratic governments across the world betrays a remarkable capacity for tyranny when specific protests against specific policies are interpreted as challenging the fundamental authority of the government and its right to govern.

6   'Representation' has tended to become self-reflexive, often overriding or neglecting altogether the requirements of 'responsibility'. That is, responsibility to the electorate has been subsumed by the 'right' of governments to govern. Responsibility has become a mutant communication activity conducted through advertising, public relations and other forms of televisual language games.

7   Governments have tended to homogenize social difference and diversity. The institutions of government were formed around the economic and political interests of the middle classes, and these interests tend to marginalize interests that cannot be contained within the morals and ideologies of the ruling elite. The willingness of governments to exert control over people's personal lives and preferences indicates a clear desire to centralize and homogenize citizenship and the discourse of freedom.

The democratic imagination in contemporary culture is formed primarily through these mediated representations. In this sense, representation has accrued wider meaning, referring both to the process of 'the government representing the people' and to 'the media representing politics'. In this chapter we will discuss the ways in which cultural studies is seeking to overcome the limitations of modernist democracy, paying particular attention to questions of identity, emancipation and governmentalism. The chapter concludes with a discussion of transcultural democracy as an alternative formation in the politics of the cultural future.

CULTURAL STUDIES: IDEOLOGY AND POSTSTRUCTURALISM

As we have noted throughout Part Two, the subject, subjectivity, difference and identity have become key aspects of recent cultural analysis. While notions of individual freedom have been present throughout the development of cultural studies, the question of individual identity becomes unavoidable as the focus of cultural analysis broadens from class to other social categories: gender, ethnicity, youth, sexuality and recreational sub-cultures. Stuart Hall, one of the early directors of the Birmingham Centre, drew on his own experiences as a West Indian migrant to alert cultural studies to the limits of a class-based analysis. American sub-cultural studies, emergent postcolonial studies and the extremely pervasive effects of feminism all contributed to a distinct broadening of the Althusserian and Gramscian reformist projects. In this sense, the emergence of diverse social movements during the 1970s and 1980s was accompanied by a significant widening of the ways in which culture was conceived and studied.

Identity Politics

In particular, the concept of identity has become central to the development of cultural politics. While theorists like Edward Said and Stuart Hall were making significant theoretical advances in the study of identity politics, powerful forces were themselves contributing to the reshaping and redrawing of cultural boundaries. This reshaping of culture, of course, served to problematize the whole notion of individual subjectivity and the formation of individual and collective identities. In particular, the very rapid increase in globalist processes – migration, tourism, business travel, trade and media communication (Held et al., 1999) – has tended to destabilize assumptions about a permanent and integrated subjectivity. The constant exposure of individual subjects to new and alien cultural elements has threatened the fixity of the self while providing new options for the formation and re-formation of a 'chosen' identity. The collective effects of this destabilization of the subject are manifest in processes like cultural hybridization and the construction of new social groupings and styles. The emergence of a 'Gothic' youth style, for example, hybridizes aspects of European Gothic culture (morbidity, vampires, black magic) with aspects of more recent British punk culture (working-class, anti-authority, anti-materialism). Individuals select from a portfolio of cultural elements in order to create an identity which subscribes to a more generalized cultural code. The Gothic individual, therefore, creates a local identity from the global code.

There are, of course, a number of cultural theorists who regard this form of hybridization as mere language play. Stuart Hall (1991a, 1991b), for example, is suspicious of a global postmodern which is founded on international cuisine and capitalist commodification. Similarly, Edward Said (1993) rejects a liberationism that is not constructed around genuine and deeply felt modes of identity politics. West (1993) argues that the recovery of diaspora (dispossessed peoples) can only be achieved through the reclamation of ethnic discourses from the regulatory and hegemonic controls of dominant, especially anglophone, interests. A number of neo-Marxist commentators (e.g., Harvey, 1989) see the opening up of identity as a new phase of cultural homogenization where First World (esp. American) capitalist and cultural imperialism emerges as the unassailable dominant for which there are no ideological alternatives. For others, however, the rupture of modernist subjectivity opens culture to new possibilities of individual agency and subjectivity. Even within this final group, however, there is considerable debate over how the reform and radicalization of the self should proceed.

Neo-Gramscian Cultural Politics

Gramscian-based hegemony theory argues basically that leadership, power and ideological domination are constituted through processes of negotiation and resistance. The difficulty for Gramscian analysis in dealing with the 'de-centring' of the subject and the 'de-bordering' of culture, however, resides in the inclination of hegemony theory to analyse power in terms of fixed structures and discourses. In hegemony theory, ideology is formed and maintained through various forms of institutionally regulated modes of production and representation. For example, educational, commercial and media institutions are able to control the scarce resources of public discourse and hence ideology. Even though it may be resisted, this ideology is nevertheless able to constitute the specific interests of power elites as the common-sense knowledge of ordinary people. The principal strategy of more recent Gramscian cultural politics is to challenge both common

sense and ideology in order to replace a faulty social system with a superior and reformed system: feminism, ethnicism and gay liberation have at various times adopted this approach to cultural and social change. New, liberated identities overthrow identities that have been imposed by power elites and their ideologies.

The limitations of this structuralist approach have been discussed in detail in earlier chapters (esp. 5, 6 and 7). Clearly, however, poststructuralist and postmodernist approaches to language and cultural formation seriously challenge the assumptions underlying analyses based on notions of hegemony and ideology. In particular, the following characteristics of poststructuralism and postmodernism cast doubt over the whole idea of a symbolic order that is regulated in social institutions and power structures.

1 Power is basically unstable and interchangeable. It is never fixed in structure but is experienced at the level of the individual body. Power is inevitably challenged at the moment of its appearance; it is always changing, mutating, being transformed.

2 Power is shaped through language, which is itself incomplete and always in transition.

3 Grand narratives like Marxism and Romanticism falsify the dispersed and incomplete nature of language. If truth exists at all, it is only a locally constituted phenomenon that operates temporarily and can never be universal.

4 Without an origin, centre or ultimate cause, language is predisposed toward the margins.

5 Culture is formed in language, so it too is transitory, unstable and dynamic.

6 Postmodernism celebrates diversity, difference, multiculturalism and the unfixing of identity and subjectivity.

7 There are no alternative systems or fixed identities, because these would simply substitute one dominant ideology for another. Postmodern culture always retreats to the margins and away from the centre.

The challenge posed by postmodernist and poststructuralist ideas has led to various forms of review and reappraisal of the Gramscian analytical paradigm. As we shall see in the discussions that follow in this chapter, a number of attempts have been made to neutralize or avoid altogether the threats posed by poststructuralist precepts, most especially through the embrace of various forms of materialist politics. Other theorists have extended the notions of difference and marginality in order to develop a radical theory of dispersal and separation. Still others have embraced the relativism enshrined in poststructuralism, producing a postmodern political perspective which abandons economic critique in favour of the celebration of capitalist-derived pleasures and textualization. For Ernesto Laclau and Chantal Mouffe (Laclau and Mouffe, 1985; Laclau, 1996), however, poststructuralism provides new resources for the development of a theory of radical democracy, governance and individual emancipation. Laclau and Mouffe seek to reconcile the problematic of individual and collective interests.

Beginning from a poststructuralist reading of language, Laclau and Mouffe argue that meanings are persistently deferred through the operations of what Jacques Derrida calls 'supplementarity' (see Chapter 5). That is, meaning cannot be fixed to a particular word but must be constantly referred to other words which supplement or add to the original word's meaning potential. This instability of meaning is reflected through the association of language to social power. Words are different and elusive, so the idea

that language can be fixed in power structures is fundamentally unsustainable. The Gramscian model, which sets language inside the primary structures of economy and class, needs to take account, therefore, of the multiply forming nature of discourse. Laclau and Mouffe characterize the 'social' in terms of 'agonism', the competing voices, meanings and interests that operate through social formations.

Undoubtedly, this agonism (of 'agonistic') is part of what Stuart Hall calls the struggle to signify. In other words, individuals and collectives engage in a broadly based competition for the right to articulate or express themselves and their particular interests. This celebration of an antagonistic perspective, however, is mediated in terms of the practical necessities of collective identification. Individuals articulate individual interests, just as words articulate individual meaning potential. However, for those interests or meanings to be fully functional in the social context, they must operate in conjunction with other interests and meanings. To this extent, social and discursive elements may form temporary allegiances or juxtapositions. Individuals may participate in such unstable collective formations through a process of identification. Individuals, therefore, might identify with collective formations such as 'nation' or 'society' by temporarily parenthesizing the significant differences which might otherwise distinguish or separate the group. For example, class, gender, sexual orientation, ethnicity and political allegiances may be juxtaposed in order for the individual to identify temporarily with the discourse of 'nation'.

Emancipation and radical democracy are formed, according to Laclau and Mouffe, through the release of these subsumed differences in a context of mediated and agonistic pluralism. Governance and government are possible only when the emancipation of the individual and his or her identity is assured. A radical democracy, therefore, is one which emerges through a wide field of identity formations, social movements and participative endeavours. Democracy of this kind must operate through feminist, environmentalist, anti-racist, sexual liberationist and various modes of urban renewal movements. Laclau and Mouffe's reworking of Gramsci's hegemony leaves open the possibility of a governance which is expressed through diversity and radical overhaul. As Laclau explains, this form of democracy is created by the interests of individual agents rather than by rationally imposed structures:

> Three conclusions follow. ... The first is that politics, far from being confined to a superstructure, occupies the role of what we can call an *ontology of the social*. If politics is the ensemble of the decisions taken in an undecidable terrain – that is in a terrain in which power is constituitive – then the social can consist only in the sedimented forms of a power that has blurred the traces of its own contingency. The second conclusion is that if the movement from modernity to postmodernity takes place at the level of their intellectual and social horizons, this movement will not necessarily involve the collapse of all the objects and values contained within the horizon of modernity but, instead, will involve their reformulation from a different perspective. ... Finally, the previous reflections show, I think, the direction into which the construction of a postmodern social imaginary should move: to indicate the positive communitarian values that follow from the limitation of historical agents, from the contingency of social relations, and from those political arrangements through which society organizes the management of its own impossibility. (1996: 103–4)

Laclau's conclusions here express an underlying commitment to the efficacy of social organization and governance which are outcomes of diversity, individual emanciption and small-scale community. The positive values that have survived as the legacy of modernity – individualism, good governance and social responsibility – are thus reworked and reintegrated into a new, postmodern political 'horizon'. This, however, is not the horizon imposed through logical, self-interested and self-sustaining structures, but is forged through the interests of individuals and community groups themselves.

CULTURAL POLICY AND CULTURAL GOVERNMENTALITY

Jürgen Habermas (1984, 1987), who rejects the nomenclature of postmodernism, seeks a similar emancipation of the democratic ideal. As a rationalist liberal humanist, Habermas prescribes a reconciliation of the individual–collective divide through the formation of a consensual public sphere. He sees culture as a consistently forming project where individualized codes are integrated into the greater good of mutual understanding and communication. In many respects, his approach is symptomatic of a broader dissatisfaction with the inability of poststructuralism and postmodernism to theorize the reconciliation of individual and collective interests. Habermas argues that pleasure and individualism are important but not sacrosanct. Inevitably, humans need to construct community. They need to communicate effectively and rationally in order to resolve the quotidian particularities that drive their emotional and psychological needs. An ordered 'intersubjectivity' will produce an appropriate and consensual reality. This reality is not fixed or immobile, but represents an ideal speech situation in which humans can congregate for the mutual satisfaction of their mutual interests. The state, Habermas argues, is to be formed as an occasional and evanescent forum – the servant of the public, rather than its master. In this sense, the ideals of democracy and modernism will finally be realized.

Foucault and Governmentality

Habermas's rationalism remains pertinent to various zones of political and cultural enquiry, especially those interested in promoting the idea of a public sphere and influencing government policy. However, his work is deeply ontological (interested in 'essential' qualities), leaving little space for a more flexible reading of postmodern culture and cultural activities. In particular, he remains suspicious of sensate or popular aesthetics which may contribute to the effective termination of democratic communication. To this extent, cultural theorists like Tony Bennett (1999) have sought to liberate the notion of governance and democracy from the rationalist order defined by Habermas. Bennett, in fact, argues that contemporary, postmodern culture is thoroughly infused by the conditions of regulatory processes and practices – these processes and practices can be conscripted into the cause of democratization and liberation. In other words, matters of governance and government policy are inevitable, and so cultural analysis needs to engage thoroughly with regulatory processes in order to enhance democratic potential and the freedom and life quality of citizens.

In support of these arguments, Bennett invokes the work of poststructural theorist Michel Foucault, most particularly his work on state power and governmentality. For some (e.g., see McGuigan, 1996), this use of Foucault's writing is a misappropriation, since Bennett's aim is to provide some normative values and principles for the practical analysis of government cultural policy and Foucault is regarded by many of his followers as something of an anarchist. Jim McGuigan points out, however, that Foucault's slippery and generally ungrounded historical analyses render his work available for quite contrary theoretical readings:

> Because he refused to ground his subtle and compelling analyses of power in norms of critical judgement, Foucault's work lends itself to radically dissimilar forms of interpretation and application. That the anarchist Foucault should have become, in effect, a theoretical source for a kind of management consultancy in the service of cultural administration is oddly plausible. (1996: 176)

Plausible or not, the application of Foucault's ideas is constituted around a fundamental belief that 'governmentalism' is pervasive throughout culture: that is, throughout the processes by which meanings are formed, distributed and consumed. For Bennett, it is the institutions and material effects of this process that need to be central to the cultural studies project.

If we return to Foucault's essays on 'governmentality', we can certainly identify a preoccupation with the pervasiveness of power. However, the notion of governmentality is only partially developed, unlike Foucault's more substantive theorizations on the state, populations, administrative technologies, power, discourse and knowledge (see Chapter 5). In fact, Foucault's 'writings' on governmentality are based on a particular series of lectures, most of which have been prohibited from publication by the literary executors of his estate (Burchell et al., 1991). The somewhat disproportionate interest being expressed in the concept indicates the seriousness with which political and cultural theory are attempting to reconcile the precepts of poststructural and postmodern theory with the demands of practical political action. Perhaps the development of the concept in the first instance was motivated by Foucault's own desire to accomplish the reforms his major writings simply intimated. In effect, governmentality is distinguished as a modern political practice which deviates from pre-modern, sovereignty-based theories of legitimation. That is, governmentality dislodges sovereignty as the essential fabric of the state from the rise of the Enlightenment. While sovereignty was concerned with obedience to law (and hence to the sovereign), governmentality is concerned with the tactics of governance: governmentality is about the filtering through of regulatory practices, including the practices of self-regulation and the management of material products or things.

> Government is defined as a right manner of disposing things so as to lead not to the form of the common good, as the jurists' texts would have said, but to an end which is 'convenient' for each of the things that are to be governed. This implies a plurality of specific aims: for instance, government will have to ensure that the greatest possible quantity of wealth is produced, that the people are provided with sufficient means of subsistence, that the population is enabled to multiply. ... [W]ith government it is not a matter of imposing laws on men, but of disposing things: that is to say, of employing tactics rather than laws, and even of using laws themselves as tactics – to arrange things in such a way that, through a certain number of means, such and such ends may be achieved. (Foucault, 1991: 95)

The Cultural Policy Debate

Governmentality, in this sense, may be regarded as a form of material management. Foucault reviews the notion in various lectures, seminars and interviews, suggesting at one point that the 'contact

between technologies of domination of others and those of the self I call governmentality' (1988: 19). In this discussion, however, Foucault concedes that his study of governmentality has overemphasized tactics of domination over those of self-management. In his essay 'Technologies of the self' (1988) he makes clear that subjects employ various 'tactics' (technologies, techniques) in order to govern themselves. To this extent, governmentality is not merely about institutionally elected governments, but rather about the ubiquity of governance, management and control. It should also be emphasized that Foucault's application of the concept of governmentality is historically focused, designed to distinguish between the Enlightenment and previous historical phases.

Tony Bennett (1999), nevertheless, is undeterred in his adaptation of Foucault's concept for a polemical account of contemporary cultural studies. Bennett expresses his deep dissatisfaction with the Gramscian approach to culture and cultural analysis, arguing that studies based around ideology and hegemony tend to reproduce simplistic notions of a centre of power. Foucault's arguments, by contrast, treat power as decentralized and pervasive in all human relations. Bennett makes several claims against a cultural studies which is preoccupied with theoretical and representational issues. A policy-driven cultural studies would redress a number of the problems that continue to limit the practical efficacy of cultural studies and cultural politics. To this extent, a policy-based cultural studies would:

(a) focus on institutions and institutional practices;

(b) recognize that cultural studies is practised within educational institutions which are in turn instruments of government and governmentality;

(c) acknowledge that cultural studies is not a renegade activity but exists within the framework of govern-mentality and so engages in specific regulatory practices (e.g., what is to be studied, what is not to be studied); and

(d) interrogate various technologies of power as they are exercised through institutional practices.

Bennett's essay, produced out of the Australian Key Centre for Cultural and Media Policy, polemicizes the issue of cultural policy analysis in contemporary cultural studies. Along with other scholars associated with the Centre – Ian Hunter, Colin Mercer and Stuart Cunningham – Bennett maintains that questions of policy and governmentality need to be central to the cultural studies project if it is to reach beyond the limited borders of textual analysis.

Similarly, Jim McGuigan (1992) argues that cultural studies' infatuation with language and discourse theory has led to an overemphasis on textual shaping and consumption. According to McGuigan, the deviation of cultural inquiry into various forms of cultural populism has limited its critical efficacy, as it surrenders to the reactionary interests of global capitalism. McGuigan, in fact, questions not only the populism of cultural analysts like John Fiske (see Chapter 8), but also a policy focus which is not grounded in normative critical values. To this extent, McGuigan distinguishes his own work from that of authors like Tony Bennett. McGuigan presents his own analysis in terms of critical values of 'democratic egalitarianism' which are applied to a number of concrete and substantive issues of cultural policy, including questions of evaluative judgement and public administration; culture, economy, geography and history, cultural identity, citizenship, censorship and morality (1996:

177). For McGuigan, Habermas's notion of a consensual communicative action within the public sphere provides the basis for understanding the actual conditions of ordinary people's everyday struggles. The ultimate question for cultural studies, McGuigan argues, is how to construct an expressive citizenship.

Within Gramscian-derived cultural studies, commentators like Angela McRobbie (1994) and Ien Ang (1996) have also identified the limits of textual analysis, suggesting that the study of culture and the media must always return to the industrial and regulatory contexts in which media are formed, operate and are consumed. McRobbie insists that cultural studies is losing its critical focus and that cultural politics must always refer to the conditions of 'hegemony' outlined by Antonio Gramsci and adapted for cultural analysis by Stuart Hall. Ang, meanwhile seeks to take her own studies of textual consumption out of the apolitical zones of reader pleasure and into the more critically fertile zones of media industries.

Graeme Turner (1994, 1997) has claimed that much of the recent integration of post-structural and postmodern theoretics into cultural studies has been brought about by the forces of globalization. According to Turner, there are two parts to this move. First, poststructuralism and postmodernism treat all texts as 'discourse', whatever their source and cultural derivation; an analytical model which applies a common strategy, 'deconstruction', to all texts sits well with the imperatives of cultural globalization. Secondly, Turner argues, academics themselves have limited opportunities to write books or papers about national conditions, industries or cultural formations since publications and publishers have become far more globalist in their outlook. A national perspective which interrogates the national conditions of a national industry is difficult to sustain in a postmodern global context. According to Turner, the dissolution of national interests seriously depletes the efficacies and freedoms constituted in 'democracy' as local interests succumb to international (especially American) cultural and economic priorities. Cultural studies must retain this level of national perspective, Turner claims, if it is to sustain its affiliations with progressive and critical politics.

Borrowing from During (1999: 480), we can identify three levels within the cultural policy debate:

1 Policy should be studied in cultural analysis.
2 Culture is characterized by governmentality and regulatory processes.
3 Policy should be the central focus of cultural studies.

There can be little argument with the first level of this debate: that policy issues should be part of the cultural studies ambit. It is certainly true that some areas of cultural studies restrict their analysis to problems of aesthetics and representation, and are less interested in issues of power and injustice. It is equally true, however, that many cultural analysts enter public and policy debates quite directly, applying modes of Gramscian or Foucauldian discourse-based cultural analysis. Stuart Hall and Edward Said, for example, have often engaged in matters of governmental policy formulation as well as direct political action. Hall (1991a, 1991b, 1996) makes it clear that his theoretical work is always and necessarily focused toward practical political outcomes. His explicit criticism of Thatcherism in Britain, and Said's opposition to US foreign policy initiatives in the Middle East, demonstrate clear continuities between various forms of textual analysis

and participation in public policy debates. Of course, Bennett objects to the putative oppositionalism of Gramscian-style cultural studies, but it is nevertheless clear that cultural studies critique reaches well beyond a simple opposition for opposition's sake. Through its Gramscian and Foucauldian incarnations cultural studies continues to make major contributions to the ways in which culture and politics can be considered; in this sense, it can be critical (or 'negative') as well as offering positive suggestions for policy formulation.

The problem for Bennett's approach – and here we encounter the second level of the policy debate – is that the whole notion of governmentality is so complete that it appears inescapable. In other words, there seems to be nothing an individual subject can achieve through a critical or ideological distance from the processes of being governed or regulated. In this sense, opposition, resistance and even rejection seem merely to be cultural articulations that are comfortably contained within the general context of citizenship. While at one level this may seem reassuring, at another level the risk of serious political dilution emerges since radical resistance becomes fatuous, meaningless or absurd. In this sense, there seems little value in a scholar (or any other subject) resisting or rejecting the threat of injustice or oppression except through the available mechanisms of democratic participation and regulation. Protest must be contained within a general discourse of participation since 'to be a citizen' is the complete lexicon of rights and political determinations. In fact, in Bennett's scheme, there appears to be no legitimate subjectivity that is not contained within the borders of the citizenry.

At the third level of this debate, then, it seems clear that the situating of policy at the centre of cultural studies seriously limits the possibilities of thinking new thoughts and exploring new horizons of culture and cultural politics. Specifically, the centralization of policy, governmentality and citizenship privileges the state and its right to govern, control and regulate. It tends to reinscribe the problems associated with representative democracy as we have outlined them above. To reverse Turner's argument, cultural policy studies tend to fix their liberation in the constituency of the nation-state; the nation is restored against the flow of diversity and multitudinous cultural forms associated with globalization, identity and cultural difference. In particular, cultural policy studies are predisposed toward regulation and protection, which inevitably compromises or diminishes the potentialities of new modes of cultural expression, subjectivity and identity. In repudiating postmodernist interests in difference and customized forms of pleasure and emancipation, the national policy approach frequently threatens to restore the authority and homogenizing tendencies of the state. The pragmatism which is often celebrated by cultural policy studies may be viewed more broadly as an unmitigating faith in governance and the humanist ideal, a faith which inevitably reconstitutes the limiting effects of rationalized order and the homogenization of individual and community desires – a faith, that is, in the social collective over the personal.

Fredric Jameson (1993) argues that the policy-primacy approach is highly localized, emerging in a context of high levels of state intervention. While such policy studies may be pertinent to a country like Australia, Jameson argues, they have far less relevance in the United States, where there is little ideological or historical support for state engagement in cultural activities. Adding to this, we might suggest that this highly localized conception of the state and state regulation seriously limits the policy scholars' view of broader global,

cultural issues. Simon During suggests something similar in his discussion of the policy debate, claiming that Australian policy scholars have been well positioned to contribute to government policy formulation designed to support local culture and cultural industries: 'But this means that the hot issues on the American culture/government interface – censorship, and the withholding of public funding for so-called obscene or blasphemous works, the attack on multiculturalism, the questioning of the public funding of culture at all – do not really appear in Bennett's work' (1999: 480). In other words, the policy-primacy argument is very much fixed within the national borders of its source.

POSTHUMANISM AND RADICAL SEPARATIONISM

Throughout this book we have argued that contemporary culture is being formed through new modes of televisual and digital media. For a number of commentators, this move toward a mediated televisual culture has fundamentally changed the relationship between humans and their 'reality'. Jean Baudrillard, most notably, has claimed that the proliferation of sensate televisual imagery is producing a 'hyperreality' which fractures the relationship between a sign and its meanings. In Baudrillard's reading of contemporary culture everything is an imitation (simulation) of everything else; meanings simply travel at the hyper-velocity of things already known, already digested and already wasted. While Baudrillard talks quite specifically about advertising and the vacuousness of propaganda television, rock video clips provide perhaps the most spectacular examples of hyperreality. The 'meanings' of the clips are usually constituted through rapidly shifting and dissociative lyrical and visual fragments. The desire that is stimulated by these fragments, however, is never fixed or directional, but will always vaporize through the very instant of their appearance, the very instant of their 'consumption'.

This radical disjunction between signs and their meanings accords with various forms of poststructural theory. Poststructuralism (see Chapter 4) calls into question the whole nature of discourse, arguing that knowledge is merely the product of a culturally constructed sign system. Deconstruction methods expose the cultural and historical assumptions which inform these systems, leaving bare the highly particulated meanings which texts artificially construct. Various forms of postmodern cultural analysis (see Chapter 7) have applied deconstruction methods to dismantle the assumptions and discourse practices that inform 'humanism'. In many respects, humanism is the ethical and ideological underpinning of political democracy. It aims to provide universal explanations for, and solutions to, the 'human condition'. Like the great religions, humanism seeks to enhance all human life through the formation of universal values and principles of governance which are not limited through national, ethnic or 'cultural' boundaries.

Postmodern deconstructionism rejects this universalism, arguing that individual humans and their chosen community formations are the primary constituents of meaning-making and culture. However, this separationism is often modulated, as we shall see, by a reinvigorated postmodern communalism (or pluralism) which inevitably restores democratic liberal humanism (e.g., Laclau and Mouffe, 1985; Poster, 1995). A more literal reading of poststructural theory has been developed by various cultural commentators, most specifically those interested in forming a genuine posthumanism or radical separationism.

For these theorists, there can be no restoration of a generalized human experience since all experiences are unique and highly individualized. Any attempt to produce a generalized ethic or political principle, indeed any attempt to produce a generalized community, necessarily transgresses the interests of individuals. For these radical theorists, the past must be ruptured and the future must be seized in a language war that can have no completion. Echoing the radical precepts of Marx and Althusser, though without the structuralist solutions, these radical theorists argue that the past is the province of the dominant social groups. Powerful groups control the material and discursive resources of culture; their own particular interests are presented as universal ideologies and values which would supposedly benefit all humanity. Humanism is merely another variation of these propagated interests.

Posthumanism is constructed out of a sense of dismay and disquiet. Like Baudrillard's critical pessimism, post-humanism abandons the possibility of meaningful communication – except in terms of ephemera and the transient formation of sub-cultures, cyborgs and the partiality of bodily pleasure. For authors like Donna Haraway (1991, 1997), post-humanism offers the possibility of an evolutionary leap, a move toward a new cyborgian identity that is not fixed by the precepts of gender, age, ethnicity or sexuality. Judith Halberstam and Ira Livingston celebrate the disillusion that is inherent in posthumanism since it provides the conduit for a new and more radical social exigency:

The gridlock of signifiers and signifieds at the juncture of gender, class, ethnicity and sexuality in the night world of voguing is a traffic jam of posthuman proportions, where the drivers may as well abandon their vehicles. The Human wanders, lost, into a maze of sex changes, wardrobe changes, make-overs, and cover versions that imbricate human reality into post-human realness. (1995: 7)

The Baudrillardian postmodern poetica is unmistakable. The apocalyptic hedonism of this passage resonates in much of the science fiction futurism from which posthuman theoretics draw their inspiration. However, a vision of radical separationism and its prescient 'realness' seriously misreads the processes of meaning-making which continue to drive and motivate contemporary culture. Separationism, displeasure and non-meaning are certainly present in current discourses and media experiences, but so too are the communalizing and communicative experiences which continue to congregate around discourses like love, freedom, nation, democracy, pleasure, family, television and music. We continue, that is, to congregate around our various formations of culture and meaning. Thus, just as the cultural policy and governance theorists might overstate the possibilities of systematic communication, so the separationists overstate its implausibility.

POSTMODERN CELEBRATIONAL FUTURISM

Posthumanism's unrelenting separationism contrasts in many respects to the more optimistic vision of other postmodern futurists. While the emphasis and intellectual heritage of these theories vary somewhat, they share a common commitment to a democratic politics based on diversity and communitarian values. Laclau and Mouffe's absorption of postmodern language theory into a neo-Gramscian democratic political framework parallels the work of political scientists interested in issues of culture and citizenship. Anthony

Giddens (1994), for example, has suggested that contemporary politics has moved beyond simple divisions of social class and the representational party politics of Left and Right. For Giddens, the new modernity is characterized by the ascent of multinational corporations and the integration of multifarious nations, peoples and cultures into a pre-eminent economic and political system; this global political and economic system is pragmatic, rationalistic, privatized and ideologically centralist, if not conservative. The neutralization of this 'neo-liberalist' ethos is possible, Giddens argues, only through the formation of a cultural politics which extends the reach, definition and experience of modern democracy. Thus, while the modern era has concerned itself with the representative and institutional dimensions of power, a contemporary reform agenda must engage with the personal, 'everyday' and symbolic dimensions of what Michel Foucault calls the 'microphysics' of power.

Giddens, like David Held (1987, 1992; Held et al., 1999), argues that the democratic experience needs to be rendered beyond, as well as within, the framework of the formal legal and political sphere. According to Giddens, a new democracy should be dialogic and relational at all levels of human experience: the personal and domestic, through social movements and self-help groups, businesses and professional organizations, and at the global level of international relations. This is not to surrender collective responsibilities and forums, but to modulate them through the immediacies of human meaning-making and pleasures. Pluralism becomes a central issue here. While authors like Stuart Hall (1991a, 1991b) have repudiated American political pluralism for its tendency to control rather than liberate 'difference', others insist that a genuine pluralism would prove dialogic. That is, pluralism facilitates a complete dialogue between the operations of the collective whole (the democratic state) and the individual interests and freedoms which constitute that whole. To a degree, this question of the cultural value of 'pluralism' is a semantic issue. Giddens' pluralistic model for the future of radical politics seeks genuinely to dismantle the binary formations that had dominated modernist political processes, facilitating a revolution of diverse social, economic and cultural interests. Mark Poster (1995) calls this dialogic 'postmodern multiculturalism': the centre is deconstructed through the emancipation of individual identities and their particular social designs and pleasures.

Poster's analysis of postmodern democracy, like Ernesto Laclau's, combines a profound interest in Western society's political heritage with a broader interest in post-structuralist language theory. Another group of postmodern futurists, however, explore democracy more directly through various forms of aesthetics and textual theory. These 'celebrational postmodernists' (see Chapter 7) apply the theories of Roland Barthes and Michel de Certeau in order to explain the increasing differentiation of cultural styles and everyday practices as modes of political expression. Popular media are presented as the pre-eminent resource for everyday creativity and expression, contributing to both individual and community identity formation. The exchange and consumption of capitalist products, therefore, is seen not as submission to powerful agencies, but as a potentially transgressive act of self-expression. That is, the 'reading' or 'consuming' of popular media texts becomes a political activity in which the interests of the individual are privileged over the interests of the social whole. Consumption becomes a political facility for the exercise of individual choice and the satisfaction of 'visceral' pleasure. The aggregation of these individual pleasures resolves

finally the problematics of modernism: the reconciliation of mind and body, individual and community, present and past, self and other, nature and culture. Postmodern populism condenses social tensions through an apotheosis of the individual.

Considered globally, celebrational postmodernism idealizes the dissolution of nations and national borders. In particular, a postmodern futurism envisages a new permutation of global culture which is formed around a myriad of cultural constituencies. That is, the global postmodern is formed through the interests and pleasures of individuals who will participate variously in culture without recourse to fixed and fundamental typologies. Individuals will choose who they want to be and with whom they will associate. The ethos of 'difference' will increasingly inform our thinking, our identity formation, our cultures, our social policies and our modes of governance. We may congregate in tele-visual spaces in order to experience the funeral of a princess; otherwise we will be free to seek out the media texts which we ourselves can form in relation to our personal or micro-community needs, pleasures and interests. Culture, like power, will be evanescent, offering its communion of meanings for a given purpose and constituency within a given context. Unlike the separationists, there is no recourse to phantasms of absolute separation, but there will always be a dialogue between conjoinment and separation.

Networked Culture

Future culture, therefore, will extend the positive conditions of contemporary postmodernism. Capitalism will continue to distribute itself across the globe, dispensing with the impalatable and the inhumane while transforming difference into commodifiable pleasures for all to share. Democracy and democratic institutions will also be transformed. The representative process which removes power from individuals and fixes it in impenetrable oligarchies and which constantly reinforces the power of the state will inevitably dissolve itself through the increasing primacy of the global–micro community dialogue. The nation, which, like religion, had been the dominant social formation and cultural referent, will be radically reduced by the greater cultural propinquities of globalization. Moreover, the stifling and bloated systems of government management will necessarily be dissolved through the dual assaults of globalization and enhanced individualism. Thus, while the bureaucracies of welfare, the arts, defence, education, policing and industrial relations may have been necessary modes of mediating state and corporate power during the period of modernity, they will no longer be necessary in a truly liberated social future. The new social and cultural spaces provided by the global postmodern will dissolve the structural premise for social management systems based primarily on divisions of class.

This new culture will be conceived, according to postmodern futurism, through the formations of computer networked communication (CNC). Indeed, the notion of network provides an ideal metaphor for futurists, who imagine a utopia which harmonizes social differences and structured differentials of power. Networks are decentralized matrices which incorporate all their nodes into a single communicational fabric. The Internet, as the primary facility of contemporary CNC, provides a spectacular example of how contemporary culture can be formed through the community of users, flows, discourses, wires and nodes. Hypertext users are both creators and consumers of meanings. Texts are enabled, modified, transformed and exchanged by the connected CNC user. As a supplement and alternative to broadcast media, CNC provides users with enormous informational access and choice. Information is the primary resource of postmodern politics and political expression; its more evenly distributed and accessible form inevitably enhances the conditions of freedom and democracy. The great media conglomerates are present on the Net but not dominant; their relevance is formed through the choices and interests of the everyday users. For the postmodern futurist, the networking of culture enhances democratic participation as it reduces the capacity of the broadcast media to control informational orientation, style and distribution.

Networked communication, therefore, is seen as an evolutionary democratic advance. The postmodern futurists' emphasis on the liberational potential of CNC parallels a broader enthusiasm for capitalist economics, most particularly as it is articulated by government, corporations and conservative economists. Thus, while the postmodernists are seeking a critical political space which deconstructs the nodalized powers of capitalist hegemony, their emphasis on individual freedom, pleasure and consumerism nevertheless places their theories within a more generalized ideological space: one which embraces capitalist expansionism, market sovereignty and the utilities of social and economic progress. The divide between postmodern futurism and the neoliberalism it would critique becomes blurred since both celebrate the individual and his/her capacity to consume and choose.

To this extent, CNC becomes a facility not merely for new modes of subjective expression and communicative exchange, but it is also a major facility for the exchange of international capital and finance. These financial flows may well operate for the broader distribution of media 'products' for consumption by individuals and micro-communities and for the exercise of subjectivity and individuated pleasure, but they are also facilities for the extension of hegemony as well as state and corporate power. The new knowledge celebrated by Anthony Giddens and other postmodern futurists is formed around the ongoing and homogenizing power of capitalist economics and ideologies. Postmodernist celebrationism, that is, has no way of distinguishing between strategic and emancipatory consumption and the unfettered embrace of hierarchical and dominant social values and ideologies. Postmodern futurism surrenders its critical space to the invisible forces it can no longer identify. It flounders as it embraces the community of consumption. Its radical intent dissolves as global 'Difference' becomes a commodifiable and consumable 'difference'. Humanism and universalism are, again, reawakened through the inevitable pursuit of a centralist value system, one which is clearly attached to the homogenizing force of capital, but which lacks the force of mind to reconstruct democratic institutions and precepts.

TRANSCULTURALISM: AN ALTERNATIVE CULTURAL STUDIES

How, then, can cultural politics and future culture be conceived or theorized? The overriding problem with the four versions of a 'democratic' cultural future rests largely on their tendency to utopianize, sentimentalize or simplify the complex formations of culture and meaning-making. In particular, the ongoing problematic of the individual–collective tension remains unresolved. In this final section I would like to offer some comments on how this problematic might be more adequately addressed. From this point we might progress toward a more complete explanation of culture and cultural processes.

Relocating Culture

From their early investigations, cultural theory and cultural studies have often assumed that culture is a more or less homogeneous and unitary formation. Each of the distinct phases of cultural analysis evolves through an attempt to explain, confirm and enhance 'social order':

1   Culture as civilization, where social progress was achieved through the intellectual and social achievements of particularly talented individuals.
2   Culture as similar to the previous category only with a greater emphasis on the refinement and elevation of aesthetic expression. The arts will lead to the humanizing and enlightenment of all citizens.
3   Culture as an anthropological category, where a society was formed around symbolic artefacts, discourses and practices. This category refers originally to homogeneous tribal communities.
4   Culture as the symbolic codes which unify a nation's people and which validate the authority of the state. The anthropological category is transformed through its application to mass society.
5   Culture as community of difference, where the symbolic codes are formed through social organizations other than nation. These symbolic codes unify social groupings such as transnational religious communities (e.g., Islamic, Jewish, Mormon) or intranational communities (e.g., biker gangs, indigenous and ethnic groups, returned servicemen, family).

This last application of the concept of culture has certainly become predominant in cultural analysis influenced by poststructuralism and postmodernism. Even Jürgen Habermas's 'public sphere' is a consensus of different parts. Theories of pluralism, multiculturalism (see Poster, 1995) or transnationalism (Ang and Stratton, 1996) are formed around a consensual, liberalist model, albeit one which defines community in relatively broad terms. In either case, the emphasis is on a form of social order where the meaning of difference becomes a modulation for a generally incorporative but respectful social order. The new democracy of postmodernism seeks the realization of the old democratic imagining; individuals are centralized in a mutually respectful community of others.

As we have noted above, however, the great weakness of a celebrational postmodern futurism rests in its inability to resolve the individual–collective tension. If it moves to separationism, it loses its capacity to engage with the broader community; if it fixes itself to notions of consumerist pleasures, it remains adhered to the homogenizing and hegemonic impulses of capitalism, including ideologies of technological and economic progressivism. Even an emphasis on identity politics (see Chapter 10) arouses the suspicions of critics who argue that postmodern difference is formed around very specific and limited ideologies – including the simplest ideology of self-interest and self-gratification. A postmodern identity politics, that is, must be formed through capitalist consumerism and it must subscribe to particular social values: sexual liberationism, tolerance, compassion, pluralism, and so on. Particular social theorists argue, in fact, that these values constitute a new humanism which is formed around personal pleasures and a globalist perspective which Stuart Hall disparagingly describes as 'the international cuisine' (Hall, 1991a). While this international cuisine or cosmopolitan consumerism is pleasant enough for the

members of the new professional classes, it hardly constitutes a radical mode of social reformism. Difference is pluralized, commodified and homogenized. In this class-bound consensus of difference we will not see a celebration of terrorists, xenophobics, thieves, murderers, rapists, Nazis, Islamic fundamentalists, the homeless or Marxists. These forms of social difference cannot, it seems, be admitted into the community of celebrational difference. In other words, the celebrational postmodernism retreats from a radical difference or separationaism in order to form a new consensus, a new ideology of humanist pluralism.

Willock (1999) has complained that postmodern politics constructed around difference and identity is unsustainable because it reduces all power to a game of subjectivity. Even if there is no consensus at the end of this identity politics but just a series of separational contingencies, the politics remain flaccid and unimpressive, according to Willock:

> In its most basic form identity politics is a strategy that aligns select groups of people by promoting differences between themselves and others. ... The result is an isolationist rhetoric that precludes groups from finding some common ground to produce some greater act that would promote the common good. (1999: 9)

This common good, in Willock's mind, is the sort of consensual public sphere advocated by Habermas and others, a space in which the relative differences between social members and sub-communities could be resolved through rational and respectful democratic debate. Willock, like Jim McGuigan (1996), despairs of postmodernism's disingenuous celebration of difference and subjectivity, arguing that a practical and inclusive communicational sphere would more honestly address the social and political problems of our day.

Transculturalism

Our own approach in this book has been to accept the problematic of the individual–collective tension. Consistently, we have treated culture as a series of imaginings, symbols and discourses which operate through a range of overlapping, sometimes consonant, sometimes dissonant, levels of meaning. Our working definition of culture, as developed in Chapter 1, reads:

> Culture is an assemblage of imaginings and meanings that may be consonant, disjunctive, overlapping, contentious, continuous or discontinuous. These assemblages may operate through a wide variety of human social groupings and social practices. In contemporary culture these experiences of imagining and meaning-making are intensified through the proliferation of mass media images and information.

During the course of this book, we have tried to explore these consonances and dissonances without necessarily trying to reconcile them. Most particularly, we have tried to avoid the presumption that culture is any one thing, or is a unitary formation which exists in some sort of fixed or ideal relationship with society, social organization or social order. Indeed, we have been careful to avoid the assumption that there is an actual 'culture' that can be simply located, interrogated and known. Rather, we have tried to present culture in terms of its evanescent and dynamic character – as multiple and always forming cultures. In many ways, we might draw the conclusion that the whole notion of 'culture' should be replaced by a new concept, one which is freed of the assumptions of its cognitive heritage. My own preference for the concept of 'transculturalism' expresses a general desire to interrogate the forming processes of meaning- making and the instabilities which characterize their operation.

Thus, in avoiding the presumption of a unitary culture, transculturalism may be summarized in the following terms:

1 Transculturalism acknowledges the instability of all cultural formations, discourses and meaning-making processes. Transculturalism avoids the assumptions which place culture beside nation, state or other fixed ideologies. 'Transculturalism' suggests its own transitory or transient nature. Unlike similar concepts (trans-nationalism, cross-cultural communication, post-colonialism), transculturalism does not assume a pre-existing or dominant cultural condition or political formation. Rather, it opens the door to all possible cultural forms and processes. It limits, therefore, notions of fixed power, social order and structure. It also acknowledges power's propensity for volatility and transition; in a theory of transculturalism, power is seen to function through processes of formation, exchange, reversal and subversion. These processes, as we will discuss below, may form concentrations of control, but these are never assured or presumed.

2 Transculturalism acknowledges in the contemporary context that cultural contiguity is inevitable, and that this contiguity may be good, bad or both. It suggests further that the epistemological, discursive and political intensification of the concept of 'difference' in fact limits the heuristic and ideological potential of cultural propinquity. That is, 'difference', like 'community', may be generative and positive, or it may be grotesque and oppressive, depending on the specific conditions of its discursive deployment. Globalization processes bring particular cultural formations together to form new hybrid

formations at an international and micro-community level. Transculturalism will always allow for transitions and mutations; these hybridities may increase or diminish human misery simultaneously or alternatively. Transculturalism offers no guarantees. Transculturalism, therefore, is a theory of perpetual exchange.

3 Transculturalism embraces the condition Lyotard (1991; see also Lewis, 1997a) calls 'the inhuman', Deleuze (1992) calls 'the imagination', Mouffe (1996) calls 'agonism', and Baudrillard (1994) calls the 'malefficient ecology'. This is a condition of multiple opposites and contradictions, both terrifying and pleasing, dissatisfied with systematized, orderly and organized liberal humanism (Lyotard, 1991) and the forces of domestication (Deleuze, 1992). This is to say, transculturalism is deeply suspicious of itself and its own theoretical tendencies to synthesis and illumination. It seeks to articulate the opposite intensities of the human and inhuman condition, the complex and chaotic, the logical and imaginative, the emotional and intellectual – acknowledging at all times that these intensities remain ultimately elusive and at critical times entirely indistinguishable. At this moment of acknowledgement comes the living and withering of true imagination and creativity. This is determined not by technology but by discursive gesture. It is a matter of distinguishing not between print and electronic media (Deleuze, 1992), but between an encompassing creativity or imagination (which is self-threatening) and a deficient, confining regularity – even a regularity that promotes itself as postmodern. Transculturalism would not seek to privilege posthumanism over humanism, nor humanism over posthumanism.

Rather, transculturalism allows the voices to speak and express their fears and hopes; it would give the terror of their irresolvability a voice.

4 The imagination of transculturalism is not easily conscripted into the capitalist project, but is intensely spontaneous, aberrant, subversive, dangerous and unpredictable. Transculturalism participates in mediation processes in order to form communities and meanings, but it also works to destabilize these formation both through the construction of alternative meanings and through the deconstructive imperatives of existing meanings. Transculturalism provides the space for meaning and undoing meaning.

5 Transculturalism is therefore political in that it promotes the discursive multiplicities of power exchange, though it insists that power – like meanings – is inevitably partial. Power intensities must be challenged with the greater might of the inhuman as much as the human, with imagination as much as intelligent conviction. Identity and difference should not, therefore, be essentialized but must be seen as ideological fragments, matters of everyday pleasure and resistance at the most immediate level, and matters of revulsion and revolution at the most brutal. The cyborg, in this sense, can only proclaim its potential in the light of a myriad alternative voices. Transculturalism is iconoclastic – as much in dispute as in dialogue with the invention of the future, refusing always to comply with the designation or determination of others.

6 That is, transculturalism rejects the essentialization of technology or progress. It rejects a utopianism which is not conditional, inhuman, imaginative or clouded by doubt. Transculturalism is a theory of change and its politics admit the possibility of social improvement via

the de-bordering potentialities of televisual and networked media. However, the visions of the cyborg, of the bit-driven world, of the 'harmonizing' superhighway, seem as terrible as they are hopeful. Transculturalism liberates identity from prescription and certainty. It allows culture to shape itself and deal with its own internal contradictions and haggling. It doesn't condemn the subject to an externally imposed order, but recognizes that this emancipation must always be threatened by disorder and doubt. This is what freedom is.

We have little expectation that a concept like transculturalism will replace the long-loved concept of culture (which has many fewer syllables for a start). However, our understanding of the concept of culture needs to be released from its past and the privileging of systematized order, common ground and a shared code. Communication and community are necessary and inevitable; however, these are constituencies of social order and the centralizing ideologies of a collectivist humanism. Celebrational postmodern politics has contributed to the extension and refinement of these forms of homogenized humanism. However, as with nineteenth-century forms of humanism, celebrational postmodern humanism is limited in its capacity to analyse culture critically since its own codes and ideologies are in fact highly localized and self-reflexive. Postmodern humanism constitutes a delusory utopianism which engages collectivist ideals through the intensification of the individual. This delusion has to be surrendered. Emancipation needs to be understood in terms of what a mind can possibly imagine more than just what emancipation is imagined to be. Our freedom, that is, should be expressed not in terms of a

false separation from collective codes, but as something that we might conceive in relation to and against those codes.

The Gulf War Did Take Place: The World is Burning (Brightly?)

As Ernesto Laclau (1996) has so forcefully demonstrated, the collective and the individual are not alternatives but interdependent elements of the same problematic. Transculturalism is not concerned to reconcile these two competing and supplementary parts; rather, it accepts the inevitability of their dispute and the possibility of achieving the best possible outcomes through the specific instance of their engagement. A transcultural analysis, that is, seeks to illuminate language wars which are formed through multiple discourses or 'heterodictions'. It deciphers the problematics of discourse claims and counter-claims, seeking always to deconstruct the various particulates that form around these wars. That is, rather than reduce to binary structures the complex of heterodictions that form culture in order to resolve them, transculturalism gives voice to the complexities and contradictions without the expectation of a resolution, conclusion or the analyst's consummate recommendation. The form and content of these language wars becomes available, therefore, to a more complete cultural and political analysis.

Some language wars are formed through extreme conditions, manifesting themselves in armed combat. As discussed in Chapter 10, the Gulf War and the US–Afghanistan war ('war against terrorism') are examples of ongoing imperialism and language struggles which erupted into physical conflict. In this sense, Jean Baudrillard's (1995) claim that the 'Gulf War did not take place' suggests that the armed conflict on the Persian peninsula was an event that had already been played out through the media. The complaints against Baudrillard's reading of the Gulf War (see Norris, 1992) reflect deeper misgivings about a 'postmodernist' privileging of symbols over the material and political conditions of lived experience. According to critics like Christopher Norris, Noam Chomsky and Edward Herman, the media functions primarily as a propaganda tool in America's military engagements in places like Iraq, Kosovo and Afghanistan; the media serves the interests of powerful elites, obscuring from the vision of American audiences the deaths and injuries inflicted on real people in a real war zone. In this sense, Baudrillard's mischievous claim that the Gulf War did not take place distracts from the realities of war and of the inimical role of the media.

As we have suggested, however, the Gulf War, like all modern televisual and digital wars, was formed and continues to be formed around critical language disputes. It is not a question of privileging the material over the symbolic, or vice versa. Rather, these wars are conducted through language which produces a range of effects. Baudrillard's apparent capitulation to the vacuousness of contemporary culture and the 'death of nature' thesis, is simply another manifestation of the language wars of contemporary culture generally and of imperialism in particular. Baudrillard remains trapped in language and must deploy it as his primary weapon. Baudrillard, like the deconstructionists and separationists discussed above, forms meanings (and ultimately non-meanings) around what he believes to be meaninglessness. He presents his claim to be heard, his claim to persuade, through a multi-layered poetic discourse – he establishes a dialogue between meanings and non-meanings, but even his non-meanings, like avant-garde postmodernism, are constituent of meaning-making – the

binary dissolved because the two, meaning/non-meaning, are operating simultaneously and often indistinguishably.

The wars in Persia, Kosovo and Afghanistan are resonances of colonialism and forms of continuing American imperialism. The Gulf War, in particular, was a battle waged over oil and territory. Simultaneously, it was a propaganda war fought out on First World television and through the American Congress. We now know that the Kuwaiti Ambassador paid millions of dollars to an American public relations company in order to elicit support from the Congress and the American public. We know that the Ambassador's daughter posed as a hospital 'worker' and told lies to the American Congress about Iraqi atrocities. We know that the presentation of the War on television was filtered through the media liaison department of the American military. Computerised images of so-called 'smart missiles', the heroic imagery of Operation Desert Storm, and the seemingly bloodless advance of the UN–US troops on the ground – all gave a sense of a brilliant, sanitized and bloodless war. But Baudrillard's claim that this was a war without adversaries or cause is as misleading as the American propaganda. The war was a serious, if complex, political engagement. It involved power, blood, oppression, the past and the future. The adversaries were formed through multiple and precarious associations with each of these elements. The rights of the Kuwaitis were infringed; the rights of the Iraqis were infringed. People died and were seriously maimed. Children were killed and orphaned. In Iraq today ordinary people are still starving to death.

In Afghanistan these alliances, agonisms and multiplying truth-claims seem even more elusive. US foreign policies, cultural and economic expansionism and the clandestine activities of the CIA have made

America a 'military' target for particular political factions in the Middle East. This culpability, however, does not justify the atrocities of the New York and Washington attacks. Nor, indeed, can America's reprisals against Afghanistan be justified, most particularly as they seem merely to perpetuate the cycle of retribution. In this context, power continues to function, even through disputes which are difficult to comprehend and even more difficult to advance toward some resolution. We might, that is, seek the redress of particular territorial and expansionist actions. We might also engage in the language wars of persuasion and propaganda as Edward Said found it necessary to do during the Gulf War. We might seek, that is, to decipher the 'differends' – equal and competing claims around which the language wars are fought. In any case, these extreme wars are rarely resolved and closed but will resonate into the future no matter which course we take. Our options in engaging with language wars are often to make the most of these complexities, to minimize harm, to advance the dispute through engagement. Most often the quickest and simplest strategies – as in Yugoslavia and Afghanistan – might achieve a short-term 'solution' which merely extends the dispute through a more unstable future.

These physical and bloody wars are among the more extreme or spectacular examples of a common cultural condition. Language wars exist through every moment of utterance: from personal relationships, through mass-mediated discourse, to governments and global engagements. The 'struggle to signify', as Stuart Hall calls it, is the primary characteristic of human cultural formations. As Michel Foucault rightly demonstrates, discourse and power are cohorts of the same inevitable human desire. Where there is language there is power, and where there is power there is challenge – culture is formed, that is,

around the necessities of language wars. The outcome of these wars is not a given, nor is it necessarily good nor bad, but may be either or both simultaneously. The same people who may congregate to watch the funeral of Princess Di or gaze repeatedly on the simulated sinking of the *Titanic* may be tearing each other apart over a divorce settlement, or over their different understanding of the teaching of God. These same people may have ancestors who fought over territory or who no longer feel nurtured by the land they love. They may be maddened by a trigger-happy media, a culture which lays out its fantasies in a seamless but senseless stream of images and sounds. These cultures each day grow bigger, wealthier and grander but leave the individual in a daze of desire and uncertainty.

This uncertainty is produced through the splitting or dissociating of our signifiers and their constituent reality. Cultures are formed through signification or meaning-making. However, as these cultures grow into self-referencing megaliths – corporations, institutions, ideologies, the state – they seek to establish themselves as a permanent and ultimate reality. This 'force-reality' is fallacious since it is removed from the immediacies of the everyday experiences which formed the signifier/reality/culture in the first place. The power that is formed through meaning concentration becomes increasingly erratic and increasingly unstable. Thus, while presenting itself as a stable reality, the nodal concentrations of culture are already collapsing, they are already hollowed out. The signifier has already split from its signified. The language wars are already dismantling the meanings and power which formed the nodal intensities. Personal dissatisfactions, mental breakdowns, divorce, social change, changes of government, military battles – all are symptoms of an

Figure 12.1 Andre the Giant

beat the dead beast into submission, to forge a new presence. This is not an act of simple utopianism, a remodelling of pleasure or despair. Rather, it is an engagement with the language wars, a seeking of victory through the Pyrrhic reconstruction of the signifier.

DISCUSSION: ANDRE THE GIANT AND OTHER Y2K DEMOCRATIC AVATARS

Andre the Giant is an image (see Figure 12.1). After a stellar career as a TV wrestler, the Andre image was reinscribed in the skateboard parks of the US, where graphics student and graffiti artist Shepard Fallrey adopted Andre as his personal skater ensign. 'The Giant has a Posse', Fairey quizzically remarked, and in the early 1990s the ensign was transformed into a popular sticker campaign; the Andre image appeared under railway bridges, in telephone booths and in nightclub toilets. The Giant and his posse are restless. They are in the street, in the shadows, seeking you out, watching you sleep. Eventually, when Andre made his way onto the Internet, slipping silently through the electronic gates, he became a global totem – unsanctioned, pervasive, postmodern, parodic, an unsettling manifestation of the new dreaming of the new youth.

Fairey, however, claims that there is no subversive intent, other than 'the presence' (omnipresence) itself. On the official Giant website, Fairey explains that the adoption of the Giant image by others is nothing more than the art of 'being here':

> The GIANT sticker campaign can be described as an experiment in Phenomenology. Heidegger describes Phenomenology as 'the process of letting things manifest themselves.' Phenomenology attempts to enable people to see clearly

already collapsing culture (transculture). This is not the random floating signifiers about which Baudrillard writes, but a strategic collapse through an authority which is inevitably hollowed out by its own fallacious and unsustainable intensity.

In many respects, therefore, the great formations and the power they imagine for themselves are simply an artifice, a display. The supernova of contemporary cultural institutions has already burnt out, but the gravity of its leaden mass must continue to be battled. Individuals and formations of micro-community have no choice but to deal with the mass, while simultaneously forging new meanings, new identities and new experiential discourses. The transcultural analyst must assist in that forging – must contribute to the deconstruction of the mass while providing some of the tools and blueprints for its replacement and the regeneration of new meanings. In this sense, we cannot wait for the stellar nodes of cultural power to burn out on their own. We must act. We must imagine. We must constantly re-create the culture. A multinational corporation is a supernova, a dying star, but it is the task of the political agent to something that is right before their eyes but obscured; things that are so taken for granted that they are muted by abstract observation.

The FIRST AIM OF PHENOMENOLOGY is to reawaken a sense of wonder about one's environment. The Giant sticker attempts to stimulate curiosity and bring people to question both the sticker and their relationship with their surroundings. (Fairey, 2000)

This unspecified radicalism is typical of 'culture jamming', (see Chapter 11) whereby the popular image is reappropriated by users and distributed through subterranean networks. Against the cultural noise of imposed and proliferating codes and icons, the Giant is issued with an amorphic and unfixable political identity.

Of course, there are those political commentators who would regard the Giant campaign and other forms of unspecified political activism as fatuous populism – an empty gesture which elicits little more than delinquent titillation and anti-authoritarianism (see McGuigan, 1996; Bennett, 1997; Kellner, 1997). For others, however, the Andre image would reflect a new promise, a reinvigoration of democratic and posthumanist ideals in the midst of a generally declining public sphere (see Bender and Druckrey, 1994; Redhead, 1997). To understand the political implications of the Andre campaign and other forms of populist culture jamming, we need to reconsider, as Robert Dahl (1989) urges, the underlying assumptions of contemporary democracy and democratic theory. Along these lines, Danilo Zolo (1992) argues that contemporary culture is characterized by increasing complexity and social differentiation. While this complexity brings the possibilities of an enhanced social and cultural diversity, it also problematizes many of the assumptions and underlying principles that inform contemporary democracy:

The central concern ... [is] the relationship between democratic institutions and the increasing complexity of post-industrial societies. ... [O]ur present theories of democracy fail to offer us conceptual instruments sufficiently complex to permit a realistic interpretation of that relationship. ... Western political theory appears increasingly unable to cope with the massive transformations which 'the information revolution' is bringing about in the primary subsystems of industrialized society. These transformations seem certain to speed up the processes of functional specialization and consequently ... to bring about still further large-scale growth of social complexity. (Zolo, 1992: 54)

Part of the problem for political theory, however, is the privileging of politics over culture and hence their separation from each other. Zolo's prescience concedes as much in suggesting that political theory generally and democratic theory specifically transgress the general empirical trajectory of modernity toward increasing levels of differentiation, specialization and social complexity. Democratic government, according to Zolo, is formed against this trend since the 'general function of a modern political system is that of reducing fear through a selective regulation of social risks and a competitive distribution of "security values"' (1992: 55). This 'amelioration of social risk' operates hegemonically, privileging the interests of particular social groups over others in a competitive cultural and economic context. To this extent, 'the central categories of the political code are the inclusion/exclusion principle and the asymmetric power/subordination relation' (Zolo, 1992: 55).

These complexities, as many other political theorists have recognized, are implicated in the increasing differentiation of cultural forms. Concepts like 'postmodernism', 'post-Fordism', 'post-industrialism', 'multiculturalism', and 'fragmentation' all refer to the disaggregating impulses of current society and culture. This increasing differentiation or disaggregation has led some theorists to emphasize the constituent nature of personal politics (Giddens, 1990, 1994), while others have sought to extend the political imperatives of democracy into a global condition (Held, 1987; Held et al., 1999). What is clear, however, is that contemporary democracy and democratic theory are implicated in communications processes which are the fundamental fabric of culture. In this very imporatant sense, culture is communication. Meanings cluster and shape themselves through the context and conduit of their medium; the medium is itself formed in terms of technological, spatial and historical conditions.

The complexity of contemporary (trans)culture is directly related to the complexity of these communicative forms: that is, to the density and differentiation associated with proliferating media discourses and texts. The image of Andre the Giant is implicated in new modes of democratic cultures that are themselves formed around assemblages of meaning. In this sense, democracy is not merely a fixed set of principles or institutions; rather, it needs to be understood as a lived experience, a work in progress, which has as its defining quality the possibility and actuality of individual liberation. Part of this liberation, of course, is the possibility and actuality of a self-governance which is facilitated through processes of cultural engagement. The freedom implied in democracy is not a single or overriding objective in the politics of power/domination, but is a series of creative gestures, some of which are complementary and others of which are antagonistic. In this way, a complex identity or liberated subjectivity is shaped through the intricate interplay of communicative experiences.

This broadened definition of democracy and the democratic subject expands the cultural policy and governmentality approaches discussed earlier in the chapter. McGuigan's (1996) desire for an 'expressive citizenship' is supplanted by the broader objective of an expressive and liberated subjectivity that is not determined in relation to the state alone. Citizenship may be a part of this democratic culture, though it is not an end so much as one political means amongst many others. A transcultural democratic mode of expression, in fact, privileges the potentiality of self-governance over the 'pragmatics' and 'imperatives' of institutional governance. In this way, Foucault's (1988) regret that his analyses of governmentality have paid too much attention to technologies of domination to the neglect of technologies of the self may be redressed; 'government by the people' is understood as an entirely ambiguous precept which vacillates arhythmically between the constituencies of the individual 'person' and the collective 'persons'. The idea of governmentality loses its cogency as the notion of domination is challenged from within its own borders. Individuals slip outside the instrumental logics of state management when they have no need of its discipline, care or observation. Foucault's schema fails us when we consider the idiomatic and sensate liberations that individuals create for themselves beyond the borders of constituent institutions and their power.

Thus, while Foucault alerts us to the dangers and gratifications associated with state-oriented management processes, his commentary never releases the subject from the limits of these technologies: Foucault never provides for us the means by which these controls may be reduced or evaded. In this sense, the technologies (techniques or apparatuses) of statutory management contribute to the essential formations of the subject, limiting individuals' scope for excess or overflow and emancipation. Of course, there are those postmodern celebrational cultural theorists, borrowing from Mikhail Bakhtin and Michel de Certeau, who have invented a politics of pleasure which situates liberation outside the discourses of governmentality, institutional democracy and conscious radical sedition. This celebration of everyday practice locates politics in various forms of social and cultural 'reversal': pilfering, bodily sense, popular aesthetics, personal use of worktime, and so on.

This type of everyday resistance, supposedly residing outside the determinations of discourse (culture, language, consciousness), struggles to distinguish itself from a type of anarchic hedonism. As it hurtles itself into a particulate self-absorption, it struggles, that is, to constitute its politics in terms of a participative or collective ideal which would enhance the possibilities of emancipation and social improvement. Among many others, McGuigan (1992) is particularly critical of this notion of a playful and unconscious politics, arguing that these reversals constitute a mere 'populism' that is implicated within the system it seeks to disrupt (see Chapter 8). That is, as subjects seek to maximize their personal advantage within the capitalist consumer system, they are actually perpetuating its seductive and pervasive power. The peripheral resistance to capitalist instrumentalism is never significant to the overall operation of systematic discipline, discrimination and subjugation.

In fact, McGuigan's expressive citizenship and de Certeau's consumer raiding respectively offer only partial explanations for the formation of contemporary cultural politics. In this sense, the Andre the Giant image and its deployment through various discursive modes represent a coalescence of democratic cultures. The Andre the Giant website is replete with playful anarchic chicanery as well as conscious and direct criticism of social and political institutions. The mysterious 'posse' is a rampant and rambunctious cultural avatar which has neither clear focus nor point of departure; the posse roams the Web and the material environments seeking some unspecified redress for an unspecified villainy. Contributors to the site may wish to fill in the meaning of the posse by directing their political vigil against multinational corporate profiteers. More often, however, this delinquent pleasure finds expression in a graffiti-ist reversal of authority where Andre is the anti-hero whose own 'authority' and 'strength' are always a pretence, an ironic and reflexive manifestation which deconstructs itself as it deconstructs the social power of others. This fiction is deployed in order to articulate the absurdity of hierarchical structures and a social order which fixes itself on prestige, consumption and social discrimination.

As already noted, there are a good many political theorists who would regard the Andre imagery and chicanery subversion generally as fatuous iconoclasm, an inconsequential distraction from genuine political critique. According to this view, the serious business of governance, social reform and democracy is somewhat undermined by an irrational or cynical populism which serves merely to gratify a personal aesthetic or light-minded anarchy. We would suggest, however, that the Andre imagery, along with various permutations of cultural jamming, constitutes an important part of the democratic cultural mosaic. Democratic cultures assemble around various modes of meaning-making and social practices associated with the liberation of subjectivity. Conceived in this way, democracy can be identified in terms of specific mediations and media-making processes. Specifically, democratic cultures are shaped and formed in relation to the major communicative media of print and electronic (audio and televisual) media. As we shall see below, these categories of democratic culture operate within and through one another, forming a volatile discursive mix in which 'democracy' becomes the central prize in the language wars of contemporary cultural politics.

Print Culture Democracy

The emergence of representative institutional democracy is clearly associated with the technology of printing. The 'rationality' of government, government bureaucracy and capitalism is facilitated by the organization and storage capacity of printed writing. More than this, however, print as a mass medium is profoundly implicated in the underlying problematics of capitalism and its related discourses. Print enables the subject and the patterns of subjective experience to be externalized, 'objectified' and 'represented' as text. This textualization constitutes a sort of presence-in-absence whereby the world appears to be present in the text, even though, of course, it is actually absent. The text is merely the representation of what is outside the text.

The notion of 'representation', therefore, appears to resolve this central ambiguity of modern societies. This concept of representation applies also to governmental processes based on democracy. 'Government' is the juridical text which seeks to resolve the interests of individuals and groups within an institutional framework of social order. Representatives who are elected are a presence-in-absence, a means by which individual citizens who are excluded from decision-making appear to be present. The interests and power of the representatives are formed around rationalist discourses; the citizenry appears to be

free and powerful because the institution of democratic government and its discourses obscure the absent–present dichotomy.

A significant part of this obscuration is the elevation of discourses of freedom and participation. Representation is supported through the oblique but nevertheless significant discourse of democratic participation. Print-based democracy articulates participation through officiated modes of citizenship. In this sense, participative democracy is both a critical alternative and a supplement to representational democracy. In either case, participation is rationalized through regulated processes. Electoral participation, lobbying, petition, legal protest, parliamentary enquiry committees, talkback radio, opinion polling, objective journalism – all constitute forms of print-based, participative democratic culture.

Broadcast Democratic Culture

As numerous writers from Heidegger to McLuhan and Baudrillard have noted, the emergence of electronic broadcast systems has led to the intensification and extensification of mediated communications. Time and space have been transformed into a kind of experiential 'instantaneity'. This instantaneity, while continuing the problematic of representation, is formed through the proliferation of words and the sensory ephemera of images and music. To this extent, the rationalism of print-based democratic discourse is not replaced by televisual and digital 'knowledge'; rather, the politics of print culture is immersed in new discursive forms, new modes of representation. Meanings proliferate as the social formation becomes increasingly complex, differentiated and discursively incommensurable.

As with print-based democratic culture, two more or less distinct categories of broadcast democracy can be identified:

celebrity democratic culture and visceral democratic culture. Celebrity politics is constituted around images of individuals who are prominent in the broadcast media and who are appropriated into the lives of viewers. In a sense, these images or 'celebrity politicians' are constituted through the institutional star system: that is, they are commodities constructed by media institutions for capitalist consumption.

Celebrity politics cannot be simply analysed in terms of differentials of power whereby the celebrity is part of a powerful media institution and necessarily expresses the interests of plutocracies. Rather, we need to conceive of celebrities as politicians who are constituted through the imaginings and instantaneities which televisual culture fosters. In this sense, the celebrity is another absent-present, a complex of power relationships that are both meaningful and vacated of meaning. The celebrity represents the individual viewer/consumer in much the same way as a politician will do. However, the relationship with the celebrity is more personal inasmuch as the presence of the celebrity is always and necessarily constituted through the imaginings and personal projections of the individual viewer. The celebrity is a fantastic presence which obscures the absence of a fleshly person with whom the viewer will have a fleshly relationship.

Thus, the celebrity is 'of the people', but removed 'from the people' by the miracle of mediated fame. Moreover, the celebrity is a complex of authority and subversion. He or she can only exist at the behest of the viewer, and yet this behest delegates and represents 'exceptional' authority: the authority to act, dress and speak in remarkably autonomous ways but in the service of other people's imaginings, interests and fantasies. Celebrities matter in democratic terms because they articulate this freedom and authority for others while being bound

to the context of instantaneity, fashion and ephemera. The meanings they have accumulated and generate are already bereft, already absent in the presence of their fantasy of authority.

Andre the Giant is a celebrity politician who is being forced to acknowledge this absent-present in his reinscribed demeanour. His meanings as a commodity televisual star have been surrendered in actuality so in a sense Andre's iconoclasm is the supernova, the dead star, of a celebrity politician. Even so, Andre the Giant succeeds as a popular figure partly because his ghostliness resonates with the celebrity culture from which he originates. Andre is therefore a complex icon/iconoclasm as his meanings oscillate between his celebrity origins and his new presence within the new cultural realm of anti-authority that has adopted him.

In either case, the Andre image has been made available for appropriation and reinscription within a visceral democratic culture. This visceral democratic culture operates in a variety of ways, though it is most characteristically a reflex of external authority which constitutes itself through modes of self-determination, self-expression and creative practices and meaning-making. Very often, the aesthetic of televisual culture is appropriated and deployed for the formation of a personal aesthetics and bodily pleasure.

Visceral democratic culture, therefore, begins from the position and perspective of the individual subject constituted through forms of self-authority. Unlike participative print-based democracy, however, visceral democracy is unspecified and begins and ends with the experience of the 'viscera' and bodily gratification. Thus, the unpredictability or unreliability of what is savagely demeaned as 'populism' is not a matter of regret, but a matter of necessity since for the self-interested viscera all external authority is to be suspected, abjured, endured and overcome. The individual interacts with televisual texts in order to experience a sensory aesthetic which becomes part of the cultural-political armoury for the self-determination of the viscera.

Ephemera, in this sense, is not the enemy of democracy, but its necessary conduit. Andre is the voice of this pursuit of freedom and self-governance. Andre is a 'relationship' that opens the self to inward and outward flows that always have as their central impetus the undoing of external authority.

Part of our problem in discussing democracy is the frequent insistence on an ideal of governmentality. Often this ideal has been expressed in terms of the legitimacy of authority and social order. Our argument here has been that democracy as the political expression of the people needs to be measured in terms of everyday meaning-making and everyday practices, some of which challenge the imposition of externally constituted modes of authority and order. It may be, of course, that an authoritative and rationalistic mode of democracy is necessary for the articulation of individual freedom, self-determination and self-expression. However, the very significant dangers that are implicated in this mode of democratic and rationalistic authority need also to be acknowledged. At least some aspects of the freedom which conventional democracy is supposed to have delivered may remain locked away within the walls of this authority; the alternative democratic cultures discussed above may provide important codes for its release.

In this sense, freedom may be marked by the facility of choice. But the value of that freedom is not confined to the provision of choice in itself; it is the expression of the choice, the actual choices that are made, which distinguishes our liberation. The increasing complexity of modern society requires individual subjects to live within and through various levels of culture. The democratic cultures outlined here operate through and within one another, often shaping our lives through various modes of consonance and dispute. In either case, the concept of democracy needs to escape older forms of critical condensation which reduce it to an idealized institutional paradigm. Rather, democracy must be understood in terms of how people live and make meaning. Andre the Giant and other Y2K cultural avatars may lack the dignity of Rousseau or Tom Paine, but they nevertheless have much to tell us about the condition of our freedom.

Genealogy of Cultural Studies

Cultural analyst	Principal texts (original date)	Contribution to the development of cultural studies
Social Enquiry		
René Descartes	*Meditations on First Philosophy* (1640)	Descartes theorised the split between the subject (I) and the object (all things outside the self). He also believed that maths should constitute a universal language.
John Locke	*Essay Concerning Human Understanding* (1690)	Humans are a blank sheet upon which things are written.
Immanuel Kant	*The Critique of Pure Reason* (1781), *Critique of Judgement* (1790)	Humans are born with frameworks of knowledge which connect with the frameworks of nature in order to produce knowledge. The mind is the rational dominion in which time, causality and spirit are reconciled.
G.W.F. Hegel	*The Phenomenology of Spirit* (1807)	The universe and the human mind are dialectically structured. Opposite poles clash and then are reconciled or synthesized. This process also defines the ascendance of the human mind to ultimate knowledge and morality.
Emile Durkheim	*The Rules of Sociological Method* (1895), *Suicide* (1897)	Defines social structure. Analyses the symbolism and culture of particular social groups. Focuses research on religious practices, art and artefacts.
Max Weber	*The Protestant Ethic and the Spirit of Capitalism* (1905), *The Religion of China* (1916)	Examines social action and the meanings that individual 'actors' attach to their actions. Society is constituted around a cohesive, symbolic system.
Robert Park	*Introduction to the Science of Sociology* (1921, with E. Burgess)	Takes an interest in the poor, immigrants and underprivileged. Directs sociological interest into the everyday experiences and personal lives of 'lower' social strata.
Martin Heidegger	*Being and Time* (1927)	Argues that the important thing about existence is that things are simply present in the world. Different from Romantics who believed that things have an 'essential' nature and that human consciousness (mind, reason) is the fount of deep knowledge.
Peter Berger	*The Social Construction of Reality* (1966, with T. Luckman)	Becomes interested in individual experiences of the world of objects and everyday experiences. Retains an interest in human consciousness; consciousness informs individual actions, meaning-making and choices.
Clifford Geertz	'Deep play: notes on the Balinese cockfight' (1972)	Is interested in the 'web of meaning' which constitutes non-modern, non-Western cultures. Geertz provides an interpretive framework for studying everyday practices as 'symbolic'.

Cultural analyst	Principal texts (original date)	Contribution to the development of cultural studies
Marxist and Critical Theory		
Karl Marx (and Frederick Engels)	*The Communist Manifesto* (1848), *Contribution to the Critique of the Political Economy* (1859)	Marx sees culture as the outcome of political economy. The notions of base-super-structure and ideology refer to the symbolic and social mechanisms which support economic inequalities.
Georg Lukács	*History and Class Consciousness* (1920)	Opposes avant-garde art. Prefers a literature which exposes the real conditions of social inequality, conflict and suffering.
Bertold Brecht	*The Threepenny Opera* (1928), *The Caucasian Chalk Circle* (1948)	Experimental art liberates humans from conformity and oppression. Humour, compassion, experimentation and sexuality are at the centre of the revolutionary project.
Theodor Adorno	*The Authoritarian Personality* (1950), *Dialectic of Enlightenment* (1944, with M. Horkheimer)	The mass media controls human thinking and creates the pseudo individual. Liberation through complex art.
Louis Althusser	*For Marx* (1963)	Dominant ideology affects all levels of culture. Ideology is the symbolic dimension of a society's thinking and action. Culture can work independently of political economy.
Antonio Gramsci	*Selections from Political Writings* (1921–26)	Oppressed social groups negotiate their subjugation with organic intellectuals. Hegemony is a negotiated leadership.
Jugen Habermas	*The Theory of Communicative Action* (1984)	Social reform is facilitated by consensus and communicative action.
Paul Ricoeur	*Political and Social Essays* (1974)	In-depth interpretation of texts releases the reader's mind to alternative worlds and liberations.
Fredric Jameson	*The Political Unconscious* (1981)	Adapts Althusser and deconstruction techniques to explain contemporary culture. Postmodern consumerism destabilizes the reform agenda since it removes the frameworks of history.
British Studies		
Matthew Arnold	*Culture and Anarchy* (1869)	Culture is a collection of the best and most worthy texts produced by a society. Fears the anarchic and sensate predisposition of the industrial working classes. Recommends universal education and the general elevation of the working-classes to a state of culture.

Cultural analyst	Principal texts (original date)	Contribution to the development of cultural studies
F.R. Leavis	*The Great Tradition* (1948)	Wants all classes to be exposed to the morality and sublime aesthetics of the great tradition of English literature (high culture).
Richard Hoggart	*The Uses of Literacy* (1958)	Uses an anthropological model to explore working class culture and meaning-making. Tracks the effects of American mass produced culture on the urban, working classes of England.
Raymond Williams	*Culture and Society* (1958), *The Long Revolution* (1961), *Culture* (1981)	Seeks to reconcile culture as a 'way of life' and as 'meaning-making'. Implies a dissolution of high art – popular art divide, though never adequately theorised. Retains an interest in complex literature.
E.P. Thompson	*The Making of the English Working Class* (1963)	Focuses history on the everyday practices and meaning-making of the English working class. Writes a Marxist interpretation of class. Culture is not a single way of life. Culture is struggle between different ways of living.
Stuart Hall	'Encoding/decoding' (1980), 'The rediscovery of ideology: the return of the repressed in cultural studies' (1982)	Brings French structural and Gramscian theory into British cultural studies. Focuses on the popular media. Broadens the concept of culture to include the media consumption practices of all social groups. Politics is central to cultural studies. Foregrounds the pleasure of popular culture consumption. Pleasure becomes a central part of cultural politics.
John Fiske	*Television Culture* (1987), *Understanding Popular Culture* (1989)	Foregrounds popular culture through the adoption of theories of pleasure, play and consumption.
John Hartley	*Popular Reality* (1996)	Emphasizes the significance of popular consumption and the construction of 'news'.
Language theories Ludwig Wittgenstein	*Tractatus Logico-Philosophicus* (1922), *Zettel (The Blue Book)* (1967)	Accepts that language and objects have an entirely arbitrary relationship. Explains language as a system of logical propositions. Later, language operates like 'games'.
Charles (C.S.) Peirce	*Collected Papers* (1931–58)	Language and other meaning systems can be understood as signs.
Ferdinand de Saussure	*Course in General Linguistics* (1915)	The sign is constituted through signifiers and signifieds. Individual signs operate in relation to the 'system' of signs. The system marks discrete differences in meaning (signification).

451

Cultural analyst	Principal texts (original date)	Contribution to the development of cultural studies
Claude Levi-Strauss	*Structural Anthropology* (1968)	Narrative patterns (language structures) or myths are common to all cultures. They are deployed to resolve complex social tensions.
Roland Barthes	*Mythologies* (1957), *The Pleasure of the Text* (1973)	Myths operate in contemporary culture. Pleasure is central to reading texts. Bliss extends the reading experience beyond structure.
Jacques Derrida	*Of Grammatology* (1974), *Writing and Difference* (1976)	Meaning (origin) is always deferred. Writing forms itself around the presence of an imagined origin of meaning. Writing should be 'deconstructed' in order to expose its false origin.
Michel Foucault	*Discipline and Punish* (1975), *The History of Sexuality Vol. I* (1976)	Discourse, power and knowledge are mutually supportive. Power functions at the level of micro-physics (particular and personal). Power and discourse are unstable and exchangeable.
Jacques Lacan	*The Four Fundamental Concepts of Psycho Analysis* (1973)	The subject is unstable and 'open'. Subjects enter the 'symbolic' as they learn and use language. Subjects discover 'lack' and the inevitability of unsatisifed desire. Meanings are perpetually deferred.
Gilles Deleuze and Felix Guattari	*Anti-Oedipus* (1972), *A Thousand Plateaus* (1980)	Psychological disturbances represent meaning gaps and adventures in the creation of new meanings. Seek to liberate subjects' bodies and minds from authoritarian and anti-pleasurable discourses (such as medical pathology, conservatism, Marxism).

Cultural feminism

Harriet Taylor-Mill	*Essays on Sex Equality* (1970)	A Suffragette who believes in the values of social and economic utility. Personal happiness would contribute to social improvement.
Virginia Woolf	*A Room of One's Own* (1929)	Seeks to re-order Mathew Arnold's conception of culture through development of a distinctively female literary voice. Women's style and interests are more flexible than men's.
Simone de Beauvoir	*The Second Sex* (1949)	A socialist feminist who believed that capitalist patriarchy was centrally responsible for women's oppression. Seeks to liberate women's desire from male control and romantic idealism.
Kate Millett	*Sexual Politics* (1970)	Critiques the representation of women and women's sexuality in male literature. Rejects patriarchal images of femininity; rejects images of women as 'sex objects'.

Cultural analyst	Principal texts (original date)	Contribution to the development of cultural studies
Laura Mulvey	'Visual pleasure and narrative cinema' (1975)	The shape, style and industrial context of narrative cinema have been constructed around males' visual pleasure: men gaze upon women.
Julia Kristeva	*Desire in Language* (1980)	Applies poststructural theory to a form of feminist analysis. Seeks the liberation of sex and desire without recourse to prescribed, pre-existing patriarchal structures. Liberates the unconscious and its rhythms. Privileges poetic language.
Angela McRobbie	'*Jackie:* an ideology of adolescent feminism' (1978), *Feminism and Youth Culture* (1991)	Earlier girls' magazines reinforce patriarchal attitudes and images. More recent girls' magazines provide opportunities for more sexually adventurous subjectivities.
Ien Ang	*Watching Dallas* (1985), *Living Room Wars* (1996)	Feminism must account for women's emotional and lifestyle predispositions. Romantic ideals may be a source of genuine liberation for women.
Postmodernism Susan Sontag	*Against Interpretation* (1966)	Rejects formal interpretation as the normalization of art's radical potential. Seeks the inclusion of popular culture as enlivening, transgressive (avant-garde) art.
Ihab Hassan	*The Dismemberment of Orpheus* (1971)	Praises twentieth century literature which reaches beyond modern nihilism. Includes literature of Samuel Becket and William Burroughs – destabilizes form, sanity and sexuality.
Andreas Huyessen	*After the Great Divide* (1986)	There is a great divide between modern and postmodern culture.
Daniel Bell	*The Coming of Post-Industrial Society* (1973)	Society is entering a new phase based on the cognitive modes of science and information exchange.
Jean Francois Lyotard	*The Postmodern Condition* (1984)	In the postmodern condition, modern 'metanarratives' are challenged by new ways of thinking and representation.
Fredric Jameson	*Postmodernism or, the Cultural Logic of Late Capitalism* (1991)	Televisual, consumer culture compresses time and space, creating an historical amnesia with no reference for reform.
Jean Baudrillard	Simulations (1983), *The Illusion of the End* (1994)	Reality has been replaced by a televisual hyperreality. Everything is an imitation of an imitation (simulacrum).
Charles Jencks	*What is Postmodernism?* (1986)	Postmodern aesthetics best represents contemporary human imaginings and pleasures.

Cultural analyst	Principal texts (original date)	Contribution to the development of cultural studies
Jurgen Habermas	'Modernity – an incomplete project' (1983), 'The French path to postmodernity' (1984)	Rejects postmodernism. Offers the alternative of a consensual speech situation and the democratic public sphere.
Audiences		
Payne Fund studies	From 1933	Examines the effects of the media (especially cinema) on individuals.
James Lull	'The social uses of television' (1980)	Audiences use and derive gratification from watching television. Uses ethnographic techniques.
Colin MacCabe	*High Theory/Low Culture* (1986)	Audiences are 'positioned' by the text and its ideology.
Stuart Hall	'Encoding/decoding' (1980)	Producers 'encode' meanings into text; readers 'decode' them. Gramsci's hegemony informs this meaning-making 'negotiation'.
David Morley	*The 'Nationwide' Audience* (1980), *Family Television* (1986)	Seeks direct information about decoding practices through enthnographic-empirical studies of audiences (including families).
Pierre Bourdieu	*Distinction* (1979)	Cultural 'taste' is determined by social conditions (including class).
Michel de Certeau	*The Practice of Everyday Life* (1974), *The Writing of History* (1975)	Freedom is achieved through the everyday practices (tactical raiding) of ordinary people.
John Fiske	*Reading the Popular* (1989)	Audiences consume texts tactically. Audience pleasure is the source of transgressive freedom. Audiences 'raid' textual meaning.
Janice Radway	*Reading the Romance* (1987)	Women's freedom comes from text selection and reading pleasures.
Ien Ang	*Dallas* (1985), *Living Room Wars* (1996)	Soap operas like *Dallas* provide women with a resource for personal pleasure and community-building. Uses empirical methods.
Henry Jenkins	*Textual Poachers* (1992)	Fans constitute a community (culture) of meaning-makers.

References

Acker, J. (1991) 'Hierarchies, jobs, bodies: a theory of gendered organizations' in J. Lorber and S. Farrell, eds, *The Social Construction of Gender*, Sage, London.

Adamse, M. and Motta, S. (1996) *Online Friendship, Chat Room Romance and Cybersex*, Health Communications Inc., Deerfield Beach, FL.

Adorno, T. (1994) 'On popular music' in J. Storey, ed., *Cultural Theory and Popular Culture: A Reader*, Harvester Wheatsheaf, Hemel Hempstead.

Adorno, T., Frenkel, B., Levinson, D. and Sanford, N. (1950) *The Authoritarian Personality*, Norton, New York.

Agger, B. (1992) *Cultural Studies as Critical Theory*, Falmer Press, London.

Alasuutari, P. (1995) *Researching Culture: Qualitative Method and Cultural Studies*, Sage, London.

Alexander, J., ed. (1988) *Durkheimian Sociology: Cultural Studies*, Cambridge University Press, Cambridge.

Althusser, L. (1969) *For Marx*, Allen Lane, London.

Althusser, L. (1971) 'Ideology and ideological state apparatuses' in L. Althusser, *Lenin and Philosophy and Other Essays*, New Left Books, London.

Althusser, L. (1971) 'Letter on art' in L. Althusser, *Lenin and Philosophy*, trans. B. Brewster, New Left Books, London.

Althusser, L. (1984) *Essays on Ideology*, Verso, London.

Anderson, B. (1990) *Language and Power: Exploring Political Cultures in Indonesia*, Cornell University Press, Ithaca, NY.

Anderson, B. (1991) *Imagined Communities: Reflections on the Origin and Spread of Nationalism*, rev. edn, Verso, London.

Ang, I. (1985) *Watching Dallas: Soap Opera and the Melodramatic Imagination*, Methuen, London.

Ang, I. (1990) *Desperately Seeking the Audience*, Routledge, London.

Ang, I. (1991) 'Stalking the wild viewer,' *Continuum*, 42.

Ang, I. (1996) *Living Room Wars: Rethinking Media Audiences for a Postmodern World*, Routledge, London.

Ang, I. and Stratton, J. (1996) 'Asianing Australia: notes toward a critical transnationalism in cultural studies', *Cultural Studies*, 10 (1).

Appadurai, A. (1990) 'Disjuncture and difference in the global cultural economy' in M. Featherstone, ed., *Global Culture: Nationalism, Globalization and Modernity*, Sage, London.

Appadurai, A. (1996) *Modernity at Large: The Cultural Dimensions of Globalization*, University of Minnesota Press, Minneapolis.

Arac, J. ed. (1988) *After Foucault: Humanistic Knowledge, Postmodern Challenges*, Rutgers University Press, New Brunswick, NJ.

Arnold, M. (1949) *Culture and Anarchy*, Everyman's Library, London.

Background Briefing (1999) 'Culture jamming: how to make trouble and influence people', ABC National Radio, 18 October.

Baker, R. (1999) *Sex in the Future: Ancient Urges Meet Future Technology*, Macmillan, Basingstoke.

Bakhtin, M. (1984) *Problems of Dostoevsky's Poetics*, trans. C. Emerson, Manchester University Press, Manchester.

Bakhtin, M. and Medvedev, P.N. (1978) *The Formal Method in Literary Scholarship*, trans. A.J. Wehrie, Johns Hopkins University Press, Baltimore.

Barney, D. (2000) *Prometheus Wired: The Hope for Democracy in the Age of Network Technology*, University of Chicago Press, Chicago.

Barthes, R. (1967) *Elements of Semiology*, trans. A. Lavers and C. Smith, Jonathan Cape, London.

Barthes, R. (1973) *Mythologies*, trans. A. Lavers, Paladin, St Albans.

Barthes, R. (1975) *The Pleasure of the Text*, trans. R. Miller, Hill and Wang, New York.

Barthes, R. (1977) *Image–Music–Text*, trans. S. Heath, Fontana, London.

Barthes, R. (1982) *The Fashion System*, trans. M. Ward and R. Howard, Hill and Wang, New York.

Baudrillard, J. (1975) *The Mirror of Production*, trans. M. Poster, Telos Press, St Louis.

Baudrillard, J. (1981) *For a Critique of the Political Economy of the Sign*, trans. C. Levin, Telos Press, St Louis.

Baudrillard, J. (1983a) *In the Shadow of the Silent Majorities*, trans. P. Foss, S. Johnson and P. Pallon, Semiotext(e), New York.

Baudrillard, J. (1983b) 'The ecstasy of communication' in H. Foster, ed., *The Anti-Aesthetic: Essays on Postmodern Culture*, Bay Press, Seattle.

Baudrillard, J. (1984a) *Simulations*, trans. P. Foss, Semiotext(e), New York.

Baudrillard, J. (1984b) 'The procession of simulacra' in H. Wallis, ed., *Art After Modernism: Rethinking Representation*, Museum of Modern Art, New York.

Baudrillard, J. (1985a) 'The masses: the implosion of the social in the media', trans. M. McLean, *New Literary History*, 16 (3), Spring.

Baudrillard, J. (1985b) *Jean Baudrillard: Selected Writings*, ed., M. Poster, Polity, Cambridge.

Baudrillard, J. (1987) *Forget Foucault*, Semiotext(e), New York.

Baudrillard, J. (1988) *The Ecstasy of Communication*, trans. B. Schutze and C. Schutze, Semiotext(e), New York.

Baudrillard, J. (1990) *Seduction*, trans. B. Singer, Culturetext, New York.

Baudrillard, J. (1994) *The Illusion of the End*, trans. C. Turner, Polity, Cambridge.

Baudrillard, J. (1993) *Symbolic Exchange and Death*, trans. I. Hamilton, Sage, London.

Baudrillard, J. (1995) *The Gulf War Did Not Take Place*, trans. P. Paron, Power Publications, New South Wales.

Baudrillard, J. (1996) *The System of Objects*, trans. J. Benedict, Verso, London.

Baudrillard, J. (1998) *The Consumer Society: Myths and Structures*, trans. C. Turner, Sage, London.

Becker, H. and McCall, M. (1990) *Symbolic Interaction and Cultural Studies*, University of Chicago Press, Chicago.

Bell, D. (1973) *The Coming of Post-Industrial Society*, Basic Books, New York.

Bell, D. (1976) *The Cultural Contradictions of Capitalism*, Basic Books, New York.

Bender, G. and Druckrey, D. (1994) *Culture on the Brink: Ideologies of Technology*, Bay Press, Seattle.

Benjamin, W. (1977) 'The work of art in the age of mechanical reproduction' in *Illuminations*, trans. M. Zohn, Fontana, London.

Bennett, T. (1985) 'The politics of the popular' in V. Beechey and J. Donald, eds, *Subjectivity and Social Relations*, Open University Press, Milton Keynes.

Bennett, T. (1986) 'Hegemony, ideology, pleasure: Blackpool' in T. Bennett, C. Mercer and J. Woollacott, eds, *Popular Culture and Social Relations*, Open University Press, Milton Keynes.

Bennett, T. (1997) 'Towards a pragmatics of cultural studies' in J. McGuigan, ed., *Cultural Methodologies*, Sage, London.

Bennett, T. (1999) 'Putting policy into cultural studies' in S. During, ed., *The Cultural Studies Reader*, 2nd edn, Routledge, London.

Bennett, T., Mercer, C. and Woollacott, J., eds (1986) *Popular Culture and Social Relations*, Open University Press, Milton Keynes.

Bennett, T., Frith, S., Grossberg, L., Shepherd, J. and Turner, G., eds (1993) *Rock and Popular Music: Politics, Policies, Institutions*, Routledge, London.

Berger, M., Wallis, B. and Watson, S., eds (1995) *Constructing Masculinity*, Routledge, New York.

Berger, P. (1967) *The Sacred Canopy*, Doubleday, Garden City, NY.

Berger, P. and Luckmann, T. (1966) *The Social Construction of Reality*, Doubleday, Garden City, NY.

Bernstein, R., ed. (1985) *Habermas and Modernity*, Blackwell, Oxford.

Bersani, L. (1995) *Homos*, Harvard University Press, Cambridge, MA.

Bertilsson, M. (1991) 'Love's labour lost? A sociological view' in M. Featherstone, M. Hepworth and B.S. Turner, eds, *The Body: Social Process and Cultural Theory*, Sage, London.

Best, K. and Lewis, J. (2000) 'Hacking the democratic mainframe: (Dis)Organising transgressive computing', *Media International Australia*, 95, May.

Bhabha, H. (1987) 'Interrogating identity' in H. Bhabha, ed., *Identity: The Real Me*, ICA, London.

Bhabha, H. (1990) *Nation and Narration*, Routledge, London.

Bhabha, H. (1994) *The Location of Culture*, Routledge, London.

Bleitch, D. (1978) *Subjective Criticism*, Johns Hopkins University Press, Baltimore.

Blount, M. and Cunningham, G. (1996) *Representing Black Men*, Routledge, New York.

Blumer, H. (1933) *The Movies and Conduct*, Macmillan, New York.

Bogard, W. (1996) *The Simulation of Surveillance*, Cambridge University Press, Cambridge.

Boller, D. (1992) 'Literature in the electronic writing space' in M. Tuman, ed., *Literacy Online*, University of Pittsburgh Press, Pittsburgh.

Boller, D. (1993) 'The information superhighway: roadmap for renewed public purpose', *Tikkum*, 8 (4).

Bourdieu, P. (1977) *Outline of a Theory of Practice*, trans. R. Nice, Cambridge University Press, Cambridge.

Bourdieu, P. (1984) *Distinction: A Social Critique of the Judgement of Taste*, Routledge, London.

Bourdieu, P. (1990) *Language and Symbolic Power*, Polity, Cambridge.

Bourdieu, P. (1991) 'Sport and social class' in C. Mukerji and M. Schudson, eds, *Rethinking Popular Culture*, University of California Press, Berkeley.

Boyne, R. and Rattansi, A., eds (1990) *Postmodernism and Society*, St Martin's Press, New York.

Bradbury, M. and McFarlane, J., eds (1978) *Modernism*, Penguin, Harmondsworth.

Brunsdon, C. (1981) '"Crossroads", Notes on soap opera', *Screen*, 22 (4).

Bryman, A. (1995) *Disney and His Worlds*, Routledge, London.

Buchbinder, D. (1998) *Performance Anxieties: Reproducing Masculinity*, Allen & Unwin, Sydney.

Burchell, G., Gordon, C. and Miller, P., eds (1991) *The Foucault Effect: Studies in Governmentality*, University of Chicago Press, Chicago.

Burroughs, W. (1966) *Exterminator*, Viking, New York.

Butter, J. (1995) 'Melancholy gender/refused identification' in M. Berger, B. Wallis and S. Watson, eds, *Constructing Masculinity*, Routledge, London.

Carey, J. (1989) *Communication as Culture*, Unwin Hyman, Boston.

Carlyle, T. (1967) *Essays: English and Other Critical Essays*, Everyman's Library, London.

Carruthers, S. (2000) *The Media at War: Communication and Conflict in the Twentieth Century*, Macmillan, London.

Castells, M. (1997) *The Power of Identity*, Blackwell, London.

Caygill, H. (1990) 'Architectural postmodernism: the retreat of an avant-garde?' in R. Boyne and A. Rattasnsi, eds, *Postmodernism and Society*, St Martin's Press, New York.

Chambers, I. (1988) *Popular Culture: The Metropolitan Experience*, Routledge, London.

Childs, K. (1991) 'Daimaru man defends his vision of the future', *The Age*, 28 October.

Chomsky, N. (1988) *Manufacturing Consent: The Political Economy of the Media*, Pantheon, New York.

Chomsky, N. (2001) *September 11*, Allen & Unwin, Crow's Nest.

Cixous, H. and Clément, C. (1986) *The Newly Born Woman*, trans. B. Wing, University of Minnesota Press, Minneapolis.

Clarke, D. (1993) '"With my body, I thee worship": the social construction of marital sexual problems' in S. Scott and D. Morgan, eds, *Body Matters: Essays on the Sociology of the Body*, Falmer Press, London.

Coleridge, S. (1962) *Coleridge: Selected Poetry and Prose*, Nonesuch Press, London.

Collins, J. (1989) *Uncommon Cultures: Popular Culture and Post-modernism*, Routledge, New York.

Connor, S. (1989) *Postmodernist Culture: An Introduction to Theories of the Contemporary*, Blackwell, New York.

Cornell, R.W. (1990) 'An iron man: the body and some contradictions of hegemonic masculinity' in M. Messner and Donald Sabo, eds, *Sport, Men and the Gender Order*, Human Kinetics Books, Champaign.

Cowie, E. (1984) 'Fantasia', *m/f*, 9.

Coyne, R. (1999) *Technoromanticism: Digital Narrative, Holism, and the Romance of the Real*, MIT Press, Massachussets.

Crary, J. and Kwinter, S., eds (1992) *Incorporations*, Zone Books, New York.

Creed, B. (1997) 'Screen sex: from television to teledildonics' in J. Matthews, ed., *Sex in Public*, Allen & Unwin, Sydney.

Culler, J. (1975) *Structuralist Poetics: Structuralism, Linguistics and the Study of Literature*, Routledge and Kegan Paul, London.

Dahl, R. (1989) *Democracy and its Critics*, Yale University Press, New Haven.

Darwin, C. (1859) *On the Origin of Species by Means of Natural Selection, or the Preservation of Favoured Races in the Struggle for Life*. John Murray: London.

Davies, C. (1993) 'Aboriginal rock music: space and place' in T. Bennett, S. Frith, L. Grossberg, J. Shepherd and G. Turner, eds, *Rock and Popular Music: Politics, Policies, Institutions*, Routledge, London.

Davies, J. (1999) *Diana: Constructing the People's Princess*, Macmillan, Melbourne.

Davies, P. (1983) *God and the New Physics*, Penguin, Harmondsworth.

Davies, P. (1987) *The Cosmic Blueprint*, Heinemann, London.

de Beauvoir, S. (1972) *The Second Sex*, trans. H.M. Parshley, Penguin, Harmondsworth.

de Certeau, M. (1984) *The Practice of Everyday Life*, trans. S. Rendall, University of California Press, Berkeley.

de Certeau, M. (1988) *The Writing of History*, trans. T. Conley, Columbia University Press, New York.

de Lauretis, T. (1987) *Technologies of Gender: Essays on Theory, Film and Fiction*, Macmillan, London.

de Man, P. (1971) *Blindness and Insight: Essays in the Rhetoric of Contemporary Criticism*, Oxford University Press, New York.

de Saussure, F. (1974) *Course in General Linguistics*, Fontana, London.

Deleuze, G. (1977) 'Discussion with Michel Foucault' in M. Foucault, *Language, Counter-Memory and Practice: Selected Essays and Interviews*, trans. D.F. Bouchard and S. Simon, Blackwell, Oxford.

Deleuze, G. (1992) 'Mediators', trans. M. Joughin, in J. Crary and S. Kwinter, eds, *Incorporations*, Zone Books, New York.

Deleuze, G. and Guattari, F. (1983) *Anti-Oedipus: Capitalism and Schizophrenia*, trans. R. Hurley, M. Seem and H. Lane, University of Minnesota Press, Minneapolis.

Deleuze, G. and Guattari, F. (1987) *A Thousand Plateaus: Capitalism and Schizophrenia*, trans. B. Massumi, University of Minnesota Press, Minneapolis.

Denzin, N. (1992) *Symbolic Interactionism and Cultural Studies: The Politics of Interpretation*, Blackwell, Cambridge, MA.

Derrida, J. (1970) 'Discussion' in *The Structuralist Controversy: The Languages of Criticism and the Sciences of Man*, R. Macksey and E. Donato, eds, John Hopkins University Press, Baltimore.

Derrida, J. (1974) *Of Grammatology*, trans. G.C. Spivak, Johns Hopkins University Press, Baltimore.

Derrida, J. (1979) *Writing and Difference*, trans. A. Bass, Routledge and Kegan Paul, London.

Derrida, J. (1981) *Dissemination*, trans. B. Johnson, University of Chicago Press, Chicago.

Dery, M. (1996) *Escape Velocity: Cyberculture at the End of the Millennium*, Hodder & Stoughton, New York.

Descombes, V. (1980) *Modern French Philosophy*, Cambridge University Press, Cambridge.

Dews, P. (1984) *Logics of Disintegration: Post-structuralist Thought and the Claims of Critical Theory*, Verso, London.

Docker, J. (1994) *Postmodernism and Popular Culture: A Cultural History*, Cambridge University Press, Cambridge.

Docker, J. (1995) 'Rethinking postcolonialism and multiculturalism in the *fin de siècle*', *Cultural Studies*, 9 (3).

Douglas, M. (1978) *Implicit Meanings: Essays in Anthropology*, Routledge and Kegan Paul, London.

Drew, A. (1998) 'Elizabeth Tudor and Diana Spencer: Charming an image; Recovering a life' in A. Hall, ed., *Delights, Desires and Dilemmas: Essays on Women and the Media*, Praeger, Westport, Conn.

Driscoll, C. (1995) 'Who needs a boyfriend? The homocentric virgin in adolescent women's magazines' in P. van Toorn and D. English, eds, *Speaking Positions: Aboriginality, Gender and Ethnicity in Australian Cultural Studies*, Victoria University of Technology, Melbourne.

Drummond, M. (1998a) 'When size matters: confusions and concerns over the ideal male body', *Body Image Research Forum* (Conference proceedings), Body Image and Health Inc. Melbourne.

Drummond, M. (1998b) 'Bodies: an emerging issue for boys and young men', *Everybody*, 2, August.

During, S. (1999) 'Popular culture on a global scale: a challenge for cultural studies?' in H. Mackay and T. O'Sullivan, eds, *The Media Reader: Continuity and Transformation*, Sage, London.

Durkheim, É. (1960) 'Preface to *L'Année sociologique 2*' in K. Wolff, ed., *Émile Durkheim et al. on Sociology and Philosophy*, Free Press, New York.

Durkheim, É. (1977) *The Evolution of Educational Thought*, Routledge and Kegan Paul, London.

References

Dyer, R. (1985) *Heavenly Bodies: Filmstars and Society*, Macmillan, Basingstoke.

Eagleton, T. (1978) *Criticism and Ideology*, Verso, London.

Eagleton, T. (1984) *The Function of Criticism*, Verso, London.

Eco, U. (1984) 'Postmodernism, irony and the enjoyable' in *Postscript to The Name of the Rose*, trans. W. Weapon, Harcourt Brace Jovanovich, New York.

Ehrenreich, B. (1995) 'The decline of patriarchy' in M. Berger, B. Wallis and S. Watson, eds, *Constructing Masculinity*, Routledge, New York.

Eisenstein, E. (1983) *The Printing Revolution in Early Modern Europe*, Cambridge University Press, Cambridge.

Elliott, G. (1994) *Louis Althusser: A Critical Reader*, Blackwell, Oxford.

Engels, F. (1994) 'Letter to Joseph Bloch' in J. Storey, ed., *Cultural Theory and Popular Culture: A Reader*, Harvester Wheatsheaf, Hemel Hempstead.

Ess, C. (1994) 'The political computer: hypertext, democracy and Habermas' in G. Landow, ed., *Hyper/Text/Theory*, Johns Hopkins University Press, Baltimore.

Fairey, S. (2000) 'A social and psychological explanation of Giant has a Posse', at <http://www.obeygiant.com/>.

Featherstone, M. (1991) *Consumer Culture and Postmodernism*, Sage, London.

Featherstone, M. (1996) 'Globalism, localism and cultural identity' in R. Wilson and W. Dissanayake, eds, *Global Local: Cultural Production and the Transnational Imaginary*, Duke University Press, London.

Featherstone, M. and Hepworth, M. (1991) 'The mask of ageing and the postmodern life course' in M. Featherstone, M. Hepworth and B. Turner, eds, *The Body: Social Process and Cultural Theory*, Sage, London.

Featherstone, M., Hepworth, M. and Turner, B., eds (1991) *The Body: Social Process and Cultural Theory*, Sage, London.

Fiske, J. (1987) *Television Culture*, Methuen, London.

Fiske, J. (1989a) *Reading the Popular*, Unwin Hyman, Boston.

Fiske, J. (1989b) *Understanding Popular Culture*, Unwin Hyman, Boston.

Fiske, J. (1996) *Media Matters: Race and Gender in US Politics*, University of Minnesota Press, Minneapolis.

Fiske, J. and Glynn, K. (1995) 'Trials of the postmodern', *Cultural Studies*, 9 (3).

Fiske, J., Hodge, B. and Turner, G. (1987) *Myths of Oz: Reading Australian Popular Culture*, Allen & Unwin, Sydney.

Flood, J. (1989) *The Archaeology of the Dreamtime*, new edn, W. Collins, Sydney.

Flood, J. (1990) *The Riches of Ancient Australia: A Journey into Prehistory*, University of Queensland Press, St Lucia.

Forester, T. (1992) 'Megatrends or megamistakes? Whatever happened to the information society?', *The Information Society*, 8 (3).

Foster, H. ed. (1983) *The Anti-aesthetic: Essays on Postmodern Culture*, Bay Press, Seattle.

Foucault, M. (1972) *The Archaeology of Knowledge and the Discourse on Language*, trans. A.M. Sheridan, Pantheon, New York.

Foucault, M. (1974) *The Order of Things: An Archaeology of the Human Sciences*, Tavistock, London.

Foucault, M. (1977a) *Discipline and Punish: The Birth of the Prison*, trans. A.M. Sheridan, Penguin, New York.

Foucault, M. (1977b) *Language, Counter-memory, Practice: Selected Essays and Interviews*, trans. D.F. Bouchard and S. Simon, Blackwell, Oxford.

Foucault, M. (1980) *Power/Knowledge: Selected Interviews and Other Writings*, Pantheon, New York.

Foucault, M. (1981) *The History of Sexuality, Volume One: An Introduction*, trans. R. Hurley, Penguin, New York.

Foucault, M. (1984) 'What is Enlightenment?' trans. C. Porter in P. Rabinow, ed., *The Foucault Reader*, Penguin, London.

Foucault, M. (1988) 'Technologies of the self' in L. Martin, H. Gutman and P. Hutton, eds, *Technologies of the Self*, University of Massachusetts Press, Amherst.

Foucault, M. (1991) 'Governmentality' in G. Burchell, C. Gordon and P. Miller, eds, *The Foucault Effect: Studies in Governmentality*. University of Chicago Press, Chicago.

Frampton, K. (1985) 'Towards a critical regionalism' in H. Foster, ed., *Postmodern Culture*, Pluto Press, London.

Frith, S. (1996) *Performing Rites: On the Value of Popular Music*, Harvard University Press, Cambridge, MA.

Frith, S. and Horn, D. (1987) *Art into Pop*, Methuen, London.

Frow, J. (1991) 'Michel de Certeau: the practice of representation', *Cultural Studies*, 5 (1).

Frow, J. (1995) *Cultural Studies and Cultural Value*, Oxford University Press, Oxford.

Gans, H. (1973) *Popular Culture and High Culture*, Basic Books, New York.

Geertz, C. (1973) *The Interpretation of Cultures*, Basic Books, New York.

Geertz, C. (1976) 'Art as a cultural system', *MLN*, 91.

Geertz, C. (1988) *Works and Lives: Anthropologist as Author*, Stanford University Press, Stanford.

Geertz, C. (1991) 'Deep play: notes on the Balinese cockfight' in C. Mukerji and M. Schudson, eds, *Rethinking Popular Culture: Contemporary Perspectives in Cultural Studies*, University of California Press, Berkeley.

Giddens, A. (1992) *The Transformation of Intimacy: Sexuality, Love and Eroticism in Modern Societies*, Polity, Cambridge.

Giddens, A. (1990) *The Consequences of Modernity*, Polity, Cambridge.

Giddens, A. (1994) *Beyond Left and Right: The Future of Radical Politics*, Polity, Cambridge.

Gilbert, S. and Gubar, S. (1988) *No Man's Land: The Place of the Woman Writer in the Twentieth Century, Volume 1*, Yale University Press, New Haven.

Giles, J. and Middleton, T. (1999) *Studying Culture: A Practical Introduction*, Blackwell, Oxford.

Goffman, E. (1959) *The Presentation of Self in Everyday Life*, Doubleday, New York.

Gouldner, A. (1976) *The Dialectic of Ideology and Technology*, Macmillan, London.

Gramsci, A. (1971) *Selections from the Prison Notebooks*, trans. Q. Hoare and G. Nowell-Smith, Lawrence and Wishart, London.

Gray, A. and McGuigan, J. (1993) *Studying Culture: An Introductory Reader*, Edward Arnold, London.

Grossberg, L., Fry, T. and Curthoys, A. (1988) *It's a Sin: Essays on Postmodernism, Politics and Culture*, Power Publications, Sydney.

Grossberg, L. (1997) *Bringing it All Back Home: Essays on Cultural Studies*, Duke University Press, Durham and London.

Grossberg, L., Nelson, G. and Treichler, P. (1992) *Cultural Studies*, Routledge, New York.

Grosz, E. (1994) *Volatile Bodies: Toward a Corporeal Feminism*, Allen & Unwin, Sydney.

Guattari, F. (1992) 'Regimes, pathways, subjects', trans. B. Masumi in J. Crary and S. Kwinter, eds, *Incorporations*, Zone Books, New York.

Gunew, S. (1993) 'Multicultural multiplicities: US, Canada, Australia', *Meanjin*, 32 (3).

Habermas, J. (1981) 'Modernity versus postmodernity', *New German Critique*, 22, Winter.

Habermas, J. (1983) 'Modernity – an incomplete project' in H. Foster, ed., *The Anti-aesthetic: Essays on Postmodern Culture*, Bay Press, Seattle.

Habermas, J. (1984a) *The Theory of Communicative Action, Volume One*, trans. T. McCarthy, Beacon, Boston.

Habermas, J. (1984b) 'The French path to postmodernity: Bataille between eroticism and general economics', *New German Critique*, 33.

Habermas, J. (1986) 'Taking aim at the heart of the present' in D.C. Hoy, ed., *Foucault: A Critical Reader*, Blackwell: Oxford.

Habermas, J. (1987a) *The Theory of Communicative Action, Volume Two*, trans. T. McCarthy, Beacon, Boston.

Habermas, J. (1987b) *The Philosophical Discourse of Modernity*, trans. F. Lawrence, MIT Press, Cambridge, Mass.

Habermas, J. (1989) *The Structural Transformation of the Public Sphere: An Inquiry into a Category of Bourgeois Society*, MIT Press, Cambridge, MA.

Halberstam, J. and Livingston, I. (1995) *Posthuman Bodies*, Indiana University Press, Bloomington.

Hall, S. (1980) 'Encoding/decoding' in S. Hall, D. Hobson, A. Lowe and P. Willis, eds, *Culture, Media, Language*, Hutchinson, London.

Hall, S. (1982) 'The rediscovery of ideology: the return of the repressed in media studies' in M. Gurevitch, T. Bennett, J. Curran and J. Woollocat, eds, *Culture, Society and the Media*, Methuen, London.

Hall, S. (1987) 'Minimal selves' in L. Appignanesi, ed., *Identity*, ICA Documents, No. 6, ICA Publications, London.

Hall, S. (1988) 'Recent developments in theories of language and ideology: a critical note' in S. Hall, D. Hobson, A. Lowe and P. Willis, eds, *Culture, Media, Language*, Hutchinson, London.

Hall, S. (1991a) 'The local and the global: globalization and ethnicity' in A. King, ed., *Culture, Globalization and the World-System*, State University of New York at Binghampton, Binghampton.

Hall, S. (1991b) 'Old and new identities, old and new ethnicities' in A. King, ed., *Culture, Globalization and the World-System*, State University of New York at Binghampton, Binghampton.

Hall, S., Critcher, C., Jefferson, T., Clarke, J. and Roberts, B. (1978) *Policing the Crisis: Mugging, the State and Law and Order*, Macmillan, London.

Hall, S., Hobson, D., Lowe, A. and Willis, P., eds (1988) *Culture, Media, Language*, Hutchinson, London.

Hall, S. (1996) 'Cultural studies and its theoretical legacies' in D. Morley and K.H. Chen, eds, *Stuart Hall: Critical Dialogues in Cultural Studies*, Routledge, London.

Hall, S., Held, D. and McGraw, T. (1992) *Modernity and its Futures*, Open University Press, Milton Keynes.

Hannerz, U. (1991) 'Scenarios for peripheral cultures' in A. King, ed., *Culture, Globalization and the World-System*, State University of New York at Binghampton, Binghampton.

Haraway, D. (1991) *Simians, Cyborgs and Women: The Reinvention of Nature*, Free Association Books, London.

Haraway, D. (1997) *Modest_Witness@Second_Millennium.FemaleMan_Meets_OncoMouse: Feminism and Technoscience*, Routledge, New York.

Hardy, C. (1997) 'Lesbian erotica and impossible images' in J. Matthews, ed., *Sex in Public*, Allen and Unwin, Sydney.

Harris, G. (1995) 'Perving on perversity: a nice night in front of the tele', *Media International Australia*, 78, November.

Hart, L. (1994) *Fatal Women: Lesbian Sexuality and the Mark of Aggression*, Routledge, London.

Hartley, J. (1987) 'Invisible fictions: television audiences, paedocracy, pleasure', *Textual Practice*, 1 (2).

Hartley, J. (1992) *Tele-ology: Studies in Television*, Routledge, London.

Hartley, J. (1996) *Popular Reality: Journalism, Modernity, Popular Culture*, Arnold, London.

Harvey, D. (1989) *The Condition of Postmodernity: An Enquiry into the Origin of Cultural Change*, Blackwell, Oxford.

Hassan, I. (1982) *The Dismemberment of Orpheus: Towards a Postmodern Literature*, Oxford University Press, New York.

Hassan, I. (1985) 'The culture of postmodernism', *Theory, Culture and Society*, 2 (3).

Hassan, I. (1987) *The Postmodern Turn: Essays in Postmodern Theory and Culture*, Ohio State University Press, Columbus.

Hebdige, D. (1979) *Sub-culture: The Meaning of Style*, Methuen, London.

Hebdige, D. (1988) *Hiding in the Light: On Images and Things*, Comedia, London.

Hegel, G.W.F. (1975) *Hegel's Aesthetics*, trans. T.M. Knox, Clarendon Press, Oxford.

Heidegger, M. (1952) *Being and Time*, trans. J. Macquarie and E. Robinson, Harper, New York.

Hekman, S., ed. (1996) *Feminist Interpretations of Michel Foucault*, Pennsylvania University Press, University Park.

Held, D. (1987) *Prospects for Democracy*, Polity, Cambridge.

Held, D. (1992) 'Democracy: from a city state to a cosmopolitan order?' in D. Held, ed., *Prospects for Democracy, Political Studies Special Issue*, Volume 40.

Held, D., McGrew, A., Goldblatt, D. and Perraton, J. (1999) *Global Transformations: Politics, Economics and Culture*, Polity, Cambridge.

Hellyer, P. (1999) *Stop: Think*, Chimo Media, Toronto.

Hendel, C. (1937) *Citizen of Geneva: Selections from the Letters of Jean-Jacques Rousseau*, Oxford University Press, New York.

Herman, E. and McChesney, R. (1999) 'Global media in the late 1990s' in H. Mackay and T. O'Sullivan, eds, *The Media Reader: Continuity and Transformation*, Sage: London.

Heywood, L. (1998) *Bodymakers: A Cultural Anatomy of Women's Body Building*, Rutgers University Press, New Brunswick, NJ.

Heywood, L. and Drake, J., eds (1997) *Third Wave Agenda: Being Feminist, Doing Feminism*, University of Minnesota Press, Minneapolis.

Hoggart, R. (1958) *The Uses of Literacy*, Penguin, London.

Horkheimer, M. and Adorno, T. (1972) 'The culture industry: Enlightenment as mass deception' in *Dialectic of Enlightenment*, Seabury Press, New York.

Horne, D. (1993) *The Intelligent Tourist*, Margaret Gee Publishing, Sydney.

Hoy, D.C., ed. (1986a) *Foucault: A Critical Reader*, Blackwell, Oxford.

Hoy, D.C. (1986b) 'Power, repression, progress: Foucault, Lukács and the Frankfurt School' in D.C. Hoy, ed., *Foucault: A Critical Reader*, Blackwell, Oxford.

Hoy, D.C. (1988) 'Foucault: modern or postmodern?' in J. Arac, ed., *After Foucault: Postmodern*

Challenges, Rutgers University Press, New Brunswick, NJ.

Hume, M. (1998) *Televictims: Emotional Correctness in the Media AD (After Diana)*, Informinc, London.

Husserl, E. (1931) *Ideas: General Introduction to Pure Phenomenology*, trans. W.R. Boyce, Macmillan, New York.

Hutcheon, L. (1988) *A Politics of Postmodernism: History, Theory, Fiction*, Routledge, New York.

Hutcheon, L. (1995) *Metafiction*, Longman, New York.

Huyessen, A. (1986) *After the Great Divide: Modernism, Mass Culture, Postmodernism*, Indiana University Press, Minneapolis.

Inglis, F. (1993) *Cultural Studies*, Blackwell, Oxford.

Iser, W. (1978) *The Act of Reading: A Theory of Aesthetic Response*, Johns Hopkins University Press, Baltimore.

Jacka, E. (1994) 'Researching audiences: a dialogue between cultural studies and social science', *Media International Australia*, 73, August.

Jackson, S. (1996) 'Ignorance is bliss: when you are *Just Seventeen*', *Trouble and Strife*, 33.

Jameson, F. (1981) *The Political Unconscious: Narrative as a Socially Symbolic Act*, Methuen, London.

Jameson, F. (1983) 'Postmodernism and consumer society' in H. Foster, ed., *The Anti-aesthetic: Essays on Postmodern Culture*, Bay Press, Seattle.

Jameson, F. (1984) 'Postmodernism, or, the cultural logic of late capitalism', *New Left Review*, 46.

Jameson, F. (1991) *Postmodernism, or, the Cultural Logic of Late Capitalism*, Verso, London.

Jameson, F. (1993) 'On cultural studies', *Social Text*, 34.

Jameson, F. (1998) *The Cultural Turn*, Verso, London.

Jarrett, L. (1997) *Stripping in Time: A History of Erotic Dancing*, HarperCollins, London.

Jencks, C. (1986) *What is Postmodernism?* Academy Editions, London.

Jencks, C. (1987a) *Post-Modernism: The New Classicism in Art and Architecture*, Academy Editions, London.

Jencks, C. (1987b) *The Language of Post-Modern Architecture*, Academy Editions, London.

Jencks, C. (1995) *The Architecture of the Jumping Universe*, Academy Editions, London.

Jenkins, H. (1992) *Textual Poachers: Television Fans and Participatory Culture*, Routledge, New York.

Johnson, R. (1979) 'Elements of a theory of a theory of working class culture' in J. Clarke, ed., *Working Class Culture's Studies in History and Theory*, Hutchinson, London.

Katz, E. (1959) 'Mass communication research and the study of popular culture', *Studies in Public Communication*, 2.

Kellner, D. (1989) *Jean Baudrillard: From Marxism to Postmodernism and Beyond*, Polity, Cambridge.

Kellner, D. (1997) 'Cultural theory and cultural studies: the missed articulation' in J. McGuigan, ed., *Cultural Methodologies*, Sage, London.

Kerby, M. (1997) 'Babes on the web: sex, identity and the home page', *Media International Australia*, 84 May.

King, A., ed. (1991) *Culture, Globalization and the World-System*, State University of New York at Binghampton, Binghampton.

Kollock, P. and Smith, M., eds (1999) *Communities in Cyberspace*, Routledge, New York.

Kristeva, J. (1980) *Desire in Language: A Semiotic Approach to Literature and Art*, trans. T. Gora, Columbia University Press, New York.

Kroker, A. and Kroker, M. (1997) 'Code warriors' in C. *Theory* <http://www.ctheory.com/a36-code_warriors.html>, 19 September.

Kuhn, T. (1970) *The Structure of Scientific Revolutions*, Chicago University Press, Chicago.

Lacan, J. (1977) *Ecrits: A Selection*, Tavistock, London.

Laclau, E. (1996) *Emancipation(s)*, Verso, London.

Laclau, E. and Mouffe, C. (1985) *Hegemony and Socialist Strategy: Towards a Radical Democratic Politics*, Verso, London.

Laing, S. (1986) *Representations of Working-class Life*, Macmillan, London.

Landow, G. (1992) *Hypertext: The Convergence of Contemporary Critical Theory and Technology*, Johns Hopkins University Press, Baltimore.

Lanham, R. (1993) *The Electronic Word: Democracy, Technology and the Arts*, University of Chicago Press, Chicago.

Lash, S. and Urry, J. (1987) *The End of Organized Capitalism*, Polity, Cambridge.

Leavis, F.R. (1948) *The Great Tradition*, Chatto and Windus, London.

Leavis, F.R. (1952) *D.H. Lawrence: Novelist*, Chatto and Windus, London.

Leavis, F.R. and Thompson, D. (1977) *Culture and Environment*, Greenwood Press, Westport, CT.

Leavis, Q.D. (1978) *Fiction and the Reading Public*, Chatto and Windus, London.

Lee, G. (1995) 'The "East is Red" goes pop: commodification, hybridity and nationalism in Chinese popular song and its televisual performance', *Popular Music*, 14 (1).

Lefebvre, H. (1991) *The Production of Space*, trans. D. Nicholson-Smith, Blackwell, Oxford.

Lefebvre, H. (1992) *Critique of Everyday Life*, trans. J. Moore, Verso, London.

Leonard, M. (1997) '"Rebel girl you are the queen of my world"': feminism, subculture and grrrl power' in S. Whitely, ed., *Sexing the Groove: Popular Music and Gender*, Routledge, London.

Lewis, J. (1994) 'Putu goes to Paris: global communication and Australian imaginings of the East', *Kunapipi*, XVI (3).

Lewis, J. (1997a) 'The inhuman state: nature, media, government', *Media International Australia*, 83, February.

Lewis, J. (1997b) 'Shot in the dark: Australia's industrial culture', *Cultural Studies*, 11 (3).

Lewis, J. (1998) 'Between the lines: surf texts, prosthetics and everyday theory', *Social Semiotics*, 8 (1).

Locke, J. (1950) *An Essay Concerning Human Understanding*, Oxford University Press, Oxford.

Long, E. (1997) *From Sociology to Cultural Studies*, Blackwell, Malden, MA.

Longley, L. (1997) *The Lusty Lady*, Scalo Zurich, New York.

Lowery, S. and De Fleur, M. (1983) *Milestones in Mass Communications Research: Media Effects*, Longman, New York.

Lukács, G. and Kahn, A. (1970) *Writer and Critic and Other Essays*, Merlin Press, London.

Lull, J. (1980) 'The social uses of television', *Human Communication Research*, 6 (3).

Lull, J. (1995) 'Meaning in motion', *Media, Communication, Culture: A Global Approach*, Cambridge University Press, New York.

Lumby, C. (1997) *Bad Girls*, Allen & Unwin, Sydney.

Luow, E. (2001) *The Media and Cultural Production*, Sage, London.

Lyon, D. (1994) *The Electronic Eye: The Rise of Surveillance Society*, University of Minnesota Press, Minneapolis.

Lyon, D. (1999) 'The world wide web of surveillance: the Internet and off-world power flows' in H. Mackay and T. O'Sullivan, eds, *The Media Reader: Continuity and Transformation*, Sage, London.

Lyotard, J. (1984a) *The Postmodern Condition: A Report on Knowledge*, trans. G. Bennington and B. Massumi, University of Minnesota Press, Minneapolis.

Lyotard, J (1984b) 'Answering the question: what is postmodernity?' in *The Postmodern Condition: A Report on Knowledge*, trans. G. Bennington and B. Massumi, University of Minnesota Press, Minneapolis.

Lyotard, J. (1986) *The Differends: Phases in Dispute*, trans. G. Van Dan Abbeole, University of Minnesota Press, Minneapolis.

Lyotard, J. (1991) *The Inhuman: Reflections on Time*, trans. G. Bennington and R. Bowlby, Polity, Cambridge.

MacCabe, C. (1974) 'Realism and the cinema: notes on some Brechtian theses', *Screen*, 15 (2).

McClintock, A., Mufti, A. and Shohat, E., eds (1997) *Dangerous Liaisons: Gender, Nation and Postcolonial Perspectives*, University of Minnesota Press, Minneapolis.

MacDonald, N. (2001) *The Graffiti Subculture: Masculinity, Youth, and Identity*, Palgrave, New York.

McGuigan, J. (1992) *Cultural Populism*, Routledge, London.

McGuigan, J. (1996) *Culture and the Public Sphere*, Routledge, London.

McGuigan, J., ed. (1997) *Cultural Methodologies*, Sage, London.

McHale, B. (1987) *Postmodernist Fiction*, Methuen, London.

Macherey, P. (1978) *A Theory of Literary Production*, trans. G. Wall, Routledge and Kegan Paul, London.

Mackay, H. and O'Sullivan, T., eds (1999) *The Media Reader: Continuity and Transformation*, Sage, London.

McLuhan, M. (1964) *Understanding Media*, Routledge and Kegan Paul, London.

McLuhan, M. (1969) *Counterblast*, Rapp and Whiting, London.

McRobbie, A. (1982) '*Jackie*: an ideology of adolescent femininity' in B. Waites, T. Bennet and G. Martin, eds, *Popular Culture: Past and Present*, Croom Helm, London.

McRobbie, A. (1991) *Feminism and Youth Culture: from Jackie to Just Seventeen*, Macmillan, London.

McRobbie, A. (1994) *Postmodernism and Popular Culture*, Routledge, London.

McRobbie, A. (1997) '*More:* new sexualities in girl's and women's magazines' in A. McRobbie, ed., *Back to Reality: Social Experience and Cultural Studies*, University of Manchester Press, Manchester.

McRobbie, A., Cohen, P. and Nana, M. (1989) *Gender and Generation*, Macmillan, London.

Maltsby, B. (1996) 'The homogenization of Hollywood', *Media Studies Journal*, 10 (2–3), Spring/Summer.

Marcuse, H. (1964) *One Dimensional Man: Studies in the Ideology of Advanced Industrial Society*, Beacon Press, Boston.

Marshall, P.D. (1997) *Celebrity and Power: Fame in Contemporary Culture*, University of Minnesota Press, Minneapolis.

Marvin, C. (1988) *When Old Technologies were New*, Oxford University Press, New York.

Marx, K. (1963) *Early Writings*, trans. T.B. Bottomore, McGraw-Hill, New York.

Marx, K. and Engels, F. (1970) *The German Ideology*, Lawrence and Wishart, London.

Marx, K. (1976) *A Contribution to a Critique of the Political Economy*, Foreign Language Press, Peking.

Marx, K. (1970) *Critique of Hegel's 'Philosophy of Right'*, trans. A.J. and J. O'Malley, Cambridge University Press, London.

Matthews, J., ed. (1997) *Sex in Public*, Allen & Unwin, Sydney.

Merleau-Ponty, M. (1974) *Adventures of the Dialectic*, trans. J. Bien, Heinemann, London.

Messner, M. and Sabo, D. (1990) *Sport, Men and the Gender Order: Critical Feminist Perspectives*, Human Kinetics Books, Champaign, IL.

Meyrowitz, J. (1985) *No Sense of Place: The Impact of Electronic Media on Social Behaviour*, Oxford University Press, New York.

Michaels, E. (1985) 'Constraints on knowledge in the economy of oral information', *Current Anthropology*, 26 (4).

Michaels, E. (1986) *The Aboriginal Invention of Television*, The Australian Institute of Aboriginal Studies, Canberra.

Michaels, E. (1994) *Bad Aboriginal Art: Tradition, Media and Technological Horizons*, Allen & Unwin, Sydney.

Mill, J.S. (1971) *Utilitarianism, On Liberty and Considerations on Representative Government*, Everyman's Library, London.

Mill, J.S. and Taylor Mill, H. (1970) *Essays on Sex Equality*, University of Chicago Press, Chicago.

Millett, K. (1971) *Sexual Politics*, Rupert Hart-Davis, London.

Mitchell, J. (1984) *Women: The Longest Revolution. Essays in Feminism, Literature and Psychoanalysis*, Virago, London.

Moores, S. (1993) *Interpreting Audiences: The Ethnography of Media Consumption*, Sage, London.

Morley, D. (1980a) *The Nationwide Audience*, British Film Institute, London.

Morley, D. (1980b) 'Texts, readers, subjects' in S. Hall, D. Hobson, A. Lowe and P. Willis, eds, *Culture, Media, Language*, Hutchinson, London.

Morley, D. (1986) *Family Television: Cultural Power and Domestic Leisure*, Comedia, London.

Morley, D. (1992) *Television Audiences and Cultural Studies*, Routledge, London.

Morley, D. and Chen, K., eds (1993) *Stuart Hall: Critical Dialogues in Cultural Studies: New Perspectives*, Routledge, London.

Morley, D. and Silverstone, R. (1990) 'Domestic communication – technologies and meanings', *Media, Culture and Society*, 12 (1).

Morris, M. (1988) *The Pirate's Fiancée: Feminism, Reading, Postmodernism*, Verso, London.

Morris, M. (1993) 'Panorama: The live, the dead, the living' in G. Turner, ed., *Nation, Culture, Text: Australian Cultural and Media Studies*, Routledge, London.

Morris, M. (1998) *Too Soon, Too Late: History in Popular Culture*, Indiana University Press, Bloomington.

Mouffe, C. (1996) 'Agonistic pluralism or deliberative democracy?' Paper delivered at the 1996 Cultural Studies Association of Australia Conference *In Search of the Public*, Fremantle, Western Australia.

Mukerji, C. and Schudson, M., eds (1991) *Rethinking Popular Culture*, University of California Press, Berkeley.

Mulvey, L. (1975) 'Visual pleasure and narrative cinema', *Screen*, 16 (3), Autumn.

Nancy, J. (1991) *The Inoperative Community*, trans. P. Conner, Minneapolis University Press, Minneapolis.

Neale, R.S. (1987) 'E.P. Thompson: a history of culture and culturalist history' in D.A. Broos, ed., *Creating Culture*, Allen & Unwin, London.

Negroponte, N. (1995) *Being Digital*, Hodder and Stoughton, Rydalmere, New South Wales.

Nietzsche, F. (1956) *The Birth of Tragedy and the Genealogy of Morals*, trans. F. Golffing, Doubleday, Garden City, New York.

Nightingale, V. (1989) 'What's ethnographic about audience research?', *Australian Journal of Communication*, 16.

Norris, C. (1987) *Derrida*, Fontana, London.

Norris, C. (1990) 'Lost in the funhouse: Baudrillard and the politics of postmodernism' in R. Boyne and A. Rattansi, eds, *Postmodernism and Society*, St Martin's Press, New York.

Norris, C. (1992) *Uncritical Theory: Postmodernism, Intellectuals and the Gulf War*, University of Boston Press, Boston.

Numberg, G. (1996) 'Farewell to the information age' in G. Numberg, ed., *The Future of the Book*, University of California Press, Berkeley.

Ogden, C. and Richards, I. (1923) *The Meaning of Meaning*, Routledge and Kegan Paul, London.

O'Toole, L. (1998) *Pornocopia: Porn, Sex, Technology and Desire*, Serpent's Tail, London.

Park, R. (1969) 'The city: suggestions for the investigation of human behaviour in the urban environment' in R. Sennett, ed., *Classic Essays on the Culture of Cities*, Appleton Century Crofts, New York.

Park, R. and Burgess, E. (1921) *Introduction to the Science of Sociology*, University of Chicago Press, Chicago.

Parsons, T. (1961) 'An outline of the social system' in T. Parsons, E. Shils, K. Naegele and J. Pitts, eds, *Theories of Society, Volume 1*, Free Press, Glencoe, IL.

Parsons, T. (1967) *Essays in Sociological Theory*, Free Press, New York.

Paxton, S. (1998) 'Do men get eating disorders?', *Everybody*, 2, August.

Peirce, C.S. (1958) *Collected Papers*, Harvard University Press, Cambridge, MA.

Poster, M. (1989) *Critical Theory and Poststructuralism*, Cornell University Press, New York.

Poster, M. (1995) *The Second Media Age*, Polity, Cambridge.

Postman, N. (1993) *Technopoly: The Surrender of Culture to Technology*, Vintage Books, New York.

Prendergast, C. and Knottnerust, J. (1990) 'The astructural bias and presuppositional form of symbolic interactionism: a noninteractionist evaluation of the new studies in social organization' in L. Reynolds, ed., *Interactionism: Exposition and Critique*, General Hall: New York.

Rabinow, P., ed. (1991) *The Foucault Reader*, Penguin, London.

Radway, J. (1987) *Reading the Romance: Women, Patriarchy and Popular Literature*, Verso, London.

Redhead, S., Wynne, D. and O'Connor, J., eds (1997) *The Clubcultures Reader: Readings in Popular Cultural Studies*, Blackwell, Oxford.

Reynolds, L., ed. (1990) *Interactionism: Exposition and Critique*, General Hall, New York.

Rheingold, H. (1993) *The Virtual Community: Homesteading on the Electronic Frontier*, Addison Wesley, Reading, MA.

Richards, J., Wilson, S. and Woodhead, L. (eds) (1999) *Diana: The Making of a Media Saint*, I.B. Tauris, London.

Ricoeur, P. (1974) *Political and Social Essays*, D. Stewart and J. Bien, eds, Ohio University Press, Ohio.

Ricoeur, P. (1981) *Hermeneutics and the Human Sciences*, Cambridge University Press, Cambridge.

Ritzer, G., ed. (1990) *Frontiers of Social Theory: The New Synthesis*, Columbia University Press: New York.

Rorty, R. (1984) 'Habermas and Lyotard on postmodernity', *Praxis International*, 4, April.

Rose, G. (1988) 'Architecture to philosophy – the postmodern complicity', *Theory, Culture and Society*, 5 (2–3), June.

Rose, M.A. (1990) *The Postmodern and the Postindustrial: A Critical Analysis*, Cambridge University Press, Cambridge.

Ross, A. (1991) *Strange Weather: Culture, Science and Technology in the Age of Limits*, Verso, London.

Said, E.W. (1978) *Orientalism*, Pantheon Books, New York.

Said, E.W. (1986) 'Foucault and the imagination of power' in D.C. Hoy, ed., *Foucault: A Critical Reader*, Blackwell, Oxford.

Said, E.W. (1993) *Culture and Imperialism*, Chatto and Windus, London.

Said, E. (1999) *Out of Place: A Memoir*, Knopf, New York.

Sawicki, J. (1991) *Disciplining Foucault: Feminism, Power and the Body*, Routledge, London.

Scammell, P. (1989) 'Public service broadcasting and modern public life', *Media, Culture and Society*, 11 (2).

Schatz, T (1981) *Hollywood Genres: Formulas, Filmmaking and the Studio System*, Temple University Press, Philadelphia.

Shilling, C. (1993) *The Body and Social Theory*, Sage, London.

Silverstone, R. (1990) 'Television and everyday life: toward an anthropology of the television audience' in M. Ferguson, ed., *Public Communication: The New Imperatives*, Sage, London.

Silverstone, R., ed. (1997) *Visions of Suburbia*, Routledge, London.

Skelton, T. and Valentine, G., eds (1998) *Cool Places: Geographies of Youth Culture*, Routledge, London.

Slavin, J. (2000) *The Internet and Society*, Polity, Cambridge.

Smith, N. (1997) 'The Satanic geographies of globalization: uneven development in the 1990s', *Public Culture*, 10 (1), Fall.

Snyder, I. (1996) *Hypertext: The Electronic Labyrinth*, Melbourne University Press, Melbourne.

Soja, E. (1989) *Postmodern Geographies: The Reassertion of Space in Critical Social Theory*, Verso, London.

Soja, E. (1996) *ThirdSpace: Journeys to Los Angeles and other Real-and-Imagined Places*, Blackwell, Cambridge.

Sontag, S. (1966) *Against Interpretation*, Deli, New York.

Sontag, S. (1978) 'The double standard of ageing' in V. Carver and P. Liddiard, eds, *An Ageing Population*, Hodder and Stoughton, London.

Spender, D. (1995) *Nattering on the Net: Women, Power and Cyberspace*, Spinifex, Melbourne.

Spinoza, B. (1989) *Ethics*, trans. A. Boyle, Dent, London.

Spivak, G.C. (1987) *In Other Worlds*, Methuen, London.

Spivak, G.C. (1988) 'Can the subaltern speak?' in G. Nelson and L. Grossberg, eds, *Marxism and the Interpretation of Culture*, Macmillan, London.

Spivak, G.C. (1992) 'Teaching for the times', *MMLA Journal for the Mid-West Modern Language Association*, 25 (1), Spring.

Stacey, J. (1994) *Star Gazing: Hollywood and Female Spectatorship*, Routledge, London.

Stark, R. (1996) *The Rise of Christianity: A Sociologist Reconsiders History*, Princeton University Press, Princeton, New Jersey.

Stauber, J. (1995) *Toxic Waste is Good for You*, Common Courage Press, Monroe, ME.

Storey, J. (1998) *An Introduction to Cultural Theory and Popular Culture*, Prentice Hall, Harvester Wheatsheaf.

Strinati, D. (1995) *An Introduction to Theories of Popular Culture*, Routledge, London.

Taylor, C. (1985) *Philosophical Papers* (2 Vols), Cambridge University Press, Cambridge.

Taylor, J. (2000) *Diana, Self-interest and British National Identity*, Praeger, Westport, Conn.

Thade, D. (1991) 'Text and the new hermeneutics' in D. Wood, ed., *On Paul Ricoeur: Narrative and Interpretation*, Routledge, London.

Thomas, W.I. and Znaniecki, F. (1918–20) *The Polish Peasant in Europe and America*, R.G. Badger, Boston.

Thompson, E.P. (1976) 'Interview', *Radical History Review*, 3.

Thompson, E.P. (1980) *The Making of the English Working Class*, Penguin, Harmondsworth.

Thompson, J. and Held, D., eds (1982) *Habermas: Critical Debates*, MIT Press, Cambridge, MA.

Thussu, D.K., ed. (1998) *Electronic Empires: Global Media and Local Resistance*, Arnold, London.

Tomkins, R. (1996) 'U.S. tops poll on cultural exports', *The Financial Times*, 4 December.

Tomlinson, J. (1997) 'Cultural globalisation: placing and displacing the west' in H. Mackay and T. O'Sullivan, eds, *The Media Reader: Continuity and Transformation*, Sage, London.

Tomlinson, J. (1999) *Globalization and Culture*, Polity, Cambridge.

Tompkins, J., ed. (1980) *Reader Response Criticism: From Formalism to Poststructuralism*, Johns Hopkins University Press, Baltimore.

Touraine, A. (1971) *The Post-Industrial Society, Tomorrow's Social History: Classes, Conflicts and Culture in the Programmed Society*, Random House, New York.

Turkle, S. (1999) 'Identity in the age of the Internet' in H. Mackay and T. O'Sullivan, eds, *The Media Reader: Continuity and Transformation*, Sage, London.

Turner, C. (1992) *Modernity and Politics in the Work of Max Weber*, Routledge, London.

Turner, G. (1991) 'Return to Oz: populism, the academy, and the future of Australian Studies', *Meanjin*, 1.

Turner, G. (1994) *Making it National: Nationalism and Australian Popular Culture*, Allen & Unwin, Sydney.

Turner, G. (1996) *British Cultural Studies: An Introduction*, 2nd edn, Routledge, London.

Turner, G. (1997) 'Two faces of Australian nationalism', *Sydney Morning Herald*, 25 January.

Turnock, R. (2000) *Interpreting Diana: Television Audiences and the Death of a Princess*, British Film Institute, London.

van Zoonen, L. (1994) *Feminist Media Studies*, Sage, London.

Vertinsky, P. (1998) 'Run, Jane, run: central issues in the current debate about enhancing women's health through exercise', *Women and Health*, 27 (4).

Vickers, A. (1990) *Bali: Paradise Created*, Penguin, Ringwood.

Walch, J. (1999) *In the Net: An Internet Guide for Activists*, Zed Books, London.

Wallis, B., ed. (1984) *Art After Modernism: Rethinking Representation*, Museum of Modern Art, New York.

Weber, M. (1930) *The Protestant Ethic and the Spirit of Capitalism*, trans. T. Parsons, Unwin, London.

Weber, M. (1946) *From Max Weber: Essays in Sociology*, Oxford University Press, New York.

Weber, M. (1949) *The Methodology of the Social Sciences*, Free Press, New York.

West, C. (1993) *Keeping Faith*, Routledge, London.

Wijeyesinghe, C. and Jackson, B. (2001) *New Perspectives on Racial Identity Development: A Theoretical and Practical Anthology*, New York University Press, New York.

Williams, F. (1982) *The Communications Revolution*, Sage, London.

Williams, L. (1989) *Hard Core: Power, Pleasure and the Frenzy of the Visible*, University of California Press, Berkeley.

Williams, L. (1992) 'When the woman looks' in G. Mast, M. Cohen and L. Braudy, eds, *Film Theory and Criticism*, Oxford University Press, New York.

Williams, R. (1958) *Culture and Society*, Chatto and Windus, London.

Williams, R. (1965) *The Long Revolution*, Penguin, London.

Williams, R. (1968) *Communications*, Penguin, Hammondsworth.

Williams, R. (1974) *Television, Technology and Cultural Form*, Fontana, London.

Williams, R. (1976) *Keywords*, Fontana, London.

Williams, R. (1981) *Culture*, Fontana, London.

Williamson, J. (1978) *Decoding Advertising*, Marion Boyars, London.

Willock, R. (1999) 'Giant sucking sounds: politics as illusion' in D. Slayden and R. Willock, eds, *Soundbite Culture: The Death of Discourse in a Wired World*, Sage, Thousand Oaks.

Wilson, T. (1993) *Watching Television: Hermeneutics, Reception and Popular Culture*, Polity, Cambridge.

Wilson, T. (1995) 'Horizons of meaning: the breadth of television narrowcasting', *Media International Australia*, 75, February.

Winship, J. (1987) *Inside Women's Magazines*, Pandora, London.

Wittgenstein, L. (1922) *Tractatus Logico-Philosophicus*, trans. C.K. Ogden, Routledge and Kegan Paul, London.

Wittgenstein, L. (1967) *Zettel (The Blue Book)*, Blackwell, Oxford.

Wittgenstein, L. (1975) *Philosophical Remarks*, trans. R. Hargreaves and R. White, Blackwell, Oxford.

Wolf, N. (1991) *The Beauty Myth: How Images of Beauty are used against Women*, Vintage, London.

Wolff, J. (1990) 'Feminism and modernism' in A. Milner and C. Worth, eds, *Discourse and Difference*, Monash University Press, Clayton.

Woolf, V. (1978) *A Room of One's Own*, Hogarth Press, London.

Woolf, V. (1979) 'Dorothy Richardson' in M. Barrett, ed., *Virginia Woolf: Women and Writing*, The Women's Press, London.

Wright, W. (1975) *Sixguns and Society: A Structural Study of the Western*, University of California Press, Berkeley.

Yodice, G. (1995) 'What's a straight white man to do?' in M. Berger, B. Wallis and S. Watson, eds, *Constructing Masculinity*, Routledge, New York.

Young and Jesser (1997) *The Media and the Military*, Macmillan, Melbourne.

Zolo, D. (1992) *Democracy and Complexity*, Polity, Cambridge.

Index

Index

Index

Index

racism 35, 135, 342, 344, 346, 404
radical eclecticism 241, 360
radical politics 31, 107, 373, 406, 417–18, 433
radical sociology 73, 100
radio 90, 254, 282, 283, 388–9
Radway, Janice 209, 251, 282–4, 454
Rambo 391
Ranson, W. K. 129
rap music 353
rationalism 46, 59, 60, 84, 93, 246, 296, 394
rationality 54, 77, 299
  communicative 245, 246
  Habermas 102, 245–6
  instrumental 44, 90, 99, 102, 245–6, 254, 297, 308
  see also reason
readers *see* audiences
reading 158, 194
  cultural patterns 264–5
  preferred and dominant 29, 31, 137, 263, 264–5, 280
  women 284
Reagan, Ronald 397
realism 85, 258–9
reality
  cultural studies 40, 140
  Habermas 101, 102, 425–6
  Hegel 44
  language 67, 148–9, 156, 270
  literature 221
  Marxism 85, 86
  mediation through discourse 175
  modernism 23, 40, 41–5
  phenomenology 177, 290–1
  postmodernism 216
  poststructuralism 163, 237
  representational 137
  shared 44–5
  signifiers 441
  structuralism 237, 271
  Weber 51
  see also hyperreality
reason 23, 41, 42, 44, 53, 299–300
  critique of 246
  Hegel 77, 79
  language 147
  print culture 385, 394
  Weber 51
  see also rationality
reception studies 58, 391
  see also audiences, active

Redhead, S. 285, 443
reggae music 355
regionalism 357
relativism 52, 68, 123–4, 183–4, 208, 211, 231
  politics 288
  postmodernism 292
  poststructuralism 424
religion
  Durkheim 46, 48–9
  Marx 84
representation 7, 8, 11, 13, 137, 269–70
  discourse 25
  female body 316
  identity 34, 100
  ideology 94–5
  male body 328
  Marxism 75, 94–5, 96
  political 205, 420, 421, 446
  postmodernism 215, 217
  textual analysis 36, 201
  women 189–91, 194, 199–200, 202, 208–9, 212–14, 278–9
resistance 31, 34, 99, 100, 134, 271–2
  to capitalism 374, 445
  globalization 377, 378
  identity 374, 376
  pleasure 273, 275
  political 138, 376, 377, 429
  postcolonialism 349, 350
  women 284
  working-class 132
Rheingold, Howard 401–2, 406
Richardson, Dorothy 191
Ricoeur, Paul 64, 103–4, 169, 291, 450
ritual 15, 48, 71, 383
Road to Bali 375
Rocky films 323
The Rolling Stones 4
Roman Empire 297
Romance 307
romance reading 209, 282–4
Romanticism 22, 23, 40, 43, 54, 91
  aesthetics 293
  Althusser comparison 95
  Barthes 164
  British 39, 109–10, 112–15, 117–18, 120, 130, 300
  critique of 45
  Geist 44

Romanticism *cont.*
  German 39, 110
  Hegel 79
  language 423
  Leavisite 117, 118, 119, 129
  literary criticism 169–70
  Marx 81
  naturalism 78
  progress 44
  subject 177
  technology 380
  tourism 120–1
Rorty, Richard 247
Rose, Gillian 226
Ross, Andrew 211, 242, 402–3
Rousseau, Jean-Jacques 24, 79, 112, 120, 167–8, 448
Rubin, Gail 197
Russell, Bertrand 145, 147, 148, 166
Russian formalism 84–5, 119
Russian Revolution 85, 93
Ryle, Gilbert 70

Sabo, D. 321
Said, Edward 21, 35, 67–8, 73, 147, 174, 176
  cultural imperialism 346, 349
  deconstruction 248
  on Foucault 269
  Gulf War 441
  identity politics 422
  Orientalism 208, 340–2
  political action 429
  racism 344
Sartre, Jean-Paul 60, 119, 182, 192
satellite and cable technology 26, 289, 321, 337, 354, 397, 400
Sawicki, J. 200
Scammell, P. 390
Schatz, Thomas 154
schizophrenia 44, 180, 181, 233, 234, 385
Schmidt, Hermolt 27, 28
Schoenberg, 91
Schütz, Alfred 60–1, 101
science 9, 23, 45, 51, 52, 103, 156–7
  architecture 360
  body 294
  cultural studies 264
  postmodernism 224, 226, 227–9, 242, 246
  separation from art and morality 102, 245